Fodor's 95
Italy

PRAISE FOR FODOR'S GUIDES

"Fodor's guides . . . are an admirable blend of the cultural and the practical."

—The Washington Post

"Researched by people chosen because they lived or have lived in the country, well-written, and with good historical sections . . . Obligatory reading for millions of tourists."

—The Independent, *London*

"Usable, sophisticated restaurant coverage, with an emphasis on good value."

—Andy Birsh, Gourmet restaurant columnist, quoted by Gannett News Service

"Packed with dependable information."

—Atlanta Journal Constitution

"Fodor's always delivers high quality . . . thoughtfully presented . . . thorough."

—Houston Post

"Valuable because of their comprehensiveness."

—Minneapolis Star-Tribune

Fodor's Travel Publications, Inc.
New York • Toronto • London • Sydney • Auckland

ISBN 0–679–02728–9

Fodor's Italy

Editors: Joan Fisher Carroll, Kristin Moehlmann, Alison Stern
Editorial Contributors: Steven Amsterdam, Robert Andrews, Barbara Walsh Angelillo, Barbara Lazear Ascher, Sheila Brownlee, Harry Eyres, Echo Garrett, Laura M. Kidder, Bevin McLaughlin, Roderick Conway Morris, Mary Ellen Schultz, George Sullivan, Phoebe Tait, Robert Tine, Nancy van Itallie
Creative Director: Fabrizio La Rocca
Cartographer: David Lindroth
Illustrator: Karl Tanner
Cover Photograph: Peter Guttman

Design: Vignelli Associates

Special Sales

Fodor's Travel Publications are available at special discounts for bulk purchases for sales promotions or premiums. Special editions, including personalized covers, excerpts of existing guides, and corporate imprints, can be created in large quantities for special needs. For more information, contact your local bookseller or write to Special Markets, Fodor's Travel Publications, 201 E. 50th Street, New York, NY 10022. Inquiries from Canada should be directed to your local Canadian bookseller or sent to Random House of Canada, Ltd., Marketing Department, 1265 Aerowood Drive, Mississauga, Ontario L4W 1B9. Inquiries from the United Kingdom should be sent to Fodor's Travel Publications, 20 Vauxhall Bridge Road, London, England SW1V 2SA.

MANUFACTURED IN THE UNITED STATES OF AMERICA
10 9 8 7 6 5 4 3 2

Contents

Maps

Foreword

We would like to express our gratitude to Barbara Walsh Angelillo, Rob Andrews, and Roderick Conway Morris for their patience, enthusiasm, and hard work in preparing this new edition.

While every care has been taken to ensure the accuracy of the information in this guide, the passage of time will always bring change, and consequently, the publisher cannot accept responsibility for errors that may occur.

All prices and opening times quoted here are based on information supplied to us at press time. Hours and admission fees may change, however, and the prudent traveler will avoid inconvenience by calling ahead.

Fodor's wants to hear about your travel experiences, both pleasant and unpleasant. When a hotel or restaurant fails to live up to its billing, let us know and we will investigate the complaint and revise our entries where the facts warrant it.

Send your letters to the editors of Fodor's Travel Publications, 201 E. 50th Street, New York, NY 10022.

Highlights'95 and Fodor's Choice

Highlights '95

As 1995 approached, local and national elections confirmed that Italy is on a new political course. The most encouraging signs of change can be seen on local levels, where reforms and innovations tend to affect tourists more directly. New administrations in cities such as Rome, Milan, and Naples, though of differing political stamp, are attempting to improve the quality of urban life for residents and visitors alike. Italians regard their efforts with some optimism, and frequent visitors to Italy are noticing signs of increased efficiency, better public transport, cleaner streets, more orderly traffic, and better air quality—all relatively speaking, of course.

If the U.S. dollar remains as strong in relation to the Italian lira in 1995 as it has been for the past two years or so, Italy will continue to be a very good value for American travelers. As the recession persisted into 1994, hoteliers and restaurateurs continued their policy of attracting customers by maintaining stable prices and promoting money-saving offers. The Jolly and Forte hotel chains, for instance, feature special weekend and vacation packages. On request, many hotels will quote discount rates; always inquire about them, especially when traveling during the slack season. Gastronomic shrines such as **Savini** in Milan and **Le Jardin** (restaurant of the Lord Byron Hotel) in Rome offer fixed-price menus (often in the form of a "business lunch") at 50% off à la carte prices. In many otherwise expensive restaurants in Rome, Florence, and Venice, similar menus are making gourmet dining more affordable.

Also more accessible are Italy's state museums, among them the **Galleria Nazionale di Arte Antica** in Rome; the **Galleria degli Offizi** in Florence; and the **Galleria dell'Accademia** in Venice, thanks to the current implementation of a 1993 law. About 30 major museums throughout Italy have extended their hours and are now open from 9 AM to 7 PM; in smaller museums, hours and closing days are being tailored to accommodate the public. The law also provides for the opening of museum shops and bookshops where visitors can buy reproductions of works of art, videos, and publications. Where possible, museum cafés and cafeterias are being installed.

Longer hours are not the only news in Rome's Galleria Nazionale di Arte Antica in Palazzo Barberini. For decades the Ministry of Culture has been trying to evict the officer's club, which has occupied part of the magnificent 17th-century palace, taking up space sorely needed for the gallery's collections, part of which has been shunted off to Palazzo Corsini, across the Tiber in the Trastevere section of Rome. In 1994 the ministry won its battle, and by 1995 the Galleria's extensive collections of Italian art from the 13th to 18th centuries will be reunited under the glorious Baroque ceilings painted for the Barberinis by artist Pietro da Cortona.

The Ministry of Culture evicted an even more illustrious tenant when it served final notice in 1994 that the **Rome Opera** would have to find another venue for its summer season, until now staged in the spectacular setting of the ancient Roman Baths of Caracalla. The motive was serious enough: The heavy stage apparatus was weakening the 2,000-year-old structure. At press time, the superintendent of the Rome Opera was still looking for a suitable site. In Verona, fortunately, the ancient Roman Arena will continue to be the impressive venue of summer opera and ballet. And the **Verona Arena Opera Company** has organized a brand-new spring festival of Baroque music, inaugurated in 1994 in the restored 18th-century Teatro Filarmonico.

By 1995, Rome's new trio of archaeological museums will be open, bringing another saga of bureaucratic dithering to a happy end. The trio consists of the original **Museo Nazionale delle Terme** (in the former monastery of Santa Maria degli Angeli, on the site of the ancient Roman Baths of Diocletian), **Palazzo Massimo** (near Termini Station), and **Palazzo Altemps** (near Piazza Navona). At last Rome has a suitable showcase for the wealth of antiquities in the Museo Nazionale Romano collections, which have been divided among the three buildings.

In Turin, the **Museo Nazionale del Cinema** (National Cinema Museum), closed for more than a decade, should reopen by 1995 in new premises in the city's landmark Mole Antonelliana. Although further work may be required on the wing of the **Uffizi** in Florence that was damaged by the 1993 bombing, no evidence of that tragic event should be evident to visitors in 1995. In Rome, the same wave of bombings severely damaged part of St. John Lateran and demolished the facade of the very old church of San Giorgio in Velabro, where restoration will probably continue into 1995. In Rome, Florence, Milan, and Venice, indefatigable museumgoers can save on admission fees by purchasing Museum Cards.

After the unveiling of the restoration of Michelangelo's *Last Judgment* in April 1994, you can get an unfettered view of the Sistine Chapel in the Vatican, with no scaffolding to detract from its awesome beauty. Restorers have now turned their attention to Giotto's 700-year-old frescoes in the Scrovegni Chapel in Padua. The chapel will remain closed during restoration and is expected to reopen in late 1995, when a system of limited access will be put into effect, probably allowing only a score of visitors at a time. The colossal job of cleaning the Colosseum continues through 1995, but the ancient Roman amphitheater can be admired even while work goes on. The larger-than-life bronze Warriors of Riace, those famous Greek statues that were recovered from the floor of the sea off the Calabrian coast, have been restored and are back on their pedestals in the Museo Nazionale Archeologico (National Archaelogical Museum) in Reggio Calabria.

U.S. hotel chains are consolidating their presence in Italy. After lengthy negotiations, Sheraton won out over other bidders for ownership of the prestitious Ciga chain of deluxe properties, which formerly belonged to the Aga Khan. They include such famous hotels as the Danieli in Venice and the Excelsior in Rome. In Naples, a four-star **Holiday Inn** opened in the city's new and modernistic **Centro Direzionale,** a forward-looking development located in the heart of the city, overlooking the bay.

Fodor's Choice

No two people will agree on what makes a perfect vacation, but it's fun and helpful to know what others think. We hope you'll have a chance to experience some of Fodor's Choices yourself while visiting Italy. For detailed information about each entry, refer to the appropriate chapters (given in parentheses) within this guidebook.

Picturesque Villages and Towns

Alberobello (Apulia)

Asolo (The Venetian Arc)

Cinque Terre (Liguria)

Dobbiaco/Toblach (The Dolomites)

Orta San Giulio (Milan, Lombardy, and the Lakes)

San Gimignano (Tuscany)

Positano (Campania)

Taormina (Sicily)

Classical Sites

Agrigento (Sicily)

Aosta (Piedmont/Valle d'Aosta)

Fiesole (Florence)

Herculaneum (Campania)

Nora (Sardinia)

Ostia Antica (Excursions from Rome)

Paestum (Campania)

Pompeii (Campania)

Roman Forum (Rome)

Siracusa (Sicily)

Works of Art

Byzantine mosaics in Ravenna (Emilia-Romagna)

Donatello's *Judith and Holofernes* (Florence)

Duccio di Boninsegna's *Maestà* in Siena (Tuscany)

Giotto's paintings in the Cappella Scrovegni, Padua (The Venetian Arc)

Raphael's *Betrothal of the Virgin*, Milan (Milan, Lombardy, and the Lakes)

Michelangelo's *David* and *Slaves* (Florence)

Michelangelo's Sistine Chapel ceiling (Rome)

Raphael's Vatican *Stanze* (Rome)

Tintoretto's *Scuola di San Rocco* cycle (Venice)

Tiepolo's Villa Valmarana frescoes (Vicenza)

Churches

Basilica di Santa Croce, Lecce (Apulia)

Basilica di San Salvatore, Spoleto (Umbria and the Marches)

Basilica di San Marco (Venice)

Duomo, Milan (Milan, Lombardy, and the Lakes)

Frari (Venice)

Il Gesù (Rome)

Basilica of San Francesco, Assisi (Umbria)

San Miniato al Monte (Florence)

San Vitale, Ravenna (Emilia-Romagna)

Santa Maria Maggiore (Rome)

Museums

Accademia (Venice)

Galleria degli Uffizi (Florence)

Museo Archeologico, Cagliari (Sardinia)

Museo Archeologico, Naples (Campania)

Museo Egizio, Turin (Piedmont/Valle d'Aosta)

Museo Etrusco Guarnacci, Volterra (Tuscany)

Museo Nazionale, Taranto (Apulia)

Museo Nazionale, Urbino (Umbria and the Marches)

Vatican Museums (Rome)

Villa Giulia (Rome)

Architectural Gems

Baptistery (Florence)

Castel del Monte (Apulia)

Castello di Buonconsiglio, Trento (The Dolomites)

Castello Sforzesco, Milan (Milan, Lombardy, and the Lakes)

Duomo, Siena (Tuscany)

Palazzo Barberini (Rome)

Palazzo Ducale (Venice)

The Pantheon, Rome

Villa La Rotonda, Vicenza (The Venetian Arc)

Hotels

Hassler (Rome) *$$$$*

Villa d'Este, Cernobbio (Milan, Lombardy, and the Lakes) *$$$$*

Villa Igiea, Palermo (Sicily) *$$$$*

Santa Caterina, Amalfi (Campania) *$$$–$$$$*

Baglioni (Florence) *$$$*

Metropole (Venice) *$$$*

La Residenza (Rome) *$$*

Alpino Monte Rota/Alpengasthof Ratsberg, Dobbiaco (The Dolomites) *$–$$*

Pescille, San Gimignano (Tuscany) *$$*

Stella Maris, Levanto (Liguria) *$*

Restaurants

Les Etoiles (Rome) *$$$$*

Savini (Milan, Lombardy, and the Lakes) *$$$$*

Alberto, Messina (Sicily) *$$$*

La Smarrita, Turin (Piedmont/Valle d'Aosta) *$$$*

Tiffany Grill/Schloss Maur, Merano (The Dolomites) *$$$*

Beccherie, Treviso (The Venetian Arc) *$$*

Il Cibreo (Florence) *$$*

Da Fiore (Venice) *$$*

Le Logge, Siena (Tuscany) *$$*

Ristorante Tornasacco, Ascoli Piceno (Umbria and the Marches) *$–$$*

Cafés

Baratti e Milano, Turin (Piedmont)

Calflisch, Naples (Campania)

Florian (Venice)

Pedrocchi, Padua (The Venetian Arc)

Tre Scalini (Rome)

Taste Treats

Biscottini di Prato (Tuscany)

Bistecca alla fiorentina (Florence)

Canederli (The Dolomites)

Cardi in bagna cauda (Piedmont/Valle d'Aosta)

Cotoletta alla bolognese (Emilia-Romagna)

Orecchiette (Apulia)

Porcheddu (Sardinia)

Risotto alla milanese (Milan, Lombardy, and the Lakes)

Tiramisù (Venice)

Zuppa di datteri (Liguria)

Off the Beaten Track

Bussana Vecchia (Liguria)

Catacombs of San Gennaro, Naples (Campania)

Earth Pyramids, Renon (The Dolomites)

Elba (Tuscany)

Island of Torcello (Venice)

Riace bronzes, Reggio di Calabria (*see* Sicily)

Tremiti Islands (Apulia)

Valnerina (Umbria and the Marches)

Times to Treasure

Attending the open-air opera performances in Verona's Roman Arena (The Venetian Arc)

Cheering for the boats in Venice's Historic Regatta (Venice)

Experiencing the pageantry and excitement of Siena's Palio (Tuscany)

Following the four-day folklore procession of Sant'Efisio (Sardinia)

Looking down on the Bay of Naples from Villa Jovis, Capri (Campania)

Monte Cervino (the Matterhorn) seen from Breuil-Cervinia (Piedmont/Valle d'Aosta)

Peeping through the Knights of Malta keyhole to see St. Peter's dome (Rome)

Rose-colored walls in Assisi catching the autumn sun (Umbria and the Marches)

The pink peaks of the Catinaccio in the Dolomites at dusk (The Dolomites)

The sleepy view of Florence and the Arno valley from Via San Francesco, Fiesole (Florence)

Italy

World Time Zones

Numbers below vertical bands relate each zone to Greenwich Mean Time (0 hrs.).
Local times frequently differ from these general indications,
as indicated by light-face numbers on map.

Algiers, **29**	Berlin, **34**	Delhi, **48**	Istanbul, **40**
Anchorage, **3**	Bogotá, **19**	Denver, **8**	Jerusalem, **42**
Athens, **41**	Budapest, **37**	Djakarta, **53**	Johannesburg, **44**
Auckland, **1**	Buenos Aires, **24**	Dublin, **26**	Lima, **20**
Baghdad, **46**	Caracas, **22**	Edmonton, **7**	Lisbon, **28**
Bangkok, **50**	Chicago, **9**	Hong Kong, **56**	London (Greenwich), **27**
Beijing, **54**	Copenhagen, **33**	Honolulu, **2**	Los Angeles, **6**
	Dallas, **10**		Madrid, **38**
			Manila, **57**

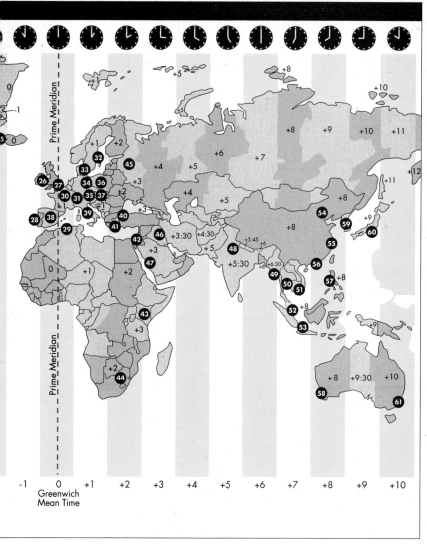

-1 | 0 | +1 | +2 | +3 | +4 | +5 | +6 | +7 | +8 | +9 | +10

Greenwich Mean Time

Introduction

By Barbara Lazear Ascher

A frequent writer about Italy for the New York Times, Barbara Lazear Ascher is also the author of a collection of essays, Playing After Dark.

They went for the light, they went for culture, they went for inspiration. Above all, they went to discover something that was missing in themselves. Passion, perhaps. A heightened sense of awareness. They came not simply to find themselves but to become their best selves.

Keats, Shelley, Byron, James, Goethe, Wagner, Prendergast, Renoir, Monet, and centuries of tourists who did not record their inspiration for the ages, but who, like Miss Lavish in E. M. Forster's *Room with a View*, knew that "one doesn't come to Italy for niceness . . . one comes for life."

And how is this life delivered unto one? If you ask the traveler of this decade, the answers will be various. For some it is the layers of history, physically present to walk upon, the reassuring sense of place and continuity that comes from a casual coexistence with antiquity. Twentieth-century businessmen and women stroll through the Roman Forum, swinging their briefcases and chatting of today's deals as they pass between the 5th-century-BC Corinthian columns of the Temple of Castor and Pollux.

It is as if one could hold out a hand and feel the touch of Pliny the Elder, Livy, or Catullus. A young woman, fresh from college Latin, made the mistake of visiting the Forum at high noon in August, suffered heat stroke, and was certain she heard Cicero speak before she fainted. There are those who would tell you that it wasn't the heat—Cicero *had* spoken.

Another woman, seven months pregnant when she and her husband traveled to Ravenna, swears that as she beheld the dazzling gold and lapis lazuli of San Vitale's 5th-century mosaics her unborn child leapt for joy. There is no guarding against it; life will fill you to brimming as Italy has its way with you.

For the sybarite, the palate is awakened by the clear, true flavors of wine and food that taste faintly of the earth and sea from which they came. Buckwheat pasta in Bormio; polenta, black with squid ink, in Venice; creamy gelato at Giolitti in Rome; or the perfectly comforting bowl of risotto in Siena, served by a family in their nameless restaurant. You will hear, on the other side of the Atlantic, the longings of travelers returned home, who, as the light begins to change in early September, yearn for *gamberetti*, Venetian shrimps the size of a baby's fingertip. Summer causes them to recall the simple delight of sitting beneath large shade trees on the banks of Lake Como, drinking cool wine from earthenware pitchers. Winter's winds bring memories of Alpine chills chased by a fiery draft of grappa.

It is the dream that takes you back, just as it was the dream that enveloped you while you were there. You will notice that those who travel in Italy seem to do so in a state of reverie. Perhaps it is the diaphanous gauze of light that softens physical outlines and blurs the distinction between past and present. A light conducive to daydreams. A light that both intensifies life and makes it gentler to the touch.

Of course, there are those who have been rudely awakened from the dream by a revved-up 1990s state-of-the-art motorcycle outside their 19th-century Roman hotel. They will grumpily tell of the shocking presence of 20th-century blight in a land that seemed impervious to such intrusion. In the heat of disillusion, they will complain of the "real" Italy, of Roman traffic jams, thefts in Naples, Venice as Disneyland, a highway system around Milan as attractive as the New Jersey Turnpike. They will warn that you, a woman, must not be persuaded by the charms of an Italian gentleman who commits his heart and future within a three-minute walk across a piazza.

There is truth in what they say, but the generosity of the Italians and the striking physical beauty of their land make it possible to live in the dream alongside the blight. You cannot arrive in Venice without driving through the gray air of Mestre, polluted by oil refineries. But once your water taxi is negotiating the Grand Canal, you lose yourself in time and space. And that is what Italy is about . . . losing and finding yourself in time and space. By morning, as the rudely awakened dreamer stands on the Palatine Hill and smells the wild fennel just as Horace did, all is forgiven.

It is the natural as well as the man-made wonders that entrance. In the Valtellina Valley you will sit in grottoes where the caesars sat to soak in hot mineral springs, and you will feel the curing effects of waters that were said to ease the pain of gout, arthritis, and politics. You can indulge in the mindless delights of the Amalfi Coast exactly as 19th-century English travelers did when they came to rest their minds, weary from the obligatory acquisition of culture in the north. Here, where rocky cliffs are caught in a perpetual dive to the sea, nothing seems more important than tonight's dinner or lovemaking.

Italy may be the most sensual of countries. Perhaps it is the basic simplicity that returns one to the simplest human emotions: the organic nature of all that surrounds you, each century seeming to grow from the land. Or perhaps it is the heightened sense of romance that comes from the constant reminders of the very best of which people are capable; the serenity of Bellini's altarpiece in San Zaccaria, the compassion of Michelangelo's Pietà in St. Peter's, the symmetry of a Palladian villa rising from the earth of the Veneto. Or it could be living among people for whom life's pleasures are celebrated rather than guiltily indulged.

Whatever it is, to experience Italy one needs time, not necessarily in days but in solitude. It is in the silent times that Italy will be revealed to you. Early morning, watching the light shine on the Pantheon, while strong Italian coffee wakens your senses. Dawn on the Grand Canal as dark green water is sprayed with gold and the only sound is a gondolier's oar breaking the silent surface. Midnight in the Forum, Daisy Miller's undoing and

Byron's inspiration. Sunrise in Stelvio National Park, where eagles soar overhead and you are knee-deep in wildflowers.

And one must believe in that elusive commodity, happiness. This is a country that, through the ages, in fact and fiction, has promised that possibility. Goethe, having fled the restrictive court life of Weimar, wrote from Rome in September 1788: "I can honestly say I have never been so happy in my life as now." And in *Room with a View*, Forster observed that when his young provincial heroine, Lucy, finally dared forfeit her Baedeker for experience, "then the pernicious charm of Italy worked on her, and, instead of acquiring information, she began to be happy."

You, too, should relinquish this book from time to time and observe with an uninstructed eye, drift into the dream, and allow yourself to be charmed.

1 Essential Information

Before You Go

Government Tourist Offices

In the United States Contact the Italian Government Travel Office at 630 5th Avenue, Suite 1565, New York, NY 10111, tel. 212/245–4822, fax 212/586–9249; 500 N. Michigan Avenue, Chicago, IL 60611, tel. 312/644–0990, fax 312/644–3019; 12400 Wilshire Boulevard., Suite 550, Los Angeles, CA 90025, tel. 310/820–0098, fax 310/820–6357.

U.S. Government Travel Briefings The U.S. Department of State's **Overseas Citizens Emergency Center** (Room 4811, Washington, DC 20520; enclose S.A.S.E.) issues Consular Information Sheets, which cover crime, security, political climate, and health risks, as well as embassy locations, entry requirements, currency regulations, and other routine matters. For the latest information, stop in at any U.S. passport office, consulate, or embassy; call the interactive hotline (tel. 202/647–5225; fax 202/647–3000); or, with your PC's modem, tap into the Bureau of Consular Affairs' computer bulletin board (tel. 202/647–9225).

In Canada 1 Place Ville Marie, Montreal, Quebec H3B 3M9, tel. 514/866–7667.

In the United Kingdom 1 Princes Street, London W1R 8AY England, tel. 071/408–1254.

Tours and Packages

Should you buy your travel arrangements to Italy already packaged or should you do it yourself? There are advantages either way. You can save money by buying a package, particularly if you find one that includes exactly what you want, and you will have a pretty good idea what your trip will cost from the outset. As to most destinations, packages to Italy come in two forms: fully escorted tours and independent packages. Escorted tours are generally the most hassle-free way to see a country, as well as generally the least expensive. Taking a tour means traveling with strangers, most often via motorcoach, with a tour director in charge. Your baggage is handled, your time rigorously scheduled, and most meals are planned. Independent packages allow flexibility. They generally include airline travel and hotels, with other options available, such as sightseeing, car rental, and excursions. They are usually more expensive than escorted tours, but your time is your own.

Travel agents are the best source of information for both tours and independent packages. They should have a large selection available, and the cost to you is the same as buying direct. Whatever program you ultimately choose, be sure to find out exactly what is included: taxes, tips, transfers, meals, baggage handling, ground transportation, entertainment, excursions, sports, or recreation (and rental equipment if necessary). Ask about the level of hotel used, its location, the size of its rooms, the kind of beds, and amenities such as pools, room service, or programs for children, if they're important to you. Find out the operator's cancellation penalties. Nearly everyone charges them and the only way to avoid them is to buy trip-cancellation insurance (*see* Trip Insurance, *below*). Also ask about the single supplement, a surcharge assessed to solo travelers. Some operators do not make you pay it if you agree to be matched with a roommate of the same sex, even if one is not found by departure time. Remember that a program that has features you won't use, whether for rental sporting equipment or discounted museum admissions, may not be the most cost-wise choice for you. Don't buy a Rolls-Royce, even at a reduced price, if all you want is a Chevy!

Fully Escorted Tours Escorted tours are usually sold in three categories: deluxe, first-class, and tourist or budget class. The most important differences are the price, of course, and the level of accommodations. Some operators specialize in one category, while others offer a range.

In the deluxe category, try **Maupintour** (Box 807, Lawrence, KS 66044, tel. 800/255–4266 or 913/843–1211) or **Tauck Tours** (11 Wilton Rd., Westport, CT 06881, tel. 800/468–2825 or 203/226–6911). In the first-class category, which has the broadest selection of tours, offerings include **Brendan Tours** (15137 Califa St., Van Nuys, CA 91411, tel. 818/785–9696 or 800/421–8446), **Caravan** (401 N. Michigan Ave., Chicago, IL 60611, tel. 800/227–2826), **Central Holiday Tours** (206 Central Ave., Jersey City, NJ 07307, tel. 800/935–5000 or 201/798–5777), **Certified Vacations** (Box 1525, Ft. Lauderdale, FL 33302, tel. 305/522–1414 or 800/233–7260), **CIT Tours Corp.** (342 Madison Ave., Suite 207, New York, NY 10173, tel. 212/697–2100 or 800/248–8687; 310/670–4269 or 800/248–7245 in western U.S.), **Donna Franca Tours** (470 Commonwealth Ave., Boston, MA 02215, tel. 800/225–6290 or 617/227–3111), **Globus** (5301 S. Federal Circle, Littleton, CO 80123, tel. 303/797–2800 or 800/221–0090), **Trafalgar Tours** (21 E. 26th St., New York, NY 10010, tel. 800/854–0103 or 212/689–8977), and **Travcoa** (Box 2630, Newport Beach, CA 92658, tel. 714/476–2800 or 800/992–2003). Escorted programs from **Perillo Tours** (577 Chestnut Ridge Rd., Woodcliff Lake, NJ 07675, tel. 800/431–1515 and 201/307–1234), particularly those that feature as many as four nights in one city, have some flexibility. Budget offerings include programs from **AESU Travel** (2 Hamill Rd., Suite 248, Baltimore, MD 21210, tel. 410/323–4416 or 800/638–7640), **Cosmos Tourama**, a sister company of **Globus** (*see above*), and the "Cost Savers" of **Trafalgar Tours** (*see above*).

Most itineraries are jam-packed with sightseeing, so you see a lot in a short amount of time (usually one place per day). To judge just how fast-paced the tour is, review the itinerary carefully. If you are in a different hotel each night, you will be getting up early each day to head out, travel to your next destination, do some sightseeing, have dinner, and go to bed, then you'll start all over again. If you want some free time, make sure it's mentioned in the tour brochure; if you want to be escorted to every meal, confirm that any tour you consider does that. Also, when comparing programs, be sure to find out if the motorcoach is air-conditioned and has a rest room on board. Make your choice based on price and stops on the itinerary.

Independent Packages Independent packages, which travel agents call FITS (for foreign independent travel), are offered by airlines, tour operators who may also do escorted programs, and any number of other companies from large, established firms to small, new entrepreneurs. Among the many programs with a wide choice of hotels and sightseeing options, some with car rentals, are **Abercrombie & Kent** (1520 Kensington Rd., Oak Brook, IL 60521, tel. 708/954–2944 or 800/323–7308), **American Airlines Fly AAway Vacations** (tel. 800/321–2121), **Certified Vacations** (*see above*), **CIT Tours** (tel. 800/248–8687), **Continental's Grand Destinations** (tel. 800/634–5555), **DER Tours** (11933 Wilshire Blvd., Los Angeles, CA 90025, tel. 800/782–2424 or 310/479–4140), **Italiatour** (tel. 800/237–0517), **TWA Getaway Vacations** (tel. 800/438–2929), **United Airlines' Vacation Planning Center** (tel. 800/328–6877), and **V E Tours** (1150 N.W. 72nd Ave., Suite 450, Miami, FL 33126, tel. 800/222–8383).

These programs come in a wide range of prices based on levels of luxury and options—in addition to hotel and airfare, sightseeing, car rental, transfers, admission to local attractions, and other extras may be offered. Again, base your choice on what's available at your budget for the destinations you want to visit.

Special-Interest Travel Italy caters to the special-interest traveler, particularly if your special interest is eating well. But everything from ballooning to biking is also available. Special-interest programs may be fully escorted or independent. Some require a certain amount of expertise, but most are for the average traveler with an interest in the subject, and they are usually hosted by experts. When the program is escorted, it enjoys the advantages and disadvantages of all escorted programs; because your fellow travelers are apt to be passionate or knowledgeable about the subject, they can prove as enjoyable a part of your travel experience as the destination itself. The price range is wide, but the cost is usually higher—sometimes a lot higher—than for ordinary escorted tours and packages, because of the expert guiding and special activities.

Adventure **Mountain Travel Sobek** (6420 Fairmount Ave., El Cerrito, CA 94530, tel. 510/527–8100 or 800/227–2384) and **Wilderness Travel** (801 Allston Way, Berkeley, CA 94710, tel. 510/548–0420 or 800/368–2794) take you on hiking tours from the medieval hill towns of Tuscany, off the beaten path in Piemonte or the island of Elba, or to the spectacular Dolomites circuit. If you prefer wheels, try **World Motorcycle Tours** (14 Forest Ave., Caldwell, NJ 07006, tel. 201/226–9107 or 800/443–7519) for guided motorcycle or car tours of the Alpine region.

Art and Architecture **Amelia Tours** (280 Old Country Rd., Hicksville, NY 11801, tel. 516/433–0696 or 800/742–4591) and **Archaeological Tours** (271 Madison Ave., New York, NY 10016, tel. 212/986–3054) have art and archaeological tours of southern Italy and Sicily. **Earthwatch** (680 Mt. Auburn St., Watertown, MA 02272, tel. 617/926–8000) recruits volunteers to serve in its EarthCorps as short-term assistants to scientists on research expeditions. **Esplanade Tours** (581 Boylston St., Boston, MA 02116, tel. 617/266–7465 or 800/426–5492) has art-treasure tours and cruises with guest lectures.

Ballooning **Buddy Bombard Balloon Adventures** (6727 Curran St., McLean, VA 22101–3804, tel. 703/448–9407 or 800/862–8537) include fine meals and accommodations and trips aloft for breathtaking views of the Italian countryside.

Biking **Backroads** (1516 5th St., Suite Q333, Berkeley, CA 94710–1740, tel. 510/527–1555 or 800/245–3874) has trips for all levels of ability, with inn accommodations and a sag wagon just in case the hills are too much for you.

Gardens **Coopersmith's England** (6441 Valley View Rd., Oakland, CA 94611, tel. 510/339–2499) spends an "Enchanted June" visiting the floral delights of Venice and the lake region. **Endless Beginnings** (9825 Dowdy Dr., Suite 105, San Diego, CA 92126, tel. 619/566–4166 or 800/822–7855) visits gardens and villas around Rome and Tuscany.

Horseback Riding **FITS Equestrian** (685 Lateen Rd., Solvang, CA 93463, tel. 805/688–9494 or 800/666–3487) has a trio of "City Slickers Go Italian" tours.

Music **Dailey-Thorp Travel** (330 W. 58th St., New York, NY 10019, tel. 212/307–1555), a performing arts specialist, offers music and opera tours to Italy. **Mozart's Europe** (Deer La., Pawlet, VT, tel. 802/325–3656) traces the composer's footsteps on tours featuring concerts and festivals, including the Rovereto Mozart Festival. **Smolka Tours** (Box 856, Frederick, MD 21705, tel. 301/695–3661 or 800/722–0057) has a summer Italian opera, concert, and music festivals tour.

Pilgrimages **Pilgrimage Tours and Travel** (39 Beechwood Ave., Manhasset, NY 11030, tel. 516/627–2636 or 800/669–0757) arranges pilgrimages to the shrines of Rome, Lanciano, Loreto, Assisi, and San Giovanni.

Shopping **Serious Shoppers** (5402 Silva Ave., El Cerrito, CA 94530, tel. 510/215–1534) has fully escorted tours visiting stores, factory outlets, and clearance houses in and around Milan.

Wine and Food **Donna Franca Tours** (*see above*) has a strong Italian cooking program in Venice, and **Amelia Tours** (*see* Art and Architecture, *above*), a Sicily specialist, has a wine tour of the island. **Diana Folonari** (E&M Assoc., 211 E. 43rd St., New York, NY 10017, tel. 212/599–8280 or 800/223–9832) gives Italian country cooking classes at the Resort Center in Positano. **Hazan Classics** (Box 285, Circleville, NY 10919, tel. 914/692–7104) are master classes in Italian food and wine held at a 16th-century Venetian palazzo several times a year by the much-in-demand Marcella Hazan.

When to Go

The main tourist season runs from mid-April to the end of September. The best months for sightseeing are April, May, June, September, and October, when the weather is generally pleasant and not too hot. The hottest months are July and August, when brief afternoon thunderstorms are common in inland areas. Winters are relatively mild in most places on the main tourist circuit but always include some rainy spells. In general, the northern half of the peninsula and the entire Adriatic Coast, with the exception of Apulia, are rainier than the rest of Italy.

Foreign tourists crowd the major art cities at Easter, when Italians flock to resorts and to the country. From March through May, bus loads of eager schoolchildren on excursions take cities of artistic and historical interest by storm.

If you can avoid it, don't travel at all in Italy in August, when much of the population is on the move. The heat can be oppressive, and vacationing Italians cram roads, trains, and planes on their way to shore and mountain resorts. All this is especially true around Ferragosto, the August 15 national holiday, when cities such as Rome and Milan are deserted and many restaurants and shops are closed. Except for a few year-round resorts, such as Taormina and some towns on the Italian Riviera, coastal resorts usually close up tight from October or November to April; they're at their best in June and September, when everything is open but uncrowded.

Major cities, such as Rome, Florence, and Milan, have no official off-season as far as hotel rates go, though some hotels will reduce rates during the slack season upon request. Always inquire about special rates. You can save considerably on hotel rooms in Venice and in such resorts as Sorrento and Capri during their off-seasons.

You may want to plan your trip to take in some spectacular local *festa* (festival) or to satisfy a special interest—in opera, food, or wine, for instance. From May through September the calendar is dotted with local folkloric festivals and other special events; outdoor music and opera festivals are held mainly in July and August (*see* Festivals and Seasonal Events, *below*).

Climate The following are average daily maximum and minimum temperatures for Italy.

Milan	**Jan.**	40F	5C	**May**	74F	23C	**Sept.**	75F	24C
		32	0		57	14		61	16
	Feb.	46F	8C	**June**	80F	27C	**Oct.**	63F	17C
		35	2		63	17		52	11
	Mar.	56F	13C	**July**	84F	29C	**Nov.**	51F	10C
		43	6		67	20		43	6
	Apr.	65F	18C	**Aug.**	82F	28C	**Dec.**	43F	6C
		49	10		66	19		35	2

Rome	**Jan.**	52F	11C	**May**	74F	23C	**Sept.**	79F	26C
		40	5		56	13		62	17
	Feb.	55F	13C	**June**	82F	28C	**Oct.**	71F	22C
		42	6		63	17		55	13
	Mar.	59F	15C	**July**	87F	30C	**Nov.**	61F	16C
		45	7		67	20		49	10
	Apr.	66F	19C	**Aug.**	86F	30C	**Dec.**	55F	13C
		50	10		67	20		44	6

Venice	**Jan.**	42F	6C	**May**	70F	21C	**Sept.**	75F	24C
		33	1		56	13		61	16
	Feb.	46F	8C	**June**	76F	25C	**Oct.**	65F	19C
		35	2		63	17		53	12
	Mar.	53F	12C	**July**	81F	27C	**Nov.**	53F	12C
		41	5		66	19		44	7
	Apr.	62F	17C	**Aug.**	80F	27C	**Dec.**	46F	8C
		49	10		65	19		37	3

Information Sources For current weather conditions and forecasts for cities in the United States and abroad, plus the local time and helpful travel tips, call the **Weather Channel Connection** (tel. 900/932–8437; 95¢ per minute) from a touch-tone phone.

Festivals and Seasonal Events

Italy's top seasonal events are listed below, and any one of them could provide the stuff of lasting memories. Contact the **Italian Government Travel Office** for exact dates and further information.

January 5–6 **Epiphany Celebrations.** Roman Catholic Epiphany celebrations and decorations are evident throughout Italy. Notable is the Epiphany Fair at Piazza Navona in Rome.

February **Carnival in Viareggio.** Masked pageants, fireworks, a flower show, and parades are among the festivities along the Tuscan Riviera.
Carnival in Ivrea, near Turin. Three days of folklore, costumes, and parades, culminating in the Battle of the Oranges, with real fruit flying through the air.

Early February **Almond Blossom Festival** in Agrigento. A week of folk music and dancing, with groups from many countries, in the Valley of the Temples.
Carnival in Venice. A big do in the 18th century, revived in the last half of the 20th century, this includes plays, masked balls, fireworks, and indoor and outdoor happenings of every sort.

Good Friday (April 14, 1995) In Rome, a torchlit nighttime **Good Friday Procession** led by the Pope winds from the Colosseum past the Forum and up the Palatine Hill.

Easter Sunday (April 16, 1995)	The **Scoppio del Carro,** or "Explosion of the Cart," in Florence, is a cartful of fireworks in the Cathedral Square, set off by a mechanical dove released from the altar during High Mass.
Late April– Early July	The **Florence May Music Festival** is the oldest and most prestigious Italian festival of the performing arts.
May 1	The **Feast of Sant'Efisio** in Cagliari sees a procession of marchers and others in splendid Sardinian costume.
Mid-May	**Race of the Candles.** This procession, in local costume, leads to the top of Mount Ingino in Gubbio.
May 20	**Sardinian Cavalcade.** A traditional procession of more than 3,000 people in Sardinian costumes makes its way through Sassari.
Late May	The **Palio of the Archers** is a medieval crossbow contest in Gubbio.
Early June	The **Battle of the Bridge,** in Pisa, is a medieval parade and contest. The **Flower Festival,** in Genzano (Rome), is a religious procession along streets carpeted with flowers in magnificent designs. The **Regatta of the Great Maritime Republics** sees keen competition among the four former maritime republics—Amalfi, Genoa, Pisa, and Venice.
Late June	**Soccer Games in 16th-Century Costume,** in Florence, commemorate a match played in 1530. Festivities include fireworks displays.
Late June– Early July	The **Festival of Two Worlds,** in Spoleto, is a famous performing-arts festival.
June and July	The **Summer Operetta Festival** is held in Trieste.
Early July and Mid-August	The **Palio Horse Race,** in Siena, is a colorful bareback horse race with participants competing for the *palio* (banner).
Early July– Late August	The **Arena of Verona Outdoor Opera Season** heralds spectacular productions in the 22,000-seat Roman amphitheater of Verona.
Mid-July	The **Feast of the Redeemer** is a procession of gondolas and other craft, commemorating the end of the epidemic of 1575 in Venice. The fireworks over the lagoon are spectacular.
Early August	The **Joust of the Quintana** is a historical pageant in Ascoli Piceno.
Late August– Early September	The **Siena Music Week** features opera, concerts, and chamber music. The **Venice Film Festival,** oldest of the international film festivals, takes place mostly on the Lido.
Late August– Mid-September	The **Stresa Musical Weeks** comprise a series of concerts and recitals in Stresa.
Early September	The **Historic Regatta** includes a traditional competition between two-oar gondolas in Venice. The **Joust of the Saracen** is a tilting contest with knights in 13th-century armor in Arezzo.
Mid-September	The **Joust of the Quintana** is a 17th-century-style joust and historical procession in Foligno.
Early October	Alba's **100 Towers Tournament** features costumes and races and is held simultaneously with the **Truffle Fair,** a food fair centered on the white truffle.
October 4	The **Feast of St. Francis** is celebrated in Assisi, his birthplace.
Early December	The **Feast of St. Ambrose,** in Milan, officially opens La Scala Opera House.

| December–June | The **Opera Season** is in full swing at La Scala in Milan and elsewhere, notably in Turin, Rome, Naples, Parma, and Genoa. |

What to Pack

Clothing The weather is considerably milder in Italy all year round than it is in the north and central United States or Great Britain. In summer, stick with clothing that's as light as possible, although a sweater or woolen stole may be necessary in the cool of the evening, even during the hot months. Brief summer afternoon thunderstorms are common in Rome and inland cities, so carry a folding umbrella. And if you go into the mountains, you will find the evenings there quite chilly. During the winter a medium-weight coat and a raincoat will stand you in good stead in Rome and farther south. Northern Italy calls for heavier clothes, gloves, hats, and boots. Even in Rome and other milder areas, central heating may not be up to your standards and interiors can be cold and damp; take wools rather than sheer fabrics, flannel rather than flimsy nightwear, and boots or shoes that can accommodate socks rather than dainty pumps. As a matter of fact, pack sturdy walking shoes, preferably with crepe or rubber soles, at any time of the year, because cobblestone streets and gravel paths are common and can be murder on both feet and footwear.

In general, Italians dress well and are not sloppy. They do not usually wear shorts in the city, unless longish bermudas happen to be in fashion. Even when dressed casually or informally, they are careful about the way they look, which is why so few restaurants establish dress codes. Men aren't required to wear ties or jackets anywhere, except in some of the grander hotel dining rooms and top-level restaurants. Formal wear is the exception rather than the rule at the opera nowadays, though people in expensive seats usually do get dressed up.

Dress codes are strict for visits to churches—especially St. Peter's in Rome and St. Mark's in Venice—and to the Vatican Museums. Women must cover bare shoulders and arms—a shawl will do—but no longer need cover their heads. Shorts are taboo for both men and women. For the huge general papal audiences, no rules of dress apply other than those of common sense. For other types of audience, the Vatican Information Office will give requirements.

Miscellaneous To protect yourself against purse snatchers and pickpockets, take a handbag with long straps that you can sling across your body bandolier-style and with a zippered compartment for your money and other valuables. Better yet, wear a money belt. Take your own soap if you stay in budget hotels. Many do not provide soap or else give guests only one tiny bar per room. Also, travel with a wash cloth, or face flannel, if you use one; Italian hotels generally supply only towels. Bring an extra pair of eyeglasses or contact lenses in your carry-on luggage. If you have a health problem that requires a prescription drug, pack enough to last the duration of the trip or have your doctor write a prescription using the drug's generic name, because brand names vary from country to country. Always carry prescription drugs in their original packaging to avoid problems with customs officials. Don't pack them in luggage that you plan to check, in case your bags go astray. Pack a list of the offices that supply refunds for lost or stolen traveler's checks.

Electricity The electrical current in most of Italy is 220 volts, 50 cycles alternating current (AC); the United States runs on 110-volt, 60-cycle AC current. Unlike wall outlets in the United States, which accept plugs that have two flat prongs, Italian outlets take Continental-type plugs, with two round prongs.

Adapters, To use U.S.-made electric appliances abroad, you'll need an adapter
Converters, plug. Unless the appliance is dual-voltage and made for travel, you'll
Transformers also need a converter. Hotels sometimes have 110-volt outlets for low-wattage appliances (marked "For Shavers Only") near the sink; don't use them for a high-wattage appliance like a blowdryer. If you're traveling with an older laptop computer, carry a transformer. New laptop computers are auto-sensing, operating equally well on 110 and 220 volts, so you need only the appropriate adapter plug. For a copy of the free brochure "Foreign Electricity is No Deep Dark Secret," send a stamped, self-addressed envelope to adapter-converter manufacturer Franzus Company (Customer Service, Dept. B50, Murtha Industrial Park, Box 142, Beacon Falls, CT 06403, tel. 203/723–6664).

Luggage Free airline baggage allowances depend on the airline, the route,
Regulations and the class of your ticket; ask in advance. In general, on domestic flights and on international flights between the United States and foreign destinations, you are entitled to check two bags—neither exceeding 62 inches, or 158 centimeters (length + width + height), or weighing more than 70 pounds (32 kilograms). A third piece may be brought aboard as a carryon; its total dimensions are generally limited to less than 45 inches (114 centimeters), so it will fit easily under the seat in front of you or in the overhead compartment. In the United States, the Federal Aviation Administration (FAA) gives airlines broad latitude to limit carry-on allowances and tailor them to different aircraft and operational conditions. Charges for excess, oversize, or overweight pieces vary, so inquire before you pack.

If you are flying between two foreign destinations, note that baggage allowances may be determined not by the piece method but by the weight method, which generally allows 88 pounds (40 kilograms) of luggage in first class, 66 pounds (30 kilograms) in business class, and 44 pounds (20 kilograms) in economy. If your flight between two cities abroad *connects* with your transatlantic flight, the piece method still applies.

Safeguarding Before leaving home, itemize your bags' contents and their worth in
Your Luggage case they go astray. To minimize that risk, tag them inside and out with your name, address, and phone number. (If you use your home address, cover it so that potential thieves can't see it.) Put a copy of your itinerary inside each bag, so that you can easily be tracked. At check-in, make sure that the tag attached by baggage handlers bears the correct three-letter code for your destination. If your bags do not arrive with you, or if you detect damage, immediately file a written report with the airline before you leave the airport.

Taking Money Abroad

Traveler's Traveler's checks are preferable in metropolitan centers, although
Checks you'll need cash in rural areas and small towns. The most widely recognized are **American Express, Citicorp, Diners Club, Thomas Cook,** and **Visa,** which are sold by major commercial banks. Both American Express and Thomas Cook issue checks that can be counter-signed and used by you or your traveling companion. Typically the issuing company or the bank at which you make your purchase charges 1% to 3% of the checks' face value as a fee. Some foreign banks charge as much as 20% of the face value as the fee for cashing traveler's checks in a foreign currency. Buy a few checks in small denominations to cash toward the end of your trip, so you won't be left with excess

foreign currency. Record the numbers of checks as you spend them, and keep this list separate from the checks.

Currency Exchange Banks offer the most favorable exchange rates. If you use currency-exchange booths at airports, rail and bus stations, hotels, stores, and privately run exchange firms, you'll typically get less favorable rates, but you may find the hours more convenient.

You can get good rates and avoid long lines at airport currency-exchange booths by getting a small amount of currency at **Thomas Cook Currency Services** (630 5th Ave., New York, NY 10111, tel. 212/757–6915 or 800/223–7373 for locations in major metropolitan areas throughout the U.S.) or **Ruesch International** (tel. 800/424–2923 for locations) before you depart. Check with your travel agent to be sure that the currency of the country you will be visiting can be imported.

Getting Money from Home

Cash Machines Many automated-teller machines (ATMs) are tied to international networks such as **Cirrus** and **Plus**. You can use your bank card at ATMs away from home to withdraw money from an account and get cash advances on a credit-card account if your card has been programmed with a personal identification number, or PIN. Check in advance on limits on withdrawals and cash advances within specified periods. Ask whether your bank-card or credit-card PIN will need to be reprogrammed for use in the area you'll be visiting. Four digits are commonly used overseas. Note that Discover is accepted only in the United States. On cash advances you are charged interest from the day you receive the money from ATMs as well as from tellers. Although transaction fees for ATM withdrawals abroad may be higher than fees for withdrawals at home, Cirrus and Plus exchange rates are excellent, because they are based on wholesale rates only offered by major banks.

Plan ahead: Obtain ATM locations and the names of affiliated cash-machine networks before departure. For specific foreign Cirrus locations, call 800/424–7787; for foreign Plus locations, consult the Plus directory at your local bank.

Wiring Money You don't have to be a cardholder to send or receive a **MoneyGram from American Express** for up to $10,000. Go to a MoneyGram agent in retail and convenience stores and American Express travel offices, pay up to $1,000 with a credit card and anything over that in cash. You are allowed a free long-distance call to give the transaction code to your intended recipient, who needs only present identification and the reference number to the nearest MoneyGram agent to pick up the cash. MoneyGram agents are in more than 70 countries (call 800/926–9400 for locations). Fees range from 3% to 10%, depending on the amount and how you pay.

You can also use **Western Union.** To wire money, take either cash or a cashier's check to the nearest office or call and use your MasterCard or Visa. Money sent from the United States or Canada will be available for pick up at agent locations in Italy within minutes. Once the money is in the system it can be picked up at *any* one of 22,000 locations (call 800/325–6000 for the one nearest you).

Currency

The unit of currency in Italy is the lira. There are bills of 100,000, 10,000, 5,000, 2,000, and 1,000 lire. Coins are 500, 200, 100, 50, 20, and 10, but the last two are rarely found, and prices are often rounded out to the nearest 50 lire. At press time (June 1994) the exchange rate was about 1,595 lire to the U.S. dollar, 1,157 lire to the Canadian dollar, and 2,402 lire to the pound sterling.

What It Will Cost

Italy's prices are in line with those in the rest of Europe, with costs in its main cities comparable to those in other major capitals, such as Paris and London. The days when the country's high-quality attractions came with a comparatively low Mediterranean price tag are long gone. With the cost of labor and social benefits rising and an economy struggling to emerge from recession, Italy is therefore not a bargain, but there is an effort to hold the line on hotel and restaurant prices that had become inordinately expensive by U.S. standards. Depending on season and occupancy, you may be able to obtain unadvertised lower rates in hotels; always inquire. Among major cities, Venice and Milan are the most expensive; resorts such as the Costa Smeralda, Portofino, and Cortina d'Ampezzo cater to the rich and famous and charge top prices. Though Capri is generally considered a millionaire's playground, it can accommodate the less affluent also. Everywhere in Italy, if you want the luxury of four- and five-star hotels, be prepared to pay top rates.

As in most countries, prices vary from region to region and are a bit lower in the countryside than in the cities. Good value for the money can be had in the scenic Trentino–Alto Adige region and in the Dolomites, in Umbria and the Marches, and on the Amalfi Coast. With a few exceptions, southern Italy, Sicily, and Sardinia also offer good values, but hotels are not always up to par.

When you make hotel reservations, ask explicitly whether breakfast is included in the rate. By law, breakfast is optional, but some hotels pressure guests to eat breakfast on the premises—and then charge a whopping amount for it. Find out what breakfast will cost at the time you book, or at least when you check in, and if it seems high, avoid misunderstanding by clearly stating that you want a room without breakfast.

Taxes
Both U.S. and Italian airport departure taxes are charged on a U.S.–Italy round-trip by air; these and other fees, such as a U.S. Customs users fee, are added to the total you pay when you buy the ticket. The Value-Added Tax (VAT, or IVA in Italy) is a sales tax levied in European Community countries; the amount varies from country to country, and also within a country depending on the nature of the goods or services. In Italy the amount is 12% on clothing and shoes, 19% on luxuries. On most consumer goods, it is already included in the amount shown on the price tag, whereas on services, it may not be. The 9% IVA is generally included in the price quoted for hotel rooms, but some five-star hotels quote rates that are *not* inclusive of the 13% IVA applicable to the luxury category; the 19% IVA on car rentals is also usually an extra charge, added when you settle the bill. The IVA paid on consumer goods can be refunded to travelers in some cases (*see* Shopping in Staying in Italy, *below*).

A service charge of approximately 15% is added to all restaurant bills; in some cases the menu may state that the service charge is already included in the menu prices. A similar service charge applies to hotels and is included in the rates quoted.

Sample Prices These sample prices are meant only as a general guide.

Admission to the Vatican Museums: 13,000 lire; the Uffizi Gallery: 10,000 lire

Inexpensive hotel room for two, including breakfast, in Rome: 140,000 lire (Margutta)

Inexpensive Rome dinner: 35,000 lire (Polese)

Cheapest seat at Rome's Opera House: 26,000 lire

Coca-Cola (standing) at a café: 2,200 lire

Cup of coffee: 1,100 to 1,400 lire

Bowl of pasta: 11,000 lire

Cover charge in an inexpensive restaurant: 2,000 lire

½ liter carafe of house wine: 4,000 lire

Rome taxi ride (1 mile): 10,000 lire

McDonald's Big Mac in Rome: 4,500 lire

Entrance to a Milan disco: 35,000 lire

Movie ticket: 10,000 lire

Daily English-language newspaper: 2,400 lire

Pint of beer in a pub: 7,000 lire

Rosticceria lunch: 14,000 lire (Il Delfino, Rome)

Round-trip train (IC) from Rome to Florence: 62,600 lire

Long-Distance Calling

AT&T, MCI, and Sprint have several services that make calling home or the office more affordable and convenient when you're on the road. Use one of them to avoid pricey hotel surcharges. **AT&T Calling Card** (tel. 800/225–5288) and the **AT&T Universal Card** (tel. 800/662–7759) give you access to the service. With **AT&T's USADirect** (tel. 800/874–4000 for codes in the countries you'll be visiting) you can reach an AT&T operator with a local or toll-free call. **MCI's Call USA** (MCI Customer Service, tel. 800/444–4444) allows that service from 85 countries or from country to country via MCI WorldReach. **Sprint Express** (tel. 800/793–1153) has a toll-free number travelers abroad can dial to reach a Sprint operator in the United States.

Passports and Visas

If your passport is lost or stolen abroad, report the loss immediately to the nearest embassy or consulate and to the local police. If you can provide the consular officer with the information contained in the passport, he or she will usually be able to issue you a new passport promptly. For this reason, keep a photocopy of the data page of your passport separate from your money and traveler's checks. Also leave a photocopy with a relative or friend at home.

U.S. Citizens All U.S. citizens, even infants, need a valid passport to enter Italy for stays of up to three months. You can pick up new and renewal application forms at any of the 13 U.S. Passport Agency offices and at some post offices and courthouses. Although passports are usually mailed within four weeks of your application's receipt, allow five weeks or more from April through summer. Call the Department of

State Office of Passport Services' information line (tel. 202/647–0518) for fees, documentation requirements, and other details.

Canadian Citizens Canadian citizens need a valid passport to enter Italy for stays of up to three months; check with the nearest Italian consulate regarding longer stays. Application forms are available at 23 regional passport offices as well as post offices and travel agencies. Whether for a first or subsequent passport, you must apply in person. Children under 16 may be included on a parent's passport but must have their own to travel alone. Passports are valid for five years and are usually mailed within two weeks of an application's receipt. For more information in English or French, call the passport office (tel. 514/283–2152 or 800/567–6868).

U.K. Citizens Citizens of the United Kingdom need a valid passport to enter Italy for purposes of tourism. Applications for new and renewal passports are available from main post offices as well as at the six passport offices, located in Belfast, Glasgow, Liverpool, London, Newport, and Peterborough. You may apply in person at all passport offices, or by mail to all except the London office. Children under 16 may travel on an accompanying parent's passport. All passports are valid for 10 years. Allow a month for processing.

A British Visitor's Passport is valid for holidays and some business trips of up to three months to Italy. It can include both partners of a married couple. Valid for one year, it will be issued on the same day that you apply. You must apply in person at a main post office.

Customs and Duties

On Arrival There are two levels of duty-free allowances for visitors to Italy.

For goods obtained anywhere outside the EU or for goods purchased in a duty-free shop within an EU country, the allowances are: (1) 200 cigarettes or 100 cigarillos or 50 cigars or 250 grams of tobacco; (2) 2 liters of still table wine plus (3) 1 liter of spirits over 22% volume or 2 liters of spirits under 22% volume (fortified and sparkling wines); and (4) 60 milliliters of perfume and 250 milliliters of toilet water.

For goods obtained (duty and tax paid) within another EU country, the allowances are: (1) 300 cigarettes or 150 cigarillos or 75 cigars or 400 grams of tobacco; (2) 5 liters of still table wine plus (3) 1.5 liters of spirits over 22% volume or 5 liters of spirits under 22% volume (fortified or sparkling wines) or 3 more liters of table wine; and (4) 75 milliliters of perfume and 375 milliliters of toilet water.

Other items including cameras and films can be brought in duty-free up to a value of £136 for non-EU citizens, £71 for EU citizens. Officially, two still cameras with 10 rolls of film each and one movie camera with 10 rolls of film may be brought in duty-free. Other items intended for personal use are generally admitted, as long as the quantities are reasonable.

Returning Home
U.S. Customs Provided you've been out of the U.S. for at least 48 hours and haven't already used the exemption, or any part of it, in the past 30 days, you may bring home $400 worth of foreign goods duty-free. So can each member of your family, regardless of age; and your exemptions may be pooled, so that one of you can bring in more if another brings in less. A flat 10% duty applies to the next $1,000 of goods; above $1,400, the rate varies with the merchandise. (If the 48-hour or 30-day limits apply, your duty-free allowance drops to $25, which may *not* be pooled.)

Travelers 21 or older may bring back one liter of alcohol duty-free, provided the beverage laws of the state through which they reenter the U.S. allow it. In addition, 100 non-Cuban cigars and 200 cigarettes are allowed, regardless of age. Antiques and works of art over 100 years old are duty-free.

Gifts valued at less than $50 may be mailed to the United States duty-free, with a limit of one package per day per addressee, and do not count as part of your exemption (do not send alcohol or tobacco products or perfume valued at more than $5); mark the package "Unsolicited Gift" and write the nature of the gift and its retail value on the outside. Most reputable stores will handle the mailing for you.

For a copy of "Know Before You Go," a free brochure detailing what you may and may not bring back to the United States, rates of duty, and other pointers, contact the **U.S. Customs Service** (Box 7407, Washington, DC 20044, tel. 202/927–6724).

Canadian Once per calendar year, when you've been out of Canada for at least
Customs seven days, you may bring in C$300 worth of goods duty-free. If you've been away less than seven days but more than 48 hours, the duty-free exemption drops to C$100 but can be claimed any number of times (as can a C$20 duty-free exemption for absences of 24 hours or more). You cannot combine the yearly and 48-hour exemptions, use the C$300 exemption only partially (to save the balance for a later trip), or pool exemptions with family members. Goods claimed under the C$300 exemption may follow you by mail; those claimed under the lesser exemptions must accompany you on your return.

Alcohol and tobacco products may be included in the yearly and 48-hour exemptions but not in the 24-hour exemption. If you meet the age requirements of the province through which you reenter Canada, you may bring in, duty-free, 1.14 liters (40 imperial ounces) of wine or liquor *or* two dozen 12-ounce cans or bottles of beer or ale. If you are 16 or older, you may bring in, duty-free, 200 cigarettes, 50 cigars or cigarillos, and 400 tobacco sticks or 400 grams of manufactured tobacco. Alcohol and tobacco must accompany you on your return.

An unlimited number of gifts valued up to C$60 each may be mailed to Canada duty-free. These do not count as part of your exemption. Label the package "Unsolicited Gift—Value under $60." Alcohol and tobacco are excluded.

For more information, including details of duties on items that exceed your duty-free limit, ask the Revenue Canada Customs and Excise Department (2265 St. Laurent Blvd. S, Ottawa, Ont., K1G 4K3, tel. 613/957–0275) for a copy of the free brochure "I Declare/Je Déclare."

U.K. Customs If your journey was wholly within EU countries, you no longer need to pass through customs when you return to the United Kingdom. According to EU guidelines, you may bring in 800 cigarettes, 400 cigarillos, 200 cigars, and 1 kilogram of smoking tobacco, plus 10 liters of spirits, 20 liters of fortified wine, 90 liters of wine, and 110 liters of beer. If you exceed these limits, you may be required to prove that the goods are for your personal use or are gifts.

No animals or pets of any kind can be brought into the United Kingdom without a lengthy quarantine. The law is strictly enforced with severe penalties.

For further information or a copy of "A Guide for Travellers," which details standard customs procedures as well as what you may bring into the United Kingdom from abroad, contact HM Customs and Excise (Dorset House, Stamford St., London SE1 9PY, tel. 0171/928–3344).

Traveling with Cameras, Camcorders, and Laptops

Film and Cameras
If your camera is new or if you haven't used it for a while, shoot and develop a few rolls of film before leaving home. Store film in a cool, dry place—never in the car's glove compartment or on the shelf under the rear window.

Airport security X-rays generally aren't harmful to film with ISO below 400. To protect your film, carry it with you in a clear plastic bag and ask for a hand inspection. Such requests are honored at U.S. airports; abroad, it's up to the inspector. Don't depend on a lead-lined bag to protect film in checked luggage—the airline may increase the radiation to see what's inside. Call the Kodak Information Center (tel. 800/242–2424) for details.

Camcorders
Before your trip, put camcorders through their paces, invest in a skylight filter to protect the lens, and check all the batteries. Most newer camcorders are equipped with batteries that can be recharged with a universal or worldwide AC adapter charger (or multivoltage converter) usable whether the voltage is 110 or 220. All that's needed is the appropriate plug.

Videotape
Videotape is not damaged by X-rays, but it may be harmed by the magnetic field of a walk-through metal detector, so ask for a hand-check. Airport security personnel may ask you to turn on the camcorder to prove that it's what it appears to be, so make sure the battery is charged. Note that rather than the National Television System Committee (NTSC) video standard used in the United States and Canada, Italy uses PAL technology. You will not be able to view your tapes through the local TV set or view movies bought there in your home VCR. Blank tapes bought in Italy can be used for NTSC camcorder taping, but they are pricey.

Laptops
Security X-rays do not harm hard-disk or floppy-disk storage, but you may request a hand-check, at which point you may be asked to turn on the computer to prove that it is what it appears to be. (Check your battery before departure.) Most airlines allow you to use your laptop aloft except during takeoff and landing (so as not to interfere with navigation equipment). For international travel, register your foreign-made laptop with U.S. Customs as you leave the country. If your laptop is U.S.-made, call the consulate of the country you'll be visiting to find out whether it should be registered with customs upon arrival. Before departure, find out about repair facilities at your destination, and don't forget any transformer or adapter plug you may need (*see* Electricity, *above*).

Language

In the main tourist cities, language is no problem. You can always find someone who speaks at least a little English, albeit with a heavy accent; remember that the Italian language is pronounced exactly as it is written (many Italians try to speak English as it is written, with disconcerting results). You may run into a language barrier in the countryside, but a phrase book and close attention to the Italians' astonishing use of pantomime and expressive gestures will go a long way.

Try to master a few phrases for daily use, and familiarize yourself with the terms you'll need to decipher signs and museum labels. You will find the basics in the Vocabulary and Menu Guide in the back of this book.

The exhortation "Va via!" (Go away!) is useful in warding off beggars.

Staying Healthy

There are no serious health risks associated with travel to Italy and no inoculations are needed to enter the country. However, the Centers for Disease Control (CDC) in Atlanta caution that most of Southern Europe is in the "intermediate" range for risk of contacting traveler's diarrhea. Part of this risk may be attributed to an increased consumption of olive oil and wine, which can have a laxative effect on stomachs used to a different diet. (Pepto Bismol is recommended for minor cases of traveler's diarrhea.) The CDC also advises all international travelers to swim only in chlorinated swimming pools, unless they are absolutely certain the local beaches and fresh-water lakes are not contaminated.

Finding a Doctor
The **International Association for Medical Assistance to Travellers** (IAMAT, 417 Center St., Lewiston, NY 14092, tel. 716/754–4883; 40 Regal Rd., Guelph, Ontario N1K 1B5; 57 Voirets, 1212 Grand-Lancy, Geneva, Switzerland) publishes a worldwide directory of English-speaking physicians whose qualifications meet IAMAT standards and who have agreed to treat members for a set fee. Membership is free.

Assistance Companies
Pretrip medical referrals, emergency evacuation or repatriation, 24-hour telephone hot lines for medical consultation, dispatch of medical personnel, relay of medical records, up-front cash for emergencies, and other personal and legal assistance are among the services provided by several membership organizations specializing in medical assistance to travelers. Among them are **International SOS Assistance** (Box 11568, Philadelphia, PA 19116, tel. 215/244–1500 or 800/523–8930; Box 466, pl. Bonaventure, Montréal, Qué. H5A 1C1, tel. 514/874–7674 or 800/363–0263), **Medex Assistance Corporation** (Box 10623, Baltimore, MD 21285, tel. 410/296–2530 or 800/874–9125), **Near Services** (450 Prairie Ave., Suite 101, Calumet City, IL 60409, tel. 708/868–6700 or 800/654–6700), and **Travel Assistance International** (1133 15th St. NW, Suite 400, Washington, DC 20005, tel. 202/331–1609 or 800/821–2828), part of Europ Assistance Worldwide Services, Inc. Because these companies will also sell you death-and-dismemberment, trip-cancellation, and other insurance coverage, there is some overlap with the travel-insurance policies discussed under Insurance, *below*.

Insurance

U.S. Residents
Most tour operators, travel agents, and insurance agents sell specialized health-and-accident, flight, trip-cancellation, and luggage insurance as well as comprehensive policies with some or all of these features. But before you make any purchase, review your existing health and home-owner policies to find out whether they cover expenses incurred while traveling.

Health-and-Accident Insurance
Specific policy provisions of supplemental health-and-accident insurance for travelers include reimbursement for up to $150,000 worth of medical and/or dental expenses caused by an accident or illness during a trip. The personal-accident, or death-and-dismember-

ment provision pays a lump sum to your beneficiaries if you die or to you if you lose one or both limbs or your eyesight; the lump sum awarded ranges from $15,000 to $500,000. The medical-assistance provision may reimburse you for the cost of referrals, evacuation, or repatriation and other services, or it may automatically enroll you as a member of a particular medical-assistance company (*see* Assistance Companies, *above*).

Flight
Insurance

Often bought as a last-minute impulse at the airport, flight insurance pays a lump sum when a plane crashes—either to a beneficiary if the insured dies or sometimes to a surviving passenger who loses eyesight or a limb. Like most impulse buys, flight insurance is expensive and basically unnecessary. It supplements the airlines' coverage described in the limits-of-liability paragraphs on your ticket. Charging an airline ticket to a major credit card often automatically entitles you to coverage and may also embrace travel by bus, train, and ship.

Baggage
Insurance

In the event of loss, damage, or theft on international flights, airlines' liability is $20 per kilogram for checked baggage (roughly about $640 per 70-pound bag) and $400 per passenger for unchecked baggage. On domestic flights, the ceiling is $1,250 per passenger. Excess-valuation insurance can be bought directly from the airline at check-in for about $10 per $1,000 worth of coverage. However, you cannot buy it at any price for the rather extensive list of excluded items shown on your airline ticket.

Trip Insurance

Trip-cancellation-and-interruption insurance protects you in the event you are unable to undertake or finish your trip, especially if your airline ticket, cruise, or package tour does not allow changes or cancellations. The amount of coverage you purchase should equal the cost of your trip should you, a traveling companion, or a family member fall ill, forcing you to stay home, plus the nondiscounted one-way airline ticket you would need to buy if you had to return home early. Read the fine print carefully, especially sections defining "family member" and "preexisting medical conditions." **Default** or **bankruptcy insurance** protects you against a supplier's failure to deliver. Such policies often do not cover default by a travel agency, tour operator, airline, or cruise line if you bought your tour and the coverage directly from the firm in question. Tours packaged by one of the 33 members of the United States Tour Operators Association (USTOA, 211 E. 51 St., Suite 12B, New York, NY 10022; tel. 212/ 750–7371), which requires members to maintain $1 million each in an account to reimburse clients in case of default, are likely to present the fewest difficulties. Even better, pay for travel arrangements with a major credit card, so that you can refuse to pay the bill if services have not been rendered—and let the card company fight your battles.

Comprehensive
Policies

Companies supplying comprehensive policies with some or all of the above features include **Access America, Inc.** (Box 90315, Richmond, VA 23230, tel. 800/284–8300); **Carefree Travel Insurance,** (Box 310, 120 Mineola Blvd., Mineola, NY 11501, tel. 516/294–0220 or 800/ 323–3149); **Tele-Trip** (Mutual of Omaha Plaza, Box 31762, Omaha, NE 68131, tel. 800/228–9792); **The Travelers Companies** (1 Tower Sq., Hartford, CT 06183, tel. 203/277–0111 or 800/243–3174); **Travel Guard International,** (1145 Clark St., Stevens Point, WI 54481, tel. 715/345–0505 or 800/782–5151); and **Wallach and Company, Inc.** (107 W. Federal St., Box 480, Middleburg, VA 22117, tel. 703/687–3166 or 800/237–6615).

U.K. Residents Most tour operators, travel agents, and insurance agents sell specialized policies covering accident, medical expenses, personal liability, trip cancellation, and loss or theft of personal property. You can also buy an annual travel-insurance policy valid for every trip (usually of less than 90 days) you make during the year in which it's purchased. Make sure you will be covered if you have a preexisting medical condition or are pregnant.

For advice by phone or a free booklet, "Holiday Insurance," that sets out what to expect from holiday-insurance policies and gives price guidelines, contact the Association of British Insurers, a trade association representing 450 insurance companies (51 Gresham St., London EC2V 7HQ, tel. 0171/600–3333; 30 Gordon St., Glasgow G1 3PU, tel. 0141/226–3905; Scottish Providence Bldg., Donegall Sq. W, Belfast BT1 6JE, tel. 01232/249176; call for other locations).

Car Rentals

Most major car-rental companies are represented in Italy, including **Avis** (tel. 800/331–1212, 800/879–2847 in Canada); **Budget** (tel. 800/527–0700); **Eurodollar Rent A Car Ltd.** (tel. 800/800–6000); **Hertz** (tel. 800/654–3131, 800/263-0600 in Canada); and **National** (tel. 800/227–7368), known internationally as InterRent and Europcar. In cities, weekly unlimited-mileage rates range from about $250 to $400. This does not include VAT tax, which in Italy is 19% on car rentals. Many rental companies impose mandatory theft coverage on all rentals; this amounts to about $10–$15 per day.

Requirements Your own driver's license is acceptable, although an International Driver's Permit, available from the American or Canadian Automobile Association, is a good idea.

Extra Charges Picking up the car in one city and leaving it in another may entail substantial drop-off charges or one-way service fees. The cost of a collision or loss-damage waiver (*see below*) can be high, also. Some rental agencies will charge you extra if you return the car *before* the time specified on your contract. Ask before making unscheduled drop-offs. Fill the tank when you turn in the vehicle to avoid being charged for refueling at what you'll swear is the most expensive pump in town. In Europe manual transmissions are standard, and air-conditioning is a rarity and often unnecessary. Asking for an automatic transmission or air-conditioning can significantly increase the cost of your rental. Find out what the standard rentals are in the country you'll be visiting and weigh that factor when making your reservation.

Cutting Costs Major international companies have programs that discount their standard rates by 15% to 30% if you make the reservation before departure (anywhere from 24 hours to 14 days), rent for a minimum number of days (typically three or four), and prepay the rental. More economical rentals may come as part of fly/drive or other packages, even bare-bones deals that only combine the rental and an airline ticket (*see* Tours and Packages, *above*).

Several companies operate as wholesalers—they do not own their own fleets but rent in bulk from those that do and are thus able to pass on advantageous rates to their retail customers. Rentals through such companies must be arranged and paid for before you leave the United States. Among them are **Auto Europe** (Box 1097, Camden, ME 04843, tel. 207/236–8235 or 800/223–5555; 800/458–9503 in Canada); **Europe by Car** (mailing address, 1 Rockefeller Plaza, New York, NY 10020; walk-in address, 14 W. 49th St., New York,

NY 10020, tel. 212/581–3040 or 212/245–1713; 9000 Sunset Blvd., Los Angeles, CA 90069, tel. 213/252–9401 or 800/223–1516 in CA); **Foremost Euro-Car** (5430 Van Nuys Blvd., Suite 306, Van Nuys, CA 91401, tel. 818/786–1960 or 800/272–3299); and **The Kemwel Group** (106 Calvert St., Harrison, NY 10528, tel. 914/835–5555 or 800/678–0678). You won't see these wholesalers' deals advertised; they're even better in summer, when business travel is down. Always ask whether the prices are guaranteed in U.S. dollars or foreign currency and if unlimited mileage is available. Find out about any required deposits, cancellation penalties, and drop-off charges, and confirm the cost of any required insurance coverage.

Insurance and Collision Damage Waiver Before you rent a car, find out exactly what coverage, if any, is provided by your personal auto insurer and the rental company. Don't assume that you are covered. If you do want insurance from the rental company, secondary coverage may be the only type offered. You may already have secondary coverage if you charge the rental to a credit card. Note that some credit-card companies do not cover cars rented in Italy.

In general, if you have an accident, you are responsible for the automobile. Car rental companies may offer a collision damage waiver (CDW), which ranges in cost from $4 to $14 a day. You should decline the CDW only if you are certain you are covered through your personal insurer or credit-card company.

Rail Passes

For those planning on doing a lot of traveling by train, rail passes can be a bargain. They allow unlimited travel within a given period of time, and they usually come in versions for first- and second-class travel. They are generally available only to foreign travelers visiting a country and sometimes must be bought before you leave the United States. Their validity begins on the first day of their use, which must be validated by a station official. A further advantage of rail passes is that they spare you time spent waiting in line to buy tickets, and holders are often exempt from paying supplements for seat reservations and for riding special trains (although if seat reservations are necessary, you will still be obliged to make them).

Italy has three rail passes, which can be bought at main train stations in Italy or in the United States through travel agents or the official representative for **Italian State Railways, CIT Tours Corp.** (342 Madison Ave., Room 207, New York, NY 10173, tel. 212/697–2100 or 800/223–7987; tel. 310/670–4269 or 800/248–7245 in western United States). **DER Tours** (Box 1606, Des Plaines, IL 60017, tel. 800/782–2424) is another source for all except the Italian Kilometric ticket. In the past, you saved money buying the passes in the United States, but at press time, with an improved rate of exchange for the dollar, it was more economical to buy them in Italy. A few lire prices are given for purposes of comparison.

The **Italian Tourist Ticket (BTLC)**—the country's basic unlimited-travel rail pass—is an excellent value because it covers the entire system, including Sicily. The pass is available in a first-class version for periods of eight days ($236 in United States/269,000 lire in Italy), 15 days ($294), 21 days ($340), and 30 days ($406). For second-class travel, the prices for the same periods are $162 (or 179,000 lire), $200, $230, and $274.

A variation on the BTLC is the **Italy Flexi Railcard,** which entitles purchasers to four days of travel within nine days of validity; eight days of travel within 21 days; and 12 days of travel within 30 days. Rates for the three types for first-class travel are $180 in the United States (220,000 lire in Italy), $260, and $324; for second-class travel, $126 (148,000 lire), $174, and $220.

The third Italian rail pass is the **Italian Kilometric Ticket,** which is a good bet for families. It is valid for 20 train trips, up to a total of 3,000 kilometers (1,875 miles) of train travel, within a two-month period, and it can be used by up to five people (related or not). Children under 12 are counted for only half the distance, those under 4 travel free. A first-class ticket costs $274 and a second-class ticket $166 if bought in the United States, or 312,000 lire and 183,000 lire if bought at main train stations and CIT offices in Italy.

The **EurailPass,** valid for unlimited first-class train travel through 17 countries, including Italy, is an excellent value if you plan on traveling around the Continent. Standard passes are available for 15 days ($498), 21 days ($648), one month ($728), two months ($1,098), and three months ($1,398). **Eurail Saverpasses,** valid for 15 days, cost $430 per person, 21 days for $550, one month for $678 per person; you must do all your traveling with at least one companion (two companions from April through September). **Eurail Youthpasses,** which cover second-class travel, cost $578 for one month, $768 for two; you must be under 26 on the first day you travel. **Eurail Flexipasses** allow you to travel first class for five ($348), 10 ($560), or 15 ($740) days within any two-month period. **Eurail Youth Flexipasses,** available to those under 26 on their first travel day, allow you to travel second class for five ($255), 10 ($398), or 15 ($540) days within any two-month period. Another option is the **Europass,** featuring a minimum of five and a maximum of 15 days (within a two-month period) of unlimited rail travel in your choice of three to all five of the participating countries (France, Germany, Italy, Spain, and Switzerland); cost for five days is $280 first class, $198 second class (3 countries); for 8 days, $394 first class, $284 second class (4 countries); and for 11 days, $508 first class, $366 second class (all five countries). Each extra rail day costs $38 for first class and $28 for second class. Apply through your travel agent or **Rail Europe** (226–230 Westchester Ave., White Plains, NY 10604, tel. 914/682–5172 or 800/848–7245; or 2087 Dundas East, Suite 105, Mississauga, Ont. L4X 1M2, tel. 416/602–4195), **DER Tours** (Box 1606, Des Plaines, IL 60017, tel. 800/782–2424), or **CIT Tours Corp.** (342 Madison Ave., Suite 207, New York, NY 10173, tel. 212/697–2100 or 800/248–8687; 310/670–4269 or 800/248–7245 in western United States).

Once in Italy, travelers under 26 who have not invested in any of the above passes should inquire about the **Carta Verde,** or Green Card (40,000 lire for one year), which entitles the holder to a 20% discount on all first- and second-class tickets. Travelers over 60 are entitled to similar discounts with the **Carta d'Argento** (*see* Hints for Older Travelers, *below*). Those under 26 should also inquire about discount travel fares under the Billet International Jeune (BIJ) scheme. The special one-trip tickets are sold by **EuroTrain International** (no connection with EurailPass) at its offices in various European cities, including Rome, and by travel agents, mainline rail stations, and youth travel specialists (*see* Centro Turistico Studentesco, *below*).

Student and Youth Travel

Travel Agencies   The **Centro Turistico Studentesco** (CTS) is a student and youth travel agency with offices in major Italian cities; CTS helps its clients find low-cost accommodations and bargain fares for travel in Italy and elsewhere and also serves as a meeting place for young people of all nations. The main Rome office is at Via Genova 16, near the railroad station (tel. 06/467–9271). CTS is also the Rome representative for **EuroTrain International.**

Council Travel Services (CTS), a subsidiary of the nonprofit Council on International Educational Exchange (CIEE), specializes in low-cost travel arrangements abroad for students and is the exclusive U.S. agent for several discount cards. Also newly available from CTS are domestic air passes for bargain travel within the United States. CIEE's twice-yearly *Student Travels* magazine is available at the CTS office at CIEE headquarters (205 E. 42nd St., 16th Floor, New York, NY 10017, tel. 212/661–1450) and in Boston (tel. 617/266–1926), Miami (tel. 305/670–9261), Los Angeles (tel. 310/208–3551), and at 43 branches in college towns nationwide (free in person, $1 by mail). **Campus Connections** (1100 E. Marlton Pike, Cherry Hill, NJ 08034, tel. 800/428–3235) specializes in discounted accommodations and airline fares for students. The **Educational Travel Centre** (438 N. Frances St., Madison, WI 53703, tel. 608/256–5551) offers low-cost domestic and international airline tickets, mostly for flights departing from Chicago, and rail passes. Other travel agencies catering to students include **TMI Student Travel** (1146 Pleasant St., Watertown, MA 02172, tel. 617/661–8187 or 800/245–3672) and **Travel CUTS** (187 College St., Toronto, Ont. M5T 1P7, tel. 416/979–2406).

Discount Cards For discounts on transportation and on museum and attractions admissions, buy the **International Student Identity Card** (ISIC) if you're a bona fide student, or the **International Youth Card** (IYC) if you're under 26. In the United States the ISIC and IYC cards cost $15 each and include basic travel accident and sickness coverage. Apply to **CIEE** (*see above*, tel. 212/661–1414; the application is in *Student Travels*). In Canada the cards are available for $15 each from **Travel CUTS** (*see above*). In the United Kingdom they cost £5 and £4 respectively at student unions and student travel companies, including Council Travel's London office (28A Poland St., London W1V 3DB, tel. 071/437–7767).

Hosteling A **Hostelling International** (HI) membership card is the key to more than 6,000 hostels in 70 countries; the sex-segregated, dormitory-style sleeping quarters, including some for families, go for $7 to $20 a night per person. Membership is available in the United States through **Hostelling International/American Youth Hostels** (HI/AYH, 733 15th St. NW, Suite 840, Washington, DC 20005, tel. 202/783–6161), the United States link in the worldwide chain, and costs $25 for adults 18 to 54, $10 for those under 18, $15 for those 55 and over, and $35 for families. Volume 1 of the *AYH Guide to Budget Accommodation* lists hostels in Europe and the Mediterranean ($13.95, including shipping). HI membership is available in Canada through **Hostelling International-Canada** (205 Catherine St., Suite 400, Ottawa, Ont. K2P 1C3, tel. 613/748–5638) for $26.75, and in the United Kingdom through the **Youth Hostel Association of England and Wales** (Trevelyan House, 8 St. Stephen's Hill, St. Albans, Herts. AL1 2DY, tel. 01727/855215) for £9.

Traveling with Children

Although Italians love children and are generally very tolerant and patient with them, they provide few amenities for them. In restaurants and trattorias you may find a high chair or a cushion for the child to sit on, but there is no such thing as a children's menu. Order a half-portion (*mezza porzione*) of any dish, or ask the waiter for a child's portion (*porzione da bambino*).

Discounts do exist. Always ask about a *sconto-bambino* before purchasing tickets. Children under 6 or under a certain height ride free on municipal buses and trams. Children under 18 are admitted free to state-run museums and galleries, and there are similar privileges in many municipal or private museums.

Publications ***Family Travel Times,*** published 10 times a year by Travel With Your
Newsletter Children (TWYCH, 45 W. 18th St., 7th Floor Tower, New York, NY 10011, tel. 212/206–0688; annual subscription $55), covers destinations, types of vacations, and modes of travel.

Books *Traveling with Children—And Enjoying It,* by Arlene K. Butler ($11.95 plus $3 shipping; Globe Pequot Press, Box 833, Old Saybrook, CT 06475, tel. 800/243–0495 or 800/962–0973 in CT), helps you plan your trip with children, from toddlers to teens. *Innocents Abroad: Traveling with Kids in Europe,* by Valerie Wolf Deutsch and Laura Sutherland ($15.95 or $4.95 paperback, Penguin USA, *see above*), covers child- and teen-friendly activities, food, and transportation.

Tour **Grandtravel** (6900 Wisconsin Ave., Suite 706, Chevy Chase, MD
Operators 20815, tel. 301/986–0790 or 800/247–7651) offers international and domestic tours for people traveling with their grandchildren. The catalogue, as charmingly written and illustrated as a children's book, positively invites armchair traveling with lap-sitters aboard. **Families Welcome!** (21 W. Colony Pl., Suite 140, Durham, NC 27705, tel. 919/489–2555 or 800/326–0724) packages and sells family tours to Europe.

Getting There On international flights, the fare for infants under age 2 not occupy-
Air Fares ing a seat is generally either free or 10% of the accompanying adult's fare; children ages 2 through 11 usually pay half to two-thirds of the adult fare. On domestic flights, children under 2 not occupying a seat travel free, and older children currently travel on the "lowest applicable" adult fare.

Baggage In general, infants paying 10% of the adult fare are allowed one carry-on bag, not to exceed 70 pounds or 45 inches (length + width + height) and a collapsible stroller; check with the airline before departure, because you may be allowed less if the flight is full. The adult baggage allowance applies for children paying half or more of the adult fare.

Safety Seats A certain amount of confusion surrounds children's car seats aloft. The FAA recommends their use and details approved models in the free leaflet **"Child/Infant Safety Seats Recommended for Use in Aircraft"** (available from the Federal Aviation Administration, APA–200, 800 Independence Ave. SW, Washington, DC 20591, tel. 202/267–3479). Airline policy varies. U.S. carriers allow FAA-approved models bearing a sticker declaring their FAA approval. Because these seats are strapped into a regular passenger seat they may require that parents buy a ticket even for an infant under 2 who would otherwise ride free. Foreign carriers may not allow infant seats, may charge the child's rather than the infant's fare for their use, or may require you to hold your baby during takeoff and landing, thus defeating the seat's purpose.

Facilities Aloft Some airlines provide other services for children, such as children's meals and freestanding bassinets (only to those with seats at the bulkhead, where there's enough legroom). Make your request when reserving. The annual February/March issue of *Family Travel Times* gives details of the children's services of dozens of airlines. "Kids and Teens in Flight" (free from the U.S. Department of Transportation, tel. 202/366–2220) offers tips for children flying alone.

Lodging   Children are generally welcome in Italian hotels, which will set up extra beds in the parents' room or give families adjoining rooms. The charge for an extra bed should be no more than 35% of the double room rate. If you are traveling with an infant, it is best to bring along your own folding crib.

CIGA Hotels (reservations: tel. 800/221–2340) has more than 20 properties in Italy, all of which welcome families. Notable are the two on the Lido in Venice, which are right on the beach and have a parklike area for children to enjoy. **Club Med** (40 W. 57th St., New York, NY 10019, tel. 800/CLUB–MED) has a Mini Club (for ages 4–9) and Kids Club (for ages 10 and 11) at its ski village in Sestriere; there are also Baby Clubs, Mini Clubs, and Kids Clubs (the applicable ages vary) at summer resort villages in Metaponto (Basilicata) and on the islands of Sicily and Sardinia, marketed mainly to Europeans. Some of the Valtur vacation villages (Via Milano 42, Rome, tel. 06/482–1000, fax 06/470–6334) also have special facilities and activities for children in various age groups.

(For information on alternative lodgings, *see* Home Exchange and Apartment and Villa Rentals in Staying in Italy, *below*).

Hints for Travelers with Disabilities

Italy has only recently begun to provide facilities such as ramps, telephones, and toilets for people with disabilities; such things are still the exception, not the rule. ENIT (Italian Government Travel Office) can provide travelers with disabilities with a list of accessible hotels and with the addresses of Italian associations for the disabled. Travelers' wheelchairs must be transported free of charge, according to Italian law, but the logistics of getting a wheelchair on and off trains and buses can make this requirement irrelevant. Seats are reserved for people with disabilities on public transportation, but buses have no lifts for wheelchairs. High, narrow steps for boarding trains create additional problems. In many monuments and museums, even in some hotels and restaurants, architectural barriers make it difficult, if not impossible, for those with disabilities to gain access. In Rome, however, St. Peter's, the Sistine Chapel, and the Vatican Museums are all accessible by wheelchair.

To bring a Seeing Eye dog into Italy requires an import license, a current certificate detailing the dog's inoculations, and a letter from your veterinarian certifying the dog's health. Contact the nearest Italian consulate for particulars.

Organizations   Several organizations provide travel information for people with disabilities, usually for a membership fee, and some publish newsletters and bulletins. Among these are the **Information Center for Individuals with Disabilities** (Fort Point Pl., 27–43 Wormwood St., Boston, MA 02210, tel. 617/727–5540 or 800/462–5015 in MA between 11 and 4, or leave message; TDD 617/345–9743); **Mobility International USA** (Box 10767, Eugene, OR 97440, tel. and TDD 503/343–1284, fax 503/343–6812), the U.S. branch of an international organization based in Britain and present in 30 countries; **MossRehab Hospital Travel Information Service** (1200 W. Tabor Rd., Philadelphia, PA 19141, tel. 215/456–9603, TDD tel. 215/456–9602); **Travel**

Industry and Disabled Exchange (TIDE, 5435 Donna Ave., Tarzana, CA 91356, tel. 818/368–5648, fax 818/344–0078); and **Travelin' Talk** (Box 3534, Clarksville, TN 37043, tel. 615/552–6670, fax 615/552–1182).

Travel Agencies and Tour Operators **Flying Wheels Travel** (143 W. Bridge St., Box 382, Owatonna, MN 55060, tel. 507/451–5005 or 800/535–6790) is a travel agency specializing in domestic and worldwide cruises, tours, and independent travel itineraries for people with mobility impairments. Adventurers should contact **Wilderness Inquiry** (1313 Fifth St. SE, Minneapolis, MN 55414, tel. and TDD 612/379–3838), which orchestrates action-packed trips like white-water rafting, sea kayaking, and dog sledding for those challenged with disabilities. Tours are designed to bring people who are physically challenged together with those who aren't.

In the United Kingdom Main sources include the **Royal Association for Disability and Rehabilitation** (RADAR, 12 City Forum, 250 City Rd., London ECIV 8AF, tel. 0171/250–322), which publishes travel information for the disabled in Britain, and **Mobility International** (228 Borough High St., London SE1 1JX, tel. 0171/403–5688), the headquarters of an international membership organization that serves as a clearinghouse of travel information for people with disabilities. **Holiday Care Service** (2 Old Bank Chambers, Station Rd., Horley, Surrey RH6 9HW, tel. 01293/774535) is a charity that provides guides, accommodation listings, and general information for tourists with special needs.

Publications Several free publications are available from the Consumer Information Center (Pueblo, CO 81009): "New Horizons for the Air Traveler with a Disability," a U.S. Department of Transportation booklet describing changes resulting from the 1986 Air Carrier Access Act and those still to come from the 1990 Americans with Disabilities Act (include Department 608Y in the address), and the Airport Operators Council's *Access Travel: Airports* (Dept. 5804), which describes facilities and services for the disabled at more than 500 airports worldwide.

Travelin' Talk Directory (*see* Organizations, *above*) was published in 1993. This 500-page resource book ($35) is packed with information for travelers with disabilities. Twin Peaks Press (Box 129, Vancouver, WA 98666, tel. 206/694–2462 or 800/637–2256) publishes the *Directory of Travel Agencies for the Disabled* ($19.95), listing more than 370 agencies worldwide and *Wheelchair Vagabond* ($14.95), a collection of personal travel tips. Add $2 per book for shipping.

Hints for Older Travelers

In Italy, travelers over 60 can purchase the **Carta d' Argento,** a rail pass good for a 30% discount on the Italian State railway system. It costs 40,000 lire and is valid for one year, except for June 26–August 14 and December 18–28. Travelers over 60 are also entitled to free admission to state museums, as well as to many other museums—always ask at the ticket office. Older travelers planning to visit Italy during the hottest months should be aware that few public buildings, restaurants, and shops are air-conditioned. Public toilets are few and far between, other than those in coffee bars, restaurants, and hotels. Older travelers may find it difficult to board trains and some buses and trams with very high steps and narrow treads.

Organizations The **American Association of Retired Persons** (AARP, 601 E St. NW, Washington, DC 20049, tel. 202/434–2277) offers independent travelers who are members of the AARP (open to those age 50 or older; $8 per person or couple annually) with the Purchase Privilege Program, which provides discounts on hotels, car rentals, and sightseeing. AARP also arranges group tours, cruises, and apartment living through AARP Travel Experience from American Express (400 Pinnacle Way, Suite 450, Norcross, GA 30071, tel. 800/927–0111 or 800/745–4567).

Two other organizations offer discounts on lodgings, car rentals, and other travel products, along with such nontravel perks as magazines and newsletters: the **National Council of Senior Citizens** (1331 F St. NW, Washington, DC 20004, tel. 202/347–8800; membership $12 annually) and **Mature Outlook** (6001 N. Clark St., Chicago, IL 60660, tel. 800/336–6330; $9.95 annually).

Note: Mention your senior-citizen identification card when booking hotel reservations for reduced rates, not when checking out. At restaurants, show your card before you're seated; discounts may be limited to certain menus, days, or hours. If you are renting a car, ask about promotional rates that might improve on your senior-citizen discount.

Educational Travel The nonprofit **Elderhostel** (75 Federal St., 3rd Floor, Boston, MA 02110, tel. 617/426–7788) has offered inexpensive study programs for people 60 and older since 1975. Held at more than 1,800 educational institutions, courses cover everything from marine science to Greek myths and cowboy poetry. Participants usually attend lectures in the morning and spend the afternoon sightseeing or on field trips; they live in dorms on the host campuses. Fees for two- to three-week international trips—including room, board, and transportation from the United States—range from $1,800 to $4,500.

Interhostel (University of New Hampshire, 6 Garrison Ave., Durham, NH 03824, tel. 800/733–9753), a slightly younger enterprise than Elderhostel, caters to a slightly younger clientele—50 and over—and runs programs overseas in some 25 countries. The idea is similar: Lectures and field trips mix with sightseeing, and participants stay in dormitories at cooperating educational institutions or in modest hotels. Programs are usually two weeks in length and cost $1,500–$2,100, excluding airfare.

Tour Operators The following tour operators specialize in older travelers: **Evergreen Travel Service** (4114 198th St. SW, Suite 3, Lynnwood, WA 98036, tel. 206/776–1184 or 800/435–2288), has introduced the "Lazy Bones" tours for those who like a slower pace. If you want to take your grandchildren, look into **Grandtravel** (*see* Traveling with Children, *above*); **Saga International Holidays** (222 Berkeley St., Boston, MA 02116, tel. 800/343–0273), caters to those over age 60 who like to travel in groups.

Publications *The 50+ Traveler's Guidebook: Where to Go, Where to Stay, What to Do*, by Anita Williams and Merrinec Dillon ($12.95; St. Martin's Press, 175 Fifth Ave., New York, NY 10010), is available in bookstores and offers many useful tips. "The Mature Traveler" (Box 50820, Reno, NV 89513, tel. 702/786–7419; $29.95), a monthly newsletter, contains many travel deals for older travelers.

Hints for Gay and Lesbian Travelers

Organizations The **International Gay Travel Association** (Box 4974, Key West, FL 33041, tel. 305/292–0217 or 800/999–7925 or 800/448–8550), which has 700 members, will provide you with names of travel agents and tour operators who specialize in gay travel. The **Gay & Lesbian Visi-**

tors Center of New York Inc. (135 W. 20th St., 3rd Floor, New York, NY 10011, tel. 212/463–9030 or 800/395–2315; $100 annually) mails a monthly newsletter, valuable coupons, and more to its members.

Tour Operators and Travel Agencies
The dominant travel agency in the market is **Above and Beyond** (3568 Sacramento St., San Francisco, CA 94118, tel. 415/922–2683 or 800/397–2681). Tour operator **Olympus Vacations** (8424 Santa Monica Blvd., Suite 721, West Hollywood, CA 90069; tel. 310/657–2220 or 800/965–9678) offers all-gay-and-lesbian resort holidays. **Skylink Women's Travel** (746 Ashland Ave., Santa Monica, CA 90405, tel. 310/452–0506 or 800/225–5759) handles individual travel for lesbians all over the world and conducts two international and five domestic group trips annually.

Publications
The premiere international travel magazine for gays and lesbians is **Our World** (1104 N. Nova Rd., Suite 251, Daytona Beach, FL 32117, tel. 904/441–5367; $35 for 10 issues). **Out & About** (tel. 203/789–8518 or 800/929–2268; $49 for 10 issues) is a 16-page monthly newsletter with extensive information on resorts, hotels, and airlines that are gay-friendly.

Further Reading

The Italians, by Luigi Barzini, is a comprehensive and lively analysis of the Italian national character, still worthy reading although published in 1964 (Atheneum). More recent musings on Italian life include *Italian Days*, by Barbara Grizzuti Harrison (Ticknor & Fields), and *That Fine Italian Hand*, by Paul Hofmann (Henry Holt), for many years *New York Times* bureau chief in Rome. Matthew Spender's *Within Tuscany* (Viking) and Tim Parks' *Italian Neighbors* (Grove) are accounts of life in rural Tuscany and Verona by British expatriates.

Classics of the travel essay genre include James Morris's *The World of Venice* (Harcourt Brace Jovanovich), Mary McCarthy's *Venice Observed* and *The Stones of Florence* (both HBJ also), and Lawrence Durrell's *Sicilian Carousel* (out of print).

For historical background, Edward Gibbon's *Decline and Fall of the Roman Empire* is available in three volumes (Modern Library). Consult Giorgio Vasari's *Lives of the Artists*, *The Autobiography of Benvenuto Cellini*, and Machiavelli's *The Prince* (all available in Penguin Classics) for eyewitness accounts of the 16th century. Otherwise, many still consider *The Civilization of the Renaissance in Italy*, by 19th-century Swiss historian Jacob Burckhardt (Modern Library), must reading. Christopher Hibbert's *The House of Medici* (Quill/William Morrow) details the family's rise and fall.

For lively historical fiction, pick up Irving Stone's *Agony and the Ecstasy* (NAL) based on the life of Michelangelo. Susan Sontag's *The Volcano Lover* (Farrar Straus Giroux), set in 18th-century Naples, is about Sir William Hamilton, his wife Emma, and Lord Nelson. *The Leopard*, by Giuseppe di Lampedusa (Pantheon), is a compelling portrait of Sicily during the political upheavals of the 1860s. Historical fiction set in World War II includes *History: A Novel*, by Elsa Morante (Vintage Aventura), about the fate of inhabitants of Rome's Jewish ghetto, and *Bread and Wine* by Ignazio Silone (Signet Classics), about Italian peasants under the control of the Fascists. Anne Cornelison's nonfiction *Women of the Shadows*, portrays the life of peasant women in early post-WWI southern Italy (Vintage).

Waverley Root's *The Food of Italy* (Vintage), published in 1977, is not a cookbook but an unsurpassed region-by-region exploration of the subject. Marcella Hazan's new *Essentials of Classic Italian Cooking* (Knopf) is an update, with modern sensibilities and lowfat diets in mind, of her earlier cookbooks. It goes well with *Italian Wine* (Knopf), by her husband, Victor Hazan, or with *Vino*, by Burton Anderson (Little Brown). *Made in Italy*, a shopper's guide by Annie Brody and Patricia Schultz (1988, Workman) is unrevised but still valuable for its knowledge of Italian products and producers.

What about a video? The delightful *Roman Holiday* (1953), in which a young princess plays hooky from her royal entourage to go "slumming" with Gregory Peck, won Audrey Hepburn an Oscar. In *Summertime* (1955), a visiting American (Katharine Hepburn) falls in love with Venice and a handsome Venetian shopkeeper (Rossano Brazzi). Federico Fellini's *La Dolce Vita* (1961), with Marcello Mastroianni discovering the decadence of high society in Rome, gave its name to an era. *Fellini's Roma* (1972) is the director's paean to the city; *Amarcord* (1974), his paean to the small Adriatic town of his childhood. Merchant/Ivory's *Room with a View* (1986), a period piece based on the E.M. Forster novel of the same name, is good cinema with good views of Florence.

A magazine for Italophiles, *Italy Italy*, published in Italy in English, is available in the United States (Italian American Multimedia Corporation, 138 Wooster St., New York, NY 10012, tel. 212/674–4132, fax 212/674–4933; $30 for 6 yearly issues).

Arriving and Departing

From North America by Plane

Flights are either nonstop, direct, or connecting. A nonstop flight requires no change of plane and makes no stops. A direct flight stops at least once and can involve a change of plane, although the flight number remains the same; if the first leg is late, the second waits. This is not the case with a connecting flight, which involves a different plane and a different flight number.

Airports and Airlines Airlines serving Italy nonstop from the United States are **Alitalia** (tel. 800/223–5730), **Delta** (tel. 800/241–4141), and **TWA** (tel. 800/892–4141), which all fly to Rome and Milan; and **American** (800/624–6262), which flies to Milan only. These flights land at Rome's **Leonardo da Vinci Airport,** better known as Fiumicino (from its location outside the city) and at Milan's **Malpensa Airport.**

Flying Time The flying time to Rome from New York is 8½ hours; from Chicago, 10–11 hours; from Los Angeles, 12–13 hours.

Cutting Flight Costs The Sunday travel section of most newspapers is a good source of deals. When booking, particularly through an unfamiliar company, call the Better Business Bureau and your local or state Consumer Protection Bureau to find out whether any complaints have been registered against the company, pay with a credit card if you can, and consider trip-cancellation and default insurance (*see* Insurance, *above*).

Promotional Airfares Less expensive fares, called promotional or discount fares, are round-trip and involve restrictions, which vary according to the route and season. You must usually buy the ticket—commonly called an APEX (advance purchase excursion) when it's for international travel—in advance (seven, 14, or 21 days are usual), although some of the major airlines have added cheap, no-frills flights to compete with new bargain airlines on certain routes.

With the major airlines the cheaper fares generally require minimum- and maximum-stays (for instance, over a Saturday night or at least seven and no more than 30 days). Airlines generally allow some return date changes for a $25 to $50 fee, but most low-fare tickets are nonrefundable. Only a death in the family would prompt the airline to return any of your money if you cancel a nonrefundable ticket. However, you can apply an unused nonrefundable ticket toward a new ticket, again with a small fee. The lowest fare is subject to availability, and only a small percentage of the plane's total seats will be sold at that price. Contact the U.S. Department of Transportation's Office of Consumer Affairs (I–25, Washington, DC 20590, tel. 202/366–2220) for a copy of "Fly-Rights: A Guide to Air Travel in the U.S." *The Official Frequent Flyer Guidebook*, by Randy Petersen ($14.99 plus $3 shipping; 4715-C Town Center Dr., Colorado Springs, CO 80916, tel. 719/597–8899 or 800/487–8893, 800/485–8893), yields valuable hints on getting the most for your air-travel dollars.

Consolidators Consolidators or bulk-fare operators–"bucket shops"–buy blocks of seats on scheduled flights that airlines anticipate they won't be able to sell. They pay wholesale prices, add a markup, and resell the seats to travel agents or directly to the public at prices that still undercut the airline's promotional or discount fares (higher than a charter ticket but lower than an APEX ticket, and usually without the advance-purchase restriction). Moreover, some consolidators sometimes give you your money back. Carefully read the fine print detailing penalties for changes and cancellations. If you doubt the reliability of a company, call the airline once you've made your booking and confirm that you do, indeed, have a reservation on the flight.

The biggest U.S. consolidator, C.L. Thomson Express, sells only to travel agents. Well-established consolidators selling to the public include **UniTravel** (Box 12485, St. Louis, MO 63132, tel. 314/569–0900 or 800/325–2222), **Council Charter** (205 E. 42nd St., New York, NY 10017, tel. 212/661–0311 or 800/800–8222), and **Travac** (989 6th Ave., New York, NY 10018, tel. 212/563–3303 or 800/872–8800).

Charter Flights Charters usually have the lowest fares and the most restrictions. Departures are limited and seldom on time, and you can lose all or most of your money if you cancel. (The closer to departure you cancel, the more you lose, although sometimes you will be charged only a small fee if you supply a substitute passenger.) The charterer, on the other hand, may legally cancel the flight for any reason up to 10 days before departure; within 10 days of departure, the flight may be canceled only if it becomes physically impossible to operate it. The charterer may also revise the itinerary or increase the price after you have bought the ticket, but if the new arrangement constitutes a "major change," you have the right to a refund. Before buying a charter ticket, read the fine print for the company's refund policy and details on major changes. Money for charter flights is usually paid into a bank escrow account, the name of which should be on the contract. If you don't pay by credit card, make your check payable to the escrow account (unless you're dealing with a travel agent, in which case, his or her check should be payable to the escrow account). The U.S. Department of Transportation's Office of Consumer Affairs (I–25, Washington, DC 20590, tel. 202/366–2220) can answer questions on charters and send you its "Plane Talk: Public Charter Flights" information sheet.

Charter operators may offer flights alone or with ground arrangements that constitute a charter package. You typically must book charters through your travel agent. One good source is **Charterlink** (988 Sing Sing Rd., Horseheads, NY 14845, tel. 607/739–7148 or 800/221–1802), a no-fee charter broker that operates 24 hours a day.

Discount *Travel Clubs* Travel clubs offer members unsold space on airplanes, cruise ships, and package tours at as much as 50% below regular prices. Membership may include a regular bulletin or access to a toll-free hot line giving details of available trips departing from three or four days to several months in the future. Most also offer 50% discounts off hotel rack rates, but double check with the hotel to make sure it isn't offering a better promotional rate independent of the club. Clubs include **Discount Travel International** (114 Forrest Ave., Suite 203, Narberth, PA 19072, tel. 215/668–7184; $45 annually, single or family), **Entertainment Travel Editions** (Box 1014, Trumbull, CT 06611, tel. 800/445–4137; $28–$48 annually), **Great American Traveler** (Box 27965, Salt Lake City, UT 84127, tel. 800/548–2812; $29.95 annually), **Moment's Notice Discount Travel Club** (425 Madison Ave., New York, NY 10017, tel. 212/486–0503; $45 annually, single or family), **Privilege Card** (3391 Peachtree Rd. NE, Suite 110, Atlanta, GA 30326, tel. 404/262–0222 or 800/236–9732; domestic annual membership $49.95, international, $74.95), **Travelers Advantage** (CUC Travel Service, 49 Music Sq. W, Nashville, TN 37203, tel. 800/548–1116; $49 annually, single or family), and **Worldwide Discount Travel Club** (1674 Meridian Ave., Miami Beach, FL 33139, tel. 305/534–2082; $50 annually for family, $40 single).

Enjoying the **Flight** Fly at night if you're able to sleep on a plane. Because the air aloft is dry, drink plenty of beverages while on board; remember that drinking alcohol contributes to jet lag, as do heavy meals. Sleepers usually prefer window seats to curl up against; restless passengers ask to be on the aisle. Bulkhead seats, in the front row of each cabin, have more legroom, but since there's no seat ahead, trays attach awkwardly to the arms of your seat, and you must stow all possessions overhead. Bulkhead seats are usually reserved for the disabled, the elderly, and people traveling with babies.

Smoking Since February 1990, smoking has been banned on all domestic flights of less than six hours' duration; the ban also applies to domestic segments of international flights aboard U.S. and foreign carriers. On U.S. carriers flying overseas, a seat in a no-smoking section must be provided for every passenger who requests one, and the section must be enlarged to accommodate such passengers if necessary, as long as they have complied with the airline's deadline for check-in and seat assignment. Foreign airlines are exempt from these rules but do provide no-smoking sections, and some nations, including Canada as of July 1, 1993, have gone as far as to ban smoking on all domestic flights; other countries may ban smoking on flights of less than a specified duration. The International Civil Aviation Organization has set July 1, 1996, as the date to ban smoking aboard airlines worldwide, but the body has no power to enforce its decisions.

From North America by Ship

Ships that sail the Caribbean in winter and European waters in summer periodically make transatlantic repositioning cruises. Sometimes rates are reduced, and fly/cruise packages are usually available. Check the travel pages of your Sunday paper for cruise lines that have ships sailing to Europe, or contact **Cunard Line** (555 Fifth Ave., New York, NY 10017, tel. 212/880–7545 or 800/221–

4770), which operates the *Queen Elizabeth II (QE2)*, the only ocean liner that makes regular transatlantic crossings (Apr.–Dec., between Baltimore, MD; New York City, NY; and Southampton, England). The line's *Vistafjord* sails between Ft. Lauderdale, Florida, and Genoa, Italy, in repositioning crossings.

From the United Kingdom by Plane, Car, Train, and Bus

By Plane **Alitalia** (tel. 0171/602–7111) and **British Airways** (tel. 0181/897–4000) operate direct flights from London (Heathrow) to Rome, Milan, Venice, Pisa, Turin, Genoa, Bologna, Florence, and Naples. Flying time is 2½ to three hours. There's also one direct flight a day from Manchester to Milan, and one a week from Manchester to Rome. Standard fares are extremely high. Both airlines offer less expensive APEX tickets (usual booking restrictions apply) and PEX and Super-PEX tickets (which don't have to be bought in advance). The Eurobudget ticket (no length-of-stay or advance-purchase restrictions) is another option.

Less expensive flights are available: It pays to look around in the classified advertisements of reputable newspapers and magazines such as *Time Out*. But remember to check the *full* price, inclusive of airport taxes and surcharges. Some of the bargains are not as inexpensive as they seem at first glance.

By Car The distance from London to Rome is 1,810 kilometers (1,125 miles) via Calais/Boulogne/Dunkirk and 1,745 kilometers (1,085 miles) via Oostende/Zeebrugge (excluding sea crossings). Milan is about 575 kilometers (360 miles) closer. The drive from the Continental ports takes about 24 hours; the trip in total takes about three days. The shortest and quickest channel crossings are via Dover or Folkestone to one of the French ports (Calais or Boulogne); the ferry takes around 75 minutes and the Hovercraft just 35 minutes. Crossings from Dover to the Belgian ports take about four hours, but Oostende and Zeebrugge have good road connections. The longer crossing from Hull to Zeebrugge is useful for travelers from the north of England. The Sheerness-Vlissingen (Holland) route makes a comfortable overnight crossing; it takes about nine hours.

Fares on the cross-channel ferries vary considerably from season to season. Until the end of June and from early September onward, savings can be made by traveling midweek. Don't forget to budget for the cost of gas and road tolls, plus a couple of nights' accommodations.

The Channel Tunnel opened officially in May 1994, providing the fastest route across the Channel—35 minutes from Folkestone to Calais, or 60 minutes from motorway to motorway. It consists of two large 50-kilometer (31-mile)-long tunnels for trains, one in each direction, linked by a smaller service tunnel running between them. Le Shuttle (tel. 01345/353535 in the U.K., 800/388–3876 in the U.S.), a special car, bus, and truck train, which was scheduled to begin service in June 1994, operates a continuous loop, with trains departing every 15 minutes at peak times and at least once an hour through the night. No reservations are necessary, although tickets may be purchased in advance from travel agents. Most passengers stay in their own car throughout the "crossing"; progress updates are provided on display screens and radio. Motorcyclists park their bikes in a separate section with its own passenger compartment, while foot passengers must book passage by coach.

The Tunnel is reached from exit 11a of the M20/A20. Drivers purchase tickets from toll booths, then pass through frontier control before loading onto the next available service. Unloading at Calais takes 8 minutes. Ticket prices start at £130 for a low-season 5-day round trip in a small car and are based on season, time of day, length of stay, and car size regardless of the number of passengers. Peak-season fares are not always competitive with ferry prices.

Roads from the channel ports to Italy are mostly toll-free. The exceptions are French autoroutes, the road crossing the Ardennes, the Swiss superhighway network (for which a special tax sticker must be bought at the frontier or in advance), the St. Gotthard Tunnel, and the road between the tunnel and the Italian superhighway system. The reduced-price petrol coupons once offered by the Italian government have been discontinued, but it won't hurt to check with the AA or RAC before departure to be sure they haven't become available again.

If these distances seem too great to drive, there's always the Motorail from the channel ports. However, no car/sleeper expresses run beyond Milan, 575 kilometers (360 miles) north of Rome.

By Train   Visitors traveling to Italy by train have several options. You can leave London's Victoria train station at 9:25 AM for the Folkestone-Boulogne Seacat catamaran service; from Boulogne Maritime, you take the train to Gare du Nord in Paris (arrival time 4:15 PM) and then a taxi or metro across town to Gare de Lyons. From there, you pick up the 8:56 PM "Napoli Express" for Rome. There are first- and second-class sleeping cars and second-class couchettes for the overnight run into Italy. From Paris to Dijon there's a refreshment service, and a buffet car is attached in the morning. The train reaches Turin at 6:10 AM the next day and Rome at 2:19 PM.

Alternatively, the 8:55 AM Victoria service catches the Dover–Calais ferry crossing; arrival time in Paris is 5:20 PM. The "Palatino" leaves Paris at Gare de Lyons and travels via Chambéry and the Mont Cenis tunnel to Turin, arriving about 2:50. You reach Rome by 9:35 AM. The train has first- and second-class sleepers and second-class couchettes, but no ordinary day cars for sitting up overnight. There's a buffet car from Paris to Chambéry and from Genoa to Rome.

A year-round service leaves Victoria at 1:25 PM, catching the Jetfoil for Oostende in plenty of time to take the 8:53 PM train to Brig, Switzerland, arriving at about 9 AM. Change there for the 10:31 AM Milan train. At Milan there's a 12:55 PM departure for Bologna, Florence, and Rome, arriving at Rome at 5:50 PM.

Since the Channel Tunnel opened, train journeys between London Waterloo to Paris Gare du Nord take only three hours, or 3¼ hours to Brussels. Departures are hourly from 6:30 AM to 8 PM. Check-in about 20 minutes before departure time. Call (tel. 0181/784–1333) for more information.

Train, ferry, and hovercraft schedules are subject to change, so consult with **French Railways** (tel. 0171/409–3518) and **British Rail** (tel. 0171/834–2345) before you leave.

By Bus   **Eurolines** (52 Grosvenor Gdns., London SW1W 0AU, tel. 0171/730–8235 or 0171/730–3499, or any National Express agent) runs a weekly bus service to Rome that increases to three times a week between June and September. Buses leave on Monday, Wednesday, and Friday over the summer, and on Saturdays the rest of the year. The trip takes about 30 hours. Buses travel via Dover, Calais, Paris, and Lyon and make stops en route at Turin, Milan, Bologna and Florence. Have a few French francs for spending en route. Fares are quite high, especially when you consider the long and tiring overnight journey and compare the price with that of a charter flight.

Staying in Italy

Getting Around

By Plane **Alitalia** and its domestic affiliate **ATI**, in addition to smaller, privately run companies such as **Meridiana,** complete an extensive network of internal flights in Italy. Apart from the major international airports, you can find frequent flights between smaller cities, such as Bologna, Genoa, Naples, Palermo, Turin, and Verona. Flight times are never much more than an hour (long flights usually are those going from the extreme north to Naples or Sicily), and most of these smaller airports are close to the cities and linked by good bus services. Italian travel agents will inform you of the discounts available, which include a 50% family reduction for a spouse and/or children traveling with you, or up to 30% for certain night flights.

By Train The fastest trains on the **Ferrovie dello Stato (FS),** the Italian State Railways, are the ETR 450 trains (listed on schedules under "P" for Pendolino), operating on a few main lines, including Rome–Milan, via Florence and Bologna; seat reservations are required, and you must pay an extra charge for the airline-type meals and service. Next fastest trains are the Intercity (IC) trains, for which you pay a supplement and for which seat reservations may be required and are always advisable. *Interregionale* trains usually make more stops and are a little slower. *Regionale* and *locale* trains are the slowest; many serve commuters.

To avoid long lines at station windows, buy tickets and make seat reservations at least a day in advance at travel agencies displaying the FS emblem. If you have to reserve at the last minute, reservation offices at the station accept reservations up to three hours before departure. You can also get a seat assignment just before boarding the train; look for the conductor on the platform. Trains can be very crowded on weekends and during holiday and vacation seasons; we strongly advise reserving seats in advance or, if the train originates where you get on, getting to the station early to find a seat. A card just outside the compartment or over the seat indicates whether it has been reserved. Carry compact bags for easy overhead storage. You can buy train tickets for destinations close to main cities at tobacconists and at ticket machines in stations; they must be stamped in the little machines near the track before you board the train.

Note that in some Italian cities (including Milan, Turin, Genoa, Naples, and Rome) there are two or more main-line stations, although one is usually the principal terminus or through-station. Be sure of the name of the station at which your train will arrive, or from which it will depart.

There is refreshment service on all long-distance trains, with mobile carts and a cafeteria or dining car. Tap water on trains is not drinkable.

Rail Passes For those planning on doing a lot of traveling by train, the **Italian Tourist Ticket (BTLC)** is an excellent value. (*See* Rail Passes in Before You Go, *above.*)

By Bus Italy's bus network is extensive, although not as attractive as those in other European countries, partly because of the low cost of train travel. Schedules are often drawn up with commuters and students in mind and may be sketchy on weekends. Regional bus companies often provide the only means of getting to out-of-the-way places. Even when this is not the case, buses can be faster and more direct than local trains, so it's a good idea to compare bus and train schedules. Among the major Italian long-distance bus companies are **SITA** (Viale Cadorna 105, Florence, tel. 055/278611), which operates throughout Italy; **Autostradale** (Piazzale Castello 1, Milan, tel. 02/801161), serving much of northern Italy; and **Lazzi** (Via Mercadante 2, Florence, tel. 055/363041), operating in Tuscany and central Italy. Bus information is available at local tourist offices and travel agencies.

Local bus companies operate in many regions (*see* Getting Around, By Bus in most chapters). In the hillier parts of Italy, particularly in the Alpine north, they take over when the gradients become too steep for train travel. A village shop or café will sometimes double as the ticket office and bus stop for these. You should have your ticket before you board.

Most of the major cities have urban bus services, usually operating on a system involving the prepurchase of tickets (from a machine, a newsstand, or a tobacco store). These buses are inexpensive, but they can become unbearably jammed at rush hours. Remember that there are also lunchtime rush hours in the hotter periods, particularly in the south, when people go home for a siesta.

By Car There is an extensive network of *autostrade* (toll highways), complemented by equally well-maintained but free *superstrade* (expressways). All are clearly signposted and numbered. The ticket you are issued upon entering an autostrada must be returned when you exit and pay the toll; on some shorter autostrade, mainly connecting highways, the toll is paid upon entering. Viacard cards, on sale at many autostrada locations, make paying tolls easier and faster. A *raccordo* is a connecting expressway. *Strade statali* (state highways, denoted by S or SS numbers) may be single-lane roads, as are all secondary roads; directions and turnoffs are not always clearly marked. Information is obtainable from **ACI** (Automobile Club of Italy, Via Marsala 8, 00185 Rome, tel. 06/499–8389) and from ACI offices throughout Italy.

Rules of the Road Driving is on the right, as in the United States. Regulations are largely as in Britain and the United States, except that the police have the power to levy on-the-spot fines. In most Italian towns the use of the horn is forbidden in certain, if not all, areas; a large sign, *Zona di Silenzio*, indicates where. Speed limits are 130 kmh (80 mph) on autostrade and 110 kmh (70 mph) on state and provincial roads, unless otherwise marked. Fines for driving after drinking are heavy, with the additional possibility of six months' imprisonment, but there is no fixed blood-alcohol regulation and no official test.

Parking In most cities, parking space is at a premium; historic town centers are closed to most traffic, and peripheral parking areas are usually full. Parking in a *Zona Disco* is allowed for limited periods (30 minutes to 2 hours or more—the limit is posted); if you don't have the cardboard disk to show what time you parked, you can use a piece of paper. It's advisable to leave your car only in guarded parking areas; many are run by ACI. Unofficial parking attendants can help you find a space but offer no guarantees. In major cities your car may be towed away if illegally parked.

Gas Gas ranges from 1,550 lire to 1,600 lire per liter, the equivalent of about $4 a U.S. gallon (*see* Conversion Tables at the back of this book). Only a few gas stations are open on Sunday, and most close for a couple of hours at lunchtime and at 7 PM for the night. Self-service pumps may be few and far between outside major cities. Gas stations on autostrade are open 24 hours.

Breakdowns **ACI Emergency Service** (Servizio Soccorso Stradale, Via Solferino 32, 00185 Rome, tel. 06/44595) offers 24-hour road service. Dial 116 to reach the nearest ACI service station.

Telephones

Local Calls Pay phones take either a 200-lire coin, two 100-lire coins, a *gettone* (token), or a *scheda* (prepaid calling card). The gettone-only phones are being phased out; if you happen upon one, buy tokens from the nearest cashier or the token machine near the phone. Insert the token (which doesn't drop right away), dial your number, wait for an answer, then complete the connection by pushing the knob at the token slot. When the token drops, the other party is able to hear you. Scheda phones are becoming common everywhere. You buy the card (values vary—2,000 lire, 5,000 lire, etc.) at Telefoni offices and tobacconists. Insert the card as indicated by the arrow, and its value will be visible in the window. After you hang up, the card is returned so you can use it until its value runs out. Don't forget it. The card makes long-distance direct dialing (*teleselezione*) much easier than it used to be. Without it, insert at least five coins and have more handy; unused coins will be returned.

International Calls Since hotels tend to overcharge, sometimes exorbitantly, for long-distance and international calls, it is best to make such calls from Telefoni offices, where operators will assign you a booth, help you place your call, and collect payment when you have finished, at no extra charge. There are Telefoni offices, designated *SIP* (sometimes also *ASST*), in all cities and towns. You can make collect calls from any phone by dialing 170, which will get you an English-speaking operator. Rates to the United States are lowest round the clock on Sunday and 11 PM–8 AM, Italian time, on weekdays.

See also Long Distance Calling in Before You Go, *above.*

Operators and Information For general information in English on calling in Europe and the Mediterranean area, dial 176. For operator-assisted service in those areas, dial 15. For operator-assisted service and information regarding intercontinental calls, dial 170.

Mail

Postal Rates Airmail letters (lightweight stationery) to the United States and Canada cost 1,100 lire for the first 19 grams and an additional 1,700 lire for up to 50 grams. Airmail postcards cost 950 lire if the message is limited to a few words and a signature; otherwise, you pay the letter rate. Airmail letters to the United Kingdom cost 750 lire; postcards, 650 lire. You can buy stamps at tobacconists.

Receiving Mail Mail service is generally slow; allow up to 14 days for mail from Britain, 21 days from North America. Correspondence can be addressed to you care of the Italian post office. Letters should be addressed to your name, "c/o Ufficio Postale Centrale," followed by "FERMO POSTA" on the next line, and the name of the city (preceded by its postal code) on the next. You can collect it at the central post office by showing your passport or photo-bearing ID and paying a small fee. American Express also has a general-delivery service. There's no charge for cardholders, holders of American Express Traveler's checks, or anyone who booked a vacation with American Express.

Tipping

Tipping practices vary, depending on where you are. The following guidelines apply in major cities, but Italians tip smaller amounts in smaller cities and towns. Tips may not be expected in cafés and taxis north of Rome.

In restaurants a service charge of about 15% usually appears as a separate item on your check. A few restaurants state on the menu that cover and service charge are included. Either way, it's customary to leave an additional 5%–10% tip for the waiter, depending on the service. Checkroom attendants expect 500 lire per person. Restroom attendants are given from 200 lire in public restrooms, and more in expensive hotels and restaurants. Tip 100 lire for whatever you drink standing up at a coffee bar, 500 lire or more for table service in a smart café, and less in neighborhood cafés. At a hotel bar tip 1,000 lire for a round or two of cocktails.

Taxi drivers are usually happy with 5%–10% of the meter amount. Railway and airport porters charge a fixed rate per bag. Tip an additional 500 lire per person, but more if the porter is very helpful. Theater ushers expect 500 lire per person, but more for very expensive seats. Give a barber 2,000–3,000 lire and a hairdresser's assistant 3,000–8,000 lire for a shampoo or cut, depending on the type of establishment.

On sightseeing tours, tip guides about 2,000 lire per person for a half-day group tour, more if they are very good. In museums and other places of interest where admission is free, an offering is expected; give anything from 500 to 1,000 lire for one or two persons, more if the guardian has been especially helpful. Service station attendants are tipped only for special services.

In hotels, give the *portiere* about 15% of his bill for services, or 5,000–10,000 lire if he has been generally helpful. For two people in a double room, leave the chambermaid about 1,000 lire per day, or about 4,000–5,000 a week, in a Moderate ($$) hotel (*see* Dining and Lodging in individual chapters for a definition of price categories); tip a minimum of 1,000 lire for valet or room service. Increase these amounts by one-half in an Expensive ($$$) hotel, and double them in a Very Expensive ($$$$) hotel. Tip doormen in a Very Expensive hotel 1,000 lire for calling a cab and 2,000 lire for carrying bags to the check-in desk. In a Very Expensive hotel tip a bellhop 2,000–5,000 lire for carrying your bags to the room and 2,000–3,000 lire for room service. In a Moderate hotel tip a bellhop 1,000–2,000 lire for carrying your bags and 1,000–2,000 for room service.

Opening and Closing Times

Banks Branches are open weekdays 8:30–1:30 and 2:45–3:45.

Churches Most are open from early morning until noon or 12:30, when they close for two hours or more; they open again in the afternoon, closing about 7 PM or later. Major cathedrals and basilicas, such as St. Peter's, are open all day. Sightseeing in churches during religious rites is usually discouraged. Be sure to have a fistful of 100-lire coins handy for the *luce* (light) machines that illuminate the works of art in the perpetual dusk of ecclesiastical interiors. A pair of binoculars will help you get a good look at painted ceilings and domes.

Museums Hours vary and may change with the seasons. Many important national museums have short hours and are closed one day a week, often on Monday. They are open on some holidays, closed on others. Check individual listings in the individual chapters and always check locally. Remember that ticket offices close from 30 minutes to one hour before official closing time.

Shops There are individual variations, depending on climate and season, but most are open 9:30–1 and 3:30 or 4–7 or 7:30. Food shops open earlier in the morning and later in the afternoon. In all but resorts and small towns, shops close on Sunday and one half-day during the week. Some tourist-oriented shops in places such as Rome and Venice are open all day, as are some department stores and supermarkets. Post offices are open 8–2; central and main district post offices stay open until 8 or 9 PM for some operations. Barbers and hairdressers, with some exceptions, are closed Sunday and Monday.

National Holidays January 1 (New Year's Day); January 6 (Epiphany); April 16, 17, 1995 (Easter Sunday and Monday); April 25 (Liberation Day); May 1 (Labor Day or May Day); August 15 (Assumption of Mary, also known as Ferragosto); November 1 (All Saints Day); December 8 (Immaculate Conception); December 25, 26 (Christmas Day and Boxing Day).

The feast days of patron saints are also holidays, observed locally. Many businesses and shops may be closed in Florence, Genoa, and Turin on June 24 (St. John the Baptist); in Rome on June 29 (Sts. Peter and Paul); in Palermo on July 15 (Santa Rosalia); in Naples on September 19 (San Gennaro); in Bologna on October 4 (San Petronio); in Trieste on November 3 (San Giusto); and in Milan on December 7 (St. Ambrose). Venice's feast of St. Mark is April 25, the same as Liberation Day.

Shopping

The best buys in Italy are leather goods of all kinds—from gloves to bags to jackets—in addition to silk goods, knitwear, gold jewelry, ceramics, and local handicrafts. Every region has its specialties. Venice is known for glassware, lace, and velvet; Milan and Como for silk; the Dolomites and the mountainous regions of Calabria and Sicily for hand-carved wooden objects; Florence for straw goods, gold jewelry, leather, and paper products; Naples for coral and cameos; Assisi for embroidery; and Deruta, Gubbio, Vietri, and many towns in Apulia and Sicily for ceramics.

Unless your purchases are too bulky, avoid having them shipped home; if the shop seems extremely reliable about shipping, get a written statement of what will be sent, when, and how. (*See* Shopping in individual chapters for details.)

IVA (VAT) Refunds Under Italy's IVA-refund system, a non-EU resident can obtain a refund of tax paid after spending a total of 300,000 lire in one store (before tax—and note that price tags and prices quoted, unless otherwise stated, include IVA). Shop with your passport and ask the store for an invoice itemizing the article(s), price(s), and the amount of tax. At departure, take the still-unused goods and the invoice to the customs office at the airport or other point of departure and have the invoice stamped. (If you return to the United States or Canada directly from Italy, go through the procedure at Italian customs; if your return is, say, via Britain, take the Italian goods and invoice to British customs.) Once back home—and within 90 days of the date of purchase—mail the stamped invoice to the store, which will forward the IVA rebate to you. A growing number of stores in Italy (and Europe) are members of the Tax-Free Shopping System, which expedites things by providing an invoice that is actually a Tax-Free Cheque in the amount of the refund. Once stamped, it can be cashed at the Tax-Free Cash refund window at major airports and border crossings.

Bargaining The notice *Prezzi fissi* (fixed prices) means just that; in shops displaying this sign it's a waste of time to bargain unless you're buying a sizable quantity of goods or a particularly costly object. Always bargain, instead, at outdoor markets and when buying from street vendors.

Participant Sports

Italians are sports lovers, and there are several daily newspapers devoted solely to sports. The climate makes it almost impossible to resist the temptation to try a cannonball serve on the red-clay tennis courts, sink a birdie putt on a scenic green, or just hike up a hill to savor the fresh air and views. Winters see ski enthusiasts trying their luck on the slopes of the Apennines and the Alps.

Canoeing The swift rivers rushing down the slopes of the Alps and Apennines make for exciting canoeing. Kayak races are held in the Dolomites and on the Aniene River near Subiaco in Lazio. For information, get in touch with the **Federazione Italiana Canoa e Kayak** (Viale Tiziano 70, 00196 Rome, tel. 06/368–58525).

Golf Relatively new to Italy, golf is catching on, and more courses are being laid out near major cities. For information, contact the **Federazione Italiana Golf** (Viale Tiziano 74, 00196 Rome, tel. 06/36851).

Horseback Riding An excursion on horseback is a pleasant way to see the countryside, and many types of tours are offered. Some include overnight stays in country estates in Lazio, Tuscany, and other regions. For information, contact the **Associazione Nazionale per il Turismo Equestre** (Via A. Borelli 5, 00161 Rome, tel. 06/444–1179).

Sailing It is especially popular on the major lakes, off the Ligurian Riviera, off northern Sardinia, and the coasts of Tuscany and Lazio. For information, contact the **Federazione Italiana Vela** (Viale Brigata Bisagno 2, 16129 Genoa, tel. 010/589431).

Windsurfers should head for Lake Garda (*see* Sports in Chapter 10, Milan, Lombardy, and the Lakes).

Skiing One of the country's most popular participant sports, skiing, is practiced along the Alpine arc and in the Apennines, as well. (*See* regional chapters for recommended resorts and package deals.)

Tennis Tennis is one of Italy's most popular sports, and most towns have public courts available for a booking fee. Many hotels have courts that are open to the public; some private clubs offer temporary visitors' memberships to travelers. Contact local tourist information offices for information.

Spectator Sports

Basketball Many Americans play on Italian pro teams, and basketball is gaining a big following around the country. For information, contact the **Federazione Italiana Pallacanestro** (Via Fogliano 15, 00199 Rome, tel. 06/886–3071).

Horse Racing There are tracks in Milan, Rome, Palermo, and many other cities. Inquire locally for the best racing days.

Soccer *Calcio* (soccer) is the most popular spectator sport in Italy. All major cities, and most smaller ones, have teams playing in one league or another. Big-league games are played on Sunday afternoons from September through May. Inquire locally or write to the **Federazione Italiana Giuoco Calcio** (Via Gregorio Allegri 14, 00198 Rome, tel. 06/84911).

Tennis A major international Grand Prix tennis tournament is held in Rome in May.

Beaches

Italy isn't the place for an exclusively "beach" holiday. With the exception of Sardinia, you'll find cleaner water and better beaches at lower prices in other parts of the world. The waters that are least polluted and best for swimming are in Sardinia (except around Cagliari, Arbatax, and Porto Torres); off portions of the coasts of Calabria and Apulia; and off the islands of Elba, Capri, Ischia, Ustica, the Aeolian group, and western Sicily. Topless bathing is widespread, except for a few staid family-type beaches near large cities. Nudism is discreetly practiced on out-of-the-way beaches, mainly on the islands and on deserted stretches of the mainland coast. Singles will find the liveliest resorts on the Adriatic Coast and on the coasts of Tuscany and Calabria.

Dining

Dining in Italy is a pleasant part of the total Italian experience, a chance to enjoy authentic Italian specialties and ingredients. Visitors have a choice of eating places, ranging from a *ristorante* (restaurant) to a *trattoria, tavola calda,* or *rosticceria.* A trattoria is usually a family-run place, simpler in decor, menu, and service than a ristorante, and slightly less expensive. Some rustic-looking spots call themselves *osterie* but are really restaurants. (A true *osteria* is a wineshop, a very basic and down-to-earth tavern.) The countless fast-food places opening up everywhere are variations of the older Italian institutions of the tavola calda or rosticceria, which offer a selection of hot and cold dishes to be taken out or eaten on the premises. At either a tavola calda or rosticceria, some items are priced by the portion, others by weight. You usually select your food, find out how much it costs, and then pay the cashier, who will give you a stub to be given to the counterman when you pick up the food.

None of the above eateries serves breakfast; in the morning you go to a coffee bar, which is where, later in the day, you will also find sandwiches and pastry and other snacks. Tell the cashier what you want, pay for it, and then take the stub to the counter, where you order. Remember that table service is extra, and you are expected not to occupy tables unless you are being served; on the other hand, you can linger as long as you like at a table without being pressed to move on.

In eating places of all kinds, the menu is posted in the window or just inside the door so you can see what you're getting into (in a snack bar or tavola calda the price list is usually displayed near the cashier). In all but the simplest places there's a *coperto* (cover charge) and usually also a *servizio* (service charge) of 10%–15%, only part of which goes to the waiter. A *menù turistico* (tourist menu) includes taxes and service, but beverages are usually extra.

Generally speaking, a typical Italian meal in a restaurant or trattoria consists of at least two courses: a first course of pasta, risotto, or soup; and a second course of meat and fish. Side dishes, such as vegetables and salads cost extra, as do desserts. There is no such thing as a side dish of pasta; pasta is a course in itself and Italians would never think of serving a salad with it; the salad comes later. Years ago, pasta dishes were inexpensive because restaurateurs made their profit on the total of first and second course. Now, tourists and even some diet-conscious Italians, tend to order only one course—usually a pasta, perhaps followed by a salad or vegetables—so hosts have jacked up the price of first courses. Now, about antipasto: Many a misunderstanding arises over a lavish offering of antipasto. The term *antipasto* means, literally, "before the meal." No matter how generous and varied the antipasto, the host expects those who have one to order at least one other course. Pizza is in a category by itself and is a one-dish meal, even for the Italians. But some like to have a small pizza as a starter, as an alternative to a pasta course.

Beware of menu items marked "SQ" (according to quantity), which means you will be charged according to the weight of the item, or "L. 18,000 hg," which means the charge will be 18,000 lire per hectogram (3½ ounces). Pricing by weight usually refers to items such as fresh fish or Florentine steaks.

Mealtimes Lunch is served in Rome from 1 to 3, dinner from 8 to 10, or later in some restaurants. Service begins and ends a half-hour earlier in Florence and Venice, an hour earlier in smaller towns in the north, a half-hour to one hour later in the south. Almost all eating places close one day a week and for vacations in summer and/or winter.

Precautions Tap water is safe almost everywhere unless labeled "*Non Potabile.*" Most people order bottled *acqua minerale* (mineral water), either *gassata* (carbonated) or *naturale*, or *non gassata* (without bubbles). In a restaurant you order it by the *litro* (liter) or *mezzo litro* (half-liter); often the waiter will bring it without being asked, so if you don't like it, or want to keep your check down, make a point of ordering *acqua semplice* (tap water). You can also order *un bicchiere di acqua minerale* (a glass of mineral water) at any bar. If you are on a low-sodium diet, ask for everything (within reason) *senza sale* (without salt).

Ratings Restaurants in our listings are divided by price into four categories: Very Expensive ($$$$), Expensive ($$$), Moderate ($$), and Inexpensive ($). (*See* Dining in individual chapters for specific prices, which vary from region to region.) Prices quoted are for a three-course meal with house wine, including all service and taxes; particularly recommended establishments are indicated by a star ★.

Lodging

Italy offers a good choice of accommodations, especially in the main tourist capitals of Rome, Florence, and Venice. It is becoming more difficult to find satisfactory accommodations in the lower categories in these cities, however, as more and more hotels are being refurbished and upgraded. Throughout Italy you will find everything from deluxe five-star hotels to charming country inns, villas for rent, camping grounds, and hostels, in addition to well-equipped vacation villages in resort areas.

Hotels Italian hotels are classified from five-star (deluxe) to one-star (guest houses and small inns). Stars are assigned according to standards set by regional boards (Italy has 20 regions), but rates are set by each hotel. In the major cities, room rates are on a par with other European capitals: Deluxe and four-star rates can be downright extravagant. In those categories, ask for one of the better rooms, since less desirable rooms—and there usually are some—don't give you what you're paying for. Hotels are justifying higher rates by refurbishing rooms and bathrooms and installing such accessories as hair dryers and personal safes. During slack periods, or when a hotel is not full, it is often possible to negotiate a discounted rate.

In all hotels you will find a rate card inside the door of your room, or inside the closet door; it tells you exactly what you will pay for that particular room (rates in the same hotel may vary according to the location and type of room). On this card, breakfast and any other optionals must be listed separately. Any discrepancy between the basic room rate and that charged on your bill is cause for complaint to the manager and to the local tourist office. The service charge and the 9% IVA, or VAT tax, are included in the rate except in five-star deluxe hotels, where the IVA (13% on luxury hotels) may be a separate item added to the bill at departure.

Although, by law, breakfast is supposed to be optional, most hotels quote room rates including breakfast. When you book a room, ask specifically whether the rate includes breakfast (*colazione*). You are under no obligation to take breakfast at your hotel, but in practice most hotels expect you to do so. Considering that Italian hotel breakfasts usually are very simple, even skimpy, this is not good value for the money; you can eat better for less at the nearest coffee bar.

Hotels that we list as Moderate ($$) and Inexpensive ($) may charge extra for optional air-conditioning. In older hotels the quality of rooms may be very uneven; if you don't like the room you're given, ask for another. This applies to noise, too. Front rooms may be larger and have a view, but they also may get a lot of street noise. Specify if you care about having either a bath or shower, since not all rooms have both. In the ($$) and ($) categories, showers may be the drain-in-the-floor type, guaranteed to flood the bathroom. Such amenities as porters, room service, and in-house cleaning and laundering are disappearing in hotels of these same categories, which, in general, are not up to U.S. standards of comfort and facilities.

Among the best-known chains operating in Italy are: **CIGA** (745 Fifth Avenue, New York, NY 10151, tel. 800/221–2340, fax 212/421–5929), which has more than 20 Italian properties, almost all five-star deluxe; **Jolly** (800/247–1277 in New York State, 800/221–2626 elsewhere, 800/237–0319 in Canada), with 32 four-star hotels in Italy; **Atahotels** (Via Lampedusa 11/A, 20141 Milano, tel. 02/895261, fax 02/8465568, or toll free in Italy 1678/23013; some bookable through E & M Associates, 212/599–8280 or 800/223–9832), with 20 mostly five- and four-star hotels; and **Starhotels** (Via Belfiore 27, 50144 Florence, tel. 055/36921, fax 055/36924, or book through 800/44–UTELL), with 14 mainly four-star hotels. **Space Hotels** (toll-free in Italy 1678/13013; or book through Supranational, 416/927–1133 or 800/843–3311) has about 50 independently owned five- and four-star (some three-star) hotels. **Italhotels** (toll-free in Italy 1678/01004) also has about 50 independently owned five-and four-star hotels.

AGIP Motels (reservations in Italy: 06/444–0183) is a chain of about 50 motels on main highways, mostly four-star (these are commercial, functional digs for traveling salesmen and tourists needing forty winks, but they—and the Jolly hotels—can be the best choice in many out-of-the-way places). **The Forte** group has taken over some top-of-the-line AGIP properties, as in Rome. **Best Western,** an international association of independently owned hotels, has some 75 mainly four- and three-star hotels in Italy (tel. 800/528–1234 for reservations or to request the *Europe and Middle East Atlas* that lists them).

Family Hotels (Via Faenza 77, 50123 Florence, tel. 055/217975, fax 055/238–1905), grouping about 75 independently owned, family-run three- and two-star hotels (some one-star), offers good value. For information in Italy, contact the address above (not a central booking service, however).

Major cities have hotel-reservation service booths in train stations.

Home Exchange
You can find a house, apartment, or other vacation property to exchange for your own by becoming a member of a home-exchange organization, which then sends you its annual directories listing available exchanges and includes your own listing in at least one of them. Arrangements for the actual exchange are made by the two parties to it, not by the organization. For more information contact the **International Home Exchange Association** (IHEA, 41 Sutter St., Suite 1090, San Francisco, CA 94104, tel. 415/673–0347 or 800/788–2489). Principal clearinghouses include: **HomeLink International** (Box 650, Key West, FL 33041, tel. 800/638–3841), with thousands of foreign and domestic listings, publishes four annual directories plus updates; the $50 membership includes your listing in one book. **Intervac International** (Box 590504, San Francisco, CA 94159, tel. 415/435–3497), which publishes three annual directories; membership is $62, or $72 if you want to receive the directories but remain unlisted. **Loan-a-Home** (2 Park La., Apt. 6E, Mount Vernon, NY 10552, tel. 914/664–7640) specializes in long-term exchanges; there is no charge to list your home, but the directories cost $35 or $45 depending on the number you receive. **Villa Leisure** (Box 209, Westport, CT 06881, tel. 407/624–9000 or 800/526–4244) facilitates swaps.

Apartment and Villa Rentals
If you want a home base that's roomy enough for a family and comes with cooking facilities, a furnished rental may be the solution. It's generally cost-wise, too, although not always—some rentals are luxury properties (economical only when your party is large). Home-exchange directories do list rentals—often second homes owned by prospective house swappers—and there are services that not only look for a house or apartment for you, but also handle the paperwork. Some send an illustrated catalogue and others send photographs of specific properties, sometimes at a charge; up-front registration fees may apply. In Italy, the possibilities include rustic, converted stone farmhouses, seaside villas, city apartments, and even quarters in a 16th-century Renaissance palace or two.

Among the companies are **At Home Abroad** (405 East 56th St., Suite 6H, New York, NY 10022, tel. 212/421–9165); **Interhome Inc.** (124 Little Falls Rd., Fairfield, NJ 07004, tel. 201/882–6864); **Europa-Let** (92 N. Main St., Ashland, OR 97520, tel. 503/482–5806 or 800/462–4486); **Overseas Connection** (31 North Harbor Dr., Sag Harbor, NY 11963, tel. 516/725–9308); **Property Rentals International** (1 Park

West Circle, Suite 108, Midlothian, VA 23113, tel. 804/378–6054 or 800/220–3332); **Rent a Home International** (7200 34th Ave. NW, Seattle, WA 98117, tel. 206/789–9377 or 800/488–7368); **Vacation Home Rentals Worldwide** (235 Kensington Ave., Norwood, NJ 07648, tel. 201/767–9393 or 800/633–3284); **Villas and Apartments Abroad** (420 Madison Ave., Suite 1105, New York, NY 10017, tel. 212/759–1025 or 800/433–3020); and **Villas International** (605 Market St., Suite 510, San Francisco, CA 94105, tel. 415/281–0910 or 800/221–2260). **Hideaways International** (15 Goldsmith St., Box 1270, Littleton, MA 01460, tel. 508/486–8955 or 800/843–4433) functions as a travel club. Membership ($99 yearly per person or family at the same address) includes receipt of two annual guides plus quarterly newsletters; rentals are arranged directly between members, not by the club staff.

All of the above represent properties in Italy along with other locations worldwide. Two companies that focus on Italy nearly exclusively are **Cuendet USA** (165 Chestnut St., Allendale, NJ 07401, tel. 201/327–2333), the U.S. representative of Cuendet of Italy, and **Vacanze in Italia** (Box 297, Falls Village, CT 06031, tel. 413/528–6610 or 800/533–5405).

Also of interest is **Italy Farm Holidays** (547 Martling Ave., Tarrytown, NY 10591, tel. 914/631–7880, fax 914/631–8831), which specializes in Agriturismo properties. These are working farms that supplement their income by renting out furnished bed-and-breakfast rooms or apartments or separate houses with kitchens. The accommodations, which range from $366 to $630 per couple per week in a B&B (more for larger quarters holding more people), can be too rustic for some or unreliable in quality, but IFH represents fewer than 50 properties (Umbria, Toscany, with Piedmont and the Veneto to come), all of which they have inspected personally.

Two companies in England with a good selection of rentals on their books are **Villas Italia Ltd.** (Astral Towers, Betts Way, Crawley, West Sussex RH10 2GX, tel. 01293/599988) and **CV Travel** (43 Cadogan St., London SW3 2PR, tel. 0171/581–0851).

Camping Camping is becoming a popular choice for Italians themselves, who take to the road and can avail themselves of some 1,700 official campsites. Apart from cost considerations, camping is a good way to find accommodations in otherwise overcrowded resorts. Make sure you stay only on authorized campsites (camping on private land is frowned upon). You must also have an international camping *carnet* (permit), which you can obtain from your local camping association before you leave home. You can obtain a directory of campgrounds in Italy by writing to the **Federazione Italiana del Campeggio e del Caravanning** (Federcampeggio, Casella Postale 23, 50041 Calenzano, Florence, fax 055/882–5918) and requesting *Campeggiare in Italia;* send three international reply coupons to cover mailing. (This directory is also available through the Italian Government Travel Office in the United States or at tourist information offices in Italy, until supplies run out.) The Touring Club Italiano publishes a multilingual *Guida Camping d'Italia* (campsite directory), available in bookstores in Italy for about 30,000 lire, with more detailed information on the sites. Camp rates for two persons, with tent, average about 30,000 lire a day. **Camper rental agencies** operate throughout Italy: Contact your travel agency for details.

Hostels The Italian Youth Hostels Association operates about 50 hostels in Italy, some in such beautiful settings as the 14th-century castle of Rocca degli Alberi at Montagnana, near Padua, and the Castello di

Scilla, on the Straits of Messina. Hostel rates are about 18,000 lire per person per night, including breakfast, but it's not easy to find accommodations, especially in tourist centers, unless you have reservations. Access to international hostels comes with membership in the International Youth Hostel Federation, which, in turn, is provided by membership in any national association; guidebooks listing the hostels worldwide are available through these same associations. (*See* Hosteling in Student and Youth Travel, *above* for particulars.) In Italy, contact the **Associazione Italiana Alberghi per la Gioventù** (Via Cavour 44, Rome, tel. 06/487–1152), the Italian member of the International Youth Hostel Federation.

Ratings Hotels in our listings are divided by price into four categories: Very Expensive ($$$$), Expensive ($$$), Moderate ($$), and Inexpensive ($). (*See* Lodging sections in individual chapters for specific prices, which differ according to region.) Hotels in some regions, particularly the northern mountainous areas, offer attractive half- and full-board packages (in which some or all meals are included in the price) and usually require that you stay a number of days. These deals can often "lower" an establishment into a less expensive classification in real terms because the inclusive deal is a bargain. Particularly recommended places are indicated by a star ★.

Credit Cards

The following credit card abbreviations are used: AE, American Express; DC, Diners Club; MC, MasterCard; V, Visa.

Great Itineraries

Rome to Florence

This itinerary offers you the chance to experience a wide range of scenery and historical influences in a relatively short distance. The route and terrain would be equally familiar to an Etruscan nobleman, Roman centurion, or medieval cardinal because the main lines of communication in central Italy have always run along, or parallel to, the Apennines.

Heading north from Rome along the coast, you pass the Etruscan city of Tarquinia before reaching Viterbo, still guarded by its medieval walls and full of crafts shops. The next stop is Orvieto, perched on the top of a rocky peak and living up to its reputation as a romantic medieval city. The area also boasts one of Italy's most famous white wines, and the surrounding countryside, made up of jagged outcrops of volcanic rock, is as dramatic as Orvieto itself.

A few miles north and you're in Tuscany, with its rolling countryside of olive groves and cypresses that captivated the Renaissance painters. The next stop is welcoming Siena, the beautiful art city famous for its motto on the city gates: *Cor Magis tibi Sena pandit* (Siena opens its heart to you). Siena's medieval past comes alive twice a year when the colorful riders in the Palio horse race charge round the fan-shaped Piazza del Campo. North of Siena lies Chianti country, a hilly district producing Italy's most famous wines. There are plenty of chances to stop and sample a glass in one of many medieval stone villages.

The last stop is Florence, the cradle of the Renaissance and the highlight of many trips to Italy. Birthplace of artistic and literary giants, Renaissance Florence nurtured its native talents and attracted others from all over Italy and Europe. The result is one of the world's greatest concentrations of art and architecture, crammed into what is really a compact city along the banks of the river Arno. Just northeast of Florence is Fiesole, a hilltop village that dates as far back as the Etruscans and provides some of the best views of the Arno Valley and Florence itself.

Duration   Seven days.

Getting   The most direct route from Rome to Florence is 277 kilometers (160
Around   miles), but to appreciate the scenery you should add to that figure
By Car   by keeping off the direct superhighway (A1). Instead, take S2 almost all the way, leaving it only to head east to Orvieto along S71.

By Public   Take an express bus to Viterbo and then another bus from Viterbo
Transportation   to Orte, where you can get a fast train to Orvieto. A slower train makes the scenic trip to Siena, passing through Montepulciano. Take the local train north from Siena, changing at Empoli for Florence.

The Main   **One Night: Viterbo.** Either stop in Tarquinia en route (taking S1
Route   from Rome to Tarquinia) or make a side trip to the Etruscan settlement from Viterbo. In Viterbo explore Piazza San Lorenzo and the San Pellegrino quarter, one of the best preserved and most hauntingly medieval cores in any Italian city.

One Night: Orvieto. Stop a few miles west of Orvieto, on S71, to appreciate the best view of the cliff-top city. In Orvieto, visit the Duomo, one of Italy's most dramatically sited cathedrals, noted for its stunning, intricately multicolored facade. Make sure to sample some of the local white wine.

Two Nights: Siena. You could spend a whole day relaxing in the beguiling Piazza del Campo, which is bathed in a warm and everchanging light. Visit the Palazzo Pubblico, the Pinacoteca Gallery, and the Duomo (Cathedral). Try to be on hand for one of the two runnings of the Palio.

Three Nights: Florence. This is the minimum stay in one of the world's great cities. If you do nothing else, visit the Duomo, Baptistery, Piazza della Signoria, Uffizi Gallery, Palazzo Pitti, Galleria dell'Accademia, and the charming church of San Miniato al Monte. If all the art is overwhelming, make a side trip to Fiesole and relax while overlooking the entire valley of the Arno.

Information   See Chapters 3, 4, 5, and 13.

From the Ligurian Sea to the Adriatic

Italy's sea trade in the Middle Ages was dominated by two maritime republics—Genoa, on the Ligurian Sea, and Venice, on the Adriatic. It was inevitable that these two powers would eventually clash over supremacy in the eastern Mediterranean: The Venetian victory at the Battle of Chioggia, in 1381, settled more than 100 years of conflict.

The development of the two cities since the decisive battle in the 14th century would have been hard to predict at the time. Genoa, defeated militarily, developed economically into one of the world's great ports. Powerful Venice remained in ascendancy for more than a century, amassing colonies along the eastern Adriatic Coast and as far east as Cyprus before sinking into a languid decline.

This west-to-east itinerary offers a chance to explore these contrasting cities—one a busy, modern port and the other the caretaker of a gilded past. In between you'll pass spectacular scenery along the Ligurian coastline, culminating in the remote fishing villages of the Cinque Terre. After turning inland across mountains, you'll reach Parma, known for its harmonious medieval cathedral and majestic baptistry as much as for its famous ham and cheese. Farther east, along the banks of the fast-flowing Adige River, is Verona, with its Roman arena and attractive medieval quarter—the setting for Shakespeare's *Romeo and Juliet.* Between Verona and Venice is Padua, noted for its famous university and the Scrovegni Chapel, decorated with magnificent wall paintings by Giotto. Finally there is glorious Venice, a city that has learned to cope with the tides of visitors and of the waters of its lagoon in equal measure.

Duration Eight to 11 days.

Getting Around *By Car*
The total distance is about 450 kilometers (270 miles). The coastal S1 route is the most scenic way to get to La Spezia from Genoa, although you'll need to hike or take a train if you want to visit the Cinque Terre. From there to Parma, Verona, Padua, and Venice, you have the choice of fast superhighways or good secondary roads the entire way.

By Public Transportation
Good trains connect all the destinations on the tour. The slowest, but most scenic, are from Genoa to La Spezia (the route follows the coast, winding along cliffs and through mountains); between La Spezia and Parma the train crosses some dramatic Apennine passes.

The Main Route
Two Nights: Genoa. Visit the port, with its 16th-century lighthouse (La Lanterna), and admire the view from above the city at Monte Righi. Visit Genoa's well-preserved medieval quarter around Piazza San Matteo; see Via Garibaldi and the Palazzo Bianco.

Two Nights: La Spezia. Leave your city concerns behind as you hike along Italy's most imposing coastline, with the fishing villages of the Cinque Terre as your aim. Visit the coastal towns of Lerici and Portovenere.

One Night: Parma. Sample the excellent Parma ham and cheeses and meander through the old streets around Piazza del Duomo. Satisfy your artistic yearnings with visits to the Galleria Nazionale and the medieval baptistery. See Correggio's frescoes in the cathedral and the church of San Giovanni Evangelista.

Two Nights: Verona. Visit the Roman Arena and the spacious Piazza Brà that abuts it. Wander through the medieval quarter and see the Castelvecchio and the church of San Zeno.

One Night: Padua. See the famous university and Giotto's masterpiece, the Cappella Scrovegni. Join the pilgrimage to the Basilica di San Antonio, patron saint of Padua, and stop for coffee at the grand Caffè Pedrocchi.

Three Nights: Venice. This is the minimum stay for the world's most romantic city. Not-to-be-missed sights include St. Mark's Basilica and all the rest of Piazza San Marco, the Doge's Palace, the church of the Frari, the Accademia, and the entire length of the Grand Canal, seen from the decks of a *vaporetto* (water bus).

Information See Chapters 6, 7, 8, and 12.

Lake Route to the Dolomites

This itinerary takes you into the lakes and mountains north of Milan, the busy financial and fashion capital of northern Italy. Starting on the Lombard plain, you begin to climb as you head north toward Bergamo in the foothills of the Alps. From there it's an off-the-beaten-track circuit around Lake Iseo and then a breathtaking drive along the western shore of Lake Garda, Italy's largest lake, on your way to Riva del Garda on the northern shore.

A direct and attractive road takes you from there to Trento, an important trading post on the north-south trade route to Germany and Austria and famous for the Council of Trent, which formulated the Catholic response to the Reformation. The road from Trento (either main highway or equally direct S road) goes almost due north to Bolzano, also known as Bozen because of the large German-speaking population in this region. Bolzano has some intriguing medieval architectural gems, but its main attraction is its handy location, on the doorstep of the dramatic Dolomite mountain range.

Duration Five days.

Getting Around **By Car** The total distance to Bolzano is 380 kilometers (210 miles). Take autostrada A4 to Bergamo. From there, S42 runs up the west coast of Lake Iseo, and S510 goes down the east to Brescia. Join S45bis along Lake Garda and continue into Trento. From there you can take either S12 or A22 north to Bolzano.

By Public Transportation Good train service takes you as far as Brescia (east of Bergamo), where you can take the bus to Riva del Garda and Trento. From Trento to Bolzano you can either continue on the bus or go by train.

The Main Route **One Night: Bergamo.** Visit the Colleoni chapel and the Piazza Vecchia in the Città Alta (Upper Town) and the Carrara Academy in the lower. Make an early start the next day to wind your way past Lake Iseo. Stop at Gardone Riviera along Lake Garda to see Il Vittoriale, the imaginatively designed mansion built by the poet Gabriele D'Annunzio.

One Night: Riva del Garda. Relax in this attractive town, which is one of Europe's best windsurfing centers. Visit the Torre Apponale, in the town center overlooking the lake.

One Night: Trento. Wander through the medieval quarter of town before climbing one of the narrow streets to the Castello del Buonconsiglio, which commands an excellent view of the city and surrounding valley.

Two Nights: Bolzano (Bozen). Savor the German-Italian atmosphere of the capital of the Alto Adige part of Italy's autonomous Trentino-Alto Adige region. Make the best of the dramatic scenery and the hiking and skiing options of the nearby Dolomites. Savor the view from the plateau of the Renon.

Information See Chapters 10 and 11.

Classical Highlights

Well colonized by the ancient Greeks, then epicenter of the Roman Empire, Italy has a wealth of classical sites, many of them quite well-preserved, thanks in part to the Italian appreciation for history and heritage. Rome was, of course, the glorious capital of the Roman Empire, and a number of ancient sites remain there today, seemingly plunked down in the middle of the bustling modern metropolis. It is quite an experience to turn a corner and see a famous building, such as the Colosseum, across the street, with Fiats and Vespas buzzing blithely past its crumbling arches. Campania, too, has a number of important classical landmarks, from both the Roman and the Greek eras. Below the volcanic cone of Mount Vesuvius, the buried ruins of Pompeii are the most famous, but even better-preserved relics are still being unearthed from the lava at nearby Herculaneum. Farther down the coast is Paestum, the remains of an ancient town with both Greek and Roman buildings; some classicists enjoy uncrowded Paestum more than either Pompeii or Herculaneum.

Those with more time or a more intense interest in ancient times will want to follow this itinerary all the way to Sicily, the large island just off the toe of Italy's boot. Heavily colonized by the Greeks, Sicily was a center of trade and culture in the Hellenic world, and it still is richly endowed with remarkable sites, most notably Agrigento and Siracusa.

Duration Seven to 17 days.

Getting Around *By Car* On the A2 autostrada, it takes about three hours to drive from Rome to Naples. Most of the classical sites in Campania can be seen on day trips from Naples; the farthest away is Paestum, 99 kilometers (60 miles) down the coast on S18. If you choose to continue on to Sicily, take either the overnight car ferry from Naples to Palermo, Sicily, or drive down the A3 autostrada (488 kilometers/302 miles) to Villa San Giovanni in Calabria, where frequent ferry service crosses the strait in a half hour to Messina, Sicily, 235 kilometers (145 miles) east of Palermo. Sicily's main sites are spread out to every corner of the large island, so you will have to stop overnight near each site. It's a 128-kilometer (80-mile) drive south from Palermo to Agrigento, on the island's southwest coast; Selinunte is up the coast from Agrigento, along S115 about 100 kilometers (60 miles). Agrigento is 212 kilometers (132 miles) from Siracusa.

By Public Transportation Train service between Rome and Naples is fast and frequent, taking less than two hours on express trains. The Circumvesuviana train line can take you conveniently from Naples to Pompeii and Herculaneum, and there is a train station right in Paestum. There is a ferry from Naples to Palermo, Sicily, and a main train line runs from Palermo to Siracusa. Other sites on Sicily are better reached by bus than by the unreliable local train service.

The Main Route **Two–Three Nights: Rome.** Spend at least a day exploring Ancient Rome—the Capitoline Hill, the Roman Forum, the Circus Maximus, the Colosseum, the Pantheon—and on subsequent days, venture out to the Appian Way and the Catacombs, or study classical sculptures in the Vatican museums and antiquities in the Museo Nazionale.

Three–Five Nights: Naples. After arriving from Rome, spend the afternoon at the Museo Archeologico Nazionale. Herculaneum and Pompeii can be visited in one day from Naples, but it would be a very full day, and some travelers may want to break it into two separate excursions. On another day, enjoy an excursion down the Amalfi coast to Paestum, with its well-preserved Greek temples. An optional day can be spent touring the area just west of Naples, taking in the Roman amphitheater at Pozzuoli, spooky Lake Avernus, the Roman resort town at Baia with its excavated baths, and the Sibyl's Cave at Cumae, perhaps the oldest Greek colony in Italy.

One Night: Ferry to Sicily.

One Night: Palermo. Visit the National Archeological Museum and nearby Segesta, with its fine Doric Greek temple.

One–Two Nights: Agrigento. Explore the Valley of the Temples, an extensive Greek site, and if you have time, make your way up the coast to see the Greek temple complex at Selinunte.

One–Two Nights: Siracusa. Visit the Archaelogical Park in town, the splendid Archeological Museum, and, if there's time, take an excursion to the Imperial Roman Villa at Casale, just north of Piazza Amerina.

One Night (Optional): Taormina. Get a fine view of Mount Etna and see the town's Greek theater, still used for the summer arts festival.

One Night: Ferry to Naples.

One Night: Return to Rome.

Information See Chapters 3, 14, and 16.

2 Portraits of Italy

Italy at a Glance: A Chronology

c. 1000 BC	Etruscans arrive in central Italy.
c. 800	Rise of Etruscan city-states.
753	Traditional date for the founding of Rome.
750	Greek city-states begin to colonize Sicily and southern Italy.
600	Latin language becomes dominant in Etruscan League; Rome becomes established urban center.
510	Foundation of the Roman republic; expulsion of Etruscans from Roman territory.
410	Rome adopts the 12 Tables of Law, based on Greek models.
343	Roman conquest of Greek colonies in Campania.
312	Completion of Appian Way to the south of Rome; an extensive Roman road system begins to develop.
264–241	First Punic War (with Carthage): Increased naval power helps Rome gain control of southern Italy and then Sicily.
218–200	Second Punic War: Hannibal's attempted conquest of Italy, using elephants, is eventually crushed.
176	Roman Forum begins to take shape as the principal civic center in Italy.
146	Third Punic War: Rome razes city of Carthage and emerges as the dominant Mediterranean force.
133	Rome rules entire Mediterranean Basin except Egypt.
49	Julius Caesar conquers Gaul.
45	Civil War leaves Julius Caesar as sole ruler (dictator); Caesar's Forum is established.
44	Julius Caesar is assassinated.
31	The Battle of Actium resolves the power struggle that continued after Caesar's death; Octavian becomes sole ruler.
27	Rome's Imperial Age begins; Octavian (now named Augustus) becomes the first emperor and is later deified. The Augustan Age is celebrated in the works of Virgil (70 BC–AD 19), Ovid (43 BC–AD 17), Livy (59 BC–AD 17), and Horace (65 BC–AD 27).
AD 14	Augustus dies.
29	Jesus Christ crucified in the Roman colony of Judea.
43	Rome invades Britain.
50	Rome is now the largest city in the world, with a population of a million.
65	Emperor Nero begins the persecution of Christians in the empire; saints Peter and Paul are executed.
70–80	Vespasian builds the Colosseum.

98–117 Trajan's Imperial military successes are celebrated with his Baths (98), Forum (110), and Column (113); the Roman Empire reaches its apogee.

165 A smallpox epidemic ravages the Empire.

c 150–200 Christianity gains a foothold within the Empire, with the theological writings of Clement, Tertullian, and Origen.

212 Roman citizenship is conferred on all nonslaves in the Empire.

238 The first wave of Germanic invasions penetrates Italy.

293 Diocletian reorganizes the Empire into West and East.

313 The Edict of Milan grants toleration of Christianity within the Empire.

330 Constantine founds a new Imperial capital in the East (Constantinople).

410 Rome is sacked by Visigoths.

476 The last Roman Emperor, Romulus Augustus, is deposed.

552 Eastern Emperor Justinian (527–565) recovers control of Italy.

570 Lombards gain control of much of Italy, including Rome.

590 Papal power expands under Gregory the Great.

610 Heraldius revives the Eastern Empire, thereafter known as the Byzantine Empire.

774 Frankish ruler Charlemagne invades Italy under papal authority and is crowned Holy Roman Emperor by Pope Leo III (800).

c 800–900 The breakup of Charlemagne's (Carolingian) realm leads to the rise of Italian city-states.

811 Venice founded by mainlanders escaping Barbarian invasions.

1054 The Schism develops between Greek (Orthodox) and Latin churches.

c 1060 Europe's first university founded in Bologna.

1077 Pope Gregory VII leads the Holy See into conflict with the Germanic Holy Roman Empire.

1152–1190 Frederick I (Barbarossa) is crowned Holy Roman Emperor (1155); punitive expeditions by his forces (Ghibellines) are countered by the Guelphs, creators of the powerful Papal States in central Italy. Guelph-Ghibelline conflict becomes a feature of medieval life.

1204 Crusaders, led by Venetian Doge Dandolo, capture Constantinople.

1257 The first of four wars is declared between Genoa and Venice; at stake is the maritime control of the eastern Mediterranean.

1262 Florentine bankers issue Europe's first bills of exchange.

1264 Charles I of Anjou invades Italy, intervening in the continuing Guelph-Ghibelline conflict.

1275 Marco Polo reaches the Orient.

1290–1375 Tuscan literary giants Dante Alighieri (1265–1321), Francesco Petrarch (1304–74), and Giovanni Boccaccio (1313–75) form the basis of literature in the modern Italian language.

1309 The pope moves to Avignon in France, under the protection of French kings.

1355 Venetian Doge Marino Falier is executed for treason.

1376 The pope returns to Rome, but rival Avignonese popes stand in opposition, creating the Great Schism until 1417.

1380 Venice finally disposes of the Genoese threat in the Battle of Chioggia.

1402 The last German intervention into Italy is repulsed by the Lombards.

1443 Brunelleschi's dome is completed on Florence's Duomo (Cathedral).

1447 Nicholas V founds the Vatican Library. This begins an era of nepotistic popes who devalue the status of the papacy but greatly enrich the artistic and architectural patronage of the Holy City.

1469–92 Lorenzo "Il Magnifico," the Medici patron of the arts, rules in Florence.

1498 Girolamo Savonarola, the austere Dominican friar, is executed for heresy after leading Florence into a drive for moral purification, typified by his burning of books and decorations in the "Bonfire of Vanities."

1499 Leonardo da Vinci's *Last Supper* is completed in Milan.

1508 Michelangelo begins work on the Sistine Chapel.

1509 Raphael begins work on his *Stanze* in the Vatican.

1513 Machiavelli's *The Prince* is published.

1521 The Pope excommunicates Martin Luther of Germany, precipitating the Protestant Reformation.

1545–63 The Council of Trent formulates the Catholic response to the Reformation.

1546 Andrea del Palladio, architectural genius, wins his first commission in Vicenza.

1571 The combined navies of Venice, Spain, and the Papacy defeat the Turks in the Battle of Lepanto.

1626 St. Peter's is completed in Rome.

1633 Galileo Galilei faces the Inquisition.

1652 The church of Sant'Agnese, Borromini's Baroque masterpiece, is completed in Rome.

1667 St. Peter's Square, designed by Bernini, is completed.

c 1700 Opera develops as an art form in Italy.

1720–90 The Great Age of the Grand Tour. Northern Europeans visit Italy and start the vogue for classical studies. Among the famous visitors are Edward Gibbon (1758), Jacques-Louis David (1775), and Johann Wolfgang von Goethe (1786).

1778 Teatro alla Scala is completed in Milan.

1796 Napoleon begins his Italian campaigns, annexing Rome and imprisoning Pope Pius VI four years later.

1809 Napoleon annexes papal states to France.

1815 Austria controls much of Italy after Napoleon's downfall.

1848   Revolutionary troops under Risorgimento (Unification) leaders Giuseppe Mazzini (1805–72) and Giuseppe Garibaldi (1807–82) establish a republic in Rome.

1849   French troops crush rebellion and restore Pope Pius IX.

1860   Garibaldi and his "Thousand" defeat the Bourbon rulers in Sicily and Naples.

1870   Rome finally captured by Risorgimento troops and declared capital of Italy by King Victor Emmanuel II.

1900   King Umberto I is assassinated by an anarchist; he is succeeded by King Victor Emmanuel III.

1915   Italy enters World War I on the side of the Allies.

1922   Fascist "black shirts" under Benito Mussolini march on Rome; Mussolini becomes prime minister and later "Duce" (head of Italy).

1929   The Lateran Treaty: Mussolini recognizes Vatican City as a sovereign state, and the Church recognizes Rome as the capital of Italy.

1940–44   In World War II Italy fights with the Axis powers until its capitulation (1943), when Mussolini flees Rome. Italian partisans and Allied troops from the landings at Anzio (January 1944) win victory at Cassino (March 1944) and force the eventual withdrawal of German troops from Italy.

1957   The Treaty of Rome is signed, and Italy becomes a founding member of the European Economic Community.

1966   November flood damages much of Florence's artistic treasure.

1968–1979   The growth of left-wing activities leads to the formation of the Red Brigades and provokes right-wing reactions. Bombings and kidnappings culminate in the abduction and murder of Prime Minister Aldo Moro in 1980.

1980   Southern Italy is hit by a severe earthquake.

1991   Waves of refugees from neighboring Albania flood southern ports on the Adriatic. Mount Etna erupts, spewing forth a lava stream that threatens the Sicilian town of Zafferana.

1992   The Christian Democrat Party, in power throughout the postwar period, loses its hold on a relative majority in Parliament.

1993   Italians vote for sweeping reforms after the Tangentopoli (Bribe City) scandal exposes widespread political corruption, including politicians' collusion with organized crime. A bomb outside the Uffizi Gallery in Florence kills five, but spares the museum's most precious artworks; authorities blame the Mafia, flexing its muscles in the face of a crackdown.

1994   A center-right coalition wins the spring elections, and media magnate Silvio Berlusconi becomes premier. Italian politics seem to be evolving into the equivalent of a two party system.

Italian Art through the Ages

By Sheila Brownlee

A long-time contributor to Fodor's Guides, Sheila Brownlee is an art historian who writes regularly on the arts for many publications.

Italy is the nursery of Western art. The discoveries that Italian artists made in the 14th and 15th centuries about how to render a realistic image of a person or an object determined the course of art in the Western world right up until the late 19th century, when, with the introduction of photography, representational art became less fashionable.

Art in the Middle Ages

The eastern half of the Roman Empire, based in Constantinople (Byzantium) remained powerful long after the fall of Rome in AD 476: Italy remained influenced—and at times ruled—by the Byzantines. The artistic revolution began when artists started to rebel against the Byzantine ethic, which dictated that art be exclusively Christian and that its aim be to arouse a sensation of mystical awe and reverence in the onlooker. This ethic forbade frivolous pagan portraits, bacchanalian orgy scenes, or delicate landscapes with maidens gathering flowers, as painted and sculpted by the Romans. Instead, biblical stories were depicted in richly colored mosaics—rows of figures against a gold background. (You can see some of the finest examples of this art at Ravenna, once the Western capital of the Empire, on the Adriatic coast.) Even altarpieces, painted on wood, followed the same model—stiff figures surrounded by gold, with no attempt made at an illusion of reality.

In the 13th century, the era of St. Francis and of a new humanitarian approach to Christianity, artists in Tuscany began to make an effort to portray real people in real settings. Cimabue was the first to feel his way in this direction, but it was Giotto who broke decisively with the Byzantine style. Even if his sense of perspective was nowhere near correct and his figures still had typically Byzantine slanting eyes, he was painting palpably solid people who, presumably, experienced real emotions.

By the end of the 14th century the International Gothic Style (which had arrived in Italy from France) had made further progress toward realism, but more with depictions of plants, animals, and clothes than with the human figure. And, as you can see from Gentile da Fabriano's *Adoration of the Magi*, in the Uffizi Gallery in Florence, it was mainly a decorative art, still very much like a Byzantine mosaic.

Italian architecture during the Middle Ages followed a number of different trends. In the south, the solid Norman Romanesque style was predominant; towns such as Siena and Pisa in central Italy had their own individual Romanesque style, more graceful than its northern European counterparts. Like northern Romanesque, it was dominated by simple geometrical forms, but buildings were covered with decorative toylike patterns done in multicolored marble. In northern Italy building was in a more solemn red brick.

In Tuscany, the region around Florence, the 13th century was a time of great political and economic growth, and there was a desire to celebrate the new wealth and power in the region's buildings. This is why such civic centers as the Palazzo Vecchio in Florence are so big and fortresslike. Florence's cathedral, the Duomo, was built on a colossal scale mainly in order to outdo the Pisans and the Sienese, Florence's rivals. All these Tuscan cathedrals are in the Italian version of Gothic, a style that originated in France and found its expression there in tall, soaring, light-and-airy verticality, intended to elevate the soul. The spiritual aspect of Gothic never really caught on in Italy, where the top priority for a church (as representative of a city) was to be grander and more imposing than the neighboring cities' churches.

Art in the Renaissance

The Renaissance, or "rebirth," did not evolve simply from a set of newfound artistic skills; the movement represented a revolution in attitudes, whereby each individual was thought to have a specific role to play in the divine scheme of things. By fulfilling this role, it was believed, the individual gained a new dignity. It was no coincidence that this revolution should have taken place in Florence, which in the 15th century was an influential, wealthy, highly evolved city-state. Artists here had the leisure, the prestige, and the self-confidence to develop their talent and produce works that would reflect this new dignity and strength as well as their own prowess.

The sculptor Donatello, for instance, wanted to astound, rather than please, the spectator with his defiant warts-and-all likenesses and their intense, heroic gazes. In painting, Masaccio's figures have a similarly assured air.

Art had changed gears in the early Renaissance: The Classical Age was now the model for a noble, moving, and realistic art. Artists studied ancient Roman ruins for what they could learn about proportion and balance. They evolved the new science of perspective and took it to its limits with sometimes bizarre results, as in Uccello's dizzily receding *Deluge* (in Florence's church of Santa Maria Novella), or his carousel-like *Battle of San Romano* (in the Uffizi in Florence). One of the most frequently used perspective techniques was that of foreshortening, or making an object seem smaller and more contracted, to create the illusion of distance. From this technique emerged the *sotto in su* effect—literally, "from below upwards," meaning that the action in the picture takes place above you, with figures, buildings, and landscapes correspondingly foreshortened. It's a clever visual trick that must have delighted the visitors who walked into, for example, Mantegna's Camera degli Sposi, in Mantua, and saw what appeared to be people looking curiously down at them through a gap in the ceiling.

The concept of the universal man was epitomized by the artist who was at home with an array of disciplines, including the science of perspective, Greek, Latin, anatomy, sculpture, poetry, architecture, philosophy—even engineering, as in the case of Leonardo da Vinci, the universal man par excellence. Not surprisingly, there was a change in attitude toward artists: Whereas previously they had been considered merely anonymous workmen trained to carry out commissions, now they were seen as giant personalities, immensely skillful, with highly individual styles.

The new skills and realistic effects of Florentine painting rapidly found a sympathetic response among Venetian painters. Gentile Bellini and Antonio Carpaccio, just two of the many whose work fills the Accademia, took to covering their canvases with crowd scenes, buildings, canals, processions, dogs, ships, parrots, chimneys. These were generally narrative paintings, telling the story of a saint's life or simply depicting everyday scenes.

It was its emphasis on color, though, that made Venetian art Venetian, and it was the 15th-century masters of color, preeminently Giovanni Bellini and Giorgione, who began to use it no longer as decoration but as a means to create a particular atmosphere. How different the effect of Giorgione's *Tempest* (in the Accademia) would be with a sunny blue sky instead of the ominous grays and dark greens that fill the background! For the first time, the atmosphere, not the figures, became the central focus of the painting.

In architecture the Gothic excesses of the 13th century were toned down in the 14th, while the 15th ushered in a completely new approach. The humanist ideal was expressed through classical Roman design. In Florence, Brunelleschi used Roman columns for the basilica of San Lorenzo; Roman-style rustication (massive rough-surfaced exterior blocks) for the Pitti Palace; and Roman round arches—as opposed to pointed Gothic ones—for his Spedale degli Innocenti (Foundling Hospital), which is generally considered the first truly classical building of the Renaissance. Leon Battista Alberti's treatise on ideal proportion was even more influential as a manifesto of the Renaissance movement. Suddenly, architects had become erudite scholars, and architecture correspondingly far more earnest.

High Renaissance and Mannerism

Florence in the late 15th century, and Rome in the early 16th (following its sacking in 1527), underwent a traumatic political and religious upheaval that naturally came to be reflected in art. Classical proportion and realism no longer seemed enough. The heroic style suddenly looked hollow and out of date. Tuscan artists such as Pontormo and Rosso Fiorentino found expression for their unease in discordant colors, elongated forms, tortured looks in staring eyes. Giambologna carved his *Hercules and the Centaur* (in Florence's Museo del Bargello) at the most agonizing moment of their battle, when Hercules bends the Centaur's back to the point where it is about to snap. This is Mannerism, a style in which optimism and self-confidence are gone. What remains is a self-conscious, stylized show of virtuosity, the effect of which is neither to please (like Gothic) nor to impress (like Renaissance art), but to disquiet. Even Bronzino's portraits are cold and unsmiling and far removed from the relaxed mood of the Renaissance portrait. By the 1530s an artistic exodus from Florence had taken place; Michelangelo had left for Rome, and Florence's golden age was over.

Venice meanwhile was following its own path. Titian's painting was a more virtuoso version of Bellini's and Giorgione's poetic style, but Titian later shifted the emphasis back to the figures, rather than the atmosphere, as the central focus of his paintings. Titian's younger contemporaries in Venice—Veronese, Tintoretto, and Bassano—wanted to make names for themselves. They started working on huge canvases—which gave them more freedom of movement—playing all sorts of visual games, juggling with viewpoints and perspective and using dazzlingly bright colors. This visual trickery suggests a natural parallel with the self-conscious artifice of Florentine painting of the same period, but the exuberance of these Venetian painters, and the increasingly emotional quality of their work, chiefly their mysterious and subtle use of color, remained significantly more vital than the arid and ever more sterile works of central Italy toward the end of the 16th century.

Mannerism found a fairly precise equivalent in architecture. In Florence the rebellious younger generation (Michelangelo, Ammanati, Vasari) used the same architectural vocabulary as the Renaissance architects, but distorted it deliberately and bizarrely in a way that would have made Alberti's hair stand on end. Michelangelo's staircase at the Biblioteca Laurenziana, in Florence, for instance, spreads out like a stone fan, filling almost the entire floor space of the vestibule. Likewise, the inside walls are treated as if they were facades, though with columns and niches disproportionately large for the size of the room.

Andrea del Palladio, whose theories and elegant palaces were to be immensely influential on architecture elsewhere in Europe and as far north as England, was one of the greatest architects of the period.

The 17th and 18th Centuries

In the second half of the 16th century, Italy was caught up in the Counter-Reformation. This movement was a reaction against the Protestant Reformation of the Christian church that was sweeping through Europe. The Counter-Reformation enlisted art as a weapon: an instrument for the diffusion of the Catholic faith. Artists were discouraged from expressing themselves as freely as they had before and from creating anything that was not of a religious nature. But within this religious framework, they were able to evolve a style that appealed to the senses.

The Baroque—an emotional and heroic style that lasted through most of the 17th century—was propaganda art, designed to overwhelm the masses through its visual illusion, dramatic lighting, strong colors, and violent movement. There was an element of seduction in this propaganda: The repressive religiosity of the Counter-Reformation went hand in hand with a barely disguised eroticism. The best-known example of this ambiguity is Bernini's sculpture of the *Ecstasy of Santa Teresa*, in Rome, in which the saint sinks back in what could be a swoon, of either pain or pleasure, while a smiling angel stands over her, holding an arrow in his hand. Both the painting and architecture of this period make extensive use of sensuous curves.

The cradle of the Baroque was Rome, where Pietro da Cortona and Bernini channeled their genius into spectacular theatrical frescoes, sculptures, palaces, and churches. Rome had become the artistic center of Italy. Florence was politically and artistically dead by this time, and Venice was producing only hack imitations of Titian's and Tintoretto's paintings.

In the 18th century Venice came back into its own, and Rome was practically finished as an artistic center. Venetian artists adopted the new Rococo style, which had originated in France and was a softer, overripe version of the Baroque—a style that celebrated sensuality for its own sake, without the strength of Baroque. Although Venice was nearing the last stages of its political decline, there was still immense wealth in the city, mostly in the hands of families who wished to make the world know about it—and what better way than through vast, dazzling Rococo canvases, reassuringly stylized and removed from reality? The revival began with Sebastiano Ricci and was expertly elaborated on by Tiepolo. But it could never have taken place had there not been a return to the city's great artistic traditions. Late-16th-century color technique and expertise were drawn on and fused with what had been learned from the Baroque to create the breathtaking, magical, decadent world of the Venetian Rococo.

This was the final flowering of Venetian painting. The death of Francesco Guardi in 1793, compounded by the fall of the Republic of Venice in 1797, marked the effective end of the city's artistic life. Neoclassicism found no champion here, except for the sculptor Canova, who, in any case, did his finest work after he left Venice. Italy had made its contribution to the world of art and went into an inexorable decline.

The Wines of Italy

By Harry Eyres

A freelance journalist and wine writer, Harry Eyres is a regular contributor to the Times of London *and the* Spectator. *He is a frequent visitor to Italy's wine-producing regions.*

The Roman poets liked to speak of Italy as *"oenotria tellus,"* the land of wine (the phrase fits well at the end of a hexameter); Oenotria, in fact, was the old Greek name for southeast Italy. Long before the time of those poets, the Greeks (who colonized southern Italy from around 800 BC) and the Etruscans had established viticulture in this land, which offers, throughout its 800-mile length, so many sites favorable to the vine. In terms of quantity Italy still is the land of wine, heading the list of wine-producing countries in four years out of five; but in terms of quality, few people would think of comparing it with the world's second-largest wine producer, France.

There is a tendency to regard Italian wines as cheap and cheerful, limited to Chianti in a wicker *fiasco* (the taste often a fiasco as well); sweet, frothy Lambrusco, and little more, and Italian wine exporters, who have concentrated on the bulk, cut-price end of the market, have only themselves to blame. But just as those who explore Italian cuisine find that it is far, far more than pasta in *bolognese* sauce, so those prepared to go beyond the liter bottle of cheap Valpolicella into the lesser-known names will be rewarded by some of the most exciting and varied taste experiences in the whole world of wine. They will also discover that the Italian wine industry, for so long introverted and stagnant, has been galvanized by a new, dynamically progressive spirit.

If Italian wines have lagged far behind the French in international repute, that is partly because Italy itself is such a recent creation. The regionalism of Italy is reflected in its wines: Just as a Florentine may consider him or herself a Tuscan first, an Italian very much second, so the wine of the region is considered a Chianti first, then a Tuscan wine. The wines of each region have developed more or less independently of others. And whereas a gastronomic visit to Bordeaux, for instance, can be a severe disappointment, the wines of Italy have developed, to a greater extent than in other countries, in close association with the regional cuisine. The tough, austere red wines of Piedmont, Barolo and Barbaresco come into their own in combination with the rich game and beef dishes of the region; Piedmont's more lowly Barbera, often harsh and rough seeming, is the perfect match for *fasoeil al furn*, the sturdy country staple of red haricot beans. The pale white Verdicchio dei Castelli di Jesi, which often seems dull and neutral, can suddenly taste deliciously fresh and crisp when drunk with seafood in an Adriatic resort like Riccione or Ancona. In Tuscany, you might progress from a simple, early-drinking Chianti Putto with a starter of *funghi porcini* (porcini mushrooms) to a more subtle aged Riserva with the main course of, say, *bistecca* (steak) *alla fiorentina*. The Romans, it seems, drink Frascati with everything, but the soft, deep yellow wine that can be such a disappointment in SoHo is perfect with, say, fettuccine Alfredo.

Given Italy's regional diversity and the legendary individualism of the Italians, it is hardly surprising that wine legislation in Italy was slow to be enacted and that, to some leading producers, it still seems more of a hindrance than a help. It was only in 1963 that the system of *denominazione di origine controllata* (DOC) was instituted, specifying more than 200 delimited areas and laying down rules about approved grape varieties, yields, and periods of aging. Even today, though, only 10%–12% of Italian wine production qualifies for DOC. A growing feeling that these rules were not sufficiently stringent led to the establishment in 1979 of another category, DOCG, standing for the same as DOC but with the addition of the word *garantita* (guaranteed). The first denominations to achieve the DOCG standard include Barolo, Barbaresco, Chianti Classico, and Brunello di Montalcino. Some of Italy's very finest wines, however, stand outside both systems of classification, which their makers—artists and individualists—consider impossibly restrictive: The 100% cabernet sauvignon Tuscan Sassicaia, marketed by Antinori; the fine Trentino Muller-Thurgau of Pojer & Sandri; and Volpaia's blend of Sangioveto and Mammolo, Coltassala, are all incongruously called *vini da tavola* (table wine), the lowest category of Italian wine. This does not stop them from fetching twice the price of a DOCG. The old maxim about wine, that the only true guarantee of quality is the name of a trustworthy producer, is particularly valid in Italy. In 1986 a small group of Italian wine producers committed a murderous breach of trust by boosting the alcoholic degree of certain wines with poisonous methanol; they claim that these wines were intended for distillation into industrial alcohol and not to be sold as wine. The fact was that the wines got onto the market, and 20 people lost their lives. Horrific though this incident was, two points should be made: First, that the wine concerned was of the lowest quality and, second, that none of the contaminated wine ever left Italy.

The methanol scandal certainly had an effect on the market for Italian wine both at home and overseas. Italians are now drinking substantially less wine than previously, but they are also becoming more discriminating. Higher-quality Italian wines are also gaining ground in most of the export markets, such as the United States, Germany, and Holland; in Britain, the cheap and cheerful image is proving harder to shake off. But in the better Italian restaurants, both in Italy itself and overseas, the sight of a bottle of Chianti Classico Riserva, Barolo, or high-class white from Friuli or Alto Adige, rather than the standard carafe of house wine, is becoming increasingly common.

This development reflects the enormous changes, the great majority of them changes for the better, that have been taking place in Italian cellars and vineyards over the past 10 or 15 years. The most far-reaching change has certainly been the widespread introduction of temperature-controlled fermentation, enabling producers to make consistently clean, healthy, lively red, and especially white, wines in place of the dull, flat oxidized stuff of yesteryear. Furthermore, attention has turned to the vineyards, and to the awesome task of sorting out the myriad varieties of vine that old Oenotria had allowed to flourish, often with little control or even knowledge. A few years ago there was a rush to plant the fashionable French varieties, like chardonnay and cabernet sauvignon. That has now abated somewhat, and there are encouraging signs of a return to old native varieties capable of bearing high-quality, but distinctively Italian, fruit. Arneis and Grecchetto are notable among the whites, and Sangiovese is notable among the reds. Italy's wine makers are rediscovering a pride in themselves and the potential of the old heartland of the vine.

The Wine Regions of Italy

The Northwest
Piedmont. Together with Tuscany, the Piedmont region is Italy's premier producer of quality wines. Its most famous wine is probably the semisweet sparkling Asti Spumante. This, as well as its slightly less fizzy brother, Moscato d'Asti, is a deliciously fresh grapey wine, which no one should feel ashamed of finding enjoyable. Piedmont is proudest, though, of the stern tannic reds made from the Nebbiolo grape near the town of Alba: Barolo and Barbaresco. These are something of an acquired taste. First-timers might be advised to try the less austere Nebbiolo-based wines called Gattinara, Ghemme, and Spanna. They are also considerably cheaper. The two other red wines worth looking for are Barbera, often rough, but delicious in the hands of a good producer, and the deep purple, softly fruity Dolcetto. Piedmont's only DOC white wine of note is the clean but somewhat neutral (and overpriced) Gavi, sometimes called Cortese di Gavi. Watch, though, for the subtle, rich Arneis (still only vino da tavola). Fine producers include Gaja, Pio Cesare, Ceretto, and the Conterno family.

Lombardy. Lombardy has never made much fuss about its wines, which are some of Italy's most underrated. Try the vigorous, almost Bordeaux-style, reds from Franciacorta and the fruity white Lugana from the southern shore of Lake Garda.

The Northeast
Trentino-Alto Adige. The Alto Adige is also known as the Südtirol, a German-speaking former province of Austria consisting of high Alpine valleys. The wine-making tradition is more Germanic than Latin: Aromatic white varieties like Riesling, Gewürztraminer, and Muller-Thurgau flourish and make crisp perfumed dry whites unlike any others in Italy. Notable chardonnays are made by producers like Lageder and Tiefenbrunner. The light red from the local Lagrein grape is worth a try. Trentino, the southern half of the area, makes similar wines, with more emphasis on red (cabernet and an attractive Beaujolais-style local variety called Teroldego Rotaliano), a little softer and fuller in style. The Veneto's three most famous wines are the light reds Valpolicella and Bardolino and the crisp dry white Soave—all names tarnished by industrial mass production. Good examples can still be found: The Bardolino of

Wine Regions

Fraterna Portalupi is deliciously fresh and cherry scented; Masi's Valpolicella has a distinctive bitter tang; and the Soaves of Anselmi and Pieropan are fine and fruity. Veneto's *vino di meditazione* (to be drunk reflectively on its own) is the strong, deep, bitter Recioto Amarone della Valpolicella made from selected half-dried grapes.

Friuli-Venezia Giulia. Italy's most highly prized whites, not much seen on the export markets, are made in this eastern province bordering Slovenia. Pinot Bianco and Pinot Grigio give wines with great depth of fruit and richness of texture. The native Tocai makes a full dry white with an intriguingly herbaceous character. Among the reds, grassy cabernet Franc and supple Merlot can be excellent. Jermann, Collavini, Schiopetto, and EnoFriulia are good producers.

Central Italy   **Emilia-Romagna.** This is a better region for food than for wine, though Lambrusco can be dry and delicious, not just sweet and frothy.

Tuscany. This region produces the Italian red wines closest in structure to great red Bordeaux: These are the top wines of Chianti Classico, from the hill country between Florence and Siena and Brunello di Montalcino, a little farther south. It must be said that the name of Chianti was besmirched in the '60s and '70s by a lot of very dull, astringent wine sold under its appellation. The region is now going through a dynamic phase of self-regeneration. Lighter, less serious Chianti is a delicious wine for everyday consumption; the Riservas can age for at least 10 years and acquire a fascinating complexity of flavor. Recently arrived on the scene are the so-called super-Tuscans, premium wines often made from a blend of Sangiovese and cabernet (and therefore qualifying only as vini da tavola) and aged in small oak barriques. Some of the best are Sassicaia (100% cabernet sauvignon), Tignanello, and Coltassala. Brunello di Montalcino (DOCG) is one of Italy's most powerful (and expensive) reds: The most famous producer is Biondi-Santi, but an excellent lighter and cheaper version is made by Altesino. Another Tuscan specialty is *vin santo*, an extraordinary sweet, liquorous white made from grapes dried on straw mats and fermented over many years.

Umbria. The most famous wine is white Orvieto, which can be either sweet (*abboccato*) or dry. The best wine, though, is Lungarotti's Rubesco Torgiano Riserva: a rich, complex red from near Perugia.

The provinces of **Marche, Abruzzi,** and **Molise** in the central east do not produce much distinguished wine, though dry white Verdicchio and the sturdy reds of Rosso Conero and Montepulciano d'Abruzzo are worth investigating.

Latium, the area around Rome, is notable above all, for soft, golden Frascati.

The South and Islands   Huge quantities of strong, mainly red, wine, high in alcohol and generally undistinguished in quality, pour out of the southern provinces of Campania, Apulia, Basilicata, and Calabria, and the two large islands of Sicily and Sardinia. Mastroberardini, in Campania, produces excellent red Taurasi and remarkably

fruity and refined white Greco di Tufo and Fiano di Avellino.
The powerful red Aglianico del Vulture, from a mountain in Ba-
silicata, can be excellent. Sicily's most famous wine used to be
the tangy fortified Marsala. It is now most unfashionable, but
De Bartoli's (dry) Vecchio Samperi is of high quality. Some good
Sicilian table wine is being made, from the reliable, commercial
Corvo to the more classy Regaleali. Sardinia's fruity, sturdy
reds, especially Cannonau, can be an excellent value.

Useful Terms

Rosso, bianco, and **rosato** are easy enough; **chiaretto** can also be
used for pink.
The words **annata** and **vendemmia** are both used for vintage.
Secco and **asciutto** both mean dry. **Abboccato, amabile,** and **dolce**
indicate three grades of sweetness, from medium to very sweet.
Passito means a sweet wine made from partially dried grapes,
and **liquoroso** means a fortified dessert wine.
Frizzante means slightly sparkling, and **spumante** decidedly
fizzy.
Vigna and **vigneto** are both used for vineyard; **tenuta** and
azienda agricola both mean estate; and **fattoria** means farmstead (not factory). **Azienda vinicola** means winery, **cantina**
means cellar, and **cantina sociale** means cooperative winery.
Classico indicates that the wine comes from a privileged zone
within a wider controlled appellation. The most famous example
is Chianti Classico, whose active **consorzio** (association of growers) uses the symbol of the **gallo nero** (black rooster) to identify
every bottle made by its members. **Enoteca** is a wine library,
with bottles instead of books: Two leading ones are in Siena and
the small town of Greve, in Chianti.

3 Rome

From ancient times, Romans have been piling the present on top of the past, blithely building, layering, and overlapping their more than 2,500 years of history to create the haphazard fabric of modern Rome. The result is a city where antiquity is taken for granted, where you can have coffee in a square designed by Bernini and go home to a Renaissance palace. Normal life in Rome is carried on in the most extraordinary setting.

Don't be self-conscious in your wanderings about the city. Poke and pry under the surface of things. Walk boldly through gates that are just ajar to peek into the hidden world of Roman courtyards. But do it with a smile, to show the people you meet that you're truly interested in them. Warm and straightforward, the Romans are pleased to show you the nooks and crannies of their hometown.

The good-humored Romans have their problems, of course. The city is noisy, polluted, afflicted with hellish traffic, and exasperatingly inefficient. But at least the traffic problem is being tackled. Sizable areas of the city center have been designated for pedestrians only. The pollution problem is less easy to cure, and far too many of the monuments you will want to see are shielded in fine green netting, while work proceeds on cleaning and repairing them.

Keep your sightseeing flexible. You'll have to plan your day to take into account the wide diversity of opening times—which will mean mixing classical sites with Baroque, museums with parks, the center with the environs. However you do it, be sure to take plenty of time off for simply sitting and observing the passing pageant of the city's teeming streets.

Inevitably, the environs of Rome are overshadowed by the five-star attractions of the Eternal City. However, the surrounding region, known as Lazio (Latium), has plenty to offer in its own right—ancient art and archaeology, medieval hill towns and abbeys, Renaissance pleasure gardens, lake and mountain scenery, and an easygoing pace, not to mention great local wines and homemade pasta. Intersperse city sightseeing with jaunts into the countryside. A breath of country air and a change of scenery can enhance your enjoyment of Rome and give you a new perspective on its many delights.

Essential Information

Arriving and Departing by Plane

Airports and Airlines Most international flights and all domestic flights arrive at **Leonardo da Vinci** airport, also known as **Fiumicino,** 30 kilometers (18 miles) outside the city. Some international charter flights land at **Ciampino,** a military airport on the Via Appia Nuova, 15 kilometers (9 miles) from the center of Rome.

Between Leonardo da Vinci Airport and Downtown
By Train To get to downtown Rome from Fiumicino airport you have a choice of two trains. Inquire at the airport (at EPT or train information counters) as to which takes you closest to your hotel. The non-stop Airport-Termini express takes you directly to Track 22 at Termini station, Rome's main train station, well served by taxis and the hub of Metro and bus lines. The ride to Termini takes 30 minutes; departures are hourly, beginning at 7:50 AM from the airport, with a final departure at 10:55 PM. Tickets cost 12,000 lire. The other airport train has its terminal at Tiburtina train station, east of downtown Rome. It makes several stops, including Trastevere and Ostiense stations, on

the southern fringes of downtown Rome. This train runs from 6 AM to 10 PM, with departures every 20 minutes. The ride to Tiburtina takes 40 minutes. Tickets cost 7,000 lire. For either train you buy your ticket at automatic vending machines (you need Italian currency). There are ticket counters at some stations (Termini Track 22, Trastevere, Tiburtina).

By Taxi A taxi from the airport to the center of town costs about 60,000 lire, including supplements for airport service and luggage, and the ride takes 30–40 minutes, depending on traffic. Private limousines can be hired at booths in the arrivals hall; they charge a little more than taxis but can take more passengers. Ignore gypsy drivers; stick to yellow or white cabs. A booth inside the arrivals hall provides taxi information.

By Car Follow the signs for Rome on the expressway, which links with the Grande Raccordo Anulare (GRA), the beltway around Rome. The direction you take on the GRA depends on where your hotel is located, so get directions from the car-rental people at the airport.

Arriving and Departing by Car, Train, and Bus

By Car The main access routes from the north are A1 (Autostrada del Sole) from Milan and Florence or the A12/E80 highway from Genoa. The principal route to or from points south, including Naples, is the A2. All highways connect with the GRA, which channels traffic into the center. Markings on the GRA are confusing: Take time to study the route you need.

By Train Termini Station is Rome's main train terminal; the Tiburtina and Ostiense stations serve a few long-distance trains. Some trains for Pisa and Genoa leave Rome from, or pass through, the Trastevere Station. For train information, call tel. 06/4775, 7 AM–10:40 PM. You can find English-speaking staff at the information office at Termini Station, or ask for information at travel agencies. If you purchase tickets and book seat reservations in advance either at the main stations or at travel agencies bearing the FS (Ferrovie dello Stato) emblem, you'll avoid long lines at ticket windows. Additionally, ticket windows on the lower concourse in Termini Station sell tickets and reserve seats for all trains, and also sell subway, bus, and airport train tickets. Tickets for train rides within a radius of 100 kilometers of Rome can be purchased at tobacco shops as well as at ticket machines on the main concourse.

By Bus There is no central bus terminal in Rome. COTRAL is the suburban bus company that connects Rome with outlying areas and other cities in the Lazio region. Long-distance and suburban buses terminate either near Termini Station or near Metro stops. For COTRAL bus information, call tel. 06/591–5551, Mon.–Fri. 7 AM–6 , Sat. 7 AM–2 PM.

Getting Around

Although most of Rome's sights are in a relatively circumscribed area, the city is too large to be seen solely on foot. Take the Metro (subway), a bus, or a taxi to the area you plan to visit, and expect to do a lot of walking once you're there. Wear a pair of comfortable, sturdy shoes, preferably with rubber or crepe soles to cushion the impact of the *sampietrini* (cobblestones). Heed our advice on security and get away from the noise and polluted air of heavily trafficked streets by taking parallel streets whenever possible. You can buy transportation-route maps at newsstands and at ATAC (Rome's public transit authority) information and ticket booths. The free city map distributed by Rome EPT offices is good; it also shows Metro and bus routes, although bus routes are not always marked clearly.

By Metro This is the easiest and fastest way to get around, but it's limited in extent. The Metro opens at 5:30 AM, and the last trains leave the farthest station at 11:30 PM. There are two lines—A and B—which intersect at Termini Station. The fare is 1,000 lire. There are ticket booths at major stations, but elsewhere you must use ticket machines. It's best to buy single tickets or books of 10 at newsstands and tobacconists. The "BIG" daily tourist ticket, good on buses as well, costs 4,000 lire at present and is sold at Metro and ATAC ticket booths.

By Bus Orange ATAC city buses and tram lines run from about 6 AM to midnight, with skeleton (*notturno*) services on main lines through the night. Remember to board at the back and exit at the middle. The ticket, 1,200 lire, is valid on all ATAC bus lines for a total of 90 minutes. Buy it before boarding, and time-stamp it in the machine on the first bus you board. Tickets are sold at tobacconists and newsstands. A weekly tourist ticket costs 18,000 lire and is sold at ATAC booths. The BIG tourist ticket is also valid on the Metro for one day (*see above*).

By Taxi Taxis wait at stands and can also be called by phone, in which case you're charged a small supplement. The meter starts at 6,400 lire, a fixed rate for the first 3 kilometers (1.8 miles); there are supplements for service after 10 PM and on Sunday or holidays, as well as for each piece of baggage. Use only metered yellow or white cabs. To call a cab, telephone 3875, 3570, 4994, or 8433. **Radio Taxi** (tel. 06/3875) accepts American Express and Diners Club credit cards, but you must specify when calling that you will pay that way.

By Bicycle Pedaling through Villa Borghese, along the Tiber, and through the center of the city when traffic is light is a pleasant way to see the sights, but remember: Rome is hilly. (For bicycle rentals, *see* Sports and Fitness in Exploring Rome, *below.*)

By Scooter You can rent a moped or scooter and mandatory helmet at **Scoot-a-Long** (Via Cavour 302, tel. 06/678–0206) or **St. Peter's Moto** (Via di Porta Castello 43, tel. 06/687–5714).

Important Addresses and Numbers

Tourist Information The main **EPT** (Rome Provincial Tourist Office) is at Via Parigi 5, tel. 06/488–3748. Open Mon.–Fri. 8:15–7:15, Sat. 8:15–1:15. There are also EPT booths at Termini Station and Leonardo da Vinci airport.

For information on places other than Rome, there is a booth at **ENIT** (National Tourist Board), Via Marghera 2, tel. 06/497–1293. Open Mon., Wed., Fri. 9–1, 4–6; Tues., Thurs. 9–1.

Consulates **U.S. Consulate** (Via Veneto 121, tel. 06/46741). **Canadian Consulate** (Via Zara 30, tel. 06/440–3028). **U.K. Consulate** (Via Venti Settembre 80A, tel. 06/482–5441).

Emergencies **Police,** tel. 06/4686.

Ambulance (Red Cross), tel. 06/5100.

Doctors and Dentists: Call your consulate or the private Salvator Mundi Hospital (tel. 06/589–4867) or Rome American Hospital (tel. 06/22551), which have English-speaking staff, for recommendations.

Late-Night Pharmacies You will find American and British products—or their equivalents—and English-speaking staff at **Farmacia Internazionale Capranica** (Piazza Capranica 96, tel. 056/679–4680), **Farmacia Internazionale Barberini** (Piazza Barberini 49, tel. 06/482–5456), and **Farmacia Doricchi** (Via Venti Settembre 47, tel. 06/487–3880), among others. Most are open 8:30–1, 4–8; some are open all night. Pharmacies take turns opening on Sunday. A schedule is posted in each pharmacy.

English-Language Bookstores English-language paperback books and magazines are available at newsstands in the center of Rome, especially on Via Veneto. For all types of books in English, visit the **Economy Book and Video Center** (Via Torino 136, tel. 06/474–6877), the **Anglo-American Bookstore** (Via della Vite 27, tel. 06/679–5222), or the **Lion Bookshop** (Via del Babuino 181, tel. 06/322–5837).

Travel Agencies **American Express** (Piazza di Spagna 38, tel. 06/67641), **CIT** (Piazza della Repubblica 64, tel. 06/47941), **Wagons Lits** (Via Boncompagni 25, tel. 06/481–7655).

Opening and Closing Times

Rome's churches have erratic and unpredictable opening times; they are *not* open all the time. Most are open from about 7 to 12 and 3 to 7, but don't be surprised if the church you were especially keen on seeing is closed even during these times. Many that are shut during the week can, however, be visited on Sunday. Appropriate dress—no shorts—is required.

Banks are open weekdays from 8:30 to 1:30 and 3 or 3:30 to 4 or 4:30. Shops are open Monday through Saturday, 9:30 to 1 and 3:30 or 4 through 7 or 7:30. Many are closed Monday mornings from September through June and Saturday afternoons from July through August.

Guided Tours

Orientation **American Express** (tel. 06/67641), **CIT** (tel. 06/47941), **Appian Line** (tel. 06/488–4151), and other operators offer three-hour tours in air-conditioned 60-passenger buses with English-speaking guides. There are four standard itineraries: "Ancient Rome" (including the Roman Forum and Colosseum), "Classic Rome" (including St. Peter's Basilica, Trevi Fountain, and the Janiculum Hill), "Christian Rome" (some major churches and the Catacombs), and "The Vatican Museums and Sistine Chapel." Most cost about 36,000 lire, but the Vatican Museums tour costs about 48,000 lire. American Express tours depart from Piazza di Spagna, and CIT from Piazza della Repubblica, both with some hotel pick-ups; Appian Line picks you up at your hotel.

American Express and other operators can provide a luxury car for up to three people, a limousine for up to seven, and a minibus for up to nine—all with English-speaking driver—but guide service is extra. A minibus costs about 450,000 lire for three hours. Almost all operators offer "Rome by Night" tours, with or without pizza or dinner and entertainment. You can book tours through travel agents.

The least-expensive organized sightseeing tour of Rome is run by **ATAC,** the municipal bus company. Tours leave from Piazza dei Cinquecento, in front of Termini Station, last about three hours, and cost about 10,000 lire. There's no running commentary, but you're given an illustrated guide with which you can easily identify the sights. Buy tickets at the ATAC information booth in front of Termini Station; there is at least one tour daily, departing at 2:30 (3:30 in summer). The least expensive sightseeing of all are the routes of bus no. 119 downtown, bus no. 56 across Rome to Trastevere, or the circle route of the no. 19 tram. For each, the cost is 1,200 lire one way.

Special- You can make your own arrangements (at no cost) to attend a public
Interest papal audience in the Vatican or at the pope's summer residence at Castel Gandolfo. Or you can book through **CIT** (tel. 06/47941), **Appian Line** (Via Barberini 109, tel. 06/488–4151), or **Carrani Tours** (Via Vittorio Emanuele Orlando 95, tel. 06/488–0510). These agencies take you by bus to the Vatican for the audience, showing you some sights along the way and returning you to or near your hotel, for about 36,000 lire. The excursion for the pope's noon blessing on summer Sundays at Castel Gandolfo costs about 40,000 lire.

Excursions Most operators offer half-day excursions to Tivoli to see the fountains and gardens of the Villa d'Este. **Appian Line's** (tel. 06/488–4151) and **CIT's** half-day tours to Tivoli include a visit to Hadrian's Villa, with its impressive Roman ruins. Most operators also have full-day excursions to Florence, Assisi, Pompeii, and Capri, among other places of interest.

Personal You can arrange for a personal guide through **American Express** (tel.
Guides 06/67641); **CIT** (tel. 06/47941); or the main **EPT Tourist Information Office** (tel. 06/488–3748).

Walking If you have a reasonable knowledge of Italian, you can take advantage of the free guided visits and walking tours organized by Rome's cultural associations and the city council for museums and monuments. These usually take place on Sunday mornings. Programs are announced in the daily newspapers.

Exploring Rome

Our exploration of Rome is divided into 10 tours. We begin where Rome itself began, amid the ancient ruins, and follow with a look at the Vatican and its museums—two separate tours. The next six tours explore various places of interest in central Rome, while Tour 10 takes you on a short trip outside the city walls. With the exception of Tours 2 and 3, which concentrate on the Vatican, Tour 8, which explores the Villa Borghese, Tour 9, which crosses the Tiber to the Trastevere district, and Tour 10, out the Appian Way to the Catacombs, these Rome tours begin in or around Piazza Venezia.

The MuseidonCard, valid for two, four, or seven days and costing from 13,000 lire to 48,000 lire, provides entrance to city museums and some monuments. It's sold at participating museums, APT offices, and some hotels and tobaconnists, but think twice before buying it because not many of the major museums are city run.

At the end of the chapter are three excursions into the surrounding countryside. Although all the places we suggest visiting could be seen on a day's trip from Rome, some itineraries combine several destinations and could be broken by an overnight stop somewhere along the way, to maintain an easy pace. If you're driving, you'll find good roads, but you may run into pockets of local traffic in the suburbs. Try not to schedule your excursions for Sundays, when the Romans make their weekly exodus and create traffic jams on their return.

A (repeat) word of caution: Gypsy children, present around sites popular with tourists throughout Europe, are rife in Rome and are adept pickpockets. One modus operandi is to approach a tourist and proffer a piece of cardboard with writing on it. While the unsuspecting victim attempts to read the message *on* it, the gypsy children's hands are busy *under* it, making like piranhas with the contents of a purse. If you see such a group (recognizable by their unkempt appearance, often with cigarettes hanging from prepubescent mouths), do not even allow them near you—they are quick and know more tricks than you do. Also be aware of Italian perpetrators who ride by on motorbikes, grab the shoulder strap of your bag, and step on the gas. Keep your bag well under your arm, especially if you're walking on the street edge of the sidewalk, or wear a money belt. Don't carry more money than you need, and don't carry your passport unless you need it to exchange money.

Highlights for First-Time Visitors

Campidoglio (Tour 1: Ancient Rome).

Castel Sant'Angelo (Tour 2: The Vatican).

Colosseum (Tour 1: Ancient Rome).

Piazza Navona (Tour 4: Old Rome).

Roman Forum (Tour 1: Ancient Rome).

St. Peter's (Tour 2: The Vatican).

Santa Maria Maggiore (Tour 6: Historic Churches).

Sistine Chapel (Tour 3: The Vatican Museums).

Spanish Steps (Tour 5: The Spanish Steps
and the Trevi Fountain).

Trevi Fountain (Tour 5: The Spanish Steps and the Trevi Fountain).

Tour 1: Ancient Rome

*Numbers in the margin correspond to points of interest on the Rome
map.*

Rome, as is common knowledge, was built on seven hills. Its legendary founders, the twins Romulus and Remus, were abandoned as infants but were suckled by a she-wolf on the banks of the Tiber and adopted by a shepherd. Encouraged by the gods to build a city, the twins chose a site in 735 BC, fortifying it with a wall that has been identified by archaeologists digging on the Palatine, the first hill of Rome to be inhabited. During the building of the city, the brothers quarreled, and in a fit of anger Romulus killed Remus. Excavations on the Palatine and in the Forum area have revealed hard evidence of at least some aspects of the city's legendary beginnings.

The ruins on the two most historic hills—the Capitoline and the Palatine—mark the center of ancient Rome, capital of the classical world and center of a vast empire. The former hill held the seat of government, the Capitol, whose name is commemorated in every capital city in the world, as well as in government buildings, such as the Capitol in Washington, DC.

If you stand on the Capitoline and gaze out over the ruins of the Forum to the Palatine, with the Colosseum looming in the background, you can picture how Rome looked when it was the center of the known world. Imagine the Forum filled with immense, brightly painted temples. Picture the faint glow from the temple of Vesta, where the vestal virgins tended their sacred fire, and the glistening marble palace complex on the Palatine, its roof studded with statues, where the emperors and their retinues lived in incredible luxury. Then think of how the area looked in the Dark Ages, when Rome had sunk into malaria-ridden squalor.

The **Capitoline hill** is a good place to begin when exploring the city. Rome's first and most sacred temples stood here. The city's archives were kept in the Tabularium (hall of records), the tall, gray stone
❶ structure that forms the foundations of today's city hall, the **Palazzo Senatorio.** By the Middle Ages, the Campidoglio, as the hill was then known, had fallen into ruin. In 1537, Pope Paul III called on Michelangelo to restore it to grandeur, and the artist designed the ramp, the buildings on three sides of the **Campidoglio** Square, the slightly convex pavement and its decoration, and the pedestal for the bronze equestrian statue of Marcus Aurelius. A work of the 2nd century AD, the statue stood here from the 16th century to just recently, when it was removed for restoration and reinstallation in a more friendly environment inside the Palazzo dei Conservatori (*see below*). Eventually, a copy of the statue will occupy the original pedestal outdoors.

The palaces flanking the Palazzo Senatorio contain two museums, the **Museo Capitolino** and the **Palazzo dei Conservatori,** whose collections were assembled in the 15th century by Pope Sixtus V, one of the earliest of the great papal patrons of the arts. Those with a taste for Roman and Greek sculpture will appreciate both museums; others may find the collections dull but the setting impressive. Many of the statues were restored by overconscientious 18th- and 19th-century collectors who added heads and limbs with considerable aban-

Rome

Acqua Paola
Fountain, **64**
Aracoeli, **4**
Ara Pacis, **56**
Arch of Constantine, **9**
Campo dei Fiori, **24**
Castel Sant'Angelo, **12**
Circus Maximus, **8**
Colosseum, **10**
Column of Marcus
Aurelius, **29**
Domus Aurea, **11**

Fountain of the
Barcaccia, **31**
Fountain of the Four
Rivers, **21**
Fountain of the
Naiads, **46**
Fontana delle
Tartárughe (Turtle
Fountain), **58**
Galleria Borghese, **50**
Galleria Nazionale
(Palazzo Barberini), **41**
Galleria Nazionale
d'Arte Moderna, **51**

Il Gesù, **16**
Janiculum Park, **65**
Mamertine Prison, **6**
Museo Capitolino, **2**
Museo Nationale
Romano, **48**
Museo di
Villa Giulia, **52**
Palazzo dei
Conservatori, **3**
Palazzo Farnese, **25**
Palazzo del
Quirinale, **38**

Palazzo Senatorio, **1**
Palazzo Venezia, **27**
Pantheon, **18**
Piazza Navona, **20**
Piazza del Popolo, **54**
Piazza San Pietro, **13**
Piazza Santa Maria in
Trastevere, **61**
Pincio, **53**
Porta Pinciana, **49**
Roman Forum, **7**
St. Peter's, **14**

don. Originally, almost all these works were brilliantly colored and gilded. Remember that many of the works here and in Rome's other museums are copies of Greek originals. For hundreds of years, craftsmen of ancient Rome prospered by producing copies of Greek statues on order; they used a process called "pointing," by which exact copies could be made.

Portraiture, however, was one area in which the Romans outstripped the Greeks. The hundreds of Roman portrait busts in the **②** **Museo Capitolino** are the highlight of a visit here. In the courtyard, the reclining river god is one of the "talking statues" to which citizens of ancient Rome affixed anonymous political protests and satirical barbs. The most interesting pieces, on display upstairs, include the poignant *Dying Gaul* and the delicate *Marble Faun*, which inspired novelist Nathaniel Hawthorne's tale of the same name. Then you'll come upon the rows of portrait busts, a kind of ancient *Who's Who*, though rather haphazardly labeled. Look for cruel Caracalla, vicious Nero, and haughty Marcus Aurelius.

③ Across the square is the **Palazzo dei Conservatori,** which contains similar treasures. The huge head and hand in the courtyard are fragments of a colossal statue of the emperor Constantine; these immense effigies were much in vogue in the later days of the Roman empire. The resplendent Salone dei Orazi e Curiazi upstairs is a ceremonial hall with a magnificent gilt ceiling, carved wooden doors, and 16th-century frescoes. Farther on, you'll see the famous *Capitoline Wolf*, a 6th-century BC Etruscan bronze; the twins were added during the Renaissance to adapt the statue to the legend of Romulus and Remus. *Museo Capitolino and Palazzo dei Conservatori, Piazza del Campidoglio, tel. 06/671–02071. Admission: 10,000 lire. Open May–Sept., Tues. 9–1:30 and 5–8, Wed.–Fri. 9–1:30, Sat. 9–1:30 and 8–11, Sun. 9–1; Oct.–Apr., Tues. and Sat. 9–1:30 and 5–8, Wed.–Fri. 9–1:30, Sun. 9–1.*

④ The Capitoline's church of **Aracoeli** was one of the first in the city built by the emerging Christians. It's known for Pinturicchio's 16th-century frescoes in the first chapel on the right and for a much-revered wooden figure of the Christ Child, kept in a small chapel in the sacristy.

The Campidoglio gardens offer the best view of the sprawling ruins of ancient Rome. **Caesar's Forum** lies below the garden, to the left of Palazzo Senatorio. It is the oldest of the Imperial Fora, those built by the emperors, as opposed to those built during the earlier, Republican period (6th–1st centuries BC), as part of the original Roman Forum.

Across Via dei Fori Imperiali, the broad avenue created by Premier Benito Mussolini for his triumphal parades, are, from the left, **⑤** **Trajan's Column,** in the base of which the emperor Trajan's ashes were buried, **Trajan's Forum,** with its huge semicircular market building, and the ruins of the **Forum of Augustus.**

Now turn your attention to the Roman Forum, in what was once a marshy valley between the Capitoline and Palatine hills. The shortest way down is Via San Pietro in Carcere—actually a flight of stairs **⑥** descending to the church that stands over the **Mamertine Prison,** a series of gloomy, subterranean cells where Rome's vanquished enemies were finished off. Legend has it that St. Peter was held prisoner here and that he miraculously brought forth a spring of water in order to baptize his jailers. *Donation requested. Open daily 9–12:30, 2–7:30.*

From the main entrance on Via dei Fori Imperiali, descend into the
➐ extraordinary archaeological complex that is the **Roman Forum.**
This was the civic heart of Republican Rome, the austere Rome that
preceded the hedonistic society that grew up under the emperors in
the 1st to the 4th century AD. Today it seems no more than a baffling
series of ruins, marble fragments, isolated columns, a few worn
arches, and occasional paving stones. Yet it once was filled with
stately and extravagant buildings—temples, palaces, shops—and
crowded with people from all corners of the world. What you see are
the ruins not of one period, but of almost 900 years, from about 500
BC to AD 400. As the original buildings became too small or old-fashioned, they were pulled down and replaced by more lavish structures. Making sense of these scarred and pitted stones is not easy;
you may want just to wander along, letting your imagination dwell
on Julius Caesar, Cicero, and Mark Antony, who delivered the funeral address in Caesar's honor from the rostrum just left of the
Arch of Septimius Severus. *Entrances on Via dei Fori Imperiali,
Piazza Santa Maria Nova, and Via di San Gregorio, tel. 06/699–
0110. Admission: 10,000 lire. Open Apr.–Sept., Mon., Wed.–Sat.
9–6, Tues. and Sun. 9–1; Oct.–Mar., Mon., Wed.–Sat, 9–3, Tues.
and Sun. 9–1.*

Leave the Forum by the exit at Arco di Tito (Arch of Titus), which is
at the end of the Forum away from the Capitoline. From here, the
Clivus Palatinus, an ancient path, leads up the Palatine hill, where
the emperors built their palaces. From the belvedere you can see the
➑ **Circus Maximus,** where more than 300,000 spectators could watch
chariot and horse races while the emperors looked on from this very
spot. The Italian garden on the Palatine was laid out during the Renaissance. Leaving the Palatine by way of the Via di San Gregorio
➒ exit, you'll come upon the imposing **Arch of Constantine,** erected in
AD 315 to commemorate Constantine's victory over Maxentius.

➓ Just beyond is the **Colosseum,** the most famous monument of ancient
Rome. Begun by the Flavian emperor Vespasian in AD 72, it was inaugurated by Titus eight years later with a program of games and
shows lasting 100 days. On the opening day alone, 5,000 wild beasts
perished in the arena. More than 50,000 spectators could crowd into
the 573-yard circumference, which was faced with marble and
boasted an ingenious system of awnings to shade them from the sun.
Originally known as the Flavian Amphitheater, in later centuries it
came to be called the Colosseum, after a colossal gilded bronze statue of Nero that stood nearby. It served as a fortress during the 13th
century and then as a quarry from which materials were filched to
build sumptuous Renaissance churches and palaces. Finally it was
declared sacred by the popes, in memory of the many Christians believed martyred there. You must pay admission to the upper levels.
*Piazza del Colosseo, tel. 06/700–4261. Admission free; admission to
upper levels: 6,000 lire. Open Mon., Tues., Thurs.–Sat. 9–one hour
before sunset, Wed. and Sun. 9–1.*

Behind the Colosseum at the Colle Oppio (Oppian Hill) on the
⓫ Esquiline Hill is what's left of Nero's fabulous **Domus Aurea,** a sumptuous palace later buried under Trajan's Baths.

Time Out About half a block from the Colosseum is **Pasqualino,** a reasonably
priced neighborhood trattoria with a few sidewalk tables with a
view of the arena's marble arches. (Via Santi Quattro 66. Closed
Mon.)

If you head back toward Piazza Venezia on Via dei Fori Imperiali, you can get a good look at the Imperial Fora and Trajan's Market.

Tour 2: The Vatican

While the ancient Roman emperors presided over the decline of their empire, a vibrant new force emerged. Christianity came to Rome, the seat of the popes was established over the tomb of St. Peter, and the Vatican became the spiritual focus of the Roman Catholic Church. There are two principal reasons for seeing the Vatican. One is to visit St. Peter's, the largest church in the world and the most overwhelming architectural achievement of the Renaissance. The other is to visit the Vatican Museums, which contain collections of staggering richness and diversity, including, of course, the Sistine Chapel. There's little point in trying to take it all in on just one visit. See St. Peter's first, and come back later to see the Vatican Museums.

⓬ Start at **Castel Sant'Angelo,** the fortress that guarded the Vatican for hundreds of years. One of Rome's most beautiful bridges, **Ponte Sant'Angelo,** spans the Tiber in front of the fortress and is studded with copies of the graceful angels designed by Giovanni Lorenzo Bernini (1598–1680). The distinctive silhouette of Castel Sant'Angelo is a throwback to its original function; it was built as a mausoleum, or tomb, for the Emperor Hadrian in AD 135. By the 6th century, it had been transformed into a fortress, and it remained the military stronghold of Rome and a refuge for the popes for almost 1,000 years.

According to legend, the castle got its name during the plague of 590, when Pope Gregory the Great, passing by in a religious procession, had a vision of an angel sheathing its sword atop the stone ramparts. He interpreted this as a sign that the plague would end immediately, and, after it did, he had a chapel built on the highest level of the fortress, where he had seen the angel. Visit the lower levels, the base of Hadrian's mausoleum, and then climb ancient ramps and narrow staircases to explore the castle's courtyards and frescoed halls; the collection of antique arms and armor; and the open loggia, where there's a café. Climb to the upper terraces for views of the city's rooftops and the lower bastions of the castle, as well as of the Passetto, the fortified corridor connecting Castel Sant'Angelo with the Vatican. *Lungotevere Castello 50, tel. 06/687–5036. Admission: 8,000 lire. Open Apr.–Sept., Mon.–Sat. 9–7, Oct.–Mar., Mon.–Sat. 9–6, Sun. 9–noon. Closed 2nd and 4th Mon. of month.*

From Castel Sant'Angelo, turn right onto Via della Conciliazione, a broad, rather soulless avenue conceived by Mussolini in the 1930s to celebrate the "conciliation" between the Vatican and the Italian government under the Lateran Pact of 1929. The pact ended 60 years of papal protest against the Italian state, which the Vatican had never recognized. Indeed, after Italian troops wrested control of Rome from the pope in 1870 to make it the capital of a newly united Italy, the popes refused to leave the Vatican.

The Via della Conciliazione approach to St. Peter's gives your eye time to adjust to the enormous dimensions of the square and the church, although the intent of Baroque artist Bernini, who designed the square, was to surprise the visitor emerging suddenly from shadowy alleys into the square's immense space and full light.

⓭ **Piazza San Pietro** (St. Peter's Square) is one of Bernini's masterpieces, completed after 11 years' work—a relatively short time in those days, considering the vastness of the job. The square can hold as many as 400,000 people and is surrounded by a pair of quadruple colonnades, which are topped by a balustrade and 140 statues of saints. Look for the two stone disks set into the pavement on each side of the obelisk, between the obelisk and the fountains. If you stand on one disk, a trick of perspective makes the colonnades seem to consist of a single row of columns.

⓮ The history of **St. Peter's** goes back to the year AD 319, when the emperor Constantine built a basilica here over the site of the tomb of St. Peter. The original church stood for more than 1,000 years, undergoing a number of restorations, until it threatened to collapse. Reconstruction began in 1452 but was soon abandoned due to a lack of funds. In 1506 Pope Julius II instructed the architect Donato Bramante (1444–1514) to raze the existing structure and build a new and greater basilica, but it wasn't until 1626 that the new church was completed and dedicated. Five of Italy's greatest Renaissance artists died while working on it—Bramante, Raphael, Peruzzi, Antonio Sangallo the Younger, and Michelangelo. Bramante outlined a basic plan for the church and built the massive pillars that were to support the dome. After his death in 1514, his successors made little progress with the work and altered his master plan. In 1546 Pope Paul III more or less forced the aging Michelangelo to take on the job of completing the building. Michelangelo returned to Bramante's ground plan and designed the dome to cover the crossing, but his plans, too, were modified after his death. The result is nevertheless breathtaking. As you approach the church, look at the people going in and out of the portico, and note the contrast between their size and the immense scale of the building. Now climb the broad steps yourself and enter the portico. Notice Filarete's 15th-century bronze doors, salvaged from the old basilica.

Persons wearing shorts, miniskirts, sleeveless T-shirts, or other revealing clothing (it's advisable for women to carry a scarf to cover bare upper arms) will not be allowed into St. Peter's. If you pass inspection, pause a moment, once inside, to consider the size of this immense temple. Look at the massive pillars, the holy-water stoups borne by colossal cherubs, the distance to the main altar. Look for the brass inscriptions in the central marble pavement, indicating the approximate length of the world's principal Christian churches, all of which fall far short of St. Peter's. The chapel immediately to your right holds Michelangelo's *Pietà*, one of the world's most famous statues. It is now behind shatterproof glass, after a serious incident of vandalism (and a masterful restoration in the Vatican workshops). This is the only sculpture Michelangelo ever signed, although the signature—on the sash across the Virgin's chest—is too high up behind the glass to be seen.

Four massive piers support the dome at the crossing, where the mighty Bernini *baldacchino* (canopy), made of bronze stripped from the Pantheon by order of the Barberini Pope Urban VIII, rises high above the papal altar. The pope celebrates mass here, over the grottoes holding the tombs of many of his predecessors and over what is believed to be the tomb of St. Peter, deep in the excavations under the foundations of the original basilica. A very old bronze statue of the saint stands at the last pillar on the right before the crossing, its foot worn and burnished by the kisses of the faithful over the centuries. Beautiful bronze vigil lights flicker around the ceremonial entrance to the crypt in front of the papal altar. In the niche below is an antique casket containing the *pallia* (bands of white wool conferred by the pope on archbishops as a sign of authority). The splendid gilt-bronze throne above the altar in the apse was designed by Bernini and contains a wooden-and-ivory chair that St. Peter was supposed to have used, though in fact it dates back no further than the Middle Ages. You can see a copy of the chair in the Treasury.

Stop in to see the small collection of Vatican treasures in the little **museum** in the sacristy, among them priceless antique chalices and the massive 15th-century bronze tomb of Pope Sixtus V by Antonio Pollaiuolo (1429–98). *Admission: 3,000 lire. Open Apr.–Sept., daily 9–6:30; Oct.–Mar., daily 9–5:30.*

Save the visit to the **Vatican Grottoes,** to see the tombs of the popes, for last. The only exit from the grottoes leads outside St. Peter's, near the entrance to the roof and dome. *Entrance at St. Longinus Pier but alternatively at one of the other piers. Admission free. Open Apr.–Sept., daily 7–6; Oct.–Mar., daily 7–5.*

Take the elevator or climb the stairs to the **roof** of the church, an interesting landscape of domes and towers. From here, climb a short interior staircase to the base of the dome for a dove's-eye view of the interior of the church. And from here, it's a taxing climb to the lantern—the architectural term for the delicate structure crowning the dome; the stairs are steep and narrow and one-way only, so there's no turning back. We emphasize that it's a strenuous, claustrophobic climb. Those who make it are rewarded with views embracing the Vatican gardens and all Rome. *Entrance to roof and dome in courtyard on left as you leave the church. Admission: 6,000 lire if you use elevator to roof, 5,000 if you use stairs. Open Apr.–Sept., daily 8–6; Oct.–Mar., daily 8–5.*

For many, a **papal audience** is a highlight of a trip to Rome. The pope holds mass audiences on Wednesday mornings at 11, in a modern audience hall. Rarely, on special occasions during the summer, a second audience may be held in St. Peter's Square. You must apply for tickets in advance, and it may be easier to arrange for them through a travel agency. Of course, you can avoid the formalities by seeing the pope when he makes his weekly appearance at the window of the Vatican Palace, every Sunday at noon when he is in Rome, to address the crowd and give a blessing. On summer Sundays he may give the blessing at his summer residence at Castel Gandolfo. *For audience tickets, apply in writing well in advance to the Prefettura della Casa Pontificia, 00120 Vatican City, indicating the date you prefer, the language you speak, and the hotel where you will be staying; or go to the prefecture yourself through the bronze door in the right-hand colonnade, tel. 06/6982. Open Mon. and Tues. 9–1 for the Wed. audience, though last-minute tickets may not be available. You can also pick up free tickets at the North American College, Via dell'Umiltà 30, tel. 06/678–9184, or through Santa Susanna American Church, Piazza San Bernardo, tel. 06/482–7510. For a fee, travel agencies make arrangements that include transportation (see Guided Tours in Essential Information, above).*

Tour 3: The Vatican Museums

The Vatican Palace, which has been the residence of the popes on and off since 1377, is made up of several interlocking buildings containing 1,400 rooms, chapels, and galleries. The pope and his household occupy only a small part of the palace, most of which is given over to the Vatican Library and Museums. The main entrance to the museums, on Viale Vaticano, is a long walk from Piazza San Pietro, but there is bus service between the square and a secondary museum entrance. It goes through the Vatican gardens and costs 2,000 lire, and although it deposits you at a side entrance, it saves a lot of walking and allows a glimpse of some of Vatican City that would be off-limits otherwise. More than a glimpse—a two-hour jaunt through the pope's backyard, half by bus and half on foot—is possible by taking the Vatican gardens tour. *Bus service 8:45–12:45 on the half-hour, except Sun. and Wed. Tour of Vatican gardens Mon., Tues., and Thurs.–Sat. Cost: 16,000 lire. Tickets are available at the Vatican Information Office in Piazza San Pietro. It's best to reserve two or three days in advance.*

Time Out Borgo Pio, a street a block or two from St. Peter's Square, has several trattorias offering economical tourist menus. For about 20,000 lire you can have a simple meal at **Il Pozzetto** (Borgo Pio 167. Closed Mon.).

---

⑮ The collections of the **Vatican Museums** are immense, covering about 4½ miles of displays. Special posters at the entrance and throughout the museum plot a choice of four color-coded itineraries, the shortest taking approximately 90 minutes and the longest five hours. You can rent a taped commentary in English, explaining the Sistine Chapel and the Raphael Rooms. You're free to photograph what you like, although if you want to use a flash, tripod, or other special equipment, you have to get permission. The main entrance is on Viale Vaticano and can be reached by the No. 49 bus from Piazza Cavour, which stops right in front; on foot from the No. 81 bus or No. 19 tram, which stop at Piazza Risorgimento; or from the Ottaviano stop on the Metro Line A. Pick up a leaflet at the main entrance to the museums in order to see the overall layout. The Sistine Chapel, the main attraction for most visitors, is at the far end of the complex, and the leaflet charts two abbreviated itineraries through other collections to reach it. It would be a shame to miss the collections en route to the Sistine Chapel, and below we give some of the highlights, whether or not you follow the itineraries suggested by the curators. *Viale Vaticano, tel. 06/698–3333. Admission: 13,000 lire; free on last Sun. of month. Open Easter week and July–Sept., weekdays 8:45–5 (no admission after 4), Sat. 8:45–2; Oct.–June (except Easter), Mon.–Sat. 9–2 (no admission after 1). Closed Sun. year-round, except last Sun. of month (open 9–2, admission free), and religious holidays: Jan. 1, Jan. 6, Feb. 11, Mar. 19, Easter Sun. and Mon., May 1, Ascension Thurs., Corpus Christi, June 29, Aug. 15–16, Nov. 1, Dec. 8, Dec. 25–26.*

Among Vatican City's many riches, probably the single most important is the Sistine Chapel. However, unless you're following one of the two abbreviated itineraries, you'll begin your visit at the recently rearranged **Egyptian Museum** and go on to the **Chiaramonti** and **Pio Clementino Museums,** which are given over to classical sculptures (among them some of the best-known statues in the world—the *Laocoön,* the *Belvedere Torso,* and the *Apollo Belvedere*—works that, with their vibrant humanism, had a tremendous impact on Renaissance art). Next come the **Etruscan Museum** and three other sections of limited interest. All itineraries merge in the **Candelabra Gallery** and proceed through the **Tapestry Gallery,** which is hung with magnificent tapestries executed from Raphael's designs.

The **Gallery of Maps** is intriguing; the **Apartment of Pius V,** a little less so. After them you'll enter the **Raphael Rooms,** second only to the Sistine Chapel in artistic interest. In 1508, Pope Julius II employed Raphael Sanzio, on the recommendation of Bramante, to decorate the rooms with biblical scenes. The result was a Renaissance masterpiece. Of the four rooms, the second and third were decorated mainly by Raphael; the others, by Giulio Romano and other assistants of Raphael. The lovely Loggia (covered balcony) was designed and frescoed by the master himself. Next you pass through the Chiaroscuro Room to the tiny **Chapel of Nicholas V,** aglow with frescoes by Fra Angelico (1387–1455), the Florentine monk whose sensitive paintings were guiding lights for the Renaissance. If your itinerary takes you to the **Borgia Apartments,** you'll see their elaborately painted ceilings, designed and partially executed by Pinturicchio (1454–1513). The Borgia Apartments have been given over to the Vatican's large, but not particularly interesting, collection of modern religious art, which continues at a lower level. Once you've seen the Borgia Rooms, you can skip the rest in good conscience and get on to the Sistine Chapel.

In 1508, while Raphael was put to work on his series of rooms, Pope Julius II commissioned Michelangelo to fresco the more than 10,000 square feet of the **Sistine Chapel** ceiling single-handedly. The task took four years of mental and physical anguish. It's said that for years afterward Michelangelo couldn't read anything without holding it up over his head. The result, however, was the masterpiece that you can now see, its colors cool and brilliant after recent restoration. Bring a pair of binoculars to get a better look at this incredible work, and if you want to have some leisure to study it, try to beat the tour groups by getting there early in the day. Some 20 years after completing the ceiling, Michelangelo was commissioned to paint the *Last Judgment* on the wall over the altar. The aged and embittered artist painted his own face on the wrinkled human skin in the hand of St. Bartholomew, below and to the right of the figure of Christ, which he clearly modeled on the *Apollo Belvedere*. Like the ceiling, the **Last Judgment** has been cleaned, surprising viewers with its clarity and color after restorers unveiled their work in April 1994.

After this experience, which can be marred by the crowds of tourists, you pass through some of the exhibition halls of the **Vatican Library.** Look in on Room X, Room of the Aldobrandini Marriage, to see its beautiful Roman frescoes of a nuptial rite. You can see more classical statues in the new wing and then, perhaps after taking a break at the cafeteria, go on to the **Pinacoteca** (Picture Gallery). It displays mainly religious paintings by such artists as Giotto, Fra Angelico, and Filippo Lippi. The **Raphael Room** holds his exceptional *Transfiguration, Coronation*, and *Foligno Madonna*.

In the **Pagan Antiquities Museum,** modern display techniques enhance another collection of Greek and Roman sculptures. The **Christian Antiquities Museum** has Early Christian and medieval art, while the **Ethnological Museum** shows art and artifacts from exotic places throughout the world. The complete itinerary ends with the **Historical Museum**'s collection of carriages, uniforms, and arms, which may still be temporarily closed in 1995.

In all, the Vatican Museums offer a staggering excursion into the realms of art and history. It's foolhardy to try to see all the collections in one day, and it's doubtful that anyone could be interested in everything on display. Simply aim for an overall impression of the collections' artistic and cultural riches. If you want to delve deeper, you can come back another day.

Time Out   Neighborhood trattorias that are far better and far less popular with tourists than those opposite the Vatican Museum entrance include **Hostaria Dino e Toni** (Via Leone IV 60, closed Sun.), where you can dine on typical Roman fare at moderate, even inexpensive, prices, and **La Caravella,** which serves Roman specialties and has pizza on the lunch menu (Via degli Scipioni 32, corner Via Vespasiano, off Via Leone IV. Closed Thurs.).

Tour 4: Old Rome

A district of narrow streets with curious names, airy Baroque piazzas, and picturesque courtyards, Old Rome *(Vecchia Roma)* occupies the horn of land that pushes the Tiber westward toward the Vatican. It has been an integral part of the city since ancient times, and its position between the Vatican and the Lateran palaces, both seats of papal rule, put it in the mainstream of Rome's development from the Middle Ages onward. Today it's full of old artisans' workshops, trendy cafés and eating places, and offbeat boutiques. On weekends and summer evenings Old Rome is a magnet for crowds of young people.

⑯ Start at Piazza Venezia and take Via del Plebiscito to the huge Baroque **Il Gesù,** comparable only to St. Peter's for sheer grandeur. Inside it's encrusted with gold and precious marbles and topped by a fantastically painted ceiling that flows down over the pillars to become three-dimensional, merging with painted stucco figures in a swirling composition glorifying the Jesuit order. Then head for ⑰ nearby Piazza della Minerva to see **Santa Maria Sopra Minerva,** a Gothic church with some beautiful frescoes, in a side chapel, by Filippo Lippi (1406–69), the monk who taught Botticelli. The tomb of another great artist-monk, Fra Angelico (c.1400–1455), stands to the left of the altar. Bernini's charming elephant bearing an obelisk stands in the center of the piazza.

⑱ The huge brick building opposite is the **Pantheon,** one of the most harmonious and best-preserved monuments of antiquity. It was first erected in 27 BC by Augustus's general Agrippa and completely redesigned and rebuilt by Hadrian, who deserves the credit for this fantastic feat of construction. At its apex, the dome is exactly as tall as the walls, so that you could imagine it as the upper half of a sphere resting on the floor; this balance gives the building a serene majesty. The bronze doors are the original ones; most of the other decorations of gilt bronze and marble that covered the dome and walls were plundered by later Roman emperors and by the popes. The Pantheon gets light and air from the apex of the dome—another impressive feature of this remarkable edifice. *Piazza della Rotonda, tel. 06/ 654–3311. Admission free. Open Mon.–Sat. 9–2, Sun. 9–1.*

Time Out The café scene in the square in front of the Pantheon rivals that of nearby Piazza Navona. The area is ice-cream heaven, with some of Rome's best *gelaterie* (ice-cream parlors) within a few steps of one another. Romans consider nearby **Giolitti** superlative and take the counter by storm. Remember to pay the cashier first and hand the stub to the man at the counter when you order your cone. Giolitti has a good snack counter, too (Via Uffizi del Vicario 40. Closed Mon.).

From Piazza della Rotonda in front of the Pantheon, take Via ⑲ Giustiniani onto Via della Dogana Vecchia to the church of **San Luigi dei Francesi.** In the last chapel on the left are three stunning works by Caravaggio (1571–1610), the master of the heightened approach to light and dark. A light machine (operated with a couple of 100-lire coins) provides illumination to view the paintings. *Open Fri.–Wed. 7:30–12:30 and 3:30–7, Thurs. 7:30–12:30.*

In the church of **Sant'Agostino,** close by (Piazza di Sant'Agostino), there is another Caravaggio over the first altar on the left. Just be-

⑳ yond these churches is **Piazza Navona,** a beautiful Baroque piazza that traces the oval of Emperor Domitian's stadium. It still has the carefree air of the days when it was the scene of Roman circus games, medieval jousts, and 17th-century carnivals. Bernini's

㉑ splashing **Fountain of the Four Rivers,** with an enormous rock squared off by statues representing the four corners of the world, makes a fitting centerpiece. Behind it stands the church of

㉒ **Sant'Agnese in Agone.** Its Baroque facade is by Francesco Borromini (1599–1667), a contemporary and sometime rival of Bernini. One story has it that the Bernini statue nearest the church is hiding its head because it can't bear to look upon the inferior Borromini fa-cade; in fact, the facade was built after the fountain, and the statue hides its head because it represents the Nile River, whose source was unknown until relatively recently.

Time Out The sidewalk tables of the **Tre Scalini** café offer a grandstand view of the piazza. This is the place that invented the *tartufo*, a luscious chocolate ice-cream specialty (Piazza Navona 30. Closed Wed.).

Leaving Piazza Navona by way of the Corsia Agonalis, the street op-posite Tre Scalini, you'll see the 17th-century **Palazzo Madama,** now the Senate, on Corso Rinascimento. To the right, at the end of the

㉓ street, the huge church of **Sant'Andrea della Valle** looms mightily over a busy intersection. Puccini set the first act of his opera *Tosca* here.

㉔ Now make your way through side streets to **Campo dei Fiori.** Once the scene of public executions (including that of philosopher-monk Giordano Bruno, whose statue broods in the center), it now holds one of Rome's busiest, most colorful morning food markets. *Mon.–Sat. 8–2.*

Continue on to Piazza Farnese, where Michelangelo had a hand in

㉕ building **Palazzo Farnese,** now the French Embassy and perhaps the most beautiful of the Renaissance palaces in Rome. (Puccini set the second act of *Tosca* here.) The twin fountains in the piazza are made with basins of Egyptian granite from the Baths of Caracalla. Behind Palazzo Farnese, turn onto Via Giulia, where you'll see some elegant palaces (step inside the portals to take a look at the courtyards), old churches, and a number of antiques shops.

Tour 5: The Spanish Steps and the Trevi Fountain

The walk up Via del Corso from Piazza Venezia takes you to Rome's classiest shopping streets and to two visual extravaganzas: the Spanish Steps and the Trevi Fountain.

㉖ Start at the **Vittorio Emanuele Monument** in Piazza Venezia. Rome's most flamboyant landmark, it was erected in the late 19th century to honor Italy's first king, Vittorio Emanuele II, and the unification of Italy. This vast marble monument, said to resemble a wedding cake or a Victorian typewriter, houses the **Tomb of the Unknown Soldier,** with its eternal flame. Although the monument has been closed to the public for many years, plans are in the works to reopen it; the views from the top of the steps are among Rome's best.

㉗ On the left, as you look up the Corso, is **Palazzo Venezia,** a blend of medieval solidity and Renaissance grace. It contains a good collec-tion of paintings, sculptures, and objets d'art in handsome salons, some of which Mussolini used as his offices. Notice the balcony over the main portal, from which Il Duce addressed huge crowds in the square below. *Via del Plebiscito 118, tel. 06/679–8865. Admission: 8,000 lire. Open Tues.–Sat. 9–1:30, Sun. 9–12:30.*

㉘ Along the Corso are some fine old palaces and a church or two. Detour to the left to see the church of **Sant'Ignazio,** where what seems to be the dome is really an illusionist canvas. Put some coins in the light machine to illuminate the dazzling frescoes on the vault of the nave. Next you'll come to Piazza Colonna, named for the ancient **Col-**
㉙ **umn of Marcus Aurelius,** with its extraordinarily detailed reliefs spiraling up to the top.

Time Out **Alfio,** on the corner of Via Bergamaschi, is popular for a stand-up lunch of sandwiches at the counter or a more relaxing meal in the upstairs dining room (Via della Colonna Antonina 33. Closed Sun.).

From Largo Goldoni, on Via del Corso, you get a head-on view of the Spanish Steps and the church of Trinità dei Monti as you start up Via Condotti, an elegant and expensive shopping street. Look for the historic **Caffè Greco** on the left. More than 200 years old, it was the haunt of Goethe, Byron, and Liszt; now it's a hangout for well-dressed ladies carrying Gucci shopping bags.

㉚ Piazza di Spagna and the **Spanish Steps** get their names from the Spanish Embassy to the Holy See (the Vatican), opposite the American Express office, though they were built with French funds. This was once the core of Rome's bohemian quarter, especially favored by American and British artists and writers in the 18th and 19th
㉛ centuries. At the center of the square is Bernini's **Fountain of the Barcaccia** (Old Boat), and just to the right of the steps is the house where Keats and Shelley lived. Sloping upward in broad curves, the Spanish Steps are perfect for socializing, and they draw huge crowds on weekend and holiday afternoons. From mid-April to early May, the steps are blanketed with azaleas in bloom.

From the narrow end of the piazza, take Via Propaganda Fide to Sant'Andrea delle Fratte, swerving left on Via del Nazareno, then crossing busy Via del Tritone to Via della Stamperia. This street
㉜ leads to the **Trevi Fountain,** one of Rome's most spectacular fountains when it's gushing. It was featured in the 1954 film *Three Coins in the Fountain.* And legend has it that you can ensure your return to Rome by tossing a coin in the fountain. Unfortunately, legend doesn't tell you how to cope with the souvenir vendors and aggressive beggars who are looking for a share of your change.

Tour 6: Historic Churches

Three churches are the highlights of this walk, two of them major basilicas with roots in the early centuries of Christianity. Not far from Piazza Venezia and the Roman Forum off Via Cavour is the
㉝ church of **San Pietro in Vincoli.** Look for Via San Francesco da Paola, a street staircase that passes under the old Borgia palace and leads to the square in front of the church. Inside are St. Peter's chains (under the altar) and Michelangelo's *Moses,* a powerful statue almost as famed as his frescoes in the Sistine Chapel. The *Moses* was destined for the tomb of Julius II, but Michelangelo was driven to distraction by the interference of Pope Julius and his successors, and the tomb was never finished. The statue, intended as part of the tomb, is a remarkable sculpture and a big tourist attraction, but crass commercialism has ruined the starkly majestic effect of this memorial.

The church is usually jammed with tour groups, and the monument itself is a front for a large and ugly souvenir shop.

❸❹ Continue along Via Cavour to **Santa Maria Maggiore,** one of the oldest and most beautiful churches in Rome. Built on the spot where a 3rd-century pope witnessed a miraculous midsummer snowfall, it is resplendent with gleaming mosaics—those on the arch in front of the main altar date from the 5th century; the apse mosaic dates from the 13th century—and an opulent carved wood ceiling supposed to have been gilded with the first gold brought from the New World.

Via Merulana runs straight as an arrow from Santa Maria Maggiore
❸❺ to the immense cathedral of Rome, **San Giovanni in Laterano,** where the early popes once lived and where the present pope still officiates in his capacity as Rome's bishop. The towering facade and Borromini's cool Baroque interior emphasize the majesty of its proportions.

The adjoining **Lateran Palace,** once the popes' official residence and still technically part of the Vatican, now houses the offices of the Rome Diocese and the **Vatican Historical Museum** (admission 6,000 lire; open first Sun. of each month, 8:45–1). Restoration of the frescoes in the Benediction Loggia, damaged by a 1993 terrorist bomb, continues. Across the street, opposite the Lateran Palace, a small
❸❻ building houses the **Scala Santa** (Holy Stairs), claimed to be the staircase from Pilate's palace in Jerusalem. Circle the palace to see the 6th-century octagonal **Baptistery of San Giovanni,** forerunner of many similar buildings throughout Italy, and Rome's oldest and tallest obelisk, brought from Thebes and dating from the 15th century BC.

❸❼ One more church awaits you just down Via Carlo Felice. **Santa Croce in Gerusalemme,** with a pretty Rococo facade and Baroque interior, shelters what are believed to be relics of the True Cross found by St. Helena, mother of the emperor Constantine and a tireless collector of holy objects.

Tour 7: The Quirinale and Piazza della Repubblica

Although this tour takes you from ancient Roman sculptures to early Christian churches, it's mainly an excursion into the 16th and 17th centuries, when Baroque art—and Bernini—triumphed in Rome. The **Quirinale** is the highest of Rome's seven original hills (the others are the Capitoline, Palatine, Esquiline, Viminal, Celian, and Aventine) and the one where ancient Romans and later the popes built their residences in order to escape the deadly miasmas and the ma-
❸❽ laria of the low-lying area around the Forum. **Palazzo del Quirinale,** the largest on the square, belonged first to the popes, then to Italy's kings, and is now the official residence of the nation's president. The fountain in the square boasts ancient statues of Castor and Pollux reining in their unruly steeds and a basin salvaged from the Roman Forum.

Along Via del Quirinale (which becomes Via XX Settembre) are two interesting little churches, each an architectural gem. The first
❸❾ you'll come upon is **Sant'Andrea,** a small but imposing Baroque church designed and decorated by Bernini, who considered it one of his finest works and liked to come here occasionally just to sit and
❹❶ enjoy it. The second is the church of **San Carlo alle Quattro Fontane** (Four Fountains) at the intersection. It was designed by Bernini's rival, Borromini, who created a building that is an intricate exercise in geometric perfection, all curves and movement.

Turn left down Via delle Quattro Fontane to a splendid 17th-century
41 palace, **Palazzo Barberini.** Inside, the **Galleria Nazionale** offers
some fine works by Raphael (the *Fornarina*) and Caravaggio and a
salon with gorgeous ceiling frescoes by Pietro da Cortona. Upstairs,
don't miss the charming suite of rooms decorated in 18th-century
fashion. *Via delle Quattro Fontane 13, tel. 06/481–4591. Admission:
6,000 lire. Open Tues.–Sat. 9–2, Sun. 9–1.*

42 Down the hill, Piazza Barberini has Bernini's graceful **Tritone Fountain,** designed in 1637 for the sculptor's munificent patron, Pope Urban VIII, whose Barberini coat of arms, featuring bees, is at the
base of the large shell.

Time Out Located on Via Barberini, next to a movie house, **Italy Italy** offers
the Italian version of fast food, tasty and inexpensive (Via Barberini
19. Closed Sun.).

---

43 Via Veneto winds its way upward from Piazza Barberini past **Santa
Maria della Concezione,** a Capuchin church famous for its crypt,
where the skeletons and assorted bones of 4,000 dead monks are artistically arranged in four macabre chapels. *Via Veneto 27, tel. 06/
462850. Donation requested. Open daily 9–noon, 3–6.*

The avenue curves past the American Embassy and Consulate; the
luxurious Excelsior Hotel; and Doney's and the Café de Paris, famous from the days of la dolce vita in the 1950s. At the U.S. Embas-
44 sy, take Via Bissolati to Piazza San Bernardo. The church of **Santa
Maria della Vittoria,** on the corner, is known for Bernini's sumptuous Baroque decoration of the Cornaro Chapel, an exceptional fusion
of architecture, painting, and sculpture, in which the *Ecstasy of St.
Theresa* is the focal point. The statue represents a mystical experience in what some regard as very earthly terms. This could be a good
point at which to interrupt this tour and pick it up again after a rest.

An interesting side trip from Piazza San Bernardo takes you to the
45 Early Christian churches of **Sant'Agnese** and **Santa Costanza,** about
a mile beyond the old city walls. Take bus No. 36, 37, 60, or 136 along
Via Nomentana to get there. Santa Costanza, a church-in-the-
round, has vaults decorated with bright 4th-century mosaics. The
custodian of the catacomb of Sant'Agnese accompanies you up the
hill to see it. Art buffs should make this side trip; others may find it
unrewarding. *Via di Sant'Agnese, tel. 06/832–0743. Admission to
Sant'Agnese catacombs: 6,000 lire. Admission to Santa Costanza is
free, but a tip is in order if you do not buy a ticket to Sant'Agnese.
Open Mon., Wed., Thurs.–Sat. 9–noon and 4–6, Tues. 9–noon,
Sun. 4–6.*

From Piazza San Bernardo, it's not far to Piazza della Repubblica,
46 where the pretty **Fountain of the Naiads,** a turn-of-the-century addition, features voluptuous bronze ladies wrestling happily with marine monsters. On one side of the square is an ancient Roman brick
47 facade, which marks the church of **Santa Maria degli Angeli,** adapted
by Michelangelo from the vast central chamber of the colossal Baths
of Diocletian, built in the 4th century AD, the largest and most impressive of the ancient baths. The baths were on such a grandiose
scale that the church and its former monastery, around the corner to
the right, account for only part of the area they occupied. Inside the
church, take a good look at the eight enormous columns of red granite; these are the original columns of the baths' central chamber and
are 45 feet high and more than 5 feet in diameter.

㊽ The collections of ancient Roman art of the **Museo Nazionale Romano** are now divided among the old museum in the former monastery of Santa Maria degli Angeli (entrance behind the church); a new museum in the Palazzo Massimo (the peach-colored building across the square from the old museum); and the small Planetario annex (next to the church in a building that was part of the ancient baths but served more recently as a movie theater). Another annex, Piazza Navona, will open this year. In addition to the statues in the Planetario, most of the museum's sculpture, including the *Ludovisi Throne*, the *Lancellotti Discus Thrower*, and the *Castelporziano Discus Thrower*, is destined for Palazzo Massimo. A delightful fresco from Empress Livia's villa outside Rome, depicting a garden in bloom, is being restored and is not on view. *Museo Nazionale Romano: Monastery of Santa Maria degli Angeli, Viale E. De Nicola 79, tel. 06/488–0530. Admission: 3,000 lire. Open Tues.–Sat. 9–2, Sun. 9–1. Palazzo Massimo, Piazza dei Cinquecento, admission and hours not available at press time; Planetario, admission free, open daily 10–1, 3–5.*

Tour 8: The Villa Borghese to the Ara Pacis

A half-mile walk northwest from Piazza della Repubblica up Via Orlando and Via Vittorio Veneto leads to **Porta Pinciana** (Pincian Gate), one of the historic city gates in the Aurelian Walls surrounding Rome. The Porta itself was built in the 6th century AD, about three centuries after the walls were built to keep out the barbarians. These days it is one of the entrances to the **Villa Borghese,** Rome's large 17th-century park, built as the pleasure gardens of the powerful Borghese family.

㊿ Once inside the park, turn right up Viale del Museo Borghese and make for the **Galleria Borghese,** which holds the family art collection. At the time of this writing, the gallery was undergoing extensive renovations, so parts of it may be closed. There is a sculpture collection on the first floor, where you can see Canova's famous statue of Pauline Borghese, wife of Camillo Borghese and sister of Napoleon. Officially known as *Venus Vincitrix*, it is really a depiction of a haughty (and very seductive) Pauline, lying provocatively on a Roman sofa. The next two rooms hold two important Baroque sculptures by Bernini: *David* and *Apollo and Daphne*. In each you can see the vibrant attention to movement that marked the first departure from the Renaissance preoccupation with the idealized human form. Daphne is being transformed into a laurel tree while fleeing from a lecherous Apollo: Twigs sprout from her fingertips while her pursuer recoils in amazement. The gallery's important picture collection has been moved to the large San Michele a Ripa complex in Trastevere, where the paintings are now hung in a former church; it will probably be there through 1995. *San Michele a Ripa complex: Via di San Michele 22, tel. 06/581–6732. Admission: 4,000 lire. Open Tues.–Sat. 9–7, Sun. 9–1. During renovation, use the Galleria Borghese entrance off Via Raimondi. Tel. 06/858577. Admission: 4,000 lire. Open May–Sept. Tues.–Sat. 9–7, Sun. 9–1; Oct.–Apr. Tues.–Sat. 9–2, Sun. 9–1.*

From the Galleria Borghese, if you cross the park taking Viale dell'Uccelleria and then go left on Viale del Giardino Zoologico, you
㋒ will come to the **Galleria Nazionale d'Arte Moderna** (National Gallery of Modern Art), a large white building boasting Italy's leading collection of 20th-century works. *Viale delle Belle Arti 131, tel. 06/322–4151. Admission: 8,000 lire. Open Tues.–Sat. 9–2, Sun. 9–1.*

(During frequent temporary exhibitions, open Tues.–Sat. 9–7, Sun. 9–1.)

☻ Close by is the **Museo di Villa Giulia,** housing one of the world's great Etruscan collections. The villa is a former papal summer palace set in lovely gardens. This is the place to study the strange, half-understood Etruscan civilization, for here are magnificent terra-cotta statues, figurines, jewelry, household implements, sarcophagi—a whole way of life on display. Among the most precious gems are the *Apollo of Veio* and the *Sarcophagus of the Sposi*. When you have had your fill of these treasures, step out into the nymphaeum (the architectural term for this place of cool recesses and fern-softened fountains) and take a close look at the full-scale reconstruction of an Etruscan temple in the garden. *Piazza di Villa Giulia 9, tel. 06/320–1951. Admission: 8,000 lire. Open Wed. 9–7, Tues. and Thurs.–Sat. 9–2, Sun. 9–1.*

☻ The **Pincio** is an extension of Villa Borghese, with gardens on a terrace overlooking much of Rome. It was laid out by the early 19th-century architect Valadier as part of his overall plan for Piazza del Popolo. The Pincio offers a superb view, absolutely spectacular when there is a fine sunset, and it's also a vantage point from which **☻** you can study Valadier's arrangement of **Piazza del Popolo.**

This is one of Rome's largest squares and a traditional place for mass meetings and rallies. At the center, four dignified stone lions guard an obelisk relating the life and times of Ramses II in the 13th century BC. Next to the 400-year-old **Porta del Popolo,** Rome's northern **☻** city gate, stop in at the church of **Santa Maria del Popolo** to see a pair of Caravaggios and some Bernini sculptures in a rich Baroque setting.

From here, it's a short walk down Via Ripetta to the large **Augusteum,** the mausoleum Augustus built for himself and his family. **☻** Next to it is an unattractive modern edifice that shelters the **Ara Pacis** (Altar of Augustan Peace), erected in 13 BC to celebrate the era of peace ushered in by Augustus's military victories. The reliefs on the marble enclosure are magnificent. *Via Ripetta, tel. 06/671–0271. Admission: 3,750 lire. Open May–Sept., Wed.–Fri. 9–1:30, Tues. and Thurs. 9–1:30 and 4–7, Sun. 9–1; Oct.–Apr., Tues.–Sat. 9–1:30, Sun. 9–1.*

Tour 9: The Jewish Ghetto and Trastevere

For the authentic atmosphere of Old Rome, explore the old Jewish ghetto and the narrow streets of Trastevere, two tightly knit communities whose inhabitants proudly claim descent—whether real or imagined—from the ancient Romans. Then climb the Janiculum, a hill with views over the whole city, a vantage point beloved of all Romans.

The shadowy area bounded by Piazza Campitelli and Lungotevere Cenci constituted Rome's old Jewish ghetto. Within this cramped quarter, until 1870, all Rome's Jews (and they were many, tracing their presence in the city to ancient Roman times) were confined under a rigid all-night curfew. At the little church opposite Quattro Capi bridge, they were forced to attend sermons that aimed to convert them to Catholicism, and to pay for the privilege.

Many Jews have remained here, close to the bronze-roofed **☻** **synagogue** on Lungotevere Cenci and to the roots of their community. Among the most interesting sights in the ghetto are the pretty **☻** **Fontana delle Tartarughe** (Turtle Fountain) on Piazza Mattei; the old

houses on Via Portico d'Ottavia, where medieval inscriptions and ancient friezes testify to the venerable age of these buildings; and
59 the **Teatro di Marcello,** hardly recognizable as a theater now, but built at the end of the 1st century BC by Julius Caesar to hold 20,000 spectators.

Time Out Stop to indulge in American and Austrian baked goods at **Dolceroma** (Via Portico d'Ottavia 20/b. Closed Sun. afternoon and Mon.).

60 Cross the Tiber over the ancient Ponte Fabricio to the **Tiberina Island,** where a city hospital stands on a site that has been dedicated to healing ever since a temple to Aesculapius was erected here in 291 BC. If you have time, and if the river's not too high, go down the stairs for a different perspective on the island and the Tiber, which has begun to undermine the island in recent years, threatening its structures.

Then continue across Ponte Cestio into **Trastevere,** a maze of narrow streets that, despite creeping gentrification, is still one of the city's most authentically Roman neighborhoods (for another, explore the jumble of streets between the Roman Forum, Santa Maria Maggiore, and the Colosseum). Among self-consciously picturesque trattorias and trendy tearooms, you'll also find old shops in alleys festooned with washing hung out to dry and dusty artisans' workshops. Trastevere's population has become increasingly diverse, and it has acquired a reputation for purse-snatching and petty thievery, much to the chagrin of the authentic *trasteverini*, so keep purses and cameras out of sight as you stroll these byways. Be sure
61 to see **Piazza Santa Maria in Trastevere,** the heart of the quarter, with one of Rome's oldest churches, decorated inside and out with 12th- and 13th-century mosaics.

Follow Via della Scala to Via della Lungara, where Raphael deco-
62 rated the garden loggia of **Villa Farnesina** for extravagant host Agostino Chigi, who delighted in impressing guests by having his servants clear the table by casting precious gold and silver dinnerware into the Tiber. Naturally, the guests did not know of the nets he had stretched under the water line to catch everything. *Via della Lungara 230, tel. 06/654–0565. Admission free. Open Mon.–Sat. 9–1.*

From Porta Settimiana you can follow Via Garibaldi as it curves up
63 to the Janiculum, past the church of **San Pietro in Montorio,** known for its views and for the Tempietto, Bramante's little temple in the
64 cloister. Beyond the impressive **Acqua Paola Fountain,** you'll come
65 upon the **Janiculum Park,** which offers splendid views of Rome.

Tour 10: The Catacombs and the Appian Way

This tour offers a respite from museums, though it's no easier on the feet. Do it on a sunny day and take along a picnic or have lunch at one of the pleasant restaurants near the catacombs. The Rome EPT office offers a free, informative pamphlet on this itinerary. Take Bus
66 118 from San Giovanni in Laterano to the **Via Appia Antica** ("the Queen of Roads"), completed in 312 BC by Appius Claudius, who also built Rome's first aqueduct. (Stay on the bus until you reach the catacombs; the most interesting walk along the ancient road lies beyond them.) You pass Porta San Sebastiano, which gives you a good idea of what the city's 5th-century fortifications looked like, and farther along you'll see the little church of **Domine Quo Vadis,** where tradi-

tion says that Christ appeared to St. Peter, inspiring him to return to Rome to face martyrdom.

There are two important **catacombs** on the Via Appia Antica. The first you come upon is that of **San Callisto,** one of the best preserved of these underground cemeteries. A friar will guide you through its crypts and galleries. *Via Appia Antica 110, tel. 06/513–6725. Admission: 6,000 lire. Open Apr.–Sept., Thurs.–Tues. 8:30–noon, 2:30–5:30; Oct.–Mar., Thurs.–Tues. 8:30–noon, 2:30–5.*

The 4th-century catacomb of **San Sebastiano,** a little farther on, which was named for the saint who was buried here, burrows underground on four levels. The only one of the catacombs to remain accessible during the Middle Ages, it is the origin of the term "catacomb," for it was located in a spot where the road dips into a hollow, a place the Romans called *catacumbas* (near the hollow). Eventually, the Christian cemetery that had existed here since the 2nd century came to be known by the same name, which was applied to all underground cemeteries discovered in Rome in later centuries. *Via Appia Antica 136, tel. 06/788–7035. Admission: 6,000 lire. Open Fri.–Wed. 9–noon and 2:30–5.*

On the other side of Via Appia Antica are the ruins of the **Circus of Maxentius,** where the obelisk now in Piazza Navona once stood. Farther along the ancient road is the circular **Tomb of Cecilia Metella,** mausoleum of a Roman noblewoman who lived at the time of Julius Caesar. It was transformed into a fortress in the 14th century.

Time Out There are several trattorias along the Via Appia Antica, most of them moderately priced (*see* Dining, *below*). For a sandwich or a snack, the bar on the corner of Via Appia Antica and Via Cecilia Metella, just beyond the tomb, can provide sustenance and a relaxing pause in the adjoining garden.

The Tomb of Cecilia Metella marks the beginning of the most interesting and evocative stretch of the Via Appia Antica, lined with tombs and fragments of statuary. Cypresses and umbrella pines stand guard over the ruined sepulchers, and the occasional tracts of ancient paving stones are the same ones trod by triumphant Roman legions.

Rome for Free

Sightseeing in many capital cities can lead to a steady draining of your resources. Rome is an exception because most of its sights are either inexpensive or, more commonly, free of charge. You could construct several memorable itineraries devoted exclusively to architecture and religious art—taking in dozens of piazzas, churches, streets, and fountains—and not part with a single lira. Museums and galleries, of course, usually do charge admission, but it's rarely steep, and there are some surprising exceptions, such as the following:

The Colosseum—Lower Level (Tour 1: Ancient Rome).
The Tombs of the Popes (Tour 2: The Vatican).
The Vatican Museums on the Last Sunday of the Month (Tour 3: The Vatican Museums).
The Pantheon (Tour 4: Old Rome).
Villa Farnesina (Tour 9: The Jewish Ghetto and Trastevere).

What to See and Do with Children

There's a lot to do in Rome that children will enjoy. Take them to a **pizzeria** with a wood-burning oven, where they can see the chef work with the dough. Take a ride in a **horse and carriage**—it's fun and feels a lot less silly than it looks. Climb or take the elevator to the roof of **St. Peter's**—and look down on the main altar from above. Spend some time in the **Villa Borghese,** perhaps taking in a **Punch and Judy show** on the Pincio. There's another Punch and Judy show on the **Janiculum** hill, where there is also a colorful stand selling puppets.

In December and early January, visit the big **Christmas bazaar** at Piazza Navona, then stop at the huge toy store at the north end of the square. For an almost comical display of orchestration, pause awhile to watch the policeman directing traffic from his little podium in the middle of **Piazza Venezia.** A small-scale spectacle, but completely serious, is the daily **changing of the guard** at the Quirinale Palace, the residence of the president of Italy. Every day at 4 PM there's a military band and parade as the guards change shifts.

Rome's residential EUR (Esposizone Universal Roma; begun in the late 1930s as a site of a World's Fair that never happened because of World War II) suburb is the home of the well-run **Luna Park** amusement center. The park's big Ferris wheel is an attraction, as are the roller coaster and other rides and games. It can be reached by bus No. 707 from San Paolo fuori le Mura. *Via delle Tre Fontane, tel. 06/ 592–5933. Admission free, but you pay for each ride. Closed Tues.*

There's usually a **circus** somewhere in town: Check billboards and newspaper listings. Also check listings for cartoon films at the movies and for puppet shows and other children's programs at theaters.

Explore **Castel Sant'Angelo** (*see* Tour 2: The Vatican, *above*). It's got dungeons, battlements, cannons, and cannonballs, and a collection of antique weapons and armor.

Rent **bicycles** and ride around Villa Borghese and the center of town on Sunday, when the traffic is lighter.

Off the Beaten Track

Stroll through the quiet, green neighborhood of the **Aventine Hill,** one of the seven hills of ancient Rome that most tourists don't see. It has several of the city's oldest and least-visited churches, as well as a delightful surprise: the view from the keyhole in the gate to the garden of the Knights of Malta (Piazza Cavalieri di Malta).

Visit the excavations under St. Peter's for a fascinating glimpse of the underpinnings of the great basilica, which was built over the cemetery where archaeologists say they have found **St. Peter's tomb.** *Apply a few days in advance (or try in the morning for the same day) to the Ufficio Scavi (Excavations Office), to the right beyond the Arco delle Campane entrance to the Vatican, which is left of the basilica. Just tell the Swiss guard you want the Ufficio Scavi, and he will let you by. Tel. 06/698–5318. Admission: 10,000 lire with guide, 6,000 lire with taped guide. Ufficio Scavi open Mon.–Sat. 9–5.*

See the **Protestant Cemetery** behind the Piramide, a stone pyramid built in 12 BC at the order of the Roman praetor (senior magistrate) who was buried there. The cemetery is reminiscent of a country churchyard. Among the headstones you'll find Keats's tomb and the place where Shelley's heart was buried. *Via Caio Cestio 6, tel. 06/*

574–1141. Ring for the custodian. An offering of 500–1,000 lire is customary. Open daily 8–11:30 and 3:20–5:30.

Explore the subterranean dwellings under the church of **San Clemente.** *Via San Giovanni in Laterano, tel. 06/704–51018. Donation requested. Open Mon.–Sat. 9–noon and 3:30–6, Sun. 10–noon.*

Have an inexpensive lunch at **L'Eau Vive,** run by lay Catholic missionary workers, whose mission in this case is running a restaurant. Though it's elegant and fairly expensive for an evening meal, the good fixed-price lunch is a bargain. *Via Monterone 85 (off Piazza Sant'Eustachio), tel. 06/654–1095. AE, DC, V. Closed Sun.* Or join the Romans who lunch downstairs at the **Savoy Hotel's** reasonably priced self-service buffet. *Via Ludovisi 15 (the glass door next to the main entrance). Open for lunch only. Closed Sun.*

Shopping

Shopping in Rome is part of the fun, no matter what your budget. You're sure to find something that suits your fancy *and* your pocketbook, but don't expect to get bargains on Italian brands, such as Benetton, that are exported to the United States; prices are about the same on both sides of the Atlantic.

Shops are open from 9 or 9:30 to 1 and from 3:30 or 4 to 7 or 7:30. There's a tendency in Rome for shops in central districts to stay open all day, but for many this is still in the experimental stage. Department stores and centrally located UPIM and Standa stores are open all day. Remember that most stores are closed Sunday and, with the exception of food and technical-supply stores, also on Monday mornings from September to June and Saturday afternoons in July and August. Most Italian sizes are not uniform, so always try on clothing before you buy, or measure gift items. Glove sizes are universal. In any case, remember that Italian stores generally will *not* refund your purchases and that they often cannot exchange goods because of limited stock. *Always* take your purchases with you; having them shipped home from the shop can cause hassles. If circumstances are such that you can't take your goods with you, and if the shop seems reliable about shipping, get a firm statement of *when* and *how* your purchase will be sent.

Prezzi fissi means that prices are fixed, and it's a waste of time bargaining unless you're buying a sizable quantity of goods or a particularly costly object. Most stores have a fixed-price policy, and most honor a variety of credit cards. They will also accept foreign money at the current exchange rate, give or take a few lire. Ask for a receipt for your purchases; you may need it at customs on your return home. Bargaining is still an art at Porta Portese flea market and is routine when purchasing anything from a street vendor.

It's possible to obtain a refund on the VAT tax, which is included in the selling price. To be eligible, you must spend at least 300,000 lire in one store. (For more information, *see* Shopping in Staying in Italy, *above*.)

Shopping Districts The most elegant and expensive shops are concentrated in the **Piazza di Spagna** area especially along **Via Condotti** and **Via Borgognona**. **Via Margutta** is known for art galleries and **Via del Babuino** for antiques. There are several high-fashion outlets on **Via Gregoriana** and **Via Sistina**. Bordering this top-price shopping district is **Via del Corso**, which—along with **Via Frattina** and **Via del Gambero**—is

Rome Shopping

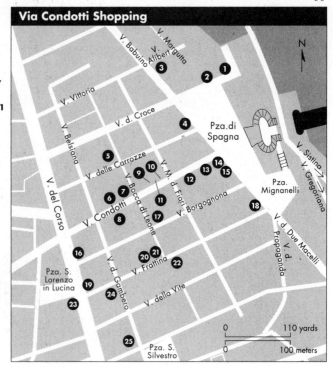

Via Condotti Shopping

lined with shops and boutiques of all kinds where prices and goods are competitive.

Via del Tritone, leading up from Piazza Colonna off Via del Corso, has some medium-priced, and a few expensive, shops selling everything from fashion fabrics to trendy furniture. Still farther up, on **Via Veneto,** you'll find more high-priced boutiques and shoe stores, as well as newsstands selling English-language newspapers, magazines, and paperback books. **Via Nazionale** features shoe stores, moderately priced boutiques, and shops selling men's and women's fashions. **Via Cola di Rienzo** offers high-quality goods of all types; it's a good alternative to the Piazza di Spagna area.

In Old Rome, **Via dei Coronari** has antiques and designer home accessories. **Via Giulia** and **Via Monserrato** also feature antiques dealers galore, plus a few art galleries. In the **Pantheon** area there are many shops selling liturgical objects and vestments. But the place to go for religious souvenirs is, obviously, the area around St. Peter's, especially **Via della Conciliazione** and **Via di Porta Angelica.**

Department Stores Rome has only a handful of department stores. **Rinascente,** near Piazza Colonna, sells clothing and accessories only. Another Rinascente, at Piazza Fiume, has the same stock. **Coin,** on Piazzale Appio, near San Giovanni in Laterano, has fashions for men and women. There is another Coin store in the U.S.-style shopping mall at CinecittàDue (*see* Shopping Malls, *below*). The **UPIM** and **Standa** chains offer low to moderately priced goods. They're the place to go for a pair of slippers, a sweater, a bathing suit, or such to see you through until you get home. In addition, they carry all kinds of toiletries and first-aid needs. Most Standa and UPIM stores have invaluable while-you-wait shoe-repair service counters.

Food and Flea Markets Rome's biggest and most colorful outdoor food markets are at **Campo dei Fiori** (just south of Piazza Navona), **Via Andrea Doria** (about a quarter mile north of the entrance to the Vatican museums), and **Piazza Vittorio** (just down Via Carlo Alberto from the church of Santa Maria Maggiore). There's a flea market on Sunday morning at **Porta Portese**; it now offers mainly new or secondhand clothing, but there are still a few dealers in old furniture and intriguing junk. Bargaining is the rule here, as are pickpockets; beware. To reach Porta Portese, take Via Ippolito Nievo, off Viale Trastevere. All outdoor markets are open from early morning to about 2, except Saturday, when they may stay open all day.

Shopping Malls The **CinecittàDue** mall was the first of several mega-malls now catering to Roman consumers, and it is the handiest—just take Metro Line A to the Subaugusta stop. The mall has 100 shops, including a **Coin** department store branch, a big supermarket, snack bars, and cafés (Piazza di Cinecittà, Viale Palmiro Togliatti, tel. 06/722–0902).

Clothing Boutiques All the big names in Italian fashion—Versace, Ferre, Valentino, Armani, Missoni—are represented in the Piazza di Spagna area. **Sorelle Fontane** (Salita San Sebastianello 6), one of the first houses to put Italy on the fashion map, has a large boutique with an extensive line of ready-to-wear clothing and accessories. **Carlo Palazzi** (Via Borgognona 7) has elegant men's fashions and accessories. **Mariselaine** (Via Condotti 70) is a top-quality women's fashion boutique. **Camomilla** (Piazza di Spagna 85) has trendy styles for women. Bargain hunters will love **Labels-for-Less** (Via Viminale 35), a discount store in the Termini Station vicinity.

Specialty Stores
Antiques and Prints For old prints and antiques, the **Tanca** shop (Salita dei Crescenzi 10, near the Pantheon) is a good hunting ground. Early photographs of Rome and views of Italy from the archives of **Alinari** (Via Aliberti 16/a) make interesting souvenirs. **Nardecchia** (Piazza Navona 25) is reliable for prints.

Handicrafts For pottery, handwoven textiles, and other handicrafts, **Myricae** (Via Frattina 36, with another store at Piazza del Parlamento 38) has a good selection. **La Galleria** (Via della Pelliccia 29) in Trastevere is off the beaten track but well worth a visit; it has a wealth of handicrafts, beautifully displayed in a rustic setting. A bottle of liqueur, jar of marmalade, or bar of chocolate handmade by Cistercian monks in several monasteries in Italy makes an unusual gift to take home; they are all for sale at **Ai Monasteri** (Piazza Cinque Lune 2).

Household Linens and Embroidery **Frette** (Piazza di Spagna 11) is a Roman institution for fabulous trousseaux. **Cesari** (Via Barberini 1 and Via Babuino 195) is another; it also has less-expensive gift items, such as aprons, beach towels, and place mats. **Lavori Artigianali Femminili** (Via Capo le Case 6) offers exquisitely embroidered household linens, infants' and children's clothing, and blouses.

Jewelry **Bulgari** (Via Condotti 10) is to Rome what Cartier is to Paris; the shop's elegant display windows hint at what's beyond the guard at the door. **Buccellati** (Via Condotti 31) is a tradition-rich Florentine jewelry house famous for its silverwork; it ranks with Bulgari for quality and reliability. **Fornari** (Via Frattina 71) and **Frugoni** (Via Arenula 83) have tempting selections of small silver objects. **Bozart** (Via Bocca di Leone 4) features dazzling costume jewelry geared to the latest fashions.

Knitwear **Luisa Spagnoli** (Via del Corso 382, with other shops at Via Frattina 116 and Via Veneto 130) is always reliable for good quality at the right price and styles to suit American tastes. **Miranda** (Via Bocca di Leone 28) is a treasure trove of warm jackets, skirts, and shawls, handwoven in gorgeous colors of wool or mohair, or in lighter yarns for summer.

Leather Goods **Gucci** (Via Condotti 8 and 77) is the most famous of Rome's leather shops. It has a full assortment of accessories on the first floor; a fashion boutique for men and women and a scarf department on the second floor; and a full complement of Japanese customers, who line up to get in on busy days. **Roland's** (Piazza di Spagna 74) has an extensive stock of good-quality leather fashions and accessories, as well as stylish casual wear in wool and silk. **Ceresa** (Via del Tritone 118) has more reasonably priced fine-leather goods, including many handbags and leather fashions. **Volterra** (Via Barberini 102) is well stocked and offers a wide selection of handbags at moderate prices. **Sermoneta** (Piazza di Spagna 61) shows a varied range of gloves in its windows, and there are many more inside. **Di Cori**, a few steps away, also has a good selection of gloves; there's another Di Cori store at Via Nazionale 183. **Merola** (Via del Corso 143) carries a line of expensive top-quality gloves and scarves.

Nickol's (Via Barberini 21) is in the moderate price range and is one of the few stores in Rome that stocks shoes in American widths. **Ferragamo** (Via Condotti 73) is one of Rome's best stores for fine shoes and leather accessories, and its silk scarves are splendid; you pay for quality here, but you can get great buys during the periodic sales. **Mario Valentino** (Via Frattina 58) is a top name for stylish shoes and leather fashions. **Magli** (Via del Gambero 1 and Via Veneto 70) is known for well-made shoes and matching handbags at high to moderate prices. **Campanile** (Via Condotti 58) has four floors of shoes in the latest, as well as classic, styles, and other leather goods.

Silks and Fabrics **Galtrucco** (Via del Tritone 18) and **Meconi** (Via Cola di Rienzo 305) have the best selections of world-famous Italian silks and fashion fabrics. You can find some real bargains when remnants *(scampoli)* are on sale.

Sports

Biking You can rent a bike at Via di Porta Castello 43 (tel. 06/687–5714) and at Piazza Navona 69. There are rental concessions at the Piazza di Spagna and Piazza del Popolo metro stops, at Largo San Silvestro, Largo Argentina, Viale della Pineta in Villa Borghese, and at Viale del Bambino on the Pincio.

Bowling There's a large American-style bowling center, **Bowling Brunswick** (Lungotevere Acqua Acetosa, tel. 06/808–6147), and a smaller one, **Bowling Roma** (Viale Regina Margherita 181, tel. 06/855–1184).

Fitness Facilities The **Cavalieri Hilton** (Via Cadlolo 101, tel. 06/31511) offers a 600-meter jogging path on the hotel grounds as well as an outdoor pool, two clay tennis courts, an exercise area, a sauna, and a steam room. The **Sheraton Roma** (Viale del Pattinaggio, tel. 06/5453) has a heated outdoor pool, a tennis court, two squash courts, and a sauna, but no gym. The **Sheraton Golf** (Viale Parco de' Medici 22, tel. 06/659788) has a fitness center and golf course. The **St. Peter's Holiday Inn** (Via Aurelia Antica 415, tel. 06/6642) has two tennis courts on the hotel grounds. It also has a 25-meter outdoor pool.

The **Roman Sport Center** (Via del Galoppatoio 33, tel. 06/320–1667) is a full-fledged sports center occupying vast premises next to the underground parking lot in Villa Borghese; it has two swimming pools, a gym, aerobic workout areas, squash courts, and saunas. It is affiliated with the **American Health Club** (Largo Somalia 60, tel. 06/862–12411).

Golf The oldest and most prestigious golf club in Rome is the **Circolo del Golf Roma** (Via Acqua Santa 3, tel. 06/784–3079). The newest are the **Sheraton Golf** course (Viale Parco de' Medici 22, tel. 06/655–3477 for clubhouse) and the **Country Club Castel Gandolfo** (Via Santo Spirito 13, Castel Gandolfo, tel. 06/931–2301). The **Golf Club Fioranello** (Viale della Repubblica, tel. 06/713–8212) is at Santa Maria delle Mole, off the Via Appia Antica. There is an 18-hole course at the **Olgiata Golf Club** (Largo Olgiata 15, on the Via Cassia, tel. 06/378–9141). Nonmembers are welcome in these clubs but must show membership cards of their home golf or country clubs.

Horseback Riding There are several riding clubs in Rome. The most central is the **Associazione Sportiva Villa Borghese** (Via del Galoppatoio 23, tel. 06/360–6797). You can also ride at the **Società Ippica Romana** (Via Monti della Farnesina 18, tel. 06/396–6214) and at the **Circolo Ippico Olgiata** (Largo Olgiata 15, tel. 06/378–8792), outside the city on the Via Cassia.

Jogging The best bet for jogging in the inner city is the **Villa Borghese.** A circuit of the Pincio, among the marble statuary, measures half a mile. A longer run in the park itself might include a loop around **Piazza di Siena,** a grass horse track measuring a quarter of a mile. Although most traffic is barred from Villa Borghese, government and police cars sometimes speed through. Be careful to stick to the sides of the roads. For a long run away from all traffic, try **Villa Ada** and **Villa Doria Pamphili** on the Janiculum. On the other hand, if you really love history, jog at the old **Circus Maximus,** or along Via delle Terme di Caracalla, which is flanked by a park. (Also, *see* **The Cavalieri Hilton** in Fitness Facilities, *above.*)

Swimming The outdoor pools of the **Cavalieri Hilton** (Via Cadlolo 101, tel. 06/31511) and the **Hotel Aldovrandi** (Via Ulisse Aldovrandi 15, tel. 06/322–3993) are lush summer oases open to nonguests. The **Roman Sport Center** (Via del Galoppatoio 33, tel. 06/320–1667) has two swimming pools, and there's another one at the **American Health Club** (Largo Somalia 60, tel. 06/862–12411).

Tennis Increasingly popular with Italians, tennis is played in private clubs and on many public courts that can be rented by the hour. Your hotel *portiere* will direct you to the nearest courts and can book for you. A prestigious Roman club is the **Tennis Club Parioli** (Largo de Morpurgo 2, Via Salaria, tel. 06/862–00882).

Spectator Sports

Basketball Basketball continues to grow in popularity in Italy, with many American pros now playing on Italian teams. In Rome, games are played at the **Palazzo dello Sport** in the EUR district (Piazzale dello Sport, tel. 06/592–5107).

Horseback Riding The **International Riding Show,** held the last few days of April and the first week in May, draws a stylish crowd to the amphitheater of Piazza di Siena in Villa Borghese. The competition is stiff, and the program features a cavalry charge staged by the dashing mounted corps of the *carabinieri.* For information, call the **Italian Federation of Equestrian Sports** (Viale Tiziano 70, tel. 06/323–3806).

Horse Racing There's flat racing at the lovely century-old **Capannelle** track (Via Appia Nuova 1255, tel. 06/718–3143), frequented by a chic crowd on big race days. The trotters meet at the **Tor di Valle** track (Via del Mare, tel. 06/529–0269).

Soccer Italy's favorite spectator sport stirs passionate enthusiasm among partisans. Games are usually held on Sunday afternoon throughout the fall–spring season. Two teams—Roma and Lazio—play their home games in the Olympic Stadium at **Foro Italico.** Tickets are on sale at the box office before the games; your hotel portiere may be able to help you get tickets in advance. The Olympic Stadium is on Viale dei Gladiatori, in the extensive Foro Italico sports complex built by Mussolini on the banks of the Tiber (tel. 06/333–6316).

Tennis A top-level international tournament is held at the Tennis Stadium at **Foro Italico** in May. For information, call the **Italian Tennis Federation** (Viale Tiziano 70, tel. 06/368–58510).

Beaches

The beaches nearest Rome are at **Ostia,** a busy urban center in its own right; **Castelfusano,** nearby; **Fregene,** a villa colony; and **Castelporziano,** a public beach area maintained by the city. At Ostia and Fregene, you pay for changing cabins, cabanas, umbrellas, and such, and for the fact that the sand is kept clean and combed. Some establishments, such as **Kursaal** (Lungomare Catullo 36 at Castelfusano, tel. 06/562–1303) have swimming pools, strongly recommended as alternatives to the notoriously polluted waters of the Mediterranean. You can reach Ostia by train from Ostiense Station, Castelfusano and Castelporziano by bus from Ostia, and Fregene by COTRAL bus from the Via Lepanto stop of Metro Line A in Rome. All beaches are crowded during July and August.

For cleaner water and more of a resort atmosphere, you have to go farther afield. To the north of Rome, **Santa Marinella** and **Santa Severa** offer shoals, sand, and attractive surroundings. To the south, **Sabaudia** is known for miles of sandy beaches, **San Felice Circeo** is a classy resort, and **Sperlonga** is a picturesque old town flanked by beaches and pretty coves.

Dining

There was a time when you could predict the clientele and prices of a Roman eating establishment by whether it was called a *ristorante,* a *trattoria,* or an *osteria* (tavern). Now these names are interchangeable. A rustic-looking spot that calls itself an osteria or hostaria may turn out to be chic and expensive. Generally speaking, however, a trattoria is a family-run place, simpler in decor, menu, and service—and slightly less expensive—than a ristorante. A true osteria is a wine shop, very basic and down to earth, where the only function of the food is to keep the customers sober.

As the pace of Roman life quickens, more fast-food outlets are opening, offering tourists a wider choice of light meals. There are variations of the older Italian institutions of the *tavola calda* (hot table) and the *rosticceria* (roast meats), both of which offer hot and cold dishes to be taken out or eaten on the premises, some sold by the portion, others by weight. You usually select your food and pay for it at the cashier, who gives you a stub to give to the counter person when you pick up the food. Newer snack bars are cropping up, and *pizza rustica* outlets selling slices of various kinds of pizza seem to have sprouted on every block.

Despite these changes, many Romans stick to the tradition of having their main meal at lunch, from 1 to 3, although you won't be turned away if hunger strikes shortly after noon. Dinner is served from 8 or 8:30 until about 10:30 or 11. Some restaurants stay open much later, especially in summer, when patrons linger at sidewalk tables to enjoy the cool breeze *(ponentino)*. Almost all restaurants close one day a week (it's usually safest to call ahead to reserve) and for at least two weeks in August, when it can sometimes seem impossible to find sustenance in the deserted city. This is not a bad time to picnic. You can buy provisions in any *alimentari* (grocery store) that's not also on vacation.

The typical Roman pasta is fettuccine, golden egg noodles that are at their classic best when freshly made and laced with *ragù*, a thick, rich tomato and meat sauce. *Pasta alla carbonara* is usually made with spaghetti or thicker, spaghetti-like *bucatini;* the cooked pasta is tossed with raw egg, chunks of fried *guanciale* (unsmoked bacon), and lots of freshly ground black pepper. *Spaghetti all'amatriciana* has a piquant sauce of tomato, unsmoked bacon, and hot red pepper. Gnocchi, a Roman favorite for Thursday dinner, are tiny dumplings of semolina and potatoes and are served with a tomato sauce and a sprinkling of grated cheese.

Abbacchio, baby lamb, is at its best in the spring; a summer favorite is *pollo coi peperoni*, stewed chicken with peppers. *Fritto misto* usually includes morsels of zucchini, artichokes, and *baccalà* (codfish) fried in batter. *Carciofi*, or artichokes, are served *alla romana*, sautéed whole with garlic and mint, or *alla giudia*, fried whole with each petal crisp and light enough to melt in your mouth. Tender peas are sautéed with prosciutto to make *piselli al prosciutto*.

Local cheeses are mild *caciotta* and sharp pecorino. Fresh ricotta is also used in a number of dishes. Typical wines of Rome are those of the Castelli Romani: Frascati, Colli Albani, Marino, and Velletri.

Tap water is safe everywhere in Rome, so if you're on a budget, order it *(acqua semplice)* rather than mineral water *(acqua minerale)*. Expect a bread and cover charge *(pane e coperto)* in all but the simplest places, as well as a service charge *(servizio)* of 10%–15%. A fixed-price tourist menu *(menù turistico)* includes taxes and services, but usually not drinks.

Highly recommended restaurants are indicated by a star ★.

Category	Cost*
$$$$	over 120,000 lire
$$$	65,000–120,000 lire
$$	40,000–65,000 lire
$	under 40,000 lire

per person, for a three-course meal, including house wine and taxes

Central Rome

$$$$ **Les Etoiles.** Memorable is the word for a meal here, both for the
★ food, which is very good indeed, and for the unique, close-up view of

Rome Dining

the dome of St. Peter's from many tables. The rooftop restaurant of the Atlante Star hotel, adjacent to the Vatican, in the Prati section of Rome, has big window walls to frame the breathtaking view, which is especially magic in the evening when the cupola's graceful curves are illuminated. The menu varies, depending on what the chef chooses at the market. There are interesting pasta dishes with porcini mushrooms or seasonal vegetables, classic or creative risotto (for two), fresh seafood and choice grilled meats. *When you reserve, ask for a table with a view of St. Peter's. Hotel Atlante Star, Via dei Bastioni 1, tel. 06/689–3434, toll-free in Italy 1678–62038. Reservations advised. Jacket and tie preferred. AE, DC, MC, V.*

Le Jardin. Located in the Parioli residential district, this restaurant is one of Rome's classiest establishments. It's in the exclusive Lord Byron hotel, itself a triumph of studied interior decoration. The imaginative menu is a tempting compendium of seasonal specialties served with style. If they are on the menu, try the risotto with seafood and vegetable sauce or the fillet of beef with morels. *Hotel Lord Byron, Via Giuseppe De Notaris 5, tel. 06/322–0404. Reservations required. Jacket and tie preferred. AE, DC, MC, V. Closed Sun.*

El Toulà. Take a byway off Piazza Nicosia in Old Rome to find this prestigious restaurant, one of a number in Italy of the same name; all are spin-offs of a renowned restaurant in Treviso in northern Italy (*see* Dining and Lodging in Chapter 7). Rome's El Toulà has the warm, welcoming atmosphere of a 19th-century country house, with white walls, antique furniture in dark wood, heavy silver serving dishes, and spectacular arrangements of fruits and flowers. There's a cozy bar off the entrance, where you can sip a *prosecco* (Venetian semi-sparkling white wine), the aperitif best suited to the chef's Venetian specialties, which include risotto with artichokes and *fegato alla veneziana* (liver with onions). *Via della Lupa 29/b, tel. 06/687–3750. Reservations required. Jacket and tie required. AE, DC, MC, V. Closed Sat. lunch, Sun., Aug., Dec. 24–26.*

$$$ **Andrea.** Ernest Hemingway and King Farouk used to eat here; now-
★ adays, you're more likely to hear the murmured conversation of Italian powerbrokers. Half a block from Via Veneto, this restaurant offers classic Italian cooking in an intimate, clubby setting, in which snowy table linens gleam against a discreet background of dark-green paneling. The menu features such delicacies as homemade *tagliolini* (thin noodles) with shrimp and spinach sauce, spaghetti with seafood and truffles, and mouth-watering *carciofi all'Andrea* (artichokes simmered in olive oil). *Via Sardegna 26, tel. 06/482–1891. Reservations advised. Dress: casual but neat. AE, DC, MC, V. Closed Sun. and most of Aug.*

Da Checcho er Carrettiere. You'll find Da Checcho tucked away behind Piazza Trilussa in Trastevere. It has the look of a country inn, with hanging braids of garlic and an antipasto table that features some unusual specialties, such as a well-seasoned mashed potato-and-tomato mixture. Among the hearty pasta offerings are *spaghetti alla carrettiera*, with black pepper, sharp cheese, and olive oil, and linguine with scampi. Seafood (which can be expensive) is the main feature on the menu, but traditional Roman meat dishes are offered, too. This is a great place to soak up genuine Trastevere color and hospitality at prices that are slightly above moderate. *Via Benedetta 10, tel. 06/581–7018. Reservations advised. Dress: casual. AE, DC, MC, V. Closed Sun. dinner, Mon., and Aug. 10–Sept. 10.*

Coriolano. The only tourists who find their way to this classic restaurant near Porta Pia are likely to be gourmets looking for quintessential Italian food, and that means light homemade pastas, choice olive oil, and market-fresh ingredients, especially seafood. The small dining room is decorated with antiques, and tables are set with immaculate white linen, sparkling crystal, and silver. Although seafood dishes vary, *tagliolini all'aragosta* (thin noodles with lobster sauce) is usually on the menu, as are porcini mushrooms in season (cooked according to a secret recipe). The wine list is predominantly Italian, but includes some French and California wines, too. *Via Ancona 14, tel. 06/855–1122. Jacket and tie preferred. Reservations advised. AE, DC, MC, V. Closed Sun. and Aug. 1–25.*

Il Convivio. Don't be intimidated by the opaque glass, closed door, and doorbell at the entrance. This, as its name suggests, is a convivial little restaurant, and it is earning a reputation as one of Rome's best. Reservations are essential, for it accommodates only 30 diners. The food is what it's all about: classic Italian (and Roman) dishes prepared with flair and a brilliant use of herbs, as in shellfish with tarragon and lamb with thyme. The *menù degustazione* (fixed menu) is good value. *Via dell'Orso 44, tel. 06/686–9432. Reservations necessary. Dress: casual. AE, DC, MC, V. Closed Sun.*

Passetto. Benefiting from a choice location near Piazza Navona, Passetto has been a favorite with Italians and tourists for many years: It's a place you can rely on for classic Italian food and courteous service. If you can, eat on the terrace—it's especially memorable at night; the mirrored dining room is more staid. Roman specialties, such as *cannelloni* (stuffed pasta tubes) and abbacchio, are featured. *Via Zanardelli 14, tel. 06/654–0569. Reservations advised. Jacket and tie preferred. AE, DC, MC, V. Closed Sun., Mon. lunch.*

Piperno. A favorite, located in the old Jewish ghetto next to historic Palazzo Cenci, Piperno has been in business for more than a century. It is *the* place to go for Rome's extraordinary *carciofi alla giudia* (crisp-fried whole artichokes, Jewish-style). You eat in three small wood-paneled dining rooms or at one of a handful of tables outdoors. Try *filetti di baccalà* (cod fillet fried in batter), *pasta e ceci* (a thick soup of pasta tubes and chickpeas), *fiori di zucca* (stuffed zucchini flowers), and artichokes. *Monte dei Cenci 9, tel. 06/654–2772. Reservations advised. Dress: casual. AE, DC, MC, V. Closed Sun. dinner, Mon., Christmas, Easter, Aug.*

★ **Ranieri.** Walk down a quiet street off fashionable Via Condotti, near the Spanish Steps, to find this historic restaurant, founded by a one-time chef of Queen Victoria. Ranieri remains a favorite with tourists for its traditional atmosphere and decor, with damask-covered walls, velvet banquettes, crystal chandeliers, and old paintings. The Italian-French cuisine is excellent: Portions are abundant, and checks remain comfortably within the lower range in this category. Among the many specialties on the vast menu are *gnocchetti alla parigina* (feather-light dumplings with cheese sauce) and *mignonettes alla Regina Vittoria* (veal with pâté and an eight-cheese sauce). *Via Mario dei Fiori 26, tel. 06/678–6505. Reservations advised. Dress: casual but neat. AE, DC, MC, V. Closed Sun.*

$$ **Dal Bolognese.** Long a favorite with the art crowd, this classic restaurant on Piazza del Popolo is a handy place for a leisurely lunch between sightseeing and shopping. While dining, feast your eyes on an extensive array of contemporary paintings, many of them by customers, both illustrious and unknown. As the name of the restaurant promises, the cooking here adheres to the hearty tradition of Bologna, with homemade pastas in creamy sauces and steaming trays of boiled meats. For dessert, there's *dolce della mamma*, a concoction of ice cream, zabaglione, and chocolate sauce. *Piazza del*

Popolo 1, tel. 06/361–1426. Reservations advised. Dress: casual. DC, V. Closed Mon. and Aug. 7–22.

La Campana. This inconspicuous trattoria off Via della Scrofa has a centuries-old tradition: There has been an inn on this spot since the 15th century, and the two plain dining rooms occupy what were once stables. It's a homey place, with friendly waiters, snowy white linens on close-set tables, and good Roman food at reasonable prices. The menu offers specialties like *vignarola* (sautéed fava beans, peas, and artichokes), rigatoni with prosciutto and tomato sauce, and *olivette di vitello con purée* (tiny veal rolls with mashed potatoes). *Vicolo della Campana 18, tel. 06/686–7820. Dinner reservations advised. Dress: casual. AE, MC, V. Closed Mon. and Aug.*

Cannavota. Located on the square next to San Giovanni in Laterano, Cannavota has a large and faithful following and has fed generations of neighborhood families over the years. Seafood dominates, but carnivores are catered to, also. Try one of the pastas with seafood sauce—fettuccine with shrimp and scampi is a good choice—and then go on to grilled fish or meat. The cheerful atmosphere and rustic decor make for an authentically Roman experience. *Piazza San Giovanni in Laterano 20, tel. 06/772–05007. Reservations advised. Dress: casual. AE, DC, MC, V. Closed Wed. and Aug. 1–20.*

Colline Emiliane. Not far from Piazza Barberini is this unassuming trattoria offering exceptionally good food. Behind an opaque glass facade are a couple of plain dining rooms, where you are served light homemade pastas, a special chicken broth, and meats ranging from boiled beef to *giambonetto di vitella* (roast veal) and *cotoletta alla bolognese* (veal cutlet with cheese and tomato sauce). Family run, it's quiet and soothing, a good place to rest after a sightseeing stint. Service is cordial and discreet. *Via degli Avignonesi 22, tel. 06/481–7538. Reservations advised. Dress: casual. No credit cards. Closed Fri. and Aug.*

Fortunato al Pantheon. Just a block away from the House of Representatives, Fortunato is a favorite of politicos. (It's also a couple of paces from Piazza della Rotonda by the Pantheon.) With politicians around, there is, of course, a back room, but you can happily settle for the largest of the three dining rooms or even a table outside in good weather. For his faithful and demanding clientele, Fortunato varies his specialties, offering several pastas—such as *penne all'arrabbiata*, with piquant tomato sauce—and *risotto alla milanese*, with saffron, or risotto with porcini mushrooms. He also serves many types of fish and meat dishes, some with expensive truffles. *Via del Pantheon 55, tel. 06/679–2788. Reservations advised. Dress: casual but neat. AE. Closed Sun. and Aug.*

Le Maschere. For a taste of southern Italian (Calabrian) fare, look for this cellar restaurant hidden away between Largo Argentina and Piazza Campo dei Fiori. A couple of planters, with a few outdoor tables in summer, mark this informal spot. Downstairs you pass an impressive antipasto buffet, and a pizza oven glows in a corner of the dining room. Dark rustic walls are hung with everything from paper garlands to old utensils; there are pottery wine jugs and rush-bottom chairs. Order spicy Calabria salami to start and then go on to pizza or southern favorites such as pasta with broccoli or with tomato and eggplant sauce. Grilled meat and seafood make up the list of second courses. Music on weekends and efficient service make for a pleasant evening. *Via Monte della Farina 29, tel. 06/687–9444. Reservations advised. Dress: casual. AE, DC, MC, V. Dinner only. Closed Mon. and mid-Aug.–mid-Sept.*

Orso 80. This bright and bustling trattoria is located in Old Rome, on a street famed for artisans' workshops. It has both a Roman and an international following, and is known, above all, for a fabulous antipasto table. Try the homemade egg pasta or the *bucatini all'amatriciana* (thin, hollow pasta with tomato sauce and bacon); there's plenty of seafood on the menu, too. For dessert, the ricotta cake, a genuine Roman specialty, is always good. *Via dell'Orso 33, tel. 06/686–4904. Reservations advised. Dress: casual. AE, DC, MC, V. Closed Mon. and Aug. 10–20.*

Osteria da Nerone. Between the Colosseum and the church of San Pietro in Vincoli, this family-run trattoria features a tempting antipasto table and fresh pastas. The specialty is *fettuccine al Nerone* (noodles with peas, salami, and mushrooms), but homemade ravioli are good, too. In fair weather you eat outdoors with a view of the Colosseum. *Via Terme di Tito 96, tel. 06/474–5207. Dinner reservations advised. Dress: casual. No credit cards. Closed Sun. and mid-Aug.*

Otello alla Concordia. The clientele in this popular spot—it's located off a shopping street near Piazza di Spagna—is about evenly divided between tourists and workers from shops and offices in the area. The former like to sit outdoors in the courtyard in any weather; the latter have their regular tables in one of the inside dining rooms. The menu offers classic Roman and Italian dishes, and service is friendly and efficient. Since every tourist in Rome knows about it, and since the regulars won't relinquish their niches, you may have to wait for a table; go early. *Via della Croce 81, tel. 06/678–1454. No reservations. Dress: casual. AE, DC. Closed Sun. and Christmas.*

Paris. On a small square just off Piazza Santa Maria in Trastevere, Paris (named after a former owner, not the city) has a reassuring, understated ambience, without the hokey, folky flamboyance of so many eating places in this gentrified neighborhood. It also has a menu featuring the best of classic Roman cuisine: homemade fettuccine, delicate *fritto misto* (zucchini flowers and artichokes, among other things, fried in batter) and, of course, *baccalà* (fried cod fillets). In fair weather you eat at tables on the little piazza. *Piazza San Callisto 7/a, tel. 06/581–5378. Dinner reservations advised. Dress: casual. AE, DC, MC, V. Closed Sun. dinner, Mon., and 3 weeks in Aug.*

Pierluigi. Pierluigi, in the heart of Old Rome, is a longtime favorite with foreign residents of Rome and Italians in the entertainment field. On busy evenings it's almost impossible to find a table, so make sure you reserve well in advance. Seafood dominates (if you're in the mood to splurge, try the lobster), but traditional Roman dishes are offered, too, including *orecchiette con broccoli* (ear-shaped pasta with greens) and simple spaghetti. Eat in the pretty piazza in summer. *Piazza dei Ricci 144, tel. 06/686–8717. Reservations advised. Dress: casual. AE, V. Closed Mon. and 2 weeks in Aug.*

★ **Romolo.** Generations of Romans and tourists have enjoyed the romantic garden courtyard and historic dining room of this charming Trastevere haunt, reputedly the one-time home of Raphael's lady love, the Fornarina. In the evening, strolling musicians serenade diners. The cuisine is appropriately Roman; specialties include *mozzarella alla fornarina* (deep-fried mozzarella with ham and anchovies) and *braciolette d'abbacchio scottadito* (grilled baby lamb chops). Alternatively, try one of the new vegetarian pastas featuring *carciofi* (artichokes) or radicchio. Meats are charcoal-grilled; there's also a wood-burning oven. *Via di Porta Settimiana 8, tel. 06/581–8284. Reservations advised. Dress: casual. AE, DC, V. Closed Mon. and Aug. 2–23.*

Tullio. This Tuscan trattoria off Via Veneto and Piazza Barberini opened in the dolce vita days of the 1950s, when this area was the center of Roman chic and bohemian life. It soon acquired a faithful clientele of politicians, journalists, and creative people, and it has changed little over the years. Decor and menu are simple. The latter offers typically Tuscan *pasta e fagioli*, grilled steaks and chops, and *fagioli all'uccelletto* (beans with tomato and sage). *Via San Nicolò da Tolentino 26, tel. 06/481–8564. Reservations advised. Dress: casual but neat. AE, DC, MC, V. Closed Sun. and Aug.*

$ **Armando.** One of the best of the many trattorias in this authentic Roman blue-collar district in the shadow of the Vatican, Armando's is a family-run favorite of neighborhood regulars and tourists-in-the-know. The menu offers Roman dishes such as pasta e ceci and *petto alla fornara* (roast veal breast) served with potatoes. *Via degli Ombrellari 41 (at Borgo Vittorio), tel. 06/686–1602. Dinner reservations advised. Dress: casual. AE, DC, MC, V. Closed Wed.*

Abruzzi. Here's a simple trattoria off Piazza Santi Apostoli near Piazza Venezia that specializes in the regional cooking of the mountainous Abruzzo region, southeast of Rome. *Tonnarelli* (square-cut pasta) is served with mushrooms, peas, and ham or with a meat sauce. Abbacchio is another classic regional dish. *Via del Vaccaro 1, tel. 06/679–3897. Lunch reservations advised. Dress: casual. V. Closed Sat. and Aug.*

Baffetto. The emphasis here is on good old-fashioned value: Baffetto is Rome's best-known inexpensive pizza restaurant, plainly decorated and very popular. You'll probably have to wait in line outside on the cobblestones and then share your table once inside. The interior is mostly given over to the ovens, the tiny cash desk, and the simple, paper-covered tables. *Bruschetta* (toast) and *crostini* (mozzarella toast) are the only variations on the pizza theme. Turnover is fast: This is not the place to linger over your meal. *Via del Governo Vecchio 114, tel. 06/686–1617. No reservations. Dress: casual. No credit cards. Dinner only. Closed Sun. and Aug.*

★ **Birreria Tempera.** This old-fashioned beer hall is very busy at lunchtime, when it's invaded by businesspeople and students from the Piazza Venezia area. There's a good selection of salads and cold cuts, as well as pasta and daily specials. Bavarian-style specialties such as goulash and wurst and sauerkraut prevail in the evening, when light or dark Italian beer flows freely. *Via San Marcello 19, tel. 06/678–6203. No reservations. Dress: casual. No credit cards. Closed Sun. and Aug.*

Cottini. For lunch or supper, this cafeteria on the corner of Piazza Santa Maria Maggiore is reliable; the food counter and tables are in the back, beyond the large coffee bar and pastry counters. Salads, hot pastas, and main courses are always fresh, and they are served with a smile. The in-house bakery provides such tempting desserts as crème caramel and chocolate cake. *Via Merulana 287, tel. 06/474–0768. No reservations. Dress: casual. No credit cards. Closed Mon.*

Fratelli Menghi. Neighborhood regulars frequent this trattoria that has been in the same family for as long as anyone can remember (a portrait of pop is on the wall in one dining room) and produces typical Roman fare for faithful customers. There's usually a thick hearty soup such as minestrone, pasta e ceci and other standbys, including *involtini* (meat roulades). *Via Flaminia 57, tel. 06/320–0803. No reservations. No credit cards. Closed Sun.*

Grappolo d'Oro. This centrally located trattoria off Campo dei Fiori has been a favorite for decades with locals and foreign residents, one of whom wrote it up in the *New Yorker* some years ago. This measure of notoriety has not induced the graying, courteous owners to change their two half-paneled dining rooms or menu, which features pasta all'amatriciana and scaloppine any way you want them. Inquire about the day's special. *Piazza della Cancelleria 80, tel. 06/*

686–4118. Reservations advised. Dress: casual, AE, MC, V. Closed Sun.

Hostaria Farnese. This is a tiny trattoria between Campo dei Fiori and Piazza Farnese, in the heart of Old Rome. Mama cooks; papa serves; and, depending on what they've picked up at the Campo dei Fiori market, you may find rigatoni with tuna and basil, spaghetti with vegetable sauce, *spezzatino* (stew), and other homey specialties. *Via dei Baullari 109, tel. 06/654–1595. Reservations advised. Dress: casual. AE, V. Closed Thurs.*

Polese. It's best to come here in good weather, when you can sit outdoors under trees and look out on the charming square off Corso Vittorio Emanuele in Old Rome. Like most centrally located inexpensive eateries in Rome, it is crowded on weekends and weekday evenings in the summer. Straightforward Roman specialties include *fettuccine alla Polese* (with cream and mushrooms) and *vitello alla fornara* (roast brisket of veal with potatoes). *Piazza Sforza Cesarini 40, tel. 06/686–1709. Reservations advised on weekends. Dress: casual. AE, DC, MC, V. Closed Tues., 15 days in Aug., 15 days in Dec.*

Pollarola. This typical Roman trattoria, located near Piazza Navona and Campo dei Fiori, has flowers (artificial) on the tables and—as a special feature—an ancient, authentic Roman column embedded in the rear wall, evidence of its historic site. You can eat outdoors in fair weather. Try a pasta specialty such as *fettuccine al gorgonzola* (egg pasta with creamy gorgonzola sauce) and a mixed plate from the array of fresh antipasti. The house wines, white or red, are good. *Piazza della Pollarola 24 (Campo dei Fiori), tel. 06/6880–1654. Reservations advised for groups. AE, V. Closed Sun.*

Tavernetta. The central location—between the Trevi Fountain and the Spanish Steps—and the good-value tourist menu make this a reliable bet for a simple but filling meal. The menu features Sicilian and Abruzzi specialties; try the pasta with eggplant or the *porchetta* (roast suckling pig). Both the red and the white house wines are good. *Via del Nazareno 3, tel. 06/679–3124. Dinner reservations required. Dress: casual. AE, DC, MC, V. Closed Mon. and Aug.*

Along Via Appia Antica

$$ **L'Archeologia.** In this farmhouse just beyond the catacombs, you dine indoors beside the fireplace in cool weather or in the garden under age-old vines in the summer. The atmosphere is friendly and intimate, and specialties include homemade pastas, *abbacchio scottadito* (grilled baby lamb chops), and seafood. *Via Appia Antica 139, tel. 06/788–0494. Dinner and weekend reservations advised. Dress: casual. No credit cards. Closed Thurs.*

Cecilia Metella. From the entrance on the Via Appia Antica, practically opposite the catacombs, you walk uphill to a low-lying but sprawling construction designed for wedding feasts and banquets. There's a large terrace shaded by vines for outdoor dining. Although obviously geared to larger groups, Cecilia Metella also gives couples and small groups full attention, good service, and fine Roman-style cuisine. The specialties are the searing-hot *crespelle* (crêpes), served in individual casseroles, and *pollo alla Nerone* (chicken à la Nero; flambéed, of course). *Via Appia Antica 125, tel. 06/513–6743. Reservations advised on weekends. Dress: casual. AE, MC, V. Closed Mon.*

Lodging

The wide range of Roman accommodations are graded according to regional standards, from five stars down to one. You can be sure of palatial comfort and service in a five-star establishment, but some of the three-star hotels turn out to be much more modest than expected; they are often superficially spruced up to capitalize on a central location. The old-fashioned Roman pension no longer exists as a category, but, while now graded as inexpensive hotels, some preserve the homey atmosphere that makes visitors prefer them, especially for longer stays.

There are distinct advantages to staying in a hotel within easy walking distance of the main sights, particularly now that so much of downtown Rome is closed to daytime traffic. You can leave your car at a garage and explore by foot. One disadvantage, however, can be noise, because the Romans are a voluble people—with or without cars to add to the racket. Ask for an inside room if you are a light sleeper, but don't be disappointed if it faces a dark courtyard.

Because Rome's religious importance makes it a year-round tourist destination, there is never a period when hotels are predictably empty, so you should always try to make reservations, even if only a few days in advance, by phone or fax. Always inquire about special low rates, often available in both winter and summer if occupancy is low. If you do arrive without reservations, try one of the following **EPT** information offices: Via Parigi 5 (tel. 06/488–3748), Termini Station (tel. 06/487–1270), Leonardo da Vinci Airport (tel. 06/601–1255). All can help with accommodations, and there is no charge. Avoid official-looking men who approach tourists at Termini Station: They tout for the less desirable hotels around the train station. **CTS**, a student travel agency, can help find rooms; the main office is at Via Genova 16 (10 minutes' walk from the station), tel. 06/46791.

Room rates in Rome are on a par with, or even higher than, those in most other European capitals. Ask whether the rate includes breakfast. An extra charge, anything from 7,000 to 27,000 lire depending on the category of hotel, may be added for this, but remember that you're not obliged to take breakfast in the hotel. If you won't be, make this clear when you check in. Air-conditioning in lower-priced hotels may cost extra; in more expensive hotels it will be included in the price. All hotels have rate cards on the room doors or inside the closet. These specify exactly what you have to pay and detail any extras. If business is slack, hotels in all categories may give you a discount rate. Ask for *la tariffa scontata* (the discount rate).

Highly recommended lodgings are indicated by a star ★.

Category	Cost*
$$$$	over 450,000 lire
$$$	300,000–450,000 lire
$$	150,000–300,000 lire
$	under 150,000 lire

All prices are for a standard double room for two, including tax and service.

$$$$ **Grand.** A 100-year-old establishment of class and style, this hotel caters to an elite international clientele. It's located only a few minutes

from Via Veneto. Off the richly decorated, split-level main salon—where afternoon tea is served every day—there are a smaller, intimate bar and a buffet restaurant. The spacious bedrooms are decorated in gracious empire style, with smooth fabrics and thick carpets in tones of blue and pale gold. Crystal chandeliers and marble baths add a luxurious note. The Grand also offers one of Italy's most beautiful dining rooms, called simply Le Restaurant. *Via Vittorio Emanuele Orlando 3, tel. 06/4709, fax 06/474–7307. 170 rooms and suites with bath. Facilities: 2 restaurants, bar. AE, DC, MC, V.*

★ **Hassler.** Located at the top of the Spanish Steps, the Hassler boasts sweeping views of Rome from its front rooms and penthouse restaurant; other rooms overlook the gardens of Villa Medici. The hotel is run by the distinguished Wirth family of hoteliers, which assures a cordial atmosphere and magnificent service from the well-trained staff. The public rooms are memorable—especially the first-floor bar, a chic rendezvous, and the glass-roofed lounge, with gold marble walls and a hand-painted tile floor. The elegant and comfortable guest rooms are decorated in a variety of classic styles, some with frescoed walls. The penthouse suite has a mirrored ceiling in the bedroom and a huge terrace. *Piazza Trinità dei Monti 6, tel. 06/678–2651, fax 06/678–9991. 101 rooms and suites with bath. Facilities: restaurant, bar. AE, MC, V.*

Majestic. In the 19th-century tradition of grand hotels, this establishment on Via Veneto offers sumptuous furnishings and spacious rooms, with up-to-date accessories such as CNN-TV, mini-bars, strongboxes, and white marble bathrooms. There are authentic antiques in the public rooms, and the excellent restaurant looks like a Victorian conservatory. *Via Veneto 50, tel. 06/486841, fax 06/488–0984. 95 rooms and suites with bath, many with whirlpool baths. Facilities: restaurant, bar with terrace, garage. AE, DC, MC, V.*

$$$ **Albergo del Sole al Pantheon.** This small hotel has been in its central location opposite the Pantheon since the 15th century. It was entirely renovated in 1989 and has been tastefully decorated with a blend of modern and antique furnishings. Ceilings are high, floors are tiled in terra-cotta, and there is a charming courtyard for al fresco breakfast in good weather. *Piazza della Rotonda 63, tel. 06/678–0441, fax 06/684–0689. 26 rooms with bath. Facilities: bar, nearby garage. AE, DC, MC, V.*

★ **Farnese.** A turn-of-the-century mansion, totally renovated in 1991, the Farnese is located near the Metro and within walking distance of St. Peter's. Furnished with great attention to detail in art deco style, it has dazzling modern baths and charming fresco decorations. Room rates are low for the category and include a banquet-size breakfast. *Via Alessandro Farnese 30, tel. 06/321–2553, fax 06/321–5129. 24 rooms with bath. Facilities: parking, bar, roof garden. AE, DC, MC, V.*

Flora. With its Old-World decor and style, now largely refurbished with entirely new bathrooms, the Flora has a solid position among Via Veneto hotels. The rooms are ample, and many have fine views of Villa Borghese. Potted plants bank the public rooms and marble-lined hallways. Period furniture, Oriental rugs, and old paintings add character to the rooms. Service is attentive; this, together with the unostentatious comfort, is what keeps its regular clientele coming back year after year. *Via Veneto 191, tel. 06/497821, fax 06/482–0359. 175 rooms with bath. AE, DC, MC, V.*

★ **Forum.** A centuries-old palace converted into a fine hotel, the Forum is on a quiet street within shouting distance of the Roman Forum and Piazza Venezia. Although it seems tucked away out of the main-

Rome Lodging

Albergo del Sole al Pantheon, **8**
Amalia, **1**
Britannia, **17**
Carriage, **6**
Duca d'Alba, **20**
D'Este, **19**
Farnese, **2**
Flora, **13**
Forum, **21**
Giulio Cesare, **3**
Grand, **15**
Hassler, **9**
Internazionale, **10**
La Residenza, **12**
Locarno, **4**
Majestic, **11**
Margutta, **5**
Montreal, **18**
Portoghesi, **7**
Romae, **16**
Victoria, **14**

stream, it's actually handy to all the main sights. The wood-paneled lobby and street-level bar are warm and welcoming. The smallish bedrooms are furnished in rich pink and beige fabrics; the bathrooms are ample, with either tub or shower. What's really special, though, is the rooftop restaurant and bar: The view toward the Colosseum is superb. Breakfast or a nightcap up here can be memorable. *Via Tor dei Conti 25, tel. 06/679–2446, fax 06/678–6479. 76 rooms with bath. Facilities: restaurant, bar. AE, DC, MC, V.*

Giulio Cesare. An aristocratic townhouse in the residential, but central, Prati district, the Giulio Cesare is a 10-minute walk across the Tiber from Piazza del Popolo. It's beautifully run, with a friendly staff and a quietly luxurious air. The rooms are elegantly furnished, with chandeliers, thick rugs, floor-length drapes, and rich damasks in soft colors. Public rooms have Oriental carpets, old prints and paintings, marble fireplaces, and a grand piano. *Via degli Scipioni 287, tel. 06/321–0751, fax 06/321–1736. 90 rooms with bath. Facilities: bar, garden, terrace. AE, DC, MC, V.*

Victoria. Considerable luxury in the public rooms, solid comfort throughout, and impeccable management are the main features of this hotel near Via Veneto. Oriental rugs, oil paintings, welcoming armchairs, and fresh flowers add charm to the public spaces, and the homey rooms are decorated in soothing combinations of peach, blue, and green. American businessmen, who prize the hotel's personalized service and restful atmosphere, are frequent guests. Some upper rooms and the roof terrace overlook the majestic pines of Villa Borghese. *Via Campania 41, tel. 06/473931, fax 06/487–1890. 110 rooms with bath. Facilities: restaurant, bar. AE, DC, MC, V.*

$$ **Britannia.** This fine small hotel offers superior quality at rates only
★ slightly above moderate prices. Its quiet but central location is one attraction. A caring management is another: Guests are coddled with English-language dailies and local weather reports delivered to their rooms each morning. Sybaritic marble bathrooms and well-furnished rooms, especially the clubby tartan and mahogany decor on the second floor, where halls are decorated in Pompeiian style, help make this a very special place. *Via Napoli 64, tel. 06/488–3153, fax 06/488–2343. 32 rooms with bath. Facilities: lounge, bar. AE, DC, MC, V.*

Carriage. Stay here for the location (by the Spanish Steps), the Old World elegance, and the reasonable rates. The hotel is decorated in soothing tones of blue and pale gold, with subdued Baroque accents adding a touch of luxury; rooms have antique-looking closets and porcelain telephones. Double room 402 and single room 305 have small balconies; elegant room 302 is spacious, with an oversize bathroom. Alternatively, try for one of the two rooms adjoining the roof terrace. *Via delle Carrozze 36, tel. 06/699–0124, fax 06/678–8279. 27 rooms and suites with bath. AE, DC, MC, V.*

D'Este. Within hailing distance of Santa Maria Maggiore and close to Termini Station (you can arrange to be picked up there by the hotel car), this is in a solidly renovated and distinguished 19th-century building. The fresh-looking decor evokes turn-of-the-century comfort, with brass bedsteads and lamps and dark wood period furniture. Rooms are quiet, light, and spacious; many can accommodate family groups. The attentive owner-manager likes to have fresh flowers in the halls and sees that everything works. He encourages inquiries about special rates, particularly during the slack summer months. *Via Carlo Alberto 4/b, tel. 06/446–5607, fax 06/446–5601. 37 rooms with bath. Facilities: bar, garden terrace. AE, DC, MC, V.*

Duca d'Alba. The Suburra quarter near the Colosseum is where the plebs of ancient Rome lived. The neighborhood is now in transition from shabby to chic, and this elegant little hotel comes under the latter heading. Over a refined reception area and small lounge furnished in neoclassic style are three floors of compact bedrooms stylishly decorated with light wood and soft colors, with bathrooms in beige travertine. Room rates are low in the category. *Via Leonina 14, tel. 06/484471, fax 06/488–4840. 24 rooms with bath or shower. AE, DC, MC, V.*

Internazionale. With an excellent location near the top of the Spanish Steps, the Internazionale has long been known as one of the city's best mid-size hotels. In a totally renovated building on desirable Via Sistina, it has doubly thick windows to ensure peace and quiet. Rooms on the fourth floor have terraces; the fourth-floor suite has a private terrace and a frescoed ceiling. The decor throughout is in soothing pastel tones, with some antique pieces, mirrors, and chandeliers. Guests relax in small, homey lounges downstairs and begin the day in the pretty breakfast room. *Via Sistina 79, tel. 06/ 679–3047, fax 06/678–4764. 40 rooms with bath. AE, MC, V.*

Locarno. The central location off Piazza del Popolo helps keep the Locarno a favorite among the art crowd, which also goes for its intimate mood, though some of Locarno's fine fin de siècle character has been lost in renovations. An attempt has been made to retain the hotel's original charm, however, while modernizing the rooms with such additions as electronic safes and air-conditioning. The decor features coordinated prints in wallpaper and fabrics, lacquered wrought-iron beds, and some antiques. *Via della Penna 22, tel. 06/ 361–0841, fax 06/321–5249. 38 rooms with bath. Facilities: bar, lounge. AE, V.*

Portoghesi. In the heart of Old Rome, facing the so-called Monkey Tower, the Portoghesi is a small hotel with considerable atmosphere. From a tiny lobby, an equally tiny elevator takes you to the quiet bedrooms, all decorated with floral prints and reproduction antique furniture. There's a breakfast room but no restaurant. *Via dei Portoghesi 1, tel. 06/686–4231, fax 06/687–6976. 27 rooms with bath or shower. MC, V.*

★ **La Residenza.** In a converted town house near Via Veneto, this hotel offers first-class comfort and atmosphere at reasonable rates. The canopied entrance, spacious well-furnished lounges, and the bar and terrace are of the type you would expect to find in a deluxe category. Rooms, decorated in aquamarine and beige, with bentwood furniture, have large closets, color TV, fridge-bar, and air-conditioning; bathrooms have heated towel racks. The clientele is mostly American. Rates include a generous American-style buffet breakfast. *Via Emilia 22, tel. 06/488–0789, fax 06/485721. 27 rooms with bath or shower. Facilities: bar, rooftop terrace, parking. MC, V.*

$ **Amalia.** Handy to the Vatican and the Cola di Rienzo shopping district, this small former *pensione* is owned and operated by the Consoli family—Amalia and her brothers. On several floors of a 19th-century building, it has 21 newly renovated rooms with TV sets, direct-dial telephones, pictures of angels on the walls, and gleaming marble bathrooms (hair dryers included). The remaining four guestrooms will be redone in the future. The Ottaviano stop of Metro Line A is a block away. *Via Germanico 66, tel. 06/397–23354, fax 06/397–23365. 25 rooms, 21 with bath or shower. Facilities: bar, breakfast room. AE, MC, V.*

★ **Margutta.** This small hotel is centrally located on a quiet side street between the Spanish Steps and Piazza del Popolo. Lobby and halls are unassuming, but rooms are a pleasant surprise, with a clean and airy look, attractive wrought-iron bedsteads, and modern baths.

Though it's in an old building, there is an elevator. *Via Laurina 34, tel. 06/322–3674. 21 rooms with bath or shower. AE, DC, MC, V.*

Romae. Located in the better part of the Termini Station neighborhood, the Romae has the advantages of a strategic location (within walking distance of many sights, and handy to bus and subway lines), a very friendly and helpful management, and good-size rooms that are clean and airy. The vivid pictures of Rome in the small lobby and breakfast room, the luminous white walls and light wood furniture in the bedrooms, and the bright little baths all have a fresh look. Amenities such as satellite TV and a hair dryer in every room, and breakfast included in the room rate, make this hotel a very good value. Families benefit from special rates and services. *Via Palestro 49, tel. 06/446–3554, fax 06/446–3914. 20 rooms with bath. AE, MC, V.*

Montreal. This is a compact hotel on a central avenue across the square from Santa Maria Maggiore, only three blocks from Termini Station, with bus and subway lines close by. Though on one floor of an older building, it has been totally renovated and offers fresh-looking rooms. The owner/managers are pleasant and helpful, and the neighborhood has plenty of reasonably priced eating places, plus one of Rome's largest outdoor markets. *Via Carlo Alberto 4, tel. 06/446–5522, fax 06/445–7797. 16 rooms with bath or shower. MC, V.*

The Arts and Nightlife

The Arts

Rome offers a vast selection of music, dance, opera, and film. Schedules of events are published in daily newspapers; in *Trovaroma*, the weekly entertainment guide published every Thursday as a supplement to the daily *La Repubblica*; in the *Guest in Rome* booklet distributed free at hotel desks; and in the monthly *Carnet*, available free from EPT offices. An English-language periodical, *Wanted in Rome* (1,000 lire), is available at centrally located newsstands and has good listings of events.

Concerts Rome has long hosted a wide variety of classical music concerts, although it is a common complaint that the city does not have adequate concert halls or a suitable auditorium. Depending on the location, concert tickets can cost from 10,000 to 50,000 lire. The principal concert series are those of the **Accademia di Santa Cecilia** (offices at Via dei Greci, box office tel. 06/678–0743), the **Accademia Filarmonica Romana** (Teatro Olimpico, Via Gentile da Fabriano 17, tel. 06/320–1752), the **Istituzione Universitaria dei Concerti** (San Leone Magno auditorium, Via Bolzano 38, tel. 06/361–0051), and the **RAI** Italian Radio-TV series at Foro Italico (tel. 06/368–65625). There is also the internationally respected **Gonfalone** series, which concentrates on Baroque music (Via del Gonfalone 32, tel. 06/687–5952). The **Associazione Musicale Romana** (tel. 06/656–8441) and **Il Tempietto** (tel. 06/481–4800) organize music festivals and concerts throughout the year. There are also many small concert groups. Many concerts are free, including all those performed in Catholic churches, where a special ruling permits only concerts of religious music. Look for posters outside churches announcing free concerts.

Rock, pop, and jazz concerts are frequent, especially in summer, although even performances by big-name stars may not be well advertised. Tickets for these performances are usually handled by **Orbis** (Piazza Esquilino 37, tel. 06/482–7403) and **Babilonia** (Via del Corso 185, tel. 06/678–6641).

Opera The opera season runs from November to May, and performances are staged in the **Teatro dell'Opera** (Via Firenze 72, tel. 06/488–1755). Tickets go on sale two days before a performance, and the box office is open 10–5. Prices range from 26,000 to 142,000 lire for regular performances; they can go much higher for an opening night or an appearance by an internationally acclaimed guest singer. Standards may not always measure up to those set by Milan's fabled La Scala, but, despite strikes and shortages of funds, most performances are respectable.

The summer opera season has been evicted from the ruins of the ancient **Baths of Caracalla.** At press time it is uncertain where the summer productions will take place. Check locally.

Dance The **Rome Opera Ballet** gives regular performances at the Teatro dell'Opera (*see* Opera, *above*), often with leading international guest stars. Rome is regularly visited by classical ballet companies from Russia, the United States, and Europe; performances are at the Teatro dell'Opera, Teatro Olimpico, or at one of the open-air venues in summer. Small classical and modern dance companies from Italy and abroad give performances in various places; check concert listings for information.

Film Rome has dozens of movie houses, but the only one to show exclusively English-language films is the **Pasquino** (Vicolo del Piede, just off Piazza Santa Maria in Trastevere, tel. 06/580–3622). Films here are not dubbed, but are shown in English with Italian subtitles. Pick up a weekly schedule at the theater or consult the daily papers.

Nightlife

Although Rome is not one of the world's most exciting cities for nightlife (despite the popular image of the city as the birthplace of *La Dolce Vita*), discos, live-music spots, and quiet late-night bars have proliferated in recent years. This has been true in the streets of the old city and in far-flung parts of town. The "flavor of the month" factor works here, too, and many places fade into oblivion after a brief moment of popularity. The best source for an up-to-date list of late-night spots is the weekly entertainment guide *Trovaroma*, a supplement to the Thursday edition of the daily newspaper *La Repubblica*.

Bars Rome has a range of bars offering drinks and background music. Jacket and tie are in order in the elegant **Blue Bar** of the Hostaria dell'Orso (Via dei Soldati 25, tel. 06/686–4250) and in **Le Bar** of the Grand hotel (Via Vittorio Emanuele Orlando 3, tel. 06/482931). **Jeff Blynn's** (Via Zanardelli 12, tel. 06/686–1990), near Piazza Navona, is a classic watering hole with seating at the bar or in leather-upholstered booths. Light meals are available. It's open from 7 PM to 2 AM, with happy hour from 7 to 10. (Closed Sun.) **Flann O'Brien** (Via Napoli 29, tel. 06/448–0418) has the look and atmosphere of an upscale Irish pub, but it is open all day, also functioning as an Italian coffee bar. (Closed Sat. morning and Sun.)

Informal wine bars are popular with Romans who like to stay up late but don't dig disco music. Near the Pantheon is **Spiriti** (Via Sant'Eustachio 5, tel. 06/689–2499), which also serves light lunches at midday and is open until 1:30 AM. The same atmosphere prevails at **Enoteca Roffi** (Via della Croce 76/a, tel. 06/679–0896) and at **Cavour 313** (Via Cavour 313, tel. 06/678–5496), near the Roman Forum. All three are closed Sunday. **Trimani Wine Bar,** between Piazza della Repubblica and Porta Pia (Via Cernaia 37/b, tel. 06/446–9630), is the family-run annex of one of Rome's most esteemed wine shops. You can sample some great wines at the counter or with a light, fixed-price meal at an upstairs table (open 11:30–3 and 5:30–midnight. Closed Sun.).

"In" places around Piazza Navona and the Pantheon include **Antico Caffè della Pace** (Via della Pace 3, tel. 06/686–1216), and **Le Cornacchie** (Piazza Rondanini 53, tel. 06/686–4485). Both are open until 2 AM.

Beer halls and pubs are popular with young Italians. **Birreria Marconi** (Via di Santa Prassede 9/c, tel. 06/486636), near Santa Maria Maggiore, is also a pizzeria. It is closed Sunday. **Birreria Santi Apostoli** (Piazza Santi Apostoli 52, tel. 06/678–8285), is open every day until 2 AM. Among the pubs, **Fiddler's Elbow** (Via dell'Olmata 43, no phone) is open 5 PM–midnight but is closed Monday. **Four Green Fields** (Via Costantino Morin 42, off Via della Giuliana, tel. 06/359–5091) features live music and is open daily from 8:30 PM to 1 AM.

Music Clubs   Jazz, folk, pop, and Latin music clubs are flourishing in Rome, particularly in the picturesque Trastevere neighborhood. Jazz clubs are especially popular, and talented local groups may be joined by visiting musicians from other countries. As admission, many clubs require that you buy a membership card for about 10,000–20,000 lire.

In the Trionfale district near the Vatican, **Alexanderplatz** (Via Ostia 9, tel. 06/372–9398) has both a bar and a restaurant, and features nightly live programs of jazz and blues played by Italian and foreign musicians. For the best live music, including jazz, blues, rhythm and blues, African, and rock, go to **Big Mama** (Vicolo San Francesco a Ripa 18, tel. 06/581–2551). There is also a bar and snack food. Latin rhythms are the specialty at **El Charango** (Via di Sant'Onofrio 28, tel. 06/687–9908), near Ponte Amedeo d'Aosta, a live music club.

In the trendy Testaccio neighborhood, **Caffè Latino** (Via di Monte Testaccio 96, tel. 06/574–4020) attracts a thirtysomething crowd with concerts (mainly jazz) in one room and a separate video room and bar for socializing. **Music Inn** (Largo dei Fiorentini 3, tel. 06/654–4934) is Rome's top jazz club and features some of the biggest names on the international scene. Open Thursday through Sunday evenings.

Live performances of jazz, soul, and funk by leading musicians draw celebrities to **St. Louis Music City** (Via del Cardello 13/a, tel. 06/474–5076). There is also a restaurant. Closed Thursday.

Discos and   Most discos open about 10:30 PM and charge an entrance fee of around
Nightclubs   30,000–35,000 lire, which may include the first drink. Subsequent drinks cost about 10,000–15,000 lire. Some discos also open on Saturday and Sunday afternoons for under-16s.

There's deafening disco music at **Frankie-Go** (Via Schiaparelli 29–30, tel. 06/322–1251) for the under-30 crowd, which sometimes includes young actors. Special events, such as beauty pageants, fashion shows, and theme parties, are featured, and there is a restaurant. Despite the address, the entrance is actually on Via Luciani 52. It's closed Monday.

Jackie O' (Via Boncompagni 11, tel. 06/488–5754) is again an upscale favorite with the rich and famous for dinner and/or disco dancing. Roman yuppies mingle with a trendy and sophisticated crowd while dancing to disco music at **Spago** (Via di Monte Testaccio, tel. 06/574–4999; it's hard to find, so take a taxi). **Fonclea** (Via Crescenzio 82/a, tel. 06/689–6302), near Castel Sant'Angelo, has a pub atmosphere and live music ranging from jazz to Latin American to rhythm-and-blues, depending on who's in town. The kitchen serves Mexican and Italian food.

Gilda (Via Mario dei Fiori 97, near Piazza di Spagna, tel. 06/678–4838) is the place to spot famous Italian actors and politicians. Formerly the Paradise supper club, this hot nightspot now has a new piano bar, as well as a restaurant, dance floors, and live music. It's closed Monday. **Hysteria** (Via Giovanelli 12, tel. 06/855–4587) attracts a very young crowd who come to enjoy the variety of music: disco, funk, soul, and hard rock. It's located off Via Salaria near the Galleria Borghese. It's closed Monday, also. A glittering disco, piano bar, and restaurant attracts over-25s to the **Open Gate** (Via San Nicola da Tolentino 4, tel. 06/474–6301). Dancing starts at midnight.

One of Rome's first discos, **The Piper** (Via Tagliamento 9, tel. 06/841–4459) is an "in" spot for teenagers. It has disco music, live groups, and pop videos. Occasionally, there's ballroom dancing for an older crowd. It opens weekends at 4 PM and is closed Monday and Tuesday. Funky music and huge video screens make **Scarabocchio** (Piazza Ponziani 8, tel. 06/580–0495) another popular spot. It's closed Monday.

Follia (Via Ovidio 17, tel. 06/683–08435) attracts celebrities and a sophisticated young crowd with disco music and a piano bar.

For Singles Locals and foreigners of all nations and ages gather at Rome's cafés on **Piazza della Rotonda** in front of the Pantheon, at **Piazza Navona,** or **Piazza Santa Maria in Trastevere.** The cafés on **Via Veneto** and the bars of the big hotels draw mainly tourists and are good places to meet other travelers in the over-30 age group. In fair weather, under-30s will find crowds of contemporaries on the **Spanish Steps,** where it's easy to strike up a conversation.

Excursion 1: Ostia Antica

One of the easiest excursions from the capital takes you west to the sea, where tall pines stand among the well-preserved ruins of Ostia Antica, the main port of ancient Rome. Founded around the 4th century BC. Ostia Antica conveys the same impression as Pompeii, but on a smaller scale and in a prettier, parklike setting. The city was inhabited by a cosmopolitan population of rich businessmen, wily merchants, sailors, and slaves. The great *horrea* (warehouses) were built in the 2nd century AD to handle huge shipments of grain from Africa; the *insulae*, forerunners of the modern apartment building, provided housing for the growing population. Under the combined assaults of the barbarians and the anopheles mosquito, the port was eventually abandoned, and it silted up. Tidal mud and windblown sand covered the city, which lay buried until the beginning of this century. Now extensively excavated and excellently maintained, it makes for a fascinating visit on a sunny day.

Tourist Information

The admission charge to the **Ostia Antica** excavations includes entrance to the Ostiense Museum, which is on the grounds and observes the same opening hours. *Via dei Romagnoli, tel. 06/565–1405. Admission: 8,000 lire. Open daily 9–one hour before sunset.*

Getting Around

By Car The Via del Mare leads directly from Rome to Ostia Antica; the ride takes about 35 minutes.

By Train There is regular train service from Ostiense train station, near Porta San Paolo, which is connected with the Piramide stop on Metro Line B. Trains leave every half-hour, and the ride takes about 30 minutes.

Exploring

Numbers in the margin correspond to points of interest on the Rome Environs map.

Near the entrance to the *scavi* (excavations) is a fortress built in the 15th century for Pope Julius II. The hamlet that grew up around it is charming. However, your visit to **Ostia Antica** itself starts at **Via delle Tombe,** lined with sepulchers from various periods. From here, passing through the **Porta Romana,** one of the city's three gates, you come to the **Decumanus Maximus,** the main thoroughfare crossing the city from end to end.

About 300 yards up on the right are the **Terme di Nettuno** (Baths of Neptune), decorated with black-and-white mosaics representing Neptune and Amphitrite. Directly behind the baths is the barracks of the fire department, which played an important role in a town with warehouses full of valuable goods and foodstuffs.

Just ahead, and also on the right side of the Decumanus Maximus, is the beautiful **Theater,** built by Augustus and completely restored by Septimius Severus in the 2nd century AD. Behind it, in the vast Piazzale delle Corporazioni, where trade organizations similar to guilds had their offices, is the **Temple of Ceres:** This is appropriate for a town dealing in grain imports, since Ceres, who gave her name to cereal, was the goddess of agriculture. Next to the theater, where there is a coffee bar, you can visit the **House of Apuleius,** built in Pompeiian style—containing fewer windows, and built lower, than those in Ostia. Next to it is the **Mithraeum,** with balconies and a hall decorated with symbols of the cult of Mithras. This men-only religion, imported from Persia, was especially popular with legionnaires.

On Via dei Molini, 200 yards beyond the theater, there is a mill, where grain for the warehouses next door was ground with the stones you see there. Along Via di Diana, a left turn 50 yards up Via dei Molini, you'll come upon a **thermopolium** (bar) with a marble counter and a fresco depicting the fruit and foodstuffs that were sold here. Turn right at the end of Via di Diana onto Via dei Dipinti; at the end is the **Museo Ostiense,** which displays some of the ancient sculptures and mosaics found among the ruins.

Retrace your steps along Via dei Dipinti and turn right just before Via di Diana for the **Forum,** with monumental remains of the city's most important temple, dedicated to Jupiter, Juno, and Minerva; other ruins of baths; a basilica (in Roman times a basilica served as a secular hall of justice); and smaller temples.

A continuation of the Decumanus Maximus leads from the Forum. From the crossroads, about 100 yards on, Via Epagathiana, on the right, leads down toward the Tiber, where there are large warehouses, erected in the 2nd century AD to deal with enormous

Rome Environs

amounts of grain imported into Rome during that period, the height of the Empire.

Take the street opposite the entrance to the warehouses to the **House of Cupid and Psyche,** a residential house named for a statue found there; you can see what remains of a large pool in an enclosed garden decorated with marble and mosaic motifs. It takes little imagination to notice that even in ancient times a premium was placed on water views: The house faces the shore, which would have been only about ¼ mile away. Take Via del Tempio di Ercole left and then go right on Via della Foce to see (on the left) the **House of Serapis,** a 2nd-century multilevel dwelling, and the **Baths of the Seven Wise Men,** named for a fresco found there.

Take Via del Tempio di Serapide away from Via della Foce and then the Cardo Degli Aurighi, where you'll pass—just up on the left— another apartment building. The road leads back to the Decumanus Maximus, which continues to the **Porta Marina.** Off to the left, on what used to be the seashore, are the ruins of the **Synagogue,** one of the oldest in the Western world. This is where you begin your return; Porta Marina is the farthest point in the tour. Go right at the **Bivio del Castrum,** past the slaughterhouse and the large round temple. You'll come to the **Cardine Massimo,** a road lined with ruined buildings. From here, turn left onto Via Semita dei Cippi to see the **House of Fortuna Annonaria,** the richly decorated house of a wealthy Ostian. This is another place to marvel at the skill of the mosaic artists and, at the same time, to realize that this really was someone's home. One of the rooms opens onto a secluded garden.

Continue on Via Semita dei Cippi for about 150 yards until you turn right onto the Decumanus Maximus to retrace the last leg of the tour back to the entrance.

Dining

Monumento. Handily located near the entrance to the excavations, this attractive trattoria serves Roman specialties and seafood. *Piazza Umberto I, tel. 06/565–0021. Dinner reservations advised. Dress: casual. AE, DC, MC, V. Closed Mon. and Aug. 20–Sept. 7. $$*
Sbarco di Enea. Also near the excavations, this restaurant is heavy on ancient-Roman atmosphere, with Pompeiian-style frescoes and chariots in the garden. On summer evenings you dine outdoors by torchlight, served by waiters in Roman costume. You'll probably come for lunch, when you can enjoy *farfalle con granchio* (pasta with crab sauce) or *linguine con aragosta* (with lobster sauce) and other seafood specialties, without all the hoopla. *Via dei Romagnoli 675, tel. 06/565–0034. Dinner reservations advised. Dress: casual. AE, MC. Closed Mon. and Feb. $$*

Excursion 2: Tivoli, Palestrina, and Subiaco

East of Rome lie some of the region's star attractions, which could be combined along a route that loops through the hills where ancient Romans built their summer resorts. The biggest attraction is Tivoli, which could be seen on a half-day excursion from Rome. But if you continue eastward to Palestrina, you can see a vast sanctuary famous in ancient times. And you could also fit in a visit to the site on which St. Benedict founded the hermitage that gave rise to Western monasticism. The monastery of St. Benedict is in Subiaco—not easy to get to unless you have a car, but you may want to make the effort to gain an insight into medieval mysticism.

Tourist Information

Tivoli (Largo Garibaldi, tel. 0774/293522).
Subiaco (Via Cadorna 59, tel. 0774/85397).

Escorted Tours

American Express (tel. 06/67641) and **CIT** (tel. 06/47941) have half-day excursions to Villa d'Este in Tivoli. **Appian Line** (tel. 06/488–4151) and **Carrani Tours** (tel. 06/482–4194) have morning tours that include Hadrian's Villa.

Getting Around

By Car   For Tivoli, take the Via Tiburtina or the Rome–L'Aquila autostrada (A24). From Tivoli to Palestrina, follow signs for the Via Prenestina and Palestrina. To get to Palestrina directly from Rome, take either the Via Prenestina or Via Casilina or take the Autostrada del Sole (A2) to the San Cesareo exit and follow signs for Palestrina; this trip takes about one hour. To get to Subiaco from either Tivoli or Palestrina or directly from Rome, take the autostrada for L'Aquila (A24) to the Vicovaro-Mandela exit, then follow the local road to Subiaco; from Rome, the ride takes about one hour.

By Train   The FS train from Termini Station to Palestrina takes about 40 minutes; you can then board a bus from the train station to the center of town.

By Bus   COTRAL buses leave for Tivoli every 15 minutes from the terminal at the Rebibbia stop on Metro Line B, but not all take the route that passes near Hadrian's Villa. Inquire which bus passes closest to Villa Adriana and tell the driver to let you off there. The ride takes about 60 minutes. For Palestrina, take the COTRAL bus from the Anagnina stop on Metro Line A. There is local bus service between Tivoli and Palestrina, but check schedules locally. From Rome to Subiaco, take the COTRAL bus from the Rebibbia stop on Metro Line B; buses leave every 40 minutes and those that take the autostrada make the trip in 70 minutes, as opposed to an hour and 45 minutes by another route.

Exploring

Numbers in the margin correspond to points of interest on the Rome Environs map.

The road east from Rome to Tivoli passes through some unattractive industrial areas and burgeoning suburbs. You'll know you're close when you see vast quarries of travertine marble and smell the sulphurous vapors of the little spa, Bagni di Tivoli. This was once green countryside; now it's ugly and overbuilt. But don't despair, because this tour takes you to two of the Rome area's most attractive sights: Hadrian's Villa and the Villa d'Este. The Villa d'Este is a popular destination; fewer people go to Hadrian's Villa. Both are outdoor sights, which entail a lot of walking, and in the case of the Villa D'Este, stair climbing. That also means that good weather is a virtual prerequisite for enjoying the itinerary.

② Visit **Hadrian's Villa** first, especially in the summer, to take advantage of the cooler morning sun: There's little shade. Hadrian, who succeeded Trajan as emperor in AD 117, was a man of genius and intellectual curiosity. Fascinated by the accomplishments of the Hellenistic world, he decided to re-create it for his own enjoyment by building this villa over a vast tract of land below the ancient settlement of Tibur. From AD 118 to 130, architects, laborers, and artists worked on the villa, periodically spurred on by the emperor himself, as he returned from another voyage full of ideas for even more daring constructions. After his death in AD 138, the fortunes of his villa declined. It was sacked by barbarians and Romans alike; by the Renaissance, many of his statues and decorations had ended up in the Villa d'Este. Still, it is an impressive complex.

Study the exhibits in the visitors' center at the entrance and the scale model in the building adjacent to the bar, close by. They will increase your enjoyment of the villa by helping you make sense out of what can otherwise be a maze of ruins. It's not the single elements, but the peaceful and harmonious effect of the whole, that makes Hadrian's Villa such a treat. Oleanders, pines, and cypresses growing among the ruins heighten the visual impact. *Villa Adriana. Admission: 8,000 lire. Open daily 9 AM–90 min before sunset.*

Time Out The **Adriano** restaurant, at the entrance to Hadrian's Villa, is a handy place to have lunch and to rest before heading up the hill to the Villa d'Este. The food is good, the cost moderate, and the atmosphere relaxing. (Closed Mon.)

③ From Hadrian's Villa, catch the local bus up to **Tivoli**'s main square, Largo Garibaldi. Take a left onto Via Boselli and cross Piazza Trento, with the church of Santa Maria Maggiore on your left, to reach the entrance to the **Villa d'Este.** Ippolito d'Este was an active figure in the political intrigues of mid-16th-century Italy. He was also a cardinal, thanks to his grandfather, Alexander VI, the infamous Borgia pope. To console himself at a time when he saw his political star in decline, Ippolito tore down part of a Franciscan monastery that occupied the site he had chosen for his villa. Then the determined prelate diverted the Aniene River into a channel to run under the town and provide water for the Villa d'Este's fountains. Big, small, noisy, quiet, rushing, and running, the fountains create a late-Renaissance playground, which is now, sadly, run down, with fountains halfheartedly spouting polluted water. *Villa d'Este. Admission: 5,000 lire. Open daily 9–90 minutes before sunset.*

④ Only 27 kilometers (17 miles) south of Tivoli on S636 and 37 kilometers (23 miles) outside Rome along Via Prenestina, **Palestrina** is set on the slopes of Mount Ginestro, from which it commands a sweeping view of the green plain and distant mountains. It is surprisingly little known outside Italy, except to students of ancient history and music lovers. Its most famous native son, Giovanni Pierluigi da Palestrina, born here in 1525, was the renowned composer of 105 masses, as well as madrigals, magnificats, and motets. But the town was celebrated long before the composer's lifetime.

Ancient Praeneste, modern Palestrina, was founded much earlier than Rome. It was the site of the Temple of Fortuna Primigenia, which dates from the beginning of the 2nd century BC. This was one of the biggest, richest, and most frequented temple complexes in all antiquity. People came from far and wide to consult its famous oracle, yet in modern times, no one had any idea of the extent of the complex until World War II bombings exposed ancient foundations that stretched way out into the plain below the town. It has since become clear that the temple area was larger than the town of Palestrina is today. Now you can make out the four superimposed terraces that formed the main part of the temple; they were built up on great arches and were linked by broad flights of stairs. The whole town sits on top of what was once the main part of the temple.

Large arches and terraces scale the hillside up to the **Palazzo Barberini,** built in the 17th century along the semicircular lines of the original temple. It's now a museum containing a wealth of material found on the site, some dating back to the 4th century BC. The collection of splendid engraved bronze urns was plundered by art thieves in 1991, but they couldn't carry off the chief attraction, a 1st century BC mosaic representing the Nile in flood. This delightful work—a large-scale composition in which form, color, and innumerable details captivate the eye—is alone worth the trip to Palestrina. But there's more: a model of the temple as it was in ancient times, which will help you appreciate the immensity of the original construction. *Museo Nazionale Archeologico, Palazzo Barberini. Admission: 6,000 lire. Open Tues.–Sun., spring and fall 9–6, summer 9–7:30, winter 9–4.*

5 If you are driving or if you don't mind setting out on a roundabout route by local bus, you could continue on to **Subiaco,** tucked away in the mountains above Tivoli and Palestrina. Take S155 east for about 40 kilometers (25 miles) before turning left onto S411 for the remaining 25 kilometers (15 miles) to Subiaco. Its inaccessibility was undoubtedly a point in its favor for St. Benedict: The 6th-century monastery that he founded here became a landmark of Western monasticism.

This excursion is best made by car because it's nearly a 3-kilometer (2-mile) walk from Subiaco to Santa Scolastica, and another half-hour by footpath up to San Benedetto. If you don't have a car, inquire in Subiaco about a local bus to get you at least part of the way.

The first monastery you come upon is that of **Santa Scolastica,** actually a convent, and the only one of the hermitages founded by St. Benedict and his sister Scholastica to have survived the Lombard invasion of Italy in the 9th century. It has three cloisters, the oldest dating back to the 13th century. The library, which is not open to visitors, contains some precious volumes; this was the site of the first print shop in Italy, set up in 1474. *Admission free. Open daily 9–12:30, 4–7.*

Drive up to the **monastery of St. Benedict,** or take the footpath that climbs the hill. The monastery was built over the grotto where St. Benedict lived and meditated. Clinging to the cliff on nine great arches, it has resisted the assaults of man and nature for almost 800 years. You climb a broad, sloping avenue and enter through a little wooden veranda, where a Latin inscription augurs "peace to those who enter." You find yourself in the colorful world of the upper church, every inch of it covered with frescoes by Umbrian and Sienese artists of the 14th century. In front of the main altar, a stairway leads down to the lower church, carved out of the rock, with yet another stairway down to the grotto, or cave, where Benedict lived as a hermit for three years. The frescoes here are even earlier than those above; look for the portrait of St. Francis of Assisi, painted from life in 1210, in the Chapel of St. Gregory, and for the oldest fresco in the monastery, in the Shepherd's Grotto. *Admission free. Open daily 9–12:30, 3–6.*

Back in town, if you've got the time, stop at the 14th-century **church of San Francesco** to see the frescoes by Il Sodoma. *Ring for admission.*

Dining

Palestrina ★ **Coccia.** In this dining room of a small, centrally located hotel in Palestrina's public garden, you'll find simple decor, a cordial welcome, local dishes, such as light and freshly made fettuccine, served with a choice of sauces, and more unusual items, such as *pasta e fagioli con frutti di mare* (thick bean and pasta soup with shellfish). *Hotel Stella, Piazzale Liberazione, tel. 06/953–8172. Reservations not needed. Dress: casual. AE, DC, MC, V. $$*

Subiaco **Belvedere.** This small hotel on the road between the town and the monasteries is equipped to serve crowds of skiers from the slopes of nearby Mount Livata, as well as pilgrims on their way to St. Benedict's hermitage. The atmosphere is homey and cordial. Specialties include homemade fettuccine with a tasty ragù sauce and grilled meats and sausages. *Via dei Monasteri 33, tel. 0774/85531. No reservations. Dress: casual. No credit cards. $*

Mariuccia. This modern barnlike restaurant, located close to the monasteries, caters to wedding parties and other groups but is calm enough on weekdays. There's a large garden and a good view from the picture windows. House specialties are homemade fettuccine with porcini mushrooms and *scaloppe al tartufo* (truffled veal scallops). In the summer you dine outdoors under bright umbrellas. *Via Sublacense, tel. 0774/84851. Lunch reservations advised. Dress: casual. No credit cards. Closed Mon. and Nov. $*

Tivoli **Del Falcone.** A central location—on the main street leading off Largo Garibaldi—means that this restaurant is popular and often crowded. In the ample and rustic dining rooms, you can try homemade fettuccine and cannelloni. Country-style grilled meats are excellent. *Via Trevio 34, tel. 0774/22358. Reservations advised. Dress: casual. No credit cards. Closed Mon. $*

Excursion 3: Viterbo, Cerveteri, and Tuscia

Scattered throughout the undulating countryside northwest of Rome are ancient Etruscan sites, medieval towns, and grandiose Renaissance villas. The attractions of this part of the region are not as well known as Tivoli or Ostia Antica, and they offer the promise of discovery. If you do not have a car, however, it takes some planning and determination to plot out an itinerary by bus or train that takes in more than one place at a time. If you are using public transportation you may want to limit your forays to an excursion from Rome to Viterbo and another from Rome to Cerveteri. Touring by car allows you to take in Lake Bracciano and its massive 15th-century castle, the imposing Palazzo Farnese at Caprarola, and the eccentric stone sculptures in the so-called Monster Park of Bomarzo, the folly of a Renaissance prince.

The area now known as Tuscia was Etruria, heartland of the Etruscan civilization that flourished here for almost one thousand years before it was overcome and assimilated by ancient Rome. To learn more about the Etruscans, read D. H. Lawrence's *Etruscan Places* (1932), and take in some of the collections of Etruscan art and artifacts in the Museum of Villa Giulia in Rome. Then visit Cerveteri and, if possible, Tarquinia and some of the other Etruscan sites. No homework is necessary to appreciate the charm of the walled city of Viterbo, capital of Tuscia. Viterbo's medieval quarter is well preserved and artlessly picturesque—a neighborhood where everyday life goes on in a 12th-century setting.

Tuscia's dramatically beautiful landscape hints at mystery. The rolling farmland is punctuated by forested hills and scarred by gorges where thick underbrush conceals shallow streams running swiftly in dark, rocky beds. Scenic roads trace the rims of extinct volcano craters, now receptacles of the deep waters of lakes Bracciano, Vico, and Bolsena. A drive through Tuscia holds the promise of some singular sights.

Tourist Information

Bracciano (Via Claudia 58, tel. 06/998–6782).
Cerveteri (Ladispoli, Via Duca degli Abruzzi 147, tel. 06/991–3049).
Tarquinia (Piazza Cavour 1, tel. 0766/856384).
Viterbo (Piazzale dei Caduti 14, tel. 0761/234795).

Getting Around

By Car This is the best way to see the area. From Rome, take Via Cassia (S2) to Monterosi, then turn off onto Via Cimina, a scenic road along the rim of the volcanic crater that now forms Lake Vico; you can detour east off Via Cimina to Caprarola to see the Palazzo Farnese before continuing on Via Cimina to Viterbo. If you leave Rome by way of Via Claudia (S493) you can detour to Lake Bracciano and visit the castle of Bracciano; you will also pass several Etruscan sites, including San Giuliano and Blera, before reaching Viterbo. The drive (either route) takes from 75 to 90 minutes, not counting detours for sightseeing. Another fast way to Viterbo is via Autostrada A1 to Orte, where you exit and take the Orte–Viterbo Raccordo, an expressway. Or you can stay on the Autostrada until the Attigliano exit, which is about 3 miles from Bomarzo and the Monster Park, then press on from Bomarzo via the Orte–Viterbo Raccordo. By autostrada the trip to Viterbo takes from 40 minutes to an hour (via Bomarzo).

For Tarquinia, take the Via Cassia southwest from Viterbo and turn off onto S1 bis, which takes you to Via Aurelia (S1), the main coast highway connecting Tarquinia and Cerveteri with Rome. Or drive directly from Rome to Cerveteri on the Rome–Civitavecchia expressway (A12) or Via Aurelia. The ride takes about 40 minutes. For Tarquinia, continue north on S1; the trip takes about 90 minutes.

By Bus To Viterbo, take the Ferrovia Roma Nord train to the Saxa Rubra stop, where you get the COTRAL bus to Viterbo. The ride takes 60 minutes on an express (*diretto*) bus, 90 minutes on slower buses. To Cerveteri, take the COTRAL bus from Lepanto Station on Metro Line A; the ride takes about 40 minutes. To Tarquinia, take the COTRAL bus from Lepanto Station on Metro Line A; the trip takes about 90 minutes.

By Train You can take a Ferrovia Roma Nord train directly to Viterbo, but service is infrequent and the ride takes about two hours. Local FS trains on the Rome–Pisa line stop at Ladispoli, where you may be able to get a bus to Cerveteri, but bus service is erratic and Cerveteri is 5 miles away. COTRAL buses from Rome are more direct. On the same FS line, Tarquinia is about 50 minutes away by local train, and there are buses from the station to Tarquinia, about 1 mile uphill.

Exploring

Numbers in the margin correspond to points of interest on the Rome Environs map.

⑥ **Viterbo** is about 80 kilometers (50 miles) from Rome in the heart of Tuscia, the modern name for the Etruscan domain of Etruria. Viterbo's chief attractions are its 12th-century walls and towers, the historic palace of the popes who held court here in the 13th century, and the perfectly preserved medieval quarter. At a conclave held at the **Palazzo Papale** in 1271 to elect a new pope, the people of Viterbo took a stand that has gone down in history. The conclave had dragged on for months, apparently making no progress. Weary of providing the cardinals with room and board, the people of Viterbo dismantled the roof of the conclave hall and put the churchmen on bread and water. Sure enough, a new pope—Gregory X—was elected in short order. The fine Romanesque **cathedral** next to the Papal Palace has a Renaissance facade. The interior has been restored to its original medieval style, but the chipped marble columns owe their look to a bomb that fell during World War II. To the left of the cathedral is a fine 15th-century town house.

Walk down Via San Lorenzo and follow Via San Pellegrino through the **medieval quarter of San Pellegrino,** one of the best preserved in Italy. The old buildings, towers, arches, vaults, and characteristic exterior staircases are made of the dark local volcanic stone called *peperino*. At the end of Via San Pellegrino, turn left toward Via delle Fabbriche and Piazza della Fontana Grande, where the largest and most original of Viterbo's medieval fountains still spouts steady streams of water. From the center of town, take a bus or drive to

⑦ Bagnaia to see **Villa Lante,** a splendid example of an Italian formal garden, studded with fountains and set in a lush park. *Admission: 5,000 lire. Open Tues.–Sun. 9 AM–one hour before sunset.*

⑧ If you have come by car, make a detour to **Bomarzo,** where the Parco dei Mostri (Monster Park) created in the 16th-century for Prince Vicino Orsini is characterized by eccentric architecture populated by surreal sculptures of mythical monsters. *Admission: 10,000 lire. Open daily 9 AM–one hour before sunset.*

Whether you reach Tarquinia and/or Cerveteri from Viterbo or Rome, you will find their necropolises. In these slightly unsettling cities of the dead, the Etruscans laid the deceased to rest, providing them with everything they might need to enjoy the afterlife: food, utensils, pictures, clothing, jewels, and arms. A highlight of a visit

⑨ to **Tarquinia** is the sight of the marvelous golden terra-cotta horses from a frieze that once decorated an Etruscan temple. This remarkable evidence of the artistic mastery achieved by the Etruscans is mounted in the main hall of the **Etruscan Museum** in Palazzo Vitelleschi. There are also ranks of sarcophagi and other Etruscan artifacts, together with some wall paintings that have been removed from the underground tombs that surround this sleepy provincial town. You can visit some of the underground tombs with a guide and see other paintings. *Admission: 8,000 lire, valid for both museum and necropolis. Open July–Sept., Tues.–Sun. 9–2, 4–7; Oct.–June, Tues.–Sun. 9–2.*

⑩ At **Cerveteri,** the tombs in the **Banditaccia Necropolis** outside of town are modeled on Etruscan dwellings and decorated with reliefs carved in stone. *Admission: 8,000 lire. Open May–Sept., Tues.– Sun. 9–7; Oct.–Apr., Tues.–Sun. 9–4.*

Dining

Cerveteri **La Necropoli.** Appropriately decorated with painted Etruscan motifs on the walls, this is the place most tourists head for after they have seen the tombs. In good weather you can eat outdoors. Specialties include shellfish, a reminder that the sea is nearby, and *maltagliate mare e monti* (pasta with mushrooms and shellfish). *Via Mura Castellane 54, tel. 06/995–0123. Reservations not necessary. Dress: casual. No credit cards. Closed Wed. $$*

Tarquinia **Solengo.** The restaurant is part of a modern hotel in the newer part of town, within walking distance of Palazzo Vitelleschi. From spring to fall you dine on a veranda with a sweeping view of the coastal plain and the sea. During the winter, meals are served in a rustic tavern with plaid tablecloths and walls hung with antique utensils. The menu offers seafood and local delicacies such as *papardelle al cinghiale* (homemade pasta with boar sauce) and roast boar. *Hotel Tarconte, Via Tuscia 23, tel. 0766/856141. Reservations advised. Dress: casual. AE, DC, MC, V. $$*

Viterbo **Da Ciro.** It's in the heart of the medieval San Pellegrino quarter, and the huge hearth where meat and fish are grilled is surely an authentic relic of the Middle Ages. The decor combines rustic country style and kitsch contemporary. The specialties of the house are *ombrichelle di Ciro* (homemade pasta with tomato and mushroom sauce) and *maialino* (roast suckling pig). *Via Cardinal La Fontaine 74, tel. 0761/243722. Reservations advised. Dress: casual. AE, DC, MC, V. Closed Fri. $$*

Il Richiastro. Open only from Thursday through lunch Sunday, this unusual restaurant occupies 13th-century premises, where beamed ceilings and a large stone fireplace add to the atmosphere. The menu, based on the traditional peasant cooking of Viterbo, features a variety of vegetables and herbs in soups and sauces and typical homemade pastas such as *ombrichelle*. The *zuppa di funghi* (wild mushroom soup) is a seasonal specialty. Il Richiastro is recommended for people who want to get off the beaten culinary track. *Via della Marrocca 16, tel. 0761/223609. Reservations advised. Dress: casual. No credit cards. Closed Sun. dinner and Mon.–Wed., Christmas, Easter, Aug. $$*

4 Florence

*By George
Sullivan*

Florence is one of the preeminent treasures of Europe, and it is a time-honored mecca for sightseers from all over the world. But as a city, it can be surprisingly forbidding to the first-time visitor. Its architecture is predominantly Early Renaissance and retains many of the harsh, implacable, fortresslike features of pre-Renaissance palazzi, whose facades were mostly meant to keep intruders out rather than to invite sightseers in. With the exception of a very few buildings, the stately dignity of the High Renaissance and the exuberant invention of the Baroque are not to be found here. The typical Florentine exterior gives nothing away, as if obsessively guarding secret treasures within.

The treasures, of course, are very real. And far from being a secret, they are famous the world over. The city is an artistic treasure house of unique and incomparable proportions. A single historical fact explains the phenomenon: Florence gave birth to the Renaissance. In the early 15th century the study of antiquity—of the glory that was Greece and the grandeur that was Rome—became a Florentine passion, and with it came a new respect for learning and a new creativity in art and architecture. In Florence, that remarkable creativity is everywhere in evidence.

Prior to the 15th century, Florence was a medieval city not much different from its Tuscan neighbors. It began as a Roman settlement, laid out in the first century BC, and served as a provincial capital when the Roman Empire was at its height. Its rise to real power, however, did not begin until the era of the medieval Italian city-states, beginning in the 11th century.

From the 11th to the 14th centuries, northern Italy was ruled by feudal lords, and by the 13th century Florence was a leading contender in the complicated struggle between the Guelphs and the Ghibellines. Florence was mostly Guelph, and its Ghibelline contingent ruled the city only sporadically (which did not, however, keep the Florentine Guelphs from squabbling among themselves). In those bloody days Florence was filled with tall defensive towers built by the city's leading families on a competitive anything-you-can-build-I-can-build-bigger basis; the towers (and the houses below them) were connected by overhead bridges and catwalks, constructed to allow the members of allied families access to each other's houses without venturing into the dangerous streets below. The era gave rise, possibly for the first time in history, to the concept of turf, and its urban conflicts were at times just as vicious and irrational as the gang warfare within cities today.

The Guelph–Ghibelline conflict ended, finally, with the victory of the Guelphs and the rise of the Medici in the 15th century. The famous dynasty that ruled Florence, and later all Tuscany, for more than three centuries began with Giovanni di Bicci de' Medici and his son Cosimo, who transformed themselves from bankers into rulers. The dynasty reached its zenith with Cosimo's grandson Lorenzo the Magnificent (1449–92), patron and friend of some of Florence's most famous Renaissance artists. The towers were torn down, and the city assumed a slightly softer aspect. It still looks today much as it did then.

The history of modern Florence was shaped by its six years as the capital of the Kingdom of Italy. In 1861 Tuscany united with most of the other states on the Italian peninsula, and in 1865 Florence became the new nation's capital. In 1871 Florence relinquished the honor, when the final unification of Italy was effected by the capitulation of Rome.

But the city's history was equally influenced by the flood of November 4, 1966. The citizens of Florence went to bed the night before in a heavy downpour after three days of rain and a particularly wet autumn; they awoke the next morning to confront the worst disaster in the city's history. Florence was entirely under water. Piazza del Duomo became a rushing river; the church of Santa Croce was battered by a torrent more than 20 feet deep; the Ponte Vecchio disappeared completely as the Arno broke into the walls of its shops and flowed through. Only toward midnight did the flood begin to recede.

The Ponte Vecchio—amazingly—survived. But the damage to the rest of the city, including some of its greatest artistic treasures, was horrific. Technologically and financially ill-equipped to cope with such a disaster, Florence asked for, and received, advice and help from an army of international experts. Today, most of the damage has been repaired, although little has been done to keep this kind of ruin from happening again. A more recent near disaster was the terrorist bomb that exploded near the Uffizi Gallery in 1993, killing five people, destroying a medieval tower, shattering the museum's skylights, and shredding some paintings. Fortunately, no major works were irreparably damaged.

Essential Information

Arriving and Departing by Plane

Airports and Airlines The A. Vespucci Airport, called **Peretola** (tel. 055/373498), is 10 kilometers (6 miles) northwest of Florence. Although it accommodates flights from Milan, Rome, and some European cities, it is still a relatively minor airport. **Galileo Galilei Airport** in Pisa (tel. 050/44325) is 80 kilometers (50 miles) west of Florence and is used by most international carriers; for flight information, call the Florence Air Terminal at Santa Maria Novella train station or Galilei airport information (tel. 055/500707).

International travelers flying on Alitalia to Rome's **Leonardo da Vinci Airport** can go directly nonstop to Florence's Santa Maria Novella Station via Alitalia's twice-daily airport train. Luggage is checked through to Florence, and meals and extras are available on the train. Airport train arrangements must be made when you buy your plane ticket. The service also operates in the other direction, returning from Florence to the da Vinci airport.

Between the Airports and Downtown **By Car:** From Peretola take autostrada A11 directly into the city. Driving from the airport in Pisa, take S67, a direct route to Florence.

By Train: A scheduled service connects the station at Pisa's Galileo Galilei Airport with Santa Maria Novella Station in Florence, roughly a one-hour trip. Trains start running about 7 AM from the airport, 6 AM from Florence, and continue service every hour until about 11:30 PM from the airport, 8 PM from Florence. You can check in for departing flights at the air terminal at Track 5 of the train station (tel. 055/216073).

By Bus: There is no direct bus service from Pisa's airport to Florence. Buses do go to Pisa itself, but then you have to change to a slow train service. There is a local bus service from Peretola to Florence (*see* Getting Around By Bus, *below*).

Arriving and Departing by Car, Train, and Bus

By Car Florence is connected to the north and south of Italy by the Autostrada del Sole (A1). It is about an hour's scenic drive from Bologna (although heavy truck traffic over the Apennines often makes for slower going) and about three hours from Rome. The Tyrrhenian coast is an hour away on A11 west. In the city, abandon all hope of using a car, since most of the downtown area is a pedestrian zone. For traffic information in Florence, call 055/577777.

By Train Florence is on the principal Italian train route between most European capitals and Rome and within Italy is served quite frequently from Milan, Venice, and Rome by nonstop Intercity (IC) trains. The **Santa Maria Novella** Station is near the downtown area; avoid trains that stop only at the Campo di Marte Station in an inconvenient location on the east side of the city. For train information in Florence, call 055/288785.

By Bus Long-distance buses run by **SITA** (Via Santa Caterina da Siena 15/r, tel. 055/483651 weekdays, 211487 on weekends) and **Lazzi Eurolines** (Via Mercadante 2, tel. 055/215154) offer inexpensive if somewhat claustrophobic service between Florence and other cities in Italy and Europe.

Getting Around

By Bus Maps and timetables are available for a small fee at the ATAF booth next to the train station or at the office at Piazza del Duomo 57/r, or for free at tourist information offices (*see* Important Addresses and Numbers, *below*). Tickets must be bought in advance and can be purchased at tobacco stores, newsstands, from automatic ticket machines near main stops, or at ATAF booths (next to the station and at strategic locations throughout the city). The ticket must be canceled in the small validation machine immediately upon boarding. Two types of tickets are available, both valid for one or more rides on all lines. One costs 1,200 lire and is valid for 60 minutes from the time it is first canceled; the other costs 1,500 lire and is valid for 120 minutes. A multiple ticket—eight tickets each valid for 60 minutes—costs 9,000 lire. A 24-hour tourist ticket costs 5,000 lire. Long-term visitors or frequent users of the bus should consider a monthly pass, which is sold at the ATAF office.

By Taxi Taxis usually wait at stands throughout the city (such as in front of the train station and in Piazza della Repubblica), or they can be called by dialing 055/4390 or 055/4798. The meter starts at 3,200 lire.

By Moped Those who want to go native and rent a noisy Vespa (Italian for wasp) or other make of motorcycle or moped may do so at **Motorent** (Via San Zanobi 9/r, tel. 055/490113) or **Alinari** (Via Guelfa 85/r, tel. 055/280500). Helmets are mandatory and can be rented here.

By Bicycle Brave souls many also rent bicycles at easy-to-spot locations at Fortezza da Basso, Santa Maria Novella train station, and Piazza Pitti, from **Alinari** or **Motorent** (*see above*), or from **Ciao e Basta** (Lungarno Pecori Girardi 1, tel. 055/234–2726).

By Foot This is definitely the best way to see the major sights of Florence, since practically everything of interest is within walking distance along the city's crowded, narrow streets or is otherwise accessible by bus.

Important Addresses and Numbers

Tourist Information The city information office is at Via Cavour 1/r (next to Palazzo Medici Riccardi), tel. 055/276–0382. Open 8:30–7. Another municipal information office is next to the train station (tel. 055/212245; closed after 2 PM in winter).

The **APT** (tourist office) is just off Piazza Beccaria, at Via Manzoni 16, tel. 055/234–6284. Open Mon.–Sat. 8:30–1:30. There is another information office near Piazza della Signoria, at Chiasso dei Baroncelli 17/r (tel. 055/230–2124).

Consulates **U.S.** Lungarno Vespucci 38, tel. 055/239–8276. Open weekdays 8:30–noon and 2–4.
British. Lungarno Corsini 2, tel. 055/284133. Open weekdays 9:30–12:30 and 2:30–4:30.
Canadians should contact their embassy in Rome.

Emergencies **Police.** Tel. 113. The main police station is located at Via Zara 2, near Piazza della Libertà.

Doctors and Dentists For English-speaking doctors and dentists, get a list from the U.S. consulate, or contact **Tourist Medical Service** (Viale Lorenzo Il Magnifico, tel. 055/475411).

Ambulance. Call 118 or Misericordia (Piazza del Duomo 20, tel. 055/212222). If you need hospital treatment—and an interpreter—you can call AVO, a group of volunteer interpreters who offer their services free (tel. 055/403126, or Mon., Wed., Fri. from 4–6 PM, 055/234–4567).

Late-Night Pharmacies. The following are open 24 hours a day, seven days a week. For others, call 055/110.

Comunale No. 13 (train station, tel. 055/289435).

Molteni (Via Calzaiuoli 7/r, tel. 055/289490).

Taverna (Piazza San Giovanni 20/r, tel. 055/284013).

English-Language Bookstores **Paperback Exchange** (Via Fiesolana 31/r, tel. 055/247–8154) will do just that, besides selling books outright. **BM Bookshop** (Borgo Ognissanti 4/r, tel. 055/294575) has a fine selection of books on Florence. **Seeber** (Via Tornabuoni 68, tel. 055/215697) has English-language books alongside the other titles. All are open 9–1 and 3:30–7:30. Closed Sunday and Monday morning.

Travel Agencies **American Express** (Via Guicciardini 49/r, near Piazza Pitti, tel. 055/288751) is also represented by **Universalturismo** (Via Speziali 7/r, off Piazza della Repubblica, tel. 055/217241). **CIT** has a main office (Via Cavour 56, tel. 055/294306) and also a branch near the train station (Piazza Stazione 51, tel. 055/239–6963). **Thomas Cook** is represented by **World Vision** (Via Cavour 154/r, tel. 055/579294). All agencies are open weekdays 9–12:30 and 3:30–7:30, Saturday 9–noon.

Guided Tours

Orientation Visitors who have a limited amount of time in Florence may find guided tours an efficient way of covering the city's major sights. The major bus operators (*see* Arriving and Departing by Car, Train, and Bus, *above*) offer half-day itineraries, all of which generally follow the same plan, using comfortable buses staffed with English-speaking guides. Morning tours begin at 9, when buses pick visitors up at the main hotels. Stops include the cathedral complex, with its baptistery and bell tower, the Accademia to see Michelangelo's famous statue of David, Piazzale Michelangelo for a fine view of Florence, and the Pitti Palace (or the Museo dell'Opera del Duomo on Monday when the Pitti is closed) for a guided tour. Afternoon tours stop at the main hotels at 2 PM and take in Piazza della Signoria, the Uffizi Gallery (or the Palazzo Vecchio on Monday, when the Uffizi is closed), the nearby town of Fiesole, and, on the return, the church of Santa Croce. A half-day tour costs about 45,000 lire, including museum admissions.

Excursions Contact the above operators a day in advance, if possible, because excursions are popular. Comfortable buses with English-speaking guides make full-day trips from Florence to Siena and San Gimignano (departure 9 AM, return 6 PM, lunch not included) and afternoon excursions to Pisa (departure 2 PM, return 7 PM), with pickup and return from the main hotels. The Siena excursion costs about 58,000 lire, the Pisa excursion about 38,000 lire. Good bus and train connections make it easy for you to do these on your own, however.

Exploring Florence

No city in Italy can match Florence's astounding artistic wealth. Important paintings and sculptures are everywhere, and art scholars and connoisseurs have been investigating the subtleties and complexities of these works for hundreds of years. But what makes the art of Florence a revelation to the ordinary sightseer is a simple fact that scholarship often ignores: An astonishing percentage of Florence's art is just plain beautiful. Nowhere in Italy—perhaps in all Europe—is the act of looking at art more rewarding.

But a word of warning is in order here. For some years now, Florentine psychiatrists have recognized a peculiar local malady to which foreign tourists are particularly susceptible. It's called "Stendhal's syndrome," after the 19th-century French novelist, who was the first to describe it in print. The symptoms can be severe: confusion, dizziness, disorientation, depression, and sometimes persecution anxiety and loss of identity. Some victims immediately suspect food poisoning, but the true diagnosis is far more outlandish. They are suffering from art poisoning, brought on by overexposure to so-called Important Works of High Culture. Consciously or unconsciously, they seem to view Florentine art as an exam (Aesthetics 101, 10 hours per day, self-taught, pass/fail), and they are terrified of flunking.

Obviously, the art of Florence should not be a test. So if you are not an inveterate museum goer or church collector with established habits and methods, take it easy. Don't try to absorb every painting or fresco that comes into view. There is second-rate art even in the Uffizi and the Pitti (*especially* the Pitti), so find some favorites and enjoy them at your leisure. Getting to know a few paintings well will be far more enjoyable than seeing a vast number badly.

And when fatigue begins to set in, stop. Take time off, and pay some attention to the city itself. Too many first-time visitors trudge dutifully from one museum to the next without really seeing what is in between. They fail to notice that Florence the city (as opposed to Florence the museum) is a remarkable phenomenon: a bustling metropolis that has managed to preserve its predominantly medieval street plan and predominantly Renaissance infrastructure while successfully adapting to the insistent demands of 20th-century life. The resulting marriage between the very old and the very new is not always tranquil, but it is always fascinating. Florence the city can be chaotic, frenetic, and full of uniquely Italian noise, but it is alive in a way that Florence the museum, however beautiful, is not. Do not miss the forest for the trees.

The three walking tours outlined in the following pages are best taken a day at a time. Attempts to complete them in fewer than three days will prove frustrating, for many (if not most) Florentine museums and churches close sometime between noon and 2, and only the churches reopen in the late afternoon.

A special museum ticket valid for six months at seven city museums, including the Palazzo Vecchio, the Museum of Firenze Com'Era (Museum of Florentine History), and the Museum of Santa Maria Novella, costs 10,000 lire and is a good buy if you're planning on doing some of these museums. Inquire at any city museum.

Highlights for First-Time Visitors

Duomo (Cathedral of Santa Maria del Fiore) (Tour 1: From the Duomo to the Boboli Gardens).

Battistero (Baptistery) (Tour 1: From the Duomo to the Boboli Gardens).

Museo dell'Opera del Duomo (Tour 1: From the Duomo to the Boboli Gardens).

Bargello (Museo Nazionale) (Tour 1: From the Duomo to the Boboli Gardens).

Piazza della Signoria (Tour 1: From the Duomo to the Boboli Gardens).

Galleria degli Uffizi (Tour 1: From the Duomo to the Boboli Gardens).

Galleria dell'Accademia (Tour 3: From the Duomo to Santa Croce and Beyond).

Ponte Vecchio (Tour 1: From the Duomo to the Boboli Gardens).

Santa Croce (Tour 3: From the Duomo to Santa Croce and Beyond).

Tour 1: From the Duomo to the Boboli Gardens

Numbers in the margin correspond to points of interest on the Florence map.

The first tour begins with the Cathedral of Santa Maria del Fiore,
❶ more familiarly known as the **Duomo,** located in Piazza del Duomo,
❷ with its adjacent **Battistero** (Baptistery), the octagonal building that faces the Duomo facade. The Baptistery is one of the oldest buildings in Florence, and local legend has that it was once a Roman temple of Mars; modern excavations, however, suggest its foundation was laid in the sixth or seventh century AD, well after the collapse of the Roman Empire. The round-arched Romanesque decoration on the exterior probably dates from the 11th or 12th century. The interior ceiling mosaics (finished in 1297) are justly famous, but—glitteringly beautiful as they are—they could never outshine the building's most renowned feature: its bronze Renaissance doors decorated with panels crafted by Lorenzo Ghiberti (1378–1455). The doors, on which Ghiberti spent most of his adult life (from 1403 to 1452), are on the north and east sides of the baptistery—at least copies of them are—while the south door panels, in

the Gothic style, were designed by Andrea Pisano in 1330. The originals of the Ghiberti doors were removed to protect them from the effects of pollution and acid rain and have been beautifully restored; some of the panels are now on display in the Cathedral Museum. (*see* Museo dell'Opera del Duomo, *below*). The copy of the east doors now installed on the Baptistery does not do Ghiberti's work justice. *Admission free to Baptistery interior. Open Mon.–Sat. 1:30–6, Sun. 9–1.*

Ghiberti's north doors depict scenes from the life of Christ; his later east doors, facing the Duomo facade, depict scenes from the Old Testament. They are worth a close examination, for they are very different in style and illustrate with great clarity the artistic changes that marked the beginning of the Renaissance. Look, for instance, at the far right panel of the middle row on the earlier north doors *(Jesus Calming the Waters)*. Ghiberti here captured the chaos of a storm at sea with great skill and economy, but the artistic conventions he used are basically pre-Renaissance: Jesus is the most important figure, so he is the largest; the disciples are next in size, being next in importance; the ship on which they founder is a mere toy. But you can sense Ghiberti's impatience with these artificial spatial conventions. The Cathedral Works Committee made him retain the decorative quatrefoil borders of the south doors for his panels here, and in this scene Ghiberti's storm seems to want to burst the bounds of its frame.

On the east doors, the decorative borders are gone. The panels are larger, more expansive, more sweeping, and more convincing. Look, for example, at the middle panel on the left-hand door. It tells the story of Jacob and Esau, and the various episodes of the story (the selling of the birthright, Isaac ordering Esau to go hunting, the blessing of Jacob, and so forth) have been merged into a single beautifully realized street scene. A perspective grid is employed to suggest depth, the background architecture looks far more convincing than on the north door panels, the figures in the foreground are grouped realistically, and the naturalism and grace of the poses (look at Esau's left leg) have nothing to do with the sacred message being conveyed. Although the religious content remains, man and his place in the natural world are given new prominence and are portrayed with a realism not seen in art since the fall of the Roman Empire, more than a thousand years before.

When Ghiberti was working on these panels, three of his artist friends were bringing the same new humanistic focus to their own very different work. In sculpture, Donato di Niccolò Betto Bardi, known as Donatello, was creating statuary for churches all over town; in painting, Tommaso di Ser Giovanni, known as Masaccio, was executing frescoes at the churches of Santa Maria del Carmine and Santa Maria Novella; in architecture, Filippo Brunelleschi was building the Duomo dome, the Ospedale degli Innocenti, and the church interiors of San Lorenzo and Santo Spirito. They are the fathers of the Renaissance in art and architecture—the four great geniuses who created a new artistic vision—and among them they began a revolution that was to make Florence the artistic capital of Italy for more than a hundred years.

As a footnote to Ghiberti's panels, one small detail of the east doors is worth a special look. Just to the lower left of the Jacob and Esau panel, Ghiberti placed a tiny self-portrait bust. From either side, the portrait is extremely appealing—Ghiberti looks like everyone's favorite uncle—but the bust is carefully placed so that there is a single spot in front of the doors from which you can make direct eye con-

Florence

tact with the tiny head. When that contact is made, the impression of intelligent life—of *modern* intelligent life—is astonishing. It is no wonder that when these doors were completed, they received one of the most famous compliments in the history of art, from a competitor known to be notoriously stingy with praise: Michelangelo himself declared them so beautiful that they could serve as the Gates to Paradise.

The immense Duomo—the fourth-largest church in the world—was designed by Arnolfo di Cambio in 1296 but was not consecrated until 1436. The imposing facade dates only from the 19th century; it was built in the neo-Gothic style to complement Giotto's genuine Gothic (14th-century) **Campanile** (Bell Tower), which stands to the right of the church's facade. The real glory of the Duomo, however, is Filippo Brunelleschi's dome, herald of the new Renaissance in architecture, which hovers over the cathedral (and the entire city when seen from afar) with a dignity and grace that few domes, even to this day, can match. It was the first of its kind in the world, and for many people it is still the best.

Brunelleschi's dome was epoch-making as an engineering feat, as well. The space to be enclosed by the dome was so large and so high above the ground that traditional methods of dome construction—wooden centering and scaffolding—were of no use whatever. So Brunelleschi developed entirely new building methods, which he implemented with equipment of his own devising (including the modern crane). Beginning work in 1420, he built not one dome but two, one inside the other, and connected them with common ribbing that stretched across the intervening empty space, thereby considerably lessening the crushing weight of the structure. He also employed a new method of bricklaying, based on an ancient Roman herringbone pattern, interlocking each new course of bricks with the course below in a way that made the growing structure self-supporting. The result was one of the great engineering breakthroughs of all time: Most of Europe's great domes, including St. Peter's in Rome, were built employing Brunelleschi's methods, and today the Duomo has come to symbolize Florence in the same way that the Eiffel Tower symbolizes Paris. The Florentines are justly proud, and to this day the Florentine phrase for "homesick" is *nostalgia del cupolone* (homesick for the dome).

The interior is a fine example of Italian Gothic, although anyone who has seen the Gothic cathedrals of France will be disappointed by its lack of dramatic verticality. Italian architecture, even at the height of the Gothic era, never broke entirely free of the influence of Classical Rome, and its architects never learned (perhaps never wanted to learn) how to make their interiors soar like the cathedrals in the cities around Paris.

Most of the cathedral's best-known artworks have now been moved to the nearby Cathedral Museum. Notable among the works that remain, however, are two equestrian frescoes honoring famous soldiers: Andrea del Castagno's *Niccolò da Tolentino*, painted in 1456, and Paolo Uccello's *Sir John Hawkwood*, painted 20 years earlier; both are on the left-hand wall of the nave. *Niccolò da Tolentino* is particularly impressive: He rides his fine horse with military pride and wears his even finer hat—surely the best in town—with panache.

If time permits, you may want to explore the upper and lower reaches of the cathedral, as well. Ancient remains have been excavated beneath the nave; the stairway down is near the first pier on the right. The climb to the top of the dome (463 steps) is not for the faint-hearted, but the view is superb; the entrance is on the left wall just before the crossing. *Piazza del Duomo, tel. 055/230-2885. Excavation admission: 3,000 lire. Ascent admission: 5,000 lire. Both open Mon.-Sat. 10-5. Duomo open daily 10-5.*

❹ Leave the Duomo by the right-aisle exit and turn left; at the east end of the piazza, opposite the rear of the cathedral, is the **Museo dell'Opera del Duomo** (Cathedral Museum). Its major attractions—other than the Ghiberti door panels mentioned earlier and the choir loft (*cantorie*) reliefs by Donatello and Luca della Robbia—are two: Donatello's *Mary Magdalen* and Michelangelo's *Pietà* (not to be confused with the more famous *Pietà* in St. Peter's, in Rome). The High Renaissance in sculpture is in part defined by its revolutionary realism, but Donatello's *Magdalen* goes beyond realism: It is suffering incarnate. Michelangelo's heart-wrenching *Pietà* was unfinished at his death; the female figure supporting the body of Christ on the left was added by one Tiberio Calcagni, and never has the difference between competence and genius been manifested so clearly. *Piazza del Duomo 9, tel. 055/2302885. Admission: 5,000 lire. Open Mar.-Oct., Mon.-Sat. 9-7:30; Nov.-Feb., Mon.-Sat. 9-5:30.*

Return to the Duomo facade, and turn left onto **Via dei Calzaiuoli.** This unusually wide street dates from the 14th century and probably represents Florence's first effort at modern city planning. The street received special attention because it ran directly from the city's main religious square to its main civic square, Piazza della Signoria, where the medieval city hall was located. Both the axis and the city hall remain intact to this day.

A short detour to the west (down Via degli Speziali) leads to **Piazza della Repubblica.** The piazza's location, if not its architecture, is historically important: The ancient forum that was the core of the original Roman settlement was located here. The street plan in the area around the piazza still reflects the carefully plotted orthogonal grid of the Roman military encampment. The Mercato Vecchio (Old Market), located here since the Middle Ages, was demolished at the end of the last century, and the current piazza was constructed between 1890 and 1917 as a neoclassical showpiece. Nominally the center of town, it has yet to earn the love of most Florentines.

❺ Return to Via dei Calzaiuoli and turn right. Just down the street is the rectangular church of **Orsanmichele,** containing a beautifully detailed 14th-century Gothic tabernacle by Andrea Orcagna. Of particular note here, however, is the exterior. Originally a granary, the building was transformed in 1336 into a church with 14 exterior niches. Each of the major Florentine trade guilds was assigned its own niche and paid for the sculpture the niche contains. All the statues are worth examining, though many are copies. Unfortunately, one that is particularly deserving of scrutiny—Andrea del Verrocchio's *Doubting Thomas* (ca. 1470)—has been removed for restoration (eventually to be put into a museum, perhaps even in Orsanmichele, along with the other originals). Were this niche not empty, you would see Christ, like the building's other figures, entirely framed within the niche, and St. Thomas standing on its bottom ledge, with his right foot outside the niche frame. This one detail, the positioning of a single foot, brings the whole composition to life. It is particularly appropriate that this is the only niche to be topped with a Renaissance pediment, for it is the revolutionary vitality of sculpture like this that gave the Renaissance its name.

From Via dei Calzaiuoli, follow Via dei Tavolini (which turns into Via Dante Alighieri after one block and passes the fraudulently named Casa di Dante on the left) to the intersection of Via del Proconsolo. The church on the southwest corner is the ancient **Badia Fiorentina,** built in 1285; its graceful bell tower (best seen from the interior courtyard) is one of the most beautiful in Florence. The interior of the church proper was half-heartedly remodeled in the Baroque style during the 17th century; its best-known work of art is Filippino Lippi's delicate *Apparition of the Virgin to St. Bernard* (1486), on the left as you enter. The painting—one of Lippi's finest—is in superb condition and is worth exploring in detail. The Virgin's hands are perhaps the most beautiful in the city. (To illuminate, drop a coin in the box near the floor to the painting's right).

On the opposite side of Via del Proconsolo from the Badia is the **❻ Bargello.** During the Renaissance the building was used as a prison, and the exterior served as a "most-wanted" billboard: Effigies of notorious criminals and Medici enemies were painted on its walls. Today, the building is the **Museo Nazionale** and houses what is probably the finest collection of Renaissance sculpture in Italy. Michelangelo, Donatello, and Benvenuto Cellini are the preeminent masters here, and the concentration of masterworks is remarkable, though they stand among an eclectic array of arms, ceramics, and enamels. For Renaissance art lovers, the Bargello is to sculpture what the Uffizi is to painting.

One particular display—easily overlooked—should not be missed. In 1402 Filippo Brunelleschi and Lorenzo Ghiberti competed to earn the most prestigious commission of the day: the decoration of the north doors of the baptistery in Piazza del Duomo. For the competition, each designed a bronze bas-relief panel on the theme of the Sacrifice of Isaac; both panels are on display, side by side, in the room devoted to the sculpture of Donatello on the upper floor. The judges chose Ghiberti for the commission; you can decide for yourself whether or not they were right. *Via del Proconsolo 4, tel. 055/238–8606. Admission: 6,000 lire. Open Tues.–Sat. 9–2, Sun. 9–1.*

Leaving the Bargello, continue south along Via del Proconsolo, to the small Piazza San Firenze. The church of San Firenze, on the left, is one of Florence's few Baroque structures; its steps offer a fine view of the Badia bell tower. From the north end of the piazza, go west on Via Condotta, then left onto Via dei Magazzini, which leads into **Piazza della Signoria,** recently excavated and then repaved, the most striking square in Florence. It was here, in 1497, that the famous "bonfire of the vanities" took place, when the fanatical monk Savonarola induced his followers to hurl their worldly goods into the flames; it was also here, a year later, that he was hanged as a heretic and, ironically, burned. A bronze plaque in the piazza pavement marks the exact spot of his execution.

Time Out   At the west end of Piazza della Signoria, facing the statuary on the steps of the Palazzo Vecchio, is **Rivoire,** a café famous for its chocolate (both packaged and hot). Its outdoor tables and somewhat less expensive indoor counter are stylish, if pricey, places from which to observe the busy piazza.

❼ The statues in the square and in the 14th-century **Loggia dei Lanzi** on the south side vary in quality. Cellini's famous bronze *Perseus Holding the Head of Medusa* is his masterpiece; even the pedestal is superbly executed (the statuettes in its niches are recent copies of the originals). Other works in the loggia include *The Rape of the Sabine Women* and *Hercules and the Centaur*, both late–16th-century works by Giambologna, and, in the back, a row of sober matrons dating from Roman times. The loggia recently underwent lengthy structural restorations; many of the statues have been replaced by copies.

In the square, Bartolomeo Ammannati's Neptune Fountain, dating from 1565, takes something of a booby prize. Even Ammannati himself considered it a failure, and the Florentines call it *Il Biancone,* which may be translated as "the big white man" or "the big white lump," depending on your point of view. Giambologna's equestrian statue, to the left of the fountain, pays tribute to the Medici Grand Duke Cosimo I. Occupying the steps of the Palazzo Vecchio are a copy of Donatello's proud heraldic lion of Florence, known as the *Marzocco* (the original is now in the Bargello); a copy of Donatello's *Judith and Holofernes* (the original is inside the Palazzo Vecchio); a copy of Michelangelo's *David* (the original is now in the Accademia); and Baccio Bandinelli's *Hercules* (1534).

❽ The **Palazzo Vecchio** itself is far from beautiful, but it possesses a more than acceptable substitute: character. The palazzo was begun in 1299 and designed (probably) by Arnolfo di Cambio, and its massive bulk and towering campanile dominate the piazza masterfully. It was built as a meeting place for the heads of the seven major guilds that governed the city at the time; over the centuries it has served lesser purposes, but today it is once again the City Hall of Florence. The interior courtyard is a good deal less severe, having been remodeled by Michelozzo in 1453; Verrocchio's bronze *puttino*, topping the central fountain, softens the effect considerably.

Although most of the interior public rooms are well worth exploring, the main attraction is on the second floor: two adjoining rooms that supply one of the most startling contrasts in Florence. The first is the vast **Sala dei Cinquecento** (Room of the Five Hundred), named for 500 deputies who debated here from 1865 to 1871, when Florence served as the capital of the Kingdom of Italy. The Sala was decorated by Giorgio Vasari, around 1570, with huge frescoes celebrating Florentine history; depictions of battles with neighboring cities predominate. Continuing the martial theme, the Sala also contains Michelangelo's *Victory* group, intended for the never-completed tomb of Pope Julius II, plus miscellaneous sculptures of decidedly lesser quality.

The second room is the little **Studiolo,** entered to the right of the Sala's entrance. The study of Cosimo de' Medici's son, the melancholy Francesco I, it was designed by Vasari and decorated by Vasari and Agnolo Bronzino. It is intimate; civilized; and filled with complex, questioning, allegorical art. It makes the vainglorious proclamations next door ring more than a little hollow. *Piazza della Signoria, tel. 055/276–8465. Admission: 8,000 lire. Open Mon.– Fri. 9–7, Sun. 8–1.*

❾ Just south of the Palazzo Vecchio is the **Palazzo degli Uffizi,** a U-shaped building fronting on the Arno, designed by Vasari in 1559. Built as an office building—"uffizi" means "offices" in Italian—the palazzo today houses the finest collection of paintings in Italy. Hardcore museum goers will want to purchase the English guide sold outside the entrance.

The collection's highlights include Paolo Uccello's *Battle of San Romano* (its brutal chaos of lances is one of the finest visual metaphors for warfare ever committed to paint); Fra Filippo Lippi's *Madonna and Child with Two Angels* (the foreground angel's bold, impudent eye contact would have been unthinkable prior to the Renaissance); Sandro Botticelli's *Primavera* (its nonrealistic fairy-tale charm exhibits the painter's idiosyncratic genius at its zenith); Leonardo da Vinci's *Adoration of the Magi* (unfinished and perhaps the best opportunity in Europe to investigate the methods of a great artist at work); Raphael's *Madonna of the Goldfinch* (darkened by time, but the tenderness with which the figures in the painting touch each other is undimmed); Michelangelo's *Holy Family* (one of the very few easel works in oil he ever painted, clearly reflecting his stated belief that draftsmanship is a necessary ingredient of great painting); Rembrandt's *Self-Portrait as an Old Man* (which proves that even Michelangelo could, on occasion, be wrong); Titian's *Venus of Urbino* and Caravaggio's *Bacchus* (two very great paintings whose attitudes toward myth and sexuality are—to put it mildly—diametrically opposed); and many, many more. If panic sets in at the prospect of absorbing all this art at one go, bear in mind that the three tours outlined here are structured so as to offer late-afternoon free time, and the Uffizi is, except Sunday, open late. Damage done by the tragic 1993 bombing has been largely erased, and no major works were lost. *Piazzale degli Uffizi 6, tel. 055/23885. Admission: 10,000 lire. Open Tues.–Sat. 9–7, Sun. 9–2.*

Time Out There is a coffee bar inside the Uffizi; its terrace offers a fine close-up view of the Palazzo Vecchio. For something more substantial, try **Cavallino,** the moderately priced restaurant overlooking Piazza della Signoria at Via delle Farine 6/r (closed Wed.).

Leave Piazza della Signoria at the southwest corner and follow Via Vaccereccia one block west to Via Por Santa Maria. Just north of ⑩ the intersection is an open-air loggia known as the **Mercato Nuovo** (New Market). It was new in 1551. Today it harbors mostly souvenir stands; its main attraction is Pietro Tacca's bronze *Porcellino* (Piglet) fountain on the south side, dating from around 1612 and copied from an earlier Roman work now in the Uffizi. Rubbing its drooling snout is a Florentine tradition—it is said to bring good luck.

Follow Via Por Santa Maria toward the river, and you will arrive at ⑪ the **Ponte Vecchio** (Old Bridge), which is to Florence what Tower Bridge is to London. It was built in 1345 to replace an earlier bridge that was swept away by flood, and its shops housed first butchers, then grocers, blacksmiths, and other merchants. But in 1593 the Medici Grand Duke Ferdinando I, whose private corridor linking the Medici palace (the Palazzo Pitti) with the Medici offices (the Uffizi) crossed the bridge atop the shops, decided that all this plebeian commerce under his feet was unseemly. So he threw out all the butchers and blacksmiths and installed 41 goldsmiths and eight jewelers. The bridge has been devoted solely to these two trades ever since.

In the middle of the bridge, take a moment to study the **Ponte Santa Trinita,** the next bridge downriver. It was designed by Bartolomeo Ammannati in 1567 (possibly from sketches by Michelangelo), blown up by the retreating Germans during World War II, and painstakingly reconstructed after the war ended. Florentines like to claim it is the most beautiful bridge in the world. Given its simplicity, this may sound like idle Tuscan boasting. But if you commit its graceful arc and delicate curves to memory and then begin to compare these characteristics with those of other bridges encountered in your travels, you may well conclude that the boast is justified. The Ponte Santa Trinita is a beautiful piece of architecture.

Once you've crossed the bridge, you are in Florence's Oltrarno—beyond, or across, the Arno—district. A few yards past the south end of the Ponte Vecchio (on the left side of Via dei Guicciardini) is the ⑫ church of **Santa Felicita,** in the tiny piazza of the same name. Rarely visited by sightseers, the church contains one of Florence's finest Mannerist masterpieces: Jacopo da Pontormo's *Deposition,* painted around 1526, above the altar in the Capponi Chapel, just to the right of the entrance. The painting's swirling design and contorted figures are quintessentially Mannerist. The palette, however, transcends Mannerism: Despite being ill-lit (the lights must be turned on by the sacristan), the altarpiece's luminous colors are among the most striking in Florence.

After leaving Santa Felicita, walk along Costa di San Giorgio, which starts as a tiny alley to the left of the church, passes a house once occupied by Galileo (No. 11), and continues on to the Porta San Giorgio entrance in the old city walls. The walk up this narrow street is one of Florence's least-known pleasures. The climb is steep, but just as you begin to wonder when it is going to end, a remarkable transformation takes place: The city falls away, the parked cars disappear, vine-covered walls screening olive trees appear on both sides, birds begin to chirp, and Florence becomes—of all things—tranquil. A narrow Florentine street has suddenly turned into a picturesque Tuscan country lane.

Just before the costa ends at Porta San Giorgio, turn onto the short lane on the right (Via del Forte di San Giorgio), which leads to the ⑬ main entrance of the **Belvedere Fortress** (down the steps and through the arch). The fortress, where temporary art exhibitions are sometimes held, was built in 1429 to help defend the city against siege. But time has effected an ironic transformation, and what was once a first-rate fortification is now a first-rate picnic ground. Buses carry view-seeking tourists farther up the hill to the Piazzale Michelangelo, but, as the natives know, the best views of Florence are right here. To the north, all the city's monuments are spread out in a breathtaking cinemascopic panorama, framed by the rolling Tuscan hills beyond: the squat dome of Santa Maria Novella, Giotto's proud campanile, the soaring dome of the Duomo, the forbidding medieval tower of the Palazzo Vecchio, the delicate Gothic spire of the Badia, and the crenellated tower of the Bargello. It is one of the best city-views in Italy. To the south the nearby hills furnish a complementary rural view, in its way equally memorable. If time and weather permit, a picnic lunch here on the last day of your stay is the perfect way to review the city's splendors and fix them forever in your memory. *Admission free. Open daily 9–sunset.*

Leave the Belvedere Fortress by the north exit, turn left, and you ⑭ will come to the rear entrance of the **Boboli Gardens,** adjacent to the Pitti Palace. Once inside the entrance, follow the path at the far left. The **Museo delle Porcellane** (Porcelain Museum) here holds the Medici porcelain collections from the palace. The gardens began to take shape in 1549, when the Pitti family sold the palazzo to Eleanor of Toledo, wife of the Medici Grand Duke Cosimo I. The initial landscaping plans were laid out by Niccolò Pericoli Tribolo. After his death in 1550 development was continued by Bernardo Buontalenti, Giulio and Alfonso Parigi, and, over the years, many others, who produced the most spectacular backyard in Florence. The Italian gift for landscaping—less formal than the French but still full of sweeping drama—is displayed here at its best. A description of the gardens' beauties would fill a page but would be self-defeating, for the best way to enjoy a pleasure garden is to wander about, discovering its pleasures for yourself. One small fountain deserves special note, however: the famous *Bacchino*, next to the garden exit at the extreme north end of the palace, nearest the river. It is a copy of the original, showing Pietro Barbino, Cosimo's favorite dwarf, astride a particularly unhappy tortoise. It seems to be illustrating—very graphically, indeed—the perils of too much pasta. *Admission: 5,000 lire. Open Tues.–Sun. 9–one hour before sunset. Admission to the Porcelain Museum: 6,000 lire; ticket valid also for the Museo degli Argenti in the palace* (see Pitti Palace, below). *Open Tues.– Sun. 9–2.*

Tour 2: From the Duomo to the Cascine

Tour 2 also begins at the Duomo. From the north side of the baptistery, walk west along the mostly modern Via dei Cerretani; after three blocks it forks. Take the middle fork (Via dei Banchi), which leads into Piazza Santa Maria Novella, dominated by the church of **Santa Maria Novella** on the north side.

The facade of the church looks distinctly clumsy by later Renaissance standards, and with good reason: It is an architectural hybrid. The lower half of the facade was completed mostly in the 14th century; its pointed-arch niches and decorative marble patterns reflect the Gothic style of the day. About a hundred years later (around 1456), architect Leon Battista Alberti was called in to complete the job. The marble decoration of his upper story clearly defers to the already existing work below, but the architectural features he added evince an entirely different style. The central doorway, the four ground-floor half-columns with Corinthian capitals, the triangular pediment atop the second story, the inscribed frieze immediately below the pediment—these are classical features borrowed from antiquity, and they reflect the new Renaissance era in architecture, born some 35 years earlier at the Ospedale degli Innocenti (*see* Tour 3: From the Duomo to Santa Croce and Beyond, *below*). Alberti's most important addition, however, the S-curve scrolls that surmount the decorative circles on either side of the upper story, had no precedent whatever in antiquity. The problem was to soften the abrupt transition between wide ground floor and narrow upper story. Alberti's solution turned out to be definitive. Once you start to look for them, you will find scrolls such as these (or sculptural variations of them) on churches all over Italy, and every one of them derives from Alberti's example here.

The architecture of the interior is (like the Duomo) a dignified but somber example of Italian Gothic. Exploration is essential, however, because the church's store of art treasures is remarkable. Highlights include the 14th-century stained-glass rose window depicting *The Coronation of the Virgin* (above the central entrance door); the Filippo Strozzi Chapel (to the right of the altar), containing late–15th-century frescoes and stained glass by Filippino Lippi; the chancel (the area around the altar), containing frescoes by Domenico Ghirlandaio (1485); and the Gondi Chapel (to the left of the altar), containing Filippo Brunelleschi's famous wooden crucifix, carved around 1410 and said to have so stunned the great Donatello when he first saw it that he dropped a basket of eggs.

One other work in the church is worth special attention, for it possesses great historical importance as well as beauty. It is Masaccio's *Holy Trinity with Two Donors*, on the left-hand wall, almost halfway down the nave. Painted around 1425 (at the same time Masaccio was working on his frescoes in Santa Maria del Carmine, described later in this tour), it unequivocally announced the arrival of the Renaissance era. The realism of the figure of Christ was revolutionary in itself, but what was probably even more startling to the contemporary Florentines was the coffered ceiling in the background. The mathematical rules for employing perspective in painting had just been discovered (probably by Brunelleschi), and this was one of the first paintings to employ them with utterly convincing success. As art historian E. H. Gombrich expressed it, "We can imagine how amazed the Florentines must have been when this wall-painting was unveiled and seemed to have made a hole in the wall through which they could look into a new burial chapel in Brunelleschi's modern style."

Leave Piazza Santa Maria Novella by Via delle Belle Donne, which angles off to the south where you entered the square from Via dei Banchi and leads to a tiny piazza. In the center is a curious column topped by a roofed crucifix, known as the **Croce al Trebbio.** The cross was erected in 1308 by the Dominican Order (Santa Maria Novella was a Dominican church) to commemorate a famous victory: It was here that the Dominican friars defeated their avowed enemies, the Patarene heretics, in a bloody street brawl.

Beyond the piazza, bear left onto the short Via del Trebbio, then turn right onto Via Tornabuoni. On the left side of the street is the church of **San Gaetano,** with a rather staid Baroque facade (and Albertian scrolls), finished in 1645. Florence never fully embraced the Baroque movement—by the 17th century the city's artistic heyday was long over—but the decorative statuary here does manage to muster some genuine Baroque exuberance. The cherubs on the upper story, setting the coat of arms in place, are a typical (if not very original) Baroque motif.

For those who can afford it, **Via Tornabuoni** is probably Florence's finest shopping street, and it supplies an interesting contrast to the nearby Piazza della Repubblica. There, at the turn of the century, the old was leveled to make way for the new; here, past and present cohabit easily and efficiently, with the oldest buildings housing the newest shops. Ironically, the "modern" Piazza della Repubblica now looks dated and more than a little dowdy, and it is the unrenewed Via Tornabuoni, bustling with activity, that seems up-to-the-minute.

Time Out For a mid-morning pickup, try **Giacosa,** at No. 83 Via Tornabuoni, for excellent coffee, cappuccino, and pastries, or **Procacci,** at No. 64, for finger sandwiches and cold drinks. (Both closed Mon.)

Via Tornabuoni is lined with Renaissance buildings. But its most imposing palazzo is the **Palazzo Strozzi,** a block south, at the intersection of Via Strozzi. Designed (probably) by Giuliano da Sangallo around 1489 and modeled after Michelozzo's earlier Palazzo Medici-Riccardi (*see* Tour 3: From the Duomo to Santa Croce and Beyond, *below*), the exterior of the palazzo is simple and severe; it is not the use of classical detail but the regularity of its features, the stately march of its windows, that marks it as a product of the early Renaissance. The interior courtyard (entered from the rear of the palazzo) is another matter altogether. It is here that the classical vocabulary—columns, capitals, pilasters, arches, and cornices—is given uninhibited and powerful expression. Unfortunately, the courtyard's effectiveness is all but destroyed by its outlandish modern centerpiece: a brutal metal fire escape. Its introduction here is one of the most disgraceful acts of 20th-century vandalism in the entire city.

One block west, down Via della Vigna Nuova, in Piazza Rucellai, is
⓵ Alberti's **Palazzo Rucellai,** which goes a step further than the Palazzo Strozzi and possesses a more representative Renaissance facade.
A comparison between the two is illuminating. Evident on the facade of the Palazzo Rucellai is the ordered arrangement of windows
and rusticated stonework seen on the Palazzo Strozzi, but Alberti's
facade is far less forbidding. Alberti devoted a far larger proportion
of his wall space to windows, which soften the facade's appearance,
and filled in the remainder with rigorously ordered classical elements borrowed from antiquity. The end result, though still severe,
is far less fortresslike, and Alberti strove for this effect purposely
(he is on record as stating that only tyrants need fortresses). Ironically, the Palazzo Rucellai was built some 30 years *before* the Palazzo
Strozzi. Alberti's civilizing ideas here, it turned out, had little influence on the Florentine palazzi that followed. To the Renaissance
Florentines, power—in architecture, as in life—was just as impressive as beauty.

If proof of this dictum is needed, it can be found several short blocks
away. Follow the narrow street opposite the Palazzo Rucellai (Via
del Purgatorio) almost to its end, then zigzag right and left to reach
Piazza di Santa Trinita. In the center of the piazza is a column from
the Baths of Caracalla, in Rome, given to the Medici Grand Duke
Cosimo I by Pope Pius IV in 1560. The column was raised here by
Cosimo in 1565, to mark the spot where he heard the news, in 1537,
that his exiled Ghibelline enemies had been defeated at
Montemurlo, near Prato; the victory made his power in Florence un-
challengeable and all but absolute. The column is called, with typical
Medici self-assurance, the **Colonna della Giustizia,** the Column of
Justice.

Halfway down the block to the right (toward the Arno) is the church
⓵ of **Santa Trinita.** Originally built in the Romanesque style, the
church underwent a Gothic remodeling during the 14th century (remains of the Romanesque construction are visible on the interior
front wall). Its major artistic attraction is the cycle of frescoes and
the altarpiece in the Sassetti Chapel, the second to the altar's right,
painted by Domenico Ghirlandaio, around 1485. Ghirlandaio was a
conservative painter for his day, and generally his paintings exhibit
little interest in the investigations into the laws of perspective that
had been going on in Florentine painting for more than 50 years. But
his work here possesses such graceful decorative appeal that his lack
of interest in rigorous perspective hardly seems to matter. The wall
frescoes illustrate the life of St. Francis, and the altarpiece, *The Adoration of the Shepherds*, seems to stop just short of glowing.

From Santa Trinita, cross the Arno over the Ponte Santa Trinita and
continue down Via Maggio until you reach the crossroads of
Sdrucciolo dei Pitti (on the left) and the short Via dei Michelozzi (on
the right). Here you have a choice. If the noon hour approaches, you
may want to postpone the next stop temporarily in order to see the
churches of Santo Spirito and Santa Maria del Carmine before they
close for the afternoon. If this is the case, follow the directions given
two paragraphs below and return here after seeing the churches.
Otherwise, turn left onto the Sdrucciolo dei Pitti.

As you emerge from the Sdrucciolo into Piazza Pitti, you will see un-
fold before you one of Florence's largest—if not one of its best—ar-
⓶ chitectural set pieces: the famous **Pitti Palace.** The original palazzo,
built for the Pitti family around 1460, comprised only the middle
cube (the width of the middle seven windows on the upper floors) of
the present building. In 1549 the property was sold to the Medicis,

and Bartolomeo Ammannati was called in to make substantial additions. Although he apparently operated on the principle that more is better, he succeeded only in producing proof that enough is enough.

Today the immense building houses four separate museums: the former **Royal Apartments,** containing furnishings from a remodeling done in the 19th century; the **Museo degli Argenti,** containing a vast collection of Medici household treasures; the **Galleria d'Arte Moderna,** containing a collection of 19th- and 20th-century paintings, mostly Tuscan; and, most famous, the **Galleria Palatina,** containing a broad collection of 16th- and 17th-century paintings. The rooms of the latter remain much as the Medici family left them, but, as Mary McCarthy pointed out, the Florentines invented modern bad taste, and many art lovers view the floor-to-ceiling painting displays here as Italy's most egregious exercise in conspicuous consumption, aesthetic overkill, and trumpery. Still, the collection possesses high points that are very high indeed, including a number of portraits by Titian and an unparalleled collection of paintings by Raphael, among them the famous *Madonna of the Chair. Piazza Pitti, tel. 055/210323. Admission: Royal Apartments, 8,000 lire; Museo degli Argenti, 6,000 lire; ticket also valid for Museo delle Porcellane* (see *Boboli Gardens,* above); Galleria d'Arte Moderna, 4,000 lire; Galleria Palatina, 8,000 lire. Open Tues.–Sun. 9–2.

Return to Via Maggio from the Pitti, take Via dei Michelozzi, a short street that leads into Piazza Santo Spirito; at the north end rises the
㉑ church of **Santo Spirito.** Its unfinished facade gives nothing away, but, in fact, the interior, although appearing chilly (or even cold) compared with later churches, is one of the most important pieces of architecture in all Italy. One of a pair of Florentine church interiors designed by Filippo Brunelleschi in the early 15th century (the other, San Lorenzo, is described in Tour 3: From the Duomo to Santa Croce and Beyond, *below*) it was here that Brunelleschi supplied definitive solutions to the two main problems of interior Renaissance church design: how to build a cross-shaped interior using classical architectural elements borrowed from antiquity and how to reflect in that interior the order and regularity that Renaissance scientists (of which Brunelleschi was one) were at the time discovering in the natural world around them.

Brunelleschi's solution to the first problem was brilliantly simple: Turn a Greek temple inside out. To see this clearly, look at one of the stately arch-topped arcades that separate the side aisles from the central nave. Whereas the ancient Greek temples were walled buildings surrounded by classical colonnades, Brunelleschi's churches were classical arcades surrounded by walled buildings. This was perhaps the single most brilliant architectural idea of the early Renaissance, and its brilliance overthrew the previous era's religious taboo against pagan architecture once and for all, triumphantly reclaiming that architecture for Christian use.

Brunelleschi's solution to the second problem—making the entire interior orderly and regular—was mathematically precise: He designed the ground plan of the church so that all its parts are proportionally related. The transepts and nave have exactly the same width; the side aisles are exactly half as wide as the nave; the little chapels off the side aisles are exactly half as deep as the side aisles; the chancel and transepts are exactly one-eighth the depth of the nave; and so on, with dizzying exactitude. For Brunelleschi, such a design technique would have been far more than a convenience; it would have been a matter of passionate conviction. Like most theoreticians of his day, he believed that mathematical regularity and aesthetic beauty were opposite sides of the same coin, that one was not possible without the other. The conviction stood unchallenged for a hundred years, until Michelangelo turned his hand to architecture and designed the Medici Chapel and the Biblioteca Laurenziana in San Lorenzo across town (*see* Tour 3: From the Duomo to Santa Croce and Beyond, *below*), and thereby unleashed a revolution of his own that spelled the end of the Renaissance in architecture and the beginning of the Baroque.

Leave Piazza Santo Spirito by Via Sant'Agostino, diagonally across the square from the church entrance, and follow it to Via dei Serragli. You are now in the heart of the working-class Oltrarno neighborhood, which is to Florence what Trastevere is to Rome: unpretentious, independent, and proud. Cross Via dei Serragli and follow Via Santa Monaca to Piazza del Carmine. The church of **Santa Maria del Carmine** at the south end contains, in the Brancacci Chapel, at the end of the right transept, a masterpiece of Renaissance painting, a fresco cycle that changed art forever. Fire almost destroyed the church in the 18th century; miraculously, the Brancacci Chapel survived almost intact.

The cycle is the work of three artists: Masaccio and Masolino, who began it in 1423, and Filippino Lippi, who finished it, after a long interruption during which the sponsoring Brancacci family was exiled, some 50 years later. It was Masaccio's work that opened a new frontier for painting; tragically, he did not live to experience the revolution his innovations caused, for he was killed in 1428 at the age of 27.

Masaccio collaborated with Masolino on several of the paintings, but by himself he painted *The Tribute Money* on the upper-left wall; *Peter Baptizing the Neophytes* on the upper altar wall; *The Distribution of the Goods of the Church* on the lower altar wall; and, most famous, *The Expulsion of Adam and Eve* on the chapel's upper-left entrance pier. If you look closely at the latter painting and compare it with some of the chapel's other works, you will see a pronounced difference. The figures of Adam and Eve possess a startling presence, a presence primarily due to the dramatic way in which their bodies seem to reflect light. Masaccio here shaded his figures consistently, so as to suggest emphatically a single, strong source of light within the world of the painting but outside its frame. In so doing, he succeeded in imitating with paint the real-world effect of light on mass, and he thereby imparted to his figures a sculptural reality unprecedented in its day. To contemporary Florentines his Adam and Eve must have seemed surrounded by light and air in a way that was almost magical. All the painters of Florence came to look.

These matters have to do with technique, but with *The Expulsion of Adam and Eve*, his skill went beyond technical innovation, and if you look hard at the faces of Adam and Eve, you will see more than just finely modeled figures. You will see terrible shame and terrible suffering, and you will see them depicted with a humanity rarely achieved in art. *Admission to Brancacci Chapel: 5,000 lire. Open Mon. and Wed.–Sat. 10–5, Sun. 1–5.*

Time Out A popular spot for lunch on Piazza del Carmine is **Carmine,** a moderately priced restaurant with outdoor tables during the warmer months. It is located at the end of the piazza's northern extension. *Closed Sun.*

From Piazza del Carmine, return to Via dei Serragli and walk back across the river over the Ponte alla Carraia (with a fine view of the Ponte Santa Trinita, to the right) to Piazza Carlo Goldoni, named for the 18th-century Italian dramatist. Here you again have a choice: Turn left to explore the Cascine, a vast (2-mile-long) park laid out in the 18th century on the site of the Medici dairy farms (it begins some 10 blocks downriver, at Piazza Vittorio Veneto), or, if you have not overdosed on art, turn right and return to the Uffizi, which is open all day on most days and which is usually far less crowded in the late afternoon than in the morning.

Tour 3: From the Duomo to Santa Croce and Beyond

Like the other two tours, Tour 3 begins at the Duomo. From the west side of the baptistery, follow Borgo San Lorenzo north one block to Piazza San Lorenzo, in which stands a bustling outdoor clothing market overlooked by the unfinished facade of the church of **② San Lorenzo.** Like Santo Spirito on the other side of the Arno, the interior of San Lorenzo was designed by Filippo Brunelleschi in the early 15th century. The two church interiors are similar in design and effect and proclaim with ringing clarity the beginning of the Renaissance in architecture. (If you have not yet taken Tour 2, you might want to read its entry on Santo Spirito now; it describes the nature of Brunelleschi's architectural breakthrough, and its main points apply equally well here. *See* Tour 2: From the Duomo to the Cascine, *above*.) San Lorenzo possesses one feature that Santo Spirito lacks, however, which considerably heightens the dramatic effect of the interior: the grid of dark, inlaid marble lines on the floor. The grid makes the rigorous regularity with which the interior was designed immediately visible and offers an illuminating lesson on the laws of perspective. If you stand in the middle of the nave at the church entrance, on the line that stretches to the high altar, every element in the church—the grid, the nave columns, the side aisles, the coffered nave ceiling—seems to march inexorably toward a hypothetical vanishing point beyond the high altar, exactly as in a single-point-perspective painting.

The church complex contains two other important interiors, designed by Michelangelo, which contrast markedly with the interior of the church proper and which in their day marked the end of Brunelleschi's powerful influence and the end of the High Renaissance in architecture. The first is the **Biblioteca Laurenziana,** the Laurentian Library and its famous anteroom, entered from the church cloister (exit the church through the door at the left side of the nave just before the crossing, take an immediate right, climb the stairs to the cloister balcony, and enter the first door to the right). Michelangelo the architect was every bit as original as Michelangelo the sculptor. Unlike Brunelleschi, however, he was not interested in expressing the ordered harmony of the spheres in his architecture. He was interested in experimentation and invention and in expressing a personal vision that was at times highly idiosyncratic.

It was never more idiosyncratic than here. This strangely shaped anteroom has had scholars scratching their heads for centuries. In a space more than two stories high, why did Michelangelo limit his use of columns and pilasters to the upper two-thirds of the wall? Why didn't he rest them on strong pedestals instead of on huge, decorative curlicued scrolls, which rob them of all visual support? Why did he recess them into the wall, which makes them look weaker still? The architectural elements here do not stand firm and strong and tall, as inside the church next door; instead, they seem to be pressed into the wall as if into putty, giving the room a soft, rubbery look that is one of the strangest effects ever achieved by Classical architecture. It is almost as if Michelangelo purposely set out to defy his predecessors—intentionally to flout the conventions of the High Renaissance in order to see what kind of bizarre, mannered effect might result. His innovations were tremendously influential and produced a period of architectural experimentation—the Mannerist era in architecture—that eventually evolved into the Baroque. As his contemporary Giorgio Vasari (the first art historian) put it, "Artisans have been infinitely and perpetually indebted to him because he broke the bonds and chains of a way of working that had become habitual by common usage."

Many critics have thought that the anteroom is a failure and have complained that Michelangelo's experiment here was willful and perverse. But nobody has ever complained about the room's staircase (best viewed head-on), which emerges from the library with the visual force of an unstoppable flow of lava. In its highly sculptural conception and execution, it is quite simply one of the most original and beautiful staircases in the world. *Admission free. Open Mon.– Sat. 10–1.*

The other Michelangelo interior is San Lorenzo's **New Sacristy,** so called to distinguish it from Brunelleschi's **Old Sacristy** (which can be entered from inside the church at the end of the left transept). The New Sacristy is reached from outside the rear of the church, through the imposing **Cappella dei Principi,** the Medici mausoleum that was begun in 1605 and kept marble workers busy for several hundred years.

Michelangelo received the commission for the New Sacristy in 1520 from Cardinal Giulio de' Medici, who later became Pope Clement VII and who wanted a new burial chapel for his father, Giuliano, his uncle Lorenzo the Magnificent, and two recently deceased cousins. The result was a tour de force of architecture and sculpture. Architecturally, Michelangelo was as original and inventive here as ever, but it is—quite properly—the powerful sculptural compositions of the side wall tombs that dominate the room. The scheme is allegorical: On the wall tomb to the right are figures representing day and night, and on the wall tomb to the left are figures representing dawn and dusk; above them are idealized portraits of the two cousins, usually interpreted to represent the active life and the contemplative life. But the allegorical meanings are secondary; what is most important is the intense presence of the sculptural figures, the force with which they hit the viewer. Michelangelo's contemporaries were so awed by the impact of this force (in his sculpture here and elsewhere) that they invented an entirely new word to describe the phenomenon: *terribilità* (dreadfulness). To this day it is used only when describing his work, and it is in evidence here at the peak of its power. *Piazza di Madonna degli Aldobrandini, tel. 055/213206. Admission: 9,000 lire. Open Tues.–Sun. 9–2.*

Just north of the Medici Chapel (a block up Via dell'Ariento) is Florence's busy main food market, the **Mercato Centrale.** If a reminder that Florence is more than just a museum is needed, this is the perfect place for it. There is food everywhere, some of it remarkably exotic, and many of the displays verge on the magnificent. At the Mercato Nuovo, near the Ponte Vecchio, you will see tourists petting the snout of the bronze boar for good luck; here you will see Florentines petting the snout of a real one, very recently deceased and available for tonight's dinner.

Time Out The **Mercato Centrale** has a number of small coffee bars scattered about; there is even one upstairs among the mountains of vegetables. Have a coffee, watch the activity, and enjoy the fact that for once there is not a painting in sight.

Return to the clothing market in front of San Lorenzo, and from the north end of the piazza follow Via dei Gori east one block, and turn left onto Via Cavour. As you turn the corner, you will pass the
❷ **Palazzo Medici-Riccardi** (entrance on Via Cavour). Begun in 1444 by Michelozzo for Cosimo de' Medici, the main attraction here is the interior chapel on the upper floor. Painted on its walls is Benozzo Gozzoli's famous *Procession of the Magi*, finished in 1460 and celebrating both the birth of Christ and the greatness of the Medici family, whose portraits it contains. Like his contemporary Ghirlandaio, Gozzoli was not a revolutionary painter and is today considered less than first rate because of his technique, old-fashioned even for his day. Gozzoli's gift, however, was for entrancing the eye, not challenging the mind, and on those terms his success here is beyond question. The paintings are full of activity yet somehow frozen in time in a way that fails utterly as realism, but succeeds triumphantly as soon as the demand for realism is set aside. Entering the chapel is like walking into the middle of a magnificently illustrated child's storybook, and the beauty of the illustrations makes this one of the most unpretentiously enjoyable rooms in the entire city. *Via Cavour 11, tel. 055/276–0340. Admission: 6,000 lire. Open Mon., Tues., Thurs.–Sat. 9–1 and 3–6; Sun. 9–1.*

From the Palazzo Medici-Riccardi, follow Via Cavour two blocks north to Piazza San Marco. At the north end of the square is the church of San Marco; attached to the church (entrance just to the right of the church facade) is a former Dominican monastery that
❷ now houses the **Museo San Marco.** The museum—in fact, the entire monastery—is a memorial to Fra Angelico, the Dominican monk who, when he was alive, was as famous for his piety as for his painting. When the monastery was built in 1437, he decorated it with his frescoes, which were meant to spur religious contemplation; when the building was turned into a museum, other works of his from all over the city were brought here for display. His paintings are simple and direct and furnish a compelling contrast to the Palazzo Medici-Riccardi Chapel (Fra Angelico probably would have considered the glitter of Gozzoli's work there worldly and blasphemous). The entire monastery is worth exploring, for Fra Angelico's paintings are everywhere, including the Chapter House, at the top of the stairs leading to the upper floor (the famous *Annunciation)*, in the upper-floor monks' cells (each monk was given a different religious subject for contemplation), and in the gallery just off the cloister as you enter. The latter room contains, among many other works, his beautiful *Last Judgment;* as usual with Last Judgments, the tortures of the damned are far more inventive than the pleasures of the redeemed. *Piazza San Marco 1, tel. 055/238–8608. Admission: 6,000 lire. Open Tues.–Sun. 9–2.*

From Piazza San Marco, take a short detour a half-block down Via Ricasoli (which runs back toward the Duomo from the square's east
❷ side) to the **Galleria dell'Accademia.** The museum contains a notable collection of Florentine paintings dating from the 13th to the 18th centuries, but it is most famous for its collection of statues by Michelangelo, including the unfinished *Slaves*—which were meant for the tomb of Michelangelo's patron and nemesis Pope Julius II (and which seem to be fighting their way out of the marble)—and the original *David*, which was moved here from Piazza della Signoria in

1873. The *David* was commissioned in 1501 by the Opera del Duomo (Cathedral Works Committee), which gave the 26-year-old sculptor a leftover block of marble that had been ruined by another artist. Michelangelo's success with the defective block was so dramatic that the city showered him with honors, and the Opera del Duomo voted to build him a house and a studio in which to live and work.

Today the *David* is beset not by Goliath but by tourists, and seeing the statue at all—much less really studying it—can be a trial. After a 1991 attack upon it by a hammer-wielding frustrated artist who, luckily, inflicted only a few minor nicks on the toes, the sculpture is surrounded by a plexiglass barrier. But a close look is worth the effort it takes to combat the crowd. The statue is not quite what it seems. It is so poised and graceful and alert—so miraculously *alive*—that it is often considered the definitive embodiment of the ideals of the High Renaissance in sculpture. But its true place in the history of art is a bit more complicated.

As Michelangelo well knew, the Renaissance painting and sculpture that preceded his work were deeply concerned with ideal form. Perfection of proportion was the ever-sought Holy Grail; during the Renaissance, ideal proportion was equated with ideal beauty, and ideal beauty was equated with spiritual perfection. In painting, Raphael's tender Madonnas are perhaps the preeminent expression of this philosophy: They are meant to embody a perfect beauty that is at once physical and spiritual.

But Michelangelo's *David*, despite its supremely calm and dignified pose, departs from these ideals. As a moment's study will show, Michelangelo did not give the statue ideal proportions. The head is slightly too large for the body, the arms are slightly too large for the torso, and the hands are dramatically too large for the arms. By High Renaissance standards these are defects, but the impact and beauty of the *David* are such that it is the *standards* that must be called into question, not the statue. Michelangelo was a revolutionary artist (and the first Mannerist) because he brought a new expressiveness to art: He created the "defects" of the *David* intentionally. He knew exactly what he was doing, and he did it in order to express and embody, as powerfully as possible in a single figure, an entire biblical story. David's hands *are* too big, but so was Goliath, and these are the hands that slew him. *Via Ricasoli 60, tel. 055/214375. Admission: 10,000 lire. Open Tues.–Sun. 9–2.*

From the Accademia, return to Piazza San Marco and turn right onto Via Battisti, which leads into Piazza della Santissima Annunziata. The building directly across the square as you enter is ❷ the **Ospedale degli Innocenti,** or Foundling Hospital, built by Brunelleschi in 1419. He designed the building's portico with his usual rigor, building it out of the two shapes he considered mathematically (and therefore philosophically and aesthetically) perfect: the square and the circle. Below the level of the arches, the portico encloses a row of perfect cubes; above the level of the arches, the portico encloses a row of intersecting hemispheres. The whole geometric scheme is articulated with Corinthian columns, capitals, and arches borrowed directly from antiquity. At the time he designed the portico, Brunelleschi was also designing the interior of San Lorenzo, using the same basic ideas. But since the portico was finished before San Lorenzo, the Ospedale degli Innocenti takes the historical prize: It is the very first Renaissance building. The 10 ceramic medallions depicting swaddled infants that decorate the portico are by Andrea della Robbia, done approximately in 1487.

28 The church at the north end of the square is **Santissima Annunziata;** it was designed in 1447 by Michelozzo, who gave it an uncommon (and lovely) entrance cloister. The interior is an extreme rarity for Florence: a sumptuous example of the Baroque. But it is not really a fair example, since it is merely 17th-century Baroque decoration applied willy-nilly to an earlier structure—exactly the sort of violent remodeling exercise that has given the Baroque a bad name ever since. The **Tabernacle of the Annunziata,** immediately inside the entrance to the left, illustrates the point. The lower half, with its stately Corinthian columns and carved frieze bearing the Medici arms, was built at the same time as the church; the upper half, with its erupting curves and impish sculpted cherubs was added 200 years later. Each is effective in its own way, but together they serve only to prove that dignity is rarely comfortable wearing a party hat.

29 One block southeast of the entrance to Santissima Annunziata (on the left side of Via della Colonna) is the **Museo Archeologico.** If time and interest permit, a visit here is unquestionably worthwhile. The collection contains Etruscan, Egyptian, and Greco-Roman antiquities; guidebooks in English are available. The Etruscan collection is particularly notable—the largest in northern Italy—and includes the famous bronze *Chimera*, which was discovered (without the tail, which is a reconstruction) in the 16th century. *Via della Colonna 36, tel. 055/247-8641. Admission: 6,000 lire. Open Tues.–Sat. 9–2, Sun. 9–1.*

30 Follow Via della Colonna east to Borgo Pinti and turn right, following Borgo Pinti through the arch of San Piero to the small Piazza San Pier Maggiore. The tower at the south end is the **Torre dei Corbizi,** dating from the Middle Ages. During the Guelph–Ghibelline conflict of the 13th and 14th centuries, Florence was a forest of such towers—more than 200 of them, if the smaller three- and four-story towers are included. Today only a handful survive.

Time Out   Have lunch at **I Ghibellini** (closed Wed.), a moderately priced restaurant overlooking Piazza San Pier Maggiore. For dessert, follow Via Palmieri to Via Isola delle Stinche 7/r, and have an ice cream at **Vivoli,** Florence's most famous gelateria.

From Piazza San Pier Maggiore, Via Palmieri (which becomes Via Isola delle Stinche) leads to Via Torta, which curves around to the left—it takes its shape from the outline of a Roman amphitheater once located here—and opens out onto Piazza Santa Croce.

31 Like the Duomo, the church of **Santa Croce** is Gothic, but (also like the Duomo) its facade dates only from the 19th century. The interior is most famous for its art and its tombs. As a burial place, the church is a Florentine pantheon and probably contains a larger number of important skeletons than any church in Italy. Among others, the tomb of Michelangelo is immediately to the right as you enter (he is said to have chosen this spot so that the first thing he would see on Judgment Day, when the graves of the dead fly open, would be Brunelleschi's Duomo dome through Santa Croce's open doors); the tomb of Galileo Galilei, who produced evidence that the earth is not the center of the universe (and who was not granted a Christian burial until 100 years after his death because of it), is on the left wall, opposite Michelangelo; the tomb of Niccolò Machiavelli, the Renaissance political theoretician whose brutally pragmatic philosophy so influenced the Medici, is halfway down the nave on the right; the grave of Lorenzo Ghiberti, creator of the Gates of Paradise doors to the Baptistery, is halfway down the nave on the left; the tomb of composer Gioacchino Rossini, of "William Tell Overture" fame, is at the end of the nave on the right. The monument to Dante Alighieri, the greatest Italian poet, is a memorial rather than a tomb (he is actually buried in Ravenna); it is located on the right wall near the tomb of Michelangelo.

The collection of art within the church and church complex is by far the most important of that in any church in Florence. Historically, the most significant works are probably the Giotto frescoes in the two adjacent chapels immediately to the right of the altar. They illustrate scenes from the lives of St. John the Evangelist and St. John the Baptist (in the right-hand chapel) and scenes from the life of St. Francis (in the left-hand chapel). Time has not been kind to them; over the centuries wall tombs were introduced into the middle of them, whitewash and plaster covered them, and in the 19th century they underwent a clumsy restoration. But the reality that Giotto introduced into painting can still be seen. He did not paint beautifully stylized symbols of religion, as the Byzantine style that preceded him prescribed; he instead painted drama—St. Francis surrounded by grieving monks at the very moment of his death. This was a radical shift in emphasis, and it changed the course of art. Before him, the role of painting was to symbolize the attributes of God; after him, it was to imitate life. The style of his work is indeed primitive, compared with later painting, but in the Proto-Renaissance of the early 14th century, it caused a sensation that was not equalled for another 100 years. He was for his time the equal of both Masaccio and Michelangelo.

Among the church's other highlights are Donatello's *Annunciation*, one of the most tender and eloquent expressions of surprise ever sculpted (located on the right wall two-thirds of the way down the nave); Taddeo Gaddi's 14th-century frescoes illustrating the life of the Virgin, clearly showing the influence of Giotto (in the chapel at the end of the right transept); and Donatello's *Crucifix*, criticized by Brunelleschi for making Christ look like a peasant (in the chapel at the end of the left transept). Outside the church proper, in the church museum off the cloister, is Giovanni Cimabue's 13th-century *Triumphal Cross*, badly damaged by the flood of 1966. The **Pazzi Chapel,** yet another of Brunelleschi's crisp exercises in architectural geometry, is at the end of the cloister. *Piazza Santa Croce 16, tel. 055/244619. Church open Apr.–Sept., Mon.–Sat. 8–6:30, Sun. 8–12:30. Oct.–Mar., Mon.–Sat. 8–12:30 and 3–6:30, Sun. 3–6. Church cloister and museum admission: 4,000 lire. Open Apr.–Sept., Thurs.–Tues. 10–12:30, 2:30–6:30; Oct.–Mar., Thurs.–Tues. 10–12:30, 3–5.*

After leaving Santa Croce, you have a choice. If you have a fair amount of stamina left, cross the river at the Ponte alle Grazie (west of the church complex) and climb the Monte alle Croci above it to investigate the view from **Piazzale Michelangelo** and the church of **San Miniato al Monte;** the latter is a famous example of Romanesque architecture dating from the 11th century and contains a fine 13th-century apse mosaic. If the climb seems too arduous, you can take Bus 12 to Piazzale Michelangelo or you can (as always) return to the Uffizi.

Shopping

Since the days of the medieval guilds, Florence has been synonymous with fine craftsmanship and good business. Such time-honored Florentine specialties as antiques (and reproductions), bookbinding, jewelry, lace, leather goods, silk, and straw attest to that. More recently, the Pitti fashion shows and the burgeoning textile industry in nearby Prato have added fine clothing to the long line of merchandise available in the shops of Florence.

Another medieval feature is the distinct feel of the different shopping areas, a throwback to the days when each district supplied a different product. Florence's most elegant shops are concentrated in the center of town, with Via Tornabuoni and the Galleria Tornabuoni, the world's chic-est shopping mall, leading the list for designer clothing. Borgo Ognissanti and Via Maggio across the river have the city's largest concentration of antiques shops, and the Ponte Vecchio houses the city's jewelers, as it has since the 16th century. Boutiques abound on Via della Vigna Nuova and in the trendy area around the church of Santa Croce. In the less-specialized, more residential areas near the Duomo and in the area south of the Arno, known as the Oltrarno, just about anything goes on sale.

Those with a tight budget or a sense of adventure may want to take a look at the souvenir stands under the loggia of the Mercato Nuovo, the stalls that line the streets between the church of San Lorenzo and the Mercato Centrale, or the open-air market that takes place in the Cascine park every Tuesday morning.

Shops in Florence are generally open from 9 to 1 and 3:30 to 7:30 and closed Sundays and Monday mornings most of the year. During the summer the hours are usually 9 to 1 and 4 to 8, with closings on Saturday afternoons but not Monday mornings. When locating the stores, remember that the addresses with "r" in them, which stands for "rosso," or red, and indicates a commercial address, follow a separate numbering system from the black residential addresses. Most shops take major credit cards and will ship purchases, though it's wiser to take your purchases with you.

Via Tornabuoni

Gucci (Via Tornabuoni 73/r). The Gucci family is practically single-handedly responsible for making designers' initials (in this case the two interlocking "Gs") a status symbol. This Florence store is the one that started it all, and prices on the clothing and leather goods are slightly better here than elsewhere.

Casadei (Via Tornabuoni 33/r). The ultimate fine leathers are crafted into classic shapes here, winding up as women's shoes and bags.

Ugolini (Via Tornabuoni 20/r). This shop once made gloves for the Italian royal family, but now anyone who can afford it can have the luxury of its exotic leathers, as well as silk and cashmere ties and scarves.

Settepassi-Faraone (Via Tornabuoni 25/r). One of Florence's oldest jewelers, Settepassi-Faraone has supplied Italian (and other) royalty with finely crafted gems for centuries. Its selection of antique-looking classics has been updated with a choice of contemporary silver.

Ferragamo (Via Tornabuoni 16/r). Born near Naples, the late Salvatore Ferragamo made his fortune custom-making exotic shoes for famous feet, especially Hollywood stars, and so this establishment knows about less-than-delicate shoe sizes. His palace at the end of the street has since passed on to his wife, Wanda, and displays designer clothing, but the elegant footwear still underlies the Ferragamo success.

Via della Vigna Nuova

Il Bisonte (Via del Parione 31/r). The street address is just off Via della Vigna Nuova; Il Bisonte is known for its natural-look leather goods, all stamped with the store's bison symbol.

Filpucci (Via della Vigna Nuova 14/r). This is Italy's largest manufacturer of yarns. Nearby factories produce skeins of the stuff for Italy's top designers, and the extensive stock of its retail outlet in Florence encourages the talented to create their own designs.

Laurèl (Via della Vigna Nuova 67/r). An elegant boutique, Laurèl has a reputation for the quality and understatement that is the hallmark of Florentine women's fashions.

Alinari (Via della Vigna Nuova 46/r). This outlet is one of Florence's oldest and most prestigious photographers, and in this store, next to its museum, prints of its historic photographs are sold along with books and posters.

Et Cetera (Via della Vigna Nuova 82/r). In a city of papermakers, this store has some of the most unusual such items, most of which are handmade and some of which have made it into the design collection of New York's Museum of Modern Art.

Antico Setificio Fiorentino (Via della Vigna Nuova 97/r). This fabric outlet really *is* antique, having been producing antique fabrics for over half a millenium. Swaths of handmade material of every style and description are for sale, and the decorative tassels make lovely typically Florentine presents as well.

Borgo Ognissanti

Pratesi (Lungarno Amerigo Vespucci 8/r). The name Pratesi is a byword for luxury, in this case linens that have lined the beds of the rich and famous, with an emphasis on the former.

Giotti (Piazza Ognissanti 3/r). The largest selection of Bottega Veneta's woven-leather bags are stocked at this shop, which carries a full line of the firm's other leather goods, as well as its own leather clothing.

Loretta Caponi (Borgo Ognissanti 12/r). Signora Caponi is synonymous with Florentine embroidery, and her luxury lace, linens, and lingerie have earned her a worldwide reputation.

Fallani Best (Borgo Ognissanti 15/r). The eclectic collection of antiques, while concentrating on 18th- and 19th-century Italian paintings, has enough variety to appeal to an international clientele.

Paolo Ventura (Borgo Ognissanti 16/r). Specialties here are antique ceramics from all periods and places of origin. As with the other shops, the rule of thumb is that the Italian goods are best.

Alberto Pierini (Borgo Ognissanti 22/r). The rustic Tuscan furniture here is all antique, and much of it dates back to the days of the Medici.

Duomo

Bartolini (Via dei Servi 30/r). For housewares, nothing beats this shop, which has a wide selection of well-designed, practical items.

Emilio Pucci (Via dei Pucci 6/r). A member of an aristocratic Italian family, the Marchese di Barsento was a household name in Florence, and until his death in 1992, he presided over the opening of the Renaissance *Calcio in Costume* festivities each year. He became an international name during the early 1960s, when the stretch ski clothes he designed for himself caught on with the dolce vita crowd. His prints and "palazzo pajamas" then became the rage. The shop in the family palazzo still sells the celebrated Pucci prints, along with a line of wines from the family estate in Chianti.

Calamai (Via Cavour 78/r). One of Florence's largest gift shops, Calamai carries everything from inexpensive stationery to housewares in bright, bold colors and designs in its largest of three stores.

Pineider (Piazza della Signoria 14/r and Via Tornabuoni 76/r). Pineider now has shops throughout the world, but it began in Florence and still does all its printing here. Personalized stationery and business cards are its main business, but the stores also sell fine desk accessories.

Casa dello Sport (Via dei Tosinghi 8/r). Here you'll find casual wear for the entire family—sporty clothes by some of Italy's most famous manufacturers.

Santa Croce **Salimbeni** (Via Matteo Palmieri 14/r). Long one of Florence's best art bookshops, Salimbeni specializes in publications on Tuscany; it publishes many itself.

I Maschereri (Borgo Pinti 18/r). Spurred on by the revival of Carnival in recent years, I Maschereri has begun to produce fanciful masks in commedia dell'arte and contemporary styles.

Sbigoli Terrecotte (Via Sant'Egidio 4/r). This crafts shop carries a wide selection of terra-cotta and ceramic vases, pots, cups, and saucers.

Leather Guild (Piazza Santa Croce 20/r). This is one of many such shops throughout the area that produce inexpensive, antique-looking leather goods of mass appeal, but here you can see the craftspersons at work, a reassuring experience.

Ponte Vecchio **Gherardi** (Ponte Vecchio 5). The king of coral in Florence has the city's largest selection of finely crafted and encased specimens, as well as other precious materials such as cultured pearls, jade, and turquoise.

Piccini (Ponte Vecchio 23/r). This venerable shop has literally been crowning the heads of Europe for almost a century, and combines its taste for the antique with contemporary jewelry.

Melli (Ponte Vecchio 44/r). Antique jewelry is the specialty here; it is displayed alongside period porcelains, clocks, and other museum-quality objects.

Della Loggia (Via Por Santa Maria 29/r). For a contemporary look, try this store, which combines precious and semiprecious stones in settings made of precious and nonprecious metals, such as the gold and steel pieces usually on display in its windows.

Oltrarno **Centro Di** (Piazza dei Mozzi 1). Its name stands for Centro di Documentazione Internazionale, and it publishes art books and exhibition catalogues for some of the most important organizations in Europe. Centro Di stocks its own publications along with many others.

Giannini (Piazza Pitti 37/r). One of Florence's oldest paper-goods stores, Giannini is *the* place to buy the marbleized version, which comes in a variety of forms, from flat sheets to boxes and even pencils.

Galleria Luigi Bellini (Lungarno Soderini 5). The Galleria claims to be Italy's oldest antiques dealer, which may be true, since father Mario Bellini was responsible for instituting Florence's international antiques biennial. At any rate, what matters is that the merchandise is genuine.

Via Maggio **Giovanni Pratesi** (Via Maggio 13/r). This shop specializes in Italian antiques, in this case furniture, with some fine paintings, sculpture, and decorative objects turning up from time to time.

Guido Bartolozzi (Via Maggio 18/r). Vying with Luigi Bellini as one of Florence's oldest antiques dealers, Bartolozzi's collection of predominately Florentine objects from all periods is as highly selected as it is priced.

Paolo Paoletti (Via Maggio 30/r). Look for Florentine antiques, with an emphasis on Medici-era objects from the 15th and 16th centuries.

Soluzioni (Via Maggio 82/r). This offbeat store displays some of the most unusual items on this staid street, ranging from clocks to compacts, all selected with an eye for the eccentric.

Sports

Bicycling Bikes are a good way of getting out into the hills, but the scope for biking is limited in the center of town. *See* Getting Around in Essential Information, *above*, for information on where to rent bicycles.

Canoeing Those who get the urge to paddle on the Arno can try **Società Canottieri Firenze** (Lungarno dei Medici 8, tel. 055/282130) near the Uffizi.

Golf **Golf Club Ugolino** (Via Chiantigiana 3, Impruneta, tel. 055/230–1009) is a hilly 18-hole course in the heart of Chianti country just outside town. It is open to the public.

Jogging Don't even think of jogging on city streets, where tour buses and triple-parked Alfa Romeos leave precious little space for pedestrians. Instead, head for the **Cascine,** the park along the Arno at the western end of the city. You can jog to the Cascine along the Lungarno (stay on the sidewalk), or take Bus 17 from the Duomo. A cinder track lies on the hillside just below **Piazzale Michelangelo,** across the Arno from the city center. The views of the Florence skyline are inspirational, but the locker rooms are reserved for members, so come ready to run.

Swimming There are a number of pools open to foreigners who want to beat the Florentine heat, among them **Bellariva** (Lungarno Colombo 6, tel. 055/677521), **Circolo Tennis alle Cascine** (Viale Visarno 1, tel. 055/356651), **Costoli** (Viale Paoli, tel. 055/675–744), and **Le Pavoniere** (Viale degli Olmi, tel. 055/367506).

Tennis The best spot for an open court is **Circolo Tennis alle Cascine** (Viale Visarno 1, tel. 055/356651). Other centers include **Tennis Club Rifredi** (Via Facibeni, tel. 055/432552) and **Il Poggetto** (Via Mercati 24/b, tel. 055/460127).

Spectator Sports

Horse Racing You can make your bets at the **Ippodromo Visarno** (Piazzale delle Cascine, tel. 055/360056). Check the local papers to see when they're running.

Soccer *Calcio* (soccer) is a passion with the Italians, and the Florentines are no exception. A medieval version of the game is played in costume each year on or around June 24, feast day of St. John the Baptist, but if you want to see the modern-day equivalent, go and watch the Fiorentina team at the Stadio Comunale (Viale Manfredo Fanti). The big games are played on Sunday afternoon, and the season runs from about late August to May.

Dining

Florentines are justifiably proud of their robust food, claiming that it became the basis for French cuisine when Catherine de' Medici took a battery of Florentine chefs with her when she reluctantly relocated to become Queen of France in the 16th century.

A typical Tuscan repast starts with an antipasto of *crostini* (toasted bread spread with a chicken liver pâté) or cured meats such as *prosciutto crudo* (a salty prosciutto), *finocchiona* (salami seasoned with fennel), and *salsiccia di cinghiale* (sausage made from wild boar). This is the time to start right in on the local wine—Chianti, *naturalmente*. Don't be surprised if the waiter brings an entire flask to the table. Customers are charged only for what they consume (*al consumo*, the arrangement is called), but it's wise to ask for a flask or bottle to be opened then and there, since leftover wines are often mixed together.

Primi piatti (first courses) can consist of excellent local versions of risotto or pasta dishes available throughout Italy. Peculiar to Florence, however, are the vegetable-and-bread soups such as *pappa al pomodoro* (tomatoes, bread, olive oil, onions, and basil), *ribollita* (a thick soup of white beans, bread, cabbage, and onions), or, in the summer, *panzanella* (tomatoes, onions, vinegar, oil, and bread). Before they are eaten, these soups are often christened with *un "C" d'olio*, a generous C-shaped pouring of the excellent local olive oil from the ever-present tabletop cruet.

Second to none among the *secondi piatti* (main courses) is *bistecca alla fiorentina*—a thick slab of local Chianina beef, grilled over charcoal, seasoned with olive oil, salt, and pepper, and served rare. *Trippa alla fiorentina* (tripe stewed with tomatoes in a meat sauce) and *arista* (roast loin of pork seasoned with rosemary) are also regional specialties, as are many other roasted meats that go especially well with the Chianti. These are usually served with a *contorno* (side dish) of white beans, sauteed greens, or artichokes in season, all of which can be drizzled with more of that wonderful olive oil.

Tuscan desserts are typically Spartan. The cheese is the hard pecorino, and locals like to go for the even tougher *biscottini di Prato*, which provide an excuse to dunk them in the potent, sweet dessert wine called *vin santo*, made of dried grapes, which they say will bring the dead back to life!

Remember that dining hours are earlier here than in Rome, starting at 12:30 for the midday meal and from 7:30 on in the evening. Many of Florence's restaurants are small, so reservations are a must. When going to the restaurants, note that the "r" in some of the following addresses indicates the red numbering system used for Florentine businesses, which differs from the black numbers used for residences.

Highly recommended restaurants are indicated by a star ★.

Category	Cost*
$$$$	over 110,000 lire
$$$	70,000–110,000 lire
$$	30,000–70,000 lire
$	under 30,000 lire

per person, for a three-course meal, including house wine and taxes

$$$$ ★ **Enoteca Pinchiorri.** A sumptuous Renaissance palace with high, frescoed ceilings and bouquets in silver vases is the setting for this restaurant, considered one of the best in Italy. The "enoteca" part of the name comes from its former incarnation as a wine shop under owner Giorgio Pinchiorri, who still keeps a stock of 70,000 bottles in the cellar. Wife Annie Feolde has added her refined interpretations of Tuscan cuisine—*triglie alla viareggina* (mullet with tomato

Florence Dining and Lodging

12

14 **15** Piazza Mercato Centrale

11

16

V. Panicale

V. Guelfa

V. S. Gallo

V. dell' Ariento

V. Faenza

40 **41** **42** **43** **44**

39 Piazza SS. Annunziata

V. Laura

V. Colonna

38

V. Cavour

V. Canto de Nelli

del Giglio

V. d. Conti

Piazza S. Lorenzo

V. Pucci

V. Ricasoli

V. dei Servi

V. degli Alfani

17

V. Martelli

V. Cerretani

V. Bufalini

V. della Pergola

37

Piazza di S. Giovanni

Piazza del Duomo

Borgo Pinti

V. Fiesolana

V. Pecori

V. dei Tosinghi

V. Vecchietti

V. d. Studio

V. S. Egidio

34

V. dei Pepi

18 Piazza della Repubblica

V. Strozzi

V. Anselmi

V. dei Speziali

22

V. dei Calzaiuoli

23

V. del Proconsolo

Borgo degli Albizi

33

Piazza Salvemini

36

V. dei Pandolfini

35

V. Ghibellina

V. dell' Agnolo

V. Porta Rossa

21

Piazza S. Firenze

25

24

V. Verrazzano

32

V. Ghibellina

V. delle Terme

20 Piazza della Signoria

V. d. Gondi

Via Torta

31

Borgo SS. Apostoli

Acciaioli

V. Vacchereccia

V. Leoni

Borgo dei Greci

V. Benci

Piazza Santa Croce

V. di S. Giuseppe

Via Por S. Maria

19

V. dei Neri

Borgo S. Croce

Ponte Vecchio

Lung. Archibusieri

Lung. Diaz

Corso Tintori

Arno

Piazza S. Maria Sopr' Arno

Costa dei Magnoli

Lung. Torrigiani

V. dei Bardi

Ponte alle Grazie

Lung. d. Grazie

30

Arno

Lung. Serristori

Piazza dei Mozzi

V. dei Renai

28

29

Via V. di S. Niccolò

S. Miniato

Via

Forte di Belvedere

S. Giorgio

0 ——— 440 yards

0 ——— 400 meters

26

V. di Belvedere

27

sauce) and *arrosto di coniglio* (roast rabbit)—to a nouvelle menu that includes *ravioli di melanzane* (ravioli stuffed with eggplant), *petto di piccione* (pigeon breast), and *formaggio alle erbette* (cheese with herbs). *Via Ghibellina 87, tel. 055/242777. Reservations required. Jacket and tie required. AE, MC, V. Closed Sun. and Mon. lunch, Aug., a week in Jan.*

$$$ **La Capannina di Sante.** Florence's best fish restaurant is situated,
★ not surprisingly, along a quiet stretch of the Arno, with indoor tables in an ample, unpretentious trattoria setting and tables outdoors on the terrace during the warmer months. Risotto and various types of pasta are combined with seafood, and the *grigliata mista di pesce* (mixed grill of fish) is among the standouts. *Piazza Ravenna, tel. 055/688345. Dinner reservations advised. Dress: casual. AE, DC, MC, V. Closed Sun., Mon. lunch, 10 days in Aug., Dec. 23–30.*

Il Cestello. Located across the Arno from the church of San Frediano in Cestello, the restaurant is part of the Excelsior hotel and moves to the roof during the warmer months to enjoy a stupendous view of the city. The Tuscan-based menu features delicious risotto and pasta dishes, including an exemplary *pasta e fagioli* (pasta with beans), a rare selection of seafood, and an ever-changing sampling of whatever is fresh from the market. *Hotel Excelsior, Piazza Ognissanti 3, tel. 055/264201. Reservations advised for nonguests of the hotel. Jacket and tie required. AE, DC, MC, V.*

Relais le Jardin. Another hotel restaurant, this one with a turn-of-the-century, stained-glass-and-wood-paneling setting, stands on its own. Its *crespelle*, or crêpes, come highly recommended in their infinite variety, as do the *medaglioni di vitello al rabarbo* (medallions of veal with rhubarb) and other aromatic meat dishes. *Hotel Regency, Piazza Massimo D'Azeglio 5, tel. 055/245247. Reservations required for nonguests of the hotel. Jacket and tie required. AE, DC, MC, V. Closed Sun.*

★ **Terrazza Brunelleschi.** The rooftop restaurant of the Hotel Baglioni has the best view in town. The dining room, decorated in pale blue and creamy tones, has wraparound picture windows framing a close-up of Brunelleschi's dome. The summer terrace outside is charming, with tables placed under arbors and with turrets for guests to climb to get an even better view. The menu offers some traditional Tuscan dishes, such as *minestra di fagioli* (bean soup) and other, more innovative choices, such as vegetable pâté. If you order carefully, your check may be in the $$ category. *Hotel Baglioni, Piazza Unità Italiana 6, tel. 055/215642. Reservations advised, especially in summer. Jacket and tie in evening. AE, DC, MC, V.*

Il Verrocchio. In an elegant 18th-century villa, now a deluxe hotel, the restaurant is about 20 minutes from downtown Florence by car or taxi, and well worth the ride. The dining room has a huge fireplace, columns, and a high, vaulted ceiling. Outdoors you dine on a terrace overlooking the Arno. The menu changes with the seasons but can be described as Tuscan-creative, with such offerings as *agnello con salsa di albicocche* (lamb with apricot sauce) and delicate, fresh pasta dishes. *Villa La Massa, Via La Massa 6, Candeli, tel. 055/666141. Reservations advised. Jacket and tie required. AE, DC, MC, V. Closed Mon. and Tues. lunch Nov.–Mar.*

$$ **Alle Murate.** Situated between the Duomo and Santa Croce, this is a sophisticated but informal restaurant. The menu features creative versions of classic Tuscan dishes—*anatra alle erbe* (boned duck with herb and orange sauce)—but also southern Italian specialties such as *cavatelli con broccoli* (homemade pasta with broccoli and cheese). The main dining room has an elegant, uncluttered look, with warm wood floors and paneling and soft lights. In a smaller adjacent room called the *vineria*, table settings are simpler and the menu more limited. Since the Murate is known for its wine list, this is the place to splurge on a good vintage. *Via Ghibellina 52/r, tel. 055/240618. Reservations advised. Dress: casual. No credit cards. Dinner only. Closed Mon.*

★ **Angiolino.** This bustling little trattoria in the Oltrarno district is popular with locals and visitors. It has a real charcoal grill and an old woodburning stove to keep customers warm on nippy days. The menu offers Tuscan specialties such as ribollita (thick bread soup) and a classic bistecca alla fiorentina. The bistecca can push the check up, as you pay by weight (order one for two people). *Via Santo Spirito 36/r, tel. 055/239–8976. Dinner reservations advised. Dress: casual. No credit cards. Closed Sun. dinner, Mon., and last 3 weeks in July.*

Buca dell'Orafo. One of the best of the Florentine *buca*, meaning hole, restaurants, Buca dell'Orafo is set in the cellar of a former goldsmith's shop near the Ponte Vecchio. It offers all the Florentine specialties and prides itself on its bistecca. *Via dei Girolami 28, tel. 055/213619. Reservations advised. Dress: casual. Closed Sun., Mon., and Aug.*

Cantinetta Antinori. Set on the ground floor of a Renaissance palace, this is an elegant place for lunch after shopping in nearby Via Tornabuoni. The Antinori family is best known as wine producers, and their wares may be sampled with light salads, bread, sausage, and cheese snacks or more complete meals. *Piazza Antinori 3, tel. 055/292234. Reservations advised. Dress: casual. AE, DC, MC, V. Closed Sat., Sun., and Aug.*

★ **Il Cibreo.** Located near the Sant'Ambrogio market, Il Cibreo uses the freshest ingredients to prepare updated versions of Florentine classics, presented in an upscale trattoria-style dining room or in a piazza overlooking the market during the warmer months. The pappa al pomodoro, presented as a thick red dollop on a sparkling white Ginori plate, and inventive dishes such as *anatra farcita di pinoli e uvetta* (duck stuffed with pine nuts and raisins) are two of many specialties. A café annex across the street serves drinks and snacks all day. There is also a small, inconspicuous and inexpensive tavern annex around the corner. *Via dei Macci 118/r, tel. 055/234–1100. Dinner reservations advised. Dress: casual. Closed Sun., Mon., and July 25–Sept. 5, Dec. 31–Jan. 7. AE, DC, MC, V.*

★ **Le Fonticine.** Owner Silvano Bruci is from Tuscany, wife Gianna from Emilia-Romagna, and the restaurant combines the best of both worlds in a setting liberally hung with their extensive collection of paintings. Emilia-Romagna specialties such as tortellini ready the taste buds for Tuscan grilled porcini mushrooms so meaty they provide serious competition for the bistecca alla fiorentina. *Via Nazionale 79/r, tel. 055/282106. Reservations advised. Dress: casual. AE, DC, MC, V. Closed Sun., Mon, and July 25–Aug. 25.*

La Giostra. Only about five minutes from the cathedral or from Santa Croce, the Giostra has the typically unpretentious look of a trattoria, but with a difference: the gourmet touch of the courteous owner-chef. Try his ravioli or veal *agli agrumi* (both served with an unusual and delicate citrus sauce) or *spianata di carne* (a skilletful of thinly sliced beef redolent of herbs). Like the menu, the wine list offers good value. Service is informal. *Borgo Pinti 10/r, tel. 055/241341. Reservations advised in evening. AE, MC, V. Check locally for new closing day.*

Harry's Bar. Americans love it, and it *is* the only place in town to get a perfect martini or a hamburger or a club sandwich, but it offers two typical Tuscan dishes every day. The small menu also has well-prepared international offerings, and the bar is open until midnight.

Lungarno Vespucci 22/r, tel. 055/239–6700. Reservations required. Dress: casual. AE, MC, V. Closed Sun. and Dec. 15–Jan. 8.

La Loggia. Though it may be crowded and somewhat rushed, La Loggia is worth the wait for the view of Florence from atop Piazzale Michelangelo, especially during the summer when there are tables outdoors. The food is almost incidental, but sticking to such Florentine classics as porcini mushrooms and bistecca alla fiorentina makes for a thoroughly memorable evening. *Piazzale Michelangelo 1, tel. 055/234–2832. Dress: casual. AE, DC, MC, V. Closed Wed. and Aug. 10–25.*

Mario da Ganino. On a side street between the Duomo and Palazzo Vecchio, this trattoria is informal, rustic, and cheerful. Your meal might include some of the homemade pasta on the menu. *Gnudoni* (ravioli without the pasta casing) are a specialty, as is cheesecake for dessert. Main courses uphold Florentine tradition, with grilled steak and chops and bean dishes. Get there early; it seats only about 35, and double that number in good weather at outside tables. *Piazza dei Cimatori 4/r, tel. 055/214125. Reservations advised. Dress: casual. AE, DC. Closed Sun. and Aug. 15–25.*

Pallottino. Pallottino has the look of a typical Florentine trattoria, with dark wood tables and benches and copper utensils and old photos on the walls, but here the decor is somehow improved. The menu features traditional fare, from bread or bean soup to *spaghetti alla fiaccheraia* (pasta with piquant tomato sauce). Meat courses are varied; try *involtini alla pallottino* (beef roulades with a creamy sauce). For dessert go down the street for ice cream at Vivoli. *Via Isola delle Stinche 1/r, tel. 055/289573. Reservations advised. Dress: casual. AE, DC, MC, V. Closed Mon.*

Sostanza detto Il Troia. Equally famous for its brusque service as it is for its bistecca alla fiorentina, Il Troia is Florence's oldest restaurant, founded in 1869. Its menu is still strictly Florentine, and all the local classics are served at communal tables, with no frills, to a clientele of out-of-towners and tourists. *Via del Porcellana 25/r, tel. 055/212691. Reservations advised. Dress: casual. No credit cards. Closed Sat. dinner, Sun., and Aug.*

Toscano. A small table attractively set in a show window identifies this restaurant located about five minutes from Palazzo Medici-Riccardi. It lives up to its name in ambience and cuisine. The cold-cuts counter at the entrance, terra-cotta tile floors, and beamed ceilings typify a Tuscan trattoria, but the pink tablecloths, arty photos on the walls, and a touch of creative cuisine take it out of the ordinary. The kitchen prides itself on top-quality meat; this is the place to try *tagliata* (sliced steak) or *spezzatino peposo* (beef stew with lots of black pepper and a wine sauce). The fixed-price menu is good value, at about 28,000 lire. *Via Guelfa 70/r, tel. 055/215475. Reservations not necessary. Dress: casual. AE, DC, MC, V. Closed Tues. and Aug.*

$ **Acqua al Due.** You'll find this tiny restaurant near the Bargello. It serves an array of Florentine specialties in a lively, very casual setting. Acqua al Due is popular with young Florentines, partly because it's air-conditioned in the summer and always open late. *Via dell'Acqua 2/r, tel. 055/284170. No reservations. Dress: casual. AE, DC, MC, V. Closed Mon. and Aug.*

La Maremmana. A display of garden-fresh vegetables and fruit catches your eye as you enter this popular trattoria near Santa Croce. Authentic Tuscan cuisine is offered in the dining room, which has the usual wood paneling and long tables that you will probably be asked to share. The fixed-price menu offers generous servings and good value, and it may include ribollita and *stracotto* (beef stew). *Via dei Macci 77/r, tel. 055/241226. Dress: casual. MC, V. Closed Sun.*

Mario. Clean and classic, this family-run trattoria on the corner of Piazza del Mercato near San Lorenzo offers a genuine Florentine atmosphere and cooking, with no frills. Open for lunch only, it's just around the corner from Za-Za (*see below*). *Via Rosina 2/r (Piazza del Mercato Centrale), tel. 055/218550. Dress: casual. No credit cards. Closed dinner and Sun.*

Mossacce. You share a heavy wooden trattoria table here and watch the cook in the glassed-in kitchen prepare your order, chosen from a menu of Florentine classics. *Via del Proconsolo 55/r, tel. 055/294361. No reservations. Dress: casual. AE, MC, V. Closed weekends and Aug.*

Za-Za. Sligtly more upscale than neighboring trattorias, Za-Za attracts white-collar workers and theater people. Posters of movie stars hang on wood-paneled walls, and classic Florentine cuisine is served at communal tables. *Piazza Mercato Centrale 16/r, tel. 055/215411. Reservations advised. Dress: casual. AE, DC, MC, V. Closed Sun. and Aug.*

Wine Shops In addition, there are many wine shops where you can have a snack or sandwich. Of these, **Le Cantine** (Via dei Pucci) is stylish and popular, as is **Cantinone del Gallo Nero** (Via Santo Spirito 6), which also serves meals in a brick-vaulted wine cellar. More modest are **Borgioli** (Piazza dell'Olio), **Fiaschetteria** (Via dei Neri 2, corner of Via dei Benci), **Fratellini** (Via dei Cimatori), **Nicolino** (Volta dei Mercanti), and **Piccolo Vinaio** (Via Castellani).

Lodging

Florence's importance not only as a tourist city but as a convention center and the site of the Pitti fashion collections throughout the year has guaranteed a variety of accommodations, many in former villas and palazzos. However, these very factors mean that, except during the winter, reservations are a must.

Near the A1 autostrada exits, drivers will find the Sheraton Firenze (tel. 055/64901, fax 055/680747, $$$$), the Holiday Inn (tel. 055/653–1841, fax 055/653–1806, $$$), and the Forte Agip (tel. 055/421–1881, fax 055/421–9015, $$).

If you do find yourself in Florence with no reservations, go to the **Consorzio ITA** office in the train station. It's open every day from 8:20 AM to 9 PM. If the office is shut, your best bet is to try some of the inexpensive (but clean) accommodations at a one- or two-star hotel; many are located on **Via Nazionale** (which leads east from Piazza Stazione) and on **Via Faenza,** the second left off Via Nazionale.

Highly recommended lodgings are indicated by a star ★.

Category	Cost*
$$$$	over 400,000 lire
$$$	225,000–400,000 lire
$$	150,000–225,000 lire
$	under 150,000 lire

All prices are for a double room for two, including tax and service.

$$$$ **Excelsior.** Traditional Old World charm finds a regal setting at the
★ Excelsior, a neo-Renaissance palace complete with painted wooden
ceilings, stained glass, and acres of Oriental carpets strewn over
marble floors in the public rooms. The rooms are furnished with the
chaises longues, classical decorations, and long mirrors of the Empire style. Plush touches include wall-to-wall carpeting in the rooms
and thick terrycloth towels on heated racks in the bathrooms. Its Il
Cestello restaurant serves excellent food and in summer moves up to
the roof for a wonderful view. *Piazza Ognissanti 3, tel. 055/264201,
fax 055/210278. 205 rooms with bath. Facilities: restaurant with piano bar. AE, DC, MC, V.*

Grand Hotel. Across the piazza from the Excelsior, this Florentine
classic, also owned by the CIGA chain, provides all the luxurious
amenities of its sister. Most rooms and public areas are decorated in
sumptuous Renaissance style, many with frescoes. Baths are in
marble. Some rooms have balconies overlooking the Arno. *Piazza
Ognissanti 1, tel. 055/288781, fax 055/217400. 107 rooms with bath.
Facilities: restaurant, winter garden, bar, parking. AE, DC, MC,
V.*

Grand Hotel Villa Cora. Built near the Boboli Gardens and Piazzale
Michelangelo in the mid-19th century when Florence was briefly the
capital of Italy, the Villa Cora retains the opulence of that era. The
decor of its remarkable public and private rooms runs the gamut
from neoclassical to rococo and even Moorish, and reflects the splendor of such former guests as the Empress Eugénie, wife of Napoleon
III, and Madame Von Meck, Tchaikovsky's mysterious benefac-
tress. *Viale Machiavelli 18, tel. 055/2298451, fax 055/229086. 48
rooms with bath. Facilities: restaurant, garden, pool, piano bar, car
service. AE, DC, MC, V.*

Regency. Undisturbed sleep is almost guaranteed at this hotel,
which is tucked away in a respectable residential district near the
synagogue. The rooms are decorated in richly colored and tasteful
fabrics and antique-style furniture faithful to the hotel's 19th-centu-
ry origins as a private mansion. It has one of Florence's best hotel
restaurants. *Piazza Massimo D'Azeglio 3, tel. 055/245247, fax 055/
234–2938. 33 rooms with bath. Facilities: restaurant, garden. AE,
DC, MC, V.*

Villa San Michele. The setting for this hideaway is so romantic—
nestled in the hills of nearby Fiesole—that it once attracted Brigitte
Bardot for her honeymoon. The villa was originally a monastery
whose facade and loggia have been attributed to Michelangelo. The
rooms now contain sumptuous statuary, paintings, and Jacuzzis.
Many have a panoramic view of Florence, while others face an inner
courtyard. A luxuriant garden surrounds the whole affair. The restaurant is excellent. *Via Doccia 4, Fiesole, tel. 055/59451, fax 055/
598734. 28 rooms with bath. Facilities: restaurant, piano bar, pool,
garden, courtesy bus service. AE, DC, MC, V. Open mid-Mar.–
mid-Nov.*

$$$ **Baglioni.** This large turn-of-the-century building was conceived in
★ the European tradition of grand hotels; it's located between the
train station and the cathedral. The charming roof terrace has the
best view in Florence and is home to the Terrazza Brunelleschi res-
taurant. The hotel has well-proportioned rooms decorated in an-
tique Florentine style, and many have leaded glass windows.
Fourth-floor rooms have been done in pastel tones harmonizing with
the carpeting or mellow parquet. There is a full range of conference
facilities, which makes it a favorite of businesspeople. *Piazza
dell'Unità Italiana 6, tel. 055/23580, fax 055/235–8895. 197 rooms
with bath. Facilities: roof-garden restaurant. AE, DC, MC, V.*

Beacci Tornabuoni. This is perhaps *the* classic Florentine pensione (although by law all lodgings have been reclassified as hotels of various categories). Set in a 14th-century palazzo, it contains a series of quaint, old-fashioned but modernized rooms, all presided over by a signora full of personality. Half board is required, but the food is good and can also be brought to the rooms, most of which have views of the red-tiled roofs in the neighboring downtown area. *Via Tornabuoni 3, tel. 055/212645, fax 055/283594. 30 rooms with bath. Facilities: restaurant, bar. AE, DC, MC, V.*

★ **Brunelleschi.** Architects united a Byzantine tower, a medieval church, and a later building in a stunning structure in the very heart of Renaissance Florence to make this the city's most unique hotel. This remarkable place even has its own museum displaying the ancient Roman foundations and pottery shards found during restoration. Medieval stone walls and brick arches contrast pleasingly with the plush, contemporary decor. The comfortable, soundproof bedrooms, many with good views, are done in coordinated patterns and soft colors; the ample bathrooms feature beige travertine marble. Brunelleschi ranks high for atmosphere, interest, and comfort. *Piazza Sant'Elisabetta (Via dei Calzaiuoli), tel. 055/562068, fax 055/219653. 94 rooms with bath, 7 junior suites. Facilities: restaurant, bar, conference rooms. AE, DC, MC, V.*

J&J. Away from the crowds, on a quiet street within walking distance of the sights, this unusual hotel is a converted 16th-century monastery. Its large, suitelike rooms are ideal for honeymooners, families, and small groups of friends traveling together. Some rooms are on two levels, and all are imaginatively arranged around a central courtyard and decorated with flair. There are also smaller more intimate rooms, some opening onto their own little courtyard. The gracious owners chat with guests in the elegant lounge; breakfast is served in a glassed-in Renaissance loggia or in the central courtyard. *Via di Mezzo 20, tel. 055/240951, fax 055/240282. 20 rooms with bath. Facilities: bar. AE, DC, MC, V.*

Kraft. The efficient and comfortable Kraft is modern, but it has many period-style rooms, some with balconies looking out toward the Arno. Its location near the Teatro Comunale (it is also next to the U.S. consulate) gives it a clientele from the music world. *Via Solferino 2, tel. 055/284273, fax 055/239-8267. 68 rooms with bath. Facilities: rooftop restaurant, pool. AE, DC, MC, V.*

★ **Monna Lisa.** Housed in a Renaissance palazzo, the hotel retains its original *pietra serena* staircase, terra-cotta floors, and painted ceilings. Its rooms still have a rather homey quality, and though on the small side, many have contemplative views of a lovely garden. The ground-floor lounges give you the feel of living in an aristocratic town house. *Borgo Pinti 27, tel. 055/2479751, fax 055/247-9755. 30 rooms with bath. Facilities: garden, bar. AE, DC, MC, V.*

Plaza Hotel Lucchesi. Elegant without being ostentatious, this hotel is right on the Arno near Santa Croce. Front bedrooms have views of the river and hills beyond; rear rooms on the top floor have balconies and knockout views of Santa Croce. Spacious, quiet bedrooms (double glazing throughout) are furnished comfortably in mahogany and pastel fabrics, against creamy white walls. The roomy, welcoming lounges and piano bar are favorite meeting places for Florentines. *Lungarno della Zecca Vecchia 38, tel. 055/264141, fax 055/248-0921. 100 rooms with bath. Facilities: La Serra restaurant, bar, garage. AE, DC, MC, V.*

$$ **Bencistà.** Below the luxurious Villa San Michele in Fiesole, this hotel has the same tranquil setting and is even two centuries older. The rooms are furnished with antiques, and half board is required. *Via*

Benedetto da Maiano 4, Fiesole, tel. 055/59163, fax 055/59163. 40 rooms, 30 with bath. No credit cards.

Hermitage. Comfortable and charming are suitable adjectives for this hotel occupying two floors of a palazzo next to Ponte Vecchio and the Uffizi. Inviting living rooms overlooking the Arno, bright breakfast rooms, flowered roof terrace, and well-lighted bedrooms have the decor and atmosphere of a well-kept Florentine home. Double glazing, air-conditioning, and attentive maintenance sustain the relaxing ambience. (The hotel has an elevator located at the top of a short flight of stairs from the street.) *Vicolo Marzio 1 (Piazza del Pesce, Ponte Vecchio), tel. 055/287216, fax 055/212208. 30 rooms with bath. Facilities: roof terrace. AE, MC, V.*

★ **Loggiato dei Serviti.** A relatively new hotel, the Loggiato dei Serviti is tucked away under a historic loggia in one of the city's quietest and loveliest squares. Vaulted ceilings and tasteful furnishings, some of them antiques, make this a place for those who want to get the feel of Florence in a spare, Renaissance building while enjoying modern creature comforts. The hotel has no restaurant. *Piazza Santissima Annunziata 3, tel. 055/289592, fax 055/289595. 29 rooms with bath. AE, DC, MC, V.*

★ **Morandi alla Crocetta.** Near Piazza Santissima Annunziata, this is a charming and distinguished residence in which guests are made to feel like privileged friends of the family. It is close to the sights but very quiet, in a former monastery, and is furnished comfortably in the classic style of a gracious Florentine home. The Morandi is not only an exceptional hotel but also a good value. Very small, it is worth booking well in advance. *Via Laura 50, tel. 055/234–4747, fax 055/248–0954. 9 rooms with bath. AE, DC, MC, V.*

Pendini. The atmosphere of an old-fashioned Florentine pensione is intact here, though most bedrooms have been freshly renovated. Public rooms are delightful; furnishings throughout are early 19th-century antiques or reproductions. Most bedrooms have brass or walnut beds, pretty floral wallpaper, and pastel carpeting; baths are modern. Many rooms can accommodate extra beds. The location is central, and rates are low for the category. *Via Strozzi 2, tel. 055/211170, fax 055/210156. 42 rooms with bath. AE, DC, MC, V.*

La Residenza. Located just down the street from the Beacci, on Florence's most elegant shopping street, is La Residenza: The top floor has a charming roof garden and rooms with even better views for fewer lire. The signora here is equally accommodating, the decor equally antique, and the plumbing up to date. *Via Tornabuoni 8, tel. 055/284197. 24 rooms with bath. Facilities: roof garden, garage. AE, DC, V.*

$ **Apollo.** A friendly Italian-Canadian couple owns and manages this conveniently located hotel near the station, offering good value in spacious rooms decorated in Florentine style. The gleaming new bathrooms, though compact, have such amenities as hair dryers. The staff is helpful and attentive to guests' needs. *Via Faenza 77, tel. 055/284119, fax 055/210101. 15 rooms with bath. AE, DC, MC, V.*

★ **Bellettini.** You couldn't ask for anything more central; this small hotel is on three floors (the top floor has two nice rooms with a view) of a palazzo near the Duomo. The cordial family management takes good care of guests, providing a relaxed atmosphere and attractive public rooms with a scattering of antiques. Breakfast, with homemade cakes, and air-conditioning are included in the low room rate. The good-size rooms have Venetian or Tuscan provincial decor; bathrooms are bright and modern. *Via dei Conti 7, tel. 055/213561, fax*

055/283551. 28 rooms with bath. Facilities: bar, lounge. AE, DC, MC, V.

Liana. This small hotel, located near the English Cemetery, is in a quiet 19th-century villa that formerly housed the British Embassy. Its clean and pleasant rooms all face a stately garden. *Via Vittorio Alfieri 18, tel. 055/245303, fax 055/234–4596. 23 rooms with bath or shower. AE, MC, V.*

Nuova Italia. Near the train station, within walking distance of the sights, this hotel is run by a genial English-speaking family. It has a homey atmosphere; rooms are clean and simply furnished, bright with pictures and posters, and all with private baths. Some rooms can accommodate extra beds. Low, bargain rates include breakfast. *Via Faenza 26, tel. 055/268430, fax 055/210941. 20 rooms with bath. AE, DC, MC, V.*

The Arts and Nightlife

The Arts

Theater **Estate Fiesolana.** From June through August, this festival of theater, music, dance, and film takes place in the churches and the archaeological area of Fiesole (Teatro Romano, Fiesole, tel. 055/599931).

Concerts **Maggio Musicale Fiorentina.** This series of internationally acclaimed concerts and recitals is held in the **Teatro Comunale** (Corso Italia 16, tel. 055/277–9236) from late April through June. From December to early June, there is a concert season of the Orchestra Regionale Toscana in the church of **Santo Stefano al Ponte Vecchio** (tel. 055/210804). Amici della Musica organizes concerts at the **Teatro della Pergola** (box office Via della Pergola 10/r, tel. 055/247–9652).

Opera Operas are performed in the Teatro Comunale from December through February.

Film **Florence Film Festival.** An international panel of judges gathers in late spring at the Forte di Belvedere to preside over a wide selection of new releases.

Festival del Popolo. This festival, held each December, is devoted to documentaries and is held in the Fortezza da Basso.

English-language films are shown at the **Cinema Astro** on Piazza San Simone near Santa Croce. There are two shows every evening, Tuesday through Sunday (closed in July).

Nightlife

Unlike the Romans and Milanese, the frugal and reserved Florentines do not have a reputation for an active nightlife; however, the following places attract a mixed crowd of Florentines and visitors.

Piano Bars Many of the more expensive hotels have their own piano bars, where nonguests are welcome to come for an *aperitivo* or an after-dinner drink. The best view is from the bar at the **Excelsior** (Piazza Ognissanti 3, tel. 055/264201), on a roof garden overlooking the Arno. Music is on tape at the **Champagneria** (Via Lambruschini 15/r, tel. 055/490804, a bistro-type watering hole (closed Sun.). The accent is on Brazil at **Caffè Voltaire** (Via della Scala 9/r, tel. 055/218255), where there's Latin food and music.

Nightclub **The River Club** (Lungarno Corsini 8, tel. 055/282465) has winter-garden decor and a large dance floor (closed Sun.).

Discos The two largest discos, with the youngest crowds, are **Yab** (Via Sassetti 5r, tel. 055/282018) and **Space Electronic** (Via Palazzuolo 37, tel. 055/239–3082). Less frenetic alternatives are **Jackie O'** (Via Erta Canina 24, tel. 055/234–4904) and **Full Up** (Via della Vigna Vecchia 21/r, tel. 055/293006). **Meccanò** (Viale degli Olmi 1, in Cascine Park, tel. 055/331371) is a multimedia experience in a high-tech disco with a late-night restaurant (closed Mon.).

5 Tuscany

*Lucca, Siena, and
the Hill Towns*

Rome may be the capital of Italy, but Tuscany is its heart. Stretching from the Apennines to the sea, midway between Milan and Rome, the region is quintessentially Italian, in both its appearance and its history. Its scenic variety is unmatched in Italy; its past has been ignoble (it produced the Guelph-Ghibelline conflict of the Middle Ages) and glorious (it produced the Renaissance). Its towns are justly famous for their wealth of fine architecture and art, but visitors often come home even more enthusiastic about Tuscany's unspoiled hilly landscapes, about the delicious Chianti wines produced by vineyards on those hills, and about the robust and flavorful Tuscan cooking. Be sure to allot some portion of your time here for leisurely strolls, unhurried meals, and aimless wandering around this peerless countryside, where the true soul of Tuscany is to be found.

Tuscany also produced the Italian language. It was the Tuscan dialect of Dante, Petrarch, and Boccaccio, all native sons who—given the eminence of their writings—grew to be the national tongue, a fact of which the Tuscans are rightly proud. Today the purest Italian is said to be spoken in the area between Siena and Arezzo, and even visitors with limited textbook Italian can often hear the difference. As they enter the region, the language suddenly becomes much easier to understand and takes on a bell-like clarity and mellifluous beauty unequaled throughout the rest of Italy.

It also takes on a notorious wit. As a common proverb has it, "Tuscans have Paradise in their eyes and the Inferno in their mouths" (a wry reference to Dante), and the sting of Tuscan wit is as famous throughout Italy as the beauty of Tuscan speech. Happily, the Tuscans usually reserve their wit for each other and treat visitors with complete and sincere courtesy.

For a long time, the Tuscan hill towns were notorious as well. Even its earliest civilized settlers, the Etruscans, chose their city/sites for defensive purposes (the fortress/town of Fiesole, above Florence, is a fine surviving example). With the end of the Roman Empire, the region fell into disunity, and by the 11th century Tuscany had evolved into a collection of independent city-states, each city seeking to dominate, and sometimes forcibly overpower, its neighbors. The region then became embroiled in an apparently endless international quarrel between a long succession of popes and Holy Roman Emperors. By the 13th century, Tuscany had become a battleground: The infamous conflict between the Guelphs and the Ghibellines had begun.

The Guelphs and the Ghibellines are the bane of Italian schoolchildren; their infinitely complicated, bloody history is to Italy what the Wars of the Roses are to England. To oversimplify grossly, the Ghibellines were mostly allied with both the Holy Roman Emperor (headquartered over the Alps in Germany) and the local aristocracy (dominated by feudal lords); the Guelphs were mostly allied with both the pope (headquartered in Rome) and the emerging middle class (dominated by the new trade guilds). Florence, flourishing as a trade center, was (most of the time) Guelph; its neighboring city-states Pisa and Siena were (most of the time) Ghibelline. But the bitter struggles that resulted were so Byzantine in their complexity, so full of factional disputes and treachery, that a dizzying series of conflicts within conflicts resulted. (Dante, for instance, was banished from Florence not for being a Ghibelline but for being the wrong brand of Guelph.)

Eventually the Florentine Guelphs emerged victorious, and in the 15th century the region was united to become the Grand Duchy of

Tuscany, controlled from Florence by the Medici grand dukes. Today the hill towns are no longer fierce, although they retain a uniquely medieval air, and in most of them the citizens walk the same narrow streets and inhabit the same houses that their ancestors did 600 years ago.

Tuscan art, to most people, means Florence, and understandably so. The city is unique and incomparable, and an astonishing percentage of the great artists of the Renaissance lived and worked there. But there is art elsewhere in Tuscany, and too often it is overlooked in favor of another trip to the Uffizi. Siena, particularly, possesses its own style of architecture and art quite different from the Florentine variety; the contrast is both surprising and illuminating. And even the smallest of the hill towns can possess hidden treasures, for the artists of the Middle Ages and the Renaissance took their work where they could find it. Piero della Francesca's fresco cycle in the church of San Francesco in Arezzo is perhaps the preeminent hidden treasure. Tucked away in a small church in a small town, and, sadly, faded, the frescoes are artistically the equal of almost everything Florence has to offer and are all the more appealing for their uncrowded setting.

Essential Information

Important Addresses and Numbers

Tourist Information **Regional information** on Tuscany is available in **Florence** (Via di Novoli, tel. 055/439311).

Local information is available in the following tourist offices, which are generally open 9–12:30, 3:30–7:30.

Arezzo (Piazza Risorgimento 116, tel. 0575/23952).
Cortona (Via Nazionale 72, tel. 0575/630557).
Lucca (Piazza Guidiccione 2, tel. 0583/491205).
Pisa (Piazza Duomo 8, tel. 050/560464).
Pistoia (Palazzo dei Vescovi, tel. 0573/21622).
Prato (Via Cairoli 48, tel. 0574/24112).
San Gimignano (Piazza del Duomo, tel. 0577/940008).
Siena (Via di Città 43, tel. 0577/42209; Piazza del Campo 55, tel. 0577/280551).
Volterra (Via Turazza 2, tel. 0588/86150).

Emergencies **Police, Ambulance, Fire,** tel. 113. This number will also put you in touch with the First Aid Service (Pronto Soccorso).

Travel Agencies In Florence, contact: **American Express** (Via Guicciardini 49/r, tel. 055/288751); **CIT** (Via Cavour 56, tel. 055/294306); or **Thomas Cook** (c/o World Vision, Via Cavour 154/r, tel. 055/579294).

Car Rentals Cars are for rent at the airports and in the larger cities in Tuscany; Alitalia may offer economical fly/drive packages with discounts on car rentals and hotels.

Arriving and Departing by Plane

The largest airports in the region are Pisa's **Galileo Galilei Airport** and Florence's **Peretola Airport.** There are direct flights from Paris to Pisa or Florence; from London, there are direct flights to Pisa; from the United States, you'll have to get connecting flights from Rome or Milan.

Arriving and Departing by Car and Train

By Car The Autostrada del Sole (A1), connects Florence with Bologna, 105 kilometers (65 miles) north, and Rome, 277 kilometers (172 miles) south, and passes close to Arezzo.

By Train The coastal line from Rome to Genoa passes through Pisa and all the beach resorts. The main line from Rome to Bologna passes through Arezzo, Florence, and Prato.

Getting Around

By Car The best way to see Tuscany, making it possible to explore the tiny towns and country restaurants that are so much a part of the region's charm, is by car. A11 leads west from Florence and meets the coastal A12 between Viareggio and Livorno. The A1 autostrada links Florence with Arezzo and Chiusi (where you turn off for Montepulciano). A toll-free superstrada links Florence with Siena. Drivers should be prepared to navigate through bewildering suburban sprawls around Tuscan cities; to reach the historic sections where most of the sights are located, look for signs to the *Centro Storico*.

By Train The main rail line runs past Chiusi and Cortona through Arezzo and Florence to Prato. Another main line connects Florence with Pisa. A secondary line links Florence, by way of Prato, with Pistoia and Lucca; there are a few other local lines.

By Bus Tuscany is crisscrossed by bus lines that connect the smaller towns and cities on the autostrade and superhighways. They are a good choice for touring the hill towns around Siena, such as San Gimignano; you can then take a Tra-In or Lazzi bus from Siena to Arezzo and get back onto the main Rome-Florence train line. From Chiusi on the main train line you can get a bus to Montepulciano. Buses connect Florence and Siena with Volterra.

By Boat Boat services link the islands of Tuscany's archipelago with the mainland; passenger and car ferries leave from Livorno and Piombino for Elba. The ferry to Giglio leaves from Porto Santo Stefano on the Argentario peninsula.

Guided Tours

From Florence, **American Express** (Via Guicciardini 49/r, tel. 055/288751) is part of a consortium operating one-day excursions to Siena and San Gimignano and can arrange for cars, drivers, and guides for special-interest tours in Tuscany. **CIT** (Via Cavour 56, tel. 055/294306) has a three-day Carosello bus tour from Rome to Florence, Siena, and San Gimignano, as well as a five-day tour that also takes in Venice.

Exploring Tuscany

Since most visitors to Tuscany will also spend some time in Florence (*see* Chapter 4), that city may be considered the starting point for the first two of these excursions. Tour 1 heads west from Florence toward the Tuscan coast, taking in the historic cities of Lucca and Pisa, among others; Tour 2 goes south through lovely inland valleys to several charming hill towns, with special attention given to Siena, Florence's ancient rival for Tuscan supremacy. Tour 3, which leaves the A1 autostrada or the main north–south rail line at a point roughly equidistant from Florence or Rome, explores southern Tuscany and other hill towns, such as unspoiled Montepulciano and the "ideal" Renaissance town of Pienza. No spot on any of these tours is more than a few hours' drive from Florence, but you would be hard pressed to see all the sights in a day trip—better to allow at least two or three days for each itinerary.

Highlights for First-Time Visitors

Lucca (Tour 1: En Route to Pisa).

Piazza del Duomo, in Pisa, including the Leaning Tower (Tour 1: En Route to Pisa).

San Gimignano (Tour 2: South to Siena).

Piazza del Campo, in Siena (Tour 2: South to Siena).

Duomo, in Siena (Tour 2: South to Siena).

Pinacoteca Nazionale, in Siena (Tour 2: South to Siena).

San Francesco, in Arezzo (Tour 2: South to Siena).

Piazza Grande, in Montepulciano (Tour 3: Southern Tuscany).

Tour 1: En Route to Pisa

Numbers in the margin correspond to points of interest on the Tuscany map.

❶ The tour begins at **Prato,** 21 kilometers (13 miles) northwest of Florence. A textile center since its early medieval days, Prato was known for its wool throughout Europe by the 13th century. In the 14th century, a local cloth merchant, Francesco di Marco Datini, who built his business, according to one of his surviving ledgers, "in the name of God and of profit," further stimulated the local industry; the city remains to this day one of the world's largest manufacturers of cloth.

Prato's main attraction is its 11th-century **Duomo.** Romanesque in style, it is famous for its Chapel of the Holy Girdle (to the left of the entrance), which enshrines the sash of the Virgin; it is said that the girdle was given to the apostle Thomas by the Virgin herself, when she miraculously appeared after her Assumption. The Duomo also contains 16th-century frescoes by Prato's most famous son, the libertine monk Fra Filippo Lippi; the best known depict Herod's banquet and Salome's dance. *Piazza del Duomo. Open 7–12, 4–7.*

Sculpture by Donatello that originally adorned the Duomo's exterior pulpit is now on display in the **Museo dell'Opera del Duomo.** *Piazza del Duomo 49, tel. 0574/29339. Admission: 5,000 lire (includes Galleria Comunale). Open Mon., Wed.–Sat. 9:30–12:30, 3–6:30; Sun. 9:30–12:30.*

The nearby **Galleria Comunale** contains a good collection of Tuscan and Sienese paintings, mainly from the 14th century. *Palazzo Pretorio, Piazza del Comune, tel. 0574/452302. Admission: 5,000 lire (includes Museo dell'Opera del Duomo). Open Mon., Wed.–Sat. 9:30–12:30, 3–6:30; Sun. 9:30–12:30.*

Prato's **Pecci Center of Contemporary Art** has a burgeoning collection of works by Italian and other artists. *Viale della Repubblica, tel. 0574/570620. Admission: 5,000 lire. Open Wed.–Sun. 10–7.*

Tuscany

Garfagnana
ALPI APUANE

Florence
Prato
Pistoia
Montecatini Terme
Altopascio
Lucca
Pisa
Marlia
Abetone
Strada
Greve
Livorno
La Spezia
Carrara
Seravezza
Pietrasanta
Forte dei Marmi
Viareggio

Arno
Elsa
Serchio
Panaro

Ligurian Sea

TO CORSICA

A15
A12
A1
A11
A12
S1
S12
S435
S439
S206
S67
S66
S64
S65
S63
S12
S324
S445
S302
S303
S304
S610
S429
S52
S222

❷ The town of **Pistoia,** 15 kilometers (9 miles) west of Prato, saw the beginning of the bitter Guelph-Ghibelline conflict of the Middle Ages. Reconstructed after heavy bombing during World War II, the town contains some fine Romanesque architecture. Its **Cathedral of San Zeno** in the main square (Piazza del Duomo) houses the **Dossale di San Jacopo,** a magnificent silver altarpiece. The two half-figures on its left side are by Filippo Brunelleschi (1377–1446), better known as the first Renaissance architect (and designer of Florence's magnificent Duomo dome). *Illumination of altarpiece: 2,000 lire.*

Other attractions include the **Ospedale del Ceppo** (Piazza Ospedale, a short way down Via Pacini from Piazza del Duomo), a hospital founded during the 14th century, with a superb early 16th-century terra-cotta frieze by Giovanni della Robbia; the church of **Sant'Andrea** (down Via Pappe to Via Sant'Andrea), with a fine early 14th-century pulpit by Giovanni Pisano that depicts the life of Christ; and, back in Piazza del Duomo, an unusual Gothic baptistery and the 14th-century **Palazzo del Comune,** which houses the **Museo Civico,** containing medieval art. *Palazzo del Comune, Piazza del Duomo, tel. 0573/371275. Admission: 5,000 lire. Open Tues.–Sat. 9–1 and 3–7, Sun. 9–1.*

❸ One of Europe's most famous health spas, **Montecatini Terme** is 16 kilometers (10 miles) west of Pistoia. It is renowned for its mineral springs, which flow from five sources and are used to treat liver and skin disorders. Those "taking the cure" report each morning to one of the town's *stabilimenti termali* (thermal establishments) to drink their prescribed cupful of water. The curative effects of Montecatini's water became known only in the 1800s, and the town was heavily developed at the beginning of this century, leaving a wealth of Art Nouveau buildings. The most attractive is the **Stabilimento Tettuccio,** a neoclassical edifice with colonnades. Here the water spouts from fountains set up on marble counters, the walls are decorated with bucolic scenes depicted on painted ceramic tiles, and an orchestra plays under a frescoed dome. An older town of Montecatini, called **Montecatini Alto,** sits on top of a hill near the spa town and is reached by a funicular.

❹ The town of **Lucca,** 27 kilometers (17 miles) west of Montecatini, was where Caesar, Pompey, and Crassus agreed to rule Rome as a triumvirate in 56 BC; it was later the first town in Tuscany to accept Christianity. Today it still has a mind of its own, and when most of Tuscany was voting communist recently, its citizens rarely followed suit. Lucca is more elegant and enjoyable than duller Pisa, so consider making it your base for exploring northwest Tuscany (but book ahead, as hotels are scarce). For a fine overview of the town, take a walk or a drive along its 16th-century ramparts, which are shaded by stately trees.

Numbers in the margin correspond to points of interest on the Lucca map.

Lucca is one of the most picturesque fortress towns in Tuscany and is worth exploring at length on foot. As usual, the main attraction is

❺ the **Duomo** (Piazza del Duomo, on the southern side of town). Its round-arched facade is a fine example of the rigorously ordered Pisan Romanesque style, in this case happily enlivened by an extremely disordered collection of carved columns. The decoration of the facade and of the porch below are worth a close look; they make this one of the most entertaining church fronts in Tuscany. The Gothic interior contains a moving Byzantine crucifix (called the **Volto Santo,** or Holy Face), brought here in the 8th century, and

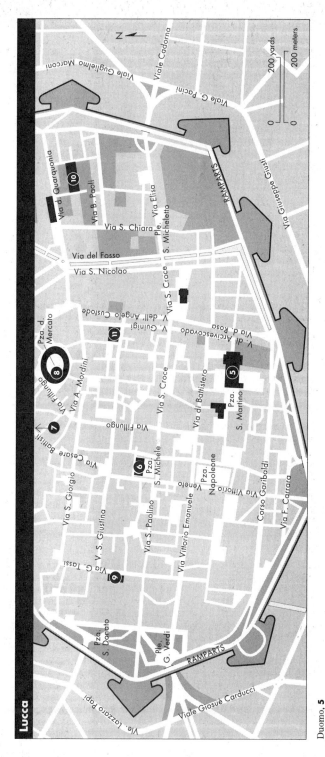

Lucca

Duomo, **5**
Museo Nazionale, **10**
Palazzo Guinigi, **11**
Piazza del Mercato, **8**
Pinacoteca
Nazionale, **9**
San Frediano, **7**
San Michele, **6**

the masterpiece of the Sienese sculptor Jacopo della Quercia, the marble *Tomb of Ilaria del Caretto* (1406).

❻ Slightly west of the center of town is the church of **San Michele** (Piazza San Michele), with a facade even more fanciful than the Duomo; it was heavily restored in the 19th century, however, and somewhat jarringly displays busts of modern Italian patriots such as Garibaldi and Cavour.

Time Out For dessert, try the local sweet cake, *buccellato*, available at **Pasticceria Taddeucci** (Piazza San Michele 34), or a coffee or ice cream at the venerable **Caffè di Simo** (Via Fillungo), a favorite of Lucca's famous son Giacomo Puccini, composer of some of the world's best-loved operas.

❼ The church of **San Frediano** (Piazza San Frediano) is just inside the middle of the north town wall; it contains more works by Jacopo della Quercia, and, bizarrely, the lace-clad mummy of the patron saint of domestic servants, Santa Zita. Near it, to the southeast, is **❽** **Piazza del Mercato,** where the **Anfiteatro Romano,** or Roman Amphitheater, once stood. The piazza takes its oval shape from the theater, but the seats disappeared when medieval houses were built on top of them.

❾ Near the west walls of the old city, the **Pinacoteca Nazionale** is worth a visit to see the Mannerist, Baroque, and Rococo art on display. *Palazzo Mansi, Via Galli Tassi 43, tel. 0583/55570. Admission: 6,000 lire. Open Tues.–Sat. 9–7, Sun. 9–2.*

Time Out For an inexpensive lunch in pleasant surroundings, try **Trattoria da Giulio** (Via delle Conce 47, near Porta San Donato), which serves orzo and *porri* (leek) soups, roasted meats, and other simple Lucchese specialties. Closed Sun. and Mon.

❿ On the eastern end of the historic center, the **Museo Nazionale** houses an extensive collection of local Romanesque and Renaissance art. *Villa Guinigi, Via della Quarquonia, tel. 0583/46033. Admission: 5,000 lire. Open May–Sept., Tues.–Sat. 9–7, Sun. 9–1; Oct.–Apr., Tues.–Sat. 9–4:30, Sun. 9–1.*

Finally, for a fine view of the surrounding countryside, climb the **⓫** tree-topped tower of the medieval **Palazzo Guinigi,** near the center of town. *Admission: 3,000 lire. Open 10–4 (9–7 in summer).*

Numbers in the margin correspond to points of interest on the Tuscany map.

⓬ The town of **Pisa,** southwest of Lucca, reached its glory as a maritime republic during the 12th century; its architects and artists strongly influenced the development of the Romanesque and Gothic styles in Tuscany. Defeated by its arch rival, Genoa (also a seaport trading center), in 1284, Pisa went into a gradual decline, its harbor filling with silt from the Arno; in the 15th century it became a satellite to Florence, when the Medici gained full control of Tuscany. During World War II, the city was virtually destroyed by Axis and Allied bombing, which miraculously spared its main attraction, **Piazza del Duomo.** Situated at the northwestern edge of town, it is also known, appropriately, as the **Campo dei Miracoli** (Field of Miracles). On it stand the **Duomo,** the **baptistery,** and the famous **Leaning Tower.** The Leaning Tower was begun in 1174, the last of the three structures to be built, and the lopsided settling began when construction reached the third story. The tower's architects attempted to compensate by making the remaining floors slightly taller on the leaning side, but the extra weight only made the problem worse. The settling continues to this day, as do efforts to prop the structure up. Legend holds that Galileo conducted an experiment on the nature of gravity by dropping metal balls from the top of the 187-foot-high tower; historians say this legend has no basis in fact (which is not quite to say that it is false). The tower is closed (it is undergoing structural reinforcement) and it will probably remain so permanently, but this hardly detracts from its allure. Just the sight of it, and of the resplendent marble monuments on the bright green lawn, is a delight.

The **Duomo** was the first building to use the horizontal marble striping pattern (borrowed from Moorish architecture in the 11th century) so common to Tuscan cathedrals. It is famous for the Romanesque panels on the transept door facing the tower, which depict the life of Christ, and for its beautifully carved 13th-century pulpit, by Giovanni Pisano. The lovely Gothic **baptistery,** which stands across from the Duomo's facade, is best known for the pulpit carved by Giovanni's father, Nicola, in 1260. *Duomo open Apr.–Sept., daily 7:45–1, 3–7; Oct.–Mar., daily 7:45–1, 3–5. Admission to baptistery: 5,000 lire (see below). Open Apr.–Sept., daily 9–7; Oct.–Mar., daily 9–5.*

The walled area on the northern side of the Campo dei Miracoli is the **Camposanto** (Cemetery), which is filled, according to legend, with earth brought back from the Holy Land during the Crusades. Its galleries contain numerous frescoes, notably *The Drunkenness of Noah,* by Renaissance artist Benozzo Gozzoli, and the disturbing *Triumph of Death* (14th century), whose authorship is disputed, but whose subject matter shows what was on people's minds in a century that saw the ravages of the Black Death. At the southeast corner of the Campo dei Miracoli, the **Museo dell'Opera del Duomo** holds a wealth of medieval sculptures and the ancient Roman sarcophagi that inspired Nicola Pisano's figures. The well-arranged **Museo delle Sinopie** across the street, on the south side of the square, holds the *sinopie,* or preparatory drawings, for the Camposanto frescoes and is of limited interest to most tourists. *Camposanto, tel. 050/ 560547. Admission: 5,000 lire. Open Apr.–Sept., daily 8–7; Oct.– Mar., daily 9–5. Museo dell'Opera del Duomo, Via Arcivescovado, tel. 050/560547. Admission: 5,000 lire. Open Apr.–Sept., daily 9–7; Oct.–Mar., daily 9–5. Museo delle Sinopie, Piazza del Duomo, tel. 050/560547. Admission: 5,000 lire. Open daily 9–1, 3–5. Combined admission to baptistery, Camposanto, and museums: 12,000 lire.*

In the center of town, **Piazza dei Cavalieri** possesses some fine Renaissance buildings: the **Palazzo dei Cavalieri,** the **Palazzo dell'Orologio,** and the church of **Santo Stefano dei Cavalieri.** The square was laid out around 1560 by Giorgio Vasari, better known for his chronicles of the lives of Renaissance artists that made him the first art historian. Along the Arno, the tiny Gothic church of **Santa Maria della Spina** (Lungarno Sonnino, south of the river) merits a visit, and the **Museo di San Matteo,** on the northern side, contains some touching examples of local Romanesque and Gothic art. *Lungarno Mediceo, tel. 050/541865. Admission: 6,000 lire. Open Tues.–Sat. 9–7, Sun. 9–1.*

Tour 2: South to Siena

Depending on how much time you have, choose between two roads leading south from Florence to Siena: the speedy modern highway

S2 if you're trying to fit Siena into a day trip from Florence, or the narrower and more meandering S222 if you really want to see the countryside. The S222 is also known as the **Strada Chiantigiana** because it runs through the heart of the Chianti wine-producing country. The most scenic section runs between **Strada in Chianti,** 16 kilometers (10 miles) south of Florence, to **Greve in Chianti,** 11 kilometers (7 miles) farther south, where rolling hillsides are planted with vineyards and olive groves. Greve is a busy provincial town that was once a medieval marketplace, and its triangular central piazza is surrounded by restaurants and vintners offering wine tastings (*degustazioni*). Many British and northern Europeans have relocated to the Chianti countryside, drawn by the unhurried life, a balmy climate, and picturesque villages. There are so many northerners, in fact, that the area is widely known as Chiantishire. Still, it remains strongly Tuscan in character and is sparsely populated. Although it is possible to visit towns in Chianti by bus from Florence or Siena, the way to get to know the district is by car. This allows you to turn off the main road to visit vineyards and perhaps stay at a "rustic-chic" country estate.

🔞 Florence's great historical rival, **Siena,** is located 68 kilometers (42 miles) south of Florence. The town was founded by Augustus around the time of the birth of Christ, although legend holds that it was founded much earlier by Remus, brother of Romulus, the legendary founder of Rome. During the late Middle Ages, the city was both wealthy and powerful (it saw the birth of the world's oldest bank, the Monte dei Paschi, still very much in business). It was bitterly envied by Florence, which in 1254 sent forces that besieged the city for over a year, reducing its population by half and laying waste to the countryside. The city was finally absorbed by the Grand Duchy of Tuscany, ruled by Florence, in 1559.

Numbers in the margin correspond to points of interest on the Siena map.

Unlike Renaissance Florence, Siena is a Gothic city, laid out over the slopes of three steep hills and practically unchanged since medieval times. Its main square, the **Piazza del Campo,** is one of the finest in Italy. Fan shaped, its nine sections of paving represent the 13th-century government of Nine Good Men, and, at the top, like an ornament, is the Fonte Gaia, so called because it was inaugurated to great jubilation. The bas-reliefs on it are reproductions of the originals by Jacopo della Quercia. Twice a year, on July 2 and August 16, the square is the site of the famous **Palio,** a horse race in which the city's 17 neighborhoods compete to possess the cloth banner that gives the contest its name. Unlike many other such in Italy, the Palio is deeply revered by the townspeople, and the rivalries it generates are taken very seriously.

🔞 Dominating the piazza is the **Palazzo Pubblico,** which has served as Siena's Town Hall since the 1300s. It now also contains the **Museo Civico,** its walls covered with pre-Renaissance frescoes, including Simone Martini's early 14th-century *Maestà* and *Portrait of Guidoriccio da Fogliano,* and Ambrogio Lorenzetti's famous *Allegory of Good and Bad Government,* painted from 1327 to 1329 to demonstrate the dangers of tyranny. The original bas-reliefs of the Jacopo della Quercia fountain, moved under cover to protect them from the elements, are also on display. The climb up the palazzo's bell tower is long and steep, but the superb view makes it worth every step. *Piazza del Campo, tel. 0577/292263. Bell tower admission: 4,000 lire. Open Mar. 15–Nov. 15, daily 10–one hour before sunset; Nov. 16–Mar. 14, daily 10–1:30. Palazzo Pubblico (Museo Civico)* *admission: 5,500 lire. Open Mar. 15–Nov. 15, Mon.–Sat 9:30–7:30, Sun. 9:30–1:30; Nov. 16–Mar. 14, daily 9:30–1:30.*

Time Out   There are several **gelaterie** on Piazza del Campo, excellent for surveying the piazza while enjoying a refreshing ice cream. More substantial sustenance may be found nearby at **Ristorante Il Verrocchio** (Logge del Papa 2, closed Wed.), which serves inexpensive Sienese specialties and is located a block east of the northern side of the campo.

⑮   Siena's **Duomo,** several blocks west of Piazza del Campo, is beyond question one of the finest Gothic cathedrals in Italy. Its facade, with its multicolored marbles and painted decoration, is typical of the Italian approach to Gothic architecture, lighter and much less austere than the French. The cathedral, as it now stands, was completed in the 14th century, but at the time the Sienese had even bigger plans. They decided to enlarge the building, using the current church as the transepts of the new church, which would have a new nave running toward the southeast. The beginnings of construction of this new nave still stand and may be seen from the steps outside the Duomo's right transept. But in 1348 the Black Death decimated Siena's population, the city fell into decline, funds dried up, and the plans were never carried out.

The Duomo's interior is one of the most striking in Italy and possesses a fine coffered and gilded dome. It is most famous for its unique and magnificent marble floors, which took almost 200 years to complete (beginning around 1370); more than 40 artists contributed to the work, made up of 56 separate compositions depicting biblical scenes, allegories, religious symbols, and civic emblems. The Duomo's carousel pulpit, which is almost as famous as the floors, was carved by Nicola Pisano around 1265 and depicts the life of Christ on its rostrum frieze (the staircase is a later addition). Finally, a door in the left-hand aisle just before the crossing leads into the **Biblioteca Piccolomini,** a room painted by Pinturicchio in 1509; its frescoes depict events from the life of native son Aeneas Sylvius Piccolomini, who became Pope Pius II in 1458. The frescoes are in fine repair and have a freshness rarely seen in work so old. *Biblioteca Piccolomini, tel. 0577/283048. Admission: 2,000 lire. Open mid-Mar.–Sept. 30, daily 9–7:30; Oct. 1–Nov. 3, daily 9–6:30; Nov. 4–Mar. 13, daily 10–1, 2:30–5.*

⑯ Next to the Duomo is its museum, the **Museo dell'Opera del Duomo,** occupying part of the unfinished new cathedral's nave and containing a small collection of Sienese art and the cathedral treasury. Its masterpiece is unquestionably Duccio's *Maestà,* painted around 1310 and magnificently displayed in a room devoted entirely to Duccio's work. *Piazza del Duomo, tel. 0577/283048. Admission: 5,000 lire. Open Mar. 14–Sept. 30, daily 9–7:30; Oct. 1–Nov. 3, daily 9–6:30; Nov. 4–Dec. 31, daily 9–1:30; Jan. 2–Mar. 13, daily 9–1.*

Steps between the cathedral and its museum lead to the **Battistero** (Baptistery), with its 15th-century frescoes. Its large bronze baptismal font (also 15th century) was designed by Jacopo della Quercia and is adorned with bas-reliefs by various artists, including two by Renaissance masters: Lorenzo Ghiberti *(The Baptism of Christ)* and Donatello *(Herod Presented with the Head of St. John).*

⑰ Chief among Siena's other attractions is the **Pinacoteca Nazionale,** several blocks southeast of the entrance to the Duomo; it contains a superb collection of Sienese art, including Ambrogio Lorenzetti's 14th-century depiction of a castle that is generally considered the first nonreligious painting—the first pure landscape—of the Christian era. *Via San Pietro 29, tel. 0577/281161. Admission: 8,000 lire. Open Apr.–Sept., Tues.–Sat. 8:30–7; Oct.–Mar., Tues.–Sat. 8:30–2, Sun. 8:30–1.*

⑱ If time permits, a visit to the church of **San Domenico,** northwest of the Duomo, is also worthwhile; its **Cappella di Santa Caterina** displays frescoes by Il Sodoma portraying scenes from the life of Saint Catherine and houses a reliquary containing her head.

Time Out Not far from the church of San Domenico, the **Enoteca Italica** is a fantastically stocked wine cellar in the bastions of the Medici fortress. Here you can taste wines from all over Italy and have a snack, too (Fortezza Medicea, Viale Maccari, tel. 0577/288497. Open 3 PM–midnight).

Numbers in the margin correspond to points of interest on the Tuscany map.

On your way north from Siena toward Colle Val d'Elsa, San Gimignano, and Volterra, be sure to visit Monteriggioni, a tiny hamlet sitting on a rise within a circle of formidable 13th-century walls. Its 14 square towers, which Dante likened to giants, were Siena's northernmost defense against Florence. And take time to make the lengthy detour around Colle Val d'Elsa's workaday lower town up to the ridge, where the medieval center remains practically intact.

⑲ The picturesque town of **San Gimignano** is 31 kilometers (20 miles) northwest of Siena. San Gimignano's high walls and narrow streets are typical of Tuscan hill towns, but it is the surviving medieval towers that set the town apart from its neighbors. Today 14 towers remain, but at the height of the Guelph-Ghibelline conflict, a forest of more than 70 such towers dominated the city. The towers were built partly for defensive purposes—they were a safe refuge and useful for pouring boiling oil on attacking enemies—and partly to bolster the egos of their owners, who competed with deadly seriousness to build the highest tower in town.

Many of the town's most important medieval buildings are clustered around the central Piazza del Duomo. They include the **Palazzo del Podestà,** with its imposing tower; the **Palazzo del Popolo,** now the municipal museum, displaying Sienese and Renaissance paintings; and the Romanesque **Collegiata,** containing fine 15th-century frescoes by Domenico Ghirlandaio in the Chapel of Santa Fina. *Admission to palazzo and chapel: 5,000 lire. Open 9:30–12:30, 2:30–5:30, summer to 7:30.*

Before leaving San Gimignano, be sure to see its most famous work of art, at the northern end of town, in the church of **Sant' Agostino:** Benozzo Gozzoli's beautiful 15th-century fresco cycle depicting the life of St. Augustine. Also try a taste of Vernaccia, the local dry white wine.

❷⓿ Continue on to **Volterra,** 29 kilometers (18 miles) southwest of San Gimignano. D. H. Lawrence, in his *Etruscan Places,* sang the praises of Volterra, "standing somber and chilly alone on her rock." The town has long been known for its alabaster, which has been mined since Etruscan times; today the Volterrans use it to make ornaments and souvenirs sold all over town. A magnificent collection of small alabaster funerary urns that once held the ashes of deceased Etruscans (along with many other Etruscan artifacts) may be seen at the **Museo Etrusco Guarnacci** (Via Don Minzoni). Later art can be found in the **Duomo,** at the **Pinacoteca** (Palazzo Minucci-Solaini, Via dei Sarti 1), and at the **Museo di Arte Sacra** (Via Roma). The town's best-known Renaissance works are the 15th-century frescoes in the Duomo by Benozzo Gozzoli and the 16th-century *Deposition* by Rosso Fiorentino in the Pinacoteca. *Combined admission to Museo Etrusco Guarnacci, Pinacoteca, and Museo di Arte Sacra: 8,000 lire. Open Mar. 16–Oct. 14, daily 9:30–6:30 (Museo Etrusco Guarnacci closes 1–3); Oct. 15–Mar. 15, daily 9:30–1 (Museo Etrusco Guarnacci 9–2). Museo di Arte Sacra open daily 9–12:30.*

The walls of Volterra also harbor one of the few pieces of Etruscan architecture that escaped Roman destruction: the **Arco Etrusco,** with its weather-worn Etruscan heads, at the Porta all'Arco.

❷❶ On the other side of Siena, a major point of interest is **Arezzo,** 88 kilometers (55 miles) northeast of Siena. (You may want to break the drive halfway with a rest stop at **Monte San Savino,** a prosperous-looking small town, with the tiny nearby fortified village of **Gargonza** that has been carefully restored into a vacation resort; *see* Dining and Lodging, *below.*) Arezzo was the birthplace of the poet Petrarch; the Renaissance artist and art historian Giorgio Vasari; and Guido d'Arezzo, the inventor of musical notation. Today the town is best known for the magnificent, but very faint, Piero della Francesca frescoes in the church of **San Francesco,** on Via Cavour in the center of town. Painted between 1452 and 1466, they depict *The Legend of the True Cross* on three walls of the choir. What Sir Kenneth Clark called "the most perfect morning light in all Renaissance painting" may be seen in the lowest section of the right wall, where the troops of the Emperor Maxentius flee before the sign of the cross. Unfortunately, part of the frescoes may be hidden from view while restoration work takes place.

With its irregular shape and sloping brick pavement, framed by buildings of assorted centuries, Arezzo's **Piazza Grande** echoes Siena's Piazza del Campo. Though not so grand, it is lively enough during the outdoor antiques fair every first Sunday of the month and when the Joust of the Saracen, featuring medieval costumes and competition, is held there on the first Sunday of September. The curving, tiered apse on Piazza Grande belongs to Santa Maria della Pieve, one of Tuscany's finest Romanesque churches. And Arezzo's medieval cathedral at the top of the hill harbors an eye-level fresco of a tender Magdalen by Piero della Francesca; look for it next to the large marble tomb near the organ.

Other attractions in Arezzo include the church of **San Domenico,** which houses a 13th-century crucifix by Cimabue, located north of Piazza Grande at Piazza Fossombroni (just inside the walls); the **house** that Giorgio Vasari designed and decorated for himself in 1540, just west of San Domenico; and the **Museo Archeologico,** with a fine collection of Etruscan bronzes. *Vasari house: Via XX Settembre 55, tel. 0575/300301. Admission free. Open Tues.–Sat. 9–7, Sun. 9–1. Museo Archeologico: Via Margaritone 10, tel. 0575/20882. Admission: 6,000 lire. Open Tues.–Sat. 9–2, Sun. 9–1.*

About 30 kilometers (18 miles) south of Arezzo on S71, the medieval ㉒ town of **Cortona** is known for its excellent small art gallery and a number of fine antiques shops, as well as for its colony of foreign residents. Cortona has the advantage of being on the main train network, though you will have to take a local bus from the station up into the town, passing the Renaissance church of **Santa Maria del Calcinaio** on the way.

The heart of Cortona is formed by **Piazza della Repubblica** and the adjacent **Piazza Signorelli.** Wander into the courtyard of the picturesque **Palazzo Pretorio,** and, if you want to see a representative collection of Etruscan bronzes, climb its centuries-old stone staircase to the **Museo dell'Accademia Etrusca** (Gallery of Etruscan Art). *Piazza Signorelli 9, tel. 0575/630415. Admission: 5,000 lire. Open Apr.–Sept., Tues.–Sun. 10–1, 4–7; Oct.–Mar., Tues.–Sun. 9–1, 3–5.*

The nearby **Museo Diocesano** (Diocesan Museum) houses an impressive number of large and splendid paintings by native son Luca Signorelli, as well as a beautiful *Annunciation* by Fra Angelico, a delightful surprise to find in this small, eclectic town. *Piazza del Duomo 1, tel. 0575/62830. Admission: 5,000 lire. Open Apr.–Sept., Tues.–Sun. 9–1, 3–6:30; Oct.–Mar., Tues.–Sun. 9–1, 3–5.*

Tour 3: Southern Tuscany

The rolling green countryside of southern Tuscany is blanketed with woods; vines grow in rich, reddish-brown earth, and cypresses stand in ranks along roads leading to isolated stone farmhouses, unspoiled hill towns, and medieval abbeys.

This tour begins at **Chiusi,** known for the frescoed tombs dating from the 5th century BC in its necropolis. One of the most powerful of the 12 ancient cities in the Etruscan federation, Chiusi is a transportation hub accessible from either the main north–south rail line or by car or bus from the A1 autostrada. From here, head 12 kilometers (7½ miles) west to **Chianciano,** a modern spa with neat parks and a host of hotels clustered around the medieval walls of the old town.

Billboards here proclaim that Chianciano's restorative waters are indispensable for a *fegato sano*, a healthy liver.

The road north from Chianciano climbs and dips, winding through woods of evergreens and oaks and affording glimpses of the vineyards that are the pride of this part of Tuscany. Two of Italy's best wines—Brunello di Montalcino and Vino Nobile di Montepulciano—originate here and bear the names of the towns where they are made. About 20 kilometers (12 miles) northwest of Chiusi, **Montepulciano** sits high on a hilltop, a pyramid of redbrick buildings set within a circle of cypress trees. At an altitude of almost 2,000 feet, it is cool in summer and chilled in winter by biting winds that sweep its spiraling streets. The town has an unusually harmonious look, the result of the work of three architects, Sangallo il Vecchio, Vignola, and Michelozzo, who endowed it with fine palaces and churches. Their work began under the aegis of Cosimo I de' Medici, who financed the rebuilding of Montepulciano after the town opted for an alliance with Florence in the early 1500s. The 16th-century Renaissance buildings blend in well with earlier medieval edifices lining the stone streets that curve upward to **Piazza Grande.** Montepulciano's many wine cellars and antiques dealers and a few trendy shops and cafés hint that this otherwise sleepy town gets its share of tourists, especially during an international arts festival in July and August. On the hillside below the town walls is the church of **San Biagio,** designed by Sangallo, a paragon of Renaissance architectural perfection that is considered his masterpiece.

Another Florentine architect, Bernardo Rossellino, had his turn at achieving perfection when he was commissioned by vainglorious Pope Pius II, subject of Pinturicchio's frescoes in the Piccolomini Library in Siena, to design an entire town. A year after his election, the pope decided to transform his native village of Corsignano into a monument to himself. **Pienza,** 12 kilometers (7 miles) west of Montepulciano, is not only a curiosity—an imperious pope's personal utopia—it is also an exquisite example of the architectural canons formulated in the early Renaissance by Leon Battista Alberti and utilized by later architects, including Brunelleschi and Michelangelo, in designing many of Italy's finest buildings and piazzas. Today the cool grandeur of Pienza's center seems almost surreal in this otherwise unpretentious village, known locally for *pienzino*, also called *cacio*, a smooth goat cheese.

About 33 kilometers (20 miles) northwest of Pienza, accessible by car but not easily by bus, is the Benedictine **Abbey of Monte Oliveto Maggiore.** The abbey is an oasis of olive and cypress trees amid the harsh landscape of a zone known as the *crete*, where erosion has sculpted the hills starkly, laying open gashes of barren rock in lush farmland. Weather and time have taken their toll on the abbey itself; in 1993 the roof of the library, long closed while awaiting overdue repairs, simply collapsed. In the main cloister of the abbey, the frescoes by Luca Signorelli and Il Sodoma on the walls of the portico relate the life of St. Benedict with earthy realism, a quality that came naturally to Il Sodoma, described by Vasari as "a merry and licentious man . . . of scant chastity." True to his nickname, Il Sodoma delighted in painting handsome young men; he also included a rendering of his pet badger and raven with a robed, black-haired figure that is a self-portrait. *Admission free. Open daily 9–12:30, 1:30–6.*

Montalcino, about 25 kilometers (15 miles) west of Pienza, is another medieval hill town with a special claim to fame. It is home of Brunello di Montalcino, one of Italy's best red wines. You can sample it in wine cellars in town or visit a nearby winery for a free guided tour and tasting. One such winery is the Fattoria dei Barbi (*see* Dining and Lodging, *below*).

The **Abbey of Sant'Antimo,** about 10 kilometers (6 miles) southeast of Montalcino, below the town of Castelnuovo dell'Abbate, is worth a visit; it is a medieval gem of pale stone set in the silvery green of an olive grove. To end this itinerary, you could return by way of San Quirico d'Orcia to Pienza and then head northeast for 20 kilometers (12 miles) to **Sinalunga,** a town on the main train line and close to the A1 autostrada. Only 8 kilometers (5 miles) north of Sinalunga, **Lucignano** is another charming old hill town. Like Cortona, Lucignano has a small foreign colony of artists and writers who live on the outskirts in converted farmhouses.

What to See and Do with Children

Just outside Pistoia is the **Giardino Zoologico,** especially laid out to accommodate the wiles of both animals and children. *Via Pieve a Celle 160, Pistoia, tel. 0573/939219. Admission: 10,000 lire adults and children over 9, 7,500 lire children 3–9. Open Apr.–Sept., daily 9–7; Oct.–Mar., daily 9–5.*

Pinocchio aficionados will be delighted by the **Parco di Pinocchio** in Collodi, near Pescia. A statue of the long-nosed puppet is the center-piece of a garden containing sculptural groups that depict scenes from Carlo Lorenzini's children's classic, *The Adventures of Pinocchio.* Close by is the beautifully kept Italian garden of Villa Garzoni. *Parco di Pinocchio, Collodi, tel. 0572/429642. Admission: 8,000 lire adults, 4,000 lire children under 12. Open May–Sept., daily 8–9; Oct.–Apr., daily 8:30–6. Villa Garzoni, tel. 0572/428400. Admission: 8,000 lire. Open daily 8–one hour before sunset.*

Walking, hiking, and **picnicking** in the inviting, hilly Tuscan coun-tryside are natural attractions for children. In the hills of Garfagnana, above Lucca, is a tennis camp, **Il Ciocco,** especially de-signed for children; there are horseback riding, swimming, and health facilities, and adults can participate as well. *Centro Turistico Internazionale, Barga, Lucca, tel. 0583/710021.*

Off the Beaten Track

Elba. The largest island in the Tuscan archipelago, Elba is an hour by ferry or a half hour by Hovercraft from Piombino, or a short hop by air from Pisa. Its main port is **Portoferraio,** fortified in the 16th century by the Medici Grand Duke Cosimo I. Victor Hugo spent his boyhood here, and Napoleon his famous exile in 1814–15, when he built (out of two windmills) the **Palazzina Napoleonica dei Mulini** and (a few miles outside town) the **Villa San Martino.** *Palazzina Napoleonica and Villa San Martino, tel. 0565/915846. Admission: 5,000 lire for both if visiting on the same day. Open Tues.–Sat. 9–1:30, Sun. 9–1.*

The island's main attractions, however, are its rough landscape and pristine beaches offering a full array of sports. Portoferraio, the liveliest town and a transportation hub, is the best base for explor-ing the island. Good beaches can be found at Biodola, Procchio, and Marina di Campo. From Elba, private visits can be arranged to the other islands in the archipelago, including **Montecristo,** which in-spired Alexander Dumas's 19th-century best-seller *The Count of Monte Cristo* and is now a wildlife refuge. Elba's restaurants offer excellent seafood, to be sampled with the local Moscato and Aleatico wines.

Forte dei Marmi. Tuscany's most exclusive beach resort, a favorite of moneyed Tuscans and Milanese, whose villas are neatly laid out in an extensive pine wood, is 65 kilometers (30 miles) northwest of Florence by car. It is near the marble-producing towns of **Carrara** (where Michelangelo quarried his stone), **Seravezza,** and **Pietrasanta.**

Marlia. Eight kilometers (5 miles) north of Lucca is the handsome Villa Reale. Its superb gardens, laid out in the second half of the 17th century and surrounded by a park, are a fine place for a break and a stroll. *Villa Reale, tel. 0583/30108. Admission: 6,000 lire. Guided tours July–Sept., Tues.–Thurs., Sun. 10, 11, 4, 5, 6; Oct., Mar.–June, Tues.–Sun. 10, 11, 3, 4, 5.*

Shopping

Specialty Items **Arezzo** is known for its production of gold, as well as a burgeoning cottage knitwear industry. (For sweaters, try *Maglierie, Piazza Grande.*) The olive oil of **Lucca** is exported throughout the world. **Prato** makes hard almond cookies called *biscottini,* ideal for dunking in the beverage of one's choice. **Siena** is known for a variety of medieval desserts—*cavallucci, panforti,* and *ricciarelli*—as well as for ceramics. **Volterra** has a number of shops selling boxes, jewelry, and other objects made of alabaster. For information and directions, contact Cooperativa Artieri Alabastro (Piazza dei Priori 2, tel. 0588/87590).

Flea Markets The first Sunday of each month, a colorful flea market selling antiques and not-so-antiques takes place in Piazza Grande in **Arezzo.** On the second Sunday of the month, another market goes to Piazza San Martino in **Lucca.** In summer, a beachcomber's bonanza takes place Wednesday mornings in **Forte dei Marmi,** near Lucca, when everything from fake designer sunglasses to plastic sandals and terrycloth towels goes on sale.

Sports

Fishing For a license, contact the **Federazione Italiana della Pesca Sportiva** (Via dei Neri 6, Firenze). The spot for tuna fishing in Tuscany is **Punta Ala,** from September to October. Fishing trips and charters may be arranged through **Renato Lessi** (Località Porto, Punta Ala, Grosseto, tel. 0564/920710).

Golf Punta Ala is also the site of the **Golf Club Punta Ala,** an 18-hole course on the sea opposite the island of Elba (Via del Golf 1, Punta Ala, Grosseto, tel. 0564/922121).

Horseback Riding Some popular riding sites are **Rendola Riding** (Rendola Valdarno, Arezzo, tel. 0575/987045), **Rifugio Prategiano** (Montieri, Grosseto, tel. 0566/997703), **Le Cannelle** (Parco dell'Uccellina, Talamone, Grosseto, tel. 0564/887020). For more information, contact the **Federazione Italiana Sport Equestre** (Via Paoletti 54, Firenze, tel. 055/480039).

Sailing Charters in Tuscany are available through the **Centro Nautico Italiano** (Piazza della Signoria 31/r, Firenze, tel. 055/287045); **Mario Lorenzoni** (Via degli Alfani 105/r, Firenze, tel. 055/284790); and **Renato Lessi** (Località Porto, Castiglione della Pescaia, Grosseto, tel. 0564/922793). For more information, contact the **Federazione Italiana Vela** (CP 49, Marina di Carrara, tel. 0585/57323) or the **Federazione Italiana Motonautica** (Via Goldora 16, 55044 Marina di Pietrasanta, tel. 0584/20963).

Skiing The best spot for skiing in Tuscany is **Abetone.** For information, contact the **Federazione Italiana Sport Invernali** (Viale Matteotti 15, Firenze, tel. 055/576987).

Spectator Sports

Horse Racing Besides the racecourses in the **Cascine** in Florence, horse racing takes place in **Montecatini** and **Punta Ala,** as well as **San Rossore** and **Follonica.**

Dining and Lodging

Dining Though Florentine cuisine now predominates throughout Tuscany, the Etruscan influence on regional food still persists after more than three millennia. Just as the ancient Etruscans were responsible for the introduction of the cypress to the Tuscan landscape, so they are also credited with the use of herbs in cooking. Basic ingredients such as tarragon, sage, rosemary, and thyme appear frequently, happily coupled with game, Chianina beef, or even seafood. Each region has its own specialties, usually based on simple ingredients, and Tuscans are disparagingly called *mangiafagioli,* or bean eaters, by other Italians. However, Tuscan chefs have recently discovered the rest of the world, and for better or worse, an "international cuisine" has been gradually making its appearance throughout the region.

Fortunately, Tuscany's wines remain unaltered. Grapes have been cultivated here since Etruscan times, and Chianti still rules the roost (almost literally when selected by the *Gallo Nero,* Black Rooster, label, a symbol of one of the region's most powerful wine-growing consortiums; the other is a *putto,* or cherub). The robust red wine is still a staple on most tables, and the discerning can select from a multitude of other varieties, including such reds as Brunello di Montalcino and Vino Nobile di Montepulciano, and whites such as Valdinievole and Vergine della Valdichiana. The dessert wine *vin santo* is produced throughout the region and is often enjoyed with biscottini di Prato, which are perfect for dunking.

Highly recommended restaurants are indicated by a star ★.

Category	Cost*
$$$$	over 110,000 lire
$$$	60,000–110,000 lire
$$	35,000–60,000 lire
$	under 35,000 lire

per person, for a three-course meal, including house wine and taxes

Lodging Highly recommended lodgings are indicated by a star ★.

Category	Cost*
$$$$	over 300,000 lire
$$$	220,000–300,000 lire

$$	100,000–220,000 lire
$	under 100,000 lire

All prices are for a double room for two, including tax and service.

Arezzo
Dining

Buca di San Francesco. A frescoed cellar restaurant in a historic building next to the church of San Francesco, this "buca" (literally "hole," figuratively "cellar") has a medieval atmosphere and serves straightforward local specialties. Vegetarians will like the *ribollita* (vegetable soup thickened with bread) and the *sformato di verdure* (spinach or chard pie), though it may be served *con cibreo* (with a giblet sauce). Meat eaters will find the lean Chianina beef a succulent treat. *Piazza San Francesco 1, tel. 0575/23271. Reservations advised. Dress: casual. AE, DC, MC, V. Closed Mon. dinner, Tues., and July. $$*

Tastevin. Close to San Francesco and to the central Piazza Guido Monaco, Tastevin has introduced creative cooking styles in Arezzo but serves traditional dishes as well, in three attractive dining rooms, two in warm Tuscan provincial style, one in more sophisticated bistro style. At the small bar the talented owner plays and sings show tunes and Sinatra songs in the evening; there is a 15% cover charge for music. The restaurant's specialties are risotto *tastevin* (with cream of truffles) and seafood or meat *carpaccio* (sliced raw). *Via dei Cenci 9, tel. 0575/28304. Dinner reservations advised. Dress: casual. AE, DC, MC, V. Closed Mon. (Sun. in summer). $$*

Spiedo d'Oro. Cheery red-and-white tablecloths add a bright note to this large, reliable trattoria near the archeological museum. This is your chance to try authentic Tuscan home-style specialties, such as *zuppa di pane* (bread soup), *pappardelle all'ocio* (noodles with duck sauce), and *osso buco all'aretina* (sautéed veal shank). *Via Crispi 12, tel. 0575/22873. No reservations. Dress: casual. V. Closed Thurs. and July 1–18. $*

Lodging

Continental. Centrally located near the train station and within walking distance of all major sights, the Continental has been a reliable and convenient place to stay since it opened in the 1950s. Recently refurbished, it now has bright white furnishings with yellow accents, gleaming new bathrooms complete with hair dryers, and a pleasant roof garden. Rates are at the low end of the $$ category. *Piazza Guido Monaco 7, tel. 0575/20251, fax 0575/340485. 74 rooms with bath or shower. Facilities: roof garden, restaurant (closed Sun. dinner, Mon. $$). AE, DC, MC, V. $$*

**Casola d'Elsa/
Pievescola**
*Dining and
Lodging*

La Suvera. This luxurious estate in the lovely valley of the river Elsa, 28 kilometers (17 miles) west of Siena and 56 kilometers (35 miles) south of Florence, was once owned by Pope Julius II. The papal villa and adjacent buildings have been restored to accommodate guests in rooms and suites that are magnificently furnished with antiques and appointed with the latest comforts. With drawing rooms, a library, Italian garden, park, pool, and the Oliviera restaurant (serving estate wines) to enjoy, guests find it hard to tear themselves away, though there is plenty to see in the vicinity. *Pievescola (Casola d'Elsa), off S541, tel. 0577/960300, fax 0577/960220. 25 rooms and 10 suites with bath. Facilities: park, heated pool, sauna, tennis, riding, restaurant, bar, heliport, conference rooms. AE, DC, MC, V. Open Mar. 15–Nov. 15. $$$–$$$$*

Colle Val d'Elsa
Dining and Lodging

Villa Belvedere. This stately villa was the residence of Ferdinand III, archduke of Austria and grand duke of Tuscany in 1820. Set in a large park, the entire villa, including the quiet bedrooms overlooking the park, is furnished in 19th-century (or even earlier) antiques. The location within 12 kilometers (about 8 miles) of both Siena and San Gimignano makes it a good choice for anyone touring by car. *Località Belvedere (Colle Val d'Elsa Sud exit on superstrada), tel. 0577/920966. 15 rooms with bath. Facilities: restaurant (closed Wed.), bar, garden, pool. AE, DC, MC, V. $$*

Cortona
Dining

La Loggetta. Located above Cortona's main medieval square, this attractive restaurant occupies a 16th-century wine cellar; its four ample dining rooms have a relaxing atmosphere and tasteful decor in keeping with the setting. In fair weather you can eat outdoors, overlooking the 13th-century town hall, dining on regional dishes and such specialties as cannelloni (crêpes filled with spinach and ricotta) and *lombatine al cartoccio* (veal chops with porcini mushrooms). The owners pride themselves on their selection of Tuscan wines. *Piazza Pescheria 3, tel. 0575/630575. No reservations. Dress: casual. AC, DC, MC, V. Closed Sun. dinner (except summer), Mon., Jan. 5–Feb. 10, 2 weeks in July. $$*

Tonino. Deservedly well known and popular with locals and visitors alike, this large modern establishment can be noisy and crowded on holiday weekends. But it is very satisfactory indeed at all other times, when you can enjoy the view of the Chiana valley and feast on host Tonino's own *antipastissimo*, an incredible variety of delectables. This is the place to taste Chiana beefsteak. *Piazza Garibaldi, tel. 0575/630500. Reservations advised, especially weekends. Dress: casual. AE, DC, MC, V. Closed Mon. dinner, Tues. $$*

Gargonza
Dining and Lodging

Castello di Gargonza. A tiny 13th-century hill town with a castle, church, and cobbled streets offers something unusual as hostelries go. All its houses—cottages, really—are for rent by the week, and rooms can be had by the night. This enchanting spot in the countryside between Siena and Arezzo, part of the fiefdom of the aristocratic Florentine Guicciardini family, was restored by the modern Count Roberto Guicciardini as a way to rescue a dying village. The houses have one to six rooms each, sleep two to seven people, and have as many as four baths. La Torre restaurant serves local specialties. *52048 Monte San Savino, tel. 0575/847021, fax 0575/847054. 18 houses with bath. Facilities: restaurant (closed Tues. $$), parking. AE, MC, V. $$ weekly; inquire about daily rate. Closed Jan. 10–Feb. 10.*

Lucca
Dining

Solferino. About 6 kilometers (4 miles) outside town, on the road to Viareggio, this pleasant restaurant serves exquisite variations of regional favorites, such as *anatra ripiena in crema di funghi* (stuffed duck with mushroom sauce), made with ingredients from the family farm. Ask for a piece of buccellato, a sweet, anise-flavored bread with raisins that is a specialty of Lucca. *San Macario in Piano, tel. 0583/59118. Reservations required. Dress: casual. AE, DC, MC, V. Closed Wed., Thurs. lunch, 2 weeks in mid-Aug., Jan. 7–15. $$$*

★ **La Mora.** Some 9 kilometers (6 miles) outside Lucca, this former country inn and coach station is worth going out of your way. The menu offers a range of local specialties, from *minestra di farro* (wheat soup) with beans to *tacconi* (homemade pasta) with rabbit sauce and lamb from the nearby Garfagnana hills. You'll be tempted by the variety of *crostini* (toast with liver pâté) and delicious desserts as well. *Via Sesto di Ponte a Moriano 1748, tel. 0583/406402.*

Reservations advised. Dress: casual. AE, DC, MC, V. Closed Wed.
dinner, Thurs. and June 25–July 8, Oct. 10–30. $$–$$$

Buca di Sant'Antonio. Near the church of San Michele, this was once a rustic inn. The specialties here are local dishes, some unfamiliar but well worth trying, such as *ravioli di ricotta alle zucchine* (cheese ravioli with zucchini) and roast *capretto* (kid) or *agnello* (lamb) with savory herb seasoning. *Via della Cervia 3, tel. 0583/55881. Dinner reservations advised. Dress: casual. AE, DC, MC, V. Closed Sun. dinner and Mon.; July 9–29. $$*

Il Giglio. Located just off Piazza Napoleone and close to the Hotel Universo, this restaurant has quiet, turn-of-the-century charm and classic cuisine. Seafood is a specialty, but it can be expensive. You may prefer to order crostini and *stracotto* (braised beef with mushrooms). *Piazza del Giglio 3, tel. 0583/494508. Dinner reservations advised. Dress: casual. AE, DC, MC, V. Closed Tues. dinner, Wed. $$*

Lodging **Villa La Principessa.** Just outside Lucca, only 3 kilometers (2 miles) from town, this is an exquisitely decorated 19th-century country mansion that has been converted into an exclusive hotel. Some rooms have beamed ceilings, and doors are individually decorated; antique furniture and portraits give an aura of gracious living. The restaurant is known for its creative cuisine. A well-manicured park and large swimming pool lure guests outdoors in fair weather. *Massa Pisana, tel. 0583/370037, fax 0583/379136. 44 rooms and suites with bath. Facilities: restaurant (closed Sun.), park, pool. AE, DC, MC, V. Closed Nov. 5–Mar. 31. $$$*

La Luna. There's an aura of Old World charm in this family-run hotel on one of Lucca's most central and historic streets. Recent extensive renovations have endowed the establishment with sparkling modern bathrooms while leaving the atmosphere intact. A plus for anyone touring by car is the hotel's own garage and parking area. *Corte Compagni 12 (corner of Via Fillungo), tel. 0583/493634, fax 0583/490021. 30 rooms with bath. AE, DC, MC, V. Closed Dec. 24–Jan. 6. $$*

Ilaria. A family-run hotel beside a minuscule canal within easy walking distance of the main sights, it has rooms that are small but fresh and functional. *Via del Fosso 20, tel. 0583/47558. 17 rooms, 12 with bath. AE, DC, MC, V. $*

Montalcino **La Cucina di Edgardo.** This tiny restaurant on Montalcino's main
Dining street seats 30 in two charming dining rooms done in off-white and beige with dark wooden beams, a fireplace, and terra-cotta floors. It offers a complete menu, including everything from antipasto to after-dinner sweets, wine, and mineral water, for about 60,000 lire. The specialties of the house are *crema contadina* (bean soup garnished with onion) and *brasato al Brunello* (beef braised in the local Brunello wine). *Via Soccorsi Saloni 33, tel. 0577/848232. Reservations advised, especially weekends and summer. Dress: casual. AE, DC, MC, V. Closed Wed. and Jan. 10–30. $$*

★ **Taverna dei Barbi.** A meal at this delightful tavern, set among vineyards and mellow brick buildings on a wine-producing country estate (Fattoria dei Barbi), may well be a highlight of your journey through this part of Tuscany. The rustic dining room features a beamed ceiling, huge stone fireplace, and arched windows. The estate farm produces practically all the ingredients used in such traditional specialties as *zuppa di fagioli* (country-style bean soup with chard) and *scottiglia di pollo* (browned chicken served with garlic bread). The estate-produced Brunello is excellent, and other wines with the Barbi label are available. *Fattoria dei Barbi, tel. 0577/*

849357. Reservations required. Dress: casual. No credit cards. Closed Tues. dinner Oct.–May and Wed., Jan. 15–31, July 1–15. $$

Montepulciano
Dining and Lodging

Il Marzocco. A 16th-century building within the town walls, it is furnished in 19th-century style, complete with dignified, old-fashioned parlors and a billiard room. Many bedrooms have large terraces overlooking the countryside, and many rooms are large enough to accommodate extra beds; they are furnished in heavy turn-of-the-century style or in spindly white wood. *Piazza Savonarola 18, tel. 0578/757262. 18 rooms, 13 with bath or shower. Facilities: restaurant (closed Wed.). AE, DC, MC, V. $$*

Monteriggioni
Dining

Il Pozzo. On the village square, this rustic tavern serves hearty Tuscan country cooking, including *maltagliati al sugo di agnello* (fresh pasta in a tomato sauce made with lamb) and *cinghiale in dolce forte* (boar with a tangy sauce). The desserts are homemade. *Piazza Roma 2, tel. 0577/304127. Reservations advised. Dress: casual. AE, DC, MC, V. Closed Sun. dinner, Mon., and Jan., July 31–Aug. 10. $$*

Pisa
Dining

Bruno. A pleasant restaurant, with beamed ceilings and the look of a country inn, Bruno is located just outside the old city walls, a short walk from the bell tower and cathedral. Dine on classic Tuscan dishes, from *zuppa alla pisana* (thick vegetable soup) to *baccalà con porri* (cod with leeks). *Via Luigi Bianchi 12, tel. 050/560818. Dinner reservations advised. Dress: casual. AE, DC, MC, V. Closed Mon. dinner, Tues., and Aug. 5–15. $$*

Osteria dei Cavalieri. Just off the beautiful old Piazza dei Cavalieri, this popular tavern has a one-course lunch menu and offers vegetarian dishes, too. The cordial owner also proposes a range of meat and fish choices, including *faraone al forno* (roast guinea hen with mushrooms). *Via San Frediano 16, tel. 050/580858. Reservations advised in the evening. Dress: casual. MC, V. Closed Sat. lunch, Sun. and Aug. $$*

La Pergoletta. In a medieval tower in the heart of the old town, La Pergoletta is on a street named for its "beautiful towers." The restaurant is small and simple and has a shady garden for outdoor dining. The signora who is the owner-cook offers traditional Tuscan minestra di farro and *grigliata* (grilled beef, veal, or lamb). *Via delle Belle Torri 36, tel. 050/542458. Reservations advised. MC, V. Closed Tues. and Aug. $$*

Lodging

Cavalieri. Opposite the railway station, in an unremarkable 1950s building, this hotel offers functional, modern comforts in completely soundproof and air-conditioned rooms, all with color TV and minibar. The restaurant specializes in homemade pasta and seafood and is open every day. *Piazza della Stazione 2, tel. 050/43290, fax 050/502242. 100 rooms with bath or shower. Facilities: bar, garage. AE, DC, MC, V. $$$*

Royal Victoria. In a pleasant palazzo facing the Arno, a 10-minute walk from the Campo dei Miracoli, this hotel is about as close as Pisa comes to Old World ambience. It's comfortably furnished, featuring antiques and reproductions in the lobby and in some rooms, in which the decor varies from functional modern to turn-of-the-century. There's a large restaurant open every day for hotel guests. *Lungarno Pacinotti 12, tel. 050/940111. 67 rooms, 46 with bath. AE, DC, MC, V. $$*

Pistoia
Dining

La Casa degli Amici. The name means "the house of friends," and that's the atmosphere that the two industrious ladies who own it succeed in creating in this restaurant located outside Pistoia's old walls, on the road toward the exit of the A11 autostrada. They offer homey specialties such as ribollita and pasta e fagioli, and some creative dishes, too. There's a terrace for outdoor dining in the summer. *Via Bonellina 111, tel. 0573/380305. Reservations advised. Dress: casual. AE, DC, MC, V. Closed Sun. dinner, Tues., and Aug. $$*

Leon Rosso. From the center of town take Via Roma, off the beautiful Piazza del Duomo, and walk straight ahead to find this small and usually crowded restaurant. It serves Tuscan cuisine, starting with appetizing crostini and *fusilli all'orto* (corkscrew pasta with seasonal vegetables). For dessert try *panna cotta* (milk custard) with caramel sauce. *Via Panciatichi 4, tel. 0573/29230. Reservations advised. Dress: casual. AE, DC, MC, V. Closed Sun., Aug. $$*

Rafanelli. *Maccheroni all'anatra* (pasta with duck sauce) and other game dishes are the specialties, served with careful attention to tradition and quality for more than half a century by the same family. The restaurant is located just outside the old city walls; prices are in the low range of this category. *Via Sant'Agostino 47, tel. 0573/ 532046. No reservations. Dress: casual. AE, DC, MC, V. Closed Sun. dinner, Mon., and Aug. $$*

Prato
Dining

Piraña. Oddly named for the cannibalistic fish swimming in an aquarium in full view of diners, this sophisticated restaurant, decorated in shades of blue with steely accents, is a favorite in Prato. Seafood is the specialty and may take the form of *ravioli di pesce* (seafood ravioli with cream of scampi sauce) or *rombo* al forno (baked turbot). It's a bit out of the way for sightseers but handy if you have a car, for it's near the Prato Est autostrada exit. *Via G. Valentini 110, tel. 0574/25746. Reservations advised. Dress: casual. AE, DC, MC, V. Closed Sat. lunch, Mon. lunch, Sun., and Aug. $$$*

La Veranda. A large antipasto buffet greets you just inside the door of this restaurant near Prato's 13th-century Castello dell'Imperatore. The decor is elegant, with pale pink walls, terra-cotta tiled floors, and Venetian glass chandeliers, but the atmosphere is friendly and family oriented. Although the large menu has several international dishes, including Spanish paella, it does not ignore Tuscan specialties: *agnello alla cacciatora* (lamb with a tangy wine-vinegar sauce) or *tagliata* (sliced beef) with rucola and truffle are two good choices. *Via dell'Arco 10, tel. 0574/38235. Dress: casual. AE, DC, MC, V. Closed Sat. lunch, Sun., and Aug. $$*

San
Gimignano
Dining

Bel Soggiorno. On the top floor of a 100-year-old inn, this rustic restaurant has a wall of windows from which to view the landscape. Tuscan specialties include *pappardelle alla lepre* (noodles with hare sauce) and risotto *del Bel Soggiorno* (with saffron and nutmeg). *Via San Giovanni 91, tel. 0577/940375. Reservations advised. Dress: casual. AE, DC, MC, V. Closed Mon. and Jan. 7–Feb. 7. $$*

Le Terrazze. This restaurant in a time-honored inn in the heart of San Gimignano has a charming view of rooftops and countryside and an ample menu featuring Tuscan dishes in seasonal variations. The specialties are served *alla sangimignanese* (finished off in the oven). *Piazza della Cisterna 23, tel. 0577/940328. Reservations advised. Dress: casual. AE, DC, MC, V. Closed Tues. and Wed. lunch and Nov. 10–Mar. 10. $$*

Stella. At this rustic, upscale trattoria, located between the main church and that of Sant'Agostino, prices are more moderate than at places with a view. The owner prides himself on farm-fresh vegetables and his own olive oil. The specialty of the house is grilled meat, including beef, lamb, and pork. *Via San Matteo 77, tel. 0577/940444. Reservations not required. Dress: casual. AE, DC, MC, V. Closed Wed. and Jan. 6–Feb. 15. $$*

Lodging
★ **Pescille.** This is a rambling farmhouse situated 8 kilometers (5 miles) outside San Gimignano that has been converted into a handsome hotel, in which restrained contemporary and country classic decors blend well. It also houses the fine Cinque Gigli restaurant. *Località Pescille, Strada Castel San Gimignano, tel. 0577/940186, fax 0577/ 940186. 33 rooms with bath. Facilities: outdoor pool, tennis, park, restaurant (closed Wed.). AE, DC, MC, V. Closed Jan.–Feb. $$*

Siena
Dining
★ **Al Marsili.** Located between Piazza del Campo and the cathedral, this 900-year-old wine cellar is an elegant place to dine, under broad, brick-vaulted ceilings. The menu offers Tuscan and Italian specialties, among them homemade pastas such as *pici* and *tortelloni burro e salvia* (large cheese-filled ravioli with butter and sage). Various meat dishes are cooked in wine, and the wine list features the finest Tuscan and Italian labels, including many from the nearby Chianti country. *Via del Castoro 3, tel. 0577/47154. Reservations advised. Dress: casual. AE, DC, MC, V. Closed Mon. $$*

★ **Le Logge.** Near Piazza del Campo, this typically Sienese trattoria has rustic dining rooms on two levels and tables outdoors from June to October. The menu features Tuscan dishes, such as *pennette all'osteria* (pasta with creamy herbed sauce) and *coniglio con pignoli* (rabbit with pine nuts). *Via del Porrione 33, tel. 0577/48013. Reservations advised. Dress: casual. MC, V. Closed Sun. and June 1–15, Nov. 1–15. $$*

Tullio Tre Cristi. This is a typical and historic neighborhood trattoria, long ago discovered by tourists and still reliable. The paintings on the walls are by famous local artists of the 1920s, but the culinary tradition here goes back even further. Try spaghetti *alle briciole*, a poor-man's dish of pasta with bread-crumbs, tomato, and garlic, or veal escalopes subtly flavored with *dragoncello* (tarragon). You can eat outdoors in summer. To find the restaurant, take Via dei Rossi from Via Banchi di Sopra. *Vicolo di Provenzano 1, tel. 0577/280608. Reservations advised. Dress: casual. MC, V. Closed Sun. dinner, Mon., and mid-Jan–mid-Feb. $$*

Lodging
★ **Certosa di Maggiano.** A former 14th-century monastery converted into an exquisite country hotel, this haven of gracious living is little more than a mile from the center of Siena. The atmosphere is that of an exclusive retreat in which a select number of guests enjoy the style and comfort of an aristocratic villa. *Via Certosa 82, tel. 0577/ 288180, fax 0577/288189. 18 rooms with bath. Facilities: outdoor pool, tennis, gardens, restaurant (closed Tues. $$$). AE, DC, MC, V. $$$$*

Park. Set among olive groves and gardens on a hillside just outside the city walls, this hotel offers solid comfort and spacious rooms with views of the grounds and countryside. A historic 16th-century villa, it has the restful atmosphere and antique charm of Tuscan country life. The Olivo restaurant is known for fine regional cuisine. *Via Marciano 18, tel. 0577/44803, fax 0577/49020. 68 double rooms with bath or shower. Facilities: pool, 2 tennis courts, riding, park, minibus service to town, 2 restaurants, poolside service, Caminetto bar. AE, DC, MC, V. $$$$*

Antica Torre. A restored 17th-century tower within the town walls in the southeast corner of Siena, Antica Torre is a 10-minute walk from Piazza del Campo. It is the work of a cordial couple who have created the atmosphere of a private home, furnished simply but in good taste and with only eight guest rooms. The old stone staircase and brick-vaulted ceilings here and there are reminders of the building's august age. *Via Fieravecchia 7, tel. 0577/222255, fax 0577/ 222255. 8 rooms with bath. MC, V. $–$$*

Chiusarelli. A handy location—near the long-distance bus terminal and a parking area and only a 10-minute walk from the main sights—makes this hotel a good choice. In a well-kept neoclassic villa, built in the early 1900s complete with caryatids, it has functional rooms that are airy and reasonably quiet. There is a small garden and a downstairs restaurant that caters to tour groups. *Viale Curtatone 9, tel. 0577/280562, fax 0577/271177. 50 rooms with bath. MC, V. $–$$*

Duomo. Occupying the top floor of a 300-year-old building in the center of Siena, near Piazza del Campo, the hotel is quiet and is furnished in a neat contemporary style, with traces of the past showing in the artfully exposed brickwork in the breakfast room. Many bedrooms have superb views of the city's towers and the hilly countryside. Two rooms are endowed with balconies. *Via Stalloreggi 38, tel. 0577/289088, fax 0577/43043. 23 rooms with bath. AE, MC, V. $–$$*

Sinalunga
Dining and Lodging
★

Locanda dell'Amorosa. A medieval hamlet set in Tuscan farmland has become a rustic retreat for jaded city folk, who reserve ahead for a meal or weekend in the country only a half-hour by car from Siena or Arezzo and even less from Montepulciano, Cortona, and Monte Oliveto Maggiore. The stone and brick buildings have been tastefully adapted for their current use, and the restaurant serves regional dishes that seem to taste even better in such apt surroundings. You can take home estate-produced wines and preserves as a souvenir of your stay. *Località Amorosa, Sinalunga, 10 km (6 mi) from the Valdichiana exit of A1, tel. 0577/679497, fax 0577/678216. 15 rooms with bath. Facilities: pool, restaurant (reservations required; dress: casual). AE, DC, MC, V. Closed Mon. and Tues. lunch and Jan. 15–Feb. 28). $$$$*

La Bandita. This attractive old farmhouse has been converted into a hotel by the Fiorini family. It has great charm, with terra-cotta floors throughout, lace curtains and antique pieces in the bedrooms, and a fireplace and grandfather's 19th-century Tuscan provincial furniture in a large, brick-vaulted living room. Some rooms can accommodate an extra bed, there is a garden, and meals are available. *Via Bandita 72, Bettolle (1 km, [.6 mi], from the Valdichiana exit of the A1 autostrada), tel. 0577/624649, fax 0577/624649. 8 rooms, 4 with bath. AE, DC, MC, V. $*

Volterra
Dining

Etruria. This restaurant on the town's main square, serves an excellent minestra di farro, an array of local game, and its own version of *panforte*, the dark, hard dessert cake that dates from medieval times. *Piazza dei Priori 8, tel. 0588/86064. No reservations. Dress: casual. AE, DC, MC, V. Closed Thurs. and Nov. 10–30, Jan. $$*

Lodging

San Lino. Located in a former convent, this hotel has modern comforts, a swimming pool, and its own regional restaurant. On top of that, it's located within the town walls, 10 minutes' walk from the main piazza. *Via San Lino 26, tel. 0588/85250, fax 0588/85250. 43 rooms with bath. Facilities: pool, restaurant (closed lunch and Wed.). AE, DC, MC, V. $$*

The Arts

Theater The seasons at the **Teatro Metastasio** (which include performances at a converted factory space called the **Capannone**), in Prato, run from January to May and October to December.

Music The Tuscan hills ring with music from July to September, when music festivals abound. These include the **Estate Musicale Lucchese,** in Lucca; the **Festival di Marlia;** and other festivals in Barga and Torre del Lago. In late July and August Siena hosts the **Settimane**

Musicali Senesi. The **Cantiere Internazionale d'Arte,** held in July and August in Montepulciano, is a multifaceted festival of figurative art, music, and theater, ending with a major theatrical production in Piazza Grande.

6 Venice

Venice is one of those cities you either love or you hate. Some people are repelled by its maze of narrow snaking streets, the faint smell of decay rising from the canals, and the hordes of pigeons and tourists in Piazza San Marco; they feel claustrophobic, longing for more grand vistas crowned with monumental architecture. But the far greater number of travelers are simply bowled over by this incredible treasure of a city. No matter how many times you have seen it in pictures or movies or TV commercials, the real thing is stranger and more lovely than you ever imagined. Its landmarks, the Basilica di San Marco and the Palazzo Ducale, are delightfully idiosyncratic, exotic mishmashes of Byzantine, Gothic, and Renaissance styles. Piazza San Marco is a true public gathering space, full of music and laughter and joy, yet only a minute's walk away are streets so quiet that your footsteps echo on the stone pavements and shuttered, crumbling facades. Sunlight shimmers here, and silvery mist softens every perspective. It is a city full of secrets, ineffably romantic, and given over entirely to pleasure.

Venice today is in one important way the same as it was more than 1,000 years ago, when inhabitants from the mainland defied the sea to build a city on forests of tree trunks driven into the mud flats of a treacherous lagoon. The intervening centuries saw the development of some of the world's most inspired architecture, but water remains the city's defining feature.

You must walk everywhere in Venice, and where you cannot walk, you go by water. Occasionally, from fall to spring, you have to walk *in* water, when extraordinarily high tides known as *acque alte* invade the lower parts of the city, flooding Piazza San Marco for a few hours. Unless you're lucky to find one of the makeshift plank bridges that appear from nowhere to keep certain busy routes open, you'll have to take off your socks and shoes, roll up your pantlegs, and wade in with everyone else. The problem of protecting Venice and its lagoon from dangerously high tides has generated extravagant plans and so many committee reports that the city may sink as much under the weight of paper as under that of the water. For centuries Venice's canals were regularly dredged to keep them clean and navigable. However, this operation has not been systematically carried out for more than 20 years. As a result, when there are *acque basse* (exceptionally low tides) some canals are left waterless and malodorous. For several years now the municipality has been promising to remedy this sad situation.

Then there are the hordes of tourists from all over the world that flow through Piazza San Marco and eddy wide-eyed around stern guides imparting succinct history lessons in a babble of tongues. Like the Venetians, you will have to adapt to the crowds, visiting the major sights at odd hours, when the tour groups are still at breakfast or have boarded buses on their return to the mainland (most of them are day-trippers). Get away from Piazza San Marco when it's crowded; you'll be surprised to find many areas of Venice practically deserted. Explore the districts of Cannaregio or Castello, quiet areas where you can find the time and space to sit and contemplate the watercolor pages of Venetian history.

The resourceful Venetians who built this island city during Europe's Dark Ages used their navigational and trading talents to turn an out-of-the-way refuge against the marauding barbarians into a staunch—and very rich—bulwark of Christendom that later held against the tides of Turkish expansion. Early in its history the city called in Byzantine artists to decorate its churches with brilliant mosaics, still glowing today. Then the influence of Lombard-Romanesque architecture from the 11th to 13th centuries gave rise to the characteristic type of palace for which Venice is famous the world over. Many of the sumptuous palaces along the Grand Canal were built at that time, strong reminders of Venice's control of the major trading routes to the East. Subsequently, Gothic styles from elsewhere in Europe were adapted to create a new kind of Venetian Gothic art and architecture.

Venice attained a peak of power and wealth in the 15th and 16th centuries. It extended its domain inland to include all of what is now known as the Veneto region and even beyond. In the last half of the 15th century, the Renaissance arrived in Venice, and its artists began to write a new and important chapter in the history of painting. Venice's greatest artists were major figures indeed—Giovanni Bellini in the late 15th century; Titian, Veronese, and Tintoretto in the 16th century—and their work covers walls and ceilings and altars all over the city still today.

The decline of Venice came slowly. For 400 years the powerful maritime city-republic had held sway. After the 16th century the tide changed. The Ottoman Empire blocked Venice's Mediterranean trade routes, and newly emerging sea powers, such as Britain and the Netherlands, broke Venice's monopoly by opening up oceanic trading routes. Like its steadily dwindling fortunes, Venice's art and culture began a prolonged decline, leaving only the splendid monuments to recall a glorious past, with the luminous paintings of Canaletto and the beautiful frescoes of Tiepolo striking a glorious swan song.

You can see the panoply of history by visiting only the major museums and churches, but if you want a fuller picture of the districts that keep this a living city, get off the beaten track as often as you can. You'll need a detailed map showing most, if not all, street names and *vaporetto* (water bus) routes, but you'll probably get lost anyway (everyone does). Ask directions from shopkeepers or at a café where locals outnumber the tourists; chances are, they will admire your initiative and put you back on the right track.

Essential Information

Arriving and Departing by Plane

Airports and Airlines
Marco Polo airport at Tessera, about 10 kilometers (6 miles) north of the city on the mainland, is served by domestic and international Alitalia flights, including service from London, Amsterdam, Brussels, Frankfurt, Munich, Paris, Vienna, and Zurich. For information, call tel. 041/661262.

Between the Airport and Downtown
By Bus
Blue **ATVO** buses make the 25-minute nonstop trip from the airport to Piazzale Roma, which is where the road ends at the entrance to Venice; from Piazzale Roma you can get a water bus to the landing nearest your hotel. ATVO fare is 5,000 lire. There are local **ACTV** buses from the airport, but you need a ticket (fare 1,000 lire) before boarding the bus, and there is no ticket office at the airport. You can buy a ticket at the tobacconist stand in the airport, but this is not always open. Also, luggage can be a problem on the ACTV bus, which is usually crowded with local commuters.

By Taxi
A yellow taxi from the airport to Piazzale Roma costs about 45,000 lire.

By Boat   Depending on where your hotel is, this may be the best way to get to Venice from the airport. The most direct way is by the **Cooperativa San Marco** launch, with regular scheduled service throughout the day, until midnight; it takes about an hour to get to the landing just off Piazza San Marco, stopping at the Lido on the way, and the fare is 15,000 lire per person, including bags. A **water taxi** (a sleek, modern motorboat known as a *motoscafo*) from the airport costs about 100,000 lire, but it is always wise to agree on a water-taxi fare before boarding.

Arriving and Departing by Car, Train, and Bus

By Car   If you bring a car to Venice, you will have to pay for a garage or parking space during your stay. Parking at Piazzale Roma (run by the city) costs between 13,000 and 23,000 lire per day, depending on the size of the car. To reach the privately-run Tronchetto parking area, follow the signs to turn right before Piazzale Roma (do not on any account allow yourself to be waylaid by illegal touts, often wearing fake uniforms, who will try to flag you down and offer to arrange parking and hotels), and continue on until you reach the automatic ticket machines. Parking here costs around 30,000 lire per day under cover and 18,000 outside. (Do not leave valuables in the car. There is a left-luggage office, open daily 8 AM–8 PM, next to the Pullman Bar on the ground floor of the municipal garage at Piazzale Roma.) The Venetian Hoteliers Association (AVA) has arranged a discount of about 40% for hotel guests who use the official Tronchetto parking facility. Ask for a voucher on checking into your hotel; it will be issued when you settle the hotel bill. Present the voucher at Tronchetto when you pay the parking fee.

There is a vaporetto (at press time, No. 82) from Tronchetto to Piazzale Roma and Piazza San Marco. (When there is thick fog or extreme tides, a bus runs to Piazzale Roma instead.) At all costs, avoid private boats—they are a rip-off. You can take your car to the Lido, the long, narrow island guarding the Venetian lagoon; the car ferry (Line 17) leaves about every 50 minutes from a landing at Tronchetto, but in summer there can be long delays.

By Train   Venice has rail connections with every major city in Italy and the rest of Europe.

Santa Lucia Station is on the Grand Canal in the northwest corner of the city. Some through trains do not terminate at Santa Lucia, stopping only at the Venezia-Mestre Station on the mainland. All trains traveling to and from Santa Lucia stop at Mestre, so to get from Venezia-Mestre to Santa Lucia, or vice versa (a 10-minute trip), take the first available train. For train information, call tel. 041/715555 from 7:10 AM to 9:30 PM.

By Bus   The bus terminal is at Piazzale Roma, near the vaporetto stop of that name. Express buses operated by SITA connect Venice with major cities and towns in the region.

Porters   Because there are no cars in Venice, people sometimes need porters to help carry their luggage and negotiate the footbridges. Porters wear badges and blue shirts or coats. You will find them at the airport and train stations and also at some of the principal vaporetto landings. They charge about 15,000 lire for one bag and about 5,000 lire for each additional piece of luggage, and there is an extra charge at night and on holidays. A porter will accompany you all the way to the vaporetto between your hotel and Santa Lucia Station or Piazzale Roma; the fee is about 50,000 lire. Since you can't always count on finding a porter when you need one, a folding luggage cart will prove invaluable (suitcases with wheels are not the answer on uneven paving stones and over bridges).

However you arrive in Venice, find out the location of your hotel beforehand and exactly how to get there. Depending on its location, regardless of whether you take a vaporetto or water taxi to the nearest landing, you may have to walk some distance from the landing to reach it, with or without the help and guidance of a porter. Be prepared to find your way on your own or to call the hotel for instructions upon arrival.

Getting Around

First-time visitors find that getting around Venice presents some unusual problems: The layout is complex; the waterborne transportation can be bewildering; the house-numbering system is baffling; street names in the six districts are duplicated; and often you must walk, whether you want to or not. It's essential that you have a good map showing all street names and vaporetto routes; buy one at a newsstand. In the areas where you're most likely to wander, signs are posted on many corners pointing you in the right direction for the nearest major landmark—San Marco, the Rialto, the Accademia, etc.—but don't count on finding such signs once you're deep into residential neighborhoods. Count on getting lost at least once—it's an essential part of the Venice experience.

By Vaporetto ACTV vaporetti run the length of the Grand Canal and circle the city. There are about 20 lines, some of which connect Venice with the major and minor islands in the lagoon. Line 1 is the Grand Canal local, calling at every stop and continuing via San Marco to the Lido. (It takes about 45 minutes from the station to San Marco.)

As the result of recent (extremely confusing and unpopular) rerouting, there are now two Line 52 routes: one runs from the railway station to San Zaccaria, skirts the north of the city, via Fondamente Nove (where boats leave for the islands of the northern lagoon) and Murano and continues via the Arsenal; the other acts as an express service via Zattere on the Giudecca Canal, south of the city, to San Marco and the Lido.

There are also two Line 82 routes from the Tronchetto: one goes via Piazzale Roma, the railway station, and Rialto, and continues, during the day, down the Grand Canal, with fewer stops than Line 1, to San Marco and, in the summer, on to the Lido; the other takes the southern route through the Giudecca Canal, via Zattere with a stop on Guidecca, to San Marco, and again, in the summer, continues to the Lido.

The fare is 2,500 on most lines, but 3,500 on the 52 Zattere–Lido route and on the 82 Grand Canal route. A 24-hour tourist ticket costs 14,000 lire, while a three-day tourist ticket costs 20,000; these are not valid on the 52 Zattere-Lido route or the 82 Grand Canal route, but can be especially worthwhile if you are planning to visit the islands (*see* Tour 5, *below*).

Timetables are posted at every landing stage, but there is not always a ticket booth operating. You may get on a boat without a ticket, but you will have to pay a higher fare. For this reason, it may be useful to buy a book of tickets (*un blochetto*) in advance. Landing stages are clearly marked with name and line number, but check before boarding, particularly with the 52, to make sure the boat is going in your direction.

By Motoscafo These stylish powerboat water taxis are extremely expensive, and the fare system is as complex as Venice's layout. A minimum fare of about 50,000 lire gets you nowhere, and you'll pay three times as much to get from one end of the Grand Canal to the other. Always agree on the fare before starting out.

By Traghetto Few tourists know about the two-man gondolas that ferry people across the Grand Canal at various fixed points. They are the cheapest and shortest gondola ride in Venice and can save a lot of walking. The fare is 500 lire, which you hand to the gondolier when you get on. Look for traghetto signs.

By Gondola No visit to Venice is complete without a gondola ride. But not many visitors know that the best time for one is in the late afternoon or early evening hours, when the Grand Canal isn't so heavily trafficked, or that it's best to start from a station on the Grand Canal because the lagoon is usually choppy. Make it clear that you want to see the smaller canals, and come to terms on the cost and duration of the ride before you start. Gondoliers are supposed to charge a fixed minimum of about 70,000 lire for up to five passengers for 50 minutes. After 8 PM the rate goes up. The official tariffs are quoted in the "Guest in Venice" booklet (*see* The Arts and Nightlife, *below*). Bargaining may get you a better price.

Important Addresses and Numbers

Tourist Information The main APT tourist office is at Calle dell'Ascensione 71C (tel. 041/522–6356, fax 041/529–8730), just off Piazza San Marco, under the arcade in the far left corner opposite the basilica. *Open every day except public holidays 8:30–6:30 (sometimes slightly later in summer).*

There are other information booths at the Santa Lucia train station (tel. 041/719078) and on the Lido (Gran Viale S. Maria Elisabetta 6A, tel. 041/526–5721, fax 041/529–8720). Another office is due to open in the newly restored, former coffeehouse pavilion in the corner of the Giardini Reali, on the waterfront near the San Marco vaporetto stop.

Consulates U.K. (Campo della Carità 1051, Dorsoduro, tel. 041/522–7207). There is no U.S. or Canadian consular service.

Emergencies **Police,** tel. 113.
Ambulance, tel. 041/523–0000.

Doctors and Dentists Dial the number for ambulances (*see above*) and ask the **Croce Azzurra** (Blue Cross) to recommend a doctor or dentist convenient to your location. The British consulate can also recommend doctors and dentists.

Late-Night Pharmacies Venetian pharmacies take turns opening late or on Sundays; dial 192 for information on which are open. Alternatively, the daily list of late-night pharmacies is posted on the front of every pharmacy. Two with English-speaking staff are **Farmacia Italo-Inglese** (Calle della Mandola 3717, in San Marco district, tel. 041/522–4837) and **Farmacia Internazionale** (Calle Larga XXII Marzo 2067, in San Marco district, tel. 041/522–2311).

English-Language Bookstores Venice's centuries of experience in dealing with foreign visitors mean that bookstores and newsstands throughout the city are well stocked with publications in English. **Fantoni,** on Salizzada San Luca, specializes in art books. **Il Libraio di San Barnaba,** on Fondamenta Gherardini, near Campo San Barnaba, has shelves full of paperbacks and books on Venice in English.

Good general-interest bookstores include **Serenissima** (Salizzada San Zulian), near San Marco; **Emiliana Editrice** (Calle Goldoni), between Piazza San Marco and Rialto; and **Studium** (Calle de la Canonica), off Piazzetta dei Leoncini. **Libreria Editrici Filippi,** on Calle della Bissa, just off Campo San Bartolomeo, near Rialto, has the best selection of books on every aspect of Venice and its history. Enrico Dori's newspaper shop on the Frezzaria shopping street, behind the post office off Piazza San Marco, has a good selection of English-language newspapers and magazines and is open from early in the morning until late at night.

Travel **American Express** (Salizzada San Moisè 1471, tel. 041/520–0844);
Agencies **Sattis Viaggi** (Calle Larga dell'Ascensione 1261, tel. 041/528–5101/2/3); **Wagons Lits/Turismo** (Piazzetta dei Leoncini 289, tel. 041/522–3405).

Guided Tours

Orientation Two-hour walking tours of the San Marco area, taking in the basilica and the Doge's Palace, can be booked through **American Express** (tel. 041/520–0844) and other travel agencies. The American Express "Jewels of the Venetian Republic" tour (about 30,000 lire) ends with a glass-blowing demonstration. From March 15 to November 15 American Express offers an afternoon walking tour that ends with a gondola ride (about 35,000 lire).

In recent years, Venice's municipal Youth Department has been running a special program to help young visitors: "Rolling Venice," as it is somewhat oddly titled, is open to everyone aged 14–29 and costs 5,000 lire to join (at Rolling Venice's offices at the Assessorato alla Gioventù, Corte Contarini 1529, behind the Piazza San Marco Post Office; the Box Office, Calle Loredan 4127, off Campo San Luca; and from July to September at the Santa Lucia railway station). Benefits include handy guidebooks to the city and (sometimes substantial) discounts in hotels, restaurants, and shops; a three-day vaporetto ticket costs about 4,000 lire less if you show your card when buying one. The Youth Department has also produced two useful leaflets, "Dormire Giovani" (Accommodations for Young People) and "Notturno Veneziano" (Venetian Nightlife) (*see* The Arts and Nightlife, *below*).

Special- American Express and other operators offer group gondola rides
Interest with serenades, daily from May through October in the evening (about 35,000 lire).

During the summer, free guided tours (some in English, including one at 11 AM) of the **Basilica di San Marco** are offered by the Patriarchate of Venice; information is available in the atrium of the church (tel. 041/520–0333). *No tours Sun.*

Excursions **American Express** can book you on to a tour of the islands of Murano, Burano, and Torcello (departing daily at 9:30 and 2:30 and costing about 20,000 lire per person). However, it is generally best to avoid organized tours to the islands, and beware of tours that operate around Piazza San Marco. Tours tend to be annoyingly commercial and emphasize glass-factory showrooms, pressuring you to buy, often at higher prices than normal. You can easily visit these islands on your own (*see* Tour 5: Islands of the Lagoon in Exploring Venice, *below*).

American Express also offers a trip by car to the Venetian villas, Padua and Asolo, available all year round (about 120,000 lire per person). Bookings should be made the day before.

Excursions aboard the Burchiello motor launch, from Venice to Padua along the Brenta Canal, are expensive (about 150,000 lire) and not necessarily the best way to see the famous villas that line the canal, since so much time is spent on the boat. *Tours Apr.–Oct., Tues., Thurs., Sat.*

Personal Guides   **American Express** and other travel agencies can provide guides for walking or gondola tours of Venice, or cars with driver and guide for tours of the mainland. You can get a list of licensed guides and their rates from the main tourist office in Piazza San Marco (tel. 041/522–6356) or contact the Guides' Association (Calle San Antonio 5448/A, Castello, tel. 041/523–9902, fax 041/523–2012).

Exploring Venice

The church of San Marco is unquestionably the heart of Venice, but venturing even 50 yards from it can sometimes lead to confusion. Although the smaller canals (a canal is called a *rio*) are spanned by frequent bridges, the Grand Canal can only be crossed on foot at three points—near the train station, at the Rialto Bridge, and at the Accademia Bridge—which decidedly complicates matters. It's supremely maddening to find yourself on the wrong bank of a canal with no bridge in sight.

A street is called a *calle*, but a street that runs alongside a canal is called either a *riva* or a *fondamenta*. The closed-in streetscapes of Venice make it hard to see any reference point, such as the spire of the Campanile, above the rooftops, and the narrow back streets often take unpredictable turnings that foul up your sense of direction. Streets and canals may look deceptively familiar, only to make sudden dead ends. Keep a map of vaporetto lines with you at all times because the best way back to Piazza San Marco or your hotel may well be along one of these routes.

Our first two tours should help you find your bearings. Tour 1 takes in the sights around the San Marco district, the geographic and spiritual center of the city. Tour 2 takes to the water along the Grand Canal, the main artery of Venice, linking many of its major sights. Tours 3 and 4 take you east and west, respectively, giving you the chance to explore some of the more offbeat sights and areas, as well as the less central churches and art collections. The last two tours take you to the other major islands of the Venetian lagoon, places where the pace of life is slower and where crafts, such as glassblowing and lace-making, are still practiced.

Highlights for First-Time Visitors

Accademia Gallery (Tour 4: The Western and Northern Districts).

Basilica di San Marco (Tour 1: The San Marco District).

Campanile of San Marco (Tour 1: The San Marco District).

Campo Santi Giovanni e Paolo (Tour 3: To the Arsenal and Beyond).

Frari Church (Tour 4: The Western and Northern Districts).

Murano, Burano, and Torcello (Tour 5: Islands of the Lagoon).

Palazzo Ducale (Tour 1: The San Marco District).

Piazza San Marco (Tour 1: The San Marco District).

Ponte di Rialto (Tour 2: The Grand Canal).

San Giorgio Maggiore (Tour 6: San Maggiore and the Giudecca).

Scuola di San Rocco (Tour 4: The Western and Northern Districts).

Tour 1: The San Marco District

Numbers in the margin correspond to points of interest on the Venice map.

❶ **Piazza San Marco** (St. Mark's Square) is the heart of Venice, perpetually animated during the day, when it's filled with people and crowds of fluttering pigeons. It can be magical at night, especially in the winter, when melancholy mists swirl around the lampposts and bell tower. Historically and geographically, it's the logical place to start exploring the city. If you stand at the piazza's far end, facing the basilica, you'll notice that rather than being a strict rectangle it opens wider at the basilica end, enhancing the perspective and creating the illusion of being even larger than it is. On your left, the long arcaded building is the **Procuratie Vecchie,** built in the early 16th century as offices and residences for the powerful Procurators of San Marco, administrators of the basilica. Across the piazza, on your right hand, is the **Procuratie Nuove,** built half a century later in a more grandiose classical style. The Procuratie Nuove has impeccable architectural lineage: It was originally planned by perhaps Venice's greatest Renaissance architect, Jacopo Sansovino (1486–1570) of Florence, to carry on the look of his **Libreria Vecchia,** where the Marciana National Library is now housed, around the corner to the right, across from the Palazzo Ducale (Doge's Palace), though Sansovino died before the building was begun. The actual designer was Vincenzo Scamozzi (*ca.* 1552–1616), a pupil of Palladio and a devout Neoclassicist; later sections were completed by Baldassare Longhena (1598–1682), Venice's other great architect, who belonged firmly to the Baroque tradition.

When Napoleon entered Venice with his troops in 1797, he called Piazza San Marco "the world's most beautiful drawing room"—and promptly gave orders to redecorate it. His architects demolished an old church that stood behind you, at the end of the square farthest from the basilica, and put up the **Ala Napoleonica** (Napoleonic Wing), or Fabbrica Nuova (New Building), to unite the two 16th-century buildings on either side.

Today the arcades of these three grand buildings shelter shops and cafés. Several of the cafés have their own small orchestras that play outdoors in fair weather; though patrons of the cafés must pay an additional charge for the entertainment, passersby in the piazza can enjoy it for free. On warm summer nights, the orchestras compete to see which can draw the biggest crowd, and the fun is infectious.

Time Out On the Procuratie Vecchie side is the historic **Café Quadri,** which was shunned by Venetians during the 19th century when the occupying Austrians made it their gathering place; loyal Venetians preferred the venerable **Café Florian,** on the Procuratie Nuove side, where Casanova, Wagner, and Proust were regular customers. Like a gondola ride, eating and drinking at these expensive cafés may be a splurge, but it's a treat you shouldn't miss. For superb sandwiches and hot dishes, too, in an area where a good, cheap eating place is hard to find, try **Snack Bar Carla** (the colorful sign over the door actually reads "Pietro Panizzolo"), at the end of a passageway, the Sotoportego Contarina, behind the Ala Napoleonica and to the right.

Venice

Sacca della Misericordia

Canale delle Navi

San Michele

31 34

0 _____ 440 yards
0 _____ 400 meters

Fondamenta

Rio S. Caterina

C. Racchetta

30

R. d. Gesuiti Nuove

Rio della Panada

C.d.Squero

Strada Nuova

Rio d. Santi Apostoli

dei Mendicanti

Campo d. Pescheria

C.d.Tesla

Erberia

16

Rio d.S.Marina

Campo Santi Giovanni e Paolo

17

R. Barbaria delle Tole

R. d. S.

R. d. S. Giustina

del Vin

9

R. d. Fava

Salì di S. Lio

Merceria

Riga

15

R. d. S. Severo

18

R.d.S. Francesco

del Carbon

C.d.Bande

Giuffa

C. Lion

22

C. d. Furlani

R. d. Scudi

Canale d. Galeazze

Campo Manin

Fabbri

R. d. Palazzo

R. d. S. Lorenzo

Fond. Osmarin

R. d. Greci

R. d. Pietà

R.d.Corna

Darsena Grande

Rio d. Vergini

Frezzaria

5 1 3 2 4

SAN ZACCARIA

Molo

Riva degli

Schiavoni

19

R. d. Arsenale

Rio d. S. Daniele

di S. Pietro

21

S. Moisè

R. d.

Piazza San Marco

20

Rio della Tana

V. Garibaldi

Rio d.S.Anna

Con

Riva dei Sette Martiri

R. d. S. Giuseppe

Canale di S. Marco

35

Isola di S. Giorgio Maggiore

Fond. delle Zitelle

Calle Michelangelo

Ci

Riva dei Partigiani

Rio d. Giardini

▲ Boat stop

At the basilica end of the piazza, on the left (north) side next to the Procuratie Vecchie, is the **Torre dell'Orologio** (Clock Tower), erected in 1496 and endowed with an enameled timepiece and animated figures of Moors that strike the hour. During Ascension Week (40 days after Easter) and on Epiphany (Jan. 6), an angel and three wise men go in and out of the doors and bow to the Virgin.

Now it is finally time to turn your attention to the piazza's crowning glory, the **Basilica di San Marco,** one of Europe's most beautiful churches. An opulent synthesis of Byzantine and Romanesque styles, it is laid out in a Greek cross topped off with five plump domes. The Basilica did not actually become the cathedral of Venice until as late as 1807, but its role as the church of the doge (the elected head of the Venetian republic) gave it immense power and wealth. It was begun in 1063, and inaugurated in 1094, to house the remains of St. Mark the Evangelist, which were filched from Alexandria two centuries earlier by two agents of the doge. The story goes that they stole the saint's remains and hid them in a barrel under layers of pickled pork to get them past Islamic guards.

That escapade is illustrated in a mosaic in the lunette (semicircular decoration) over the farthest left of the front doors. This 13th-century mosaic is the earliest one on this heavily decorated facade; look at it closely and you can see a picture of the church as it appeared in the 13th century.

Over the years this church stood as a symbol of Venetian wealth and power, and it was endowed with all the riches the Republic's admirals and merchants could carry off from the Orient, earning it the nickname Chiesa D'Oro (Golden Church). The four bronze horses that prance and snort over the central doorway (copies only, but the originals are on view indoors in the Museo di San Marco, *see below*) were classical sculptures that victorious Venetians took away from Constantinople in 1204, along with a lot of other loot that you can see inside. Just inside the central front doors in the church porch, look for a medallion of red porphyry set in the floor to mark the spot of another of Venice's political coups: the reconciliation between Barbarossa, the Holy Roman Emperor, and Pope Alexander III, brought about by Doge Sebastiano Ziani in 1177.

Entrance to the church is free, but be warned: Guards at the door turn away any visitors, male or female, wearing shorts or inappropriate attire. If you want to take a free guided tour in English (offered Mon.–Sat. at 11 AM in summer, and with less certainty in winter, since the guides are volunteers), wait on the left in the porch for a group to form. *Church open Mon.–Sat. 9:30–5:30, Sun. 2:30–5:30.*

One of the innovations of this church was a roof of brick vaulting, rather than wood, enabling the ceiling to be decorated with mosaics. As you enter the basilica, you'll find it surprisingly dark inside, compared to the soaring light-filled Gothic cathedrals of northern Europe. This is because many of the original windows were filled in and covered with even more mosaics. In the mysterious dusk, candles flicker and the gold tiles of mosaics glitter softly, sensuously. (The tiles were laid on at slight angles to achieve precisely this effect.) The earliest mosaics are from the 11th and 12th centuries; later ones were done as late as the 16th century, such as the Last Judgment on the arch between the porch and the nave, said to be based on drawings by Tintoretto. Go into the Zen Chapel (to the right just off the porch, and named after a local cardinal rather than any form of Buddhism) to see some earlier (13th-century) mosaics, telling the story of the life of St. Mark. Next to it, the **baptistery** contains a bronze font cover by Jacopo Sansovino and the tomb of Doge Andrea Dandolo (1307–1354), a friend of Petrarch and a writer in his own right. Several of the earlier doges were buried here, while later ones were interred in the church of Santi Giovanni e Paolo (*see* Tour 3, *below*).

Two more chapels, both in the left transept, are worth a special look: the **Chapel of the Madonna of Nicopeia,** which holds a precious icon (part of the loot from Constantinople) that many consider Venice's most powerful protector; and next to it, on the left, a small chapel dedicated to the Virgin Mary with fine 15th-century mosaics depicting her life, possibly based on drawings by Andrea Mantegna.

If you stand in the central aisle facing the main altar, notice the polygonal pulpit to the right, at the intersection of the nave and right transept. After the coronation ceremony, each new Doge stood here for the people to behold him in the glory of his new office.

To enter the **sanctuary,** you must pay an admission fee (2,000 lire), but it's well worth it. (Open Mon.–Sat. 10–4, Sun. 1:45–4.) The main altar, with its green marble canopy lifted high on carved alabaster columns, covers the tomb of St. Mark. Behind this is the real attraction: the **Pala d'Oro** (Golden Altarpiece), a dazzling gold-and-silver screen encrusted with precious gems and enameled panels. Originally made in Constantinople in the 10th century, it was continually embellished over the next few centuries by master craftsmen in Venice and elsewhere. Invest a few 100-lire coins to listen to a recorded description—otherwise you'll miss some of the incredible detail. The bronze door leading from the sanctuary back into the sacristy is another Sansovino work; check out the top left corner, where the artist included a self-portrait and, above that, a picture of his friend and fellow artist Titian.

The same ticket admits you to the **Treasury,** which is entered from the right transept. It contains some exquisite pieces, many of them exotic treasures borne away from Constantinople and other vanquished places.

From the atrium, climb the steep stairway to the **Museo di San Marco** (St. Mark's Museum) for a look at the interior of the church from the organ gallery and a sweeping view of Piazza San Marco and the Piazzetta dei Leoncini from the outdoor gallery. The highlight of the museum is the close-up of the four magnificent gilded bronze horses that once stood outside on the gallery. The originals were probably cast in Constantinople in the 4th century AD, but some hold that they are Greek works of the 3rd century BC. Napoleon hauled them off to Paris after he conquered Venice in 1797, but they were returned after the fall of the French Empire. *Admission: 2,000 lire. Open Apr.–Sept., daily 9:30–5:30; Nov.–Mar., daily 10–4.*

❸ Just outside the basilica is the tall brick **Campanile** (Bell Tower), a reconstruction of the original, which stood for 1,000 years before it collapsed one morning in 1912, practically without warning. In the 15th century, clerics found guilty of immoral behavior were suspended in wooden cages from the tower, sometimes to subsist on bread and water for as long as a year, sometimes to starve to death. The pretty marble loggia (covered gallery) at its base was built in the early 16th century by Jacopo Sansovino: It, too, has been carefully restored. The view from the tower on a clear day is worth the price of admission. You get a pigeon's-eye view of the city, the Lido, the lagoon, and the mainland as far as the distant Alps. Oddly, you can't see the myriad canals that snake through the 117 islets on which Venice is built. *Piazza San Marco, tel. 041/522–4064. Admission: 4,000 lire. Open Easter–Oct., daily 10–8; Nov.–Easter, daily 10–4. Closed for maintenance most of Jan.*

The square that leads from Piazza San Marco down to the waters of St. Mark's Basin is called the **Piazzetta San Marco.** This landing stage, now crowded with excursion boats, was once the grand entrance to the Republic. Two tall columns rise here on the waterfront: one is topped by the winged lion, a traditional emblem of St. Mark that became by extension the symbol of Venice itself; the other bears aloft a statue of St. Theodore (the first patron saint of Venice) and his dragon.

❹ Above the Piazzetta rises the **Palazzo Ducale,** a Gothic-Renaissance fantasia of pink-and-white marble, a majestic expression of the prosperity and power attained by Venice during its most glorious period. Its top-heavy design (the dense upper floors rest on the graceful ground-floor colonnade) has always confounded architectural purists, who insist that proper architecture be set out the other way around. The palace was not only the residence of the doge, but also the parliament house, home of the law courts, and a prison. Venice's government, set up sometime in the seventh century as a participatory democracy, provided for an elected ruler, the doge, to serve for life, but in practice he was simply a figurehead. Power really rested with the Great Council, originally an elected body but, from the 13th century on, an aristocratic stronghold, with members inheriting their seats from their noble ancestors. Laws were passed by the Senate, a group of 200 elected from the Great Council (which could have as many as 1,700 members); executive powers belonged to the College, a committee of 25 leaders. In the 14th century, the Council of Ten was formed to deal with emergency situations; this group's meetings were not open to the public, and the Council often proved more powerful than the Senate, though its members could only serve for limited terms, before new members were elected.

A fortress for the doge existed on this spot in the early ninth century; the building you see today was a product of the 12th century, although, like the basilica next door, it was continually added to and transformed throughout the centuries. You enter the palace at the ornate Gothic **Porta della Carta** (Gate of the Paper, where official decrees were traditionally posted), which opens onto an immense courtyard. Ahead is the **Scala dei Giganti** (Stairway of the Giants), guarded by huge statues of Mars and Neptune by Jacopo Sansovino. Ordinary mortals do not get to climb these stairs, however; after paying your admission fee, walk along the arcade to reach the central interior staircase. Its upper flight is called the **Scala d'Oro** (Golden Staircase), also designed by Sansovino, with its lavish gilded decoration. While it may seem odd that the government's main council rooms and reception halls would be so far upstairs, imagine how effectively foreign emissaries must have been intimidated by this arduous climb.

Visitors must have also been overwhelmed with the sumptuous decoration of these apartments, their walls and ceilings covered with works by Venice's greatest artists. Among the grand rooms you can visit are the **Anticollegio** (a waiting room outside the College's chamber), which features two fine paintings, Tintoretto's *Bacchus and Ariadne Crowned by Venus* and Veronese's *Rape of Europa;* the **Sala del Collegio** (College Chamber), its ceiling magnificently painted by Veronese; and the **Sala del Senato** (Senate Chamber), with Tintoretto's *Triumph of Venice* on the ceiling. The huge *Paradise* on the end wall of the **Great Council Hall** is by Jacopo Tintoretto

(1518–94): It is a dark, dynamic masterpiece. This is the world's largest oil painting (23 by 75 feet), a vast work commissioned for a vast hall. Don't miss the gorgeous ceiling, with Veronese's majestic *Apotheosis of Venice* filling one of the center panels. Step onto the balcony of the Great Council Hall for a view of St. Mark's Basin, its waters churning with the wakes of countless boats. Look at the frieze of portraits of the first 76 doges around the upper part of the walls. One portrait is missing: A black painted curtain near the left-hand corner of the wall opposite Tintoretto's painting marks the spot where the portrait of doge Marin Falier should be. A Latin inscription bluntly explains that Falier was executed for treason in 1355. The Republic never forgave him.

At the ticket office of the Doge's Palace you can book a guided tour (unfortunately, only given in Italian) of the palace's secret rooms; it takes you to the doge's private apartments, up into the attic and Piombi prison, and through hidden passageways to the torture chambers, where prisoners were interrogated. The 18th-century writer and libertine, Casanova, a native of Venice, was imprisoned here in 1755, having somehow offended someone in power (the official accusation was of being a Freemason); he made a daring escape 15 months later and fled to France, where he continued his career of intrigue and scandal. From the east wing of the Doge's Palace, the enclosed marble **Ponte dei Sospiri** (Bridge of Sighs) arches over a narrow canal to the cramped, gloomy cell blocks of the so-called New Prison. (The bridge was named for the sighs of those being led to prison.) *Piazzetta San Marco, tel. 041/522–4951. Admission: 8,000 lire. Open Apr.–Oct., daily 9–7; Nov.–Mar., daily 9–4 (last entry one hour before closing time). Secret Itineraries Tour (in Italian only) daily 10 AM and noon; reserve at least a day ahead if possible. Cost: 5,000 lire.*

❺ Walk back to the far end of Piazza San Marco, where a massive marble staircase in the Fabbrica Nuova leads to the **Museo Correr,** an interesting and varied collection of historical items and paintings by old masters, once the private collection of the aristocrat Teodoro Correr, who donated them to the city in 1830. Exhibits range from the absurdly high-soled shoes worn by 16th-century Venetian ladies (who had to be supported by a servant on each side in order to walk on these precarious perches) to fine artworks by the talented Bellini family of Renaissance painters. *Piazza San Marco, Ala Napoleonica, tel. 041/522–5625. Admission: 5,000 lire. Open Apr.–Oct., Wed.–Mon. 9–7; Nov.–Mar., Wed.–Mon. 9–4.*

Tour 2: The Grand Canal

Catch Vaporetto Line 1 at the San Marco landing stage for a leisurely cruise along the **Grand Canal,** Venice's main thoroughfare. This 2-mile ribbon of water loops through the city. When the canal is busiest, usually in the morning, large and small craft crisscross its waters, stirring up a maelstrom that sets gondolas rocking and sends green waves slapping at the seaweed-slippery foundations of palaces. The quietest and most romantic time to ride in a gondola along the Grand Canal is about an hour or so before sunset: This is an experience you shouldn't miss. However, for an overall sightseeing tour of the canal, you get a better, more extensive view from the vaporetto—which is both higher in the water and much less expensive. Try to get one of the coveted seats in the prow, where you have a clear view.

The Grand Canal has an average depth of about 9 feet and varies from 40 to 76 yards in width. It winds like an inverted letter *S* through Venice, from the San Marco landing to the landing at the train station (Ferrovia), passing under three bridges and between 200 palaces dating from the 14th century to the 18th century, most of them in Venetian Gothic or Renaissance style. Starting from San

❻ Marco, look left for **Santa Maria della Salute,** the huge, white, domed 17th-century Baroque church designed by Longhena. On the same side is the low white marble wall marking the never-completed **Palazzo Venier dei Leoni,** well worth a return visit (April through

❼ October) to view the **Peggy Guggenheim Collection,** a small but choice gallery of 20th-century painting and sculpture in the heiress's lavish former apartments. Guggenheim (1898–1979) used her wealth and social connections to become a serious patron of art—she was once married to the painter Max Ernst—and her holdings include several works by Picasso, Kandinsky, Ernst, Pollock, and Motherwell, among others. *Entrance on Calle San Cristoforo, Dorsoduro, tel. 041/520–6288. Admission: 10,000 lire. Open Sun., Mon., Wed.–Sat. 11–6.*

Across the canal you can see the imposing terraced front of the **Gritti Palace Hotel** (*see* Lodging, *below*), occupying the former Palazzo Pisani. English critic John Ruskin stayed here with his young wife Effie in 1851, while working on his book *Stones of Venice.* **Palazzo Corner,** otherwise known as Ca' Grande, is also on the right bank, just past the Santa Maria del Giglio stop. A Renaissance beauty designed by Sansovino, with classical details, it now houses the Prefecture. **Palazzo Barbaro,** the 15th-century Gothic villa on the right bank just before the Accademia Bridge, is where Henry James lived while writing *The Aspern Papers;* later he made it the setting for his novel *Wings of the Dove.* The **Accademia Bridge** is one of only three spanning the Grand Canal—until the first bridge was built here in 1854; in fact, the Rialto was the only bridge over the Grand Canal. The current plain wooden bridge, dating from 1934, leads on the left bank to the wonderful **Accademia Gallery,** a treasure house of Venetian painting (*see* Tour 4, *below*).

A few minutes farther on, on the left bank at the Ca' Rezzonico stop,

❽ is **Ca' Rezzonico,** a Baroque mansion begun by Longhena in the 1660s and completed by another architect, Giorgio Massari, in the 1740s. This was English poet Robert Browning's last home, where he died in 1889. Return here to visit the **Museo del Settecento Veneziano** (Museum of 18th-Century Venice). Pictures by the 18th-century Venetian painters Francesco and Gianantonio Guardi and Pietro Longhi, and a fine series of frescoes by their younger contemporary Giandomenico Tiepolo at the back of the palace, really open a window onto that charming if sometimes frivolous social era. *Fondamenta Rezzonico, tel. 041/522–4543. Admission: 5,000 lire. Open Apr.–Oct., Sat.–Thurs. 9–7; Nov.–Mar., Sat.–Thurs. 9–4.*

Just past Ca' Rezzonico, still on the left bank, are two identical 15th-century Gothic palaces designed by Bartolomeo Bon for the Giustinian family. In the second one, composer Richard Wagner lived in 1858–59 while writing his opera *Tristan und Isolde.* Next door is **Ca' Foscari,** where the second of Venice's two disgraced doges, Francesco Foscari, lived in 1457 when he was deposed by the Council of Ten. Now part of the University, it is adorned with lovely marble columns, tracery, and a frieze.

Turn to the right bank, as you round the bend in the canal, to see the **Palazzi Mocenigo,** a series of four buildings, the two central ones unified behind a double neoclassical facade, decorated with lions' heads. Byron lived in one of these from 1816 to 1819; it was here that he began his satiric epic *Don Juan,* enjoyed several reckless love affairs, and eventually stole Countess Guiccioli from her husband. A couple of years later he wrote historical dramas about the traitor doge Marin Falier and the two Foscari doges. Just past the next vaporetto stop, still on the right bank, stands **Palazzo Corner-Spinelli,** a richly decorated Renaissance palace with arched windows, probably designed by Mauro Coducci (1440–1504). On the right bank across from the next vaporetto stop, look at Renaissance architecture in full flower at the imposing white **Palazzo Grimani,** by Michele Sanmicheli (1484–1559); today the Court of Appeals sits here.

❾ The canal narrows and boat traffic increases as you approach the **Rialto Bridge,** arched high over the canal. The windows in the arch belong to the shops inside; plan to return here on foot and walk across to admire fine views up and down the Grand Canal. This is a commercial hub of the city, with open-air vegetable, fruit, and fish markets on the left, and on the right, an upscale shopping district. Just beyond the bridge on the right is the 16th-century **Fondaco dei Tedeschi,** originally used by merchants from various Germanic states as warehouses and offices for the all-important trade with Venice. Now that the Giorgione frescoes that once covered its facade have gone, it's a rather austere-looking building; today it's the city's main post office.

❿ The Ca' d'Oro landing on the right, just beyond the Rialto, identifies the lovely Venetian Gothic palace of **Ca' d'Oro,** adorned with marble traceries and ornaments that were once embellished with pure gold. Today it houses the **Franchetti Gallery,** a fine collection of tapestries, sculptures, and paintings. *Calle della Ca' d'Oro, tel. 041/523-8790. Admission: 4,000 lire. Open Mon.–Sat. 9–2, Sun. 9–1.*

⓫ A little farther up from Ca' d'Oro, over on the left bank, is the grand Baroque **Ca' Pesaro,** designed by Longhena. It's now home to two rather dull art collections, the **Galleria d'Arte Moderna** (Modern Art Gallery), containing mostly 19th-century and some 20th-century works, although the intention is also to display the gallery's large collection of contemporary art when restoration is completed, and **Museo Orientale** (Oriental Art Museum). *Galleria d'Arte Moderna: tel. 041/721127, admission: 3,000 lire; open Apr.–Oct., Tues.–Sun. 9–7; Nov.–Mar., Tues.–Sun. 9–4. Museo Orientale: tel. 041/524-1173, admission: 4,000 lire; open Tues.–Sun. 9–1, Sat. 9–2.*

⓬ Not far beyond, on the left, another white church is adorned with Baroque statues; this is **San Stae,** and the landing here is a gateway to a part of Venice that most tourists never see, a neighborhood of narrow canals and airy squares. Back on the right bank, the Renaissance **Palazzo Vendramin-Calergi** (1509), designed by Coducci in white stone with red marble medallions and an imposing carved frieze, was where Wagner died in 1883; it is now the winter home of the **Casino** (*see* The Arts and Nightlife, *below*). Turn to the left bank **⓭** to see the **Fondaco dei Turchi,** built in the Veneto-Byzantine style in the 12th–13th centuries, but very heavy-handedly restored in the 19th century; it was the trade center for the Turks from 1621–1838. Under its portico, the traitorous doge Marin Falier was buried after his execution. The **Museo di Storia Naturale** (Natural History Museum) occupies the building now. *Tel. 041/524-0885. Admission: 5,000 lire. Open Tues.–Sat. 9–1:30, Sun. 9–1.*

⓮ Another vaporetto stop away is **San Marcuola,** on the right. This unfinished brick church is guarded by cats and pigeons, and it marks the edge of another district that is off the beaten track and well worth exploring: Cannaregio and the old Jewish ghetto.

Tour 3: To the Arsenal and Beyond

To explore the city's eastern districts and see some of its most beautiful churches, head out of Piazza San Marco under the clock tower into the **Mercerie,** one of Venice's busiest streets. It's actually a five-part series of streets (Merceria dell'Orologio, di San Zulian, del Capitello, di San Salvador, and 2 Aprile) leading more or less directly from Piazza San Marco to the Rialto bridge. At Campo San Zulian and the church of San Giuliano, turn right onto Calle Guerra and
⓯ Calle delle Bande to reach the graceful white marble church of **Santa Maria Formosa.** It's on a lively square with a few sidewalk cafés and a small vegetable market on weekday mornings. Follow Calle Borgoloco into Campo San Marina, where you turn right, cross the little
⓰ canal, and take Calle Castelli to the church of **Santa Maria dei Miracoli.** Perfectly proportioned and sheathed in marble, it's an early Renaissance gem, decorated inside with exquisite marble reliefs. Notice how the architect, Pietro Lombardo, made the church look bigger with various optical illusions: varying the color of the exterior marble to create the effect of distance; using extra pilasters to make the building's canal side look longer; slightly offsetting the arcade windows to make the arches look deeper. The church was built in the 1480s to house an image of the Virgin that is said to perform miracles—look for this icon on the high altar.

Behind the church, bear right to Calle Larga Giacinto Gallina, which leads to **Campo Santi Giovanni e Paolo,** site of the massive Dominican
⓱ church of **Santi Giovanni e Paolo,** or San Zanipolo, as it's known in the slurred Venetian dialect. The powerful equestrian **monument of Bartolomeo Colleoni** by Florentine sculptor Andrea del Verrocchio (1435–88) stands in the square. Colleoni had served Venice well as a *condottiere,* or mercenary commander (the Venetians preferred to pay others to fight for them on land and had the money to do it). When he died in 1475, he left his fortune to the city on the condition that a statue be erected in his honor "in the piazza before St. Mark's." The republic's shrewd administrators coveted Colleoni's ducats but had no intention of honoring anyone, no matter how valorous, with a statue in Piazza San Marco. So they commissioned the statue and put it up before the Scuola di San Marco, which is off to the side here and is the headquarters of a charitable confraternity that happened to have the right name, enabling them to collect the loot. San Zanipolo itself contains tombs of several doges, as well as a wealth of artworks. Don't miss the Rosary Chapel, off the left transept; with its Veronese ceiling paintings, it's a sumptuous study in decoration, built in the 16th century to commemorate the victory of Lepanto in western Greece in 1571, when Venice and a combined European fleet succeeded in destroying the Turkish navy.

Continue beyond Santi Giovanni e Paolo to another large church,
⓲ **San Francesco della Vigna,** built by Sansovino in 1534. A pretty cloister opens out from the severely simple gray-and-white interior. Not many tourists find their way here, and local youngsters play ball in the square shadowed by the church's austere classical Palladian facade.

Go left as you leave the church to begin the 500-yard walk to the
⓳ **Campo dell'Arsenale,** at the main entrance to the **Arsenal,** an immense dockyard founded in 1104 to build and equip the fleet of the Venetian republic and augmented continually through the 16th cen-

tury. For a republic founded on sea might, having a huge state-of-the-art shipyard was of paramount importance, and this one was renowned for its skill and size. All subsequent dockyards were named after it (the name comes from the Arabic "d'arsina," meaning workshop). No wonder it has such a grandiose entrance, with four stone lions from ancient Greece guarding the great Renaissance gateway.

20 The **Museo Navale** (Naval Museum) on nearby Campo San Biagio has four floors of scale boat models and an annex containing actual boats, from gondolas to doges' ceremonial boats, guaranteed to fascinate children—and boat lovers. *Campo San Biagio, Castello, tel. 041/ 520–0276. Admission: 2,000 lire. Open Mon.–Sat. 9–1.*

If you still have time and energy, go east to the island and church of
21 **San Pietro di Castello.** Two footbridges lead to this island. The church served as Venice's cathedral for centuries; now it presides over a picturesque workaday neighborhood, and its tipsy bell tower leans over a grassy square.

Time Out If you're this far afield, you may need sustenance to get you back to the center of town. There are several moderately priced snack bars and *trattorie* on Via Garibaldi, midway between the Arsenal and the island of San Pietro. **Sottoprova** (closed Tues.) has tables outdoors.

About midway between the Arsenal and St. Mark's, on your way
22 back from the eastern district, is the **Scuola di San Giorgio degli Schiavoni,** one of numerous *scuole* built during the time of the Republic. These weren't schools, as the present-day Italian word would imply, but confraternities devoted to charitable works. Many scuole were decorated lavishly, both in the private chapels and in the meeting halls where work was discussed. The Scuola di San Giorgio degli Schiavoni features works by Vittore Carpaccio (ca. 1465–1525), a local artist who often filled his otherwise devotional paintings with acutely observed details of Venetian life. Study the exuberance of his *St. George* as he slays the dragon or the vivid colors and details in *The Funeral of St. Jerome* and *St. Augustine in His Study. Calle dei Furlani, tel. 041/522–8828. Admission: 5,000 lire. Open Tues.–Sat. 10–12:30, 3:30–6; Sun. 11–12:30.*

Tour 4: The Western and Northern Districts

If churches, art, and sculpture and further ramblings through the back streets and along the old canals of Venice continue to interest you, head out of Piazza San Marco under the arcades of the Fabbrica Nuova at the far end of the square. If you want to make a detour for an expensive drink at the fabled **Harry's Bar,** just turn left down Calle Vallaresso, behind the Hotel Luna Baglioni. Then head for
23 **Campo Morosini,** which everyone calls by its old name, Campo San Stefano, in honor of the 14th-century church off to one side of the square; stop in to see the ship's-keel roof, a type found in several of Venice's older churches and the work of its master shipbuilders.

Time Out **Café Paolin,** with tables occupying most of one end of the square, is reputed to have Venice's best ice cream. It's a pleasant place to sit and watch the passing parade.

Join the stream of pedestrians crossing the Grand Canal on the Accademia Bridge to the district called Dorsoduro (literally, "hard back") because of its strong clay foundation. The bridge leads you
24 directly to the **Accademia Gallery,** Venice's most important picture gallery. It has an extraordinary collection of Venetian paintings, at-

tractively displayed and well lit. Highlights include Giovanni Bellini's altarpiece from the church of San Giobbe (notice how he carried the church's architectural details right into the frame of the painting) and his moving *Madonna with St. Catherine and the Magdalen;* a fine *St. George* by Andrea Mantegna, Bellini's brother-in-law from Padua, who was much admired by later Venetian painters; the *Tempest,* by Giorgione (1477–1510); and Veronese's monumental canvas, *Feast in the House of Levi.* This last painting was commissioned as a Last Supper, but the Inquisition took issue with Veronese's inclusion of jesters and German soldiers in the painting. Veronese avoided the charge of profanity by changing the title, and the picture was then supposed to depict the bawdy, but still biblical, feast of Levi. This museum was built on what was originally the Scuola della Carità and the church of Santa Maria della Carità; the body of the church has been preserved in a large room that contains the surviving fragments of Giorgione's masterful frescoes from the facade of the Fondaco dei Tedeschi (*see* Tour 2, *above*). A room preserved from the Scuola holds on one wall its original masterpiece, Titian's *Presentation of the Virgin.* And don't miss the room containing various views of 15th- and 16th-century Venice by Giovanni Bellini's brother Gentile: Study them to see how much the city has changed since then—and how much it looks the same. *Campo della Carità, tel. 041/522–2247. Admission: 8,000 lire. Open Apr.–Oct. 9–7, Nov.–Mar. 9–2.*

Time Out   Just beside the Accademia is **Bar Belle Arti** (closed Sun.), a coffee bar and sandwich shop with a variety of tasty sandwiches, quiches, and beer.

Off Campo San Barnaba, on Fondamenta Gherardini, you'll see a floating fruit and vegetable market tied up in the canal. It's one of the few left in Venice. Continue toward Campo Santa Margherita, passing **Mondonovo**, one of Venice's best mask shops (*see* Shopping, *below*).

At **Campo Santa Margherita,** a busy neighborhood shopping square, ㉕ stop in to see Giambattista Tiepolo's ceiling paintings in the **Scuola dei Carmini.** The paintings, now displayed on the second floor, were commissioned to honor the Carmelite order by depicting prominent Carmelites in conversation with saints and angels. Of the three great Venetian painters whose names start with T (Titian, Tintoretto, and Tiepolo), Tiepolo came last chronologically (he painted in the 18th century, while the others were 16th-century artists) and achieved the greatest international fame in his own time, though an underlying melancholy in his ethereal, brightly colored paintings betrays a man of sober piety. Tiepolo's vivid techniques transformed some unpromising religious themes into flamboyant displays of color and movement. Mirrors are available on the benches to make it easier to see the ceiling without getting a sore neck. *Campo dei Carmini, tel. 041/528–9420. Admission: 5,000 lire. Open Mon.–Sat. 9–noon, 3–6.*

㉖ Continue on to the **Frari,** an immense Gothic church of russet-colored brick, built in the 14th century for the Franciscans. In keeping with the austere principles of the Franciscan order, the Frari is quite stark inside, with much less ornamentation than other Venetian churches. The relative absence of decoration gives a select feeling to the church paintings, such as Bellini's *Madonna and Four Saints* in the sacristy. The most striking is Titian's large *Assumption* over the main altar showing his clever use of the design of the church interior to frame his painting. Worldly and polished, Titian also was a fashionable portrait painter, and the Virgin's rapturous rise to heaven here is charged with very real human emotion. The *Pesaro Madonna* over the first altar on the left nave near the main altar is also by Titian; his wife, who died shortly afterward in childbirth, posed for the figure of Mary. Both of these pictures demonstrate Titian's love of robust, brilliant color and dramatic composition. The Madonna was radical for its time because the main figure was not placed squarely in the center of the painting, but look at how dynamic the picture is as a result. On the same side of the church, look at the spooky pyramid-shape monument to the sculptor Antonio Canova (1757–1822), containing his heart. Across the nave is a neoclassical 19th-century monument to Titian, executed by two of Canova's pupils. *Admission: 1,000 lire. Open Apr.–Oct., Mon.– Sat. 9–12, 2:30–6, Sun. 3–6; Nov.–Mar., Mon.–Sat. 9:30–12, 3–5:30, Sun. 3–5:30.*

㉗ Behind the Frari is the **Scuola di San Rocco,** filled with dark, dramatic canvases by Tintoretto. Born some 30 years after Titian, Jacopo Robusti—called Tintoretto because his father was a dyer— was more mystical and devout than the sophisticated Titian. Though his colors are equally brilliant, he carried Titian's love of motion and odd composition to almost surreal effects, in the same Mannerist vein as El Greco (who was at one time a pupil of Titian's!). In 1564, Tintoretto beat other painters competing for the commission to decorate this building by submitting not a sketch but a finished work, which he additionally offered free of charge. The series of more than 50 paintings that he ultimately created took a total of 23 years to complete. These works, depicting Old and New Testament themes, were restored in the 1970s, and Tintoretto's inventive use of light has once more been revealed. *Campo San Rocco, tel. 041/523–4864. Admission: 7,000 lire. Open Apr.–Oct., Mon.–Fri. 9–5:30; Nov.– Mar., 10–1; Sat. and Sun. year-round 10–4.*

The area around San Rocco is well off the normal tourist trail, with narrow alleys and streets winding alongside small canals to little squares, where posters advertising political parties and sports events seem to be the only signs of life. Head back past the Frari to
㉘ **Campo San Polo,** one of Venice's largest squares and a favorite playground for neighborhood children. From here you take Calle della Madonetta, Calle dell'Olio, Rugheta del Ravano, and Ruga Vecchia San Giovanni to the **Rialto** shopping district, where you can cross the Grand Canal for the shortcut back to San Marco. Alternatively, you can go north from Campo San Polo by way of Calle Bernardo, Calle dello Scaleter, Rio Terrà Parrucchetta, and Calle del Tintor to
㉙ **Campo San Giacomo dell'Orio,** where the 13th-century church of San Giacomo stands on a charming square that few tourists ever find (and there are a number of reasonably priced pizzerias). Here you're not far from the **San Stae** vaporetto landing, so you can take the boat back along the Grand Canal to the heart of the city.

Tour 5: Islands of the Lagoon

Conical bundles of piles, called *bricole,* mark the navigable channels to help boats negotiate the shallow waters of the Venetian lagoon, with its islands of Murano, Burano, and Torcello. These islands are famous for their handicrafts—notably glass and lace—but guided tours here usually involve high-pressure attempts to make you buy, with little time left for anything else. It's much cheaper and more adventurous to make your own way around the islands, using the good vaporetto connections. Services to and from Venice use the landing stage at Fondamenta Nuove, almost due north of San Marco.

The most distant island, Torcello, is ideal for picnics but has no food stores. Buy provisions in Venice if you plan to picnic there.

③⓪ If you're making your way on foot to Fondamenta Nuove, stop at the church of the **Gesuiti,** which dominates the Campo dei Gesuiti. This 18th-century church is built in an extravagantly Baroque style; the classical arches and straight lines of the Renaissance have been abandoned in favor of flowing, twisting forms. The marble of the gray-and-white interior is used like brocade, carved into swags and drapes. Titian's *Martyrdom of St. Lawrence,* over the first altar on the left, is a dramatic example of the great artist's feel for light and movement.

From **Fondamenta Nuove** you have a choice of vaporetti. Line 52 goes to San Michele and Murano; Line 12, which you can join at Murano, skips Venice's cemetery-island of San Michele and goes to Murano, Burano, and Torcello.

Numbers in the margin correspond to points of interest on the Venetian Lagoon map.

③① It's only a five-minute ride to **San Michele,** Venice's cypress-lined cemetery island with its pretty Renaissance church of **San Michele in Isola,** designed by Coducci in 1478, and Venice's **cemetery.** It is a moving experience to walk among the gravestones, with the sound of lapping water on all sides. The American poet Ezra Pound, the great Russian impresario and art critic Sergey Diaghilev, and the composer Igor Stravinsky are buried here.

③② Another five minutes on Line 52 takes you to **Murano,** which, like Venice, is made up of a number of smaller islands linked by bridges. Murano is known exclusively for its glassworks, which you can visit to see how glass is made. Many of these line the **Fondamenta dei Vetrai,** the canalside walkway leading away from the Colonna landing stage. The houses along this walk are simpler than many of their Venetian counterparts; traditionally they were workmen's cottages. Just before the junction with Murano's Grand Canal—250 yards up from the landing stage—is the church of **San Pietro Martire.** This 16th-century reconstruction of an earlier Gothic church has several works by Venetian masters: notably, the *Madonna and Child,* by Giovanni Bellini, and *St. Jerome,* by Veronese.

Cross the Ponte Vivarini and turn right onto **Fondamenta Cavour.** Follow the Fondamenta around the corner to the **Museo Vetrario** (Glass Museum), with a collection of Venetian glass that ranges from priceless antique to only slightly less expensive modern. The museum gives you a good idea of the history of Murano's glassworks, which were moved here from Venice in the 13th century because they were a fire risk. It's useful, too, to get a clear idea of authentic Venetian styles and patterns if you're planning to make some purchases later. *Tel. 041/739586. Admission: 5,000 lire. Open Apr.– Oct., Thurs.–Tues. 9–7; Nov.–Mar., Thurs.–Tues. 10–4.*

③③ Make your way back along the same route to the landing stage, and take Line 12 to **Burano,** which is about 30 minutes from Murano. It's a small island fishing village with houses painted in cheerful colors and a raffishly raked bell tower on the main square, about 100 yards from the landing stage and clearly visible from there. Lace is to Burano what glass is to Murano, but be prepared to pay a lot for the real thing. Stalls line the way from the landing stage to **Piazza Galuppi,** the main square; the vendors, many of them fishermen's wives, are generally good-natured and unfamiliar with the techniques of the hard sell.

Venetian Lagoon

The **Scuola di Merletti di Burano** (Lace Museum) on Piazza Galuppi is the best place to learn the intricacies of the lace-making traditions of Burano. It is also useful for learning the nature of the skills involved in making the more expensive lace, in case you intend to buy some lace on your way back to the vaporetto. *Piazza Galuppi. Tel. 041/730034. Admission: 3,000 lire. Open Tues.–Sat. 9–6, Sun. 10–4.*

Time Out | Among the pleasant trattorie on Piazza Galuppi are **Ai Pescatori** (closed Mon.) and **Romano** (closed Tues.). Both serve seafood specialties à la carte, but keep your eye on the costs.

34 Vaporetto Line 12 continues from the Burano landing stage to the sleepy green island of **Torcello,** about 10 minutes farther. This is where the first Venetians landed in their flight from the barbarians 1,500 years ago. Even after many settlers left to found the city of Venice on the island of Rivo Alto (Rialto), Torcello continued to grow and prosper, until its main source of income, wool manufacturing, was priced out of the marketplace. It's hard to believe now, looking at this almost deserted island, that in the 16th century it had 20,000 inhabitants and 10 churches.

A brick-paved lane leads up from the landing stage and follows the curve of the canal toward the center of the island. You pass **Locanda Cipriani,** an inn famous for its good food and the patronage of Ernest Hemingway, who often came to Torcello for the solitude. These days Locanda Cipriani is about the busiest spot on the island, as well-heeled customers arrive on high-speed powerboats for lunch. (Count on at least 75,000 lire for a set menu. Tel. 041/730150. Reservations advised.)

Just beyond is the grassy square that holds the only surviving monuments of the island's past splendor. The low church of **Santa Fosca,** on the right, dates back to the 11th century. Next to it is the cathedral of Santa Maria Assunta, also built in the 11th century: The ornate Byzantine mosaics are testimony to the importance and wealth of an island that could attract the best artists and craftsmen of its day. The vast mosaic on the inside of the facade depicts the Last Judgment as artists of the 11th and 12th centuries imagined it: Figures writhe in vividly depicted contortions of pain. Facing it, as if in mitigation, is the calm mosaic figure of the Madonna, alone in a field of gold above the staunch array of Apostles.

The trip back from Torcello retraces the route from Venice. Boats leave approximately every hour, and the trip takes about 50 minutes.

Tour 6: San Giorgio Maggiore and the Giudecca

Numbers in the margin correspond to points of interest on the Venice map.

Looking out across the Basin of San Marco, you can see the island of San Giorgio Maggiore, separated by a small channel from the Giudecca. A tall brick campanile on that distant bank perfectly complements the Campanile of San Marco. Behind it looms the stately dome of one of Venice's greatest churches, San Giorgio Maggiore. To reach the island, take the Line 82 vaporetto from San Zaccaria, which is near San Marco.

㉟ A church has been on this island since the late eighth century, with a Benedictine monastery added in the tenth century. The present church of **San Giorgio Maggiore** was begun in 1566 by the greatest architect of his time, Andrea Palladio, whose work is so evident throughout the Venetian Arc (*see* Chapter 7, The Venetian Arc). Two of Palladio's hallmarks are mathematical harmony and architectural elements borrowed from classical antiquity, both of which are evident in this superbly proportioned neoclassical church of red brick and white marble. Inside, the church is refreshingly airy and simply decorated. Two important late Tintoretto paintings hang on either side of the chancel: *The Last Supper* and *The Gathering of Manna.* Over the first altar on the right-hand side of the nave is an *Adoration of the Shepherds* by Jacopo Bassano (1517–1592), a painter from Bassano del Grappa on the mainland who possessed considerable originality and was especially adept at portraying nature and country life. Take the elevator up the Campanile outside (admission 2,000 lire) for a fine view of Venice and its harbor. *Open daily 9–12:30, 2–5.*

The monastery of San Giorgio Maggiore, where the conclave that elected Pope Pius VII took place in 1800, later a barracks for the occupying Austrians, now houses an artistic and cultural foundation where conferences are often held, and is usually closed to the public. Palladio designed the monastery's first cloister, and Longhena was the architect for the grand baroque library.

Catch the Line 82 vaporetto to reach the island of **Giudecca,** a crescent cupped around the southern shore of Venice. The Giudecca has always been seen as a place apart. Its name is a something of a mystery. According to some, it derives from the possible settlement of Jews on the island in the 14th century, and according to others it was so called because in the 9th century nobles condemned to exile (*giudicato* means judged or sentenced) were sent here. It became a

pleasure garden for wealthy Venetians during the long and luxurious decline of the Republic. Even today it has an atmosphere of its
own, quite distinct from the heart of Venice. In one regard it is still
the province of the wealthy, however: The exclusive **Cipriani** hotel
(*see* Lodging, *below*) lies secluded on its eastern tip.

③⑥ The main attraction here is the church of **Il Redentore,** also by Palladio. Its tranquil, stately facade is actually a series of superimposed
temple fronts, topped by a dome and a pair of slim, almost
minaretlike, bell towers. The interior, like San Giorgio Maggiore's,
is perfectly proportioned and airy, in contrast to the dusky mystery
of the Basilica di San Marco.

On the third Sunday of July, the feast of Il Redentore (the Redeemer) is celebrated with a pontoon bridge being built over the channel
to the Giudecca, commemorating the doge's annual visit to this
church to offer thanks for the end of a 16th-century plague. Traditionally, the Venetians take to the water in boats en masse, as midnight fireworks explode over the lagoon, and a good time is had by
all.

The vaporetto Line 82 will take you back in the other direction to
San Marco, or you can take Line 82 going the other way, from the
Giudecca directly across the channel to the **Zattere,** the broad waterfront promenade on Dorsoduro, where there are several pizzerias
and a casual neighborhood atmosphere.

What to See and Do with Children

The whole experience of a visit to Venice should provide excitement
for a child. For the parent it means trading one constant warning
("Look both ways before crossing") for another ("Stay away from
the edge of that canal"). Wandering over the many footbridges and
along narrow alleyways leading nowhere, children get a chance to
burn off a lot of excess energy, and sometimes their aimless rambles
lead to an unexpected square or little church. But there are not
many activities aimed at children.

Carnival. Children enjoy dressing up in masks or full costume or
having their faces painted by street makeup artists during the carnival festivities during the two weeks before Ash Wednesday.

Glassblowing. Go to one of the showrooms with demonstrations
along Fondamenta dei Vetrai in Murano (*see* Tour 5: Islands of the
Lagoon, *above*).

Gondola ride. Your child will probably have suggested this more
than once, long before you even arrive in Venice. Gondoliers usually
perform well for children, demonstrating how they steer and calling
out to other traffic as they near a junction.

Lion Statues. These guardians of the Arsenal are a reminder of
Venice's glorious naval past (*see* Tour 3: To the Arsenal and Beyond,
above). The lions in Piazzetta dei Leoncini, near San Marco, are fine
mounts for tots.

Museo Navale (*See* Tour 3: To the Arsenal and Beyond, *above*).

Torre dell'Orologio. The hourly display when the bell is struck by the
mechanical figures always draws a crowd of young and old (*see* Tour
1: The San Marco District, *above*).

Off the Beaten Track

The Ghetto. In 1516, Venice's Great Council ordered all Jews to be confined to a small island in Cannaregio. They were not allowed to leave this area after sunset, when the gates were barred until dawn. Jewish physicians, whose services were favored by the aristocrats, were the only exception. The ghetto eventually expanded to include the Ghetto Vecchio, Ghetto Nuovo, and Ghetto Nuovissimo. In 1797, when the Venetian Republic fell, Napoleon's troops pulled down the Ghetto's gates, but by then, Jewish homes and synagogues were rooted in these neighborhoods and the word "ghetto"—which perhaps derived from foundries for the casting (or "getto") of metal that had existed there—passed into the language as a place for the isolation of Jews or other minorities. The **Museo Ebraico** is in one corner of Campo Ghetto Nuovo, a pretty square with a fountain and a few trees. From the museum, you can join a guided tour of the synagogues; tours are in English and are given several times a day. *Campo del Ghetto Nuovo, tel. 041/715359. Admission: 4,000 lire, with tour 10,000 lire. Open Jun.–Sept., Sun.–Fri. 10–7; Oct.–May, Sun.–Fri. 10–4:30. Closed Sat. and Jewish holidays.*

Lido. This island, forming the north–south barrier for the Lagoon, has the best beaches for sunbathing, but although thousands swim here and at nearby Jesolo, the Adriatic is reputedly polluted. There are tennis courts, a golf course, a flying club, and a horse-riding club. Hotels Des Bains and Cipriani have exclusive clubs with lovely swimming pools. The famous Lido Casino operates during the summer months only (in the winter it returns to its palatial home on the Grand Canal—*see* Tour 2, *above*). The church and monastery of San Nicolo are on the northern end of the island; during the week, this is a pleasant place for a walk and lunch. Avoid the Sunday crowds; most restaurants are closed on Monday. *Take vaporetto Line 1, 52, or (in summer only) 82 to Piazzale Maria Elisabetta on the Lido. From there bus A goes north to San Nicolo.*

Madonna dell'Orto. In the residential Cannaregio district, north of the first loop of the Grand Canal, this was Tintoretto's parish church; he was buried just to the right of the main altar. On each side of the altar are his paintings *The Last Judgment* and *Adoration of the Golden Calf*. In the latter, he supposedly painted his own face (with a black beard) on one of the pagans holding the calf. There are several more of his paintings and work by other artists here. *Cannaregio district, Fondamenta Madonna dell'Orto.*

Palazzo Labia. This 18th-century palace, once the home of the wealthy Labia family, is located between the train station and the Ghetto, just off the Grand Canal. It is now the Venetian headquarters of RAI, Italy's National Broadcasting Corporation. The Palazzo's ballroom contains magnificent Tiepolo frescoes, including his famous scenes of Antony and Cleopatra. Other rooms contain more Tiepolos and other 17th–18th century paintings and tapestries. *Campo San Geremia, Cannaregio, tel. 041/524–2821. Admission to the ballroom: free, Mon., Thur. and Fri. 3–4; guided tour of the ballroom and other rooms (available in English): 10,000 lire, by prior arrangement, Mon.–Fri. 10–4.*

Shopping

Shopping in Venice is part of the fun of exploring the city, and you're sure to find plenty of interesting shops and boutiques as you explore. It's always a good idea to mark on your map the location of a shop that interests you; otherwise you may not be able to find it again in mazelike Venice. Shops are usually open 9–12:30 or 1 and 3:30 or 4–7:30 and are closed Sunday and on Monday morning. However, many tourist-oriented shops are open all day, every day. Food shops are closed Wednesday afternoon, except over the Christmas and New Year period, when they remain open. Some shops close for both a summer and a winter vacation.

Shopping Districts

The main shopping areas are the **Mercerie,** the succession of narrow and crowded streets winding from Piazza San Marco to the Rialto, and the area around Campo San Salvador, Calle del Teatro, Campo Manin, and Campo San Fantin. The **San Marco** area is full of shops and top-name boutiques, such as Missoni, Valentino, Fendi, and Versace.

Department Stores

The only thing approximating a department store here is **Coin,** at the Rialto Bridge, featuring men's and women's fashions. The **Standa** stores on Campo San Luca, Strada Nuova, and the Lido have a wide range of goods at moderate prices.

Food Markets

The open-air fruit and vegetable market at **Rialto** is colorful and animated throughout the morning. The adjacent fish market offers a vivid lesson in ichthyology, presenting some species you've probably never seen (open mornings Tues.–Sat.). At the other end of Venice, in the Castello district, is **Via Garibaldi,** the scene of another lively food market on weekday mornings. The **Standa** stores on Strada Nuova and on the Lido also have supermarket sections, and there are other supermarkets tucked away in the city, including **SUVE** on Salizzada San Lio, **Mega** on Campo Santa Margherita, and **CAR** at San Basilio, at the western end of the Zattere.

Specialty Stores

Glassware

Glass, most of it made in Murano, is Venice's number-one product, and you'll be confronted by mind-boggling displays of traditional and contemporary glassware, often kitsch. Take your time and be selective. Should you buy glass in Venice's shops or in the showrooms of Murano's factories? You will probably find that prices are pretty much the same; showrooms in Venice that are outlets of Murano glassworks sell at the same prices as the factories. However, because of competition, shops in Venice stocking wares from various glassworks may charge slightly lower prices.

In Venice, **Venini** (Piazzetta dei Leoncini 314), **Pauli** (Calle dell'Ascensione 72), and **Salviati** (Piazza San Marco 78 and 110) are reliable and respected firms. For chic, contemporary glassware, **Carlo Moretti** is a good choice; his signature designs are on display at **Isola** (Campo San Moisè). For stunning glass beads and jewelry, go to **Archimede Seguso** (Piazza San Marco 143); **Vetri d'Arte** (Piazza San Marco 140) offers moderately priced glass jewelry. In a category all his own is **Gianfranco Penzo** (Campo del Ghetto Nuovo 2895), who decorates Jewish ritual vessels in glass, makes commemorative plates, and takes special orders.

In Murano, most of the glass factories have showrooms where glassware is sold. The **Domus** shop (Fondamenta dei Vetrai) has a selection of smaller objects and jewelry from the best glassworks.

Lace

Venice's top name is **Jesurum,** with a shop at Piazza San Marco 60 and a much larger establishment at Ponte Canonica, behind the Basilica di San Marco. **Martinuzzi, Fabris,** and **Tokatzian,** all on Piazza San Marco, also have a good selection. Remember that much of the lace and embroidered linen sold in Venice and on Burano is made in China or Taiwan. For the same sumptuous brocades, damasks, and cut velvets used by the world's most prestigious decorators, go to **Lorenzo Rubelli** (Campo San Gallo 1089), just off Piazza San Marco. At **Norelene** (Calle de la Chiesa 727) you'll find stunning hand-printed fabrics, and at **Venetia Studium** (Campo San Fantin 1997, opposite La Fenice opera house and also at Calle Larga XXII Marzo 2430, San Marco) are beautiful Fortuny-inspired lamps, furnishings, clothes, and accessories.

Masks　These are a tradition in Venice; they were worn everywhere during the lengthy Carnival season in the 18th century. Shops throughout the city sell masks of all types. Among the most interesting are **Mondonovo** (Rio Terrà Canal), **Cà Macana** (Calle delle Botteghe, near San Barnaba), and **Laboratorio Artigiano Maschere** (Barbaria delle Tole, near Santi Giovanni e Paolo).

Prints　An old print of Venice makes a distinctive gift or souvenir. There are several print shops on Salizzada San Moisè and on the streets as you continue toward Campo Santo Stefano. Hand-printed paper and desk accessories, memo pads, and address books abound at the well-known **Piazzesi** shop (Campiello della Feltrina, near Santa Maria del Giglio).

Sports

Golf　The **Golf Club Lido di Venezia,** an 18-hole course, is located on the Lido island. *Via del Forte, Alberoni, Lido, tel. 041/731333.*

Horseback　**Circolo Ippico Veneziano** (tel. 041/526–5162) is located at Ca' Bianca Riding　on the Lido. It is open all year.

Jogging　The best spot to jog is past the public gardens (Giardini) in the Castello district and over to the pine wood on Sant'Elena; you get a magnificent view of the city as you jog back toward the center.

Swimming　Many Venetians and visitors are happy to swim from the seaward-facing side of the Lido. There is free public access to the beach at either end of the Lido (the Line C bus, leaving every 20 minutes from the Santa Maria Elisabetta landing, goes all the way to Alberoni, where there are usually fewer people). The strand in between is sectioned off in the summer season into private beaches offering various facilities—changing rooms, bar, showers—for the use of guests of hotels on the Lido and of nonguests who are charged a fixed daily or weekly rate. However, considering the reputedly polluted state of the Adriatic, you may wish to swim in a pool. Venice's only public pool is the **Piscina Gandini** (tel. 041/528–5430), located on the island of Sacca Fisola, at the far end of Giudecca (take Line 52 vaporetto to Sacca Fisola). The deluxe hotels **Excelsior** (tel. 041/526–0201) and **Hotel des Bains** (tel. 041/526–5921) are both located on Lungomare Marconi on the Lido; their pools are open to nonguests for a fee.

Tennis　The **Hotel des Bains** (*see* Swimming, *above*) and the exclusive **Sea Gull Club** of the Hotel Cipriani (tel. 041/520–7744) will let nonguests play for a fee. There are tennis clubs on the Lido: **Lido Tennis Club** (tel. 041/526–0954) and the **Tennis Union** (tel. 041/968134).

Dining

The general standard of Venetian restaurants has suffered from the onslaught of mass tourism, but it is still possible to eat well in Venice at moderate prices. Although seafood is a specialty here, the fact that the wholesale cost of fish is generally higher than meat is reflected in the prices, and you will find some fish dishes very expensive, especially those that are priced by weight (mainly baked or steamed fish). However, if you do want to eat fish, don't be shy about asking the cost. Under the auspices of the restaurant association, most of the city's restaurants offer special tourist menus, moderately priced according to the level of the restaurant and generally representing good value. It's always a good idea to reserve your table or have your hotel *portiere* do it for you. Dining hours are short, starting at 12:30 or 1 for lunch and ending at 2:30–3, when restaurants close for the afternoon, opening up again to start serving at about 8 and closing again at 11 or midnight. Most close one day a week and are also likely to close without notice for vacation or renovation. Few have signs on the outside, so when the metal blinds are shut tight, you can't tell a closed restaurant from a closed TV-repair shop. This makes them hard to spot when exploring the city. You may not find a cover charge *(pane e coperto)*, but a service charge of 10%–15% will almost surely be on the check.

Venetian cuisine is based on seafood, with a few culinary excursions inland. Antipasto may take the form of a seafood salad, *prosciutto di San Daniele* (cured ham) from the mainland, or pickled vegetables. As a first course Venetians favor risotto, a creamy rice dish that may be cooked with vegetables or shellfish. Pasta, too, is good with seafood sauces; Venice is *not* the place to order spaghetti with tomato sauce. *Pasticcio di pesce* is pasta baked with fish, usually *baccalà* (dried cod). A classic first course is *pasta e fagioli* (thick bean soup with pasta). *Bigoli* is strictly a local pasta, made of whole wheat, usually served with a salty *tonno* (tuna) sauce. Polenta, made of cornmeal, is another pillar of regional cooking. It's often served as an accompaniment to *fegato alla veneziana* (liver with onion, Venetian style). Local seafood includes *granseola* (crab), *moeche* (small, soft-shelled crabs), and *seppie* or *seppioline* (cuttlefish).

The dessert specialty in Venice is *tiramisù*, a heavenly concoction of creamy cheese (*mascarpone*), coffee, chocolate, and ladyfingers (*savoirdi*). The recipe originated on the mainland, but the Venetians have adopted it enthusiastically. Local wines are the dry white Tocai and Pinot from the Friuli region and bubbly white Prosecco, a naturally fermented sparkling white wine that is a shade less dry. The best Prosecco comes from the Valdobbiadene; Cartizze, which is similar, is considered superior by some but is expensive. Popular red wines include Merlot, Cabernet, Raboso, and Refosco. You can sample all of these and more in Venice's many *bacari*, or old-style wine bars, where wine is served by the glass and accompanied by *cicchetti* (assorted tidbits), often substantial enough for a light meal.

Highly recommended restaurants are indicated by a star ★.

Category	Cost*
$$$$	over 120,000 lire
$$$	80,000–120,000 lire

| $$ | 50,000–80,000 lire |
| $ | under 50,000 lire |

per person, including three courses, wine, and service

$$$$ **Grand Canal.** The Grand Canal restaurant at the Monaco hotel is a
★ favorite with Venetians, who enjoy eating in summer on the lovely
canalside terrace looking across the mouth of the Grand Canal to the
island of San Georgio Maggiore, and in the cosy dining room in winter. All the pasta is made fresh daily on the premises, and the
smoked and marinaded salmon are also home-produced. The traditional Venetian dishes are very well prepared, and the chef, Angelo
Maiocco, also offers delicious meat and fish dishes such as scampi
alla Ca' d'Oro (in a cognac sauce), served with rice. *Hotel Monaco,
Calle Vallaresso 1325, San Marco, tel. 041/520–0211. Reservations
advised. Dress: casual but neat; jacket required at dinner. AE, DC,
MC, V.*

La Caravella. This small and intimate restaurant with old-time sail-
ing-ship decor has a reputation for fine food and cordial, courteous
service. Among the specialties on the vast menu are the very Venetian *taglierini alla granseola* (delicate pasta with crab sauce) and
scampi in port sauce. (The same kitchen also serves the slightly less
expensive **Cortile** restaurant next door in a pretty garden courtyard
during summer and in wood-paneled salons during winter.) *Calle
Larga XXII Marzo 2397, San Marco, tel. 041/5208901. Reservations
required. Dress: casual. AE, DC, MC, V. Closed Wed.*

$$$ **Arturo.** The cordial proprietor of this tiny restaurant near Campo
Sant'Angelo has the distinction (in Venice) of not serving seafood.
Instead there are varied and delicious fresh vegetable and salad
dishes; tasty, tender, and generous meat courses, including the deli-
cately pungent *braciola alla veneziana* (pork chop schnitzel with
vinegar); and an authentic creamy, homemade tiramisù for dessert.
*Calle degli Assassini 3656, San Marco, tel. 041/528–6974. Reserva-
tions required. Dress: casual. No credit cards. Closed Sun. and 3
weeks in Aug.*

★ **Da Fiore.** Long a favorite with Venetians, Da Fiore has been discov-
ered by tourists, so it's imperative to reserve for an excellent sea-
food dinner, which might include such specialties as *pasticcio di
pesce* (fish pie) and seppioline. Not easy to find, it's near Campo San
Polo. *Calle dello Scaleter 2202, San Polo, tel. 041/721308. Reserva-
tions necessary. Dress: casual but neat. AE, DC, MC, V. Closed
Sun., Mon., Aug. 10–early Sept., Dec. 25–Jan. 15.*

Fiaschetteria Toscana. You'll soon see why this is one of the most
popular restaurants with the Venetians themselves, whether you
eat in the upstairs dining room or under the arbor on the square.
Cheerful courteous waiters may suggest the delicate *tagliolini alla
buranella* (thin noodles with shrimp) or *rombo* (turbot) with capers.
*Campo San Giovanni Crisostomo 5719, Cannaregio, tel. 041/528–
5281. Reservations advised. Dress: casual. AE, DC, MC, V. Closed
Tues. and July 1–15.*

$$ **Al Mondo Novo.** This excellent fish restaurant is owned by a fish
wholesaler in the Rialto market, who himself eats here every day, so
you can be sure that everything is absolutely fresh. Specialties prepared by Signora Trevisan, the owner's wife, include *cape sante*
(scallops) and *cape longhe* (razor clams), risottos and pasta dishes,
and the best of the day's catch grilled on charcoal. Meat dishes are
also available. The manager, Pino Calliandro, offers set menus on
request to suit your taste and pocket, and service continues until

midnight or later if there's a demand for it. *Salizzada San Lio 5409, Castello, tel. 041/520–0698. Reservations advised. Dress: casual. AE, MC, V. Closed Wed. Feb.–Mar.*

Da Gigio. An attractive, friendly, family-run trattoria on the quayside of a canal just off the Strada Nuova, Da Gigio is popular with Venetians and visiting Italians, who appreciate the affable service and excellently cooked homemade pasta, fish and meat dishes, and good-quality draft wine. It's useful, too, for a cheaper, simpler lunch at tables in the barroom. *Fondamenta de la Chiesa 3628/a, Cannaregio, tel. 041/528–5140. Dinner reservations advised. Dress: casual. AE, DC, MC, V. Closed Sun. dinner, Mon., 2 weeks in Jan., 2 weeks in Aug.*

Da Ignazio. Smallish, pleasant, and near Campo San Polo, Ignazio is reliable for good food at reasonable prices, barring expensive fish dishes. The cuisine is classic Venetian here, from pasta or risotto with seafood sauce to fegato alla veneziana, but there are standard Italian items as well. *Calle dei Saoneri 2749, San Polo, tel. 041/523–4852. Reservations advised. Dress: casual. AE, DC, MC, V. Closed Sat.*

Da Raffaele. Near Santa Maria del Giglio, this tavern has wood-beamed ceilings and serves classic Venetian specialties, such as fegato alla veneziana. In warm weather tables are set outdoors alongside a canal. *Fondamenta delle Ostreghe 2347, San Marco, tel. 041/523–2317. Reservations advised. Dress: casual. AE, DC, MC, V. Closed Thurs.*

Da Remigio. This very popular local trattoria near the church of San Giorgio dei Greci offers reliable and tasty fish and meat dishes. *Salizzada dei Greci 3416, Castello, tel. 041/523–0089. Reservations required. Dress: casual. Closed Mon. dinner and Tues.*

Montin. On a quiet canal in the Dorsoduro district, this old inn is certainly an institution but not quite the bohemian artistic hang-out it's often described as. Inside, walls are covered with paintings; outside, you dine under an elongated arbor, but the food and service can be erratic. The specialties are *rigatoni ai quattro formaggi* (with four cheeses, mushrooms, and tomato) and *antipasto Montin* (seafood antipasto). *Fondamenta di Borgo 1147, Dorsoduro, tel. 041/522–7151. Reservations advised. Dress: casual. AE, DC, MC, V. Closed Tues. dinner, Wed., 15 days in Jan., 15 days in Aug.*

$ Al Mascaron. A lively, often crowded bacaro, Al Mascaron, with its paper tablecloths and very informal atmosphere, is a regular stop for locals who like to drop in on their way home from work to gossip, drink, and eat cicchetti at the bar. There are also delicious and generous seafood pasta dishes. *Calle Lunga Santa Maria Formosa 5225, Castello, tel. 041/522–5995. Reservations advised. Dress: casual. No credit cards. Closed Sun., end Dec.–mid-Jan., last 2 weeks in Aug.*

Le Bistrot. Very central, this café-brasserie is open all day and offers tasty Venetian and French specialties, pasta dishes, and pancakes and pizzas at lunchtime and in the evening until 1 AM. Service and cover are included in the prices, and there are tables outside in the summer. *Calle dei Fabbri 4685, San Marco, tel. 041/523–6651. Reservations not necessary. Dress: casual. V, MC. Closed Tues. in winter.*

L'Incontro. This trattoria has a faithful clientele of Venetians and visitors, attracted by generous meat dishes, friendly waiters, and reasonable prices. Menu choices include juicy steaks, wild duck, boar, and (with advance notice) roast suckling pig. It is between San Barnaba and Campo Santa Margherita. *Rio Terrà Canal 3062/a,*

Venice Dining and Lodging

Dining
Al Mascaron, **23**
Al Mondo Novo, **22**
Arturo, **12**
Da Fiore, **3**
Da Gigio, **1**
Da Ignazio, **4**
Da Raffaele, **13**
Da Remigio, **27**

Fiaschetteria
Toscana, **18**
Grand Canal, **20**
L'Incontro, **5**
La Caravella, **16**
Le Bistrot, **19**
Metropole Buffet, **28**
Montin, **6**
San Trovaso, **8**
Vino Vino, **11**

Lodging
Accademia, **9**
Alboretti, **7**
Bucintoro, **30**
Cipriani, **31**
Danieli, **24**
Flora, **15**
Gritti Palace, **14**

La Residenza, **29**
Locanda Fiorita, **10**
Locanda Sturion, **2**
Londra Palace, **26**
Metropole, **28**
Paganelli, **25**
Riva, **21**
Saturnia
Internazionale, **17**

Sacca della Misericordia

Canale delle Navi

San Michele

0   440 yards

0   400 meters

C. Racchetta

Fondamenta

Rio S. Caterina

R. d. Gesuiti Nuove

Rio d. Santi Apostoli

Rio della Panada

C. d. Sauero

C. d. Testa

dei Mendicanti

Campo Santi Giovanni e Paolo

R. d. S. Giustina

R. Barbaria delle Tole

Rio d. S. Marina

18

R. d. Fava

Sal di S. Lio

Campo di S. Maria Formosa

23

R. d. S. Severo

R. S. Lorenzo

R. d. S. Francesco

Canale d. Galeazze

22

C. d. Bande

21

C. d. Specchier

19

Fabbri

R. d. Palazzo

Fond. Osmarin

C. Lion

C. d. Furlani

R. d. Pietà

C. d. Pestrin

R. d. Scudi

R. d. Corpe

27

R. d. Greci

Darsena Grande

Rio d. Vergini

Rio d. S. Daniele

Can. di S. Pietro

Frezzaria

i

20

R. d. S. Mosè

Molo

24 **25** **26**

Riva degli

28

Schiavoni

29

Piazza San Marco

R. d. Arsenale

Rio della Tana

30

V. Garibaldi

Riva dei Sette Martiri

Rio d. S. Anna

R. d. S. Giuseppe

Rio dei Giardini

Canale di S. Marco

Isola di S. Giorgio Maggiore

Fond. delle Zitelle

31

Calle Michelangelo

Riva dei Partigiani

▲ Boat stop

Dorsoduro, tel. 041/522–2404. Reservations advised. Dress: casual.
MC, V. Closed Mon.

Metropole Buffet. Here at the Hotel Metropole Buffet, in a charming
and comfortable room overlooking the waterfront by the Pietà
Church, you can eat a substantial and tasty lunch or dinner (for a
fixed price of around 45,000 lire), helping yourself from a varied selection of starters, soups, pastas, hot and cold dishes, and desserts.
The price even includes a highly drinkable Bianco di Custoza (a light
white wine from the Veneto region) on draft. *Hotel Metropole, Riva
degli Schiavoni 4149, Castello, tel. 041/520–5044. Reservations advised. Dress: casual. AE, DC, MC, V.*

San Trovaso. A wide choice of Venetian dishes and pizzas, reliable
house wines, and economical fixed-price menus make this busy tavern, conveniently near the Accademia Gallery, a good value.
*Fondamenta Priuli 1016, Dorsoduro, tel. 041/520–3703. Reserva-
tions advised. AE, DC, MC, V. Closed Mon.*

Vino Vino. The annex of the extremely expensive Antico Martini
restaurant, this is a highly informal wine bar where you can sample
Italian vintages and munch on a limited selection of (microwaved)
dishes from the kitchens of its upscale big sister, next door. It's open
nonstop 10 AM–midnight. *Calle delle Veste 2007/a, near Campo San
Fantin, San Marco, tel. 041/523–7027. No reservations. Dress: casual. AE, DC, MC, V. Closed Tues.*

Lodging

Most of Venice's hotels are in renovated palaces. The top ones are
indeed palatial, although some "Cinderella" rooms may be small and
dowdy. In lower categories, space is at a premium; some rooms may
be cramped, and not all hotels have lounging areas. Because of pre-
servation laws, some cannot install elevators. Air-conditioning is essential for survival in summer heat; many hotels charge a hefty
supplement for it. Although the city has no cars, it does have boats
plying the canals and pedestrians chattering in the streets, even
late at night. Don't be surprised if your room is noisy (earplugs
help).

The busiest times for hotels are spring and autumn; December 20–
January 2; and the two-week Carnival period leading up to Ash
Wednesday, usually in February. Book well in advance. If you don't
have reservations, you can almost always get a room in any category
by going upon arrival to the AVA (Venetian Hoteliers Association)
booths at the train station (open Apr.–Oct. 8 AM–10 PM, Nov.–Mar. 8
AM–9:30 PM), airport (open Apr.–Oct. 10 AM–9 PM, Nov.–Mar. 10:30
AM–6:30 PM), and at the municipal parking garage at Piazzale Roma
(open Apr.–Oct. 9 AM–10 PM, Nov.–Mar. 9 AM–9 PM). The 15,000–
60,000-lire deposit (depending on the category of the hotel) is rebated
on your bill.

Most hotels quote rates inclusive of breakfast. Rates are generally
comparable with Rome and Milan, but you can save considerably in
the off season. Remember that it is essential to know how to get to
your hotel when you arrive in Venice.

Highly recommended lodgings are indicated by a star ★.

Category	Cost*
$$$$	over 450,000 lire
$$$	250,000–450,000 lire

$$	160,000–250,000 lire
$	under 160,000 lire

All prices are for a standard double room for two, including taxes and service.

$$$$ Cipriani. It's impossible to feel stressed in this sybaritic oasis of
★ stunningly decorated rooms and suites, some with garden patios.
The Cipriani is located on the Giudecca, across St. Mark's Basin
from the heart of Venice, with views of San Giorgio and the lagoon.
The hotel launch whisks you back and forth to San Marco at any hour
of the day or night, but the Cipriani is not for anyone who wants to
feel Venice's heartbeat. Cooking courses and fitness programs help
keep guests occupied. The newly restored Palazzo Vendramin annex
(seven suites and three double rooms) is open all year. *Giudecca 10,
tel. 041/520–7744, fax 041/5203930. 104 rooms or suites with bath.
Facilities: bar, restaurant, outdoor pool, gardens, tennis courts.
AE, DC, MC, V. Closed Dec.–mid-Mar.*

Danieli. This famous hotel is a collage of newer buildings around a
15th-century palazzo, which is loaded with sumptuous Venetian decor and atmosphere. Some of the suites are positively palatial, but
some of the less attractive rooms may seem overpriced. The salons
and bar are chic places to relax and watch the celebrities go by, and
the dining terrace, like many rooms, has a fabulous view of San
Giorgio and St. Mark's Basin. *Riva degli Schiavoni 4196, Castello,
tel. 041/522–6480, fax 041/5200208. 235 rooms or suites with bath.
Facilities: bar, restaurant, terrace, the use of tennis court and
swimming pool at the Hotel Excelsior and/or Hotel des Bains on the
Lido. AE, DC, MC, V.*

Gritti Palace. The atmosphere of an aristocratic private home per-
vades this quietly elegant hotel. Fresh flowers, fine antiques, sumptuous appointments, and Old World service give guests the feeling of
being very special people. The dining terrace on the Grand Canal is
best in the evening when the boat traffic dies down. *Campo Santa
Maria del Giglio 2467, San Marco, tel. 041/794611, fax 041/5200942.
88 rooms or suites with bath. Facilities: bar, restaurant, canalside
terrace, the use of tennis court and swimming pool at the Hotel Excelsior and/or Hotel des Bains on the Lido. AE, DC, MC, V.*

$$$ Londra Palace. This grand hotel commands a fine view of San
Giorgio and St. Mark's Basin and has a distinguished ambience. The
rooms are decorated in dark paisley prints, with sophisticated
touches, and the rooftop suite is a honeymooner's dream. The Deux
Lions restaurant offers fine Venetian and French cuisine, and the pi-
ano bar is open late. Guest perks include a complimentary Mercedes
for one-day excursions and free entrance to the city casino. *Riva
degli Schiavoni 4171, Castello, tel. 041/520–0533, fax 041/5225032.
69 rooms and suites with bath. Facilities: piano bar, restaurant, ter-
race, solarium. AE, DC, MC, V.*

★ **Metropole.** This exceptionally well-run hotel is on a quieter part of
the waterfront near the Pietà church, but still only a few minutes'
stroll from Piazza San Marco. The spacious rooms and sitting areas
are furnished with style and panache from the owner's impressive
collection of antiques, and the efficient, courteous staff creates an
unusually pleasant and relaxed atmosphere. The management's
thoughtfulness extends to providing rubber boots for guests in case
of high water in the city. Many rooms have a view of the lagoon, but
the others overlooking a canal and peaceful gardens are also invit-
ing. Special rates—such as the best rooms at the lowest price, if the
hotel is not full—are well worth checking out. You can step from

your water taxi or gondola directly into the hotel lobby. *Riva degli Schiavoni 4149, Castello, tel. 041/520-5044, fax 041/522-3679. 73 rooms with bath. Facilities: bar, buffet restaurant (see Dining, above). AE, DC, MC, V.*

Saturnia Internazionale. There's lots of Old World charm in this historic palace, which is quietly but centrally located near Piazza San Marco. Its beamed ceilings, damask-hung walls, and authentic Venetian decor impart real character to the solid comfort of its rooms and salons. Many rooms have been extensively redecorated and endowed with more glamorous—and much larger—bathrooms. *Calle Larga XXII Marzo 2398, San Marco, tel. 041/520-8377, fax 041/520-7131. 95 rooms with bath. Facilities: bar, 2 restaurants. AE, DC, MC, V.*

$$ **Accademia.** One of Venice's most charming hotels, the Accademia is also one of its most popular, so early reservations are a must. It is located in a 17th-century villa near the Accademia Gallery and the Grand Canal. Lounges, bar, and wood-paneled breakfast room are cheery, and you can even have breakfast outside on the garden terrace in good weather. *Fondamenta Bollani 1058, Dorsoduro, tel. 041/521-0188, fax 041/523-9152. 27 rooms, 25 with bath or shower. Facilities: bar, 2 gardens, landing on canal. AE, DC, MC, V.*

Alboretti. This small hotel is simply but attractively furnished. Despite its size and central location, it has a little garden courtyard off the breakfast room and a sitting room upstairs from the tiny lobby and bar area. There is no elevator. The hotel restaurant has creative Venetian cuisine. In all, the Alboretti offers good value. *Rio Terrà A. Foscarini 882, Dorsoduro, tel. 041/523-0058, fax 041/521-0158. 19 rooms with bath or shower. Facilities: bar, restaurant. AE, MC, V.*

Flora. This hotel has what many in this category lack: plenty of sitting rooms and a pretty courtyard with wrought-iron coffee tables. It's in a quiet, though central, location near San Moisè and Piazza San Marco. Rooms have Venetian period decor, which some might find a bit dark; some are rather small, with tiny bathrooms. When booking, ask about the availability of rooms with a view of the courtyard or the garden. *Calle Bergamaschi 2283 (off Calle Larga XXII Marzo), San Marco, tel. 041/520-5844, fax 041/522-8217. 44 rooms with bath or shower. Facilities: bar, garden. AE, DC, MC, V. Closed mid-Nov.-Jan.*

La Residenza. A little out of the way, this hotel in a Gothic palace is worth the 10-minute walk from San Marco (or the vaporetto ride to the Arsenale stop). Breakfast is served in an authentic Venetian salon, and the rooms are well furnished. The atmosphere is subdued, almost staid—this is not the place to take children. *Campo Bandiera e Moro 3608, Castello, tel. 041/528-5315, fax 041/523-8859. 17 rooms, 14 with bath. AE, DC, MC, V. Closed 2nd week of Jan.-mid-Feb., 2nd week of Nov.-1st week of Dec.*

Locanda Sturion. There was a hostelry here by the Rialto Bridge as long ago as the 13th century, and its sign, showing a sturgeon (*sturion*) to illustrate its name, appears in a 1494 Carpaccio painting in the Accademia. If you don't mind a longish walk, you'll find a very friendly, pleasant hotel recently refurbished in the Venetian style. All rooms have baths, two have views over the Grand Canal, as does a bright breakfast/day room. Extra beds for shared rooms are no problem, and the pricing policy is flexible—so do ask for the best deal when booking. *Calle del Sturion 679, San Polo, tel. 041/523-6243, fax 041/522-8378. 11 rooms with bath. AE, MC, V.*

Paganelli. This charming, small hotel on the waterfront near Piazza San Marco, with an annex on the quiet square of Campo San

Zaccaria (three rooms overlook the lagoon, six face the square), is tastefully decorated in the Venetian style. *Riva degli Schiavoni 4182, Castello, tel. 041/522–4324, fax 041/523–9267. 22 rooms, 19 with bath or shower. AE, DC, MC, V.*

$ **Bucintoro.** This friendly, family-run hotel on the waterfront by the Arsenal, slightly off the tourist track, is the only hotel in Venice where every room has a view over the lagoon. The rooms are clean and simple, and the price unbeatable for such a spectacular position. *Riva San Biagio 2135, Castello, tel. 041/522–3240, fax 041/523–5224. 28 rooms, 18 with bath. No credit cards. Closed Jan.–mid-Feb.*

★ **Locanda Fiorita.** This welcoming, small hotel is tucked away in a sunny little square (where breakfast is served in the summer), just off Campo Santo Stefano, near the Accademia Bridge, and is centrally located for sightseeing. The rooms have beamed ceilings and are simply and unfussily furnished. *Campiello Novo 3457, San Marco, tel. 041/523–4754, fax 041/522–8043. 10 rooms, 7 with shower. AE, MC, V. Closed 2 weeks Nov.–Dec.*

Riva. This small hotel, close to San Marco, is in a picturesque spot at the junction of three canals much used by all manner of Venetian watercraft. While they are endlessly fascinating to watch, the boats can seem a little noisy early in the morning. The Riva has been refurbished by its enthusiastic owner. *Ponte dell'Angelo 5310, Castello, tel. 041/522–7034. 12 rooms, 10 with bath. No credit cards. Closed mid-Nov.–Feb. 1, except 2 weeks at Christmas.*

The Arts and Nightlife

The Arts

You'll find a list of current and upcoming events in the "Guest in Venice" booklet, free at your hotel, or available from the Assessorato al Turismo at Ca' Giustinian (2nd floor), Calle del Ridoto (close to Piazza San Marco). Keep an eye out for posters announcing concerts and other events. Venice hosts important temporary exhibitions in the Doge's Palace, in Palazzo Grassi at San Samuele on the Grand Canal, and in other venues. The **Biennale,** a cultural institution, organizes many events throughout the year, including the film festival, beginning at the end of August. The big Biennale international art exhibition, held from the end of June to the end of September, has been held since 1993 in odd-numbered years.

Concerts There are regular concerts at the Pietà Church, with an emphasis on Vivaldi, and also at San Stae—though prices tend to be high and the performance quality uneven. Concerts are also held in other churches, sometimes free, by visiting choirs and musicians. For information on these often short-notice events, ask at the APT office and look for posters on walls and in restaurants and shops. **Kele e Teo Agency** (San Marco 4930, tel. 041/520–8722) handles tickets for many musical events.

Opera and Ballet **Teatro La Fenice,** on Campo San Fantin, is one of Italy's oldest opera houses. The season lasts all year, except August, with opera or concert performances most months. Ballets and other musical events are also held there. For programs and tickets, write Biglietteria, Teatro La Fenice, Campo San Fantin, 30121 Venice, or call 041/521–0161, fax 041/522–1768. Tickets for opera performances go on sale at the box office about one month in advance. The box office is open Monday–Saturday 9:30–12:30, 4–6. If there is a performance on Sunday, the box office remains open, closing on Monday instead.

Nightlife

Piazza San Marco in fair weather, when the cafés stay open late, is a meeting place for visitors and Venetians, though young Venetians tend to gravitate toward Campo San Luca and Campo San Salvador and Bartolomeo, near Rialto. There is far more nightlife in Venice than meets the eye: the best up-to-date guide to live music venues, discos, and late bars is *"Notturno Veneziano"* (Venetian Nightlife), published by the Assessorato alla Gioventù (city Youth Department, Corte Contarina 1529, 4th Floor, near Piazza San Marco), and available free at APT information offices. At present, the guide is only available in Italian, but with its useful maps and easy-to-follow notes it should be decipherable to any serious nighthawk.

Bars, Discos, and Nightclubs
The top hotel bars stay open late if the customers want to linger. The **Martini Scala Club** is an elegant piano bar with restaurant. *Calle delle Veste (Campo San Fantin), San Marco, tel. 041/522–4121. Open Wed.–Mon. 8 PM (10 PM in summer)–3:30 AM.*

Among the most popular nightspots for young Venetians are **Ai Canottieri** (Fondamenta San Giobbe 690, Cannaregio, tel. 041/71548, live music Tues., closed Sun.), and **Paradiso Perduto** (Fondamenta Misericordia 2540, Cannaregio, tel. 041/720581), which serves good pizzas and other hot dishes at low prices (live music usually on the weekend, closed Wed.). **Bar Salus,** just off Campo Santa Margherita (Rio Terà Canal 3112, Dorsoduro, tel. 041/528–5279, open till 2 PM, closed Sunday) attracts a lively late-night crowd, particularly in summer.

Casino
The city-operated gambling casino is open April–September in a modern building on the Lido (Lungomare Marconi 4, tel. 041/529–7111) and in the beautiful Palazzo Vendramin Calergi (same phone) on the Grand Canal during the other months. Both are open daily 3 PM–about 4:30 AM.

7 The Venetian Arc

Verona to Trieste

The Venetian Arc encompasses the coastal crescent and inland plain that stretches from the mouths of the Rivers Po and Adige southwest of Venice over to Trieste and the Slovenian border east of Venice. It bridges two Italian regions—the Veneto and Friuli-Venezia Giulia—and is mainly flat green farmland spotted with low hills that swell and rise steeply inland in a succession of plateaus and high meadows to the snow-tipped Alps. The entire area basks in the reflected splendor of Venice, its long-time ruler, and is studded with some of Italy's most interesting cities. All of them came under Venice's domination at one time or another, and Venetian influence is evident in their art and architecture, though there's a touch of German *gemütlichkeit* (congeniality) in the mountain towns, and there are stately shades of Hapsburg grandeur in cosmopolitan Trieste.

Much of the pleasure of exploring this area comes from discovering the individual variations on the overall Venetian theme that confer special charm on each of the towns you'll visit. Some, such as Verona, Treviso, and Udine, have a solid medieval look; Asolo has an idyllic setting; Bassano combines a bit of both. If you're interested in architecture, you'll seek out the scores of villas built by Venetian aristocrats on their country estates. Several of these were designed by the architect Andrea Palladio (1508–80), and some were decorated with frescoes by Tiepolo or Veronese. If you are a confirmed or fledgling oenophile, you'll enjoy tasting local wines within view of the vineyards that produce some of the best-known Italian vintages— among them, Soave, Valpolicella, Bardolino, and Prosecco. You'll find art everywhere, from Giotto's frescoes in Padua and the great Venetian masters in Verona to single, perfect gems such as Giorgione's solemn altarpiece in Castelfranco and Veronese's light-hearted frescoes in Villa Barbaro at Maser.

Essential Information

Important Addresses and Numbers

Tourist Information
Padua (Stazione Ferroviaria [train station], tel. 049/875–2077).
Treviso (Via Toniolo 41, tel. 0422/547632).
Trieste (Stazione Centrale, tel. 040/420182).
Udine (Piazza Primo Maggio 6, tel. 0432/295972).
Verona (Via Leoncino 61, tel. 045/592828; Piazza delle Erbe 42, tel. 045/803–0086; open Apr.–Sept.).
Vicenza (Piazza Matteotti, tel. 0444/320854; Piazza Duomo 5, tel. 0444/544122).

Emergencies
Police, Ambulance, Fire, tel. 113. This number will also put you in touch with the First Aid Service (Pronto Soccorso).

Doctors and Dentists. Telephone 112, or go to the Ospedale Civile e Policlinico dell'Università, Padua, tel. 049/821-1111.

Late-Night Pharmacy. Pharmacies take turns staying open late and on Sunday. For information on which is open, call 192.

Travel Agencies
The largest area offices of **American Express** and **Wagons Lits** are located in Venice (*see* Essential Information in Chapter 6, Venice). Offices in the Venetian Arc include the following:

Padua (American Express, Via Risorgimento 20, tel. 049/666133).
Trieste (Paterniti Viaggi [American Express representative], Corso Cavour 7, tel. 040/65222).

Car Rentals **Padua.** *Avis* (Piazza Stazione 1, tel. 049/664198); *Hertz* (Piazza Stazione 5, tel. 049/657877).
Trieste. *Avis* (Via San Nicolo 12, tel. 040/68243); *Hertz* (Via Mazzini 1, tel. 040/60650).
Udine. *Avis* (Via Europa Unita 23, tel. 0432/22149); *Hertz* (Via Europa Unita 127, tel. 0432/293033).
Verona. *Avis* (Stazione FS [train station], tel. 045/26636); *Hertz* (Stazione FS, tel. 045/25832).

Getting Around

By Plane The main airport serving the Venetian Arc is **Marco Polo** in Venice (*see* Essential Information in Chapter 6, Venice), which handles international and most domestic flights to the region. Two other airports serve domestic routes. **Ronchi dei Legionari Airport,** 35 kilometers (21 miles) north of Trieste, is linked with Via Miramare in the center of town by a regular bus service. **Villafranca Airport,** 11 kilometers (7 miles) west of Verona, is connected with Porta Nuova train station by regular bus service. There are charter flights that now land at **Treviso** airport (about 20 miles north of Venice); passengers are then bused to Venice and other destinations.

By Car The main highway in the region is A4, which connects Verona, Padua, and Venice with Trieste. The distance from Verona, in the west, to Trieste is 263 kilometers (163 miles). Branches link A4 with Treviso (A27), Pordenone (A28), and Udine (A23).

By Train The main lines from Milan (via Verona and Vicenza) and from Rome (via Florence and Bologna) meet at Padua, where cars for Venice are shunted off if the train is to continue to Treviso and Gorizia or to Trieste. From Venice, it's about 20 minutes by train to Padua, about two hours to Trieste, and 1½ hours to Verona.

By Bus An efficient bus network serves the smaller centers, and frequent buses for Padua and Treviso leave Venice's bus terminal at Piazzale Roma.

Guided Tours

Orientation Many of the best tours begin and end in Venice because so much of the region is accessible from there. For Venice addresses of operators, *see* Essential Information in Chapter 6, Venice. The **Burchiello excursion boat** makes an all-day tour along the Brenta Canal, including lunch and visits to several villas but the trip is expensive and not necessarily the best way to see the villas, since so much time is spent on the boat. For those preferring to go it alone, American Express suggests itineraries that can be followed by rented car, with or without driver.

Exploring the Venetian Arc

This exploring section covers the broad Adriatic sweep of the Venetian Arc from west to east, beginning at Venice. Many of the first towns visited can be seen on one- or two-day excursions from Venice itself, although it is far better to give yourself time to appreciate the more remote spots by planning a few overnight stops en route.

The first three tours head westward to the ancient university city of Padua, Palladio's Vicenza, and the Roman city of Verona. Tour 4 picks up northeast of Verona and Vicenza and pushes into the foot-hills of the Alps and the Dolomites, where market towns cling to steep hillsides and streams rage down from the mountains. Moving farther east and then southeast, Tour 5 passes the medieval trading city of Udine before continuing into Trieste, formerly the principal port of the Hapsburg Empire and still very much a multicultural city. Trieste is Italy's easternmost outpost, fronting on the Adriatic and otherwise nearly surrounded by Slovenia, with only a narrow strip of Italian territory connecting it with the rest of the country.

Highlights for First-Time Visitors

Arena di Verona (Tour 3: Verona).
Asolo (Tour 4: High Road to Treviso).
Bassano del Grappa (Tour 4: High Road to Treviso).
Cappella degli Scrovegni (Tour 1: Villa Pisani and Padua).
Castello di San Giusto (Tour 5: East to Trieste).
La Rotonda (Tour 2: Palladian Vicenza).
Miramare Castle (Tour 5: East to Trieste).
Strada del Vino Rosso (Tour 4: High Road to Treviso).
Teatro Olimpico (Tour 2: Palladian Vicenza).
Villa Pisani (Tour 1: Villa Pisani and Padua).

Tour 1: Villa Pisani and Padua

Numbers in the margin correspond to points of interest on the Venetian Arc map.

❶ About 30 kilometers (20 miles) west of Venice, along the A4, **Villa Pisani** (or Villa Nazionale), in Strà, is typical of the stately resi-dences built for wealthy Venetians on their country estates. An im-posing 18th-century edifice, it once belonged to Napoleon, who appreciated the similarities with Versailles. See the grandiose fres-coes by Giambattista Tiepolo on the ceiling of the ballroom and ex-plore the park; also climb to the top of the little tower for a good look at the maze. *Admission: 6,000 lire. Open Apr.–Sept., Tues.–Sun. 8:30–6; Oct.–Mar., Tues.–Sun. 9–3.*

❷ Only 7 kilometers (4 miles) farther west is **Padua** (Padova in Italian), well worth a one-day stopover. It's a bustling city with a medieval nucleus, the seat of a famous university founded in 1222, but now surrounded by unattractive modern business districts. Pick up a map and brochures at the tourist office in the train station and head straight down **Corso del Popolo,** which changes its name to Corso Garibaldi about 400 yards on, when it crosses the Bacchiglione River.

To the left just across the river is the **Cappella degli Scrovegni** (Scrovegni Chapel), built in the 13th century near the site of an an-cient Roman arena. The chapel was erected by a wealthy Paduan, Enrico Scrovegni, in honor of his deceased father. Scrovegni called on Giotto to decorate its interior, a task that occupied the great art-ist and his helpers from 1303 to 1305. They created a magnificent fresco cycle, arranged in typical medieval comic-strip fashion, illus-trating the lives of Mary and Christ. *Corso Garibaldi, tel. 049/875–1153. Admission: 10,000 lire (includes admission to the Museo Civico degli Eremitani, tel. 049/875–2321, see below). Both open Apr.–Sept., Tues.–Sun. 9–7; Oct.–Mar., Tues.–Sun. 9–5:30.*

Turn left from the chapel entrance and cross the gardens that now occupy the area of the original Roman arena to reach Piazza Eremitani and the 13th-century church of the **Eremitani.** It contains

Venetian Arc

some fragments of frescoes by Andrea Mantegna (1431–1506), the brilliant locally born artist, some of whose masterpieces are in nearby Mantua: Most of these frescoes, however, were destroyed in the Allied bombing of 1944. The **Museo Civico** (Civic Museum) here has its quota of works by Venetian masters. A small road leads diagonally left from the church back to Corso Garibaldi.

Time Out About a quarter-mile farther along Corso Garibaldi is the **Caffè Pedrocchi** (Piazzetta Pedrocchi), a monumental 19th-century neoclassical coffeehouse that looks like a cross between a museum and a stage set—an impressive place for a cappuccino.

Just to the left, on a side street leading off the other side of the Corso, is the 16th-century **University** building. This is worth a visit to see the exquisite and perfectly proportioned anatomy theater and a hall harboring a lectern used by Galileo. *Via VIII Febbraio. Admission free. Guided visits only. Closed for restoration. May reopen in 1995.*

The **Municipio** (city hall) faces the University from the Caffè Pedrocchi side of the Corso. Behind it are three adjacent historic squares that form the heart of the city and are constantly crisscrossed by students on bicycles. In the largest square, scene of the city's outdoor market in the morning, is the **Palazzo della Ragione** (also called **Il Salone**), which was built in the Middle Ages as the seat of Padua's parliament. Today its street-level arcades shelter shops and cafés. In the frescoed Great Hall on the upper level is an enormous wooden horse, a 15th-century replica of the bronze steed in Donatello's equestrian statue of Gattamelata (*see below*). The hall is often used for exhibitions, and on those occasions is open to the public.

Take a look at the 15th- and 16th-century buildings on Piazza dei Signori and at the cathedral a few steps away. Then return to the University and take the second street east of the Corso—Via del Santo—south to the huge basilica of **Sant'Antonio,** one of Padua's major attractions. Standing in front of the church is Donatello's powerful statue of the *condottiere* (mercenary general) Gattamelata, which was cast in bronze—a monumental technical achievement—in about 1450 and was to have an enormous influence on the development of Italian Renaissance sculpture. A cluster of Byzantine domes and slender, minaretlike towers gives the church an Oriental look, reminiscent of San Marco in Venice. The interior is sumptuous, too, with marble reliefs by Tullio Lombardo, the greatest in a talented family of marble carvers who decorated many churches in the area—among them, Santa Maria dei Miracoli in Venice. The artistic highlights here, however, all bear Donatello's name; the 15th-century Florentine master did the remarkable series of bronze reliefs illustrating the life of Saint Anthony—whose feast day, June 13, draws pilgrims from all over Europe—as well as the bronze statues of the Madonna and saints on the high altar.

Take a left outside the museum and walk along Via Belludi to **Prato della Valle,** an unusual and attractive piazza laid out in 1775, with a wooded oval park at the center, surrounded by a canal. At the southeast end of this immense square is the church of **Santa Giustina,** with finely inlaid choir stalls and Veronese's colossal altarpiece, *The Martyrdom of St. Justine.*

Tour 2: Palladian Vicenza

Another 32 kilometers (20 miles) west of Padua by rail or autostrada **❸** is **Vicenza,** the city that bears the distinctive signature of the 16th-century architect Andrea Palladio. The architect, whose name is the basis of the term "Palladian," gracefully incorporated elements of classical architecture—columns, porticoes, and domes—into a style that reflected the Renaissance celebration of order and harmony. His elegant villas and palaces were influential in propagating classical architecture in Europe, especially Britain, and later in America.

In the mid-16th century Palladio was given the opportunity to rebuild much of Vicenza, which had suffered great damage during the bloody wars waged against Venice by the League of Cambrai, an alliance of the Papacy, France, the Holy Roman Empire, and several neighboring city-states. He imposed upon the city a number of his grand Roman-style buildings—rather an overstatement, considering the town's status. With the Basilica, begun in 1549 in the very heart of Vicenza, he ensured his reputation and embarked on a series of lordly buildings, all of which proclaim the same rigorous classicism.

From the train or bus station, Viale Roma leads straight north to Porta Castello, a gateway through a fragment of the old city wall and the starting point of the broad main avenue of Vicenza, **Corso Palladio.** Before strolling down the Corso, however, you may want to turn right just past the gate, go one block south, and turn left to see the Gothic **Duomo,** which contains a gleaming altarpiece by Lorenzo Veneziano, a 14th-century Venetian painter.

Corso Palladio is a memorable avenue, lined with a succession of imposing palaces and churches that run the gamut from Venetian Gothic to Baroque, including the striking **Palazzo del Comune,** about halfway along. Make a side trip left down Contrà Porti for a look at other splendid palaces and, back on Corso Palladio, stop in at the church of **Santa Corona** to see the exceptionally fine *Baptism of Christ* (1500) by Giovanni Bellini over the altar on the left just in front of the transept. **Palazzo Chiericati,** on a square at the end of the Corso, is an exquisite and unmistakably Palladian building. The palace houses the **Museo Civico,** with a representative collection of Venetian paintings. *Piazza Matteotti, tel. 0444/321348. Admission: 5,000 lire; includes Teatro Olimpico (see below). Open Tues.–Sat. 9:30–12, 2:30–5, Sun. 9:30–12.*

On the other side of the square is the **Teatro Olimpico,** Palladio's last, and perhaps finest, work. Based closely on the model of the ancient Roman theater, it represents an important development in theater and stage design and is noteworthy for its acoustics and the cunningly devised false perspective of a classical street in the permanent backdrop. *Piazza Matteotti, tel. 0444/323781. Admission: 5,000 lire. Open Mar. 16–Oct. 15, Mon.–Sat. 9:30–12:20, 3–5:30, Sun. 9:30–12:20; Oct. 16–Mar. 15, Mon.–Sat. 9:30–12:20, 2–4:30, Sun. 9:30–12:20.*

Retrace your steps along Corso Palladio and, halfway back, turn left onto Contrà del Monte, which leads to the elongated Piazza dei Signori, the heart of the city. This is the site of Palladio's basilica, a confusing name, since it is not a church but a courthouse, the Palazzo della Ragione. An early Palladian masterpiece, it was actually a medieval building that the architect modernized, and the skill with which he wedded the graceful two-story exterior loggias to the existing Gothic structure is remarkable. He also designed, but never completed, the **Loggia del Capitaniato,** opposite.

Time Out | **Gran Caffè Garibaldi** is a classic coffeehouse with a good restaurant upstairs. It looks out on the basilica (Piazza dei Signori 5. Closed Tues. dinner, Wed.). Or, just off the piazza, there's the cozier **Bar Firenze,** in Piazzetta Palladio.

Two of the most interesting villas of the Veneto region are a little more than a mile from the center of Vicenza, on the Este road to the southeast. You can walk to both, but it is easier to take the Bus 8 from Corso Palladio to the Via San Bastiano bus stop. From the bus stop you climb gently a quarter-mile until you reach **Villa Valmarana dei Nani,** an 18th-century country house decorated with a series of marvelous frescoes by Giambattista Tiepolo: These are fantastic visions of a mythological world. The guest house holds more frescoes, these by Tiepolo's son, Giandomenico. *Via San Bastiano 8, tel. 0444/ 321803. Admission: 8,000 lire. Open Mar.–Apr., Oct.–Nov., Tues.– Sat. 2:30–5:30; May–Sept., Wed., Thurs., Sat., Sun. 10–12, Tues.– Sat. 3–6.*

From Villa Valmarana, continue along Via San Bastiano (which narrows to the size of a path) for a few hundred yards to reach **La Rotonda,** the most famous Palladian villa of all. Serene and symmetrical, it was the model for Jefferson's Monticello. Take the time to admire it from all sides, and you'll see that it was the inspiration not just for Monticello, but for nearly every state capital in the United States. The interior is a bit of a disappointment, but that's not why you came here anyway. *Via della Rotonda 29, tel. 0444/321793. Admission: to grounds, 5,000 lire; to interior, 10,000 lire. Open Mar. 15–Nov. 4. Grounds open Tues.–Thurs. 10–12, 3–6; interior open Wed. 10–12, 3–6.*

Tour 3: Verona

4 Only about 60 kilometers (38 miles) west of Vicenza on the main autostrada and rail line is **Verona.** This attractive city, on the banks of the fast-flowing Adige river, is, after Venice, the top attraction in the region and rivals other Italian art cities. It has considerable charm; classical and medieval monuments; a picturesque town center where bright geraniums bloom in window boxes; and a romantic reputation, thanks to Shakespeare's *Romeo and Juliet,* which is set here. It is one of Italy's most alluring cities, despite extensive industrialization and urban development in its newer sections. Inevitably, with its lively Venetian air, proximity to Lake Garda, and renowned summer opera season, it attracts hordes of tourists, especially vacationing Germans and Austrians, who drive through the Brenner Pass just to the north.

Verona grew to power and prosperity within the Roman Empire as a result of its key commercial and military position in northern Italy. After the fall of the Empire, the city continued to flourish under the guidance of Barbarian kings such as Theodoric, Alboin, Pepin, and Berenger I, reaching its cultural and artistic peak in the 13th and 14th centuries, under the Della Scala dynasty. (You'll see the *scala,* or ladder, emblem all over town.) In 1404, however, Verona traded its independence for security and placed itself under the control of Venice. (The other recurring architectural motif is the lion of Saint Mark, symbol of Venetian rule.) Verona remained under Venetian protection until 1797, when Napoleon invaded. In 1814 the entire

Veneto region was won by the Austrians, and it was finally united with the rest of Italy in 1866.

Numbers in the margin correspond to points of interest on the Verona map.

⑤ The obvious place to start your visit is at **Piazza Brà,** the vast and airy square at the center of the city. Here you'll find the **Arena di Verona,** built by the Romans in the 1st century AD and one of the largest and best preserved Roman amphitheaters anywhere. Only four arches remain of the outer rings, but the main structure is so complete that it takes little imagination to picture it as the site of the cruel deaths of countless gladiators, wild beasts, and Christians. Today it hosts Verona's summer opera, famous for spectacular productions and audiences of as many as 22,000. The best operas to see here are the big splashy ones that demand huge choruses, "Cinerama" sets, lots of color and movement, and, if possible, camels, horses, and/or elephants. The music can be excellent, and the acoustics are fine, too. If you go, be sure to bring or rent a cushion—four hours on 2,000-year-old marble can be an ordeal (*see* The Arts and Nightlife, *below*). *Arena di Verona 045/800–3204. Admission: 6,000 lire; free the first Sunday of the month. Open Tues.–Sun. 8–6:30; open Tues.–Sun. 8–1:30 during opera season in July and August.*

Via Mazzini, an old and fashionable thoroughfare, leads off Piazza Brà to **Piazza delle Erbe** (Vegetable Market Square), site of the ancient Roman forum and today a colorful market in the morning, when huge rectangular umbrellas are raised to shade the neat ranks of fruits and vegetables. Off Piazza delle Erbe is **Piazza dei Signori,** enclosed on all sides by stately public buildings. The 12th-century **⑥ ⑦ Palazzo della Ragione** has a somber-looking courtyard, Gothic staircase, and medieval tower. Opposite is the graceful **Loggia del Consiglio,** built in the 12th century to house city council meetings. **⑧** At the end of the square is the **Palazzo del Governo,** the medieval stronghold from which the Della Scalas ruled Verona with an iron fist.

⑨ Just off this end of the square are the **Arche Scaligere,** the magnificent Gothic tombs of the Della Scalas, behind a 14th-century wrought-iron fence bearing the family's ladder emblem. The tomb over the door of the church is the resting place of Cangrande I, protector of Dante and patron of the arts; the equestrian statue is a copy of the one on view at the Castelvecchio Museum (*see below*). In the **⑩** same neighborhood are the Gothic church of **Sant'Anastasia** and the **⑪** Romanesque **Duomo.** The square by Sant'Anastasia leads onto a shady riverside walkway along the swift-flowing but shallow Adige, which always has a refreshingly cool breeze blowing from it, thanks to its origins in the Alpine glaciers.

⑫ Cross the Adige at Ponte Nuovo to see the **Giusti Gardens,** laid out on several levels around a 16th-century villa. There's a formal Italian garden and a fine view of the city from the terrace, from which Johann von Goethe, the German poet and dramatist, drew inspiration. *Via Giardino Giusti, tel. 045/803–4029. Admission: 5,000 lire. Open daily Apr.–Oct. 8–8, Nov.–Mar. 8–sunset.*

Time Out   **Cacciatore** (Via Seminario 4. Closed Sun.), in the Piazza Isolo section at this end of Ponte Nuovo, is one of Verona's historic *osterie* (wine shops). The fine local wines are still a big draw for habitués, but some inexpensive dishes are also available.

Verona

Arche Scaligere, **9**
Arena di Verona, **5**
Castelvecchio, **14**
Duomo, **11**
Giusti Gardens, **12**
Juliet's Tomb, **16**

Loggia del Consiglio, **7**
Museo Archeologico, **13**
Palazzo del Governo, **8**
Palazzo della Ragione, **6**
San Zeno Maggiore, **15**
Sant'Anastasia, **10**

The medieval church of Santa Maria in Organo is on the same road as the Giusti Gardens. Be sure to visit the choir and sacristy to see the inlaid-wood masterpieces of the 15th-century monk Fra Giovanni. A series of panels depicts varied scenes—local buildings, an idealized Renaissance town, wildlife, and fruit—that radiate a love of life and reveal the artist's eye for detail.

On the same bank of the river, there are good views from the terraces of the **Museo Archeologico,** located in an old monastery above a Roman theater that was built in the same era as the arena. The Roman theater is in the museum grounds and is sometimes used for dramatic productions. *Rigaste del Redentore, tel. 045/800–0360. Admission: 5,000 lire; free on the first Sunday of the month. Open Tues.–Sun. 8–1:30.*

Cross the Adige on Ponte Pietra and head back to Sant'Anastasia to pick up Corso Sant'Anastasia, which becomes Corso Porta Borsari and then Corso Cavour, which is lined with attractive old buildings and palaces and leads to **Castelvecchio,** a 14th-century castle built for Cangrande II Della Scala. A crenellated building in russet brick with massive walls, towers, turrets, and a vast courtyard, it looks like a fairy-tale castle guarding a bridge across the Adige. Inside, the **Museo del Castelvecchio** gives you a good look at the castle's vaulted halls and the treasures of Venetian painting and sculpture that they contain. *Corso Cavour, tel. 045/594734. Admission: 5,000 lire; free on the first Sunday of the month. Open Tues.–Sun. 8–6:30; hours and admission may change during special exhibitions.*

From the castle it's a short walk upstream along Rigaste San Zeno and Via Barbarani to one of Italy's finest Romanesque churches, **San Zeno Maggiore.** It's set between two medieval bell towers and has a 13th-century rose window and 12th-century portal. Inside, look for Mantegna's *Madonna* over the main altar; there's a peaceful cloister off the left nave.

Romantic souls may want to see what the astute tourist office says is **Juliet's Tomb,** on the other side of the old town; it's a pretty spot, though hardly a major attraction. Authentic or not, it is still popular with lovesick Italian teenagers, who leave notes for the tragic lover. *Via del Pontiere, tel. 800–0361. Admission: 5,000 lire; free on the first Sunday of the month. Open Tues.–Sun. 8–6:30.*

Tour 4: High Road to Treviso

Numbers in the margin correspond to points of interest on the Venetian Arc map.

If you're coming from Venice or Padua, take S47 north from the A4 for 37 kilometers (22 miles); from Vicenza, take S248 northeast into the foothills of the Alps, toward **Bassano del Grappa,** a beautifully located town directly above the swift-flowing waters of the Brenta River at the foot of the Mount Grappa massif (5,880 feet). Bassano's old streets are lined with low buildings sporting wooden balconies and eye-catching flowerpots. Bright ceramic wares produced here and in nearby Nove are displayed in shops along byways that curve uphill toward a centuries-old square, and, even higher, to a belvedere with a good view of Mount Grappa and the beginning of the Valsugana valley.

Bassano's most famous landmark is the covered bridge that has spanned the Brenta since the 13th century. Rebuilt countless times (floods are frequent), the present-day bridge is a postwar reconstruction using Andrea Palladio's 16th-century design. The great architect astutely chose to use wood as his medium, knowing that it could be replaced quickly and cheaply. Almost as famous is the characteristic Nardini liquor shop at one end of the bridge; it's redolent of the grappa that has been distilled here for more than a century. Stop in for a sniff or a snifter.

(18) A side trip of only 7 kilometers (4 miles) west takes you to **Marostica,** where a castle on the hillside overlooks the town. The main square is paved in checkerboard fashion, and a game of chess is acted out here by people in medieval costume on the second weekend in September in even-numbered years.

(19) The most romantic and charming of the towns in the vicinity is **Asolo,** 11 kilometers (7 miles) east of Bassano along S248. This hillside hamlet was the consolation prize of an exiled queen. At the end of the 15th century, Venetian-born Caterina Cornaro was sent here by Venice's doges to keep her from interfering with their administration of her former kingdom of Cyprus, which she had inherited. To soothe the pain of exile, she established a lively and brilliant court in Asolo. Over the centuries, Venetian aristocrats continued to build gracious villas on the hillside, and in the 19th century Asolo once again became the idyllic haunt of musicians, poets, and painters. In the center of town you can explore Piazza Maggiore, with its Renaissance palaces and turn-of-the-century cafés, and then continue uphill, past Caterina's ruined castle and some Gothic-style houses, to the Roman fortress that stands on the summit. Other walks will take you past the villas once inhabited by Robert Browning and the actress Eleanora Duse. Be warned that Asolo's dreamy Old World atmosphere disappears on holiday weekends when the crowds pour in.

(20) Seven kilometers (4 miles) northeast of Asolo, in Maser, is **Villa Barbaro,** a gracious Renaissance creation, the work of Palladio. Easy to reach by car, it's also accessible by bus from Bassano. The fully furnished villa is still inhabited by its owners, who make you slip heavy felt scuffs over your shoes to protect the highly polished floors. The elaborate stuccos and opulent frescoes by Paolo Veronese bring the 16th century to life. This Venetian villa is worth going out of your way to see. *Via Cornuda 2, tel. 0423/923004. Admission: 8,000 lire. Open Apr.–Sept., Tues., weekends 3–6; Oct.–Mar., Tues., weekends 2:30–5.*

(21) On your way to Treviso, you can make a slight detour south down S307 to see **Castelfranco Veneto,** girdled by crenellated walls and a moat. There's a superb Giorgione *Madonna* in the cathedral. *Open daily 9–12, 3–6.*

(22) Only 26 kilometers (16 miles) east of Castelfranco and 30 kilometers (20 miles) north of Venice is **Treviso.** It has arcaded streets, frescoed houses, and channeled streams that run through the center of town. You can explore Treviso on foot in half a day; its restaurants are good places to stop for lunch. The most important church here is **San Nicolò,** on Via San Nicolò, a few blocks north and across the river from the train station. An impressive Gothic building with an interesting vaulted ceiling, San Nicolò has frescoes of the saints by 14th-century artist Tommaso da Modena on the columns. But the best is the remarkable series of 40 portraits of Dominican friars by the same artist in the seminary next door. They are astoundingly realistic, considering that some were painted as early as 1352, and include one of the earliest-known portraits of someone wearing glasses. *Via San Nicolò. For admission, inquire at the custodian's desk at the seminary entrance.*

As you explore the town, you'll see lots of old houses with decorated facades, many of them built in the 15th century. Go left from the front of the seminary a quarter-mile to the **Duomo.** Inside, on the altar of one of the chapels to the right, is an *Annunciation* by Titian. Running alongside the cathedral are Via Canova and Via Calmaggiore, lined with some well-preserved medieval buildings. Via Calmaggiore leads to **Piazza dei Signori,** the heart of medieval Treviso and still the town's social center, with outdoor cafés and some impressive public buildings facing it. One of these, the Palazzo dei Trecento, has a small alley leading behind it. Follow the alley for about 200 yards to the **Pescheria** (Fish Market), on an island in one of the small rivers that flow through town.

㉓ A 23-kilometer (14-mile) drive north on S13 takes you to **Conegliano,** in the heart of wine-producing country. Conegliano itself is attractive, with Venetian-style villas and frescoed houses, but the real attraction is the wine. Well marked and leading southeast from Conegliano, the **Strada del Vino Rosso** (Red Wine Road) winds its way through cabernet and merlot country along the Piave River, and there are dozens of places to stop, sample, and buy the red—and some rosé—wines. It ends at **Oderzo,** where S53 takes you back to the A4, the main east–west route for the Venetian Arc.

Tour 5: East to Trieste

㉔ About 100 kilometers (65 miles) east of Venice on the A4, take A23 north for 18 kilometers (10 miles) to reach **Udine,** in Italy's Friuli-Venezia Giulia region. The city commands a view of the surrounding plain and the Alpine foothills, and legend has it that Udine stands on a mound erected by Attila the Hun so he could watch the burning of the important Roman center of Aquileia to the south. Udine flourished in the Middle Ages, thanks to its good location for trade and the rights it gained from the local patriarch to hold regular markets. There is a distinct Venetian feel to the city, noticeable in the architecture of Piazza della Libertà, under the stern gaze of the lion of St. Mark, symbol of Venetian power.

㉕ Take a 17-kilometer (9-mile) excursion east along Route 54 to **Cividale,** a city that dates from the time of Julius Caesar. It is popularly supposed (particularly by locals) that Cividale was built by Caesar when he was commander of Roman legions in the area. The city straddles the river Natisone and contains many examples of Venetian Gothic buildings, particularly the **Duomo** and the **Palazzo Comunale.**

The **Museo Archeologico Nazionale** is the best place to trace the history of the area and the importance of Cividale and Udine in the formative period following the collapse of the Roman Empire. Among the interesting exhibits is a large collection of Lombard artifacts, including weapons, jewelry, and domestic wares from this warrior race that swept into what is now Italy in the 6th century. *Piazza del Duomo. Admission: 4,000 lire. Open Tues.–Sat. 9–1:30, Sun. 9–12:30.*

Time Out Stop for a moderately priced lunch of local dishes, especially mushrooms and game. **Al Fortino** (Via Carlo Alberto 46. Closed Tues., Jan. 1–15, Aug.) is located in an old castle with vaulted ceilings and an open hearth.

You'll have to backtrack through Udine to return to the A4 and resume the trip eastward to Trieste. The road follows the coast under the shadow of the huge geological formation called the Carso, a large, barren expanse of limestone that forms a giant ledge, most of which is across the border in Slovenia. Italian territory goes only a few miles inland in this strip, and Italy's small Slovenian minority ekes out an agricultural existence in the region, which has changed hands countless times since the final days of Imperial Rome.

㉖ Little more than 7 kilometers (4 miles) before Trieste is **Miramare Castle,** a 19th-century extravaganza in white stone, built on the seafront for the Archduke Maximilian of Hapsburg (brother of Emperor Franz Josef). Maximilian spent a brief, happy time here until Napoleon III of France took Trieste from the Hapsburgs and sent the poor archduke packing. He was given the title of Emperor of Mexico in 1864 as a compensation, but met his death before a Mexican firing squad in 1867. You can visit the lush grounds and admire the memorable views over the Adriatic. *Admission: 6,000 lire; guided tour of castle costs another 2,500 lire. Grounds open Tues.– Sun. 9–5. Castle open Tues.–Sat. 9–4, Sun. 9–1.*

㉗ Surrounded by rugged countryside and beautiful coastline, **Trieste** is built on a hillside above what was once the chief port of the Austro-Hungarian Hapsburg Empire. Typical of Trieste are its turn-of-the-century cafés, much like Vienna's coffeehouses; these are social and cultural centers of the city.

The sidewalk cafés on the vast seaside Piazza dell' Unità d'Italia are popular meeting places in the summer months. The square is similar to Piazzetta San Marco in Venice; both are focal points of architectural interest that command the best views of the sea. The Palazzo Comunale (Town Hall) is at the end of the square, away from the sea; behind it, steps lead uphill, following the city's pattern of upward expansion from its roots as a coastal fishing port in Roman times. About a hundred yards beyond Palazzo Comunale, you pass two churches in dramatically different styles. The first, **San Silvestro,** is a solid Romanesque construction dating from the 11th century; just beyond it is the Baroque extravagance of **Santa Maria Maggiore,** which backs onto a network of yet more alleys (closed to traffic) heading farther up the hill.

At the top is the **Cattedrale di San Giusto,** a 14th-century church that incorporates two much older churches, one dating as far back as the 5th century. The exterior adds even more to the jumble of styles involved by using fragments of Roman tombs and temples: You can see these most clearly on the pillars of the main doorway. The highlights of the interior are the mosaics and frescoes dating from the 13th century.

Some of the best views from the hilltop are from the **Castello di San Giusto,** which is next to the church. This 15th-century castle was built by the Venetians, who always had an eye for the best vantage point in the cities they conquered or controlled. The Hapsburgs, subsequent rulers of Trieste, enlarged it to its present size. Some of the best exhibits in the Castle **Museum** are the displays of weaponry and armor. *Piazza Cattedrale 3. Admission: 2,000 lire. Open Tues.– Sun. 9–12:45.*

Time Out Two vaulted halls within the castle walls are occupied by the **Bottega del Vino** (Piazza Cattedrale 3. Closed Tues. and Jan.), which has a different entrance, so it keeps different hours from the rest of the castle, not opening until about 6 PM. For supper, try the gnocchi with porcini mushrooms while sitting on a terrace overlooking the bay.

Return downward to the port, along Via della Cattedrale, passing the **Arco di Riccardo,** a 1st-century AD Roman arch honoring Augustus. Retrace your steps toward Piazza dell'Unità d'Italia, but just before you reach it, turn right for **Piazza della Borsa,** the square containing Trieste's original stock exchange, the **Borsa Vecchia,** a neoclassical building now serving as the chamber of commerce. The statue of Leopold I, at one end of the square, marks the beginning of **Corso Italia,** Trieste's busy shopping street. As you walk along, you'll notice a variety of international shops and goods, reflecting not just the variety of rulers who have presided over this important port, but also the fact that many of the present-day shoppers in Trieste are visitors from what used to be Yugoslavia, intent on stocking up on Western consumer goods.

What to See and Do with Children

The Venetian Arc bears the distinct stamp of culture—or, in the case of Trieste, cultures—so it would be a shame not to combine a little learning with the pleasures of exploring new places. **La Rotonda** (*see* Tour 2: Palladian Vicenza, *above*) is a unique blend of classical architectural principles and Palladio's Renaissance sensibilities, but for a child it's the prototype of Monticello. Similarly, Palladio's bridge at **Bassano del Grappa** is an example of these same design ideas, but this time given a very practical purpose. And the maze at **Villa Pisani** (*see* Tour 1: Villa Pisani and Padua, *above*) should provide a good energy outlet for youngsters who are surfeited with old masters. The Roman **Arena** in Verona (*see* Tour 3: Verona, *above*) evokes the era of gladiators; children who like medieval castles will enjoy visits to **Castelvecchio** in Verona (*see* Tour 3: Verona, *above*) and **Castello di San Giusto** in Trieste (*see* Tour 5: East to Trieste, *above*).

Off the Beaten Track

Abano Terme and **Montegrotto Terme.** These two spas, about 12 kilometers (8 miles) south of Padua, are set in the dreamy landscape of the Euganean Hills. Colorful gardens and fresh summer breezes make them havens for those seeking a break from city life.

Montagnana. Take A13 then S10 southwest from Padua 50 kilometers (30 miles) to reach this medieval city. Its surrounding walls are remarkably well preserved, and there are 24 towers, a moat, and four city gates. Its former rivals, Este and Monselice, are only 20 kilometers (12 miles) east on the same road.

Praglia. This Benedictine monastery, hidden in the hills 12 kilometers (7 miles) southwest of Padua, provides guided tours of its evocative 15th-century halls and cloisters. You can also buy wine and honey produced here by the monks. *Offerings appreciated. Open for guided tours Tues.–Sun. (except major religious holidays) Apr.–Oct. every half-hour 3:30–5:30, Nov.–Mar. every half-hour 2:30–4:30.*

Check locally with the EPT and AAST offices for the opening days of the countless villas in the Venetian hinterland. Many are privately owned but are open to the public at certain times or by special request. These gracious country homes give insight into the way wealthy Venetians used to—and still do—vacation.

Shopping

Many of the goods normally associated with Venice are actually produced in the surrounding areas of the Venetian Arc—which means that with a bit of diligence or luck you can pick up a bargain from the source. Mountain towns and villages—Bassano del Grappa is one—have the strongest handicraft tradition, and you can find a wide range of goods in artisans' shops on the side streets. The main towns on the coastal plain are often associated with one or two specialties, either because of traditional skills or because of ancient trading rights that set a pattern of importing specific items from other parts of the Mediterranean.

Flea Markets Verona's **Piazza delle Erbe** market has a changing selection of food, wines, clothing, some antiques, and even pets. (Open daily.)

Padua has three Saturday-only markets featuring a wide range of goods: **Piazza Barbato, Piazza di Brenta,** and **Prato della Valle.** On the second Sunday of every month, there is an antiques market in the center of **Asolo;** get there early.

Specialty Stores
Antiques The area around the church of Sant'Anastasia in **Verona** is full of antiques shops, most of them catering to serious collectors. Near the Gothic church is a square with cool breezes, where you can picnic after a strenuous day of antiques-hunting.

Ceramics **Bassano del Grappa** and nearby **Nove** are the best bets for ceramic items (*see* Tour 4: High Road to Treviso, *above*).

Jewelry **Vicenza** is one of Italy's leading centers for the production and sale of jewelry. Each year, in January and in June, it plays host to an international trade fair for goldsmiths.

Liqueurs You can buy some of Trieste's famous **Stock** (Via L. Stock 2, tel. 040/7350) liqueur from the headquarters.

Wrought-Iron Goods Shops in **Bassano del Grappa** and **Treviso** feature wrought-iron and copper utensils, many of them made on the premises.

Sports

The Adriatic coastline and Alpine foothills provide multiple opportunities for exercise, to burn off those pasta calories. Swimming is possible at most of the area's ports, but pollution has made the prospect risky at most beaches. Most towns of even moderate size have public swimming pools. Below are some other sporting options.

Golf **Golf Club Condulmer** (Via Zermanese, 16 km, or 10 mi, south of Treviso, just outside Mogliano Veneto, tel. 041/457100); **Padriciano** (Trieste, tel. 040/226159).

Horseback Riding **Via Libia 20** (Padua, tel. 049/871–7244; **Lancenigo** (6 km, or 3½ mi, northwest of Treviso, tel. 0422/63357).

Tennis **Via Col Fagheron 24** (Bassano del Grappa, tel. 0424/31853); **Via Col Galliano** (Verona, tel. 045/566372); **Via Monte Zebio 42** (Vicenza, tel. 0444/565547).

Sailing **Club Vela d'Altura** (Via Pigafetta 7, Santa Margherita, Caorle [23 km, or 14 mi, south of A4 from Santo Stino], tel. 0421/83346).

Dining and Lodging

Dining In the main cities of the Veneto region, restaurants are in the middle to upper ranges of each price category, but in smaller towns and in the countryside you can find some real bargains in comfortable accommodations and good eating. At the eastern end of the Arc, in less trafficked Friuli-Venezia Giulia, prices are generally lower. Seafood is the specialty along the coast, of course, but inland the cuisine varies from the delicate risotto, radicchio, and asparagus of the Veneto to the more decisively flavored cooking of the Trieste area, heavily influenced by Austria. San Daniele del Friuli, near Udine, is famous for its delicious prosciutto. Polenta, made of cornmeal, is a staple throughout the area; it is served with thick, rich sauces or grilled as an accompaniment to meat dishes. In Trieste, the city's position near the Austrian and Slovenian borders has fostered a varied—and somewhat heavier—cuisine reflecting the tastes of those countries. The best local wines are Soave, Tocai, Prosecco, Riesling, and pinot—all white; Bardolino, valpolicella, merlot, cabernet, and pinot nero—reds. The Collio designation indicates wines from vineyards in the eastern part of Friuli, up against the Slovenian border. One of the best known and rarest wines produced here is the sauterne-like Picolit, made in very limited quantities. Grappa is a locally distilled aquavit.

Category	Cost*
$$$$	over 95,000 lire
$$$	70,000–95,000 lire
$$	35,000–70,000 lire
$	under 35,000 lire

**per person, including house wine, service, and tax*

Highly recommended restaurants are indicated by a star ★.

Lodging The area around Venice has been playing host to visitors for centuries, and the result is a range of comfortable accommodations at every price. As with dining, common sense should tell you that the slightly out-of-the-way small hotel will cost you less than its counterpart in a stylish Adriatic resort. Expect to pay more as you approach Venice, since many of the mainland towns absorb the overflow during the times when Venice becomes most crowded, such as Carnival (the two weeks preceding Lent) and throughout the summer.

Category	Cost*
$$$$	over 250,000 lire
$$$	160,000–250,000 lire
$$	90,000–160,000 lire
$	under 90,000 lire

**Prices are for a standard double room for two, including IVA and service.*

Highly recommended lodgings are indicated by a star ★.

Asolo
Dining

Hosteria Ca'Derton. The location is an attraction here: Ca'Derton is right on the main square. It has a pleasant, old-fashioned ambience, with early photos of Asolo on the walls and bouquets of dried flowers on each table. The friendly proprietor takes pride in the homemade pasta and desserts and in offering a good selection of both local and international dishes. *Piazza D'Annunzio 11, tel. 0423/952730. Reservations advised. Dress: casual. AE, DC, MC, V. Closed Mon. dinner, Tues., and Feb. 15–28, Aug. 17–31. $$*

Lodging
★

Villa Cipriani. A distinguished member of the CIGA chain, this historic old villa is set in a romantic garden on the hillside and surrounded by other gracious country homes. Tastefully furnished with 19th-century antiques, it offers Old World atmosphere, all creature comforts, and attentive service. The excellent restaurant has a terrace overlooking the garden. *Via Canova 298, tel. 0423/952166, fax 0432/952095. 31 rooms with bath or shower. Facilities: garden, garage, restaurant (reservations advised; jacket and tie required). AE, DC, MC, V. $$$$*

Bassano del Grappa
Dining

Al Ponte–Da Renzo. An ample family-run establishment on the Brenta River, this popular restaurant has big picture windows with a vista of the old town and the famed covered bridge. The tree-shaded garden for outdoor dining has the same view. The specialty of the house is seafood, with seafood antipasto and grilled fish fresh from the Adriatic featured on the menu, where you'll also find regional dishes according to the season. *Via Volpato 60, tel. 0424/503055. Reservations advised in summer. Dress: casual. V. Closed Mon. dinner, Tues., and Jan. $$*

Birraria Ottone. This Old World restaurant in the center of town is a favorite with the locals, who appreciate the excellent cuisine, draft wine and beer, and the friendly atmosphere created by the Wipflinger family, headed by Otto, whose Austrian forebear founded this beer hall about a hundred years ago. Equally good for a simple lunch or a more elaborate dinner, Ottone's specialties include a delicious goulash cooked with cumin. *Via Matteoti 47/50, tel. 0424/522206. Reservations advised. Dress: casual. MC, V. Closed Mon. dinner, Tues., and first 3 weeks in Aug. $–$$*

Lodging
★

Belvedere. This historic hotel has richly decorated public rooms with period furnishings and Oriental rugs. A fireplace and piano music in the lounge and an excellent restaurant with a garden make for a very pleasant stay. The bedrooms are decorated in traditional Venetian or chic contemporary style. *Piazzale G. Giardino 14, tel. 0424/529845, fax 0424/529849. 91 rooms with bath or shower. Facilities: air-conditioning, color TV, restaurant (Tel. 0424/526602. $$ Closed Sun.). AE, DC, MC, V. $$$*

Conegliano
Dining

Canon d'Oro. The town's oldest inn (19 rooms with bath or shower. Tel. as below, fax 0438/34246. $$), Canon d'Oro is in a 15th-century building in a central location near the train station. Restful classic decor lets you concentrate on the good food, mainly regional specialties such as risotto, *gnocchi alla Canon d'Oro* (potato dumplings), *baccalà alla vicentina* (creamy cod), and *fegato alla veneziana* (liver with onions). *Via XX Settembre 129, tel. 0438/34246. Reservations not required. Dress: casual. AE, MC, V. Closed Sat. $$*

Maser
Dining
★

Agnoletti. About 19 kilometers (12 miles) from Treviso in the town of Giavera del Montello near Maser, Agnoletti is an 18th-century inn with Old World atmosphere and decor. The kitchen can produce an all-mushroom menu; but if you order something else, at least try the mushroom *zuppa* (soup) or *crostata* (tart). In the summer you eat in the garden. *Giavera del Montello, Via della Vittoria 131, tel. 0422/*

776009. Reservations advised. Dress: casual. No credit cards. Closed Mon., Tues., and Jan. 1–20, July 1–15. $$

Da Bastian. A good place to stop for lunch before visiting the Villa Barbaro, this establishment has a contemporary look, a pleasant garden for outdoor dining, and an interesting menu featuring a varied antipasto of pâtés, homemade vegetarian ravioli, and broiled meat with tasty sauces. *Via Cornuda, tel. 0423/565400. Dress: casual. No credit cards. Closed Wed. dinner, Thurs., and Aug. $$*

Padua **Belle Parti.** The reincarnation of El Toulà (and still related to that
Dining prestigious chain), Belle Parti remains the best restaurant in town. The ambience is sophisticated, and the adventurous and seasonal cuisine has a Venetian accent. Specialties include risotto *al fior d'arancio con gamberi di fiume* (orange-flower and river-prawn risotto) and *quaglia tartufata in crosta* (truffled quails in pastry). The wine list offers a fine selection of the area's best bottles. *Via Belle Parti 11, tel. 049/875–1822. Reservations advised. Dress: jacket and tie or elegantly casual. AE, DC, MC, V. Closed Sun., Mon. lunch, and first 3 weeks in Aug. $$$*

Cavalca. A family-run establishment with a long tradition, Cavalca is just off Piazza dei Signori in the heart of Padua. Classic decor and simple but courteous service are hallmarks here. The specialties are *pasta e fagioli* (pasta and bean soup), roast *capretto* (kid), or a platter of *arrosti misti* (assorted roast meats). *Via Manin 8, tel. 049/ 876–0061. Reservations required. Dress: casual. AE, DC, MC, V. Closed Tues. dinner, Wed., and July 1–21, Jan. 12–22. $$*

Fagiano. Located near the basilica of Sant'Antonio, Fagiano is a popular trattoria with locals and tourists. The specialties are hearty standbys: pasta e fagioli and *fagiano farcito* (stuffed pheasant). *Via Locatelli 45, tel. 049/875–0073. Reservations advised. Dress: casual. MC, V. Closed Mon. and July 15–Aug. 15. $*

Lodging **Donatello.** Directly opposite the basilica of Sant'Antonio, the Donatello is central and popular with tourists. About half the rooms have a view of the square and church but can be noisy. The decor is contemporary; rooms have a minibar and color TV. *Via del Santo 102, tel. 049/875–0634, fax 049/875–0829. 49 rooms, 42 with bath or shower. Facilities: garage, restaurant (Closed Wed., $$). AE, DC, MC, V. Closed mid-Dec.–mid-Jan. $$$*

Europa. Located right in the center of town, the Europa is handy for sightseeing: It's a reliable 1960s commercial hotel and is furnished in undistinguished modern style. All rooms have air-conditioning, minibar, and color TV; marble-sheathed bathrooms add a touch of dated luxury. Parking space in front of the hotel is reserved for guests. *Largo Europa 9, tel. 049/661200, fax 049/661508. 59 rooms with bath or shower. Facilities: Zaramella restaurant (Closed Sat. lunch, Sun. $$). AE, DC, MC, V. $$*

Treviso **El Toulà.** Clones of this, the original Toulà, have sprouted up in un-
Dining likely places—even Japan. This is your chance to enjoy the art nou-
★ veau decor and classic international cuisine for which it became famous. There are regional dishes as well, among them risotto *con funghi* (with mushrooms) or asparagus in season. For cooking, ambience, and service, it's one of the region's best. *Via Collalto 26, tel. 0422/540275. Reservations advised. Jacket and tie preferred. AE, DC, MC, V. Closed Sun. dinner, Mon., and July 25–Aug. 25. $$$*

★ **Beccherie.** In a town known for good eating, this rustic inn is a favorite. It's in the heart of old Treviso, behind the main square, and there are tables outside for fair-weather dining under the portico. Specialties vary with the season. In winter, look for *crespelle al radicchio* (crêpes with radicchio) and *faraona in salsa peverada* (guinea hen in a peppery sauce); spring brings risotto with spring vegetables, *stinco di vitello* (roast veal shin), and *pasticcio di melanzane* (eggplant casserole). *Piazza Ancilotto 10, tel. 0422/ 540871. Reservations advised. Dress: casual. AE, DC, MC, V. Closed Sun. dinner and Mon., and July 12–30. $$*

Lodging **Continental.** You'll find this hotel within the old city walls, between the train station and the sights. It is a traditional four-star hotel offering solid comfort. The rooms have a minibar, a color TV, and air-conditioning. Rich fabrics and Oriental rugs lend an air of opulence. There is no restaurant. *Via Roma 16, tel. 0422/411216, fax 0422/ 55054. 82 rooms with bath or shower. AE, DC, MC, V. $$$$*

Al Fogher. Located on the outskirts, Al Fogher is handy if you're traveling by car. It has a bright contemporary look, with lots of modern art on the walls and room decor about equally divided between classic and modern. All rooms are equipped with a minibar and a color TV, and all are air-conditioned. *Viale della Repubblica 10, tel. 0422/432950, fax 0422/430391. 54 rooms with bath or shower. Facilities: parking, restaurant (Closed Sun., $$). AE, DC, MC, V. $$*

Trieste **Suban.** Despite its location in the hills on the edge of town, this his-
Dining toric trattoria is worth the taxi ride. The rustic decor is rich in dark
★ wood, stone, and wrought iron, and you'll find typical regional fare with imaginative variations. You can eat under an arbor in fair weather. Among the specialties are *jota carsolina* (typical local minestrone made of cabbage, potatoes, and beans) and duck breast in Tokay sauce. *Via Emilio Comici 2, tel. 040/54368. Reservations advised for dinner and Sun. lunch. Dress: casual. AE, DC, MC, V. Closed Mon., Tues., and Aug. 1–20. $$*

Lodging **Colombia.** With a convenient location near the train station, Colombia is also within walking distance of the major sights and the cog railway to Opicina. Unpretentious but adequate, it caters mainly to a business clientele. There is no restaurant, but there's a typical beer cellar restaurant close by. *Via della Geppa 18, tel. 040/369333, fax 040/369644. 40 rooms with bath or shower. AE, DC, MC, V. $$$*

Duchi d'Aosta. Located on the spacious Piazza dell'Unità d'Italia, this hotel is beautifully furnished in period style and lavish with Old World atmosphere. Its restaurant, Harry's Grill, is one of the city's most elegant. *Piazza dell'Unità d'Italia 2, tel. 040/7351, fax 040/ 366092. 50 rooms with bath or shower. Facilities: restaurant ($$$), bar. AE, DC, MC, V. $$$*

Udine **Alla Buona Vite.** This classic restaurant in the center of town specia-
Dining lizes in seafood. Tagliolini *dello chef* (with a creamy scampi sauce) and *rombo al limone e capperi* (turbot with lemon and capers) are among the many choices here. *Via Treppo 10, tel. 0432/21053. Reservations advised. Dress: casual. AE, DC, MC, V. Closed Sun. dinner, Mon., and Aug. $$*

★ **Antica Maddalena.** Just a few steps from Udine's pretty Piazza dell'Unità you'll find this elegant eating place, defined by its owner as a deluxe trattoria. Lots of warm wood tones, fresh flowers, and stained glass create a distinctive ambience to complement a menu of regional and Italian specialties, among them zuppa di funghi porcini, gnocchi *con zucca e ricotta* (with squash and ricotta cheese), and *carpaccio di salmone con rucola* (chopped salmon with lemon and arugula). *Via Pelliccerie 4, tel. 0432/25111. Reservations advised. Dress: casual. AE, DC, MC, V. Closed Sun., Mon., lunch, and 2 weeks in Feb., 2 weeks in Aug. $$*

Trattoria al Lepre. A characteristic *focolare* (hearth) in one of the dining rooms is a symbol of traditional local cooking, and that's what you'll enjoy in this simple establishment. The specialties include *tagliatelle con funghi* (homemade pasta with mushrooms) and *stinco di maiale* (roast pork shin served with polenta). *Via Poscolle 27, tel. 0432/295798. Reservations advised. Dress: casual. AE, DC, MC, V. Closed Sun. and 10 days in Aug. $$*

Lodging **Astoria Hotel Italia.** Centrally located, the Italia offers sound-proofed, air-conditioned rooms furnished in traditional style, all with minibar and color TV. Public rooms feature Venetian glass chandeliers and comfortable armchairs. *Piazza XX Settembre 24, tel. 0432/505091, fax 0432/509070. 80 rooms with bath or shower. Facilities: garage, restaurant ($$). AE, DC, MC, V. $$$*

Verona **Le Arche.** True to its name, this elegant yet informal restaurant is in
Dining a medieval building a step away from the Della Scala tombs. The dining room is furnished in art nouveau style, featuring candlelight and flowers, and it has an elegant turn-of-the-century air. Only seafood is served, absolutely fresh and superlatively prepared in the Venetian tradition. The specialties are *ravioli di branzino con vongole* (ravioli stuffed with sea bass with clam sauce) and *scorfano con olive nere* (baked sea scorpion with black olives). *Via Arche Scaligere 6, tel. 045/800–7415. Reservations advised. Dress: casual. AE, DC, MC, V. Closed Sun., Mon. lunch, the first two weeks of Jan. and July 1–21. $$$$*

Dodici Apostoli. Vaulted ceilings, frescoed walls, and a medieval ambience make this an exceptional place to enjoy classic local and regional dishes. Near Piazza delle Erbe, it stands on the foundations of a Roman temple. Specialties include *zuppa scaligera* (a soup of meat stock with vegetables and bread) and *vitello Lessinia* (veal with mushrooms, cheese, and truffles). *Corticella San Marco 3, tel. 045/596999. Reservations advised. Dress: casual. AE, DC, V. Closed Sun. dinner, Mon., and June 15–July 7, Jan. 1–7. $$$$*

La Greppia. The classic decor with vaulted ceilings sets the tone in this popular restaurant off Via Mazzini between the Arena and Piazza delle Erbe. The kitchen produces fine versions of local and regional dishes, especially *tortelli di zucca* (ravioli filled with squash) and *bolliti* (assorted boiled meats served with a choice of sauces). Service is courteous and efficient. *Vicolo Samaritana 3, tel. 045/800–4577. Reservations advised. Dress: casual. AE, DC, V. Closed Mon., first week of Jan., and June 15–30. $$*

Pizzeria Vesuvio. Between Castelvecchio and San Zeno Maggiore, this authentic Neapolitan pizzeria has tables on the riverbank in summer, with a lovely breezy view of the Adige. *Via Rigaste 41, tel. 045/595634. MC, V. Closed Mon. $*

Lodging **Colomba d'Oro.** This attractive four-star hotel, located right by the
★ arena, occupies a historic building dating from the 14th century. Repeatedly renovated over the past few years, it has retained a clubby atmosphere and European charm while providing up-to-date comfort. There is no restaurant. *Via Cattaneo 10, tel. 045/595300, fax 045/594974. 49 rooms with bath or shower, 2 suites. Facilities: garage. AE, DC, MC, V. $$$$*

★ **Gabbia d'Oro.** A historic building off Piazza delle Erbe in the ancient heart of Verona was fully and tastefully restored in 1990. Public rooms and individually furnished guest rooms have frescoes, beamed ceilings, and antique prints and furnishings. Guests can relax outdoors in the medieval courtyard or on the roof terrace. *Corso Porta Borsari 4/a, tel. 045/800–3060, fax 045/590293. 27 rooms with bath. Facilities: courtesy taxi to 24-hour garage, bar, roof terrace; restaurant for guests open on request, with buffet in courtyard, lunch and dinner, in summer. AE, DC, MC, V. $$$$*

Giulietta e Romeo. In the medieval part of Verona and very handy for sightseeing, this is a comfortable hotel with an irresistibly romantic name. The hotel was extensively renovated in 1991. *Vicolo Tre Marchetti 3, tel. 045/800–3554, fax 045/801–0862. 30 rooms with bath or shower. AE, MC, V. $$$*

Mazzanti. Just off Piazza delle Erbe, this very central, popular hotel offers good, straightforward accommodations at charmingly old-fashioned prices. *Via Mazzanti 6, tel. 045/800–6813, fax 045/801–1262. 23 rooms, 19 with bath or shower. MC, V. $$*

Vicenza **Da Remo.** Located about a mile outside town, Da Remo is worth the
Dining taxi ride simply because it is one of Vicenza's best restaurants. In an attractive country-house setting, with light, airy dining rooms and a garden terrace, you can enjoy a relaxing meal of Venetian specialties, among them *faraona al radicchio* (guinea hen with radicchio) and risotto with seasonal vegetables. *Via Ca'Impenta 14, tel. 0444/911007. Reservations advised. Dress: casual. AE, DC, MC, V. Closed Sun. dinner, Mon., the last week of July and first 3 weeks of Aug., Christmas holidays. $$*

★ **Scudo di Francia.** A Gothic palace in the heart of town houses the white vaulted dining rooms of Scudo di Francia. The regional cuisine features specialties such as *bignè caldi al prosciutto e tartufo* (hot pastry puffs with ham and truffles), pasta e fagioli, and *baccalà alla vicentina* (creamed cod). *Contrà Piancoli 4, tel. 0444/323322. Reservations advised. Dress: casual. AE, DC, MC, V. Closed Sun. dinner, Mon., and Aug. $$*

Al Paradiso. This pizzeria-trattoria just off the Piazza dei Signori is one of a pair (the other is Vecchia Guardia), right next door to each other, owned by two brothers. It's particularly attractive in summer, when you can sit at tables outside. The pizzas and other dishes are tasty and very reasonably priced. *Via Pescherie Vecchie 5, tel. 0444/322320. Closed Mon. AE, DC, MC, V. $–$$*

Lodging **Campo Marzio.** Centrally located, Campo Marzio is between the train station and the historic center, within walking distance of the sights. This contemporary hotel has functionally furnished rooms with color TV, and minibar. The buffet breakfast is abundant. *Viale Roma 21, tel. 0444/545700, fax 0444/320495. 35 rooms with bath or shower. Facilities: parking, restaurant. AE, DC, MC, V. $$$$*

Due Mori. Located in the heart of Vicenza just off Piazza dei Signori, this small hotel was recently refurbished and is a favorite with regular visitors. *Contra Do Rode 26, tel. 0444/321886, fax 0444/326217. 28 rooms, 25 with bath or shower. MC, V. $–$$*

Vicenza. Another useful hotel in the traffic-free town center, the Vicenza offers simple, clean, and pleasant accommodations. *Stradella dei Nodari 5/7, tel. 0444/321512. 37 rooms, 30 with bath or shower. No credit cards. Closed 10 days at Christmas. $*

The Arts and Nightlife

The Arts

Most of this region is within striking distance of Venice, with its own wide range of cultural attractions (*see* The Arts and Nightlife in Chapter 6), but the Arc does offer ample opportunities to satisfy a hunger for Italian culture.

Concerts and Pride of place must go to the spectacular summer opera season in the
Opera **Arena di Verona** (*see* Tour 3: Verona, *above*). The season runs from July through August, and the 22,000 in the audience sit on the original stone terraces, which date back to the time when gladiators

fought to the death. The opera stage is huge and best suited to grand operas such as *Aïda*, but the experience is memorable no matter what is being performed. *For tickets, contact Ente Lirico Arena di Verona, Piazza Brà 28, 37100 Verona, tel. 045/590109. The box office is at Arches 8–9 of the Arena, tel. 045/596517 or 800–5151. Open weekdays 8:40–12:20, 3–5:50, Sat. 8:40–12:20.*

Trieste holds an open-air operetta festival each summer (July–August). For dates, times, and prices, contact the main tourist office (*see* Important Addresses and Numbers in Essential Information, *above*).

Theater Even if your Italian is dismal, it's probably worth attending a performance of classical drama (in Italian) in the **Teatro Olimpico** in Vicenza (*see* Tour 2: Palladian Vicenza, *above*). Palladio's masterpiece was designed to be used, not just admired. For details, contact Teatro Olimpico (Vicenza, tel. 0444/323781).

Nightlife

Many visitors to the Veneto area are willing to make the trip into Venice for a big night out, but it can be more enjoyable to stay put and soak up the atmosphere where you are. Most towns have central squares where the slow ritual of the *passeggiata* (promenade) takes place. As for cities, Padua is perhaps the liveliest, given its large student population, with Verona a close second, thanks to all the tourists.

Bars **Caffè Pedrocchi** (*see* Tour 1: Villa Pisani and Padua, *above*) in Padua is probably the best-known café in the Venetian Arc. Have your drink inside or out while you admire the uninhibited mixture of architectural styles. **Piazza Brà** in Verona and **Piazza dell'Unità d'Italia** in Trieste are standout squares surrounded by outdoor cafés. Sometimes, while sipping a drink in a café at Piazza Brà, you can overhear the opera being performed inside the adjacent arena. Historic **Caffè San Marco** on Via Battisti in Trieste is a shrine of Old World atmosphere.

Discos The best bets are in Padua: **Big Club** (Via Armistizio, tel. 049/680934) and **Ippopotamus** (Via Savonarola 149, tel. 049/42108).

Jazz Club **Video Club Sisma** (Via Chiesanuova 106, Padua, tel. 049/871–6577).

8 Liguria

Genoa and the Rivieras

The region of Liguria is contained in a narrow strip of coastline stretching 349 twisting kilometers (217 miles) from the French border to Tuscany and never more than 40 kilometers (25 miles) wide. The sea that beats upon these shores has given them their character and their history. Every American schoolchild knows that Genoa, set in the heart of this rocky coast, is the birthplace of Christopher Columbus. That famous explorer was only one, and not the first or the last, in a long line of seafaring men whose activity centered in the ports of the two Rivieras of Italy.

Liguria is favored by a mild climate year-round; this, and the ease with which it can be reached from the rest of western Europe, has helped to make it one of the most popular regions in Italy for visitors. An impressive number of foreigners—British, American, French—have permanent residences here. For centuries, its charm has inspired poets and artists, many of whom came for a brief visit and stayed on. Italians from inland cities flock to its beaches in summer or maintain their villas along its length, and some areas of the western coast have become especially popular with German and other European package-tour operators, almost swamping what were once attractive small seaside towns. The flavor of the area is cosmopolitan, a mellow blend of provincial and smart set, primitive and old-fashioned, and luxurious and up-to-date. The eye is caught, the attention is held, by the contours of the coastline curving serpentinely in an arc from Ventimiglia to La Spezia; by the Ligurian Alps, plunging in sheer cliffs or sloping gradually to the sea; by the glamour and color of the resorts, the busy ports, the stately yachts against the skyline, and the grandiose view across the Gulf of Genoa from a hairpin curve on the highway.

Liguria's narrow strip of coastline, protected by mountains, varies considerably between the two Rivieras. The Riviera di Ponente (western Riviera), from the French border to Genoa, has some protected bays and wide sandy beaches and is generally more commercialized and built up than its counterpart to the east. Along the Riviera di Levante (eastern Riviera), from Genoa eastward, the coastline becomes rockier and steeper, punctuated by small bays and inlets, and the less accessible coastal villages have a more traditional way of life. Two rugged peninsulas jut out from the Levante coastline. The first is the famous Portofino promontory, a rocky outcrop 40 million years old and covered with olive trees, pines, and cypresses. A network of nature and hiking trails crosses the peninsula, rewarding the energetic with sweeping views of the coastline. Farther along the coast is the second peninsula, where the road goes inland, leaving the visitor to hike or take a train or boat to explore the Cinque Terre, five fishing or farming villages clinging to cliff faces or perched on bluffs overlooking the sea.

As Italy's largest port, Genoa itself is a bustling city, with a proud history of trade and navigation that predates Columbus. Modern container ships unload at docks that centuries before served galleons and vessels bound for the spice routes. By the 3rd century BC, when the Romans conquered Liguria, Genoa was already an important trading station, which the Romans enhanced by building the Via Aurelia to link Rome with what is now France. The Middle Ages and the Renaissance saw the rise of Genoa as a great seaport, and the city—jumping-off place for the Crusades, commercial center of tremendous wealth and prestige, strategic bone of international contention—was of key importance to Europe. Thereafter, Genoa declined in rank as a sea power. Napoleon reduced all Liguria to an ineffective "family estate of the Bonapartes," as Tolstoy speaks of it in *War and Peace.* When the emperor was finally defeated at Water-loo, the region became part of Piedmont, and reacquired its separate identity only after the unification of Italy.

People today come to Liguria less for its history and its art than for its mild climate, fine seafood, and coastal villages, many of which remain unspoiled. Tennis and bocce (Italian lawn-bowling) are played all year, while during the summer the coast sees colorful flotillas of yachts and smaller sailboats, often moored next to the boats of the hard-working local fishermen. The Mediterranean vegetation along the coast—myrtle, heather, broom, rosemary, pine, and olives—gives way to chestnut groves and terraced vineyards on the hills. Relaxed Liguria is the sort of place where knowing the difference between scrub pine and cypress means more than knowing Rococo from Renaissance.

Essential Information

Important Addresses and Numbers

Tourist Information The main APT (tourist board) offices for Genoa are in the center of town (Via Roma 11, tel. 010/581407, just off Piazza De Ferrari, and Via Porta degli Archi 10, tel. 010/541541). There are information offices at Principe Station (tel. 010/262633), at Brignole Station (tel. 010/562056), and at the airport (tel. 010/2415247). The helpful local tourist offices (listed below) are sometimes known as "Pro Loco." *APT and Pro Loco offices usually open Mon.–Thurs. 9–2, 2:30–5:30, Fri. and Sat. 8–1.*

Alassio (Palazzo Hanbury, Via Gibb 26, tel. 0182/640346).
Albenga (Via Martiri della Libertà, tel. 0182/50475).
Bordighera (Palazzo del Parco, tel. 0184/262322).
Camogli (Via XX Settembre 33r, tel. 0185/771066).
Imperia (Via Matteotti 22, tel. 0183/60730).
La Spezia (Via Mazzini 47, tel. 0187/770900).
Lerici (Via Gerini 40, tel. 0187/967346).
Levanto (Piazza Colombo 12, tel. 0187/808125).
Rapallo (Via A. Diaz 9, tel. 0185/51282).
San Remo (Corso Nuvoloni, tel. 0184/571571).
Varazze (Viale Nazioni Unite, tel. 019/97007).
Ventimiglia (Via Cavour 61, tel. 0184/351183).

Emergencies **Police,** tel. 113; Genoa municipal police, tel. 010/53631.
Ambulance, tel. 010/595951.

Doctors and Dentists In case of accident, go to the public hospital in Genoa, **Ospedale Generale Regionale San Martino** (Viale Benedetto XV, tel. 010/516748). For information on dentists and night-duty and Sunday-duty doctors, call tel. 010/354022.

Late-Night Pharmacies **Europa** (Corso Europa 676, Genoa, tel. 010/380239). **Ghersi** (Corte Lambruschini [Tower A], Genoa, tel. 010/541661).

Car Rentals **Genoa.** *Avis* (Piazza Acquaverde, tel. 010/255598, for reservations, tel. 06/4780150); *Budget* (at the airport, tel. 010/603–822); *Hertz* (Via delle Casacce 3, tel. 010/564412).
La Spezia. *Avis* (Via Fratelli Rosselli 86/88, tel. 0187/33345); *Hertz* (Via San Bartolomeo 665, tel. 0187/516712).
San Remo. *Avis* (Corso Imperatrice 96, tel. 0184/73897); *Hertz* (Via XX Settembre 17, tel. 0184/85618).

Arriving and Departing by Plane

Cristoforo Colombo International Airport, at Sestri Ponente (tel. 010/2411) is only 6 kilometers (4 miles) from the center of Genoa. It has regular service to all main European cities. The nearest airport for U.S. flights is Nice, in France, about 2½ hours west of Genoa. Volabus services (tel. 010/599–7414) from Cristoforo Colombo connect with Genoa's Brignole Station, stopping also at Piazza Acquaverde (Principe Station).

Arriving and Departing by Car, Train, Bus, and Boat

By Car Autostrada (highway) A12 south from Genoa links up with the autostrada network for all southern destinations; Rome is a six-hour drive from Genoa. The 150-kilometer (90-mile) trip north to Milan on A7 takes two hours. Nice is 2½ hours west on A10.

By Train Frequent and fast train services connect Liguria with the rest of Italy. Genoa is 1½ hours from Milan and five hours from Rome. Many services from France (in particular, the French Riviera) pass along the Ligurian Coast on the way to all parts of Italy.

By Bus Buses operated by **SITA** (tel. 010/313851) provide connections along both Ligurian coasts to Genoa, linking the region with the French Riviera and other parts of Italy. The main station is at Piazza del Principe. The **Pesci** line (Piazza della Vittoria 94/r, Genoa, tel. 010/564936) specializes in services from Genoa to all other parts of Italy, with frequent connections to Rome and Milan.

By Boat Genoa is Italy's largest port and can be reached from the United States as well as other parts of Liguria and Italy (Sardinia, La Spezia, and Savona). Ships berth in the heart of Genoa, including cruise ships of the Genoa-based **Costa Cruise Line** (Via Gabriele D'Annunzio 2, tel. 010/54831) and ferries to various ports around the Mediterranean, operated by **Tirrenia Navigazione** (Stazione Marittima, tel. 010/258606).

Getting Around

By Car Two good roads run parallel to each other along the coast of Liguria. Closer to shore and passing through all the towns and villages is S1, which has excellent views at almost every turn but which gets crowded in July and August. More direct and higher up than S1 is the autostrada, known as A10 west of Genoa and A12 to the east. This route saves a lot of time on weekends, in summer, and on days when festivals slow traffic in some resorts to a standstill.

By Train Regular service, connecting all parts of Liguria, operates from Genoa's two stations, **Stazione Principe** (for points west) and **Stazione Brignole** (for the east). All the coastal resorts are on this line, and many international trains stop along the coast west of Genoa on their way from Paris to Milan or Rome.

By Bus **SITA** and **Pesci** (*see* Arriving and Departing By Bus, *above*) buses run the length of the Ligurian Coast in both directions. Local buses serve the steep valleys that run to some of the towns along the western coast. Tickets may be bought at local bus stations, or at newsstands in the case of local buses. Buy your ticket before you board the bus.

By Boat This is the most pleasant (and, in some the cases, the only) way to get from place to place within Liguria. A busy network of local services connects many of the resorts. For general information about availability of services in Liguria, contact **Servizio Marittimo del Tigullio** (Calata Zingari, Genoa, tel. 010/265712), which connects Genoa with most of the ports to the west and provides links to the east to the Cinque Terre and Portovenere. Or contact **Camogli–San Fruttuoso Maritime Services** (Società Golfo Paradiso, Via Scalo 2, Camogli, tel. 0185/772091), which runs between Camogli and San Fruttuoso (on the Portofino promontory), as well as between Recco and Punta Chiappa, two other towns close to Camogli. Summer excursions link both ports with the Cinque Terre and Portovenere.

Guided Tours

Orientation One of the joys of visiting even the tiniest of the Ligurian coastal resorts is the chance to take an informal **harbor cruise** or excursion to the next town along the coast. Some of these tours are scheduled and operated by the main ferry lines (*see* Getting Around by Boat, *above*), but you can have as much fun—if not more—negotiating a price with a boat owner at one of the smaller ports. You're likely to get someone whose English is rudimentary at best, but that shouldn't affect your appreciation of the rugged and colorful coastal scenery.

A three-hour **bus tour** of Genoa is operated by the tourist office. Buses have English-speaking guides and are the best way to get to know the city. Buses leave from the **AMT** (municipal bus company) office at Piazza della Vittoria at 9 AM, stopping to pick up passengers at Piazza De Ferrari and at Piazza Acquaverde (about 9:20). Tickets (about 30,000 lire) can be purchased on the bus, but seats should be reserved at Cioncoloni (Via Nizza 4, tel. 010/302142). For information, inquire at the tourist booth at **Stazione Principe** (Piazza Acquaverde, tel. 010/262633).

You can also take a **boat tour** of the harbor in Genoa. The tour lasts about an hour and includes a visit to the Lanterna, the breakwater outside the harbor, the Bacino delle Grazie, and the Molo Vecchio (Old Pier). You can see extensive views of the city throughout the tour. For information, contact the **Cooperativa Batellieri** (Stazione Marittima, Ponte dei Mille, Genoa, tel. 010/265712).

Exploring Liguria

Our three exploring tours follow the coast from west to east. The scenic coastal road, S1, links every attraction discussed in this chapter, except for those villages that are inaccessible from any road and have to be reached by foot or by boat.

Tour 1 covers the Riviera di Ponente from its western border with France, at Ventimiglia, along the coast toward Genoa at the head of the broad Ligurian Gulf. Tour 2 explores Genoa itself, starting with a bird's-eye view of the city, from the top of the Granarolo funicular, and continuing through the old and new sections before finishing with the port itself. Tour 3, along the Riviera di Levante, snakes its way southward along this rocky coastline, abandoning S1 only when it explores the remoter parts of the Portofino peninsula and the Cinque Terre.

Highlights for First-Time Visitors

Camogli (Tour 3: Riviera di Levante).

Cinque Terre (Tour 3: Riviera di Levante).

Giardino Hanbury (Tour 1: Riviera di Ponente).

Museo del Tesoro di San Lorenzo, Genoa (Tour 2: Genoa).

Palazzo Reale, Genoa (Tour 2: Genoa).

Portofino (Tour 3: Riviera di Levante).

Portovenere (Tour 3: Riviera di Levante).

San Remo (Tour 1: Riviera di Ponente).

Via Garibaldi, Genoa (Tour 2: Genoa).

Tour 1: Riviera di Ponente

Numbers in the margin correspond to points of interest on the Liguria map.

The **Riviera di Ponente** is a narrow coastal strip punctuated by rocky outcrops jutting out between wide bays and sandy coves. Its other name is Riviera dei Fiori (Riviera of Flowers), because flower cultivation is a major industry here. Just past the French border, stop at ❶ Mortola Inferiore to visit the world-famous **Giardino Hanbury** (Hanbury Garden), one of the largest botanical gardens in Italy. Planned and planted by a wealthy English merchant, Sir Thomas Hanbury, and his botanist brother, Daniel, in 1867, the gardens contain a variety of species from five continents—including many palms and succulents (plants of the cactus group). There are panoramic views of the sea from the gardens. *Giardino Hanbury, Mortola Inferiore, tel. 0184/229507. Admission: 9,000 lire. Open June–Sept., daily 9–6; Oct.–May, Thurs.–Tues. 10–4.*

On the ocean side of the road are the famous **Balzi Rossi** (Red Rocks), caves in the sheer rock, in which prehistoric man left traces of his life and magic rites. You can visit the caves and a small museum containing some of the objects found there. *Tel. 0184/38113. Admission: 4,000 lire. Open July–Aug., Tues.–Sun. 9–1, 2:30–6:30; Sept.–June, 9–1, 2:30–6.*

❷ **Ventimiglia,** about 9 kilometers (6 miles) from the French border, was once a pre-Roman settlement known as Albintimilium and contains some important archaeological remains, such as a 2nd-century AD amphitheater. A vital trade center for hundreds of years, Ventimiglia declined in prestige as Genoa grew and is now little more than a frontier town that lives on tourism and the cultivation of flowers. The town is divided in two by the Roia River. The **Città Vecchia** (Old City), on the western side, is what you'll see first: It is a well-preserved and typical medieval town. The 11th-century **Duomo** (Cathedral) has a Gothic portal dating from 1222. Walk up Via del Capo to the ancient walls, which offer fine views of the coast. S1 crosses the river into the new part of town, famous for its large flower market. Avoid Ventimiglia on Friday, a chaotic market day that draws crowds of bargain hunters from France, creating traffic gridlock.

Time Out While you're in the heart of the Città Vecchia, stop at the **Cuneo** (Via Aprosio 16, closed Tues. dinner, Wed., and July) for a lunch of fresh shellfish or pasta.

From Ventimiglia, a provincial road swings up the Nervia River valley to the lovely sounding medieval town of **Dolceacqua** (Sweetwater), with its ruined castle, and beyond to **Pigna,** another medieval village built in concentric circles on a hilltop.

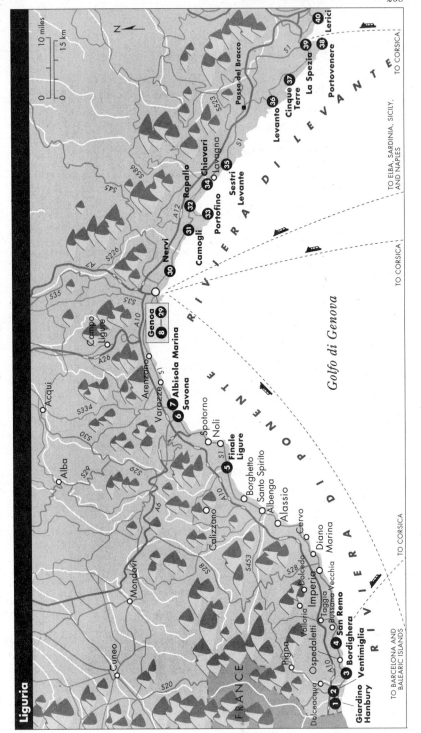

Liguria

10 miles
15 km

N

TO ELBA, SARDINIA, SICILY,
AND NAPLES

TO CORSICA

TO CORSICA

TO CORSICA

TO BARCELONA AND
BALEARIC ISLANDS

Golfo di Genova

R I V I E R A   D I   P O N E N T E

R I V I E R A   D I   L E V A N T E

FRANCE

Cuneo

Mondovì

Alba

Acqui

Campo
Ligure

Arenzano

Varazze

Albisola Marina
Savona

Spotorno
Noli

Finale
Ligure

Borghetto

Santo Spirito
Albenga

Alassio

Cervo

Diano
Marina

Imperia

Oneglia

Taggia

Bussana
Vecchia

San Remo

Bordighera

Ventimiglia

Giardino
Hanbury

Dolceacqua

Ospedaletti

Vallolio

Pigna

Dolcedo

Calizzano

Genoa

Nervi

Camogli

Rapallo
Portofino

Chiavari
Lavagna

Sestri
Levante

Levanto

Cinque
Terre

La Spezia
Portovenere

Lerici

Passo del Bracco

Golfo di Genova

Passo del Bracco

1 **2** Giardino Hanbury
3 Ventimiglia
4 San Remo · Bordighera
5 Finale Ligure
6 **7** Albisola Marina · Savona
8—**29** Genoa
30 Nervi
31 Camogli
32 Rapallo
33 Portofino
34 Chiavari
35 Sestri Levante
36 Levanto
37 Cinque Terre
38 Portovenere
39 La Spezia
40 Lerici

❸ **Bordighera,** just a few minutes down the coast from Ventimiglia, is a famous winter resort dominating a broad promontory with lush vegetation. A large English colony, still very much in evidence, developed here in the second half of the 19th century, attracted by the mild climate. Bordighera is an elegant town with a fin de siècle atmosphere; expect to find people taking afternoon tea in the cafés. This garden spot was the first town in Europe to grow date palms, and its citizens still have the exclusive right to provide the Vatican with palm fronds for Easter celebrations. Walk along the **Lungomare Argentina,** the magnificent mile-long seafront promenade, beginning at the western end of the town, for a good view westward, to the French Côte d'Azur. Thanks partly to its year-round English residents, Bordighera does not close down entirely in the winter like many Riviera resorts. With plenty of fine hotels and restaurants, it makes a good base for excursions and is quieter and less commercial than San Remo.

❹ Twelve kilometers (8 miles) east is **San Remo,** the capital of this coast and its largest resort. Renowned for its royal visitors, its famous casino (one of only four in Italy), and its romantic setting, San Remo still maintains some of the glamour of its heyday from the late 19th century to World War II. Among the rich and famous who flocked to San Remo, drawn by the mild climate and pleasant countryside, were Alfred Nobel, who built a summer house here, and Russian Empress Maria Alexandrovna, wife of Czar Alexander II. The Russian Orthodox church of **San Basilio,** with its onion domes, stands at one end of the **Corso dell'Imperatrice** and, like that imposing seafront promenade, is a legacy of the Empress. San Remo also has elegant world-class hotels, where you can stop to have a drink, and exotic gardens, in addition to its promenades.

San Remo is also famous for the **Mercato dei Fiori,** Italy's most important wholesale flower market held in a market hall between Piazza Colombo and Corso Garibaldi. More than 20,000 tons of carnations, roses, mimosa, and innumerable other cut flowers are dispatched from here each year. The old part of San Remo, **La Pigna** (meaning pine cone), is a warren of alleyways leading up to **Piazza Castello,** with a splendid view of the town.

Time Out | Join the fishermen and other locals for a lunch of freshly caught seafood at **Porto-Da Nico** (Piazza Bresca 9, closed Tues. and Nov.–Dec. 28.), a small family-run trattoria near the harbor.

The newer parts of San Remo suffer from the same epidemic of overbuilding that transformed so many towns on the western Riviera for the worse. And as center of northern Italy's flower-growing industry, the resort is surrounded by hills where once verdant terraces are now blanketed with plastic to form immense greenhouses. Fortunately, the town of **Taggia,** about 10 kilometers (6 miles) from San Remo, has survived intact. It has a medieval core and one of the most imposing medieval stone bridges in the area. The church of **San Domenico,** on a rise south of Taggia, was part of a monastery that was founded in the 15th century and was a beacon of faith and learning in western Liguria for three hundred years.

Imperia, 26 kilometers (16 miles) east along the coast, actually consists of two towns: Porto Maurizio, a medieval town built on a promontory, and Oneglia, now an industrial center for oil refining and pharmaceuticals. Obviously, Oneglia can be skipped entirely. Porto Maurizio has a virtually intact medieval center, the Parasio quarter, an intricate spiral of narrow streets and stone portals, and some imposing 17th- and 18th-century palaces.

A detour inland takes you to the well-preserved medieval villages of **Dolcedo** and **Valloria.** The 7-kilometer (4.8-mile) road to Dolcedo is narrow but fairly straight. Instead, there are about 10 kilometers (6 miles) of scenic but tortuous asphalt between Dolcedo and Valloria.

Don't pass by one of the most interesting towns on the entire western Riviera—**Cervo**, the quintessential Ligurian coastal village. About 8 kilometers (5 miles) east of Imperia, it is a remarkably well-preserved medieval town. Though much larger, **Albenga,** about 20 kilometers (12 miles) beyond Cervo, also has a medieval core, with narrow streets laid out by the ancient Romans. They form a network of alleys punctuated by centuries-old towers, surrounding the cathedral and baptistery dating back to the 5th century AD.

5 The countryside around **Finale Ligure,** 20 kilometers (12 miles) northeast along the coast, is pierced by deep, narrow valleys and caves; the limestone outcroppings provide the warm pinkish stone found in many buildings in Genoa. Here there are rare reptiles and rare species of flora. Finale Ligure itself is made up of three villages: Borgo, Marina, and Pia. The last two have fine sandy beaches and modern resort amenities. About two kilometers (1 mile) inland is the old village of **Finalborgo,** a medieval settlement planned to a rigid blueprint, with 15th-century walls. The village is crowned by the impressive ruins of the huge **Castel Gavone.** The Baroque church of **San Biagio** houses many works of art, and the 14th- to 15th-century Dominican convent of **Santa Caterina** can be visited for the shade of the courtyard or to see the museum of paleontology and natural history, which houses prehistoric remains found in the area. *Museo Civico. Tel. 019/690020. Admission free. Open May–Sept., Tues.–Fri., 10–12, 3–6, weekends 9–12; Oct.–Apr., Tues.–Fri., 9–12, 2:30–4:30.*

Time Out   Develop your taste for homemade pesto (pasta sauce made of basil and pine nuts) at the **Torchi** restaurant (Via dell'Annunziata 12, tel. 019/690531, closed Tues. and Jan.–Feb. $$–$$$), located in the center of Finalborgo.

The coast road (S1) from Finale Ligure to Savona is scenic, passing through the little towns of **Noli** and **Spotorno** (the latter can also be reached by train). If you don't have a car, a bus from Spotorno will take you to Noli, a tiny, medieval gem with the picturesque ruins of a castle above the village. It is hard to believe that Noli, like Genoa, Venice, Pisa, and Amalfi, was a prosperous maritime republic in the Middle Ages.

6 **Savona,** 9 kilometers (5 miles) east of Spotorno, is the fifth largest seaport in Italy and handles vast oil and coal cargoes, as well as car and truck ferries. Much of the town is modern and not very interesting, although a small, austere older quarter near the harbor contains some fine homes of the town's merchant class. The large **Palazzo della Rovere,** on Via Pia, was designed for Pope Julius II by the Florentine Giuliano da Sangallo in 1495; there is also the 14th-century **Palazzo degli Anziani** and three 12th-century towers. Every other year (next in 1996) on Good Friday, antique wooden carvings depicting the Passion of Christ are carried in procession. Watch for shops selling crystallized fruit, which is a local specialty.

7 Just outside Savona, to the east, is **Albisola Marina,** which preserves its centuries-old tradition of ceramic making. Numerous shops here sell these distinctive wares, and a whole sidewalk, **Lungomare degli Artisti,** has been transformed by the colorful ceramic works of local artists. It runs along the beachfront. The 17th-century **Villa Faraggiana,** located by the parish church on Via dell'Oratorio, has interesting antique ceramics and exhibits on the history of the craft. *Admission free. Open Apr.–Sept., Wed.–Mon. 3–7.*

If you'd like to take a break for a little sea and sun, stop in **Varazze,** 12 kilometers (7 miles) east, known for its fine sandy beach. The town also has well-preserved ancient ramparts, with a 10th-century church facade built into one of the rampart walls.

From Varazze, it is about 35 kilometers (22 miles) to Genoa. Just before you get to the city, you'll pass **Pegli,** a popular summer home for many patrician Genoese families. Some of the grand villas, with their well-tended gardens and parks, also function as museums.

Tour 2: Genoa

Visitors who come to Liguria for the sun and the sea generally avoid the busy, sprawling city of **Genoa,** which stretches for 20 kilometers (12 miles) along the coast. Yet Genoa can offer a fascinating, rich, and colorful experience. Known as La Superba (The Proud), Genoa was from the 13th century a great maritime center that rivaled Venice and Pisa in power and splendor. Its bankers, merchants, and princes adorned the city with palaces and churches and amassed impressive collections of art. Genoa's lively medieval center is one of Europe's largest. While brimming with historical curiosities and buildings, Genoa is also a thoroughly modern city struggling with problems of traffic, noise and air pollution, and an increasing immigrant population. Its port (Italy's largest) is being equipped to keep up with new technologies; the city is also advanced in communications, electronics, and general commerce.

Europe's biggest boat show takes place here, as does the Euroflora flower show (held every five years—next in 1996). Classical dance and music are richly represented; the new Carlo Felice Theater is a showcase (*see* The Arts and Nightlife, *below*) and the annual Niccolò Paganini Violin Contest, internationally renowned, also takes place in Genoa.

The historic harbor area was given a face-lift for the Columbus celebrations in 1992, and some of the fair installations, such as the Bigo elevator ride with harbor view, have become a permanent part of the city scene. The Acquario (Aquarium), Europe's largest, is one of Genoa's more recent attractions.

Numbers in the margin correspond to points of interest on the Genoa map.

Immediately above the coast the terrain rises steeply: Dotted around the circumference of the city are a number of huge fortresses. Start your tour of Genoa with an aerial view of the city. Take the **Granarolo funicular,** actually a cog railway, up to one of the fortified gates in the 17th-century city walls. It takes 15 minutes to hoist you from Piazza del Principe, behind the Principe Station on Piazza Acquaverde, to **Porta Granarolo,** 1,000 feet above, where you can get a good sense of the size of Genoa. *Fare: 400 lire. Leaves every ½-hour, on the ¼-hour, 6AM–midnight.*

A good way to begin exploring Genoa, once you're back on street level, is to start on **Via Balbi,** which runs southeast from the train station toward the medieval town. On the right, at No. 10, is the

Genoa

⑩ Palazzo Reale, otherwise known as **Palazzo Balbi Durazzo,** formerly the royal palace. The palace, which dates from the 17th century, contains paintings, sculptures, tapestries, and Oriental ceramics. The building was bought by the Royal House of Savoy in the early 19th century and has some magnificent rooms decorated in the lavish and frivolous rococo style. The gallery of mirrors and the ballroom on the upper floor are particularly good examples. There are also works by Sir Anthony Van Dyck, who lived in Genoa for six years, from 1621, and painted many fine portraits of the Genoese nobility. *Tel. 010/247–0640. Admission: 4,000 lire. Open daily 9–1.*

⑪ Opposite is the **Palazzo dell' Università,** built in the 1630s as a Jesuit college and the site of a university since 1803. Climb the stairway flanked by lions to visit the elegant courtyard, with its portico of double Doric columns.

A few minutes' walk along Via Balbi, on Piazza della Nunziata, is the 16th- to 17th-century church of the **Santissima Annunziata,** which has exuberantly frescoed vaults and is an excellent example of Genoese Baroque architecture.

Continue down Via Cairoli to **Via Garibaldi,** once known as the "Strada Nuova" (New Street). Genoa's leading patrician families built their residences here from 1554 onward to escape the cramped conditions of the medieval section of town; 13 palaces were built along the street in just 10 years. Via Garibaldi is one of the most impressive streets in Italy, and its palaces house some of the finest art collections in the country.

⑫ The 17th-century Baroque **Palazzo Rosso** (Red Palace), at No. 18, was one of the last palaces to be erected here. Named after the red stone used in its construction, it now contains, apart from a number of lavishly frescoed suites, works by Titian, Veronese, Caravaggio, Rubens, and Van Dyck. *Tel. 010/282641. Admission: 4,000 lire. Open Tues.–Sat. 9–7, Sun. 9–12:30.*

⑬ Opposite, at No. 10, is the **Palazzo Bianco.** Originally white, as its name suggests, the palace has become considerably darkened with age and grime. It has a fine art collection, with the Dutch and Flemish schools well represented. *Tel. 010/291803. Admission: 4,000 lire. Open Tues.–Sat. 9–7, Sun. 9–12:30.*

⑭ Palazzo Tursi (No. 9) is Genoa's Town Hall, built in the 16th century by the wealthy Nicolò Grimaldi. The palace, also known as Palazzo Municipale, is made of pink stone quarried in the region. Visitors are welcome to view the richly decorated rooms and the famous Guarnerius violin that belonged to Paganini and is played once a year on Columbus Day (October 12). However, when the rooms are in use by Genoa's officials, as is often the case, they are closed to the public. *Tel. 010/20981. Admission free. Open Mon.–Sat.; call for hours.*

Most of the other palaces on Via Garibaldi can be visited only by special application, but many have courtyards that are open to the public.

⑮ At the end of Via Garibaldi, on Piazza Portello, take the elevator to **Castelletto** for a good view of the old city. *Fare: 400 lire one way. Continuous service 6 AM–10:30 PM.*

Turn right at the end of Via Garibaldi onto the narrow streets that zigzag down into the **medieval city.** The winding, picturesque alleys—known as *caruggi*—contain many medieval buildings, some decorated with typically Ligurian black-and-white facades, that are on a more human scale than the grand, airy palaces of Via Garibaldi. But the caruggi district is also the city's most disreputable. Don't go there after dark, or on holidays, when shops are closed and the alleys deserted.

🕧 Make your way west toward the harbor and **San Siro,** Genoa's oldest church. Evidence of a church on this spot goes back to the 4th century, but the original edifice, which was Genoa's cathedral until the 9th century, was rebuilt in the 16th and 17th centuries. Nearby, just

🕧 off Via San Luca, is the **National Gallery,** housed in the richly adorned **Palazzo Spinola.** The collection contains, among other fine works, masterpieces by Luca Giordano (1634–1705) and Guido Reni (1575–1642). The *Ecce Homo,* by Antonello da Messina (1430–79), is a hauntingly beautiful painting and is also of historical interest because it was the Sicilian da Messina who first brought Flemish oil paints and techniques to Italy from his voyages in the Low Countries. *Piazza Pellicceria 1, tel. 010/294661. Admission: 4,000 lire. Open May–Sept., Tues–Sat. 9–7, Sun.–Mon. 9–1.*

🕧 Walk south down Via San Luca to Piazza Banchi to see the **Loggia dei Mercanti** (covered market). Then head back to the heart of the medieval quarter, to Via Soziglia, a street lined with shops selling handicrafts and tempting foods.

Time Out   You may want to rest your feet at the **Klanguti Tearoom** (tel. 010/296502), at the end of the street in Piazza Soziglia. Try the excellent homemade cakes and ice creams.

South of Piazza Soziglia is the quarter where wealthy Genoese built their homes in the 16th century. Prosperous guilds, such as the goldsmiths for whom Vico Indoratori and Via Orefici were named, also set up shop here. **Piazza San Matteo** is an excellently preserved medieval square, for 500 years the seat of the Doria family, who ruled Genoa and much of Liguria from the 16th to the 18th century and built fine palaces all over the city. The square is bounded by 13th- to 15th-century houses decorated with portals and loggias

🕧 (open galleries). The black-and-white church of **San Matteo** dates from the 12th century; its crypt contains the tomb of Andrea Doria, who framed a constitution for the city in 1529 and began his family's reign. Doria won his fame as an admiral, serving, in turn, the French and Spanish crowns, but managing to maintain the independence of his native city.

Leaving Piazza San Matteo, continue down toward the cathedral of

🕧 **San Lorenzo,** at the heart of medieval Genoa's political and religious center. The cathedral is embellished inside and out with the contrasting black slate and white marble so common in Liguria. It was consecrated in 1118 to St. Lawrence, who passed through the city on his way to Rome in the 3rd century; the last campanile dates from the early 16th century. For hundreds of years the building was used for state, as well as religious, purposes: Civic elections, court rulings, and religious ceremonies and festivals all took place here. Note the lively 13th-century Gothic portal and the 15th- to 17th-century frescoes inside. The **Museo del Tesoro di San Lorenzo** (San Lorenzo Treasury Museum), located in the cathedral, contains some stunning medieval pieces. The art of goldsmiths and silversmiths, for which medieval Genoa was renowned, is particularly well represented here. *Admission: 2,000 lire. Open Tues.–Sat. 9:30–11:45, 3–5:45.*

🕧 Across Piazza San Lorenzo is the **Palazzo Ducale,** built in the 16th century over a medieval hall, with a facade that was rebuilt in the late 18th century. The building has been restored and houses temporary exhibitions. Cross over the 19th-century thoroughfare, Via San Lorenzo, and head southwest into the old city center, where a settlement has existed since the 6th century BC. **Santa Maria di Castello,** one of Genoa's greatest religious buildings, was an early Christian church. It was rebuilt in the 12th century and finally completed in 1513. You can ask to visit the adjacent cloisters and see the fine artwork contained in the museum.

Take the little lane left from behind the church to reach the 12th-century Romanesque church of **San Donato,** with its original portal and octagonal campanile. The 13th-century Gothic church of **Sant'Agostino,** almost directly behind it, was damaged during World War II, but still has a fine campanile and two well-preserved cloisters, which now house an excellent sculpture museum. *Piazza Sarzano 21, tel. 010/201661. Admission: 4,000 lire. Open Tues.–Sat. 9–7, Sun. 9–12.*

At the southeastern end of the old city, the twin-towered, 12th-century **Porta di Sant'Andrea,** or Porta Soprana, stands at the old gateway to the Roman road that led through Genoa. Nearby, in Piazza Dante, is the ruined, ivy-covered house where **Christopher Columbus** spent his childhood.

Taking Via Dante northwest, you'll hit **Piazza de Ferrari,** the center of modern Genoa. The World War II–ravaged opera house, **Teatro Carlo Felice,** finally rebuilt, reopened in 1991, with a massive, much-criticized tower. It stands next to the **Academy of Fine Arts,** which contains a collection of Ligurian paintings from the 13th to the 19th century. The piazza, which also contains the Stock Exchange and part of the Ducal Palace, leads into Via XX Settembre, Genoa's chic modern shopping center. The spacious 19th-century urban layout of this part of town strongly contrasts with the narrow, crowded alleys of the medieval quarter, only a few minutes away.

A fitting end to your tour of Genoa could be a visit to the **harbor,** the layout of which dates to Roman times. The Genoa inlet, the only one of its size along the Italian Riviera, was also used by the Phoenicians and Greeks as a harbor and a vantage point from which they could penetrate inland to form settlements and to trade. Don't miss the **Acquario,** opened in 1992, with 50 tanks full of marine fauna and flora, reproducing saltwater and freshwater habitats. *Ponte Spinola. Admission 10,000 lire, free for children under 5. Open Tues., Wed., Fri. 9:30–7:30 (ticket office closes 5:30); Thurs., Sat., Sun. 9:30 AM–9:30 PM (ticket office closes 7:30).*

Take the **Bigo elevator** up to the top of this mast erected as a symbol of the 1992 Columbus Quincentennial events. The view from the top takes in the harbor, the city, and the sea. *Admission: 4,000 lire. Open Tues.–Sun. 10–1 and 2–5:30.*

The **Lanterna,** a lighthouse more than 360 feet high, stands in the middle of the harbor. Built in 1544 at the height of Andrea Doria's career, it is one of Italy's oldest lighthouses and a traditional emblem of Genoa. You can get a closer view of the Lanterna, the Molo Vecchio (the historic dock), and all Genoa's harbor from one of the informative harbor tours (*see* Guided Tours in Essential Information, *above*).

Tour 3: Riviera di Levante

Numbers in the margin correspond to points of interest on the Liguria map.

Of the two Ligurian Rivieras, the Riviera di Levante is the wilder and more rugged. Here the hills drop sharply to the sea and are pierced by compact bays and inlets. You may want to choose a base and take short day-trips or explore the area by boat from the larger towns.

㉚ **Nervi,** 10 kilometers (6 miles) east of Genoa, is an elegant turn-of-the-century resort. It's famous for the **Anita Garibaldi** promenade, with its splendid sea views, palm-lined roads, and 300 acres of parks rich in orange trees and exotics. In these grounds stand the Gropallo, Grimaldi, and Serra villas, the last of which contains the **Galleria d'Arte Moderna.** *Closed for restoration.*

Also worth seeing is the **Museo di Villa Luxoro.** It has 17th- and 18th-century Genoese furnishings, furniture, ceramics, and ornaments; Flemish and Genoese paintings and drawings; old silver and lace; and antique clocks. *Via Aurelia 29, tel. 010/322673. Admission: 4,000 lire. Open May–Sept., Tues.–Sat. 9–7, Sun. 9–12:30; Oct.–Apr., Tues.–Sat. 9–5, Sun. 9–12:30.*

㉛ **Camogli,** at the edge of the large promontory and nature reserve known as the Portofino peninsula, is the first unspoiled port you reach, about 20 kilometers (12 miles) from Genoa. Camogli has always been a town of sailors, and by the 19th century this small village was leasing its ships throughout the Continent. The festival of San Fortunato, held on the second Sunday of May each year, is noteworthy for the Sagra del Pesce, a public—and free—feast of freshly caught fish cooked in pans 12 feet wide. The village has multicolored houses, a huge 17th-century sea wall in the harbor, and the Dragone Castle, built onto the sheer rock face by the harbor. Within the castle is the **Acquario,** with good displays of local marine life. The tanks are actually built into the ramparts. *Admission: 3,000 lire adults, 1,500 lire children under 10. Open May–Sept., Tues.–Sun. 10–12, 3–7; Oct.–Apr., Sat. and Sun. 10–12, 2–6.*

From Camogli you can reach, by foot or boat, the hamlets of **San Rocco, San Nicolò,** and **Punta Chiappa,** with their remarkable sea views. They lie along the western coast of the peninsula and are more natural and less fashionable than those facing south on the eastern coast. The small Romanesque church at San Nicolò was where sailors who survived dangerous voyages came to offer thanks.

㉜ **Rapallo** lies at the extreme eastern edge of the peninsula, about 10 kilometers (6 miles) from Camogli on S1. Rapallo was once one of Europe's most fashionable resorts, but it passed its heyday before World War II and has suffered from the building boom brought on by tourism. Ezra Pound and D. H. Lawrence lived here, and many other writers, poets, and artists have been drawn to it. Today, the town's natural harbor is filled with yachts. A single-span bridge on the eastern side of the bay is named after Hannibal, who is said to have passed through the area after crossing the Alps. Two ancient buildings are highlights in the center of town: The cathedral of **Santi Gervasio and Protasio,** at the western end of Via Mazzini, was founded in the 6th century; across the road is the **Leper House of San Lorenzo,** which still retains parts of its original medieval frescoes on its exterior walls. While exploring the medieval part of town, you can browse for antique lace, for which Rapallo is famous. The **Museo Civico** has a collection of the handiwork. *Admission: 3,000 lire. Open Oct.–Aug., Tues.–Wed., Fri.–Sat. 3–6, Thurs. 10–11:30.*

From Rapallo, you can take the road onto the Portofino peninsula for about 3 kilometers (2 miles) to visit **Santa Margherita Ligure,** a quieter and more sedate resort, and then 5 kilometers (3 miles) farther,

❸❸ to **Portofino** itself, one of the most picturesque villages along the coast.

Known as the "Pearl of the Riviera," this enchanting fishing village is the refuge of some of Europe's wealthiest and most discerning pleasure-seekers. From the harbor, follow the signs for the climb to the **Castello di San Giorgio,** with its medieval relics and excellent views. *Admission: 3,000 lire. Open Apr.–Sept., Wed.–Mon. 10–6; Oct.–Mar., Wed.–Mon. 10–4.*

Across a small square is the church of **San Giorgio,** which is supposed to contain the saint's relics, brought back from the Holy Land by the Crusaders. Not surprisingly, Portofino enthusiastically celebrates St. George's day (April 23). Other excellent views can be seen from the lighthouse at **Punta del Capo,** a 15-minute walk along a marked path from the village. The best vantage point over the entire peninsula and sea, however, is from **Monte di Portofino,** which looms 2,000 feet over the village. The climb is worth it; take the road from Ruta (between Camogli and Rapallo) to Portofino Vetta.

Portofino's popularity is understandable, but trying to reach it by the single narrow road can be a nightmare in the summer. Cars are not allowed in the center (parking outside); an alternative is to take a boat from Santa Margherita.

Return to the Riviera di Levante coast for the 12-kilometer (8-mile)
❸❹ drive from Rapallo to **Chiavari,** another fishing village with narrow, twisting streets and a good harbor. Chiavari's citizens were energetic explorers, and many emigrated to South America in the 19th century. The town boomed, thanks to the wealth of the returning voyagers, but Chiavari still retains many medieval traces in its buildings. There is an interesting **Museo Archeologico** in the center of town. Here you can see finds from an 8th-century BC necropolis, or city of the dead, excavated nearby. *Palazzo Rocca, Piazza Matteotti. Admission free. Open Tues.–Thurs. 9–1, Fri.–Sun. 2–7.*

❸❺ About 6 kilometers (4 miles) along the coast is the town of **Sestri Levante,** situated at the base of another, tiny, peninsula. Follow Lungomare Descalzo to the wharf on the peninsula. From here you have excellent views of the town and the coast.

Although the center of Sestri is industrial, with steelworks and shipyards, there is a small medieval district surrounding what is known as the **Baia del Silenzio** (Bay of Silence), the small harbor just behind Piazza Matteotti at the base of the peninsula. Walk up one of the alleyways to see some of the worked slate doorways of the older houses.

From Sestri, S1 turns inland past the spectacular Passo del Bracco and does not reach the coast again until the large port of La Spezia, more than 60 kilometers (40 miles) away. The towns that lie on the less accessible coastal strip between Levanto and Portovenere (near La Spezia) are reached by narrow roads that wind down from the hills; until about 50 years ago, they could be reached only by boat. Visits can still be made by boat or by the small local train that runs from Levanto to Riomaggiore, the southeasternmost of the Cinque Terre (*see below*), and stops at each station. You can drive only as far as Levanto or Riomaggiore, but not between the two.

❸❻ It's best to make **Levanto** your base for exploring this area. Levanto is a secluded town with good beaches and a few graceful buildings that date from the 13th century. Many of the buildings are adorned with clever trompe l'oeil paintings that give the impression that real town folk are looking at you from their windows.

Some of the best attractions near Levanto are within walking distance—but the walk can be a hike of up to five hours. Make sure you wear comfortable, sturdy shoes and carry a water bottle, since it can be very hot in the summer. Your goal is the group of almost inaccessible coastal villages known as the **Cinque Terre,** built against steep cliffs and linked by walks.

The first and largest is **Monterosso,** with a 12th-century church in the Ligurian style, lively markets, and small beaches. Next is **Vernazza,** a charming village of narrow streets, small squares and arcades, and the remains of forts dating from the Middle Ages. **Corniglia,** the middle village, is perched on a hillside amid vineyards; it offers excellent views of the entire coastal strip. The last two villages, **Manarola** and **Riomaggiore,** sit on tiny harbors hemmed in by sheer cliffs. It's an adventure to visit these five villages, and the reward for your exertion is a sense of tranquillity amid the dramatic coastal scenery.

Portovenere's small colorful houses, some dating from the 12th century, were once all connected to the 12th- to 16th-century citadel, so that in times of attack the villagers could reach the safety of the battlements. The town has a strategic position at the end of a peninsula that extends southeast from the Cinque Terre and forms the western border of the Gulf of La Spezia. Lord Byron is said to have written *Childe Harold* here. The huge, strange grotto at the base of the seaswept cliff is named after the poet, whose strength and courage were much admired after he swam across the gulf to the village of San Terenzo, near Lerici, to visit his friend Shelley. Above the grotto, on a formidable solid mass of rock, is **San Pietro,** a 13th-century Gothic church built on the site of an ancient pagan shrine. With its black-and-white-striped exterior, it is a landmark recognizable from far out at sea.

About 8 kilometers (5 miles) from Portovenere is **La Spezia,** a large industrialized naval port. La Spezia lacks the charm of the smaller towns, but it does have the remains of the massive 13th-century **Castel San Giorgio.**

The road to **Lerici,** the last Ligurian town before you reach Tuscany, passes through a magnificent unspoiled coastline of gray cliffs and pine forests. The town once belonged to Tuscan Pisa, and the medieval castle that stands above the splendid bay, which has attracted lovers of nature for centuries, is 13th-century Pisan. Shelley was one of Lerici's best-known visitors and spent some of the happiest months of his life in the lovely white village of **San Terenzo,** 2 kilometers (1 mile) away. The Villa Magni, where he lived, has a collection devoted to him. After Shelley drowned at sea here in 1822, the bay was renamed Golfo dei Poeti, in honor of him and Byron.

What to See and Do with Children

Liguria itself is an attraction for children because its charm and popularity are based more on the scenery of the coastline than on museums and galleries. Watching the local fishermen can be a captivating experience for many children, and the best villages for watching nets being mended or hauls being dragged in are **Camogli, Santa Margherita Ligure,** and **Sestri Levante.** Children might also want to burn off energy with some hiking along the coastal paths; these walks provide lots of opportunities for budding naturalists to examine the local flora. The area around Portofino is ideal for these activities.

Monte di Portofino. The footpaths up to and around the mountain have a wide variety of plant species, as well as excellent views of the Riviera di Levante.

Paraggi. Walk around this eastern stretch of the Portofino peninsula to see some of the plant and tree species that are known as "living fossils" because they survived the glaciers of the Ice Ages.

Genoa Aquarium. You can combine a ride on the Bigo with an interesting visit to the aquarium, where there are displays of fish and plant life in their natural habitat (*see* Tour 2: Genoa, *above*).

Villa Doria. This villa near the train station at Pegli (just west of Genoa) has a large park that is a great place for children to run free. The villa itself, which has been converted into a naval museum, is closed indefinitely for renovation. *Villa Doria, Piazza Bonavino 7, Pegli. Park admission free. Open Oct.–Apr., daily 10–12, 2–6.*

Villa Durazzo Pallavicini. Also in Pegli, these 19th-century gardens feature temples and artificial lakes arranged to delight children and parents. The villa has an archaeological museum. *Via Pallavicini 11, Pegli. Admission to villa: 4,000 lire; park is free. Open Tues.–Sat. 9–5, Sun. 9–12:30.*

Off the Beaten Track

We have followed the west–east format of the three exploring tours in arranging these sights and attractions.

Bussana Vecchia. About 8 kilometers (5 miles) by bus or car east of San Remo, in the hills where flowers are cultivated for export, is Bussana Vecchia, a picturesque ghost town that was largely destroyed by an earthquake in 1877. The inhabitants packed up and left en masse after the quake, and for almost a century, the houses, church, and crumbling bell tower were empty shells, overgrown by weeds and wildflowers. Since the 1960s an artist's colony has grown up among the ruins. Painters, sculptors, artisans, and bric-a-brac dealers have restored dwellings for themselves and sell their wares to visitors.

Olive Museum. The story of the olive—its cultivation and the manufacture of olive oil—is the theme of this small museum in Imperia set up by the Carli olive oil company. Displays show farm implements, types of presses, and utensils used in making olive oil in many countries throughout history. *Museo dell'Ulivo, Via Garessio 11, Imperia, tel. 0183/27101. Admission free. Open Mon., Wed.–Sat. 9–12, 3–6.*

Bardinetto. From Borghetto Santo Spirito (between Albenga and Finale Liqure), drive 25 kilometers (15 miles) inland to reach this attractive village in the middle of an area rich in mushrooms, chestnuts, and raspberries, as well as local cheese. A ruined castle stands high above the village.

Museo d'Arte Orientale Chiossone. The museum, with one of Europe's most extensive collections of Oriental art, stands in a relaxing green park. The Japanese, Chinese, and Thai collections are noteworthy. *Villetta di Negro, Piazza Corvetto, Genoa, tel. 010/542285. Admission: 4,000 lire. Open Tues.–Sat. 9–5, Sun. 9–12:30.*

Shopping

Liguria is famous for its fine laces, its silver and gold filigree work, and its ceramics. Look also for bargains in velvet, macramé, olive wood, and marble. Genoa is the best spot to find all these specialties, but the coastal towns and villages along the two Ligurian Rivieras have bazaar-style markets in the central squares or along the harbor front. In these markets you can succeed with a bit of bargaining, and your chances improve if you're able to clinch your deal with a word or two in Italian.

Genoa **Codevilla** (Via Orefici 53, tel. 010/20657). This well-established shop is one of the best jewelers on a street devoted to goldsmiths.

Pescetto (Via Scurreria 8, tel. 010/593637). You'll find designer clothes, perfumes, and gifts in this elegant shop located near Codevilla.

Pietro Romanengo fu Stefano (Via Soziglia 74, tel. 010/297869). Judge for yourself whether the handmade chocolates here are the best in Genoa (the management says they are).

L'Enoteca (Via Porta degli Archi 3 [next to the tourist office], tel. 010/564071). The wine connoisseur will appreciate the selection of rare Ligurian wines on sale in this wine shop.

La Rinascente (Via Vernazza 5) and **Coin** (Via XII Ottobre 4) are Genoa's two major department stores.

Via XX Settembre and **Via Luccoli** are famous for their wide range of small, exclusive shops.

Riviera di **Taggia.** An antiques market is held here on the fourth weekend of
Ponente the month. *7 km (4 mi) east along S1 from San Remo, then 3 km (2 mi) inland from Armi di Taggia.*

Millesimo. Little rum chocolates known as *millesimi* are produced here. Look for bargains, too, in wrought-iron work, relief work on copper plate, and pieces in local sandstone. *4 km (2½ mi) west of Savona on A10, then 36 km (21 mi) inland on A6.*

Albisola. This is the center of the Ligurian ceramics industry; shops around the central square all have ceramic ware. *3 km (2 mi) inland from Albisola Marina, off S334.*

Campo Ligure. Silver filigree is the specialty of this market town in the attractive Stura Valley. *27 km (17 mi) inland from Voltri on A26 and S456.*

Riviera di **Zoagli.** This attractive coastal village is famous for its silk velvet. *On*
Levante *S1, 4 km (2½ mi) east of Rapallo.*

Chiavari. The famous wood and raffia Campanino chairs are produced here, as well as macramé lace. *On S1, 12 km (7 mi) east of Rapallo.*

Sports

In Liguria, water sports are popular all along the coast. Most resorts have good facilities for swimming, waterskiing, and sailing. The mild climate means that tennis can be played all year, and every town has public courts (usually next to the bocce area).

Biking **Albisola Marina.** *Velo Club Albisola* (Albisola Superiore, Via Italia 1).

Genoa. *Quito al Mare* (Piazza San Pietro 3/r). *Alta Val Bisogno Sports Club* (Via Benedetto da Porto 2/a, tel. 010/804771).

Levanto. *Genoa Club Levanto* (Piazza Staglieno 1, tel. 0187/808160).

Ventimiglia. *Ventimiglia Cycling Club* (Corso Genova 112, tel. 0184/352879).

Bowling **Albenga** (Piazza Corridoni, tel. 0182/52241).
Genoa (Piazza Rizzolio, tel. 010/466671; Via Gobetti 8/a, tel. 010/314102).

Fishing There is good fresh water fishing in most of the remote inland areas. Try the streams around Calizzano. Underwater spear-fishing is best at Zoagli, Bordighera, and Nervi. For information about restrictions and licenses, contact the **Federazione Italiana della Pesca Sportiva e Attività Sub-acquee** (Galleria Mazzini 7/1, Genoa, tel. 010/565273).

Golf **Alassio.** *Garlenda Club* (18 holes) (Garlenda, tel. 0182/580012).
Arenzano. *Pineta di Arenzano* (nine holes) (Arenzano, tel. 010/911–1817).
Rapallo. *Golf Club* (18 holes) (Rapallo, tel. 0185/261777).
San Remo. *Campo Golf* (18 holes) (Via Campo Golf, tel. 0184/557093).

Horseback **Arenzano** (Via Aurelia 21, tel. 010/911–0616).
Riding **Chiavari.** *Rivarola Carasco* (Via Veneto 212, tel. 0185/382204).
Boschetto Horse-Riding Club (Salita Ceiva, tel. 0185/301785).
Genoa. *Ligurian Horse-Riding Club* (Via Bosco 57/7, tel. 010/588872).
Rapallo. *Rapallo Riding Club* (Via Santa Maria Campo 196, tel. 0185/50462).

Tennis Tennis is extremely popular throughout Liguria all year long, and each town has at least one set of public courts or a private club that welcomes visitors. Local Pro Loco tourist offices (*see* Important Addresses and Numbers in Essential Information, *above*) can provide information on the availability of courts and short-term membership in local clubs.

Waterskiing **La Spezia.** *La Spezia Motorboat Club* (Via della Marina 224, tel. 0187/50401).

Beaches

Along both Ligurian Rivieras, the beaches are protected by mountains, so the climate is mild and the foliage lush. But on either Riviera, the beaches are best used for sunbathing, not swimming, because of pollution. The Riviera di Ponente, from Genoa west to the French border, has both sandy and pebbly beaches with some quiet bays. **Alassio** has a long sandy beach at the head of a bay. The villages of **Diano Marina** and **Pia** (near Finale Ligure) have fine sandy beaches with all the amenities of modern resorts. **Varazze** has a wide, sandy beach and many tall palm trees. **Arenzano,** 22 kilometers (14 miles) west of Genoa, is perhaps the last pleasant beach resort on the Riviera di Ponente before greater Genoa's industrial influence takes over. The beach is large and broad, endowed with nearly every sports facility.

The Riviera di Levante includes Genoa and the coast east as far as Portovenere. Beaches on this coast are rocky, with many spectacular cliffs near the sea. There are small coves *(ciazze)* where you can dock your boat in relatively calm water, and enjoy the enticing combination of sea and foliage. **Portofino Promontory** has one sandy beach, on the east side, at **Paraggi.** From Chiavari to Cavi di Lavagna, the coast becomes a bit gentler, with a few sandy areas. From Sestri Levante down to Portovenere, the coast is rugged; however, these areas are good for sailing.

Dining and Lodging

Dining Liguria makes the best of its coastal location by utilizing all sorts of seafood. Anchovies, sea bass, squid, and octopus are popular ingredients in the cuisine, which uses liberal amounts of olive oil and garlic. *Datteri*, tiny razor clams unique to Liguria, figure in *zuppa di datteri* (a type of chowder) and in many pasta dishes. Another famous Ligurian pasta sauce is pesto, made from pine nuts, garlic, oil, cheese, and a type of basil that grows only along the coastal hills. *Vitello* (veal) is the most popular meat and is often served stuffed, as in *cima*. You should also try the succulent *agnello* (lamb).

When not snacking on pizza sold by the slice or by weight, the Genoese and other Ligurians eat focaccia, a salty, pizzalike bread that goes well with a cool glass of wine. Local vineyards tend to produce mainly light and refreshing whites, such as Pigato, Vermentino Ligure, and Cinque Terre. Rossese and Dolceacqua are good reds. Desserts are less rich than those in other Italian regions, and the Ligurians often finish a meal with fresh fruit. Homemade gelato (ice cream) is another favorite.

Highly recommended restaurants are indicated by a star ★.

Category	Cost*
$$$$	over 85,000 lire
$$$	65,000–85,000 lire
$$	35,000–65,000 lire
$	under 35,000 lire

per person, including house wine, service, and tax

Lodging There are fewer Ligurian bargains in lodging than in dining. Constant demand combines with a limited choice to create a high average price, at least in comparison with other Italian regions. Genoa, the largest city in the region, has surprisingly few hotels, and these tend to be mainly expensive establishments geared more to the needs of business clients than to tourists. Two four-star hotels, the Sheraton (tel. 010/65491) and the Novotel (tel. 010/6484), were about to open in Genoa as we went to press. Visitors prefer to stay in the towns and resorts along the coast, where there is a better range of accommodations. Here, though, you should try to have reservations, particularly during the peak summer period. The best bargains are in the less-visited inland areas: There are few hotels in this part of Liguria, but many of them are family-run and welcoming.

Highly recommended lodgings are indicated by a star ★.

Category	Cost*
$$$$	over 300,000 lire
$$$	170,000–300,000 lire
$$	110,000–170,000 lire
$	under 110,000 lire

All prices are for a standard double room for two, including service and tax.

Alassio
Lodging

Eden. This small but well-maintained and friendly hotel has a beachfront location in a quiet part of town, about a 10-minute walk along the beach from the center. Many rooms have sea views, and the beachfront terrace has a seafood restaurant for guests only. *Passeggiata Cadorna 20, tel. 0182/640281, fax 0182/643037. 29 rooms, most with bath or shower. Facilities: beach facilities, restaurant, bar. MC, V. Closed Nov.–Jan. $–$$*

Bordighera
Dining

La Reserve Tastevin. This traditional and informal trattoria has access to the beach and excellent views of the sea from the dining room. There are even changing rooms for anyone who wants a postlunch dip. Concentrate on the seafood here: *Muscoli alla marinara* (mussel soup) is a hearty concoction that can be ordered as a starter or a main course. *Via Arziglia 20, tel. 0184/261322. No reservations. Dress: casual. AE, DC, MC, V. Closed Sun. dinner, Mon. (except July and Aug.), and Oct. 20–Dec. 20. $$$*

Le Chaudron. The charming rustic interior, with ancient Roman arches, has the look of restaurants across the French border in Provence. Ligurian specialties are featured on the predominantly seafood menu of this centrally located restaurant: Try the *branzino al sale grosso* (sea bass baked in a mold of sea salt) or spaghetti *con aragosta* (with tiny lobsters). Other specialties, such as the *coquilles St. Jacques*, reflect the French influence. *Piazza Bengasi 2, tel. 0184/263592. Reservations advised. Dress: casual. AE, DC, MC, V. Closed Mon. and Feb. 1–15, July 1–15. $$–$$$*

Piemontese. Located a block from the seaside and five minutes from the train station, this simple restaurant features typical Ligurian cooking, including minestrone with pesto and seafood fresh from the market. *Via Roseto 8, off Via Vittorio Veneto, tel. 0184/261651. Closed Tues. and Nov. 20–Dec. 20. AE, DC, MC, V. $$*

Lodging

Grand Hotel del Mare. Located at the top of a steep hill rising from the beach, this elegant hotel lives up to its name; the service and facilities are impeccable. The large rooms have panoramic views of the coastline; ask for one facing the water. The hotel restaurant enjoys a fine reputation. *Via Portico della Punta 34, tel. 0184/262201, fax 0184/262394. 109 rooms with bath. Facilities: beach, saltwater pool, garden, tennis courts, restaurant, piano bar. AE, MC, V. Closed Oct.–Dec. 22. $$$*

Grand Hotel Capo Ampelio. This hotel occupies a converted villa on a hill overlooking the town and the coastline; traditional architectural features in the reception rooms and staircases are enhanced by convenient modern features in the rooms. The hotel is somewhat outside the town center, so rooms are quiet; ask for one with a sea view. *Via Virgilio 5, tel. 0184/264333, fax 0184/264244. 104 rooms with bath. Facilities: pool, garden, restaurant, bar. AE, DC, MC, V. Closed Nov. 20–Dec. 20. $$$*

Camogli
Dining

Vento Ariel. This tiny but friendly restaurant is located right on the port, and it has informal but elegant decor and place settings. It serves seafood only and regularly runs out of items because it relies on the day's catch. Try the spaghetti *alle vongole* (with clams) or the grilled mixed fish, which differs according to the day's haul. *Calata Porto, tel. 0185/771080. Reservations advised. Dress: casual. AE, DC, MC, V. Closed Wed. and Feb. $$$*

Lodging
★

Cenobio dei Dogi. Although this hilltop villa perched over the town was once the summer home of Genoa's doges (medieval elected rulers), it now has a modern appearance. The rooms have TV and air-conditioning. Guests can relax in the colorful park gazing out on outstanding views of the Portofino peninsula, or they can enjoy numerous sporting activities. Although the rooms are not lavishly appointed, many have a balcony with panoramic view. *Via Cuneo 34, tel. 0185/770041, fax 0185/772796. 88 rooms with bath. Facilities: private beach, pool, tennis courts, park, bar, restaurant. AE, MC, V. Closed Jan. 7–Mar. 10. $$$–$$$$*

Diano Marina
Dining
★

Candidollo. Take the valley road just a couple of miles north to find this charming and good-value restaurant, which uses locally grown ingredients as well as freshly caught seafood. *Carciofi* (artichokes), peaches, and apricots—all grown on neighboring farms—accompany a selection of fish and meat dishes that vary according to the season. Portions are large. *Diano Borello, tel. 0183/43025. Reservations advised. Dress: casual. No credit cards. Closed Mon. lunch, Tues., and Nov.–Apr. (except several days around Christmas and Easter). $*

Genoa
Dining

Gran Gotto. Classic regional dishes are served in this elegant restaurant in spacious quarters decorated with soft greens and lots of wood paneling. Gran Gotto is near Brignole Station in the modern part of town. The service is quick and helpful; the waiter will proudly detail the ingredients of the day's specials. Try the *ripieni* (stuffed vegetables) and the *antica torta di mele* (apple pie), one of the many excellent homemade desserts. *Via Viale Brigata Bisagno 69/r, tel. 010/564344. Reservations advised. Jacket and tie required. AE, MC, V. Closed Sat. lunch, Sun., and Aug. 10–31. $$$*

★ **Zeffirino.** The five Belloni brothers share the chef's duties at this remarkable restaurant, which is full of odd combinations. The decor is a mixture of styles and materials, ranging from rustic wood to modern metallic. Try the *passutelli* (ravioli stuffed with ricotta cheese and fruit) or any of the homemade pasta dishes. *Via XX Settembre 20, tel. 010/591990. Reservations advised. Jacket and tie required. AE, DC, MC, V. Closed Wed. $$$*

Da Genio. On a byway in old Genoa, near Piazza Dante, this classic trattoria serves equally classic Genoese dishes, including *trenette al* pesto (pasta with pesto sauce) and minestrone, also laced with a dollop of pesto. *Salita San Leonardo 61/r, tel. 010/588463. Reservations advised. Dress: casual. No credit cards. Closed Sun. and Aug. 1–30. $$*

Marinella. This restaurant is located in Nervi, 10 kilometers (6 miles) east of the center of Genoa. It has a waterside location, which attracts regular customers as much as do its seafood specialties. (There's an inexpensive hotel annex, too.) Try *trofie al* pesto (fresh pasta with pesto, potatoes, and green beans); main dishes change from day to day, according to the fishermen's catch. *Passeggiata Anita Garibaldi 18, Nervi, tel. 010/321429. Reservations advised weekends. Dress: casual. AE, DC, MC, V. Closed Fri. and Nov. $$*

Melograno. Tuscan specialties figure prominently on the menu of this small restaurant decorated in art nouveau style. It is located in the southern part of Genoa and overlooks the harbor. In addition to the Tuscan specialties, such as *bistecca alla fiorentina* (charcoal-grilled steak, Florence-style), there are many homemade items, including pesto and gelato. *Via Maccaggi 62/r, tel. 010/546407. Reservations required. Dress: casual. No credit cards. Closed Sun. and Aug. 8–31. $$*

Osteria Oca d'Oro. In a byway near Teatro Carlo Felice, this white-walled, wood-paneled tavern feeds office workers at lunch and a more bohemian crowd of musicians, actors, and students in the evening. Homemade gnocchi and spaghetti with seafood sauce are specialties, but there are many other typical Genoese dishes on the menu. *Vico Domoculta 14/r, tel. 010/546511. Dress: casual. No reservations. MC, V. $$*

Sette Nasi. The historic Quarto dei Mille district is the setting for this large establishment, proudly supervised by its chef, Enrico Nasi, who specializes in a wide range of Ligurian seafood dishes. Homemade desserts are also recommended. Summertime meals are served on the terrace, which has an excellent view of the bustling harbor. Try the zuppa di datteri if you see it on the menu. *Via Quarto 16, tel. 010/337357. No reservations. Dress: casual. AE, DC, MC, V. Closed Tues. $$*

Trattoria Walter. This unpretentious family-run restaurant is in the heart of the city, near Palazzo Spinola. The service is simple and straightforward, and the price is right for a good, inexpensive sampling of genuine Genoese specialties. *Via Colalanza 2, corner of Via San Luca, tel. 010/290524. No reservations. Dress: casual. No credit cards. Closed Sun. and Aug. 1–21. $*

Lodging **Bristol Palace.** This grand hotel, located on a fashionable downtown shopping street, was built in the last century and maintains the old-fashioned traditions of courtesy and discretion. The rooms are large, with high ceilings, and paintings decorate the large reception rooms. There's no restaurant, but the hotel is in the heart of the downtown area. *Via XX Settembre 35, tel. 010/592541, fax 010/561756. 130 rooms with bath. Facilities: bar, no-smoking rooms. AE, DC, MC, V. $$$$*

President. This member of the Starhotel chain of comfortable and reliable business hotels is also well located for tourists. The high-rise hotel opened in 1991 as part of a large new commercial and convention center near Brignole Station. The rooms have big windows and modern decor in tones of dusty rose and blue-gray, with sparkling white baths. There's a large bar area between the desk and the terrace, which becomes an outdoor café in fair weather. *Corte Lambruschini 4, tel. 010/5727, fax 010/553-1820. 198 rooms with bath or shower. Facilities: restaurant, bar, parking. AE, DC, MC, V. $$$$*

★ **Pagoda Residence.** If you want to stay at a top-quality hotel outside the center of Genoa, try this unusual establishment in Nervi, 10 kilometers (6 miles) east of Genoa. It occupies a 19th-century building designed to look like a pagoda, built at a time when Europe was fascinated by the exotic Orient. Inside, the rooms have modern decorations and furnishings. Reception rooms are decorated in a combination of Venetian and Baroque styles, with an emphasis on dark wood. It's set next to a large, shady park. *Via Capolungo 15, Nervi, tel. 010/326161, fax 010/321218. 21 rooms with bath. Facilities: private beach, garden, restaurant, bar. AE, DC, MC, V. $$$*

★ **Agnello d'Oro.** The central location in Genoa's old quarter, about 100 yards from Principe Station, makes this modest hotel a good choice for budget travelers who want to be in the thick of things. There are simple furnishings in renovated, air-conditioned rooms. *Vico delle Monachette 6, tel. 010/262084. 40 rooms, 37 with bath. Facilities: bar, terrace, restaurant (guests only; closed Oct.–Mar.). DC, MC, V. $$*

Viale Sauli. Conveniently located in the vicinity of Brignole Station, this hotel occupies several floors of an undistinguished modern building. It has a mainly business clientele. Here you can be sure of clean and functional accommodations in one of Genoa's more secure districts. *Viale Sauli 5, tel. 010/561397, fax 010/590092. 49 rooms with bath. AE, DC, MC, V. $$*

Lerici **Florida.** A seafront hotel, this family-run establishment has bright,
Lodging simply furnished rooms with all the extras you would expect in a higher category: TV, fridge, bar, air-conditioning, and, best of all, a balcony with a sea view. For an even better view, loll in one of the deck chairs on the roof terrace. The Florida has its own beach area

and is close to tennis courts and a golf course. *Lungomare Biaggini 35, tel. 0187/967332, fax 0187/967344. 33 rooms with shower. AE, DC, MC, V. $–$$*

Levanto   **Araldo.** Arches and frescoes add to the atmosphere of this elegant
Dining   little restaurant. Food and service are outstanding; the menu, featuring creative Mediterranean cuisine, changes with the seasons and offers more than 100 wines. *Via Jacopo 24, tel. 0187/807253. Reservations advised. Jacket preferred. Closed Tues. (except July–Aug.), Nov. AE, DC, MC, V. $$–$$$*

Lodging   **Stella Maris.** Located in the center of Levanto and only a 10-minute
★   walk from the beach, this is a real find. It takes up one floor of a 19th-century palazzo (the ground floor houses a palatial bank). Seven rooms are decorated with original frescoes and 19th-century furniture, and seven are modern; the couple who run the hotel have an infectious enthusiasm for the building's history and decoration. A half-board plan is required in summer, but that's no sacrifice because the home cooking features Ligurian seafood specialties; you can have your homemade ice cream in the sunny garden. *Via Marconi 4, tel. 0187/808258. 14 rooms with shower. Facilities: garden, restaurant. No credit cards. Closed Nov. $*

Monterosso   **Il Gigante.** A good introduction to Ligurian seafood is the *zuppa di*
(Cinque Terre)   *pesce* (fish soup) served at this traditional trattoria in one of the fish-
Dining   ing villages of the Cinque Terre. This soup is usually served as a first course, but is filling enough to be an entrée. The waiters are happy to advise you on the daily specials, which can include risotto *di frutti di mare* (shellfish risotto) and spaghetti with an octopus sauce. *Monterosso al Mare, tel. 0187/817401. Reservations advised. Dress: casual. AE, DC, MC, V. Closed Tues. and Oct. 15–Mar. 15. $$*

Lodging   **Porto Roca.** Five minutes out of town and set on a hill with excellent
★   sea views, Porto Roca is removed from the crowds who visit the village, especially on weekends. It has the look of a well-kept villa; its interiors have authentic antique pieces and ample terraces. The rooms are bright and airy, with sea breezes that visitors to the town below often miss. Porto Roca is located on a network of not-too-demanding hill walks. *Via Corone 1, tel. 0187/817502, fax 0187/817692. 43 rooms with bath or shower. Facilities: terrace, gardens, restaurant, bar. AE, MC, V. Closed Oct. 15–Mar. 31. $$$*

Portofino   **Il Pitosforo.** A chic, tan clientele, many with luxury yachts in the
Dining   harbor, gives this waterfront restaurant a glamorous atmosphere. Spaghetti di frutti di mare is recommended; adventurous diners might want to try *lo stocco accomodou* (dried cod in a savory sauce of tomatoes, raisins, and pine nuts). *Portofino, tel. 0185/269020. Reservations required. Dress: casual. AE, DC, MC, V. Closed Mon., Tues. lunch and Jan.–Feb. $$$$*

Lodging   **Splendido.** Most people resort to superlatives when trying to de-
★   scribe this luxury hotel, built in the '20s on a hill overlooking the sea. The abiding impression is one of color, from the coordinated fabrics and furnishings of the rooms to the fresh flowers in the reception rooms and on the large terrace. It's like a Jazz Age film set, and you almost expect to see a Bugatti or Daimler roll up the winding drive from Portofino below. A network of footpaths leads away from the wooded grounds. The Splendido's relatively small size means you get even more personal attention than at other luxury hotels. *16034 Portofino, tel. 0185/269551, fax 0185/269614. 65 rooms with bath. Facilities: pool, tennis court, garden, terrace, restaurant, bars. AE, DC, MC, V. Closed Nov.–Mar. $$$$*

Portovenere **Da Iseo.** Try to get one of the tables outside at this waterfront res-
Dining taurant, which is decorated in the style of a local fishing hut, with
nets and buoys along the walls. Seafood is the only choice: It's fresh
and plentiful. Try the zuppa di datteri, spaghetti ai datteri, or the
fritto misto di frutti di mare (mixed grilled seafood). *Portovenere,
tel. 0187/900610. Reservations advised in summer. Dress: casual.
AE, DC, MC. Closed Wed. and Jan.–Feb. $$*

Antica Osteria del Carrugio. Near the castle built to defend the coast
from Pisan incursions, this is a hundred-year-old tavern with mari-
time decor. The menu features seafood, which varies with the catch
of the day. Specialties include trenette al pesto and focaccia. *Via
Cappellini 66, tel. 0187/900617. No reservations. No credit cards.
Closed Thurs., mid-Nov.–mid-Dec. $*

Lodging **Royal Sporting.** Appearances are deceptive at this modern hotel,
★ which is located on the beach, about a 10-minute walk from the vil-
lage. From the outside, the stone construction seems austere and
unwelcoming, but the courtyards and interior are colorful and vi-
brant. There are fresh flowers and potted plants in the reception
rooms and terraces, and the cool, airy rooms all have sea views. The
sports facilities are among the best in the area. *Via dell'Olivo 345,
tel. 0187/900326, fax 0187/529060. 62 rooms with bath. Facilities:
private beach, pool, tennis court, gardens, restaurant, bar. AE,
DC, MC, V. Closed Oct. 15–Apr. (open Easter week). $$–$$$*

Locanda San Pietro. This good-value inn occupies a castle at the
edge of the village and is five minutes from the beach. The rooms,
decorated in art-nouveau style, are quiet. Most have good views of
the coastline around Portovenere. The restaurant features local cui-
sine and stresses seafood. *Portovenere, tel. 0187/900616. 31 rooms
with bath or shower. Facilities: restaurant, bar. AE, MC. Closed
Jan. 2–Mar. 14. $*

Rapallo **Da Ardito.** This lively trattoria is in the village of San Pietro di No-
Dining vella, which is just north of Rapallo. It's extremely popular with
wine lovers, who appreciate the attention given to the wine list. For
a change from seafood, try the *pansotti alla salsa di noci,* pasta
served with creamy walnut sauce. *Via Canale 9, San Pietro di No-
vella, tel. 0185/51551. Reservations advised. Dress: casual. MC, V.
Closed Mon. and Feb. $$*

Savoia. People-watching and pizzas are the attractions of this modern restaurant occupying a sunny position just off the beach. There's
a good view of the promenade from nearly every table, and you can
relax, knowing that you won't break the bank with any of the excellent pizzas. Wash it all down with a cool glass of Pigato. *Piazza IV
Novembre 3, tel. 0185/247021. No reservations. Dress: casual. No
credit cards. Closed Sun. $*

Lodging **Grand Hotel Bristol.** This large Victorian showcase has undergone
total renovation, emerging as one of the most luxurious hotels on the
Riviera. It is in an elevated position overlooking the sea outside Rapallo, and is set in lush gardens with a huge pool. Spacious rooms,
many with balcony and sea view, are decorated in soft colors in a
smart, contemporary style and have extra-large beds. The hotel has
five restaurants, one of which is on a roof terrace. *Via Aurelia
Orientale 369, tel. 0185/273313, fax 0185/55800. 91 rooms and suites
with bath. Facilities: pool, minibus to 18-hole golf course, tennis,
riding, conference rooms, restaurants, bar. AE, DC, MC, V. $$$$*

Continental. This resort hotel by the sea is a stately mansion with a
columned portico, built in the early 1900s and set in a lush garden
shaded by tall palms and pine trees. The decor is a blend of traditional furnishings, mostly in 19th-century style, with some more func-

tional pieces. There is also a modern wing. The hotel's own cabanas and swimming area are at the bottom of the garden. Ask for a room with a sea view; many rooms have balconies, and the views are, indeed, superb. *Via Pagana 8, tel. 0185/286512, fax 0185/284463. 76 rooms with bath. Facilities: restaurant, bar, garage, beach bar. AE, DC, MC, V. $$$*

Eurotel. On the old coast road, but in an elevated position above the harbor, the Eurotel is a modern building set in a garden, with a large swimming pool. The decor is functional rather than charming, but rooms are bright, with balconies and sea views. *Via Aurelia Occidentale 22, tel. 0185/60981, fax 0185/50635. 65 rooms with bath. Facilities: pool, garden, restaurant, bar. AE, DC, MC, V. Closed Jan. 8–Feb. 15. $$$*

Giulio Cesare. Only a block from the sea, this old town house was transformed into a hotel that offers rooms with modern furnishings and sea views. Many rooms have balconies, but noise may be a problem, since the hotel is on a main street. Half board is required during high season (June–Sept. at about 100,000 lire per person). *Corso Colombo 62, tel. 0185/50685, fax 0185/50896. 33 rooms with bath. AE, DC, MC, V. Closed Nov.–Dec. 15. $–$$*

San Remo
Dining

Nuovo Piccolo Mondo. This small, centrally located trattoria has plenty of charm and a homey atmosphere—the old wooden chairs date back from the 1920s, when the place opened. Family-run, it has a faithful clientele, so get there early to grab a table and order Ligurian specialties such as cima and vegetable pies. *Via Piave 7, tel. 0184/509012. Reservations advised for lunch. No credit cards. Closed Sun., Wed. evening, and last 3 weeks in June. $$*

Lodging
★

Royal. It would take a dedicated hedonist to determine whether this deluxe hotel or the Splendido in Portofino is the most luxurious in Liguria. One major difference is the location: Only a few paces from the Casino and the train station, the Royal is definitely part of San Remo, unlike the Splendido, which is set above Portofino. Try for a room facing the sea or one of the new penthouse rooms and suites, with terrific views. The rooms have a mixture of modern appliances and antique furnishings, each with a unique feel. It is claimed that there is nearly always a member of European royalty in residence; the best place to find out is on the terrace, where an orchestra plays each night under the stars in season. *Corso Imperatrice 80, tel. 0184/5391, fax 0184/61445. 149 rooms and suites with bath. Facilities: pool, tennis courts, terrace, restaurant, bar. AE, DC, MC, V. Closed Oct. 9–Dec. 18. $$$$*

Paradiso. This small hotel is almost directly behind the Royal, so it shares some of the advantages of its grander neighbor. A quiet, palm-fringed garden gives it an air of seclusion, which is a plus in this sometimes hectic city. The rooms are modern and bright, and many have a little terrace. The hotel restaurant has a good fixed-price menu. *Via Roccasterone 12, tel. 0184/571211, fax 0184/578176. 41 rooms with bath or shower. Facilities: restaurant, bar, garden. AE, DC, MC, V. $$*

Santa Margherita Ligure
Dining
★

Da Baicin. A very friendly family runs this bright trattoria. Outdoor tables afford a view of the seaside gardens in the center of Santa Margherita. The specialties of the house are zuppa di pesce and pansotti alla salsa di noci. *Via Algeria 5, tel. 0185/286763. Reservations advised. Dress: casual. AE, DC, MC, V. Closed Mon. and Nov. 1–Dec. 15. $$*

La Bassa Prora. This waterfront restaurant is a popular spot, partly because of its central location and partly because of the fresh fish specials, usually grilled. The antipasto misto di frutti di mare is excellent, and the main courses provide good value for the money. *Via Garibaldi 7, tel. 0185/286586. No reservations. Dress: casual. AE, V. Closed Mon. dinner, Tues., and mid-Sept.–mid-Oct. $–$$*

Il Frantoio. The large, hand-carved wooden screws that turned the olive press for which this rather elegant little restaurant is named stand at the entrance. And here you not only choose wine from a list; you can also consult the olive oil list for just the right condiment for your *bruschetta* (grilled bread with or without garlic). Quality is a keynote in the food, too, as in traditional Ligurian pansotti alla salsa di noci and spaghetti with seafood sauce. The menu is varied enough to suit most tastes. *Via del Giunchetto 23/a, tel. 0185/286667. Reservations advised. Dress: casual. AE, MC, V. $*

Lodging **Grand Hotel Miramare.** Take the shore road south from town to reach this palatial turn-of-the-century hotel overlooking the bay. It has a lush garden and swimming pool, and a private swimming area on the sea. The bright and airy rooms are decorated in colonial or late–19th-century style. The best have sea views, as do the hotel terraces. *Lungomare Milite Ignoto 30, tel. 0185/287013, fax 0185/284651. 83 rooms with bath. Facilities: private beach, pool, waterskiing, garden, restaurant, bar. AE, MC, V. $$$$*

Imperial Palace. Via Pagana climbs north out of Santa Margherita Ligure on its way toward Rapallo; just outside town it passes this Old World luxury hotel, which is set in an extensive park. The rooms are furnished with antiques; many overlook the shore drive to the sea. The reception rooms are elegantly decorated with tall windows, plush chairs, and potted plants. *Via Pagana 19, tel. 0185/288991, fax 0185/284223. 101 rooms with bath. Facilities: private beach, pool, restaurant, bar, garden. AE, DC, MC, V. Closed Nov.–Mar. 15. $$$$*

★ **Fasce.** An extremely good value, this small, modern hotel is centrally located on one of the town's main thoroughfares, but from its pleasant roof garden you have views of the sea and surrounding hills. The Italian owner and his English wife take cordial interest in their guests' well-being and comfort. Rooms are attractively furnished and have satellite TV. *Via Bozzo 3, tel. 0185/286435, fax 0185/283580. 16 rooms with bath. Facilities: restaurant, parking. AE, DC, MC, V. $*

Ventimiglia **La Mortola.** Take the coast road about five minutes west from
Dining Ventimiglia, until you reach Mortola Inferiore, where you will find this elegant restaurant opposite the famous Hanbury Gardens. The menu is a sophisticated mixture of Italian, Scandinavian, and international dishes, with smorgasbord every Sunday noon, and *rombo al vapore* (steamed turbot, served with butter and radishes). *Mortola Inferiore, tel. 0184/38482. Reservations advised. Jacket and tie required. AE, DC, MC, V. Closed Sun. dinner, Mon., and Nov. $$*

Dining and **La Riserva.** Just 3 miles west of Ventimiglia, but more than 1,100
Lodging feet above sea level, is the village of Castel d'Appio, where you'll find
★ this innlike establishment. The staff is very helpful, providing, for example, regular lifts into town for those without cars. But there's no real need to leave La Riserva; apart from its excellent restaurant, it offers numerous activities and a lovely terrace for drinks or sunbathing. Full-board rates are a good value. Try for a room facing the sea. *Castel d'Appio, tel. 0184/229533, fax 0184/229712. 29 rooms with bath or shower. Facilities: tennis, garden, terrace bar, restaurant, pool, well-marked walks. AE, DC, MC, V. Closed Sept. 20–Easter (except Dec. 18–Jan. 6). $$*

The Arts and Nightlife

The Arts

Music   **Alassio.** Each September sees a **jazz festival,** with internationally renowned musicians and local bands creating a lively atmosphere in various venues around town.

Cervo. There is an **International Festival of Chamber Music** in July and August.

Dance   **Nervi.** The grounds of Villa Gropallo provide the setting for an **International Festival of Ballet** (tel. 010/542792) usually held throughout July, though it sometimes skips a year.

Opera   **Genoa.** The opera season (Oct.–May) at **Teatro Carlo Felice** (Via XXV Aprile, tel. 010/591697) attracts many lavish productions and occasionally sees the debut of a new work.

Nightlife

Even Genoa, Liguria's largest city, cannot compare with Milan or Rome in the field of organized evening entertainment, but that isn't a problem, because a lot of the fun of staying in Liguria is its informal and easygoing atmosphere. It's hard to imagine a more enjoyable activity than sipping local wine outside a café on a warm summer evening, knowing that your eardrums and wallet won't be damaged.

Casino   The **San Remo Casino** is one of only four in Italy. It is a sophisticated establishment reminiscent of the turn of the century. The view over the Ligurian coast is free, even if nothing else is. *Corso Inglese, San Remo. Open daily 2 PM–2 AM.*

Bar   **Bordighera.** Have a quiet drink in the piano bar of the **Grand Hotel del Mare** (*see* Dining and Lodging, *above*).

Nightclub   **San Remo.** The casino (*see above*) has a nightclub and restaurant, as well as gaming tables.

Discos   **San Remo.** *Nabila* (Giardino Vittorio Veneto 74, tel. 0184/80959).

Santa Margherita Ligure. *Covo di Nord Est* (Lungomare Rossetti 1, tel. 0185/286558).

9 Piedmont/ Valle d'Aosta

From Turin to the Alps and across the Po Plain

From Alpine valleys hemming the highest mountains in Europe to the mist-shrouded lowlands skirting the Po River, from pulsating industrial centers turning out the best of Italian design to tiny stone villages isolated above the clouds, from hearty peasant cooking in farmhouse kitchens to French-flavored delicacies washed down by some of the finest wines in Italy, Piedmont and the spectacular Valle d'Aosta offer the traveler a store of historical, cultural, and natural riches.

Piedmont's Italian Alps afford excellent skiing and climbing at famous resort towns such as Courmayeur and Breuil-Cervinia. In the lowlands, Turin, the regional capital, is a historical center that today also serves as the heart of Italy's booming auto industry. Nearby are Alba, home of the famous Italian white truffles, seasonal delicacies that sell for more than $1,000 per pound; Asti, Barolo, and Barbaresco, the famous wine centers; and the modern business hubs Ivrea, Novara, and Alessandria.

Tucked away at the foot of the Pennine, Graian, Cottian, and Maritime Alps (the name Piemonte, in Italian, means "foot of the mountains"), Piedmont and the autonomous region of Valle d'Aosta just north of it seem more akin to neighboring France and Switzerland. Well-dressed women in the elegant cafés of Turin are addressed more often as *madama* than *signora*, and French is often used in the more remote mountain hamlets.

Piedmont was originally inhabited by Celtic tribes who were absorbed by the Romans. As allies of Rome, the Celts held off Hannibal when he came down through the Alpine passes with his elephants but were eventually defeated, and their capital—Taurasia, the present Turin—was destroyed. The Romans rebuilt the city, giving its streets the grid pattern that survives today. Roman ruins can be found throughout both regions and are particularly abundant in the town of Aosta.

With the fall of the Roman empire, Piedmont suffered the fate of the rest of Italy and was successively occupied and ravaged by barbarians from the east and the north. In the 11th century, a feudal French family named Savoy ruled Turin briefly; toward the end of the 13th century they returned to the area, where they would remain, almost continuously, for 500 years. In 1798 the French Republican armies invaded Italy, but when Napoleon's empire fell, the House of Savoy returned to power.

Beginning in 1848, Piedmont was one of the principal centers of the Risorgimento, the movement for Italian unity. In 1861 the Chamber of Deputies of Turin declared Italy a united kingdom. Rome became the capital in 1870, marking the end of Piedmont's importance in the political sphere. Nevertheless, the architectural splendors of Turin continue to draw travelers.

Piedmont became one of the first industrialized regions in Italy, and the automotive giant FIAT—the Fabbrica Italiana Automobili Torino—was established here in 1899. Today the region is the center of Italy's automobile, metalworking, chemical, and candy industries, having attracted thousands of workers from Italy's impoverished south.

The Valle d'Aosta, to the north, is famous for its impressive fortified castles and splendid Alpine beauty. It was settled in the 3rd millennium BC by people from the Mediterranean and later by a Celtic tribe known as the Salassi, who eventually fell to the Romans. The Saracens were here in the 10th century; by the 12th century, the Savoy family had established itself, and the region's feudal nobles moved into the countryside, building the massive castles that still stand. Valle d'Aosta enjoyed relative autonomy as part of the Savoy kingdom and was briefly ruled by the French four separate times. The region is still officially bilingual, speaking both Italian and French.

Essential Information

Important Addresses and Numbers

Tourist Information
Alessandria (Via Savona 26, tel. 0131/251021).
Aosta (Piazza E. Chanoux 8, tel. 0165/236627).
Asti (Piazza Alfieri 34, tel. 0141/530357).
Bardonecchia (Viale Vittoria 44, tel. 0122/99032).
Courmayeur (Piazzale Monte Bianco, tel. 0165/842060).
Ivrea (Corso Vercelli 1, tel. 0125/618131).
Novara (Via Dominioni 4, tel. 0321/623398).
Turin (Via Roma 222, tel. 011/535901; Porta Nuova train station, tel. 011/531327).

Emergencies **General Emergencies,** tel. 113. **Police,** tel. 112.

Doctors and Dentists
Call 113 and ask for "Pronto Soccorso" (First Aid); this will put you in touch with someone who can recommend a doctor or dentist.

Late-Night Pharmacies
Aosta. *Farmacia Centrale* (Piazza E. Chanoux 35, tel. 0165/262205). **Turin.** *Farmacia Internazionale* (Via Carlo Alberto 24, tel. 011/535144). Pharmacies in these cities and throughout the region take turns staying open late and on Sunday. Call 192 for the latest information on which are open.

Car Rental
Ivrea. *Avis* (Corso Botta 30, tel. 0125/424179). **Turin.** *Avis* (Corso Turati 15, tel. 011/500852); Caselle Airport, tel. 011/470–1528). *Hertz* (Corso Marconi 19, tel. 011/650–4504; Caselle Airport, tel. 011/470–1103).

Arriving and Departing by Plane

The region's only international airport, **Aeroporto Caselle,** is 18 kilometers (11 miles) north of Turin. The airport is notoriously foggy in winter, and many flights are diverted to Genoa, on the coast, with bus connections provided to Turin. Buses from Caselle Airport to Turin arrive at the bus station on Corso Inghilterra in the center of the city. For airport information, call tel. 011/577–8361.

Arriving and Departing by Car, Train, and Bus

By Car
Italy's *autostrada* (superhighway) network links the region with the rest of Italy and neighboring France. Aosta, Turin, and Alessandria all have autostrada connections, with the A4 heading east to Milan and the A6 heading south to the Ligurian coast and Genoa. If you drive in from France or Switzerland, you pass through either the Mount Blanc or Grand St. Bernard tunnels: These are two of the most dramatic entrances to Italy.

By Train
Turin is on the main Paris–Rome express line and is also connected with Milan, only 90 minutes away on the fast train. The fastest trains cover the 667-kilometer (400-mile) trip to Rome in about six hours, but most take about nine.

By Bus
Two Turin-based lines, **SADEM** (Via della Repubblica 14, Grugliasco, Turin, tel. 011/3111616) and **SAPAV** (Corso Torino 396,

Pinerolo, Turin, tel. 011/322032), offer services along the autostrada network to Genoa, Milan, and more distant destinations in Italy. **SITA** buses, part of the nationwide system, also connect Turin with the rest of Italy. The main bus station is on the corner of Corso Inghilterra and Corso Vittorio Emanuele.

Getting Around

By Car Turin is the hub of all the transportation systems in Piedmont, with autostrada connections to the north, south, and east. Well-paved secondary roads run through the rest of the region, following the course of mountain valleys in many places. Sudden winter storms can close off some of the mountain stretches: For information on road conditions, call tel. 011/5711.

By Train Services to the larger cities east of Turin are part of the extensive and reliable train network serving the Lombard Plain. West of the region's capital, however, the train services soon peter out in the steep mountain valleys. Continuing connections by bus serve these valleys, and information about train/bus mountain services can be obtained from train stations.

By Bus **SADEM** and **SAPAV** (*see* Arriving and Departing by Bus, *above*) are the specialists in bus transportation in Piedmont and the Valle d'Aosta. **SAVDA** (Strada Ponte Suaz 6, Aosta, tel. 0165/361244) specializes in mountain service, providing frequent links between Aosta, Turin, and Courmayeur.

Guided Tours

Turin's guided tours are organized by the city's tourist office at Via Roma 222 (tel. 011/535901). The range of tours is extensive, from group tours by bus, to see the main sights of Turin and its surroundings, to specialist tours led by personal guides.

Alpine guides are not only recommended, they're essential if you're planning to traverse some of the dramatic ranges outside Saint-Vincent, Courmayeur, or Breuil-Cervinia. Before embarking on an excursion (however short) into the mountains in these areas, contact the representative of the CAI (Club Alpinisti Italiani) about the risks involved and the availability of an experienced guide. The main regional office of the CAI is in Aosta, Piazza Chanoux 8, tel. 0165/40194 (open Tues. and Fri.); CAI information is also available at each tourist information office.

Exploring Piedmont/Valle d'Aosta

While certain parts of this region remain inaccessible by car or train, the roads that do exist are good and, in most cases, direct. This exploring chapter takes you along rushing streams and into the highest reaches of the mountains, as well as through cities that have borne the imprint of humans for millennia.

The first tour is a detailed examination of Turin and some of the sights that make easy day trips from the regional capital. Tour 2 begins in Turin and winds its way northeast into the Valle d'Aosta, passing Europe's most distinctive peak (the Matterhorn) before taking you to the highest (Mont Blanc). In between are the castles of the Valle d'Aosta (sometimes called Italy's Loire) and the Roman city of

Aosta itself. The last tour, which also begins in Turin, heads east across the fertile Po plain, visiting major cities and ancient towns, such as Asti, Alessandria, and Novara.

Highlights for First-Time Visitors

Breuil-Cervinia (Tour 2: The Valle d'Aosta, the Matterhorn, and Mont Blanc).

Cloister of Sant'Orso, Aosta (Tour 2: The Valle d'Aosta, the Matterhorn, and Mont Blanc).

Courmayeur (Tour 2: The Valle d'Aosta, the Matterhorn, and Mont Blanc).

Fénis Castle (Tour 2: The Valle d'Aosta, the Matterhorn, and Mont Blanc).

Mole Antonelliana, Turin (Tour 1: Turin and Its Outskirts).

Sacra di San Michele (Tour 1: Turin and Its Outskirts).

Tour 1: Turin and Its Outskirts

Numbers in the margin correspond to points of interest on the Piedmont/Valle d'Aosta and Turin maps.

1 **Turin**—in Italian, Torino—is roughly in the center of Piedmont/ Valle d'Aosta; it is situated on the Po River, in the middle of the plain that marks the beginning of the Po Valley and stretches eastward all the way to the Adriatic. Apart from its role as northwest Italy's major industrial, cultural, and administrative hub, Turin is also a center of education, science, and the arts. It also has a reputation as Italy's capital of black magic and the supernatural. This distinction is enhanced by the presence of Turin's most controversial, fascinating, and unsettling relic, the Sacra Sindone (Holy Shroud), still believed by many Catholics to be the cloth in which Christ's body was wrapped when He was taken down from the cross. The shroud, an ancient piece of linen more than four yards long, is rarely on view to the public. In 1988, after centuries of public debate about the authenticity of the cloth—which clearly shows the imprint of a human body—the Vatican agreed to have samples dated by scientists in the United States, Britain, and Italy. The tests showed the shroud to be a medieval fake, though how the human image became fused into it remains a mystery, and the shroud continues to be revered as a holy relic.

2 Start your tour of Turin at the 15th-century **Duomo** (Cathedral), where the **Holy Shroud** is housed. The building, with its white marble facade and campanile (bell tower), stands in the heart of town on Piazza San Giovanni, adjacent to the Royal Palace. Inside, two monumental black marble staircases lead to the shadowy black marble-walled **Cappella della Sacra Sindone** (Chapel of the Holy Shroud), designed by the priest and architect **Guarino Guarini** (1604–83), a genius of the Baroque style who was official engineer and mathematician to the court of Duke Carlo Emanuele II of Savoy. Unfortunately, the chapel has been closed indefinitely for restoration.

3 Adjoining the cathedral is the 17th-century **Palazzo Reale** (Royal Palace). The former Savoy royal residence, it is an imposing work of brick, stone, and marble that stands on the site of Turin's ancient Roman city gates. In contrast to its austere exterior, the palace's interior is characterized by luxurious, mostly Rococo decor, including tapestries, gilded ceilings, and sumptuous 17th- to 19th-century furniture. *Tel. 011/436-1455. Admission: 6,000 lire. Open Tues.-Sun. 9-2.*

Pass through wrought-iron gates in the adjacent Piazza Castello to
❹ **Palazzo Madama,** named for the French queen Maria Cristina, who
made it her home in the 17th century. The castle incorporates the
remains of a Roman gate, as well as medieval and Renaissance additions. The architect Filippo Juvarra (1678–1736) designed the castle's elaborate Baroque facade in the early 18th century: He was
intent on dispelling the idea that Italy's importance as a producer of
contemporary art and architecture was in decline. Juvarra's bold
use of the Baroque is also evident in the interior of the castle, where
the huge marble staircase heralds his patron's wealth and prestige.
The large assembly hall was the scene of the first Italian Senate
meetings in the mid-19th century. Today the castle houses the
Museo Civico d'Arte Antica (Civic Museum of Ancient Art), which
has a rich collection of Gothic, Renaissance, and Rococo sculpture
and paintings, as well as medieval illuminated manuscripts. This
museum has been closed for some time for extensive restorations.

❺ In the same square is the church of **San Lorenzo,** built by Guarini
from 1668 to 1680. Guarini was in his mid-60s when he began work on
the church, but the sprightly collection of domes, columns, and florid Baroque features seems more the work of a younger architect cutting his teeth with a daring display of mathematical invention. The
cupola and the vividly painted interior are standouts.

Time Out **Baratti e Milano,** located just to the east of Piazza Castello in the
glass-roofed gallery between Via Lagrange and Via Po, is one of
Turin's charming Old World cafés. It's famous for its chocolates, so
you can indulge your sweet tooth here or buy some *gianduiotti*
(hazelnut-flavored chocolates) or candied chestnuts to take home to
friends.

From Piazza Castello, the porticoed Via Roma, one of the city's main
thoroughfares, leads half a mile south to Piazza Carlo Felice, a landscaped park and fountain in front of the train station. First opened
in 1615, Via Roma was largely rebuilt in the 1930s, during the time
❻ of Premier Benito Mussolini. Halfway down are the churches of **San**
❼ **Carlo** and **Santa Cristina,** the latter with its ornate Baroque facade.
❽ The churches flank the entrance to **Piazza San Carlo,** a stately, formal expanse considered by many to be the grandest square in Italy.
In the center stands a statue of Duke Emanuele Filiberto of Savoy,
victor, in 1557, of the battle of San Quintino, which heralded the
peaceful resurgence of Turin under the Savoys, after years of bloody
dynastic fighting. The fine bronze statue, erected in the 19th century, is one of Turin's symbols.

Time Out **Café San Carlo,** located under the arcades running alongside the
square, is another historic coffeehouse where locals love to stop for
coffee and pastry at tiny marble-topped tables under the huge crystal chandelier. On the opposite side of the square is **Stratta,** one of
Turin's best-known chocolate shops.

❾ Just off Via Roma is Guarini's **Palazzo dell'Accademia delle Scienze**
(Palace of the Academy of Sciences). This large Baroque building,
prefiguring the 18th century's preoccupation with logic and science,
houses two of Turin's most famous museums. The **Museo Egizio**
(Egyptian Museum) is considered by many to be one of the finest in
scope outside Cairo. Its superb collection includes statues of pharaohs, mummies, and whole frescoes taken from royal tombs. Equal-

Piedmont/Valle d'Aosta

SWITZERLAND

Mte. Cervino
(Matterhorn)

23 Breuil-Cervinia

Monte Rosa

27 Monte Bianco

Great St. Bernard Pass

S27

Valtournenche

S406

Gressoney-la-Trinité

26 Courmayeur

S26

Dora

25 Aosta

Nus Châtillon

Saint Vincent

S26

S505

Little St. Bernard Pass

Baltéa

VALLE D'AOSTA

24 Fénis

Verrès

28 Cogne

Forte di Bard **22**

Gran Paradiso

Pont St. Martin

Ceresole Reale

S26

FRANCE

Forno Alpi Gràie

S460

Orco

Ivrea

Cuorgnè

S5

Dora Baltéa

S26

Balme

Céres

Bardonecchia

S25

Chivasso

Susa

S24

A4

S460

Sacra di San Michele **21**

20 **19** **18**

Avigliana

Rivoli

Turin

Sant'Antonio di Ranverso

1 — **16**

Sestriere

TO CLAVIERE

N

Stupinigi

17

S23

S10

S589

0   10 miles

0   15 km

S23

Carignano

A21

Pinerolo

S20

A6

S29

TO BRÀ

TO ALBA

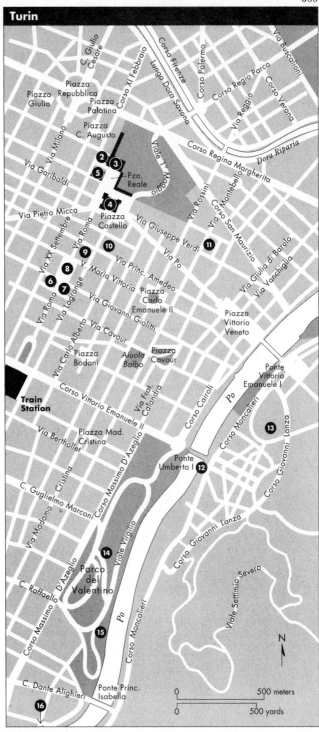

Turin

ly fascinating are the papyrus, art objects, and day-to-day utensils taken from the tombs of less noble ancient Egyptians. Look for the papyrus *Book of the Dead* and the 13th-century BC statue of Ramses II, which still glistens in its original colors. *Tel. 011/5617776. Admission: 10,000 lire. Open Tues–Sun. 9–2.*

The **Galleria Sabauda,** in the same building, houses the collections of the house of Savoy. It is particularly rich in 16th- and 17th-century Dutch and Flemish paintings: Note Jan Van Eyck's *Saint Francis with Stigmata,* with the saint receiving the marks of Christ's wounds while a companion cringes beside him as if feeling it all himself. Other Dutch masterpieces include paintings by Anthony Van Dyck and Rembrandt. Simone del Pollaiuolo's *Tobias and the Angel* is showcased, and other Italian artists featured include Fra Angelico, Andrea Mantegna, and Paolo Veronese. *Tel. 011/547440. Admission: 6,000 lire. Open Tues.–Sun. 9–2.*

⑩ Diagonally across the square is another of Guarini's Baroque triumphs, the redbrick **Palazzo Carignano,** built from 1679 to 1685. This is one of Turin's and Italy's most historic buildings. Kings of Savoy, Carlo Alberto (1798–1849) and Vittorio Emanuele II (1820–78), were born within its walls; Italy's first parliament met here from 1860 to 1865.

⑪ Take the little road behind the palazzo about 50 yards to Via Po, turn right and take the fourth left (Via Montebello) to the striking **Mole Antonelliana.** You will probably have noticed this Turin landmark already: Its unusual square dome and thin, elaborate spire jut well above the city's rooftops. This odd structure, built between 1863 and 1897, was originally intended to be a synagogue, but costs escalated and eventually it was bought by the city of Turin. In its time it was the tallest building in the world. There is an excellent view of the city, the plain surrounding it, and the Alps beyond from a terrace at the top of the dome. Take the elevator to the top. *Tel. 011/839–8314. Admission: 3,000 lire. Open Tues.–Sun. 9–7.*

⑫ Via Po leads to the large Piazza Vittorio Veneto, which slopes down to the Po River and the stone bridge, **Ponte Vittorio Emanuele.** Immediately across the bridge is the 19th-century church of **Gran Madre di Dio** (Great Mother of God), built in a neoclassical style based on the Pantheon in Rome. Turn right, along the Corso Moncalieri, to climb the Monte dei Cappuccini. At the top of this **⑬** 150-foot hill are the church and convent of **Santa Maria del Monte,** which date from 1583. Don't be surprised if you find yourself in the middle of a wedding party: Local couples often come here to have their pictures taken.

⑭ Return to Corso Moncalieri and cross the next bridge downstream, Ponte Umberto I. Running along this cityside bank of the river is the **Parco del Valentino,** opened in 1856 and one of the most beautiful in Italy. The park has many pedestrian avenues, one of which, **Viale Virgilio,** goes right along the riverbank and leads to the **Castello del Valentino.** The design of this 17th-century castle, built more for appearance than for defense, is based on models of 16th-century French châteaux. The interior is particularly elaborate, with frescoed walls and rich decoration, but the real attraction of the castle is its riverside setting amid the greenery of the park. *Tel. 011/669-9372. Admission: 3,000 lire, free Fri. Open Tues.–Sat. 9–6, Sun. 10:30–6.*

⑮ Follow the riverside to the southern edge of the park, where you'll find the **Borgo Medioevale** (Medieval Village), one of the most tranquil spots in Turin. The village, a faithful reproduction of medieval

Piedmontese buildings, was created for the Turin Exposition of 1884. A visit here is like stepping back into the Middle Ages, with craftsmen's shops, houses, churches, and stores clustered along narrow streets and lanes. *Admission free. Open daily 8–8.*

No visit to car-manufacturing Turin would be complete without a pilgrimage to the **Museo dell'Automobile** (Car Museum). Here you'll get an idea of the importance of FIAT—and automobiles, in general—to Turin's economy. A collection of antique cars dates from 1893, and displays show how the city has changed over the years as a result of its premier industry. *Corso Unita d'Italia, tel. 011/677666. Admission: 7,000 lire. Open Tues.–Sun. 10–6:30.*

The next five sights are west of the city. Start at the train station and follow Via Sacchi as it heads southwest. The road changes its name several times within the city boundaries before becoming Corso Unione Sovietica. About 8 kilometers (5 miles) out of Turin by car or on Bus 41 from Porta Nuova Station, you come to the **Palazzina di Caccia** in the town of **Stupinigi**. This elaborate building was built by Juvarra in 1729 as a hunting lodge for the House of Savoy. It is more like a royal villa, with its many wings, landscaped gardens, and surrounding forests. This regal aspect was not lost on Napoleon, who lived here before claiming the crown of Italy. The castle interior is sumptuously decorated and today houses a collection of art and furniture in the appropriately named **Museo d'Arte e Ammobiliamento.** *Tel. 011/358–1220. Admission: 6,000 lire. Open Tues.–Sat. 9:30–5, Sun 10–1, 2–5.*

The next sights are best reached by going back to Turin and taking Corso Francia west from Piazza Rivoli. You can take Tram 1 from downtown Turin, then Bus 36 (fare: 1,600 lire). After 13 kilometers (8 miles), you reach **Rivoli,** where the Savoy court was based in the Middle Ages. The 14th- to 15th-century **Casa del Conte Verde,** right in the center of town, is a good example of medieval architecture of the transitional period, when its defensive function was giving way to the decorative. The 18th-century Savoy castle, built in the Baroque style under the direction of Juvarra, now houses the **Museo d'Arte Moderna** (Modern Art Museum), which contains many examples of 20th-century Italian art. The Futurist movement is particularly well represented. *Tel. 011/958–1547. Admission: 8,000 lire. Open Tues.–Sun. 10–7.*

Roads west from Rivoli begin to climb the broad Valle di Susa, which narrows as it heads toward France. Take the road marked "Rosta" from Rivoli; at Rosta, about 6 kilometers (4 miles) west, you can park and walk to the abbey of **Sant'Antonio di Ranverso.** This building was an abbey hospital, founded in the 12th century by the Hospitalers of Saint Anthony to care for victims of Saint Anthony's Fire, a crippling disease contracted by eating contaminated grains. Pilgrims came here over the centuries for cures or, sometimes, to offer thanks for a miraculous recovery, and the 15th-century terra-cotta decorations, with their lifelike depictions of pilgrims and saints, retain the color of the originals. *Tel. 011/931–2346. Donation requested. Open Tues.–Sun. 9–noon, 2–4.*

Six kilometers (4 miles) farther along the same road that led from Rivoli, you reach the medieval town of **Avigliana.** With its attractive lakeside setting, Avigliana was a favorite of the Savoys up to the mid-15th century. Medieval houses still line the twisting and narrow streets. **Casa della Porta Ferrata,** on the street of the same name, is a well-preserved example of Piedmont Gothic domestic architecture:

Notice how the fascination with narrow pointed arches is carried through even to private houses.

㉑ A car is essential for an excursion to the **Sacra di San Michele** (Abbey of Saint Michael). Take the twisting, narrow road that leads south from Avigliana and pass between two glacier-fed lakes before going right for the rest of the 14-kilometer (8-mile) climb to the abbey. San Michele was built here in the 11th century to stand out: The location, on Monte Pirchiriano, is the most prominent for miles around. When monks came to enlarge the abbey, they had to build part of the structure on supports more than 90 feet high—an engineering feat that was famous in medieval Europe. By the 12th century, this important abbey controlled 176 churches in Italy, France, and Spain, and one of the abbeys under its influence was Mont St-Michel in France. Because of the abbey's strategic position, it came under numerous attacks over the next five centuries, and it was eventually abandoned in 1622. It was restored in the late 19th and early 20th centuries.

From Porta dello Zodiaco, a splendid Romanesque doorway decorated with the signs of the zodiac, you climb 150 steps, past 12th-century sculptures, to reach the church. The interior has 16th-century frescoes on the walls: On the left are religious subjects representing New Testament themes, while on the right are stories depicting the founding of the church. Go down to the crypt to see the 9th- to 12th-century chapels. *Donation requested. Open Apr.–Sept., daily 9–noon, 3–7; Oct.–Mar., daily 9–noon, 2–dusk.*

Tour 2: The Valle d'Aosta, the Matterhorn, and Mont Blanc

Take Autostrada A5 north from Turin; at Ivrea, 50 kilometers (30 miles) along, join S26 on its way north. The road takes you through countryside that becomes hillier and hillier, passing through steep ravines guarded by brooding, romantic castles. Another change that you may not notice from your car is the beginning of French-speaking territory, as you enter the Aosta region, about 18 kilometers (11 miles) north of Ivrea. Pont St-Martin is the first village of the region; a few minutes afterward you pass through the narrow

㉒ Gorge de Bard. Towering above the gorge is the **Forte di Bard** (closed to the public), a 19th-century reconstruction of a fort that stood for eight centuries, serving the Savoys for six of them. In 1800 Napoleon entered Italy through this valley and used the cover of darkness to get his artillery units past the castle unnoticed. Ten years later he remembered this inconvenience and had the fortress destroyed.

Continue on S26, through the town of **Saint Vincent,** a popular resort since the late 18th century. Its main claim to fame these days is the Casino de la Vallée, Europe's largest gambling site. A few kilometers farther on S26, turn right, at Châtillon, for the 30-kilometer

㉓ (19-mile) detour up a dramatic mountain valley to **Breuil-Cervinia,** the Italian-Swiss village at the base of the Matterhorn (Monte Cervino, in Italian; Mont Cervin in French). Like the village, the famous peak straddles the border between Italy and Switzerland, and all sightseeing and skiing facilities are operated jointly. Serious climbers can make the ascent of the Matterhorn from Breuil-Cervinia (having registered with the local mountaineering officials at the tourist office), but this climb is for serious and experienced climbers only. You get splendid views of the peak from Plateau Rosa and the Cresta del Furggen, both of which can be reached by cable car from the center of Breuil-Cervinia. While many locals complain that the tourist facilities and the condominiums in the village have changed the face of their beloved Breuil, most would agree that the cable car has given them access to climbing and off-trail skiing in ridges that were once inaccessible.

Return to S26 and continue west toward Aosta. About 12 kilometers (7 miles) from Châtillon is the best-preserved fortress in the Valle d'Aosta. The many-turreted castle of **Fénis** was built in the mid-14th century by Aimone di Challant, a member of a prolific family that was related to the Savoys. This castle is the sort imagined by schoolchildren, with pointed turrets, portcullises, and spiral staircases. The 15th-century courtyard has a stairway leading to a loggia (open walkway) with wooden balconies. Inside you can see the medieval kitchen, with much of the original cooking equipment, and a collection of weapons in the armory. If you have time to visit only one castle in the Valle d'Aosta, this is it, though it may be partly closed for restoration. *Tel. 0165/764263. Admission: 4,000 lire. Open Mar.–Oct., Wed.–Mon. 9–6:30 (group tour every half-hour); Nov.–Feb., Wed.–Mon. 9:30–noon, 2–5 (group tour every hour).*

S26 continues climbing through the Valle d'Aosta for the last 14 kilometers (9 miles) to Aosta itself. The road at this point is heading almost due west, with rivulets from the Parco Nazionale del Gran Paradiso (a wilderness reserve) streaming down from the left to join the Dora Baltea. Be careful driving here in late spring, when melting snow can turn some of these streams into torrents. **Aosta** stands at the junction of two important trade routes from France to Italy—from the valleys of the Rhône and the Isère. Its significance as a trading post was recognized by the Romans, who built a garrison here in the 1st century BC. The present-day layout of streets in this small city, which is tucked away in the Alps more than 400 miles from Rome, is the clearest example of Roman street planning in Italy. Well-preserved Roman walls form a perfect rectangle around the center of Aosta, and the regular pattern of streets reflects its role as a military stronghold.

At the eastern entrance to town, in a square that commands a fine view over Aosta and the mountains, is the **Arco di Augusto** (Arch of Augustus), built in 25 BC to mark Rome's victory over the Celtic Salassi tribe. Across the square, and then a right turn off Via Sant' Anselmo, is the **Collegiata di Sant'Orso** (Collegiate Church of Saint Orso): the sort of church that has layers of history in its architecture. Originally there was a 6th-century chapel on this site, founded by the Archdeacon Orso, a local saint. Most of this structure was destroyed or hidden when an 11th-century church was erected over it. This church, in turn, was encrusted with Gothic, and later Baroque, features, leaving the church a jigsaw puzzle of styles, but—surprisingly—not a chaotic jumble. The 11th-century features are almost untouched in the crypt, and if you go up the stairs on the left from the main church you can see the 11th-century frescoes (ask the sacristan for entrance). These restored frescoes depict the life of Christ and the Apostles: Although only the tops are visible, you can see the expressions on the faces of the disciples. Take the doorway by the entrance to the crypt to see the crowning glory of Sant'Orso—the 12th-century **cloister.** Beside the church, it is enclosed by some forty stone columns with masterfully carved capitals representing Old and New Testament themes and scenes from the life of St. Orso.

Continue down Via Anselmo (named for St. Anselm, who was born in Aosta and later became archbishop of Canterbury in England) through the huge Roman **Porta Pretoria.** Turn right after this three-arch gateway to see the 72-foot-high ruin of the facade of the **Teatro Romano** (Roman Theater). Just ahead are the ruins of the 1st-century BC amphitheater, which once held 20,000 spectators. Only seven of its original 60 arches remain, and these are built onto the facade of the adjacent convent of **Santa Caterina.** The convent usually allows visitors in to see these arches (ask at the entrance).

About 100 yards west of the Roman theater (down Via Monsignor de Sales) is Aosta's cathedral, which dates from the 10th century, although all that remains from that period are the campaniles. The decoration inside is mainly Gothic, but the main attraction of the cathedral predates that era by 1,000 years: the carved ivory diptych (devotional work with two images) showing the Roman Emperor Honorius and dating from AD 406. *For admission to the treasury, contact the sacristan at the Piccolo Seminario, 2 Piazza Giovanni XXIII (behind the cathedral).*

Take Via Stati Generali about 50 yards down to Piazza Chanoux, the center of Aosta and the scene of a permanent craft exhibition, in one of its arcades. Aosta and the surrounding countryside are famous for wood carvings and wrought-iron work, and this exhibition is a good place to pick up a bargain. Each year, on the last two days of January, the whole town turns out for the Sant'Orso Fair, when all sorts of handicrafts are on sale, including handmade lace from nearby Cogne, carved wood and stonework, and brightly colored woolens.

Having made a detour to see the Matterhorn on your way up from Turin, you probably won't want to leave the Valle d'Aosta without seeing Europe's tallest peak, Mont Blanc (Monte Bianco in Italian). Follow S26 west for about 40 kilometers (25 miles) from Aosta, turning right on S26D when you see the signs for **Courmayeur,** about a mile outside town. The jet-set celebrities who flock here, particularly in winter, are following a tradition that dates from the late 17th century, when Courmayeur's natural springs first began to draw visitors. The scenic spectacle of the Alps gradually surpassed the springs as the biggest drawing point (the Alpine letters of the English poet Shelley were almost advertisements for the region), but the biggest change in the history of Courmayeur came in 1965, when the Mont Blanc tunnel opened. Now Courmayeur stands on one of the main routes from France into Italy, although the planners have managed to maintain some restrictions on wholesale development within the town.

Take S26D north about 3 kilometers (2 miles) beyond Courmayeur to **La Palud,** where you can catch the cable car up to **Monte Bianco.** The cable car crosses into France, so have your passport ready. Remember, too, that the cable car depends on the weather, and that can mean being stuck on the French side, sometimes overnight: Have French money with you, in case. You ride up to the viewing platform at **Punta Helbronner** (over 11,000 feet), which is also the border post with France. Mont Blanc's attraction is not so much its shape (much less distinctive than the Matterhorn) as its expanse and the vistas from the top. The next stage, as you pass into French territory, is particularly impressive: You dangle over a huge glacial snow field (more than 2,000 feet below) and make your way slowly to the viewing station above **Chamonix.** From this point you're looking down into France, and if you change cable cars, you can make your way down to Chamonix itself. The return trip covers the same route, and the total time should be 90 minutes, weather permitting. *Funivie La Palud, tel. 0165/89925. Fare: 36,000 lire round-trip to Punta Helbronner; 43,000 lire from Punta Helbronner to Chamonix.*

As you make your way back toward Aosta, take time to explore the **Parco Nazionale del Gran Paradiso.** Take the right turn at

28 Aymavilles, about 6 kilometers (4 miles) west of Aosta, to climb into the Val di Cogne. The village of **Cogne** itself, about 20 kilometers (12 miles) up the valley, is the best place to stop and sample the peace and solitude of this huge park, once the domain of King Vittorio Emanuele II and bequeathed to the nation after World War I. Gran Paradiso is one of Europe's most rugged and unspoiled wilderness areas, with wildlife and many plant species protected by law. Try to visit in May, when spring flowers are in bloom and most of the meadows are clear of snow. This is one of the few places in Europe where you can see the ibex (a mountain goat with horns up to three feet long) or the chamois (a small antelope whose soft skin nearly drove it to extinction).

If you're in a hurry to return to Turin, you can go back via superhighway A5, which runs parallel with S26 as far as Ivrea.

Tour 3: Fortified Cities of the Po Plain

Take Autostrada A6 south from Turin for about 5 kilometers (3 miles), to the Torfarello exit, and join A21 east (left turn) for the 50-
29 kilometer (30-mile) drive to the famous wine city of **Asti.** The last few miles of this trip take you into the **Monferrato,** a hilly wooded area, rich in vineyards and truffles. Asti is one of the main cities of the Monferrato. It is known to Americans mainly because of its wines (there are excellent reds as well as the famous sparkling white spumante), but its strategic position on trade routes between Turin, Milan, and Genoa has given it a broad economic base. In the 12th century, Asti began to develop as a republic, at a time when other Italian cities were also flexing their economic and military muscles. It flourished in the following century, when the inhabitants began erecting lofty towers for its defense. Some of these towers remain, giving the city a medieval look.

Arriving on the autostrada, you enter Asti through Piazza Torino. Directly ahead is Corso Vittorio Alfieri, which runs west–east across the city. This road, known in medieval times as Contrada Maestra, was built by the Romans. About 100 yards up on the right is the 18th-century church of Santa Caterina, which has incorporated one of the medieval towers, the **Torre Romana** (itself built on an ancient Roman base), as its bell tower.

Turn left at Piazza Cairoli, about a two-minute walk ahead, and take the small road that leads to the **Duomo.** Here is a good chance to see the evolution of the Gothic style of architecture. The cathedral, built in the early 14th century, is decorated mainly in a Gothic style that emphasizes geometry and verticality: Pointed arches and narrow vaults are counterbalanced by the earlier, Romanesque, attention to balance and symmetry. Then look at the porch, on the south side of the cathedral, facing the square. This addition, built in 1470, represents Gothic at its most florid and excessive.

Return to the Corso and continue to Piazza Roma, where there is another of Asti's 13th-century towers, **Torre Comentini.** Asti's best-preserved medieval tower, **Torre Troyana,** is up Via Morelli, the third left off the Corso after Piazza Roma. This tall, thin tower is attached to the Palazzo Troya, in Piazza Medici. Go back to the Corso and take the small street opposite Via Morelli; just ahead is the Gothic church of **San Secondo.** San Secondo is the patron saint of Asti and of the city's favorite sporting event, the annual *palio*, the colorful medieval-style horse race held each year on the third Sunday of September in the Campo del Palio to the south of the church.

Take the small Via Garibaldi from the right of the church for the few steps it takes to reach Piazza Libertà, which forms the southwest edge of the large triangular **Piazza Alfieri.** This square is the heart of Asti, with its tourist office and civic administrative offices.

Time Out	The **Bottega del Vino** (open Mon.–Sat. 9–4:30), located on Piazza Alfieri (just to the left of Corso alla Vittoria), is a wine center and shop, where you can try the range of Asti vintages, buy some as souvenirs or picnic ingredients, or sample a light snack.

Take Corso Alfieri, at the northern end of Piazza Alfieri, right (east) to join S10 on its way 36 kilometers (22 miles) east to Alessandria. The road is straight, lying mainly in the southern edge of the Po plain, but for the first half of the drive you see the green hillsides covered with vineyards. If you find yourself driving along this road during a thunderstorm (quite common in late summer afternoons) don't be surprised by the sound of man-made explosions. Wine growers will often let off cannons loaded with blanks to force heavy clouds to rain, rather than build up and develop destructive hailstones.

From Alessandria, S31, a direct secondary route that was originally a military supply route for the Romans, goes almost due north. Thir-❸⓪ ty kilometers (18 miles) from Alessandria is **Casale Monferrato,** strategically situated on the southern banks of the Po. The town was held by the Gonzagas, rulers of Mantua, before falling into the hands of the Savoys: The 16th-century **Torre Civica,** marking the heart of Casale Monferrato in Piazza Mazzini, commanded extensive views up and down the Po. Casale's most enlightening sight is the **Museo Israelitico** (Jewish Museum), located in the women's section of the synagogue on Via Alessandria. Inside is a collection of documents and sacred art of a community that was vital to the prosperity of this mercantile city. The synagogue dates from the late 16th century, and neighboring buildings on the same street formed the Jewish ghetto of that period. *Admission: 5,000 lire. Open Aug.–June, Sun. 10–12, 3:30–5:30. At other times apply to the caretaker.*

S31 continues north from Casale Monferrato; the 23-kilometer (14-❸① mile) stretch from there to **Vercelli** goes past rice fields. Vercelli is the rice capital of Italy and of Europe itself: Northern Italy's mainstay, risotto, owes its existence to the crop that was introduced to this fertile area in the late Middle Ages. Arriving from Casale, you enter town along Corso De Rege. Turn left along Via Massaua to reach the parking area in the grassy square of Piazza Camana. Take Via Manzoni, and then the first left after the post office, to reach **Piazza Cavour,** the heart of the medieval city and former market square. It was to this small square that merchants across northern Italy came in the 15th century to buy bags of the novelty grain from the east—rice. Rising above the low rooftops around the square is the **Torre dell'Angelo** (Tower of the Angel), whose forbidding military appearance reflects its origins as a watchtower.

Vercelli has an unusual guided tour of the **Borsa Merci,** the rice exchange where the grain has been traded for centuries. Call first to check on tour times (Via Zumaglini 4, tel. 0161/5981).

Via Gioberti goes east from the square, leading to Via del Duomo, up on the left. Ahead of you is the campanile of the **Duomo,** which is at the end of the street, on Piazza D'Angennes. The building, mainly a late–16th-century construction on the site of what was a 5th-century church, contains tombs of several Savoy rulers in an octagonal chapel along the south (right) wall. The cathedral's *biblioteca* (chapter library—apply in the cathedral for entrance) contains the "Gospel of St. Eusebius," a 4th-century document, and the *Codex Vercellensis*, an 11th-century book of Anglo-Saxon poetry.

Cross Piazza San Eusebio, which is directly in front of the cathedral, and follow Corso De Gasperi to the **Basilica di Sant' Andrea,** on the left. This Cistercian abbey church, built in the early 13th century with funds from another Abbey of St. Andrew (in England), witnessed the growing influence of northern Europe on Italy. Sant'Andrea is one of Italy's earliest examples of Gothic architecture, which spread from the north but ran out of steam before getting much farther south than the Po plain. The church interior is a soaring flight of Gothic imagination, with slender columns rising up to the ribbed vaults of the high ceiling. Tombs along the side aisle continue the preoccupation with stylized decoration and relief work. The gardens on the north (Corso De Gasperi side) of the basilica hold the remains of the abbey itself and some of the secondary buildings. It is only here that the unadulterated Gothic style is interrupted. The buildings surround a cloister in which you can see the pointed Gothic arches resting on the severe and more solid 12th-century Romanesque column bases.

Wander back to Piazza Camana through the **Città Vecchia,** a collection of narrow streets and alleys reached by taking Via Galileo (left from the basilica) and then making your way left into the narrow streets, using the Torre dell'Angelo in Piazza Cavour as your landmark. Many of the houses are five centuries old, and you can see partly hidden gardens and courtyards beyond the wrought-iron gates.

Leaving Vercelli, follow Corso De Gregori and then Corso Palestro from the parking lot at Piazza Campana. Corso Palestro leads into S11, which turns right out of town at Piazza Cugnolio. The road heads northeast to **Novara,** 23 kilometers (14 miles) away, past intensively farmed rice fields. Novara is the easternmost city in Piedmont, only about 6 miles west of the Ticino River, which forms the border with Lombardy. Milan is only 20 miles beyond the border, and over the centuries the opposing attractions of this neighboring giant and of the regional capital, Turin, have made Novara a bit schizophrenic. In the Middle Ages, Novara's pivotal position actually made it a battlefield. A major engagement took place as recently as 1849, when the Austrian forces from the east defeated the Piedmontese armies.

Much of the present city dates from the late 19th and early 20th centuries, although there are interesting buildings from earlier periods scattered around Novara. Just after you enter the city, bear left up Corso Torino for about half a mile and turn right onto Corso XX Settembre, where there are parking lots. From here it's impossible to miss Novara's famous landmark, the tall, slender cupola of **San Gaudenzio,** which you can reach by taking a left on Baluardo Quintino Sella. The church itself, built between 1577 and 1690, conforms to a Baroque design, with twisted columns and sumptuous statues. The main attraction for most people, though, is the cupola, which was built from 1840 to 1888 and soars to a height of just under 400 feet. This spire is visible from everywhere in the city and the surrounding countryside, and has become as much a symbol of Novara as the Mole Antonelliana is of Turin.

Take a left immediately after leaving the front door of San Gaudenzio and follow the small street south (against the flow of the one-way traffic). You soon pass Corso Italia. Immediately to the left, after you've crossed this main street, is the **Broletto,** a cluster of well-preserved late-medieval buildings. Inside is the **Museo Civico,** which is full of Piedmontese military and social records from the Middle Ages through the 18th century. There are also some archaeological items going back to the Roman and early Christian (4th–5th century) periods. *Tel. 0321/623021. Admission: 2,000 lire. Open Apr.–Sept., Tues.–Sun. 9–1, 4–7; Oct.–Mar., Tues.–Sun. 9–12, 3–5.*

Novara's **Duomo** is next to the Broletto. Its Romanesque origins are impossible to detect because a major reconstruction of the past century left the building with an austere neoclassical appearance. You can delve into history more easily at the **Battistero** (Baptistery), which is just outside the entrance to the cathedral. This rotunda-shaped building dates from the 5th century, although it was substantially enlarged in the 10th and 11th centuries. Recent restoration work has uncovered pre-Romanesque frescoes, over 1,000 years old, decorating the inside walls. Their flat, two-dimensional style reflects the influence of Byzantine icons, and their restored colors add a frightening feel to the apocalyptic scenes depicted.

Just north of Novara, the A4 autostrada will take you back west to Turin (91 kilometers/56 miles) or east to Milan (51 kilometers/32 miles).

What to See and Do with Children

The Alpine landscapes of the Valle d'Aosta will impress youngsters, especially excursions to the **Matterhorn** and **Mont Blanc.** In the vast wilderness of **Parco Nazionale del Gran Paradiso,** there's plenty of wildlife to observe. Among Valle d'Aosta's many castles, the one at **Fénis** most satisfies a young person's image of what a castle should look like. Kids who are interested in ancient times can explore a number of Roman ruins in the city of **Aosta.** In **Turin,** children generally enjoy the model medieval village (Borgo Medioevale), the vintage cars in the Museo dell'Automobile, and the mummies in the Museo Egizio.

Off the Beaten Track

Alba. This moderate-size town, about 30 kilometers (18 miles) southwest of Asti, is the wine and truffle capital of the area. Visit in October for the National Truffle Fair, the Cento Torri Joust, and the Palio degli Asini (donkey races). For information, contact Tourist Information (Piazza Medford, tel. 0173/35833).

Cinzano Wine Cellars. Brà, about 50 kilometers (30 miles) south of Turin and only 16 kilometers (10 miles) west of Alba (*see above*), is the home of this world-famous wine and vermouth company. You can take a guided tour of the plant and sample some of the product at the end. *Call tel. 0172/47041 for information. Admission free.*

Shopping

Turin is the major city of Piedmont/Valle d'Aosta, and it has all the shopping that you expect to find in a metropolis. Famous Cinzano and Martini-Rossi brand wines and vermouth are particular favorites, while salamis, cheeses, and delicious gianduiotti are also appreciated as gifts. Elsewhere in the region you'll find more handicrafts, such as Borsalino hats from Alessandria and wrought-iron goods or wood carvings from Aosta. Many towns and villages have regular antiques markets.

Alessandria The Borsalino hat factory (Spinetta Marengo, tel. 0131/61880) is 6 kilometers (4 miles) southeast of town.

Aosta The capital of the Valle d'Aosta region is a handicrafts center, especially for wood carvings, stone and wrought-iron work, handmade lace, and colorful wool fabrics. There is a permanent craft exhibition in the arcade of Piazza Chanoux in the center of town, and the annual St. Orso Fair, held on the last two days of January, is a good time to find handicrafts.

Asti The Arazzeria Scassa (tel. 0141/271352) is a craft workshop specializing in tapestries.

Nizza Monferrato Take S456 southeast for 28 kilometers (17 miles) from Asti to reach this attractive medieval town, which has an antiques market every third Sunday of the month.

Turin *Antiques* Piazza San Carlo, Via Po, and Via Maria Vittoria are lined with antiques shops, some—but not all—specializing in 18th-century furniture and domestic items.

Boutiques Most people know that Turin produces more than 75% of Italy's cars, but they don't realize that it is also a clothing manufacturing city. Top-quality boutiques stocking local, national, and international lines are clustered along Via Roma and Via Garibaldi.

Food and Flea Markets Go to the famous Balon Flea Market (Piazza Repubblica) on a Saturday morning for some excellent bargains in secondhand books and clothing and some stalls selling local specialties such as gianduiotti.

Valenza Take S494 northeast from Alessandria for 13 kilometers (8 miles) to reach this historic town on the Po. Valenza is one of the world's major producers of gold and silver work, and there is a permanent display of jewelry at Piazza Don Minzoni 1 (tel. 0131/953643).

Sports

Boating The **Lega Navale di Torino** (Turin Boating League) (Corso Unione Sovietica 316, tel. 011/530979) organizes courses and special races throughout the summer.

Fishing The streams and rivers around northern Piedmont and Valle d'Aosta are good spots for trout fishing. For information on regulations and licenses, contact the **Federazione Italiana di Pesca Sportiva,** in Turin (Via Giolitti 24, tel. 011/546732).

Golf **Avigliana, Fiano** (near Turin), and **Sestriere** have championship 18-hole courses; nine-hole courses are located in **Claviere, Aosta, Turin,** and **Valenza.**

Rock Climbing Beginner and advanced courses are taught in Macugnana, sponsored by CAI Macugnana Monte Rosa (tel. 0324/65119).

Skiing This is the major sport in both Piedmont and the Valle d'Aosta. Resorts with excellent facilities abound near the highest mountains in Europe—Mont Blanc, Monte Rosa, the Cervino (Matterhorn), and the Gran Paradiso.

Breuil-Cervinia Because its slopes border the Cervino glacier, this resort at the foot of the Matterhorn offers year-round skiing.

Claviere This quaint village, with slate-roofed houses, is one of Italy's oldest ski resorts. Its slopes overlap with those of the French resort of Montgenevre.

Courmayeur This famous spot for the well heeled is well equipped and easy to reach, just outside the Italian end of the Mont Blanc tunnel. The skiing around Mont Blanc is particularly good, and the off-piste options are among the best in Europe.

Sestriere At 6,670 feet, this famous resort near the French border, just 50 kilometers (30 miles) west of Turin, gets good snow from November until May.

Spelunking Cave explorations are organized by CAI Speleological Groups (tel. 011/537983) in Turin. Contact the group for information on trips from Turin or the classes it holds from January to May.

Tennis Tennis is popular throughout the area, and most towns have public courts as well as private clubs that offer temporary membership to visitors. Contact the local tourist offices.

Dining and Lodging

Dining These two regions offer rustic specialties from farmhouse hearths and fine cuisine with a French accent—and everything in between. The favorite form of pasta is *agnolotti* (similar to ravioli), filled with meat, spinach, or cheese. Another regional specialty is *fonduta*—a local form of fondue, made with melted Fontina (a cheese from the Valle d'Aosta), eggs, and sometimes grated truffles. Alba is the home of *tartufi bianchi* (white truffles), much rarer and more expensive than black ones and considered the tastiest by connoisseurs. They sell for at least $1,000 a pound wholesale. Another local dish is *cardi in bagna cauda*, made of edible thistles *(cardi)* chopped raw, and then dipped in a hot sauce *(bagna cauda* means hot bath), made from butter, oil, anchovies, cream, and shredded garlic.

Turin is also known for delicate pastries and fine chocolates, especially for gianduiotti. Valle d'Aosta is famous for a variety of schnappslike brandies made from fruits or herbs.

Piedmont is one of Italy's most important wine-producing regions. Most of the wines are full-bodied reds, such as Barolo, Nebbiolo, Freisa, Barbera, and Barbaresco. Asti Spumante, a sparkling wine, comes from the region, as does vermouth, which was developed in Piedmont by A. B. Carpano in 1786.

Highly recommended restaurants are indicated by a star ★.

Category	Cost*
$$$$	over 85,000 lire
$$$	60,000–85,000 lire
$$	30,000–60,000 lire
$	under 30,000 lire

**per person, including house wine, service, and tax*

Lodging There is a good variety of accommodations in Piedmont and Valle d'Aosta, but remember that except for the cities, the area tends to be a two-season resort. Summer and winter occupancy rates are usually quite high, since skiers and mountaineers add to the competition for rooms then. In the following list, we have mentioned when a hotel or chalet offers attractive half-board or off-season rates that can sometimes reduce the cost by a full Fodor's category. In the mountain resorts, many hotels cater primarily to half- or full-board guests only, for stays of at least a week. It's better to take a package deal if you're coming for a ski vacation.

Highly recommended lodgings are indicated by a star ★.

Category	Cost*
$$$$	over 300,000 lire
$$$	180,000–300,000 lire
$$	100,000–180,000 lire
$	under 100,000 lire

All prices are for a standard double room for two, including service and 9% IVA (13% for luxury establishments).

Aosta
Dining
★

Piemonte. A small restaurant in the center of town, the Piemonte has a comfortable, rustic decor and offers *crespelle alla valdostana* (crêpes with cheese) and *filetto alla provenzale* (beef fillet with porcini mushrooms). *Via Porta Pretoria 13, tel. 0165/40111. Lunch reservations advised. Dress: casual. MC, V. Closed Fri. and Nov. $$*

Vecchio Ristoro. Local and Italian dishes predominate in this old mill, furnished with antiques, in the city center. Try the *trota affumicata* (smoked trout) or the *uova walzer* (eggs cooked with cream and cheese on a bed of crusty baked polenta seasoned with wild herbs). *Via Tourneuve 4, tel. 0165/33238. Reservations advised. Dress: casual. AE, DC, MC, V. Closed Sun., Mon. lunch, and July, Feb. $$*

La Brasserie du Commerce. Small, lively, and informal, it is in the heart of Aosta, near central Piazza Chanoux. On a sunny summer day try to get a table on the terrace. Typical valley dishes, such as fonduta are on the menu, together with a wide range of vegetable dishes and salads. *Via de Tillier 10, tel. 0165/35613. No reservations. Dress: casual. No credit cards. Closed Sun. $*

Taverna Nando. A wine cellar with wooden floors and vaulted ceilings, this family-run tavern is located in the center of Aosta, and it has a terrace for outdoor dining. The menu features regional specialties such as fonduta, *carbonada* (veal stew), and *cervo* (venison) with mushrooms. The wine list is impressive. *Via de Tillier 41, tel. 0165/44455. Reservations advised. Dress: casual. AE, DC, MC, V. Closed Thurs. and June. $*

Lodging

Valle D'Aosta. You'll find this comfortable, modern four-star hotel on the outskirts of town. A few rooms on the fifth floor have balconies, but virtually all rooms have big windows and splendid views of the mountains. There are rooms suitable for people with disabilities. There is no restaurant, but there is a pleasant garden. *Corso Ivrea 146, tel. 0165/41845, fax 0165/236660. 104 rooms with bath. AE, DC, MC, V. Closed mid-Nov.–mid-Dec. $$$*

Milleluci. A small, cozy, family-run hotel, it is set in its own garden on the hillside overlooking Aosta, with good views of the city and mountains. It has sunny, comfortable rooms, and there's plenty of parking space. The hotel provides breakfast only, leaving guests free to sample local restaurants. Rates are low in this category. *Località Roppoz, tel. 0165/42374, fax 0165/235284. 12 rooms with bath. Facilities: bar, tennis court. AE, MC, V. $$*

Rayon du Soleil. Saraillon, a residential district in the hills above

Aosta, is the setting for this traditional redbrick mountain hotel set in a park. There are excellent views from the rooms, which are large, bright, and quiet. The hotel interior is decorated in traditional dark wood. There are rooms suitable for people with disabilities. *Saraillon 16, tel. 0165/262247, fax 0165/236085. 45 rooms with bath. Facilities: pool, garage. AE, DC, MC, V. Closed mid-Oct.–mid-Mar. $$*

Asti
Dining
★

Gener Neuv. Family-run and one of Italy's top restaurants, the Gener Neuv offers a sumptuous menu of regional specialties in a warm, welcoming atmosphere of rustic-style elegance, highlighted by excellent service, fine linen, silver, and crystal. The position in a park on the bank of the Tanaro River is splendid. Your choices, which are limited to dishes on a "small" prix-fixe menu and another "grand" and more expensive one, may include agnolotti d'anatra (with duck filling and brown sauce), roast lamb, and, for dessert, zabaglione made with sweet moscato d'Asti wine and served with almond cake. *Lungo Tanaro 4, tel. 0141/557270, fax 0141/436723. Reservations required. Dress: casual. AE, MC, V. Closed Sun. dinner, Mon., and Aug. $$$$*

Falcon Vecchio. There's been a restaurant in this ancient house in the historic center of Asti since the year 1670. Today, in intimate surroundings, the Falcon Vecchio serves rich local dishes that vary with the season. In fall and winter there are mushroom, truffle, and game dishes. Otherwise, there's a big selection of antipasti; grilled vegetables; and mixed boiled or grilled meats *(bollito misto* or *arrosto misto). Vicolo San Secondo 8, tel. 0141/593106. No reservations. Dress: casual. MC, V. Closed Sun. dinner, Mon., and Aug. $$$*

Lodging

Hasta. Close to the autostrada, this is the best choice if you are driving. It is a full-fledged modern hotel complex in a suburb of Asti, with tennis courts, a soccer field, and a garden restaurant. *Valle Benedetta 25, tel. 0141/213312, fax 0141/219580. 26 rooms with bath. Facilities: restaurant, bar, sauna. AE, DC, MC, V. $$*

Rainero. An older hotel in the town center, near the station, Rainero has been under the same family management for three generations. It's been remodeled many times and is fitted with modern furnishings. There is no restaurant. *Via Cavour 85, tel. 0141/353866, fax 0141/594985. 49 rooms with bath. AE, DC, MC, V. $–$$*

Bardonecchia
Lodging
★

Asplenia. Skiers love this small, modern version of a mountain chalet, located near the center of town and the ski lifts. The ample rooms are comfortably furnished, with a small entryway and a balcony looking out onto beautiful views. *Viale della Vittoria 31, tel. 0122/999870, fax 0122/96192. 25 rooms with bath. MC, V. Closed Easter–May, Sept.–Nov. $$*

Des Geneys-Splendid. One of the best hotels in the area, this establishment is set in a private park near the center of town. Its 1930s style is evident in the arched windows on the ground floor, the stucco walls, and the long metal-rail balconies. The public rooms are spacious and comfortable, and there's a playroom for children. *Via Einaudi 21, tel. 0122/99001, fax 0122/999295. 57 rooms with bath. Facilities: restaurant, bar, solarium. MC, V. Closed Apr. 15–June 25, mid-Sept.–mid-Dec. $$*

Riky. This centrally located modern hotel has good service; comfortable, spacious rooms; a good restaurant; and pleasant public rooms, including a children's playroom equipped with video games. There's a solarium and a piano bar with a cozy fireplace, and almost all rooms have terraces with panoramic views. Catering mainly to longer stays at half-board rates, it has excellent low-season rates (nearly half price) for people staying at least a week. *Via della Vittoria 22, tel. 0122/9353. 76 rooms with bath. Facilities: restaurant, bar, solarium. AE, DC, V. Closed Apr.–June, Sept.–Dec. 15. $$*

Breuil- **Cristallo.** An elegantly modern hotel high above town, the Cristallo
Cervinia has spectacular views. The two restaurants serve local specialties,
Lodging such as fonduta and *bistecca alla valdostana* (chops cooked with
cheese and ham). Facilities and decorations contribute to an overall
feeling of pampering and comfort. *Via Piolet 6, tel. 0166/943411, fax
0166/948377. 100 rooms with bath. Facilities: 2 restaurants, bar, fitness center, Olympic-size indoor and outdoor pools, tennis courts.
AE, DC, MC, V. Closed May–June, Sept.–Nov. $$$–$$$$*

Bucaneve. This small, centrally located hotel is decorated in typical
mountain style, with lots of wood paneling, flowers, and terraces.
Some rooms have balconies. For après-ski activities, there's a restaurant and a cozy bar with a big fireplace. The hotel caters to longer stays at half-board rates. *Tel. 0166/949119, fax 0166/948308.
28 rooms with bath. Facilities: restaurant, bar, sauna, hydromassage. AE, MC, V. Closed May–June, Sept.–Oct. $$*

Chalet Valdotain. Located about a mile outside the town on the road
from Châtillon, this Alpine chalet has wooden balconies and snug
rooms with a terrific view of the Matterhorn. It is known for good
food and its friendly atmosphere. *Località Lago Bleu, tel. 0166/
949428, fax 0166/948874. 35 rooms with bath. Facilities: restaurant,
bar, garden, garage. AE, MC, V. Closed May 1–15, Nov. $$*

Hermitage. Skiers prefer this small, rustic hotel, located outside
town near the ski lifts. There's lots of wood decoration and country
touches, including a big fireplace in the hall. Some rooms have balconies with beautiful mountain views. The restaurant serves local specialties. Like many mountain hotels, this one caters to longer stays
at half-board rates. *Strada Cristallo, tel. 0166/948998, fax 0166/
949032. 36 rooms with bath. Facilities: restaurant, bar, indoor pool,
sauna. AE, MC, V. Closed May–early July, Sept.–Oct. $$*

Dining and **Neiges D'Antan.** Located in a pine wood at Perrères, just outside
Lodging Cervinia, this small, rustic family-run inn is quiet and cozy, with
★ lots of wood decor and three big fireplaces. There are no TVs in the
rooms: "It disturbs the atmosphere," says one of the proprietors.
There's an excellent restaurant serving local specialties, such as
fonduta, *zuppa Valpulinentza* (a peasant soup of bread, cabbage,
and Fontina cheese), and polenta served with *fressa* (stuffed cabbage). *Perrères, 2 mi outside Cervinia, tel. 0166/948775, fax 0166/
948852. 28 rooms with bath. Facilities: restaurant (reservations advised), bar. V. Closed May 4–June 25, Sept. 15–Dec. 5. $$–$$$*

Courmayeur **Maison de Filippo.** Here you'll find country-style home cooking in a
Dining character-filled mountain house furnished with antiques. Reserve
in advance, for it's one of the most popular restaurants in the Valle
d'Aosta. In summer, you can eat outside, surrounded by stunning
views. There is a set menu only, featuring a daily selection of specialties, including a wide choice of antipasti and pasta dishes, such as
tortelloni alla valdostana; agnolotti in various sauces; and spaghetti
affumicata (with salami and bacon). The inn provides ample parking. *Entreves, tel. 0165/89968. Reservations required. Dress: casual. V. Closed Tues. and June 1–July 15, Nov. $$*

Lodging **Royal.** A classic mountain hotel in the center of town, the Royal is
decorated with terraces, flowers, and wood paneling. Informal but
elegant, it has modern rooms, a restaurant, and an evening piano
bar. The hotel caters to longer stays with half- or full-board service.
*Via Roma 83, tel. 0165/846787, fax 0165/842093. 93 rooms with bath.
Facilities: restaurant, bar, outdoor pool, health center with mas-*

sage, sauna, whirlpool. AE, DC, MC, V. Closed 1 week after Easter–June; mid-Sept.–mid-Dec. $$$$

Palace Bron. A posh, comfortable hotel, Palace Bron is set in a pine wood at Plan Gorret, above the town itself. There are beautiful views, and it's ideal for relaxing. The rooms are comfortably furnished with period pieces. The restaurant has a fireplace. *Plan Gorret, tel. 0165/846742, fax 0165/844015. 27 rooms with bath. AE, DC, V. Facilities: restaurant, bar, garden, parking. Closed May–June, Oct.–Nov. $$$*

Pavillon. This is a modern version of a rustic chalet, complete with wood paneling, nostalgic decoration, and friendly service. Some rooms have views of Mont Blanc. Near cableways, it attracts a lively crowd. The atmosphere and facilities are reminiscent of old-fashioned spas. The hotel offers money-saving full-board rates. *Strada Regionale 62, tel. 0165/846120, fax 0165/846122. 50 rooms with bath. Facilities: restaurant, bar, heated indoor pool, health center with massage and sauna. AE, DC, MC, V. Closed May 1–June 20, Oct. 3–Dec. 1. $$$*

Cresta et Duc. A bright, modern Alpine hotel in the center of town, the Cresta features plenty of wooden terraces, flowers, and wooden furnishings. For relaxation there's a good restaurant, bar, billiards room, and lounges. The rooms are large and warm, and the hotel offers good full- and half-board rates. *Via Circonvallazione 7, tel. 0165/842585, fax 0165/842591. 39 rooms (no singles) with bath. Facilities: restaurant, bar. AE, DC, MC, V. Closed Easter–June, mid-Sept.–Dec. 20. $$*

Croux. This bright, comfortable hotel is located near the town center on the road leading to Mont Blanc. Many rooms have balconies with great views of the town and towering Alps. There is no restaurant. *Via Circonvallazione 94, tel. 0165/846735, fax 0165/845180. 30 rooms with bath. Facilities: bar, parking. AE, DC, MC, V. Closed mid-Apr.–June, Oct. 1–Dec. 20. $$*

Novara
Lodging

Italia. This modern hotel in the center of the city features comfortable rooms and efficient service; the facilities cater mainly to businesspeople. There is a restaurant, and some rooms have extensive views of the town. *Via Solaroli 8, tel. 0321/399316, fax 0321/399310. 62 rooms with bath. Facilities: restaurant (closed Fri.), bar, sauna, solarium. AE, DC, MC, V. $$*

Saint Vincent
Dining
★

Batezar. This tiny restaurant has only eight tables. Its simple furnishings are enhanced by local antiques and fine crystal and silver place settings. Just a few steps from the casino, it is considered one of Italy's best restaurants. There's an extensive à la carte menu, changing with the season, but also recommended are the set menus: one of local specialties, the other of international gourmet treats. Try the ravioli stuffed with *caprino* (goat cheese) or *castagne* (chestnuts); *capriccio d'anatra* (boned duck with olives); or *trota* (trout) cooked with lettuce and a basil sauce with grilled radicchio. *Via Marconi 1, tel. 0166/513164. Reservations required. Jacket and tie required. AE, DC, MC, V. Closed weekday lunch, Wed., Christmas, June 1–20. $$$$*

Lodging

Billia. A luxury Belle Epoque hotel with pseudo-Gothic touches, the Billia is set in a park in the middle of town and connected directly to the casino by a passageway. Half the rooms are done in modern and half in period decor, and all creature comforts are attended to. There's a bar, three restaurants (open-air dining in summer), and a nightclub with dancing and a midnight floor show. The hotel also offers a fully equipped conference center—not to mention a private fishing reserve on a nearby mountain stream. *Viale Piemonte 18,* *tel. 0166/5231, fax 0166/523799. 250 rooms with bath. Facilities: heated outdoor pool, tennis courts, billiards, fitness center with sauna and gym. AE, DC, MC, V. $$$$*

Elena. The central location is the selling point of this hotel near the casino. The spacious rooms are decorated with color-coordinated fabrics in a comfortable modern style and have air-conditioning. *Piazza Zerbion, tel. 0166/512140, fax 0166/537459. 48 rooms with bath. Facilities: restaurant, bar. AE, DC, MC, V. Closed Nov. $-$$*

Sestriere
Lodging

Grand Sestriere. Large, elegant, and modern, the Grand Sestiere was built in 1980 near the ski lifts. Some rooms have terraces, where you can have breakfast or just a drink while soaking up the sunshine. There is a restaurant and cozy bar for après-ski relaxation. *Via Assietta 1, tel. 0122/76476, fax 0122/76700. 93 rooms with bath. AE, DC, MC, V. Closed Easter–June, Sept.–Dec. 21. $$$*

Miramonti. Nearly every room has a terrace at this pleasant, centrally located modern chalet. The ample, comfortable rooms are done in traditional mountain style, featuring lots of wood paneling and flowers. *Via Cesana 3, tel. 0122/755333, fax 0122/755333. 30 rooms with bath. Facilities: restaurant, bar. MC, V. Closed May, mid-Sept.–mid-Nov. $$*

Turin
Dining
★

Cambio. It's hard to match the setting and atmosphere of this restaurant in the heart of Turin, set in a palace that dates from 1757. It is probably one of the most beautiful and historic restaurants in Europe, with decorative mouldings and mirrors and hanging lamps that look just as they did when Italian national hero Cavour dined here a century ago. The cuisine draws heavily on Piedmontese tradition and is served with a wide choice of fine Piedmontese wines. Recommended are pastas, such as the agnolotti in an *arrosto* (roast veal) sauce, and other traditional dishes, such as veal carbonada. *Piazza Carignano 2, tel. 011/546690. Reservations required. Jacket and tie required. AE, DC, MC, V. Closed Sun. and Aug. $$$$*

Vecchia Lanterna. Sumptuously decorated with brocades, old paintings, and rich carpets, this elegant, intimate restaurant in the center of town serves classic food, made from antique regional recipes. For a first course, try *savarin di riso al Dogaressa*, a rice dish made with seafood. For a second course, *filetto di branzino al Barolo* is a surprising combination of fish and full-bodied red wine. A set menu of local fare is offered at a special price. *Corso Re Umberto 21, tel. 011/537047. Reservations required. Jacket and tie required. DC, MC, V. Closed Sat. lunch, Sun., and Aug. $$$$*

Bue Rosso. Centrally located in an old building decorated in elegant rustic style, this popular restaurant serves Italian cuisine and a few local specialties, such as agnolotti in truffle sauce and meat grilled over an open fire. There is a friendly atmosphere, and the waiters are helpful. *Corso Casale 10, tel. 011/8191393. Reservations advised. Dress: casual. AE, DC, V. Closed Mon., Sat. lunch, and Aug. $$$*

Due Lampioni. Join the stylish clientele of this elegant Baroque-style restaurant in a 17th-century palace in the heart of the city. It serves fine classic cuisine and an excellent selection of French and Italian wines. Try the agnolotti, filled with duck and cooked with tartufi bianchi; the terrine of fish; tournedos with a purée of olives; or the *carré di cervo* (roast venison). *Via Carlo Alberto 45, tel. 011/8179380. Reservations advised. Jacket and tie required. AE, MC, V. Closed Sun. and Aug. $$$*

★ **La Smarrita.** A spin-off of the restaurant now known as Prima Smarrita, La Smarrita is located off central Piazza Carlo Alberto in the palace where statesman Cavour had his offices. The new restaurant closely resembles its big sister in quality and culinary creativity (both are owned by Moreno Grossi), while offering such simple and hearty country cooking as *minestra di farro* (wheat soup) à la carte. A set menu showcases La Nuova Cucina Italiana, light Mediterranean dishes prepared with fresh herbs and little fat or oil. Try the fresh homemade pasta with a sauce of *ortiche* (nettle shoots), *tagliatelli con fagiolini e pomodori* (noodles with green beans and tomatoes), or spaghetti *alle vongole* (with clams). There is an excellent wine cellar. *Via Cesare Battisti 17, tel. 011/8177679. Reservations required. Jacket and tie required. AE, DC, MC, V. Closed Mon. and Aug. 8–22.* $$$

Da Mauro. Try the Tuscan dishes in this lively, popular family-run trattoria. Specialties include *cannelloni alla Mirella* (stuffed rolls of noodle dough baked with mozzarella cheese), prosciutto and raw tomatoes, *castellana al* prosciutto (a thin cut of veal baked with Fontina cheese and prosciutto), and famous Florentine grilled beef. *Via Maria Vittoria 21, tel. 011/8170604. No reservations. Dress: casual. No credit cards. Closed Mon. and July.* $$

Ostu Bacu. You'll find this small rustic-style restaurant on the edge of town near the autostrada that goes to Milan. It specializes in regional Piedmontese dishes, such as agnolotti and *fritto misto di carne,* a typical Piedmontese specialty of fried mixed meats. *Corso Vercelli 226, tel. 011/2464579. Reservations advised. Dress: casual. DC, MC, V. Closed Sun. and Aug.* $$

Taverna delle Rose. The cooking of the Piedmont and Veneto regions dominates in this character-filled restaurant near the train station. One dining room has walls covered with paintings; the other is done in old bricks and candlelight. Piedmontese specialties include agnolotti and *brasato* (braised veal), cooked in Barolo wine. Dishes from the Veneto include *pasta e fagioli* (pasta and bean soup) and *baccalà* (salt cod, Venice style). *Via Massena 24, tel. 011/538345. Dinner reservations advised. Dress: casual. AE, DC, MC, V. Closed Sat. lunch, Sun., and Aug.* $$

Porto di Savona. You have to look for this centuries-old tavern under the arcades of vast Piazza Vittorio Veneto, where it served as a terminal for the Turin-Savona stagecoach line. The small street-level and upstairs dining rooms have a decidedly old-fashioned air; period photos of Old Turin grace the walls. Customers sit at long wooden tables to eat home-style Piedmontese cooking, including *pasticcio* (pasta casserole) with seasonal vegetables and brasato. The owner serves a good Barbera house wine. *Piazza Vittorio Veneto 2, tel. 011/8173500. Reservations advised. Dress: casual. No credit cards. Closed Mon., Tues. lunch, and July.* $–$$

Lodging **Principi di Piemonte.** The Principi is one of the best hotels in town, with 50 years of experience. The rooms, elegantly furnished in antique style, are spacious and light, with high ceilings. It's conveniently located and popular with famous guests. *Via Gobetti 15, tel. 011/562–9693, fax 011/562–0270. 107 rooms with bath. Facilities: restaurant, bar, parking. AE, DC, MC, V.* $$$$

Turin Palace. You're right across from the train station at this century-old building in the center of town. Quiet, spacious, and well-furnished rooms have high ceilings and feature either leather-and-wood classic modern style or Imperial Louis XV furnishings. It's the classiest in town. *Via Sacchi 8, tel. 011/562–5511, fax 011/5612187. 123 rooms with bath. Facilities: restaurant, bar, garage. AE, DC, MC, V.* $$$$

Jolly Ligure. This comfortable hotel occupies a centrally located 300-year-old restored building. The rooms are large and airy, with particularly big beds (even in singles) and lots of space for clothes. The location is ideal for sightseeing or business. *Piazza Carlo Felice 85,* *tel. 011/55641, fax 011/535438. 156 rooms with bath. Facilities: restaurant, bar, parking. AE, DC, MC, V. $$$*

Genio. This 120-year-old building in the center of town has been decorated in a smart modern style. The rooms are large and bright, with big, comfortable beds. There's no restaurant, but plenty are within easy walking distance. *Corso Vittorio Emanuele 47, tel. 011/ 650–5771, fax 011/6508264. 75 rooms with bath. Facilities: bar, parking. AE, DC, MC, V. $$*

Victoria. This is a centrally located, modern hotel. Most of the rooms are decorated in classic style with personalized touches. Room 316 has an Indian motif; 310, Old England; 206, Arabian; and so on. Some rooms have canopied beds and 15 rooms on the top floor have terraces. *Via Nino Costa 4, tel. 011/561–1909, fax 011/5611806. 90 rooms with bath. Facilities: bar. AE, DC, MC, V. $$*

Liberty. Liberty is the Italian term for the Art Nouveau style, and this small, conveniently located hotel maintains that style in turn-of-the-century furnishings and an Old World atmosphere, enhanced by the Anfossi family's attentive courtesy. The hotel is a favorite of academics, artists, and others who appreciate its solid, old-fashioned comfort. *Via Pietro Micca 15, tel. 011/5628801, fax 011/ 5628163. 34 rooms with bath. AE, DC, MC, V. $–$$*

The Arts and Nightlife

The Arts

Turin, and to a lesser extent, Aosta, dominates the world of the arts in this northwest corner of Italy. Music is especially popular among the population as a whole, with entire towns and villages flocking enthusiastically to concerts, recitals, and special exhibitions. In the Valle d'Aosta, you can hear French folk songs in Alpine surroundings, while Piedmont itself (and especially Turin) is on the Genoa–Milan concert circuit. The best source of information is Turin's daily paper, *La Stampa*.

Music **Aosta.** Each summer there is a series of concerts held in different venues around the city. Organ recitals in July and August attract performers of world renown.

Asti. September is a month of fairs and celebrations in this famous wine city, and the Asti Competition in the middle of the month brings musicians, who perform in churches and concert halls. For information, contact the tourist information office (Piazza Alfieri 34, tel. 0141/530357).

Turin. Classical music concerts are held in the famous **Conservatorio Giuseppe Verdi** (Via Mazzini 11) throughout the year, but mainly in the winter months. Sacred music and some modern religious pieces are performed in the **Duomo** on Sunday evening; these are usually advertised in the vestibule or in *La Stampa*.

Opera **Turin.** The **Teatro Regio** (tel. 011/8815241, fax 011/8815214), one of Italy's leading opera houses, begins its season in December. You can buy tickets for most performances (premieres are sold out well in advance) at the box office facing Piazza Castello.

Nightlife

As is the case with the arts, Turin is the major center for after-hours entertainment, although it has some competition from the swanky ski resorts of Courmayeur and Breuil-Cervinia. Elsewhere in Piedmont and Valle d'Aosta you'll find it best to limit yourself to sipping an after-dinner drink in a café on a busy city square or joining in the sometimes-boisterous song-fests in the mountain hotel bars.

Casino **Saint Vincent.** The Casino de la Vallée, Europe's largest gambling house, operates in this spa resort near Châtillon in the Valle d'Aosta. Remember to pack your black tie—and a lot of lire.

Bars **Breuil-Cervinia.** Go to the bar of the hotel **Bucaneve** (*see* Dining and Lodging, *above*) for après-ski atmosphere, with a blazing fire and wood paneling.

Courmayeur. There is a hushed, sophisticated feeling about the piano bar of the **Royal** hotel (*see* Dining and Lodging, *above*), in the center of town.

Nightclub **Saint Vincent.** There is a nightly floor show at midnight and a lively nightclub at the **Billia Hotel** (*see* Dining and Lodging, *above*).

Discos The large hotels of Breuil-Cervinia, Courmayeur, and Saint Vincent all have discos catering to the young, fashionable crowd that comes to these posh resorts. The names of the individual discos change as often as the latest music craze, but all of them have a cover charge (sometimes including the first drink) and a dress code that is best described as neat but eccentric.

Turin. Two good spots for unwinding to the rhythm of a disco beat are **Pick Up** (Via Barge 8) and **Patio** (Corso Moncalieri 346/14). Both are open late and cater to a mixed crowd of young Turinese, university students, and visitors.

10 Milan, Lombardy, and the Lakes

One is tempted to describe Lombardy as a place with something for everyone—Milan, capital of all that is new in Italy; the great Renaissance cities of the plain, Pavia, Cremona, and Mantua, where even the height of summer can be comparatively peaceful; and the Lakes, where glacial waters framed by the Alps have been praised by writers as varied as Virgil, Tennyson, and Hemingway.

The truth, of course, is more complicated. Milan can be disappointingly modern—rather too like the place you have come here to escape—but it is also the perfect blend of old and new, with historic buildings and art collections rivaling those in Florence and Rome. The Lakes, home to dozens of fashionable resorts, have preserved an astonishingly unspoiled beauty, often enhanced by sumptuous summer palaces and exotic formal gardens. Still, one cannot imagine Catullus returning to his "jewel" Sirmione, on Lake Garda, without being a little daunted by its development as a lively resort town. The great towns of the Lombardy plain are rich in history, but their art and architecture pale before the staggering wealth of Rome, Florence, and Venice.

More than 3,000 years ago—the date and the details are lost in the mysteries of Etruscan inscriptions—explorers from the highly civilized realm of Etruria in central Italy wandered northward beyond the river Po. The Etruscans extended their dominance into this region for hundreds of years but left little of their culture. They were succeeded by the Cenomanic Gauls, who, in turn, were conquered by the legions of Rome in the latter days of the Republic.

The region became known as Cisalpine Gaul, and under the rule of Augustus it became a Roman province. Its warlike, independent people became citizens of Rome. Virgil, Catullus, and both the Plinys were born in the region during this relatively tranquil era.

The decline of the Roman Empire was followed by the invasions of the Huns and the Goths. Attila and Theodoric, in turn, gave way to the Lombards, who ceded their iron crown to Charlemagne as the emblem of his vast but unstable empire.

Even before the fragile bonds that held this empire together had begun to snap, the cities of Lombardy were erecting walls in defense against the Hungarians and against each other. These communes did, however, form the Lombard League, which, in the 12th century, finally defeated Frederick Barbarossa.

Once the invaders had been defeated, new and even more bloody strife began. In each city the Guelphs (bourgeois supporters of the popes) and the Ghibellines (noble adherents to the so-called emperors) clashed with each other. The communes declined, and each fell under the yoke of powerful local rulers. The Republic of Venice dominated Brescia and Bergamo. Mantua was ruled by the Gonzaga, and the Visconti and Sforza families took over Como, Cremona, Milan, and Pavia.

The Battle of Pavia in 1525, when the generals of Charles V defeated the French (and gave Francis I the chance to coin the famous phrase "All is lost save honor"), brought on 200 years of Spanish occupation. The Spaniards were, on the whole, less cruel than the local tyrants and were hardly resisted by the Lombards.

The War of the Spanish Succession, in the early years of the 18th century, threw out the Spaniards and brought in, instead, the Austrians, whose dominion was "neither liked or loathed" during the nearly 100 years of its existence.

Napoleon and his generals routed the Austrians. The Treaty of Campoformio resulted in the proclamation of the Cisalpine Republic, which quickly became the Republic of Italy and, just as rapidly, the Kingdom of Italy, which lasted only until Napoleon's defeat brought back the Austrians. But Milan, as the capital of Napoleon's republic and of the Kingdom of Italy, had had a taste of glory, and the city's inherently independent citizens, along with those of the other Lombardian cities, were not slow to resent and combat the loss of "national" pride.

From 1820 on, the Lombards joined the Piedmontese and the House of Savoy in a long struggle against the Hapsburgs and, in 1859, finally defeated Austria and brought about the re-creation of the Kingdom of Italy two years later.

Milan and other cities of Lombardy have not lost their independence and their hatred of domination. Nowhere in Italy was the partisan insurrection against Mussolini (to whom they first gave power) and the German regime better organized or more successful. Milan was liberated from the Germans by its own partisan organization before the entrance of Allied troops; escaping Allied prisoners could find sanctuary there when fighting was still going on far to the south.

Lombards are a forthright people. They are as much inclined to taciturnity as any Italian is ever apt to be, and, when they do talk, they mean exactly what they say. When they quote a price, there is little use haggling about it. A Milanese is inclined to be courteous, but probably has little time for pleasantries; his or her compatriot on the rice farm or in the mountains may be less talkative, but may take more interest in you as an individual.

Our three Lombardy tours—of Milan, the cities of the plain, and the lakes—are arranged as a circuit, running counterclockwise, starting and finishing in Milan. Even without a car, it should be possible to complete all three tours in a hard-paced week. A sensible alternative would be to use Milan as a base and to approach any of our tours' single destinations as a day's or weekend's excursion.

Essential Information

Important Addresses and Numbers

Tourist Information

Bellagio (Piazza della Chiesa 14, tel. 031/950204).
Bergamo (Vicolo Aquila Nera, at Piazza Vecchia, tel. 035/232730); in lower Bergamo, Viale Papa Giovanni 106, tel. 035/242226).
Brescia (Corso Zanardelli 34, tel. 030/43418).
Como (Piazza Cavour 16, tel. 031/274064; Train station, tel. 031/267214; Provincial Tourist Board; Via Borgovico 148, tel. 031/230329).
Cremona (Piazza del Comune 8, tel. 0372/23233).
Desenzano del Garda (Via Porto Vecchio, tel. 030/914–1510).
Malcesine (Via Capitanato del Porto 6, tel. 045/740–0055).
Mantua (Piazza A. Mantegna 6, tel. 0376/350681).
Milan (Via Marconi 1, tel. 02/809662; Stazione Centrale, tel. 02/669–0432).
Pavia (Via Fabio Filzi 2, tel. 0382/22156).
Riva del Garda (Giardini di Porta Orientale 8, tel. 0464/554444).
Sabbioneta (tel. 0375/52039).
Sirmione (Viale Marconi 2, tel. 030/916245).
Stresa (Via Principe Tomaso 70, tel. 0323/30150).

Consulates Most nations maintain consulates in Milan. **Canada** (Via Pisani 19, tel. 02/669–7451); **United Kingdom** (Via San Paolo 7, tel. 02/723001); **United States** (Via Principe Amedeo 2, tel. 02/290351); **Australia** (Via Borgogna 2, tel. 02/7601–3330).

Emergencies **Como: Police,** tel. 031/272366; **Medical Emergency,** tel. 031/113.
Cremona: Police, tel. 0372/2333; **Medical Emergency,** tel. 0372/4051.
Desenzano del Garda: Police, tel. 030/113; **Medical Emergency,** tel. 030/914–4761.
Malcesine: Police, tel. 0464/552326; **Medical Emergency,** tel. 0464/554004.
Mantua: Police, tel. 0376/326341; **Medical Emergency,** tel. 0376/329261.
Milan: Police, tel. 02/113; **Carabinieri,** tel. 02/112; **Ambulance,** tel. 02/7733; **Medical Emergency,** Fatebenefratelli Hospital, Corso di Porta Nuova 23, tel. 02/63631.
Pavia: Police, tel. 0382/301204; **Medical Emergency,** tel. 0382/3901.
Sirmione: Police, tel. 0365/20179; **Medical Emergency,** tel. 0365/40361.

Late-Night Pharmacies The pharmacy on the upper level of Milan Central Station is open 24 hours. Others take turns staying open late and on weekends; call 02/192 for the location of the nearest one, or check the roster published in the *Corriere della Sera.*

English-Language Bookstores In **Milan: The American Bookshop** (Largo Cairoli at Via Camperio, tel. 02/7202–0030), **The English Bookshop** (Via Mascheroni 12, tel. 02/469–4468), **Feltrinelli Bookstore** (Via Manzoni 12, tel. 02/7600–0386).

Travel Agencies In **Milan: Compagnia Italiana Turismo** (CIT) (Galleria Vittorio Emanuele, tel. 02/866661), **American Express Travel Agency** (Via Brera 3, tel. 02/809645), **Chiariva** (Largo Domodossola 1, tel. 02/481–8366).

Arriving and Departing by Plane

Milan has two principal airports. **Malpensa,** located about 50 kilometers (31 miles) northwest of the city, handles all intercontinental air traffic, and **Linate,** located less than 10 kilometers (6 miles) east of the city, handles international and domestic air traffic. For air traffic information for both airports, call 02/74852200. Air Pullman buses run twice daily in the morning between Malpensa and Linate airports. The fare is 18,000 lire, and the trip takes about 75 minutes.

Between the Airports and Downtown *From Malpensa* **By Car:** Take Route S336 east to the A8 autostrada southeast toward Milan. The drive takes about 40 minutes, depending on traffic and destination. **By Taxi:** A taxi stand is located directly outside the arrivals building doors. Approximate fare is 110,000 lire. **By Bus:** There is bus service to Milan's Central Station. Buses usually leave every half-hour between 8:15 AM and 11:15 PM. Cost is 12,000 lire. The trip takes about one hour. Buy your ticket inside before embarking.

From Linate **By Car:** Take what was once the Old Brescia Road west into the central downtown area. **By Taxi:** A taxi stand is directly in front of the arrivals building. Approximate fare is 25,000 lire. The duration of the journey is less than 20 minutes. **By Bus:** Buses leave every 20 minutes for Milan's Central Station. The trip takes about 20 minutes. Cost is 4,000 lire. You can also take ATM municipal Bus 73 to Piazza San Babila (every 15 minutes). Cost is 1,200 lire.

Arriving and Departing by Car, Train, and Bus

By Car Two major autostrada routes cross at Milan: the A1, which leads south to Bologna, Florence, and Rome, and the A4, which runs west–east from Turin to Venice. A7 angles southwest down to Genoa from Milan. The city is ringed by a bypass road (the Tangenziale).

By Train Although Milan claims a bewildering number of railway stations, only one is of concern, unless you travel on local routes at peculiar hours—in which case service can begin or terminate in suburban stations (most notably Milano Lambrate for Bergamo, and Stazione Nord for Como). **Milano Centrale** (a bombastic neo-Babylonian creation, from what is now politely termed the era of "rational" architecture) has, since opening in 1931, been Milan's main railway station. Premium international (EC) service and premium (IC) domestic service connect Milan with major European cities. The station is located northeast of the historic center, about 5 kilometers (3 miles) from the Duomo and Galleria. Metro line 3 links it with Piazza de Duomo. For train information, call 02/67500.

By Bus Italian bus service is best avoided on intercity routes, since it is neither faster, cheaper, nor more convenient than the railways. Most bus companies use Piazza Castello as a terminus, because Milan has no central bus terminal. For bus information, call Autostradale (tel. 02/801161) or Zani Viaggi (tel. 02/867131).

Getting Around

By Car The A4 autostrada is the main east–west highway for this region, with various other major highways—A8 from the northwest, A7 from the southwest, A1 from the southeast—converging at Milan. A21 runs roughly parallel to the A4 until it curves north through Cremona and Brescia to feed into the A4. The A22 is a major north–south highway running just east of Lake Garda. Although these major highways will allow you to make good time between the cities of the plain, you'll have to follow secondary roads—often of great beauty—around the lakes. S572 goes along the southern and western shores of Lake Garda, S45bis along the northernmost section of the western shore, and S249 along the eastern shore. Around Lake Como, follow S340 along the western shore, S36 on the eastern coast, and S583 on the lower arms. S33 and S34 trace the western shore of Lake Maggiore.

Car rental agencies in Milan include **Avis** (tel. 02/668–00681), **Hertz** (tel. 02/20483), **Europcar** (tel. toll-free 1678/68088), or **Budget** (tel. 02/670–3151), or try "Autonoleggio" in the Yellow Pages. The major international companies have offices at both airports.

By Train From Milan, there is frequent direct service to Cremona, Bergamo, Pavia, Brescia, Mantua, Desenzano del Garda–Sirmione, and Como.

By Bus Trains are generally better than buses for getting around the cities of the plain. There is regular bus service between the small towns on the lakes, and it tends to be a cheaper way of getting around than ferry or hydrofoil service. The bus service around Lake Garda serves mostly towns on the western coast.

By Boat There is frequent daily ferry and hydrofoil service between towns on the lakes, and a range of round-trip excursions, with a dining service (optional) aboard. For all lakes call **Navigazione Laghi** (Via Ariosto 21, Mílan, tel. 02/481–2086. Locally, call **Navigazione Lago di Garda** (tel. 030/914–1321) for Lake Garda, **Navigazione Lago di Como** (Piazza Cavour, Como, tel. 031/304060) for Lake Como, and **Navigazione Lago Maggiore** (Piazza Matteotti, Stresa, tel. 0323/30393) for Lake Maggiore. In addition, lake tours can often be arranged by private launches at lakeside hotels.

Milan

Milan's history as a capital city goes back at least 2,500 years. Its fortunes ever since, both as a great commercial trading center and as the object of regular conquest and occupation, are readily explained by its strategic position at the center of the Lombard plain. Directly south of the central passes across the Alps, Milan is bordered by three highly navigable rivers—the Po, the Ticino, and the Adda—which for centuries were the main arteries of an ingenious network of canals crisscrossing all Lombardy (and ultimately reaching most of northern Italy).

Virtually every invader in European history—Gaul, Roman, Goth, Longobard, and Frank—as well as every ruler of France, Spain, and Austria, has taken a turn at ruling the city and the region. Milan's glorious heyday of self-rule proved comparatively brief, from 1277 until 1500, when it was ruled by its two great family dynasties, the Visconti and subsequently the Sforza. These families were known, justly or not, for a peculiarly aristocratic mixture of refinement, classical learning, and cruelty, and much of the surviving grandeur of Gothic and Renaissance art and architecture is their doing. Be on the lookout in your wanderings for the Visconti family emblem—a viper, its jaws straining wide, devouring a child.

If you are wondering why so little seems to have survived from Milan's antiquity, the answer is simple—war. Three times in the city's history, partial or total destruction has followed conflict—in AD 539, 1157, and 1944.

Getting Around
By Car Serious pollution is responsible for a rigorously enforced effort to ban all unnecessary traffic from the city's center. Cars lacking a special resident's permit will be stopped and ticketed. Parked cars may be towed. For taxi service, call 02/6767, 02/8585, or 02/8388. For limousine service, call 02/2940–0555. If age or infirmity entitle you to special dispensation, and both taxis and other forms of cars with drivers are unsuitable for your needs, inquire of your rental agency or hotel concierge about car permits for special cases.

By Public Transport Milan has an excellent system of public transport, consisting of trolley cars, buses, and a subway system, the Metropolitana, which runs on three lines. Tickets for each must be purchased before you board and must be canceled by machines located at underground station entrances and mounted on poles inside trolleys and buses. Tickets cost 1,200 lire and can be purchased from news vendors, tobacconists, and machines at larger stops. Buy several at once—they remain valid until canceled. One ticket is valid for 75 minutes on all surface lines, or for one subway trip. A 24-hour ticket valid on all public transport lines costs 3,800 lire, and one ticket valid for 48 hours costs 6,600 lire; they are sold at Duomo Metro and Stazione Centrale Metro stations.

By Bicycle As part of its campaign to ban cars from Milan's center, the city government has begun to set up a network of one-way bicycle rental stations. At first, rentals were free; now there is a small charge. Though the bicycles are clearly intended for residents who would otherwise use cars, current opinion is that tourists may use them, too (though doubtless individual proprietors of stands may arbitrarily decide to disagree, especially if you are unable to explain your rights in Italian). Look for yellow stands filled with yellow bicycles.

By Taxi Taxi fares seem expensive compared with those in American cities, but drivers are honest (to an extreme, compared with some cities). A short downtown hop averages 8,000 lire. Taxis wait at stands or can be called (tel. 02/6767, 8585, or 8388).

Museumcard The **Museumcard** is valid for six months and entitles the bearer to admission to 20 Milan museums, including the Brera, the Duomo Museum, and the Refectory of Santa Maria delle Grazie (home of the *Last Supper*). The card costs 37,000 lire and is available at Milan APT offices, museum ticket offices, and major travel agencies.

Highlights for First-Time Visitors

Pinacoteca di Brera

Duomo

Santa Maria delle Grazie (for the *Last Supper*)

Galleria Vittorio Emanuele

Exploring Milan

Numbers in the margin correspond to points of interest on the Milan map.

❶❷ There's only one logical place to begin a walking tour of **Milan**—the **Duomo** (Cathedral), which has been fascinating and exasperating visitors and conquerors alike since it was begun by Galeazzo Visconti III, first duke of Milan, in 1386. Consecrated in 1577, and not wholly completed until 1897, it is the third-largest church in the world and the largest Gothic building in Italy.

Whether you concur with travel writer H. V. Morton, writing 25 years ago, that the cathedral is "one of the mightiest Gothic buildings ever created," or regard it as a spiny pastiche of centuries, there is no denying that for sheer size and complexity it is unequaled. Its capacity—though it is hard to imagine the church filled—is reckoned to be 40,000. Usually it is empty, a perfect sanctuary from the frenetic pace of life outside and the perfect place for solitary contemplation. The poet Shelley swore by it—claiming it was the only place to read Dante.

The building is adorned with 135 marble spires and 2,245 marble statues. The oldest part is the apse (the end of the cruciform opposite the portals). Its three colossal bays of curving and counter-curved tracery, especially the bay adorning the exterior of the stained-glass windows, should not be missed.

Step inside and walk down the right aisle to the southern transept, to the tomb of Gian Giacomo Medici. The tomb owes something to Michelangelo, but is generally considered its sculptor's (Leone Leoni's) masterpiece; it dates from the 1560s.

Directly ahead is the Duomo's most famous sculpture, the rather gruesome but anatomically instructive figure of St. Bartholomew, whose glorious martyrdom consisted of being flayed alive. It is usually said the saint stands "holding" his skin, but this is not quite accurate. It would appear more that he is luxuriating in it, much as a 1950s matron might show off a new fur stole.

As you enter the apse to admire those splendid windows, glance at the sacristy doors to the right and left of the altar. The lunette on the right dates from 1393 and was decorated by Hans von Fernach. That on the left also dates from the 14th century and is ascribed jointly to Giacomo da Campione and Giovanni dei Grassi.

Don't miss the view from the Duomo's roof: Walk outside the left (north) transept to the stairs and elevator. Sad to say, late–20th-century air pollution has, on all but the rarest days, drastically reduced the view. But even in fog, the roof itself has a fairy-tale quality. As you stand among the forest of marble pinnacles, remember that virtually every inch of this gargantuan edifice, including the roof itself, is decorated with precious white marble. *Admission: 4,000 lire for stairs, 6,000 lire for elevator.*

Should you wish to learn more about the cathedral's history and see some of the treasures removed for safety from the exterior, visit the **Duomo Museum.** *Museo del Duomo, Piazza del Duomo 14B, tel. 02/860358. Admission: 7,000 lire. Open Tues.–Sun. 9:30–12:30, 3–6.*

The subterranean ruins of a 4th-century **baptistery** are located beneath the Duomo's piazza. Though opinion remains divided, it is widely believed that this may have been where Ambrose (Milan's first bishop and patron saint) baptized Augustine. *Battistero Paleocristiano. Access through the cathedral. Admission free. Open Tues.–Sun. 10–noon, 3–5.*

Time Out The best alternative to a conventional restaurant is **Peck,** one of Italy's, if not the world's, most irresistible food emporiums. In the Duomo area, it is something better than a shop—it's six shops. Best for a quick stand-up lunch is **Bottega del Vino** (Via Victor Hugo 4, tel. 02/861040), which offers almost 200 wines by the glass. **Peck Rosticceria** (Via Cantù 3, tel. 02/869–3017, closed Mon.) offers grilled takeout; for a more relaxed lunch, try **Il Restaurant** (Via Victor Hugo 4, tel. 02/876774, closed Sun. and 2 weeks in Jan.); for do-it-yourself, try the **Delicatessen** (Via Spadari 9, tel. 02/8646–1158).

❸ The great glass-topped, barrel-vaulted tunnel just beyond the northern tip of the cathedral's facade is the **Galleria Vittorio Emanuele.** Anyone who has grown up on the periphery of a contemporary American city should recognize this spectacularly extravagant late–19th-century creation for what it is—one of the planet's earliest and most elegant shopping malls, rivaled perhaps only by G.U.M., off Red Square in Moscow, for sheer Belle Epoque splendor. Its architect, Giuseppe Mengoni, accidently lost his footing and tumbled to his death on the floor of his own creation, just days before its opening.

Like its suburban American cousins, the Galleria fulfills a variety of social functions vastly more important than its ostensible commercial purpose. If you had only a half hour to spend in Milan, this would be the place to spend it. This is the city's heart, midway between the cathedral and La Scala opera house, and it is sometimes called *Il Salotto* (The Living Room). For all but a few hours of the week, it positively teems with life. If you're a bit weary from your exploration of the Duomo, stop here to enjoy that most delightful of spectator sports—people watching. Pull up a chair at one of the strategically situated tables that spill from the Galleria's bars and restaurants, and prepare to enjoy one of those monstrously surcharged coffees that are the modest price of a front-row seat at one of the best shows in Italy.

Like the cathedral, the Galleria is cruciform in shape. The space at the crossing, however, forms an octagon. If this is where you're standing, don't be afraid to look up and gawk. Even in poor weather, the great glass dome makes a splendid sight. And the mosaics, usually unnoticed, are a vastly underrated source of pleasure, even if they are not to be taken too seriously. They represent Europe, Asia, Africa, and America; those at the entrance arch are devoted to science, industry, art, and agriculture.

Books, clothing, food, wine, pens, jewelry, and myriad other goods are all for sale in the Galleria, and one of Milan's most correct and traditional restaurants, Savini, is located here. There is, in addition, one of those curious Italian institutions, an *albergo diurno* (daytime hotel), where you can take an hour's nap or a bath, get a haircut or a pedicure, and have your suit pressed or a button replaced. Most of its patrons are Italian, but it is hard to think of a better oasis for a vacationer who's worn out from sightseeing.

Continue across the transepts of the Galleria and head north into Piazza della Scala, home of the Teatro alla Scala, or **La Scala,** where Verdi's fame was established. It was completely renovated after its destruction by Allied bombs in 1943 and reopened at a performance led by Arturo Toscanini in 1946.

You need know nothing of opera to sense that, like Carnegie Hall, La Scala is something rather more than an auditorium. It looms as a symbol—both for the performer dreaming one day of singing here and for the buff who knows every note of *Rigoletto* by heart. For some, a visit to La Scala will be—even more than the Duomo—a solemn but pleasurable act of pilgrimage.

If you are lucky enough to be here during the opera season, which runs for approximately six months beginning each December 7, St. Ambrose Day, do whatever is necessary to attend—even if it requires perching among the rafters in one of the dreaded gallery seats. Hearing a Verdi or Puccini opera sung in Italian by Italians in Italy is a magical experience. For now, whet your appetite with a quick stroll through the theater's small museum, **Museo Teatrale alla Scala.** The visit allows you a peek at the gilded grandeur of the boxes. *Tel. 02/805-3418. Admission: 5,000 lire. Open year-round, Mon.–Sat. 9–noon, 2–6, plus May–Oct., Sun. 9:30–noon. Closed occasionally during rehearsals.*

At the northern end of Piazza della Scala, Via Manzoni leads straight into the heart of Milan's most luxurious shopping district, perhaps the most luxurious shopping district in all of Italy. Right here, in a few small streets laid out like a game of hopscotch—Via Monte Napoleone, Via Sant'Andrea, Via della Spiga—lie the shops of the great Italian designers, such as Armani, Versace, and Gianfranco Ferre. Don't come here looking for affordable fashion—that has been relegated to the other side of the Duomo—but even though the prices are high, it costs nothing to stroll around and drink in the distinctive look and style that makes shopping in Milan special. Milan's fortissimo occurs twice a year, in March and October (for women) and June and January (for men), when the world's fashion elite descends upon the city for the famous ready-to-wear designer shows that invariably set next season's styles around the globe.

At the northern end of Via Manzoni, you'll reach the **Giardini Pubblici,** a good park for young children. On the eastern side of the park, facing Corso Venezia, is the **Civico Museo di Storia Naturale,** with exhibits that appeal to animal and nature lovers. *Corso Venezia 55, tel. 02/6208–5407. Admission free. Open Tues.–Sun. 9:30–5:30.*

From the southwestern corner of the park, follow Via Fatebene-fratelli and then Via Pontaccio to Via Brera, where you'll find the **Pinacoteca di Brera,** on the right at No. 28. The picture collection here is star studded, even by Italian standards. As everyone knows, the only way to "do" a large collection is to start with the best, while you're still fresh, eager, and observant, and leave the charming minor masterpieces for afterward. We suggest you begin by ignoring the 20th-century work displayed along the long entrance corridor and walk to the large, well-patrolled room (No. 22) with only two big paintings, both behind glass.

Note that Raphael painted *Betrothal of the Virgin* when he was 22, a time when many of us are still struggling with the question of what to do in life. The other painting, Piero della Francesca's *Madonna with Saints and Angels,* is just as lovely, much aided by its recent and skillful restoration and cleaning.

The gallery's best-known painting is probably the somber, beautiful, and moving *Dead Christ* by Mantegna, in Room 18. Though it is by far the smallest painting in the room, it dominates, with its sparse palette of gray and terra-cotta. Mantegna's shocking, almost surgical, precision in the rendering of Christ's wounds, the face propped up on a pillow, the day's growth of beard—tells of an all-too-human agony. It is one of Renaissance painting's most quietly wondrous achievements, finding an unsuspected middle ground between the excesses of conventional gore or beauty in representing the Passion's saddest moment.

On your way out, pause a moment to view the fine paintings by Carlo Carrà (especially *La Musa Metafisica,* or *Metaphysical Muse*), suggesting Italy's confident and stylish response to the likes of Picasso and Max Ernst and to the schools of Cubism and Surrealism. *Tel. 02/864–63501 Admission: 8,000 lire. Open Tues.–Sat. 9–5:30, Sun. 9–12:30.*

Take time to wander around the lively quarter surrounding the Pinacoteca di Brera. The narrow streets, lined by boutiques, craft shops, cafés, restaurants, and music clubs, comprise what is often referred to as Milan's Greenwich Village. Longtime haunt of artists and musicians, it has a number of clubs and cafés offering live music until late at night.

The **Castello Sforzesco,** a little more than two blocks west, along Via Pontaccio, is the next stop. For the serious student of Renaissance military engineering, the imposing Castello must be something of a travesty, so often has it been remodeled or rebuilt since it was begun in 1450 by the condottiere who founded the city's second dynastic family, Francesco Sforza, fourth duke of Milan. As for the rest of us, children of all ages, it's clearly everything a storybook castle ought to be—huge, for one. It is also just across the road from what is claimed to be the best gelateria or ice cream shop, in all northern Italy: **Viel** (Largo Cairoli) is at the right of the intersection in front of the Castello's southeast face.

Though today the word "mercenary" has a strongly pejorative ring, during the Renaissance all Italy's great soldier-heroes were professionals hired by the cities and principalities that they served. Of them—and there were thousands—Francesco Sforza is considered to have been one of the greatest and most honest. It is said he could remember not only the names of all his men, but of their horses. And it is with his era, and the building of the Castello, that we know we have entered the enlightened age of the Renaissance. It took barely half a century before it and the city were under foreign rule.

Today, the Castello houses municipal museums devoted variously to Egyptian and other antiquities, musical instruments, paintings, and sculpture. Highlights are the Salle delle Asse, a frescoed room still sometimes attributed to Leonardo da Vinci, and Michelangelo's unfinished *Rondanini Pietà*, believed to be his last work: an astounding achievement for a man nearly 90, but a sad memorial to genius at the end. *Piazza Castello, tel. 02/6208–3940. Admission free. Open Tues.–Sun. 9:30–5:30.*

H.V. Morton noted that Milan might well be the only city on earth where you could give a taxi driver the title of a painting as your destination. If this appeals to you, flag one down and say, "*L'Ultima Cena*, per favore," since this is how the *Last Supper* is known here. If not, you can walk to the church and former Dominican monastery **❽** of **Santa Maria delle Grazie**, and the **Cenacolo Vinciano,** which used to be the order's refectory. It is a few blocks southwest of the Castello, on Corso Magenta.

The *Last Supper* has had an almost unbelievable history of bad luck and neglect—its near destruction in an American bombing raid in August 1943 was only the latest chapter in a series of misadventures, including, if one 19th-century source is to be believed, being whitewashed by the monks. Well-meant but disastrous attempts at restoration have done little to rectify the problem of the work's placement: It is situated on a wall unusually vulnerable to climatic dampness. Yet the artist chose to work slowly and patiently in oil pigments—which demand dry plaster—instead of proceeding hastily on wet plaster according to the conventional fresco technique. Aldous Huxley called it "the saddest work of art in the world." After years beneath a scaffold, with restorers patiently shifted from one square centimeter to another, Leonardo's famous masterpiece still is in a sad state, and studies in further methods to preserve this great fresco continue.

Despite Leonardo's carefully preserved preparatory sketches, in which the apostles are clearly labeled by name, there still remains some small debate about a few identities in the final arrangement. But there can be no mistaking Judas, small and dark, his hand calmly reaching forward toward the bread, isolated from the terrible confusion that has taken the hearts of the others. One critic, Professor Frederick Hartt, offers an elegantly terse explanation for why the composition works: It combines "dramatic confusion" with "mathematical order." Certainly, the amazingly skillful and unobtrusive repetition of threes, when first you see it—in the windows, in the grouping of the figures, and in their placement—adds a mystical aspect to what at first seems simply the perfect observation of spontaneous human gesture. *Cenacolo Vinciano, tel. 02/498–7588. Admission: 6,000 lire. Open Tues.–Sun. 8:15–1:15, but hours may vary.*

Take at least a moment to visit Santa Maria delle Grazie itself. It's a handsome church, with a fine dome by Bramante, which was added along with a cloister about the time that Leonardo was commissioned to paint the *Last Supper*. If you're wondering how it was that two such giants came to be employed decorating and remodeling the refectory and church of a comparatively modest religious order, and not, say, the Duomo, the answer lies in the ambitious but largely unrealized plan to turn Santa Maria delle Grazie into a magnificent

Sforza family mausoleum. Though Ludovico il Moro Sforza, seventh duke of Milan, was but one generation away from the founding of the Sforza dynasty, he was its last ruler. Two years after Leonardo finished the *Last Supper*, Ludovico was defeated and was imprisoned in a French dungeon for the remaining eight years of his life.

Time Out For those who don't scream for ice cream, a venerable neighborhood institution, the **Bar Magenta** (Via Carducci 13 at Corso Magenta) provides an excellent alternative en route. Luncheon, beer, or coffee provides only an excuse for coming here; the real attraction is its casual but civilized, quintessentially Milanese ambience.

Go east on Corso Magenta, across Via Carducci, to visit the city's **❾ Museo Archeologico.** Housed in a former monastery, there are some enlightening relics from Milan's Roman past here, from everyday utensils and jewelry to several fine examples of mosaic pavement. *Corso Magenta 15. tel. 02/8645–0011. Admission free. Open Tues.– Sun. 9:30–5:30.*

Next to the Museo Archeologico, Via Sant'Agnese leads to the church of **Sant'Ambrogio.** Across from the church's main doors, turn **❿** left on Via San Vittore to see the **Museo Nazionale della Scienza e della Tecnica,** which has models based on technical projects by Leonardo da Vinci and collections of locomotives, planes, and cars. *Via San Vittore 21, near Sant'Ambrogio, tel. 02/4801–0040. Admission: 8,000 lire. Open Tues.–Sun. 9:30–4:50.*

If you have time, walk back to Via Carducci, which becomes Via Edmondo de Amicis, and follow it southeast until you can turn right onto Corso Porta Ticinese, which ends at the impressive early 19th- **⓫** century arch of Porta Ticinese. Beyond lies the picturesque **Navigli district** in the southern part of the city. In medieval times a network of navigable canals, called *navigli*, crisscrossed Milan. Almost all have been covered over, except for two long canals, Naviglio Grande and Naviglio Pavese, and part of a third, Darsena. The canals are lined by quaint shops, art galleries, cafés, pubs, restaurants, and clubs. Much of Milan's nightlife is centered here, and the neighborhood has a romantic, bohemian atmosphere.

Shopping

Always beautiful, impeccably groomed, wrapped in fur and glittering jewels, the Milanese lady, the *gran signora*, is possessed of an understated elegance unequaled anywhere in the world.

Her habitat is **Via Monte Napoleone,** where she can be found lining up for fresh pasta and quail eggs in aspic at Il Salumaio (just a few steps from the spot where Verdi wrote his opera *Nabucco*), sipping cappuccino around the pink-lace-covered tables of the Bar Cova, or dropping into **Ars Rosa** for an embroidered silk-satin nightdress or a hand-smocked dress for her little girl. Via Monte Napoleone has 10 top-notch jewelers and a profusion of antique stores and designer fashion boutiques, as well. It's also prime shopping territory for shoes—all beautifully made, classic, fashionable, and expensive. Within a few steps of one another, you'll find **Ferragamo** at No. 3; **Lario 1898** at No. 21; **Fratelli Rossetti** at the corner of Corso Matteotti; and **Beltrami** at Piazza San Babila 4/a.

Her tailored suit may come from **Giorgio Armani,** just a few steps away on **Via Sant'Andrea,** or from **Gianni Versace,** on Via Montenapoleone, or **Gianfranco Ferre,** also on Via Sant'Andrea, where **Moschino** offers more unconventional styles. For amusing items for her house, there is **L'Utile e il Dilettevole,** also on Via della Spiga, with its enchanting Italian country style.

An Armani or Ferre ensemble can set you back several thousand dollars, but similar Italian taste and styling can be found at more affordable prices at **Benetton,** and **Emporio Armani,** or the department stores **La Rinascente** (in Piazza del Duomo) and **Coin** (Piazza Loreto). In between are covetable but sensible Italian fashion buys at shops like **Biffi, Komlas, Gemelli,** and **Max Mara.**

Canny Milanese regularly make the rounds of the dozens of factory outlets and discount stores in the city, often finding designer labels at 30 to 70% off. Stock changes daily, and not all accept credit cards. Some of the better-known discount stores for men's and women's fashion (and in some cases, shoes) are **Il Salvagente** (Via Fratelli Bronzetti 16, tel. 02/761–10328), **Leuce** (Via Panizzi 6, tel. 02/489–50907), **Vestistock** (Viale Romagna 19, tel. 02/749–0502), **Firme** (Via Porpora 109, tel. 02/2614–2787), **Niki** (Via Fontana 19, tel. 02/551–81284), and **Floretta Coen** (Via San Calogero 3, tel. 02/839–7708). You can find designer shoes at whopping discounts at the outdoor market at **Piazzale Martini** Wednesday morning and Saturday.

Shops are usually open 9–1 (closed Mon. morning) and 4–7:30; many are closed in August. Here are other possibilities:

Brera is an area with many unique shops. Walk along Via Brera, Via Solferino, Corso Garibaldi, and Via Paolo Sarpi.

Corso Buenos Aires is a wide avenue with a variety of shops, several offering moderately priced items.

Corso Vittorio Emanuele has clothing, leather goods, and shoe shops, some with items at reasonable prices.

Prada (Galleria Vittorio Emanuele, tel. 02/876979) is a smart leather goods store also famous for a series of turn-of-the-century murals on a travel theme (downstairs in the main sales area).

Lenci (Galleria Vittorio Emanuele, tel. 02/870376) is among the world's foremost doll shops and doubtless the only one brandishing a Latin motto from which we all can learn—*Ludus est nobis constanter industria* (play is our constant work).

Flea markets are popular in Milan and all over Lombardy. Food and a vast array of items, new and old, are displayed in open-air stalls. In many markets, bargaining is no longer the custom. You can try to haggle, but if you fear getting ripped off, go to the stalls where prices are clearly marked. On Saturdays there is the huge Mercato Papiniano, on Viale Papiniano, and the Fiera di Senigallia, on Via Calatafimi, with old and new bargains. If you collect coins or stamps, go on Sunday morning to Via Armorari, near Piazza Cordusio, where there is a specialized market. The best antiques markets are held on the last Sunday of each month along the Navigli and the third Saturday of each month on Via Fiori Chiari, near Via Brera. Antiques markets are closed in August.

Cities of the Plain

This tour takes in some of the great Lombard cities of the Po River plain south of Milan—Pavia, celebrated for its Certosa, or charterhouse, an easy day's excursion from Milan or the first stop on our trans-Lombardy itinerary; Cremona, where history's great violin makers lived and worked; Sabbioneta, a diminutive utopian Renaissance city, the fruit of one man's life-long obsession; and Mantua, home for almost 300 years of the fantastically wealthy Gonzaga dynasty.

Numbers in the margin correspond to points of interest on the Lombardy and the Lakes map.

Located at the confluence of the Ticino and Po rivers, about 38 kilometers (24 miles) south of Milan on E62, **Pavia** was once Milan's chief local rival. The city dates at least from the Roman era and was the capital of the Lombard kings for two centuries (572–774). Pavia came to be known subsequently as "the city of a hundred towers" (of which only a handful have survived). Its prestigious **university** was founded in 1361 on the site of a 10th-century law school but has claims dating to antiquity. The 14th-century **Castello Visconteo** (Piazza Castello) now houses the local Museo Civico (Civic Museum), which has an interesting archaeological collection and a picture gallery featuring works by Correggio (admission 5,000 lire, open Tues.–Sat. 9–1:30, Sun. 9–1). Go right from the castle entrance and turn right, off Via Matteotti, to visit the tomb of Christianity's most celebrated convert, St. Augustine, housed in a Gothic marble ark on the high altar of the Romanesque church of **San Pietro in Ciel d'Oro.**

The main reason for stopping in Pavia, however, is to see the **Certosa** (the Carthusian monastery), 8 kilometers (5 miles) north of the city center. Its facade is stupendous, anticipating by several hundred years, with much the same relish as the Duomo in Milan, the delightful first commandment of Victorian architecture: Always decorate the decoration.

The Certosa's extravagant grandeur was due, in part, to the plan to have it house the tombs of the family of the first duke of Milan, Galeazzo Visconti III (he died during a plague, at age 49, in 1402). And extravagant it was—almost unimaginably so in an age before modern roads and transport. Only the very best marble was used in construction, transported, undoubtedly by barge, from the legendary quarries of Carrara, roughly 150 miles away. Though the ground plan may be Gothic—a cruciform planned in a series of squares—the gorgeous fabric that rises above it is triumphantly Renaissance. On the facade, in the lower frieze, are medallions of Roman emperors and Eastern monarchs; above them are low reliefs of the life of Christ, as well as that of Galeazzo Visconti III.

The first duke was the only Visconti to be interred here, and then only some 75 years after his death, in a tomb designed by Gian Cristoforo Romano. Look for it in the right transept. In the left transept is a tomb of greater human appeal—that of a rather stern middle-aged man and a beautiful young woman. The man is Ludovico il Moro Sforza, seventh duke of Milan, who commissioned Leonardo da Vinci to paint the *Last Supper*. The woman is his wife, one of the most celebrated women of her day, Beatrice d'Este, the embodiment of brains, culture, birth, and beauty. Married when he was 40 and she was 16, they had enjoyed six happy years of marriage when she died suddenly, giving birth to a stillborn child. Ludovico commissioned the sculptor Cristoforo Solari to design a joint tomb for the high altar of Santa Maria delle Grazie in Milan. Originally much larger, the tomb for some years occupied the honored place in Santa Maria delle Grazie as planned. Then, for reasons that are still mysterious, the Dominican monks, who seemed to care no more for their former patron than they did for their faded Leonardo fresco, sold the tomb to their Carthusian brothers to the south. Sadly, part of the tomb, and its remains, were lost. *Certosa, tel. 0382/925613.*

Admission free, donation requested. Open Sept.–Apr., Tues.–Sun. 9–11:30 and 2:30–4:30; May–Aug. 9–11:30 and 2:30–5:30.

⑬ If there is only one place in Italy to buy a violin, it's **Cremona**—as true today as when Andrea Amati (1510–80) opened up shop here in the middle of the 16th century. Though cognoscenti continue to revere the Amati name, it was the apprentice of Amati's nephew, Nicolo (1596–1684), for whom the fates had reserved a wide and lasting international fame. In a career that spanned an incredible 68 years, Antonio Stradivari (1644–1737) made more than 1,200 instruments—including violas, cellos, harps, guitars, and mandolins, in addition to his fabled violins. Labeled simply with a small printed slip, "Antonius Stradivarius Cremonensis. Faciebat anno. . . ." (the date added in a neat italic hand), they remain the best, most coveted, and most expensive stringed instruments in the world.

Cremona is about 93 kilometers (58 miles) southeast of Milan, via the A1 and A21 autostradas. From Pavia, it's 86 kilometers (53 miles) east on S234.

If you would like to see the original Stradivarius instruments, go to the second floor of the **Palazzo del Comune** (City Hall), where five masterpieces by Cremonese *liutai* (violin makers), dating from the 16th to the 18th centuries, are on view. *Piazza del Comune, tel. 0372/4071. Admission: 5,000 lire, valid for all other Cremona museums, including the Museo Stradivariano (see below), Pinacoteca (Art Gallery), and Natural History Museum. Open Tues.–Sat. 8:30–5, Sun. 9–1.*

Piazza del Comune has impressed visitors as one of Italy's loveliest: The cathedral, campanile, baptistery, and City Hall are particularly distinctive and harmonious. The combination of old brick, rose- and cream-colored marble, terra-cotta and old copper roofs brings Romanesque, Gothic, and Renaissance together with unusual success. Don't miss the **Torrazzo** (Big Tower), perhaps the tallest campanile in the country, visible for a considerable distance across the Po plain. *Admission: 5,000 lire. Open Apr.–Oct., Mon.–Sat. 10–noon and 3–6:30, Sun. 10–12:30, 3–7.*

From Piazza del Comune continue along Via Solferino two blocks to what is now **Piazza Roma.** Here, in this lovely square of gardens, trees, and lawns, at No. 1, Antonio Stradivari lived, worked, and died. It is said that in addition to knowing all there was to know about woods, varnish, and the subtleties of assembling the 70-odd component parts that make up a violin, Stradivari liked to keep each new instrument in his bedroom for a month before varnishing it. This way, he claimed, by virtue of some mysterious somnolent transmigration, he gave a soul to each of his creations.

In the center of the park is **Stradivari's grave,** marked by a simple tombstone.

The small **Museo Stradivariano** (Stradivarius Museum) has an informative display of Stradivari's plans and models, as well as violins made by Cremona's more modern masters. *Via Palestro 17, tel. 0372/461886. Admission: 5,000 lire (see Palazzo del Comune, above). Open Tues.–Sat. 8:30–5, Sun. 9–1.*

Strolling about town, you may notice that violin making continues to flourish here. There are, in fact, more than 50 liutai working by traditional methods in small shops scattered throughout Cremona. Most have graduated from the **Scuola Internazionale di Liuteria** (International School of Violin Making). Some have returned there to teach. The school, too, can be an instructive place to visit and is es-

Lombardy and the Lakes

SWITZERLAND

Locarno **32**
Ascona
Brissago

Cannobio

Cannero Riv.

Verbania Pallanza **30**

Lago Maggiore

Laveno **31**

Stresa **29**

Belgirate

Orta San Giulio **33**

Lago di Orta

Arona

Angera

Lago Varese

Varese

Lugano

Lago di Lugano

Menaggio

Tremezzo **24**

Cernobbio **23**

Como

Lago di Como

Bellano **28**

Varenna **27**

Bellagio **25**

Madonna del Ghisallo **26**

Lecco

Bergamo **22**

S38

Milan **1** — **11**

TO TURIN

Novara

Abbiategrasso

Vigevano

Ticino

Certosa di Pavia

Pavia **12**

Cassano d'Ad

Treviglio

Adda

Cr

Lodi

Po

A21

S10

A7

A21

A26

N

0   20 miles
0   30 km

pecially welcoming to those contemplating the acquisition of their own ready-made or custom-built Cremonese violins. *Piazza Marconi, tel. 0372/386689. Open Mon.–Sat. 8–1.*

Time Out There are two fine restaurants in Cremona—one just in front of, the other just behind, the cathedral, both elegant and expensive. **Aquila Nera** (Via Sicardo 3, tel. 0372/25646; closed Sun. dinner, Mon.) specializes in risotto and roast duck; **Ceresole** (Via Ceresole 4, tel. 0372/23322; closed Sun. dinner, Mon.) is older and considered slightly better.

⑭ Our next stop is **Mantua,** the Gonzaga seat, 89 kilometers (55 miles) east of Cremona on S10. The Gonzagas, like the Visconti and Sforza of Milan (with whom they intermarried), lived with the regal pomp and circumstance befitting one of Italy's richest family dynasties. Their reign, first as marquesses, and later as dukes, was a long one—stretching from the first half of the 14th century into the beginning of the 18th.

Even if you've had enough of old palaces, you may still wish to come to Mantua. First, Virgil was born near here. Second, Mantegna (painter of the poignant *Dead Christ* in Milan's Brera) was the Gonzaga court painter for 50 years, and his best-known and only large surviving fresco cycle can be seen here. In addition, there are two fine churches by Leon Battista Alberti (1404–72): **Sant'Andrea** (1471, some sections earlier or later) and **San Sebastiano** (1461). Both (much like Mantegna's work here) proved highly influential and were widely emulated by lesser architectural lights later in the Renaissance.

Our tour begins at the 500-room complex that centuries of Gonzagas thought of, somehow, as home. The fortress and castle of the **Palazzo Ducale** (Ducal Palace), located at the northeast end of Mantua's Piazza Sordello, gives one the sense that the palace took centuries to build. From a distance, the group of buildings dominates the skyline, and the effect is fascinating. As with Sabbioneta's palazzo, the interiors of Mantua's Palazzo Ducale may be seen today only on a rigorous guided tour conducted in Italian by the municipality. *Piazza Sordello, tel. 0376/320283. Admission: 10,000 lire. Open Mar.–Sept., Tues.–Sat. 9–1 and 2:30–5, Sun.–Mon. 9–1; Oct.–Feb., Tues.–Sat. 9–1 and 2:30–4, Sun.–Mon. 9–1.*

Begun in the 13th century by predecessors of the Gonzagas, then expanded and remodeled by the rulers of Mantua from the 14th through the 18th centuries, the palace complex contains several buildings, courtyards, and gardens. Highlights of the tour include the following:

The **Appartamento dei Nani** (Dwarfs' Apartments) were literally that, dwarf-collecting being one of the more amusing occupations of Renaissance princes. According to historians, the dwarfs were not mistreated but were considered something between members of the family and celebrity comics. The apartments were built both for the dwarfs' enjoyment and for that of the court.

The **Appartamento del Paradiso** (Paradise) is usually praised for its view but is somewhat more interesting for its decorator and first resident, Isabella d'Este. Not only was she married at 16, like her younger sister Beatrice (the beautiful young woman of the tomb in the Certosa at Pavia), she was apparently also Ludovico il Moro Sforza's first and original choice for a wife—until he learned she was already affianced to a Gonzaga rival. Isabella, too, is regarded as one of the great patrons of the Renaissance. She survived her sister by more than 40 years, and the archives of her correspondence, totaling more than 2,000 letters, are regarded as some of the most valuable records of the era.

The high point of all 500 rooms, if not of the city, is the **Camera degli Sposi** (literally, "Chamber of the Wedded Couple," because Duke Ludovico and his wife are the focus of attention; it was actually an audience chamber). It was painted by Mantegna over a nine-year period, when he was at the height of his power, and finished when he was 44. Here, Mantegna made a startling advance in painting by organizing the picture's plane of representation in a way that systematically mimics the experience of human vision. Even now, more than five centuries after the event, you can almost sense the excitement of a mature artist, fully aware of his painting's great importance, expressing his vision with a masterly, joyous confidence.

The most serious Mantegna fancier will want to visit his house, **Casa di Andrea Mantegna** (Via Acerbi 47, tel. 0376/360506, admission free), not otherwise of great intrinsic interest. It is located diagonally across from the church of San Sebastiano, and you must phone to arrange a visit. It is occasionally open for temporary art exhibitions (daily 9–12:30, 3:30–6:30). The artist's tomb is located in the first chapel on the left in another church, **Sant'Andrea,** which itself is considered Mantua's most important Renaissance creation. *Piazza delle Erbe, south of Piazza Sordello. Open daily 8–12:30, 3–7.*

Due south, just beyond the town walls, is the **Palazzo Te,** built by Isabella d'Este's son, Federico II Gonzaga, between 1525 and 1535, for his mistress. Reopened in 1989 after restoration, it is the singular Mannerist creation of artist/architect Giulio Romano, decorated with mythological trompe l'oeil frescoes that are not to every visitor's taste. Nevertheless, the palace does not skimp on pictorial drama. *Admission: 5,000 lire. Open Tues.–Sun. 10–6.*

About 34 kilometers (21 miles) southwest of Mantua on S420 lies **⓯ Sabbioneta.** Vespasiano Gonzaga (1531–91), Sabbioneta's lord, founder, and chief architect, was not a particularly sympathetic man. The glory of his attainments in a life of public service is said to have been excelled only by the ignominy of his treatment of three wives and his only son. Upon retiring from military life at 47, he resolved to turn an old castle and a few squalid cottages into the Perfect City—a tiny, urbane metropolis where the most gifted artists and greatest writers would live in perfect harmony with a perfect patron. After some five years of planning and another five of work, the village was transformed into an elegant, star-shaped, walled fortress, with a rational grid of streets, two palaces, two squares, two churches, an exquisite theater (said to be the first in Europe with a roof), by Vincenzo Scamozzi, and a noble Gallery of Antiquities (a forerunner of today's art galleries). Gonzaga died four years later, survived only by the last of his wives.

When Aldous Huxley and his wife visited Sabbioneta in 1924, the town had reached an appalling state of neglect and decay. The Huxleys were given a tour (still the only way of seeing the interiors of most of Sabbioneta's buildings) much like the tour you take today. It began in the **Palazzo Ducale,** where they admired the four fine remaining equestrian figures of Vespasiano and his Gonzaga forebears. They were led through what had once been the Cabinet of Diana, the ducal saloon, and other rooms, only to discover that the rooms had been converted to serve the structure's new function as the town hall. They were shown the little **theater** (an adaption of

Palladio's, at Vicenza, by the man who helped him build it), but it lacked its stage, and its frescoes were covered with whitewash. Today you will find the theater restored and its frescoes uncovered. The third building on the tour, the **Palazzo del Giardino,** has a dusty but impressive gallery of antique sculptures. *Open Apr.–Sept., daily 9–noon and 2:30–6; Oct.–Mar., Tues.–Sat. 9–noon and 2:30–5, Sun. 9–noon and 2:30–5:30. Tour (8,000 lire) begins whenever enough of the willing are assembled. Apply at the Ufficio Turistico, Via Gonzaga 31 (daily 9:30–noon and 2:30–5:30, tel. 0375/52039) or at the Bar Ducale.*

The sole surviving trace of Sabbioneta's prosperous 16th-century Jewish community is a now-shuttered and derelict **synagogue,** near the center of town. You will have to ask someone to point it out.

From Sabbioneta, S420 heads southwest another 28 kilometers (17 miles) to Parma (*see* Chapter 12, Emilia-Romagna); the A1 shoots northwest from Parma to Milan, a 122-kilometer (76-mile) drive.

The Lakes

"The Lakes" actually denotes a vast region spread over the middle third of the northern border region. Though our tour is limited to the four lakes of Garda, Como, Maggiore, and Orta, the best way to see the lake country is to rent a car in fall or spring and thread a path, at as leisurely a pace as possible, along the small mountain roads linking the lakes' least-spoiled northern tips. This is splendid mountain-driving country, with some of the most beautiful and challenging roads in the world.

It is important to remember that the lakes are extremely popular seasonal resort areas. If your wish is not only to see the lakes but actually to stay at them, the throngs that descend in July and August (particularly on weekends) make reservations absolutely essential. As a rule of thumb, if you are not fond of vacation crowds, head north.

Exploring Lake Garda

Numbers in the margin correspond to points of interest on the Lombardy and the Lakes map.

Of all the curious things to be noted about Lake Garda, one is its perennial attraction for writers. Even the 16th-century essayist Michel de Montaigne, whose 15 months of travel journals contain not a single other reference to nature, paused to admire the view down the lake from Torbole, which he called "boundless."

Lake Garda is 50 kilometers (31 miles) long, ranges from 1½ to 10 miles wide, and is as much as 346 meters (1,135 feet) deep. The terrain is flat at the lake's southern base, mountainous at its northern tip. As a consequence, the standard descriptions of it vary from stormy inland sea to crystalline Nordic fjord. It is the biggest lake in the region and by most accounts the cleanest.

16 Our tour begins at **Sirmione,** an enchanting town on the southwest shore. The ruins here, at the water's edge, are a reminder that Garda has been a holiday resort for the pleasure-seeking well-to-do since the height of the Roman era. The locals will almost certainly tell you that the so-called **Grotte di Catullo** (Grottoes of Catullus) were once the site of the villa of Catullus, one of the greatest pleasure-seeking poets of all time. Present archaeological wisdom, however, does not concur, and there is some consensus that this was the site of two villas of slightly different periods, dating from about the 1st century AD. But never mind—the view through the cypresses and olive trees is lovely, and even if Catullus didn't have a villa here, he is closely associated with the area and undoubtedly did have a villa somewhere nearby. *Open Apr.–Sept., Tues.–Sun. 9-6; Oct.– Mar., Tues.–Sun. 9–4.*

Rocca Scaligera, the castle, was built, along with almost all the other castles on the lake, by the Della Scala family. As hereditary rulers of Verona for more than a century before control of the city was seized by the Visconti in 1402, they counted Garda among their possessions. You may wish to go inside (particularly if you have children with you), since there is a nice view of the lake from the tower. The old part of town, in the shadow of the fortress, is still medieval in appearance. Or you may want to go for a swim at the nearby beach before continuing on the brief clockwise circuit of Lake Garda's shore. *Admission: 6,000 lire. Open June–Sept., Tues.–Sat. 9–6; Oct.–May, Tues.–Sat. 9–1; year-round Sun. 9–1.*

Time Out **Vecchia Lugana,** at the base of the peninsula, is considered one of Italy's best restaurants, and it specializes in fish from the lake; grilled trout and fillet of perch with artichokes are especially good. There's also an elegant garden. *Via Lugana Vecchia, Lugana di Sirmione, tel. 030/919012. Reservations advised. AE, DC, MC, V. Closed Mon. dinner, Tues., and Jan. $$$*

Passing Desenzano and Salò (the tiny last-ditch republic of Mussolini's final hours), you come to **Gardone Riviera,** a once-fashionable turn-of-the-century resort, now delightfully faded, and the former home of the flamboyant Gabriele d'Annunzio (1863–1938), one of Italy's greatest modern poets. D'Annunzio's estate, the **Vittoriale,** is an elaborate memorial to himself, clogged with souvenirs of conquests in art, love, and war (of which the largest is a ship's prow in the garden), and complete with a mausoleum. *Admission: 7,000 lire, including guided tour. Open Tues.–Sun. 9–12:30, 2–6.*

Time Out **Villa Fiordaliso** is as pretty a restaurant as you will find anywhere. Grilled fish and meats are the specialty. The restaurant is in Gardone Riviera, near the Vittoriale. *Via Zanardelli 132, tel. 0365/ 20158. AE, DC, MC, V. Closed Sun. dinner, Mon., and Jan.–Feb. $$$*

Just before the village of **Toscolano-Maderno,** turn left and drive about 3 kilometers (1.8 miles) up the hill to the charming Romanesque church of **Santa Maria di Gaino.** Return to the lake and continue north to the **Villa Feltrinelli** at **Gargnano,** where Mussolini lived. Take the fork to the left about 5 kilometers (3 miles) north of Gargnano and head to **Tignale.** The view from the **Madonna di Monte Castello** church, some 2,000 feet above the lake, is spectacular. Adventurous travelers will want to follow this pretty inland mountain road to **Tremosine** and **Limone sul Garda,** back on the lake, where it is said the first lemon trees in Europe were grown.

18 **Riva del Garda** is the next town to the north. It is large and prosperous, and if you're there in summer, you may want to lodge there if the towns farther south seem too crowded. Many of the town's public buildings date from the 15th century, when it was a strategic outpost of the Venetian Republic. The heart of town, the lakeside **Piazza 3 Novembre,** is surrounded by medieval palazzi. The **Torre Apponale,** predating the Venetian period by three centuries, looms above these houses: Its crenellations recall its defensive purpose. Standing in the piazza and looking out onto the lake, you can understand Riva del Garda's importance as a windsurfing center. Mountain air currents ensure good breezes on even the sultriest midsummer days.

Time Out Several hotels and cafés line Piazza 3 Novembre. **Hotel Centrale**, at the foot of the Torre Apponale, has tables outside, where you can have a cool drink while watching the boating and windsurfing activity offshore.

About 4 kilometers (2.4 miles) north of town, on the road to Tenno, is an attractive waterfall, the 295-foot **Cascata del Varone.** Continue along the northernmost tip of the lake and head south along the eastern shore.

⑲ Continue past Torbole to **Malcesine,** one of the loveliest areas along the upper eastern shore of Lake Garda, and visit the 13th–14th-century **Castello Scaligero** (built, like the one in Sirmione, by the Della Scalas). You're in the Veneto now, and if you are fond of cable cars, take the *funivia* to the top of Monte Baldo (5,791 feet). Continue to ⑳ **Punta di San Vigilio,** which just about everyone agrees is the prettiest spot on Garda's eastern shore, with cypresses, the gardens of the 15th-century Villa Guarienti di Brenzone, and more fine views.

To the south is **Garda,** a very old port, and **Bardolino,** which makes undistinguished but famous red wine. Here, if you are feeling guilty about not entering a single church all day, there are two handsome Romanesque examples—**San Severo,** from the 11th century, and **San Zeno,** from the 9th. **Lazise,** the next town south, has another Della Scala castle, which brings you to the final few, lovely kilometers of Garda's eastern shore.

㉑ **Brescia** is a mere 19 kilometers (12 miles) west of Lake Garda. The ruins of the **Capitolino,** a Capitoline Temple built by the Emperor Vespasian in AD 73, testify to Brescia's Roman origin. Outstanding among the sculptures in the adjoining **Museo Romano** is the famed 1st-century bronze *Winged Victory. Via dei Musei 57/a, tel. 030/46031. Admission: 2,000 lire. Open Tues.–Sun. 9–12:30 and 2–4:30.*

More relics are in the **Museum of Christian Art** (also on Via dei Musei), including a remarkable collection of early medieval pieces, but the museum is only open for temporary exhibitions. Check with the tourist office (Corso Zanardelli 34, tel. 030/43418). Otherwise, to the southeast of the center, the **Pinacoteca Tosio-Martinengo** accommodates—besides the works of the Brescia School—pictures by Raphael, Tintoretto, Tiepolo, and Clouet. *Piazza Moretto, tel. 030/59120. Admission: 2,000 lire. Open Tues.–Sun. 9–12:30, 2–5.*

A network of squares in the center of town contains much that is worth savoring. Palladio and Sansovino contributed to the splendid marble **Loggia,** the great Lombard-Venetian palace overlooking Piazza della Loggia. Another palazzo is topped by the 16th-century **Torre dell'Orologio** (Clock Tower), modeled on the campanile in Venice's Piazza San Marco. On Piazza del Duomo, the 17th-century Baroque **cathedral** sits beside the simple stone 12th-century **Rotonda.** Among the churches worth visiting is the **Madonna del Carmine,** behind which a flight of stairs climbs to the ramparts of the Venetian **Castello,** high enough to give a panoramic view over the town and across the plain to the distant Alps.

㉒ From Brescia, head 43 kilometers (27 miles) west to **Bergamo,** en route to Lake Como. The old city of Bergamo lies at the foot of the

Bergamese Alps. Actually, Bergamo is two cities—Bergamo Bassa (Lower Bergamo) and Bergamo Alta (Upper Bergamo), connected by a funicular railway. High up on the hillside, walled in by the ruins of ancient Venetian fortifications, surmounted by a fortress, is Bergamo Alta. It is one of northern Italy's most charming medieval centers. The principal monuments here—the 12th-century **Palazzo della Ragione,** the massive **Torre del Comune,** the **Duomo** of Bergamo, the church of **Santa Maria Maggiore,** the **Colleoni Chapel,** and the **baptistery**—are in or near the Piazza Vecchia. The facade of the Colleoni Chapel has been cleaned, and its elaborate marble decoration is resplendent.

In Bergamo Bassa, just below the city walls, in the **Accademia Carrara,** you will find one of Italy's greatest and most important art collections. Many of the Venetian masters are represented— Mantegna, Carpaccio, Tiepolo, Guardi, Canaletto—and there are some magnificent Bellinis and Botticellis as well. *Piazza Carrara, tel. 035/399426. Admission: 3,000 lire, Sun. free. Open Wed.–Mon. 9:30–12:15, 2:30–5:15.*

Exploring Lake Como

When somebody next asks you where to spend a honeymoon, an eminently sensible thing to say would be, "Lake Como," and leave it at that. Though summer crowds do their best to vanquish the lake's dreamy mystery and civilized, slightly faded, millionaire's-row gentility, they fail. Como remains a place of consummate partnership between the beauties of nature and those of humanity. Accordingly, our tour of the lake is of gardens and villas (of which a couple of the finest are now hotels). Like so many of Italy's most beautiful villa gardens, those of Como owe their beauty to the landscape architecture of two eras: Renaissance Italian, with its taste for order; and 19th-century English, with its fondness for illusions of natural wildness. The two are often framed by vast areas of the most picturesque farmland—notably olive groves, fruit trees, and vineyards.

Como is some 47 kilometers (30 miles) long, measured north to south, and its southern half is divided into two long legs, or branches; it is also Europe's deepest lake (almost 411 meters, or 1,350 feet). Virgil liked Como at least as much as Garda, calling it simply our "greatest" lake.

㉓ **Cernobbio** is the first town you come to as you head north from the town of Como, where the lake's remarkable beauty can be seen. Though most of the villas of the southwest branch (the lake's most fashionable district) remain private and closed to the public, they can be enjoyed from a boat. From the old square at the center of Cernobbio, all paths seem to lead to the **Grand Hotel Villa d'Este.** If you're planning to say "budget be damned" in only one place, this should be it. If you possibly can, stay for a few days at this legendary lakeside resort hotel. If not, then call ahead and ask to see the grounds or enjoy a wonderful meal in the hotel's restaurant (*see* Dining and Lodging, *below*).

Originally built for Cardinal Tolomeo Gallio (who began life humbly as a fisherman) over the course of approximately 45 years (it was completed in 1615), the Villa d'Este has had a colorful and somewhat checkered history, swinging wildly between extremes of grandeur and dereliction. Its tenants have included the Jesuits, two generals, a ballerina, the disgraced and estranged wife of a future king of England (Caroline of Brunswick and George IV, respectively), a family of ordinary Italian nobles, and, finally, a czarina of Russia. Its life as a private summer residence ended in 1873, when it was turned into the fashionable hotel it has remained ever since. The name is not, as you might imagine, derived from some connection with Lombardy's famous d'Este sisters but from a distant ancestral tie of Caroline Brunswick, called Guelfo d'Este (whose name, for some reason, she evidently liked).

Though the gardens are not so grand as they are reputed to have been during the villa's best days as a private residence and though they have suffered some modification in the course of the hotel's building of tennis courts and swimming pools, they still possess an aura of stately, monumental dignity. The alley of cypresses is a fine example of a proudly repeated Italian garden theme. The fanciful pavilions, temples, miniature forts, and mock ruins make for an afternoon's walk of quietly whimsical surprises—especially once you stray from the more structured and Italian sections of the lower gardens.

If you are lucky enough to visit in late spring or very early summer, **24** you will find the **Villa Carlotta** (just up the road in **Tremezzo**) a riotous blaze of color, with more than 14 acres of azaleas and dozens of varieties of rhododendron in full bloom. The range of the garden's collection is remarkable, particularly when you consider the difficulties of transporting delicate, exotic vegetation before the age of aircraft. Palms, banana trees, cactus, eucalyptus, a sequoia, orchids, and camellias are only the beginning of a list that includes more than 500 species. The villa itself, built between 1690 and 1743 for the luxury-loving Marquis Giorgio Clerici, is slightly newer than the Villa d'Este. *Tel. 0344/40405. Admission to villa and gardens: 6,000 lire adults, 2,500 lire children. Open Apr.–Sept., daily 9–6; Mar. 15–31, Oct., daily 9–1, 2–4:30.*

According to local lore, one motive for the Villa Carlotta's magnificence was a keeping-up-with-the-Joneses sort of rivalry between the marquis's ambitious, self-made son-in-law, who inherited the estate, and the son-in-law's arch rival, who built *his* summer palace directly across the lake. Whenever either added to his villa and garden, it was tantamount to taunting the other in public. Eventually the son-in-law's insatiable taste for self-aggrandizement prevailed. The villa's last (and final) owners were Prussian royalty (including the "Carlotta" of the villa's name), and the property was confiscated during World War I.

The villa's interior is worth a visit, particularly if you have a taste for Antonio Canova's most romantic sculptures. The best known is his *Cupid and Psyche*, which depicts the lovers locked in an odd but graceful and passionate embrace, with the young god above and behind, his wings extended, while Psyche, her lips willing, waits for a kiss that will never come.

Take the ferry from the pleasant resort town of Menaggio, just **25** north of Tremezzo, to **Bellagio,** sometimes called the prettiest town in Europe. The garden of the **Villa Melzi** is open to the public; go there after a stroll along the cobblestone streets of the town. *Admission: 4,000 lire. Open Mar.–Oct., daily 9–12:30, 2–4:30.* **Villa Serbelloni,** a property of the Rockefeller Foundation, is another villa to visit for its celebrated gardens. *Villa Serbelloni. Admission: 5,000 lire. Guided visits only, mid-Apr.–mid-Oct., Tues.–Sun. at 10:30 and 4.*

If you have a car, take the panoramic drive south through the mountains between Como's two southern branches, to the church of the **26** **Madonna del Ghisallo** (the patroness of bicyclists), and then back to

Bellagio, along the edge of the lake. The mountain road goes from Bellagio to Civenna, Asso, and Valbrona and then joins the main shore road at Onno, about 10 kilometers (6 miles) south of Bellagio.

㉗ Another lovely trip is by ferry from Bellagio to **Varenna.** The principal sight here is the lovely garden of the **Villa Monastero,** which, as its name suggests, was a monastery before it was a villa. Now it's an international science center. *Admission: 4,000 lire. Open Apr.–*
㉘ *Oct., daily 9–noon, 2–5.* At **Bellano,** a few miles north of Varenna, is a dramatic gorge called the **Orrido.**

Exploring Lake Maggiore

The most beautiful and idyllic of the Italian lakes, Lake Maggiore has its less mountainous eastern shore in Lombardy, its higher western shore in Piedmont, and its northern tip in Switzerland. Never more than 5 kilometers (3 miles) wide, the lake is almost 50 kilometers (30 miles) long. The better-known resorts are on the Piedmontese shore, particularly Stresa, a well-established tourist town that is just the place to unwind and drift into a siesta, to be awakened only by a cool late-afternoon lake breeze.

㉙ **Stresa** is a small town with a lot going for it. While capitalizing on its central lakeside position, with good connections to the Borromean islands in Lake Maggiore, it has managed to retain a welcoming, relaxing atmosphere that can only be described as charming. Its period of development was about a century ago, and the architecture reflects a genteel, languorous attitude that blends in with the subtropical vegetation. Hemingway's *A Farewell to Arms* was partly set here. Your first duty, if you've driven, is to park and make your way on foot down to the water's edge. Stop at one of the two adjacent waterfront squares, Piazza Marconi or Piazza Matteotti.

Time Out Have a drink or an ice cream in one of the several cafés in Piazza Marconi. You can sit back and relax, watching the Borromean island steamers preparing to set off from the landing stage a few yards away.

Make your way away from the shore toward Corso Umberto 1, the main road that runs along the length of the lake. The buildings on each side of you are decorated in a playful fashion, with mock windows painted onto blank walls, sometimes with what appears to be nosy locals giving you the eye. Turn left and just about 50 yards up on the right is the entrance to the gardens of **Villa Pallavicino,** a stately residence built on the hill rising from the lake. As you wander around the grounds, with their palms and semitropical shrubs, don't be surprised if you're followed by a peacock or even an ostrich: They're part of the zoological garden, and they are allowed to roam almost at will. From the top of the hill you can see the gentle hills of the Lombardy shore of Lake Maggiore and, nearer and to the left, the jewellike Borromean islands (Isole Borromee). *Admission: 8,000 lire adults, 6,000 lire children 4–14. Open mid-Mar.–Oct. 30, daily 9–6.*

Boats for the **Borromean Islands** leave every few minutes from the landing stage by Piazza Matteotti: Just look for the signs for "Navigazione Lago Maggiore." Although you can hire a boatman to take you to the islands, it's cheaper and just as convenient to use the regular service. Make sure to buy a ticket allowing you to visit all the islands—Bella, Dei Pescatori, and Madre.

The islands take their name from the Borromeo family, which has owned them since the 12th century. **Isola Bella** (Beautiful Island) is the most famous of the three, and the first that you'll visit. Its name is actually a shortened form of Isabella, wife of the 16th-century Count Carlo III Borromeo who built the palace and terraced gardens for her. Few wedding presents anywhere have been more romantic. Wander up the 10 terraces of the gardens, where peacocks roam among the scented shrubs, statues, and fountains. The view of the lake is splendid from the top terrace. Before Count Carlo began his project, the island was rocky and almost devoid of vegetation, and the soil for the garden had to be transported from the mainland. Visit the **Palazzo** to see the rooms where famous guests—including Napoleon and Mussolini—stayed in 18th-century splendor. *Admission to garden and palazzo: 10,000 lire. Open Apr.–Oct., daily 8:30– noon, 1:30–5:30.*

Stop for a while at the second island, tiny **Isola dei Pescatori** (Island of the Fishermen), which is less than 100 yards wide and only about a quarter of a mile long. Of the three islands, this is the one that has remained closest to the way they all were before the Borromeos began their building projects. Little lanes twist through the island, which is nothing more than a tiny fishing village, crowded with souvenir stands in high season.

Isola Madre (Mother Island) is the largest of the three and, like Isola Bella, has a large **botanical garden** (Orto Botanico). There's not much to the island except the garden, but even dedicated nongardeners should stop to appreciate the profusion of exotic trees and shrubs running down to the shore in every direction. Two special times to visit are April (for the camellias) and May (when azaleas and rhododendrons are in bloom). *Admission: 10,000 lire. Open Apr.–Oct., daily 8:30–noon, 2– 5:30.*

30 Across the Gulf of Pallanza, in the town of **Verbania Pallanza,** the 17th-century **Palazzo Dugnani** has a splendid collection of peasant costumes. The **Villa Taranto** has magnificent botanical gardens containing some 20,000 species. Created by an enthusiastic Scotsman, Captain Neil McEachern, these gardens rank among Europe's finest. *Admission: 8,000 lire. Open Apr.–Oct., daily 8:30–7:30.*

31 From Stresa, you can take a steamer to **Laveno,** on the Lombardian side of the lake. From Laveno, there also are several other trips
32 available. Go up to **Locarno** by way of Griffa, Porto Valtravaglia, and Cannero Riviera. You'll stop, too, at the village of **Cannobio** before you enter Switzerland's waters, then at **Brissago** and **Ascona,** and finally at Locarno.

Exploring Lake Orta

A mountainous strip of land separates Lake Maggiore from Lake Orta, its smaller neighbor to the west, in Piedmont. Orta attracts fewer visitors than the three big lakes described above, and consequently a tour around this lake can be a pleasant alternative in the summer. If you're coming from Stresa, take the twisting mountain road past Mottarone, the tallest peak between the lakes, to Gignese, where you'll be about 2,300 feet above sea level and can take in a last dramatic view of Maggiore. Follow the road down to Orta, through the town of Armeno, shaded first by forests of evergreens, then oaks. In the late summer and early fall, you're likely to see whole families out in these woods, crouched down in their hunt for wild mushrooms, or—if they're particularly lucky—truffles.

③③ When you reach the lake shore, you'll be in the town of **Orta San Giulio,** at the end of a small peninsula that juts out into Lake Orta about a third of the way up its eastern shore. Intricate wrought-iron balustrades and balconies adorn the 18th-century buildings of this small and charming resort town. Small cafés and shops line the shady main square, which looks out across the lake to the small island of San Giulio. There are few more relaxing experiences than sipping a drink at one of these cafés and looking out at the languid waters being stirred by a mountain breeze, with sailboats busily making their way nowhere in particular.

Enjoy the interesting hike from Orta to the top of the **Sacro Monte** (Sacred Mountain), rising up behind Orta and looking down on the lake. Take the little street past the church of the Assumption, and just ahead you see a gateway marked "Sacro Monte." This leads to the path up the hill, a not very difficult climb taking about 40 minutes for the round-trip. As you approach the top, you pass no fewer than 20 17th-century chapels, all devoted to St. Francis of Assisi. They are decorated with frescoes and striking life-size terra-cotta statue groups (a total of almost 400 figures) that illustrate incidents in the saint's life. You can climb the campanile of the last chapel for a panoramic view over the whole lake and the town, about 350 feet below.

Back down at the lake shore you can hire a boatman to take you across to the island of **San Giulio,** just offshore. The lake is no more than 2 kilometers (1½ miles) wide, and most charge about 10,000 lire for up to four people to make the round-trip. The island takes its name from the 4th-century St. Julius, who—like St. Patrick in Ireland—is said to have banished snakes from the island. Julius is also said to have founded the **Basilica** in AD 390, although the present building shows more signs of its renovations in the 10th and 15th centuries. Inside, there is a black marble pulpit (12th century) with elaborate carvings, and downstairs you'll find the crypt containing relics of the saint. In the sacristy of the church is a large bone, which is said to be from one of the beasts destroyed by the saint, but which on closer examination seems to be a whalebone.

It only takes a few minutes to walk around the parts of the island that are open to the public: Much of the area is taken up by the grounds of private villas. The view back across the lake to Orta, with Sacro Monte behind it, is memorable, particularly in the late afternoon, when the light picks up the glint of the wrought-iron traceries.

Follow the shore drive from Orta San Giulio north to **Omegna,** at the head of Lake Orta. A couple of miles west of Omegna, in the village of **Quarna Sotto,** there's a musical instrument factory that's worth a stop. The shore drive continues around the rest of the lake, and at the southern end you can pick up S229, which will take you back to the A4 autostrada.

What to See and Do with Children

Cruises on the lakes are fun for all ages. Arrange a boat trip through local tourist offices or contact the **Gestione Navigazione Laghi** in Milan (Via L. Ariosto 21, tel. 02/481–2086).

Gardaland Amusement Park is in Castelnuovo, in the hills south of Lake Garda. *Tel. 045/644–9777. Admission: 27,000 lire; children under 10, 22,000 lires; children under 1 meter (40 inches) tall, free.*

Open Sept. 17–Nov. 4 and Mar. 24–June 30, daily 9–dusk; July 1–Sept. 11, daily 9–midnight.

Minitalia Park, between Milan and Bergamo, has a relief model of Italy, on a scale of 1:500, with about 200 replicas of the most important monuments. *On the A4 autostrada to Bergamo, 35 km (21 mi) from Milan, at Capriate San Gervasio, tel. 02/909-1341. Admission: 12,000 lire adults, 10,000 lire children 3–10. Open daily 9–dusk.*

Parco della Preistoria, 25 kilometers (15 miles) east of Milan on the road to Brescia, has a 4-kilometer (2½-mile) path with 20 full-size replicas of prehistoric animals. Children will be delighted by the 70-foot-long brontosaurus and the fierce tyrannosaurus. There is a picnic area and, for the adults, two bars. *On SS11, near Cassano d'Adda, tel. 0363/78184. Admission: 10,000 lire adults, 8,000 lire children 4–14. Open Mar.–Nov., daily 9–dusk.*

Tremosine, known as the "Garda Terrace," is a mountain forest area that is an ideal place for nature hikes. For more information, write or call the Ufficio Comunale (Via Papa Giovanni XXIII, tel. 0365/953185).

Sports

Participant Sports

Fishing   The rivers of Lombardy are known for good fishing. Check with the local tourist office or your hotel for license regulations.

Golf   The **Parco di Monza,** 15 kilometers (9 miles) from Milan, contains 18- and 9-hole courses. Contact the Golf Club Milano (tel. 039/303081). There are four more courses near Milan and seven courses near Lake Como.

Health Spas   Off the Sirmione peninsula, in Lake Garda, is the Boiola thermal spring. Three Sirmione hotels offer thermal halls with various treatments: **Grand Hotel Terme** (tel. 030/916261); **Hotel Sirmione** (tel. 030/916331); and **Hotel Fonte Boiola** (tel. 030/916431).

Hiking   Hiking is particularly good in the **Parco Nazionale dello Stelvio** and the **Val Malanca,** both in the northern province of Valtellina. (APT, Sondrio, tel. 0342/512500.)

Horseback Riding   In the Como area, contact **Centro di Equitazione Comasco,** Frazione Barella (Grandate) (tel. 031/450235).

Mountain Climbing   There is good climbing in the northern province of Valtellina (*see* Hiking, *above*).

Water Sports   Schools for sailing, scuba diving, and windsurfing are located in Riva del Garda, on Lake Garda. Torbole, 5 kilometers (3 miles) east of Riva del Garda on S240, is a prime spot for windsurfing; contact **Centro Windsurf** (Colonia Pavese, tel. 0464/505385). At Lake Como, there are well-equipped sailing and windsurfing schools.

Sea Planes   Contact the **Seaplane Club Como** (Via Masia 44, tel. 031/559882).

Skiing   Facilities are good in the mountains near **Bergamo** (APT, Bergamo, tel. 035/242226). In the province of **Como,** fine ski facilities abound: Valsassina, Val Lesina, Valvarrone, Valcavargna, and Val d'Intelvi (APT, Como, Via Borgovico 148, tel. 031/230329). Another well-equipped resort is **Malcesine,** on the east side of Lake Garda, with six lifts and more than 11 kilometers (7 miles) of runs of varying difficulty (IAT, Malcesine, tel. 045/7400044).

Sport Center The best equipped of Milan's many sport centers is the **Centro Saini** (Via Corelli 136, tel. 02/7380841), in the vast Parco Forlanini. Much like a municipal gym, it offers squash and volleyball facilities and weight rooms. It's outside the city center; take Bus 38.

Waterskiing Numerous facilities for waterskiing and all water sports can be found on Lombardy's lakes. (APT, Como, Via Borgovico 148, tel. 031/230329.)

Spectator Sports

Auto Racing A Formula 1 race is held in Monza, 15 kilometers (9 miles) from Milan, every September. The track was built in 1922, in the Parco di Monza, where there is also a hippodrome, golf course, and other facilities.

Horse Racing There are tracks near Lake Garda at Maderno and at Padenghe.

Soccer Milan's soccer teams, AC Milan and Inter Milan, are two of the best in Europe. Matches are played on Sunday, and information is available from the city tourist offices.

Dining and Lodging

Dining Unlike most Italian regions, Lombardy exhibits a northern European preference for butter rather than oil as its cooking medium, which imparts a rich and distinctive flavor to the cuisine. Among the most popular specialties is *osso bucco alla milanese,* veal knuckle served with risotto, which is rice that has been cooked until almost all the liquid has evaporated and a creamy sauce remains. Risotto alla milanese uses chicken broth and saffron, which gives the dish a rich yellow color. The lakes are a good source of fish, particularly trout and pike.

Gorgonzola, a rich veined cheese, and panettone, a raised fluffy fruitcake with raisins and candied fruit, both come from Milan and can be enjoyed throughout Lombardy. Although most of the wines in Lombardy are good accompaniments to the cuisine, try in particular to have the red Grumello or Sangue di Giuda (blood of Judas) wines or the delicious light sparkling whites from the Franciacorta area.

Highly recommended restaurants are indicated by a star ★.

Category	Milan	Other Areas
$$$$	over 120,000 lire	over 90,000 lire
$$$	80,000–120,000 lire	60,000–90,000 lire
$$	45,000–80,000 lire	35,000–60,000 lire
$	under 45,000 lire	under 35,000 lire

*per person, including a first course, main course, dessert or fruit, and house wine

Lodging Lombardy is one of Italy's most prosperous regions, and hotels cater to a clientele that demands high standards and is willing to pay for extra comfort. Most of the famous lake resorts are expensive, although more basic—and reasonably priced—accommodations can be found in the smaller towns and villages. Milan may seem to have fewer tourists than other large Italian cities, but there is always competition for rooms, generated by the nearly year-round trade fairs and other business-related bookings. It is best—and almost essential in spring and summer—to make reservations.

Many Lombardy hotels are converted from beautiful old villas and have well-landscaped grounds. Try to visit one or two, even if they are out of your price range as accommodations.

Highly recommended hotels are indicated by a star ★.

Category	Cost*
$$$$	over 400,000 lire
$$$	200,000–400,000 lire
$$	125,000–200,000 lire
$	under 125,000 lire

Prices are for standard double room for two, including tax and service.

Bellagio
Dining

La Pergola. Located in Pescallo, about a kilometer (.6 mile) from Bellagio, on the other side of the peninsula, La Pergola is a popular lakeside restaurant. Those in the know reserve a table on the lakeside terrace and order the daily special of freshly caught lake fish. You can also stay in one of the inn's 13 rooms. *Pescallo, tel. 031/ 950263. Reservations advised. Jacket advised. AE, DC, MC, V. Closed Nov.–Feb. $$*

Silvio. At the edge of town, this family-owned trattoria with a terrace on the lakeshore is for those who love fresh lake fish. Served cooked or marinated, with risotto or as a ravioli stuffing, the fish is caught by Silvio's family. This is local cooking at its best. *Via Carcano 12, tel. 031/950322. Reservations advised. Dress: casual. MC, V. Closed Jan. $$*

Lodging

Grand Hotel Villa Serbelloni. A large park surrounds this luxury establishment facing the lake. The atmosphere is one of 19th-century luxury that has not so much faded as mellowed: The rooms are immaculate and plush. The public rooms are a riot of gilt, marble, and thick, colorful carpets. Service is discreet, and the staff is particularly good about arranging transportation across and around the lake. Ask for a room facing the lake and the mountains beyond. *Lungolago Bellagio, Via Roma 1, tel. 031/950216, fax 031/951529. 95 rooms with bath or shower. Facilities: private park, private beach, tennis court, pool, bar, restaurant, terrace. AE, DC, MC, V. Closed Oct. 21–Apr. 14. $$$$*

Du Lac. Located in the center of Bellagio, by the Lake Como landing dock, Du Lac is a comfortable medium-size hotel. Most rooms have views of the lake and mountains, and there is a rooftop terrace garden for drinks or just unwinding. *Piazza Mazzini 32, tel. 031/ 950320, fax 031/951624. 48 rooms with bath or shower. Facilities: roof garden, restaurant, bar. DC, MC, V. Closed Oct. 16–Apr. 3. $$*

Bergamo
Dining
★

Dell'Angelo–Antico Ristorante. High marks could be awarded here in equal measure for the atmosphere (it's a 17th-century inn) and for the excellent cuisine. The restaurant is a 15-minute walk from the Accademia Carrara. In good weather there is dining outside in the attractive courtyard. Fish plays a prominent role on the menu: Try the ravioli *di branzino al basilico fresco* (stuffed with bass in fresh basil) and the *zuppa di porcini* (wild mushroom soup). *Via Borgo*

Santa Caterina 55, tel. 035/237103. Reservations advised. Jacket advised. AE, DC, MC, V. Closed Mon., 1 week in Jan., Aug. $$$$

Agnello d'Oro. A 17th-century tavern on a main street in Upper Bergamo, with wooden booths and walls hung with copper utensils and ceramic plates, Agnello d'Oro is a good place to imbibe the atmosphere as well as the good local wine. Specialties are typical Bergamasque risotto, polenta with game and mushrooms. *Via Gombito 22, tel. 035/249883. Reservations advised in evening. Dress: casual. AE, DC, MC, V. Closed Mon. and mid-Jan.–mid-Feb. $$*

Da Ornella. On the main street in the Upper Town, this trattoria is well-known and popular, so reservations are a must. Vaulted ceilings, wooden beams, and antique ceramic ware on the walls enhance the Old World atmosphere. Ornella herself is in the kitchen, turning out *casonsei* (large meat-filled ravioli) in butter and sage and platters of assorted roast meats. *Via Gombito 15, tel. 035/232736. Reservations advised. Dress: casual. AE, DC, MC, V. Closed Thurs., Fri. lunch, Christmas holidays, July. $$*

La Trattoria del Teatro. Traditional regional food tops the bill at this good-value restaurant in the Upper Town. Polenta, made of cornmeal and eaten throughout northern Italy, makes an appearance as an accompaniment and as an alternative to pasta. Game is recommended in season. *Fettuccine con funghi* (fettuccine with mushrooms) is a deceptively simple but rich and memorable specialty. *Piazza Mascheroni 3, tel. 035/238862. Reservations advised weekends. Jacket advised. No credit cards. Closed Mon. and July 15–30. $$*

Bernabò. From the funicular it's worth heading straight ahead, past Piazza Vecchia to the old military fortress and this corner trattoria. It has two simple rooms with vaulted ceilings, wrought-iron lamps, and wood-paneled walls. The clientele is a mix of locals and economy-minded tourists. All are treated cordially. Specialties are casonsei served with butter and sage, and veal scaloppine or game with polenta. Pizza is also served. *Via Colleoni 31, tel. 035/237692. Reservations advised weekends. Dress: casual. Closed Thurs. and July 15–Aug. 15. MC, V. $–$$*

Lodging **Cristallo Palace.** Located on the periphery of town, the Cristallo Palace offers the amenities of a modern, efficient hotel as well as the bonus of good parking and a convenient position on the *tangenziale* (the road that bypasses the center). The rooms are large and well equipped, and the service is polished and prompt. The hotel's restaurant, L'Antica Perosa, is very good, and its prices are at the lower range of this category. *Via Betty Ambiveri 35, tel. 035/311211, fax 035/312031. 90 rooms with bath or shower. Facilities: restaurant, bar, parking, conference facilities. AE, DC, MC, V. $$$*

Excelsior San Marco. The most comfortable hotel in the lower part of Bergamo, the Excelsior San Marco is only a short walk from the walls of the Upper Town. The rooms are surprisingly quiet, considering the central location of the hotel. Its restaurant, Tino Fontana, features a rooftop terrace. *Piazza della Repubblica 6, tel. 035/366111, fax 035/223201. 160 rooms with bath or shower. Facilities: restaurant (closed Sun., $$$), bar, terrace, parking, conference facilities. $$$*

Brescia **La Sosta.** Located just south of Brescia's cathedral, La Sosta occu-
Dining pies a 17th-century building. The cuisine and service suggest a more expensive establishment, and the ambience is refined. A Brescian specialty is casonsei. *Capretto alla bresciana* (roast kid with polenta) is an outstanding main course, but make sure you have room for it. *Via San Martino della Battaglia 20, tel. 030/295603. Reserva-*

tions advised. Jacket advised. AE, DC, MC, V. Closed Mon., Dec. 24–Jan. 7, Aug. 6–30. $$$

Lodging **Vittoria.** Centrally located and set among 16th-century buildings, Vittoria has more than its share of atmosphere. Built in 1933, the hotel is in the Venetian style, with a hint of Byzantium and the Spice Routes in its pointed arches and windows. The rooms have been renovated recently and are decorated with antiques. *Via delle X Giornate 20, tel. 030/280061, fax 030/280065. 65 rooms with bath or shower. Facilities: restaurant, bar, conference facilities. AE, DC, MC, V. $$$*

Cassinetta di Lugagnano
Dining
★

L'Antica Osteria del Ponte. Make your way 20 kilometers (12 miles) southwest of Milan to one of Italy's finest (and most expensive) restaurants, located in an attractive agricultural village. The Naviglio Grande (Grand Canal) flows nearby: It was built to carry the area's produce to Milan. Luckily, enough of this produce stays put to form the basis of a rich and imaginative menu that changes each season to follow the harvest cycle and sometimes the whim of chef Ezio Santin. The restaurant is set in a traditional country inn, and the inside is a cozy combination of wooden ceiling beams and a blazing fire. Inventive recipes include ravioli di aragosta (filled with lobster meat—summer only) and, in the fall, a range of specialties featuring porcini, the prized wild mushrooms. *Cassinetta di Lugagnano (3 km, or 1.8 mi, north of Abbiategrasso), tel. 02/942–0034. Reservations required. Jacket and tie required. AE, DC, MC, V. Closed Sun., Mon., Dec. 25–Jan. 15, Aug. $$$$*

Cernobbio
Dining and Lodging
★

Grand Hotel Villa d'Este. One of the most luxurious hotels in Italy (less cautious folk could extend that to Europe or even the whole world), Villa d'Este provides just about every conceivable comfort. The villa was built in the late 16th century, and the setting and decorations are enough to indulge the fantasies of a card-carrying hedonist. A broad veranda sweeps out to the lakefront, where a large swimming pool juts out above the water. Across the lake are blue, snowcapped mountains gradually blending into the deep green of the slopes that lead down to the shore. Inside, sparkling chandeliers cast their light on broad marble staircases, and the rooms are furnished in the discreet color-coordinated manner of wealthy Italians. The restaurant is on a par with every other aspect of Villa d'Este, and you can eat in the sumptuous grillroom or outside on the veranda. *Via Regina 40, tel. 031/511471, fax 031/512027. 158 rooms with bath. Facilities: indoor and outdoor pools, 8 tennis courts, sauna, gym, squash court, Turkish bath, massage room, large secluded park, restaurant, cocktail bars. AE, DC, MC, V. Closed Nov.–Mar. $$$$*

Como
Dining

Da Angela. Reservations are a must at this small and intimate restaurant serving Piedmontese specialties. The service is attentive, and the waiters will help you select from a menu that includes various homemade pasta dishes and tasty *coniglio ai capperi* (rabbit with capers). *Via Ugo Foscolo 16, tel. 031/304656. Reservations required. Jacket advised. AE, DC, MC, V. Closed Sun. and Aug. $$$*

Lodging
★

Barchetta Excelsior. Piazza Cavour, the address of this welcoming and comfortable hotel, is some of the choicest real estate in Como. The Barchetta Excelsior exploits this lakefront (and central) position; many of its rooms look directly across the well-tended piazza and over Lake Como, which is only about 100 yards away. The rooms are airy and spacious, with those on the upper floors commanding the best views. Make sure to ask for a lake view because not all rooms have one. *Piazza Cavour 1, tel. 031/3221, fax 031/302622. 85* rooms with bath or shower. *Facilities: restaurant (closed Sun.), bar, parking. AE, DC, MC, V. $$$*

Tre Re. Located only a block west of the central Piazza del Duomo, this clean, spacious, and welcoming hotel is just a few steps from the cathedral. While the exterior gives away the age of this 16th-century palazzo, the rooms inside are airy, comfortable, and modernized. The moderately priced restaurant, which shares an ample terrace with the hotel, is popular with locals for Sunday lunch. *Via Boldoni 20, tel. 031/265374. 32 rooms, 29 with bath or shower. Facilities: restaurant (closed Mon. and Dec. 10–Jan. 9), bar, parking. MC, V. Closed Dec. 10–Jan. 15. $$*

Gardone Riviera/ Fasano del Garda
Dining
★

Villa Fiordaliso. The pink-and-white lakeside Villa Fiordaliso is mainly a high-quality restaurant, but it also has seven rooms for weary travelers. The menu is tied closely to the availability of fresh local produce, with seasonal treats such as zucchini flowers or porcini mushrooms used in salads or sauces. The villa once belonged to Claretta Petacci, who got it as a present from her lover, Benito Mussolini. You can eat on the lakefront terrace in summer. *Via Zanardelli 132, tel. 0365/20158, fax 0365/290011. Reservations advised. Jacket advised. 7 rooms with bath. AE, DC, MC, V. Closed Sun. dinner, Mon., and Jan.–Feb. $$$*

Lodging
★

Villa del Sogno. A small, winding road takes you from the village to this imposing villa, which surveys the valley and the lake below it. The most popular rooms, inevitably, are those with this view, which can be savored from balconies. The large hotel terrace and the quiet surrounding grounds add to the feeling of getting away from it all, and you'll probably think twice about a busy sightseeing itinerary once you've settled into position in the sun, with a cool drink in hand. *Corso Zanardelli 107, tel. 0365/290181, fax 0365/290230. 34 rooms with bath or shower. Facilities: park, terraces, pool, tennis court, restaurant. AE, DC, MC, V. Closed Oct. 15–Easter. $$$$*

Grand Hotel Fasano. A former 19th-century hunting lodge on the lakefront, the Fasano has matured into a seasonal hotel of a high standard. The staff is friendly, as are most of the guests, who seem to be keen to make the most use of the water sports at their disposal. It's worth paying a bit extra to get one of the larger rooms with a lake view and balcony. *Corso Zanardelli 160, tel. 0365/290220, fax 0365/290221. 70 rooms with bath or shower. Facilities: restaurant, bar, lakefront terraces, private beach, pool, tennis court. MC, V. Closed Nov.–May 15. $$$*

Gargnano
Dining

La Tortuga. Gargnano is where the lakeside road leading north from Gardone Riviera begins to weave its way through a series of tunnels: La Tortuga is the best restaurant in this scenic village. Specializing in the local cuisine, it features *soufflé di verdura* (soufflé of greens) and the excellent *trota allo scalogno e tartufo* (trout with scallions and truffles). From the wine list, try the local red Lugana, which is often served chilled. *Gargnano, tel. 0365/71251. Reservations advised. Jacket advised. AE, DC, MC, V. Closed Mon. evening (except June–Sept.), Tues., and Jan.–Feb. $$$*

Goito
Dining

Al Bersagliere. One of Lombardy's best restaurants can be found in this rustic four-room inn, located in the tiny riverside hamlet of Goito, some 16 kilometers (10 miles) northwest of Mantua on Route 236 (the main Mantua—Brescia road). It is homey and has been run by a single family for more than 150 years. Fish in particular is excellent, including the Mantuan classic, frog soup. The sole terrine and scampi mayonnaise are a bit lighter and less traditional. *Via Goitese 258, Goito, tel. 0376/60007. Reservations required. AE, DC, MC, V. Closed Mon., Tues. lunch and 15 days in Jan., 15 days in Aug. $$$*

Isola **La Locanda dell'Isola.** Isola Comacina, Lake Como's only island, five
Comacina minutes by regular boat from Sala Comacina, is rustic, restful, but
Dining at times crowded. The same could be said for the Locanda, but in
each case the visit is worth it. Forget any notions of choosing from
dozens of items on the menu because here the deal is a set price for a
set meal, with drinks included in the price. The good news is that the
food is fine, the service is friendly, and the setting (eating outdoors
on a shady terrace) is relaxing. You'll have to pace yourself through
a mixed antipasto, trout, chicken, salad, and dessert. *Isola Comacina, Sala Comacina, tel. 0344/55083. No reservations. Dress: casual. No credit cards. Closed Tues. (except June–Sept.) and Nov.–
Feb.* $$$

Mantua **Trattoria dei Martini.** With a romantic setting inside a 16th-century
Dining palazzo (and featuring some walls frescoed during that period), this
restaurant scores well with atmosphere. The menu leads through
traditional Mantuan terrain, with local specialties such as *tortelli di
zucca* (pasta stuffed with pumpkin), *insalata di cappone* (capon sal-
ad), and local variations on the Lombard favorite, risotto. *Piazza
Carlo d'Arco 1, tel. 0376/327101. Reservations advised; required on
weekends. AE, DC, MC, V. Closed Mon., Tues., July 15–31.* $$
L'Aquila Nigra. Located down a small side street opposite the Palaz-
zo Ducale, this popular restaurant is set in a former medieval convent. Frescoes look down from the walls on diners making their way
through local Mantuan dishes, such as *frittata di zucchine* (zucchini
omelet) and *faraona al pepe verde* (guinea fowl with green pepper).
*Vicolo Bonacolsi 4, tel. 0376/350651. Reservations required. AE,
DC, MC, V. Closed Sun., Mon., 3 weeks in Aug., and Dec. 24–Jan.
5.* $$

Lodging **San Lorenzo.** Mantua is a compact city, and the San Lorenzo is ideal-
ly placed in its center. The rooms are large and the decor is authentic
early 19th century. Although there is no restaurant, you're within
easy walking distance of the two listed above. Some people may find
the rooms in the front a little noisy at night, when locals decide that
the streets are empty enough of tourists to begin their own
passeggio, or fashion-conscious constitutional. The San Lorenzo has
a rooftop terrace and exudes comfort and individual attention. *Piaz-
za Concordia 14, tel. 0376/220500, fax 0376/327194. 41 rooms with
bath or shower. Facilities: garage. AE, DC, MC, V.* $$$

Milan **Savini.** Red carpets and glass chandeliers characterize the classy
Dining Savini, in the Galleria Vittorio Emanuele. It's a typical old-fashioned Milanese restaurant, with dining rooms on three floors, including a "winter garden," where you can watch the people strolling
in the Galleria. This is a good place to try the Milanese specialty risotto *al salto* (rice cooked as a sort of pancake, flipped in the pan) or
costoletta di vitello (fried veal cutlets). *Galleria Vittorio Emanuele,
tel. 02/720–03433. Dinner reservations advised. Jacket advised.
AE, DC, MC, V. Closed Sun., Aug. 10–20, Dec. 23–Jan. 3.* $$$$
Scaletta. The name means "little stairway" in Italian, and the steps
leading up to the Scaletta restaurant are a little stairway to culinary
paradise. This tiny restaurant could be the dining room of a gracious
home, with cool pastel colors, book-lined walls, and a superb collection of blown glass. Host/sommelier Aldo Bellini and genius cook
Mamma Pina in the kitchen treat their guests with cordiality and
take time to discuss wines and menus with you, if you like. Pina's
cooking is a light, personalized version of traditional Italian cuisine;
menus change frequently. Reserve two weeks ahead. *Piazzale
Stazione Porta Genova 3, tel. 02/581–00290. Reservations required.*

Jacket and tie preferred. No credit cards. Closed Sun., Mon., and Christmas, Easter, Aug. $$$$

★ **Boeucc.** This restaurant (pronounced "birch") is Milan's oldest. It's located in the same square as novelist Alessandro Manzoni's house, not far from La Scala. Subtly lit, with cream-colored fluted columns, chandeliers, thick carpets, and a garden for warm-weather dining, it has come a long way from the time when it was simply a basement "hole" (*boeucc* is old Milanese for *buco*, or hole). It serves not only typical Milanese food, but also a wide range of other dishes, including *penne al branzino e zucchine* (pasta with sea bass and zucchini sauce) and *gelato di castagne con zabaglione caldo* (chestnut ice cream with hot zabaglione). *Piazza Belgioioso 2, tel. 02/760-22880. Reservations required. Jacket advised. AE. Closed Sat., Sun. lunch, and Aug., Dec. 24–28. $$$*

Al Cantinone. Opera goers still come here for an after-theater drink, just as they did a century ago. The decor is classic Milanese trattoria, the service is fast, and the food is homey and reliable. A bonus: homemade pasta. Try the *pappardelle* (noodles) or ravioli with meat sauce, Tuscan style. There's a wide selection of grilled meats and a staggering choice of wines. *Via Agnello 19, entrance on Via Ragazzi del 99, tel. 02/807666. Reservations advised. AE, MC, V. Closed Sat. lunch, Sun., and Aug., Christmas, and 1 week in Jan., Easter. $$.*

Antica Trattoria della Pesa. Turn-of-the-century decor, dark wood paneling, and old-fashioned lamps re-create the atmosphere of this restaurant from when it opened more than one hundred years ago. This is authentic Old Milan, as the menu confirms, offering risotto, minestrone, and osso buco. *Viale Pasubio 10, tel. 02/655-5741. Reservations advised in the evening. AE, DC, MC, V. Closed Sun. and 2 weeks in Aug. $$*

La Capanna. The signora cooks the food, and her husband pours the wine and sees that everything goes smoothly in this popular trattoria located near the Piola Metro stop (and the university). The food is prevalently Tuscan—Tuscan salami, papardelle and steak—but some Milanese specialties are also on the menu. *Via Donatello 9, tel. 02/2940-0884. Reservations advised. AE, DC, MC, V. Closed Sat., Mon. evening. $$*

La Libera. Although this establishment in the heart of Brera bills itself as a *birreria con cucina* (beer cellar with kitchen), its young clientele comes here as much for the excellent food and convivial atmosphere as for the draft beer. A soft current of jazz plays under the gentle ripple of conversation, and the decor is a restful dark green. Sample the imaginative cooking—*insalata esotica* (salad with avocado, chicken, rice, and papaya) or *rognone di vitello con broccoletti e ginepro* (veal kidneys with broccoli and juniper berries). *Via Palermo 21, tel. 02/805-3603. No reservations. Jacket advised. No credit cards. Closed Sat., Sun. lunch, and Aug., Dec. 22–Jan. 1. $$*

Nabucco. This is a smart restaurant in the Brera district, tastefully furnished, whose menu offers such delights as risotto con porcini, an excellent range of salads, and homemade pastries and desserts. Although moderately priced, the good prix fixe lunches take it into the lower category. *Via Fiori Chiari 10, tel. 02/860663. Reservations advised. Jacket advised. AE, DC, MC, V. Closed Sun., Mon. lunch. $$*

Antica Trattoria Milanese. In the business district near the Castello Sforzesco, this small, family-run trattoria is crowded with white-collar workers at lunch and with regulars at dinner, when lingering is allowed. Get there early. Food is regional, with risotto and *cotoletta alla milanese* (breaded veal cutlet) good choices. The menu also offers seafood. *Via Camperio 21, tel. 02/864–62333. No reservations. Dress: casual. No credit cards. Closed Sun. and Aug. $–$$*

Brunch. A large and very pleasant cafeteria atop the Rinascente department store off Piazza del Duomo, it offers a varied menu, including seafood salad, vegetarian lasagne, grilled meat, and other luncheon specialties. This is a lunchtime bargain, only open noon–2:30, with a bonus view of the Duomo's spires. *La Rinascente, Piazza Duomo, tel. 02/877–15920. No reservations. Dress: casual. AE, DC, MC, V. Lunch only. Closed Sun. $–$$*

La Bruschetta. You'll find this tiny, busy pizzeria off Corso Vittorio Emanuele, behind the Duomo; it is run by a partnership of Tuscans and Neapolitans. The wood stove is in full view, so you can see your pizza cooking in front of you, although there are plenty of nonpizza dishes available, too, such as spaghetti *alle cozze e vongole* (spaghetti with clam and mussel sauce). *Piazza Beccaria 12, tel. 02/802494. Reservations advised, but fast service means you never wait long. Dress: casual. No credit cards. Closed Mon., Aug. 1–21, Dec. 24–28, Good Fri.–Easter Mon. $–$$*

La Giara. In this Pugliese restaurant you eat tavern style, at wooden tables and benches in simple surroundings. Yet the quality of the food from the limited menu is a revelation. Start with the *antipasto sott'olio* (eggplant, artichoke, mushroom, and tomato preserved in olive oil), and try one of the grilled meat courses, cooked on a range at the front of the restaurant and eaten with nothing but the excellent Pugliese bread and olive oil provided. *Viale Monza 10, tel. 02/285–3835. Reservations not necessary, though you may be asked to share a table at busy times. Dress: casual. No credit cards. Closed Wed. $*

San Tomaso. The atmosphere of an informal beer hall, a trendy young clientele, and a self-service counter add up to pleasant, easy eating. Very busy at lunch, it's usually quieter at night. *Via San Tomaso 5, tel. 02/874510. Reservations advised in evening. Dress: casual. No credit cards. Closed Sun. $*

Taverna Moriggi. Near the stock exchange, it's a dusky, wood-paneled wine bar serving a fixed-price lunch for about 30,000 lire, or cold cuts and cheeses in the evening. *Via Moriggi 8, tel. 02/864–50880. No reservations. Dress: casual. No credit cards. Closed Sat. lunch and Sun. $*

Lodging **Duomo.** This is the obvious choice if a central location is your priority: You're only 20 yards from the cathedral itself. Rooms on the second, fourth, and fifth floors look out onto the Gothic gargoyles and pinnacles of the Duomo. The hotel is spacious and modern, with air-conditioned rooms and duplex suites, snappily furnished in golds, creams, and browns. The guests' comfort is the important thing here; celebrities may be turned away if it's thought they will attract noisy fans and paparazzi. *Via San Raffaele 1, tel. 02/8833, fax 02/864–62027. 140 rooms with bath. Facilities: cable TV, restaurant, bar. AE, DC, MC, V. Closed Aug. $$$$*

Four Seasons. This elegant restoration of a 14th-century monastery is located on an exclusive shopping street in the center of Milan and has produced a gem—a precious one—at the highest rates in the city. The hotel blends European class with American comfort. Individually decorated rooms have opulent marble bathrooms; most rooms face the quiet courtyard. Downstairs is the hotel's popular Il Teatro restaurant. *Via Gesù 8, tel. 02/77088, fax 02/77085000. 78 rooms, all with bath. Facilities: restaurant, bar, convention facilities, business center. AE, DC, MC, V. $$$$*

Hotel de la Ville. This modern hotel in the center of town is decorated in pleasingly subtle, pale colors with silk-hung walls in the guest rooms. Many of the rooms have small balconies, and some have a view of the spires of the Duomo. *Via Hoepli, 6, tel. 02/867651, fax 02/866609. 105 rooms with bath. Facilities: sitting room, bar, 5 conference rooms. AE, DC, MC, V. $$$$*

Pierre Milano. No expense was spared to furnish each room of this luxury hotel in a different style with the most elegant color-coordinated fabrics and a variety of modern and antique furniture. Everything is electronic. You can open the curtains, turn off the lights, have personal messages from the front desk appear on your TV screen—all by pressing the buttons on your remote control. The Pierre is located on the inner beltway, near the medieval church of Sant'Ambrogio. *Via De Amicis 32, tel. 02/720–00581, fax 02/805–2157. 47 rooms with bath or shower. Facilities: restaurant, bar, convenient parking. AE, DC, MC, V. $$$$*

Principe di Savoia. Of the three deluxe Ciga hotels in Milan renovated in 1991, this is the most sumptuously elegant. Behind the neoclassical facade, the decor is in 19th-century Lombard style, with lavish mirrors, drapes, and carpets. Bedrooms have been enlarged and are more comfortable than ever. In the same general location, near the central station, are Ciga's **Palace,** with interiors in Empire style, and the **Duca di Milano,** suites only, with Edwardian decor. *Piazza della Repubblica 17, tel. 02/6230, fax 02/659–5838. 287 rooms with bath. Facilities: restaurant, indoor pool, fitness center, bar, parking. AE, DC, MC, V. $$$$*

Carlton-Senato. This is the ideal choice for visitors who intend to spend time shopping—or even window shopping—in the nearby high-fashion streets, Via della Spiga, Via Sant'Andrea, and Via Monte Napoleone. The hotel is very light and airy, with air-conditioning, double-thick windows, a garage with direct access to the hotel, and lots of little touches (such as free chocolates and liqueurs) to make up for the rather functional room furnishings. Some rooms have terraces large enough for a table, chair, and potted shrubs. *Via Senato 5, tel. 02/760–15535, fax 02/783300. 79 rooms with bath. Facilities: restaurant, bar, garage. AE, MC, V. Closed Aug. $$$*

Gritti. The Picassos, Matisses, and Van Goghs in the lobby are originals—so the manager will tell you—except that they were painted quite recently "in the spirit." The Gritti is a bright hotel with a cheerful atmosphere, adequate rooms, and good views (from the inside upper floors) of tiled roofs and the gold Madonnina statue on top of the Duomo, only a few hundred yards away. *Piazza Santa Maria Beltrade 4 (north end of Via Torino), tel. 02/801056, fax 02/89010999. 48 rooms with bath or shower. Facilities: restaurant, bar. AE, DC, MC, V. $$–$$$*

Canada. This friendly small hotel is close to Piazza del Duomo on the edge of a district full of shops and restaurants. It offers good value in rooms that are furnished in anonymous style but have TV, air-conditioning, and fridge-bar. *Via Santa Sofia, 16, tel. 02/583–04844, fax 02/583–00282. 35 rooms with bath. AE, DC, MC, V. $$*

Casa Svizzera. A faithful clientele considers this one of Milan's best small hotels in its price category, so it's advisable to make reservations early. The location, adjacent to the Duomo and a few yards from the Galleria, is central and handy to Metro and bus lines. The hotel has been renovated and soundproofed, and the air-conditioned rooms, with TV and fridge-bar, are decorated in a cheery floral-printed fabric. *Via San Raffaele 3, tel. 02/8692246, fax 02/72004690. 45 rooms with bath. Facilities: bar. AE, DC, MC, V. Closed Aug. $$*

★ **London.** Close to the Duomo, the London has clean, spacious rooms and an English-speaking staff. It has an arrangement with the Opera Prima restaurant in the same building, if you want to take your meals there. *Via Rovello 3, tel. 02/720–20166, fax 02/805–7037. 29 rooms with shower. MC, V. Closed Dec. 25–Jan. 3, Aug. $*

San Francisco. Located near Metro stations on two lines (Loreto, Piola, or Pasteur stops) and not far from the Central Station, this modern hotel has a functional, flag-bedecked lobby, simply furnished rooms, and a small garden where guests can relax in fair weather. *Viale Lombardia 55, tel. 02/236–1009, fax 02/266–80377, 33 rooms, 31 with bath. AE, DC, MC, V. $*

Orta San Giulio
Dining and Lodging

Hotel San Rocco. A converted 17th-century convent in a lakeside garden on the edge of town, the San Rocco has completed a major renovation. Half of the rooms have views of the lake, garden, and surrounding mountains. Many have balconies and are furnished in modern style. The restaurant features international cuisine and beautiful views of the lake. Among the specialities is *pesce persico* (perch). *Via Gippini da Verona 11, tel. 0322/905632, fax 0322/ 905635. 74 rooms with bath. Facilities: restaurant (reservations advised), bar, pool, health club. AE, DC, MC, V. $$$*

Pavia
Dining
★

Locanda Vecchia Pavia. This attractive restaurant next to the cathedral has art nouveau decor and caters to sophisticated tastes. You'll find creative versions of traditional regional cuisine, including *rane* (frogs), the local specialty, in risotto or on a spit. *Casoncelli* (stuffed pasta) and *costoletta di vitello alla milanese* (breaded veal chop) are done with style, as are more imaginative seafood dishes. *Via Cardinale Riboldi 2, tel. 0382/304132. Reservations required. Jacket advised. AE, DC, MC, V. Closed Mon., Wed. lunch, Jan. 1–9, and Aug. $$$*

Ranco
Dining
★

Ristorante del Sole. Chef Carlo Brovelli presides over this lakeside inn on the southern, Lombardian shore of Lake Maggiore, with a cheerfulness that is infectious. You'll probably feel the same way if you get there early enough to snag one of the tables in the arbor and enjoy one of the best views of the lake, which figures in the menu, too, in the form of carpaccio made of fine slices of raw trout and perch. Pigeon is usually served caramelized in honey, while much of the menu changes with the season—artichokes, for example, in many forms in the spring, and eggplant in the summer. Take our advice on reservations to ensure the best table possible because this restaurant is memorable (there are also nine apartments). *Piazza Venezia 5, Ranco (near Angera), tel. 0331/976507, fax 0331/976620. Reservations advised. Jacket advised. AE, DC, MC, V. Closed Mon. dinner (except June–Sept.), Tues., and Jan. 1–Feb. 15. $$$$*

Sirmione
Dining

Osteria del Pescatore. The specialty of this simple and popular restaurant is lake fish. The restaurant is located in town, on the road that leads to the Grotte di Catullo, and has a rustic look. Try grilled trout with a bottle of local white wine. *Via Piana 20, tel. 030/916216. Reservations advised. Dress: casual. DC, MC, V. Closed Jan. and Wed. Oct.–May. $$*

Lodging
★

Villa Cortine Palace. An imposing former private villa set in a secluded park and entered through large iron gates, Villa Cortine treads the fine line between being ornately imposing and just plain ostentatious. It dominates a low hill, and the grounds—a colorful mixture of lawns, trees, statues, and fountains—go down to the lake. The villa itself dates from the early part of the 19th century, although a new wing (1952) has been added: The trade-off is between the more charming Old World decor in the older rooms and the better lake views from the newer ones. Either way you'll have the benefit of the extensive grounds and diverse facilities, as well as the attention of the well-trained and friendly staff. *Via Grotte 6, tel. 030/*

990–5890, fax 030/916390. 57 rooms with bath or shower. Facilities: spacious park-style grounds, lakefront beach, pool, tennis court, restaurant, terrace bar. AE, DC, MC, V. Closed Oct. 26–Mar. $$$$

Continental. Conveniently located, on the lakefront, right next to the spa, the Continental operates on a demi-pension basis only. This works to keep the cost in check, and the hotel has the amenities and feel of a much more expensive establishment. Most rooms have balconies, but ask specifically for a lake view. *Via Punta Staffalo 7, tel. 030/990–5711, fax 030/916278. 53 rooms with bath or shower. Facilities: lakeside terraces, pool, private beach. AE, DC, MC, V. Closed Dec.–Feb. $$$ ($$ off-season: Mar.–June, Oct., Nov.).*

Hotel Sirmione. Just inside the city walls, near the Castello, this charming hotel, which is also a spa, sits amid gardens and terraces beside the lake. The guest rooms are decorated with comfortable Scandinavian slat beds. Some have matching draperies and wall coverings in spriggy prints, some have superbly executed white built-in furniture, and many have balconies. The corner dining room overlooks the lake and garden, and there is outdoor dining in fine weather. Many of the guests have been coming for years, and there's a homelike feeling about the place and the attentiveness of its staff. Full and half-pension are offered. *Piazza Castello 19, tel 030/916331, fax 030/916558. 76 rooms with bath. Facilities: restaurant, bar, meeting room, pool, landing stage, parking, spa treatments. AE, DC, MC, V. $$*

Stresa
Dining

Monferrato. Centrally located, off Piazza Cadorna and close to the embarcadero, this hotel restaurant serves risotto *con filetti di persico* (rice with perch fillets) and typical Piedmontese meat dishes, such as beef braised in Barolo wine. *Via Mazzini 14, tel. 0323/31386. Dress: casual. AE, DC, MC, V. $$*

Lodging

Grand Hotel et des Iles Borromees. A palatial Old World hotel, this princely establishment has catered to a demanding European clientele since 1863. And though it still has the spacious salons and lavish decor of the turn of the century, it has also been discreetly modernized; rooms have new and luxurious bathrooms, and there is a fitness center, as well as convention facilities. *Lungolago Umberto I 167, tel. 0323/30431, fax 0323/32405. 167 rooms with bath. Facilities: restaurant, bar, pool, tennis courts, fitness center, park. AE, DC, MC, V. $$$$*

Milan e Speranza. The result of the fusion of two of Stresa's traditional hostelries, this large hotel overlooks the embarcadero, where the lake boats come in and out, and has views of the Borromean islands and lake. The decor is pleasantly old-fashioned, and many rooms have that romantic view, but they also get some noise from the dock. *Piazza Imbarcadero, tel. 0323/31190, fax 0323/32729. 159 rooms with bath. Facilities: bar, restaurant. AE, DC, MC, V. $$*

Primavera. In a plain 1950s building in the heart of Stresa, Primavera has balconies embellished with flower boxes. It has the advantage of a location in a quiet pedestrian zone only three minutes from the lake and embarcadero. Rooms are compact and simply furnished. *Via Cavour 39, tel. 0323/31286, fax 0323/33458. 32 rooms with bath. AE, MC, V. $–$$*

La Fontana. A small hotel with a friendly management, the Fontana is on the main road through town, about 20 minutes on foot from the embarcadero. Some rooms have good views of the lake, but the noise factor may make it advisable to take a back room. There is a pleasant garden, but no restaurant. *SS33 (Sempione road), tel. 0323/32707. 20 rooms with bath. AE, MC, V. $*

The Arts and Nightlife

The Arts

Opera   The season at Milan's famous **La Scala** opera house runs from December 7 (St. Ambrose Day) through May. Seats are sold out well in advance, but if you are prepared to pay the desk clerk at your hotel, you will probably be able to get hold of a pair of tickets. For information on schedules and the (unlikely) possibility of box-office tickets, contact Teatro alla Scala (Piazza della Scala, tel. 02/807041). For reservations, call 02/809126. From abroad you can book in advance by mail or fax (02/887–9297) or at CIT or other travel agencies (at agencies, no more than 10 days before performance). Consult the listings in the informative monthly *Milano Mese*, free at APT offices, or the weekly *Viva Milano*.

Concerts   La Scala opera house in Milan (*see above*) features a two-month season of **classical concerts** in October and November.

Brescia's **Teatro Grande** (tel. 030/375–0459) has a series of **classical music** concerts from November to May.

In Gardone Riviera, **Il Vittoriale,** the home of the Italian poet Gabriele d'Annunzio, has a series of concerts in its outdoor theater during July and August. For information, call 0365/20347.

Bergamo's **International Piano Festival,** held in Teatro Donizetti (Piazza Matteotti, tel. 035/249631), with some concerts in Brescia, attracts world-class musicians in May and June.

In September, music festivals are held in Como, Stresa, and Orta San Giulio.

Events   Each year, on the feast of the Assumption (Aug. 15), a **contest** is held in Mantua to determine who is the best *madonnaro* (street artist). Some of the painters can re-create masterpieces in a matter of minutes. During the first half of September, Pavia's **Settembre Pavese** festival presents street processions, displays, and concerts.

Theater   Milan's **Piccolo Teatro** (Via Rovello 2, tel. 02/877663) and **Teatro Manzoni** (Via Manzoni 40, tel. 02/790543) are noted for their excellent productions, given in Italian, of course.

Nightlife

Jazz   **Le Scimmie** (Via Ascanio Sforza 49, Milan, tel. 02/894–02874) is a good spot for cool jazz in a relaxed atmosphere.

Nightclubs   The following Milan clubs are good bets for an evening of dinner and dancing, but don't expect this entertainment to come cheap: **Stage** (Galleria Manzoni, off Via Monte Napoleone, tel. 02/760–21071, closed Mon.) and **Nepentha** (Piazza Diaz 1, tel. 02/804837, closed Sun.).

Discos   **Lizard** (Largo La Foppa, Milan, tel. 02/659–0890, closed Mon.) is trendy, loud, and expensive—a formula that doesn't deter the young Milanese crowd.

Contatto (Corso Sempione 76, Milan, tel. 02/331–4904, open daily midnight–dawn) and **After Dark** (Via Certosa 134, Milan, tel. 02/305585, closed Tues.) are gay clubs/discos for men only.

Bars **Gershwin's,** in Milan (Via Corrado il Salico 10, tel. 02/849–7722), is a relaxed piano bar, where Cole Porter and Noel Coward, along with the bar's namesake, figure in the repertoire.

El Brellin (Vicolo Lavandai at the corner of Alzaia Naviglio Grande, Milan, tel. 02/5810–1351, closed Sun.) is one of the many bars in the Navigli district.

In the Brera quarter, **Momus** (Via Fiori Chiari 8, tel. 02/805–6227) is upscale and intimate.

11 The Dolomites

Bolzano, Trento, and Cortina d'Ampezzo

Unlike other famous Alpine ranges, this vast mountainous domain in northeast Italy has remained relatively undeveloped. The virginal landscape is the ultimate playground for the family or traveler on a quest for an original adventure. Ski fanatics travel across the world to dare some of the steep slopes that test even Olympic champions. Mountaineers risk the climb up sheer rock faces. For calmer souls there is the seduction of a landscape painted from a palette of extreme colors. The lowland valleys are laced with rivers spanned by awkward bridges and are dotted with secluded villages, picturebook castles, and unexpected historic sites.

The Dolomites, sprawling over the Trentino–Alto Adige region and into parts of Lombardy by the Swiss border and the Veneto along the Austrian border, became known to Americans as a winter sports center after Cortina d'Ampezzo catapulted to fame by hosting the Winter Olympics of 1956. Today, scores of funiculars, chair lifts, and ski lifts give access to 600 miles of ski runs, as well as ski jumps and bobsled runs.

Then there are the "untouchable" zones—inaccessible by means of chair lift or ski lift. These are the famous plateaus topping some of the highest mountains, from which you can see Italy on one side and Austria or Switzerland on the other. To enjoy such a rare spectacle, you must spend arduous hours climbing beyond where the lifts leave you, and when you reach the top, you will probably see cows casually grazing on the grass. It can make you dizzy just thinking of how they got there, but contradictions are common in the Dolomites.

This expansive land of rocks and valleys has long attracted Italians and other Europeans looking for a varied natural environment. What they—and you—find is a confusion of colors, architectural styles, and languages. At sunset, the colors of the rocks are highlighted by purples and pinks, with even the snowcapped peaks reflecting the pink glow. A meander through the valleys becomes a botanical escapade, with rare plant species abounding; high above you on the cliffs are castles, protected by their size and position. The serious climber will get a closer view of these remote fortresses. There, on the higher levels, are some rarely seen animals: bears, deer, mountain goats, and birds of prey. It's perhaps not surprising that Reinhold Messer, the first man to climb Everest without oxygen, lives in the Dolomites.

Straddling the Brenner Pass—the main access point to Italy from central Europe—the Dolomites play host to a mixture of cultures and languages. The people of the Alto Adige are predominantly German speaking, and their crafts and food have an Austrian accent (until World War I, the area was Austria's South Tyrol). The Trentino, on the other hand, is Italian speaking. Reflecting this diversity, the area, since 1948, has enjoyed special status as the Autonomous Region of Trentino–Alto Adige, made up of the independent provinces of Trento and Bolzano. But there is still another language to be heard in the area: Ladin, an offshoot of Latin still spoken by a small Ladin community, can credit centuries of isolation in mountain fastnesses for its survival.

In this chapter, place names are given in Italian, with German equivalents, where relevant, in parentheses. Signs throughout much of the Dolomites are bilingual.

Essential Information

Important Addresses and Numbers

Tourist Information The Tourist Board for the autonomous province of Alto Adige is located on Piazza Parrocchia 11–12, Bolzano (tel. 0471/993808). The Trentino Tourist Board is at Via Sighele 3, Trento (tel. 0461/914444). The following are local tourist boards.

Bolzano (Piazza Walther 8, tel. 0471/975656).
Bormio (Via Stelvio, tel. 0342/903300).
Bressanone (Via Stazione 9, tel. 0472/36401).
Chiusa (Piazza Tinne 40, tel. 0472/47424).
Cortina d'Ampezzo (Piazzetta San Francesco 8, tel. 0436/3231).
Madonna di Campiglio (Via Pradalago 4, tel. 0465/42000).
Merano (Corso della Libertà 45, tel. 0473/35223).
Rovereto (Via Dante 63, tel. 0464/430363).
Trento (Via Alfieri 4, tel. 0461/983880).

Emergencies **Police, Ambulance,** tel. 113. For first aid, ask for "Pronto Soccorso," and be prepared to give your address.

Late-Night Pharmacies Pharmacies take turns staying open late or on Sundays; for the latest information, consult the current list posted on the front door of each pharmacy or ask at the local tourist office.

Car Rentals **Bolzano.** *Avis* (Piazza Verdi 18, tel. 0471/971467); *Hertz* (Via Alto Adige 30, tel. 0471/977155).

Arriving and Departing by Car and Train

By Car The most important route in the region, A22, is the main north–south autostrada linking Italy with northern Europe via the Brenner Pass.

By Train The express train line that links the towns of Bolzano, Trento, and Rovereto connects with other main lines at Verona, just south of the region.

Getting Around

By Car Autostrada A22 connects Bressanone, Bolzano, Trento, and Rovereto. Roads in the broad mountain valleys are usually wide two-lane routes, but the roads up into the highest passes can be narrow and subject to sudden closure, even in the months when they are open to drivers. A Bolzano number (tel. 0471/49000) provides information on weather-related closures.

By Train An express train line follows the course of the Adige Valley from the Brenner Pass southward past Bolzano, Trento, and Rovereto. Branch lines from Trento and Bolzano go to some of the smaller valleys, but most of the mountain attractions described in this chapter are beyond the reach of trains.

By Bus Local buses connect the train stations at Trento, Bolzano, and Merano with the mountain resorts. The service is fairly frequent between most main towns during the day, though some parts of the region remain out of the reach of public transportation.

Guided Tours

Orientation If you are without a car or if you don't care to drive over mountain
roads, guided tours from Bolzano or Trento can show you the Dolomites the easy way. However, the sudden and frequent snowfalls
mean that tours are offered in summer only.

In **Bolzano,** city sightseeing and local excursions are organized by
the **SAD** bus company (Via Conciapelli 60, near the train station, tel.
0471/971259). In July and August, full-day mountain tours include a
Great Dolomites Tour from Bolzano to Cortina and a tour of the
Venosta Valley that climbs over the Stelvio Pass into Switzerland. A
tour of the **Val Gardena** and the Siusi Alps is available from April to
October.

In **Trento,** city sightseeing can be arranged through the **Azienda
Autonoma** tourist office (Via Alfieri 4, tel. 0461/983880). From June
through September, the **Calderari e Moggioli** travel agency (Via
Manci 46, tel. 0461/980275) offers a full-day guided bus tour of the
Brenta Dolomites and the **Great Dolomites Tour,** a full-day drive over
the Pordoi and Falzarego passes to Cortina d'Ampezzo and Lake
Misurina. Also, from June through September, the Trentino APT
(Via Sighele 3, tel. 0461/980000) organizes guided tours and excur-
sions by train to castles in the region.

Exploring the Dolomites

The best—and only—way to get around in this mountainous region
is by following the course of the valleys that find their way to the
heart of the massifs that compose the Dolomites. The most important are the valleys formed by the Adige River, which begins near
the Swiss border and runs to Bolzano, then continues almost due
south, and by the Isarco River, beginning at the Brenner Pass and
running southward to Bolzano, where it flows into the Adige. Italy's
main road and rail connections to north central Europe follow the
same rivers northward en route to the Brenner Pass.

The first tour devotes most of its time to Bolzano and Trento, the
two main towns, along with a peek at Rovereto. Tour 2 sets off west
from Bolzano along the Venosta Valley, climbing to panoramic views
from the Stelvio Pass before swinging south to visit the lofty Brenta
massif.

The last tour goes east from Bolzano, following the Great Dolomite
Road to the chic ski resort of Cortina d'Ampezzo. It then goes north
to the lesser-known town of Dobbiaco, gateway to the Pusteria Valley and the best way west toward the Isarco Valley. Before completing the circuit to Bolzano, it makes a slight detour eastward into the
Val Gardena, the valley where you'll have the best chance of hearing
Ladin spoken.

Highlights for First-Time Visitors

Brunico (Tour 3: The Great Dolomites Road).

Cappella di San Giovanni, Bolzano (Tour 1: Bolzano to Trento).

Castello di Buonconsiglio, Trento (Tour 1: Bolzano to Trento).

Cornedo and the view of the Catinaccio range
(Tour 3: The Great Dolomites Road).

Cortina d'Ampezzo (Tour 3: The Great Dolomites Road).

Merano (Tour 2: West to the Stelvio Pass).

Museo Diocesano, Bressanone (Tour 3: The Great Dolomites Road).

Passo dello Stelvio (Tour 2: West to the Stelvio Pass).

Val Gardena (Tour 3: The Great Dolomites Road).

Tour 1: Bolzano to Trento

Numbers in the margin correspond to points of interest on the Dolomites and Bolzano maps.

❶ Bolzano (Bozen), the capital of the autonomous province of Alto Adige, is an ideal base for your exploration of the surrounding Dolomites. It is protected by the mountains to the north and the east and is located on the main north–south artery between northern Europe and Italy. This quiet city at the confluence of the Isarco (Eisack) and Talvera rivers has retained a provincial appeal, but it contradicts its country image with commercial features acquired to cater to the needs of tourists. There are no high rises, but McDonald's can be seen—housed, of course, in a more archaic building.

Bolzano's heart is pedestrians-only **Piazza Walther,** named after the 12th-century German wandering minstrel Walther von der Vogelweide, whose songs lampooned the papacy and praised the Holy Roman Emperor. The square serves as an open-air living room where locals and tourists alike can be found at all hours sipping a drink (perhaps a glass of chilled Riesling) at the café tables.

Time Out   The bar at the **Hotel Grifone** (Grief), on Piazza Walther, is one of the best places for a view of the square. Tables are set up outside, but the cozy interior is enticing if the weather turns bad.

---

❷ At one corner of the square is the city's Gothic **Duomo** (Cathedral), built between the 12th and 14th centuries. Its lacy spire looks down on the mosaiclike tiles covering its pitched roof. Inside the church are 14th- and 15th-century frescoes and an intricately carved stone pulpit dating from 1514.

Via Posta leads from the other side of the square to **Piazza ❸ Domenicani,** with its 13th-century **Dominican church,** renowned as Bolzano's main repository for paintings, especially frescoes. In the adjoining **Cappella di San Giovanni** you can see frescoes of the Giotto school, one of which is the *Triumph of Death* (ca. 1340). Despite its macabre title, this fresco shows the birth of a pre-Renaissance sense of depth and individuality.

❹ From here the narrow Via Goethe leads to **Piazza delle Erbe,** where a bronze statue of Neptune presides over a bounteous fruit and vegetable market (Mon.–Sat. 8–1). The stalls spill over with colorful displays of local produce; bakeries and grocery stores showcase hot breads, pastries, cheeses, and delicatessen meats—a complete range of picnic supplies. Try the *speck* (smoked ham) and the Tyrolean-style apple strudel.

The market is at the beginning of Bolzano's main shopping street, **Via dei Portici** (Lauben), lined with long, narrow arcades. The shops specialize in Tyrolean handicrafts and clothing—lederhosen, loden goods, linen suits, and dirndls.

❺ Via del Museo leads away from the market to the **Museo Civico,** which houses a rich collection of traditional costumes, wood carvings, and archaeological exhibits. The mixture of styles is a reflection of the region's cultural cross-fertilization. *Via del Museo 45. Admission: 2,000 lire. Open Tues.–Sat. 9–noon, 2:30–5:30, Sun. 10–1.*

Just across the road is **Ponte Talvera,** a bridge that extends over the Talvera River to the district of Gries. Cross over to visit the **Parrocchiale** (parish church) of Gries, with its elaborately carved 15th-century wooden altar, and the Benedictine abbey and Baroque church of **Sant'Agostino.** The churches are about a half mile beyond the bridge, along Corso Libertà. Just beyond the parish church is the Passeggiata, a pathway that leads up to the **Guncina** hill, where you get a panoramic view of Bolzano.

Recross the river and go immediately left, along the Lungotalvera Promenade, upstream to the 13th-century **Castel Mareccio** (Schloss Maretsch), nestled under the mountains and surrounded by vineyards. *Restaurant open to public; admission to castle by appointment only. Call tel. 0471/976615 or contact the Bolzano tourist office.*

Fifteen kilometers (9 miles) south of Bolzano is the vineyard village of **Caldaro,** located on the Strada del Vino (Wine Route). From here you get clear views of castles high up on the surrounding mountains, a backdrop that reflects the centuries of division that forged the unique character of the area. The Caldaro architecture is famous for the way it blends Italian Renaissance elements of balance and harmony with the soaring windows and peaked arches of the local Gothic tradition. Santa Caterina church, on the main square, is a good example.

The Wine Route traces its way through foothills and small villages where the vineyards rise up the terraced hillsides. Eight kilometers (5 miles) beyond Caldaro is **Termeno,** where there is a **Wine Museum** at Ringberg Castle just as you enter the village. Here you can taste or buy some of the specialties of the region. *Admission: 2,000 lire. Open Easter–Oct., Tues.–Sat. 10–noon and 2–6, Sun. 2–6.*

Time Out   In the fall, join the locals as they go into the hills to little taverns to taste the new wine and eat roast chestnuts. These jaunts are known as *toergglen* (from the German *toergl,* meaning winepress).

About 10 minutes past Termeno is **Ora** (Auer), where the Adige Valley broadens and you can join the autostrada A22 heading south. Half an hour of easy driving through the orchard-lined valley takes you to **Trento,** capital of the autonomous Trentino province. Somehow this city has escaped the ravages of commercialization and retains its architectural charm, artistic attractions, and historic importance.

It was here, from 1545 to 1563, that the structure of the Catholic Church was redefined, in the famous Council of Trent. This was the starting point of the Counter-Reformation, which brought half of Europe back to Catholicism. Until 1803, Trento itself was ruled by prince-bishops. You'll see the word *Consiglio* (Council) everywhere in Trento—in hotel, restaurant, and street names, and even on wine labels.

Trento is worth a visit anytime but is especially attractive in the spring, at blossom time, or during the fall harvest. The city hosts many festivals in both seasons, ranging from the agricultural fair in early spring to the *Festival Internazionale Film delle Montagne* (International Festival of Mountain and Exploring Films) in May. A

The Dolomites

Bolzano

Castel Mareccio, **8**
Dominican Church, **3**
Duomo, **2**
Museo Civico, **5**
Parrocchiale, **6**
Piazza delle Erbe, **4**
Sant'Agostino, **7**

summer bonus is the week-long San Vigilio Fair, culminating on June 26, when townspeople don medieval clothing in honor of their patron saint.

Like Bolzano, Trento has a square at its heart—**Piazza del Duomo.** In the center is a Baroque fountain of Neptune; the massive, low, Romanesque **Duomo** forms the southern edge of the square. Before entering the cathedral, pause to savor the view of the mountaintops ranged majestically around the city and visible above the rooftops in every direction. The mountain weather can change within minutes, and you can never be sure of the same visibility when you reemerge from the cathedral.

Step inside to see the unusual arcaded stone stairways on either side of the austere nave. Ahead of you is the *baldacchino* (altar canopy), a clear copy of Bernini's masterpiece in St. Peter's in Rome. In a small chapel to the right is a mournful 15th-century Crucifixion, with Mary and the Apostle John. This crucifix was a focal point of the Council of Trent: Each decree agreed on during the two decades of deliberations was solemnly read out in front of it. Outside, walk around to the back of the cathedral to see an exquisite display of 14th-century stonemasons' art, from the small porch to the intriguing knotted columns on the graceful apse.

The crenellated **Palazzo Pretorio,** which seems to be a wing of the cathedral, was built in the 13th century as the prudently fortified residence of the prince-bishops. Endowed with considerable power and autonomy, these clerics enjoyed a unique position in the medieval hierarchy. From the beginning of the 11th century, they wielded a twofold authority, administering civil and military affairs on behalf of the Holy Roman Emperor, and acting as the pope's representatives in ecclesiastical matters. At the same time other parts of Italy were at war, with each side pledging its loyalty to one or the other power. This delicate balancing act continued for 800 years, ending when Austria secularized the principality in 1802.

The Palazzo Pretorio now houses the **Museo Diocesano Tridentino,** where you can see paintings showing the seating plan of the prelates during the Council of Trent; early 16th-century tapestries by Pieter van Aelst, the Belgian artist who carried out Raphael's designs for the Vatican tapestries; carved wood altars and statues; and an 11th-century sacramentary, or book of services. These and other precious objects all come from the cathedral's treasury. *Piazza Duomo 18. Admission: 2,000 lire. Open mid-Feb.–mid-Nov., Mon.–Sat. 9:30–12:30, 2:30–6.*

Time Out Locals love the ice cream and snacks at **Bertelli** (Via Oriola 29, closed Mon.), an attractive café with tables outdoors on Piazza Lodron. It's located a few steps down Via Garibaldi from the rear of the cathedral.

Return to Piazza del Duomo to reach **Via Cavour,** which leads off from the northwest side. About 100 yards down this narrow street is the Renaissance church of **Santa Maria Maggiore,** where many sessions of the Council of Trent were held. From here it's an easy 50-yard walk up the lane behind the church to **Via Belenzani,** famous for its Renaissance *palazzi,* whose frescoed facades add a colorful note to the street. Locals sometimes call this stretch of road Trento's outdoor gallery.

Turn right onto Via Manci and begin a pleasant 200-yard climb past souvenir shops and glassware outlets to the moated **Castello del**

Buonconsiglio (Castle of Good Counsel). This huge castle was the stronghold of the prince-bishops; its position and size made it easier to defend than the Palazzo Pretorio. As you stand facing it, you can see the evolution of architectural styles, starting with the medieval fortifications of the Castelvecchio section on the far left, down to the more decorative Renaissance Magno Palazzo, built three centuries later in 1530. The Castello now houses the **Museo Provinciale d'Arte** (Provincial Art Museum), where exhibits of art and archaeology are displayed in medieval halls or under Renaissance coffered ceilings. The 13th-century **Torre dell'Aquila** (Eagle's Tower) holds the highlight of the museum, a fresco cycle of the months of the year. It is full of charming and informatively detailed scenes of 15th-century life in both court and countryside. *Via B. Clesio 5. Admission: 4,000 lire. Open Tues.–Sun. 9–noon, 2–5.*

Walk along the front of the castle to the Castelvecchio end, on the left, and cross onto Piazza Raffaello Sanzio. The **Torre Verde** (Green Tower), part of Trento's 13th-century fortifications, stands here, alongside other fragments of the walls. From this square, Via Torre Verde leads back to the center of Trento: The road changes its name to **Via Torre Vanga** as it reaches the tower of that name, another 13th-century fortification, this time guarding the medieval bridge across the Adige, Ponte San Lorenzo.

From a cable car station at the bridge, you can get a lift to **Belvedere di Sardagna,** a vantage point 1,200 feet above Trento.

⓬ Continue down A22 another 24 kilometers (15 miles) to reach **Rovereto**, a medieval town in the main north–south valley of the Adige. A 15th-century castle looks down on the town, but this district has more recent memories of warfare. Some of the fiercest fighting of World War I took place in the wooded hills around Rovereto, with Italian and Austrian troops bogged down in prolonged and costly conflict. Every night you're reminded of the thousands who fell: At nightfall the bells of the **Campana dei Caduti** (Bell of the Fallen) toll to commemorate war victims throughout the world.

Tour 2: West to the Stelvio Pass

The high mountain road running through the Stelvio Pass is closed from November to May, so if you're traveling during that period, you won't be able to follow this tour all the way. The leg from Merano to Naturno can be driven from Bolzano year-round; at times of the year when the pass is closed, you'll have to take S42 west from Bolzano 126 kilometers (78 miles) to Tresenda, in Lombardy, and head northeast on S38 another 48 kilometers (30 miles) in order to resume the tour at Bormio.

⓭ Only 28 kilometers (17 miles) north of Bolzano, along the Adige Valley, is **Merano** (Meran), the second largest town in the Alto Adige. Merano has been famous as a spa town for 150 years, known for its thermal waters, which, like those in many health spas, have natural radioactivity. It is also renowned for its "grape cure"—consisting of grapes, not wine. Sheltered by mountains, Merano has an unusually mild climate, with summer temperatures rarely exceeding 80° F and winters that usually stay above freezing, despite the skiing that is within easy reach. (Chair lifts and cable cars connect Merano with the high Alpine slopes of Avelengo and San Vigilio.)

Along the narrow streets of Merano's old town, houses sport little towers and huge wooden doors, and the pointed arches of the Gothic cathedral sit with harmony next to neoclassical and art nouveau buildings. In the heart of the old town, **Piazza del Duomo,** is the 14th-century Gothic cathedral, with a crenellated facade and an ornate campanile. The Cappella di **Santa Barbara,** just behind the cathedral, is an octagonal church containing a 15th-century *Pietà*.

Merano's main shopping street, the narrow, arcaded **Via dei Portici** (Lauben), runs west from the cathedral. A good place for souvenir shopping, it features most of the best regional products: wood carvings, Tyrolean-style clothes, embroidery, cheeses, salami, and fruit schnapps. Turn left when it ends, onto Via delle Corse and head down to the Passirio River, about a quarter-mile away. Cross the river via the Ponte del Teatro to reach the **Terme** (Municipal Baths), just on the other side. This huge complex is the nerve center of the spa facilities, although some hotels have their own. Technicians are trained to treat you with mud packs, massages, and inhalation and sauna routines, or just with the thermal waters, which are said to be especially good for coronary and circulatory problems. Other cures include the famous grape cure at harvest time in the fall, when a two-week diet of fresh grapes has since Roman times been seen as a successful way to tone up digestive, liver, and urinary tract functions.

From Merano, follow S38 west along the course of the Adige into the Val Venosta district. Tiny churches, some 1,200 years old, dot the hillsides: Distances play tricks on the eye, making some of the higher ones appear to be toys. Stop at **Naturno,** about 15 kilometers (9 miles) west of Merano, to look at **San Procolo.** This small church, which is frescoed inside and out, has wall paintings that are the oldest in the German-speaking world, dating from the 8th century.

⑭

The road climbs higher as it follows the upstream course of the Adige, which is more often called by its German name, the Etsch, in this German-speaking area. The peaks to the left are in the National Park of the Stelvio, part of the Italian government's long-term project to protect the Dolomites from the rapid development that spoiled mountainous regions in neighboring countries.

About 35 kilometers (21 miles) beyond Naturno, follow S38 as it turns sharply left at the village of **Spondigna** (Spondinig). This next stretch of road is well paved and open from June to October, but can be a bit hair-raising for anyone who doesn't like mountain driving.

⑮

Your goal is the **Passo dello Stelvio** (Stelvio Pass), at just over 9,000 feet the second-highest pass in Europe. Between Spondigna and the pass is 30 kilometers (18 miles) of winding road, with 48 hairpin turns. The view from the top is worth the effort because the pass connects the Venosta Valley with the Valtellina in neighboring Lombardy. Just to the right as you enter the pass is Switzerland. Stelvio is well known as a summer skiing center.

⑯

Time Out You'll probably want a breather once you've made it to the top of the pass. A good place for a drink is the bar of the **Hotel Passo dello Stelvio** (tel. 0342/903162), where you can enjoy the view of two valleys.

⑰

Continue along S38 as it begins its descent toward **Bormio,** the famous Lombard skiing center just 21 kilometers (13 miles) along. The road has its share of hairpins and tunnels, but is less intimidating than the road to Stelvio. At Bormio turn left onto S300; this begins a spectacular drive southward along the western border of the national park. The road is good but narrow and twisting, and for long stretches your only company will be the complacent cows in the Alpine meadows. About 25 kilometers (15 miles) beyond Bormio, you

⑱ reach the **Passo di Gavia**, a magnificent pass more than 8,500 feet above sea level. Just to your right are the cold waters of **Lago Nero** (Black Lake). This is the source of the River Messi, whose course you follow for the next 18 kilometers (10 miles) as you descend to ⑲ **Ponte di Legno**. About halfway down this part of S300, the road meets the fast-flowing river, at the tiny village of Sant'Apollonia, at the top of a series of hairpin turns.

At Ponte di Legno, turn left along S42 to head east along the Val Vermiglio. The signs will tell you you're heading back to Bolzano, but some of the best parts of this tour, the Brenta Dolomites, are off ⑳ the direct route to home base. Turn right at **Dimaro**, 37 kilometers (23 miles) east of Ponte di Legno, to begin the climb on S239 into the Brenta Dolomites. In the space of a few miles, you climb more than 2,000 feet, once more getting steering practice on the hairpin turns and switchbacks. The strange, rocky pinnacles of the Dolomites, which jut straight up like chimneys and look at times more like Monument Valley in Utah than any European ranges, loom over scattered mountain lakes.

Just above the **Carlo Magno Pass,** where Charlemagne is said to have ㉑ stopped in AD 800 on his way to Rome to be crowned emperor, is **Madonna di Campiglio,** a chic winter resort with more than 130 kilometers (80 miles) of ski runs and 39 lifts. The resort itself is 5,000 feet up, but some of the runs (and summer hiking routes) approach the heights of the surrounding peaks, including Pietra Grande, at over 9,700 feet.

㉒ At **Pinzolo,** 14 kilometers (8 miles) south of Madonna di Campiglio, you can see a remarkable 16th-century fresco on the side of a small village church. Follow the signs for the church of **San Vigilio,** which you'll come to after a short walk through the pines. On an exterior wall, the vivid fresco describes the Dance of Death, with ghoulish figures offering a stern rebuke to potential sinners.

S239 continues its descent to the Sarca Valley, where you pick up ㉓ S237 east at **Tione.** There are more signs of habitation in this lower valley, with ruins of castles looking down on modern farming settle- ㉔ ments. **Comano,** a small but locally renowned spa, is 20 kilometers (12 miles) along. You may want to turn south on S45bis to visit the famous **Lake Garda** (*see* The Lakes in Chapter 10 for an exploring route around Lake Garda). Otherwise, continue east on S237 until it meets A22 at Trento.

Tour 3: The Great Dolomites Road

This tour also begins in Bolzano but explores the area to the north and east, following an itinerary known as the **Grande Strada delle Dolomiti** (Great Dolomites Road) to the mountain resort of Cortina d'Ampezzo. The route, opened in 1909, now comprises 110 kilometers (70 miles) of easy grades and smooth driving between the two cities.

The Grande Strada begins just 6 kilometers (4 miles) east of Bolza- ㉕ no, at **Cornedo,** the beginning of the Ega Valley (Eggental). Before starting off on S241, pull over to savor the view of the Catinaccio Mountains to the left. Their craggy peaks seem to be props for a lighting display, as pink and purple reflections dance over huge rocks. The rocks are the protagonists in a local German legend that tells of King Laurin, who lived in a vast palace on the Catinaccio, at a time when the mountain was covered with roses. King Laurin be- came infatuated with the daughter of a neighboring king, Similde, and kidnapped her, but Similde, searching for his daughter, recognized her place of imprisonment by the red roses that grew there. Laurin freed the girl and was made Similde's prisoner. When Laurin finally escaped he decreed that the roses that had betrayed him should be turned to rocks, so that they could be seen neither by day nor by night. Today, the spectacular pinkish-red display is at its best at dawn and at sunset.

Continue along S241 as it climbs the Val d'Ega. About 20 kilometers (12 miles) along, just before you reach the **Passo di Costalunga** (Karerpass), you begin to see the near-vertical rock displays of the
㉖ Dolomites reflected in the clear waters of **Lake Carezza.** You can view the needlelike range on your right as the road descends into the valley. At **Vigo di Fassa** you join S48 to head left into the heart of the Dolomites.

The road snakes its way through narrow valleys and crosses a series of passes that are all over a mile high. The scenery is outstanding, but the rocky terrain means the soil is too poor for agriculture; miles go by with no farms in sight. As the road continues through the high mountain valleys of the **Cordevole** and then the **Dores** rivers, you start to see chair lifts and runs of the famous Dolomite skiing cen-
㉗ ters. Some of these, such as Nuvolau, by the **Passo di Falzarego**, are immediately off the road. The Passo di Falzarego also marks the point at which S48 begins its descent. There are more curves and steep-sided turns; the best view comes when you emerge from the Crepa Tunnel and see Cortina and the cross-shaped Ampezzo valley for the first time.

㉘ **Cortina d'Ampezzo**, known as the "Pearl of the Dolomites," is set in a lush meadow 4,000 feet above sea level. Dense forests adjoin the town, and mountains encircle the whole valley. The town sprawls on the slopes along a fast-moving stream; a public park extends along one bank. Luxury hotels and the villas of the rich are conspicuously scattered over the slopes above the town—identifiable, ironically, by their attempts to hide behind stands of firs and spruces.

The bustling center of Cortina has little nostalgia for old-time atmosphere, despite its alpine appearance. The tone is set by elegant shops and stylish cafés, as opulent as their well-dressed patrons, whose corduroy knickerbockers may well have been tailored by Armani. Cortina is the place to go for a whiff of the heady aroma of wealth and sophistication; if you want authentic Tyrolean *gemütlichkeit* (knee-slapping conviviality), pass through Cortina and stop at one of the resorts later on the tour.

The Great Dolomites Road ends at Cortina d'Ampezzo, but our tour goes north and then west, to complete a great loop back to Bolzano. From Cortina continue along S48 for an 11-kilometer (7-mile) climb over the **Passo di Tre Croci** and down again as you head toward the jewellike **Lake Misurina** below. Turn left as you reach the lake to join
㉙ S48bis, which leads northward to S51, to **Dobbiaco** (Toblach), 34 kilometers (20 miles) north of Cortina. At Dobbiaco, the influence of Austria, which is just 12 kilometers (7 miles) to the east along the Drau Valley, intensifies. Italian is spoken grudgingly here, Austrian money is accepted at most shops and restaurants, and the locals appear more blond and blue-eyed than the average Italian. It is not surprising that Gustav Mahler (1860–1911), the great Austrian composer, should have come here often for inspiration.

At Dobbiaco, head west along S49 as it runs beside the fast-flowing Rienz River in the **Pusteria** (Puster) Valley. This valley is broader than others in this tour, so you'll be able to make good time on the

30 26-kilometer (16-mile) drive west to **Brunico** (Bruneck), with its medieval quarter nestling below the 13th-century bishop's castle. Here, in the adjacent district of Teodone, just to the right of town as you enter from the Dobbiaco side, is the **Museo degli Usi e Costumi della Provincia di Bolzano** (Bolzano Province Customs and Costumes Museum, or Ethnographic Museum). This re-creation of a typical local village, built around an authentic 300-year-old mansion, reveals the functions and significance of traditional architecture. The wood-carving displays are particularly interesting. *Via Herzog Diet 24, Teodone. Admission: 4,000 lire. Open Apr. 15–Oct., Tues.– Sat. 9:30–5:30, Sun. 2–6.*

31 Continue west on S49 to **Bressanone** (Brixen), 35 kilometers (21 miles) away. Bressanone is an important artistic center of the Alto Adige and for centuries was the seat of prince-bishops. Like their counterparts in Trento, these medieval administrators had the delicate problem of serving two opposing masters—the pope (the ultimate spiritual supervisor) and the Holy Roman Emperor (the civil and military leader). Since the papacy and the Holy Roman Empire were virtually at war throughout the Middle Ages, Bressanone's prince-bishops became experts at tact and diplomacy in order to survive. As you arrive from Brunico, you enter the town on Via Mercato Vecchio, a broad road leading to the imposing **Duomo**. It was built in the 13th century but acquired a Baroque facade 500 years later, and its 14th-century cloister is decorated with medieval frescoes. The adjacent **Museo Diocesano** (Diocesan Museum) is a treasure house of local medieval art, particularly Gothic wood carving. The wooden statues and liturgical objects were all collected from the cathedral treasury. During the Christmas season the curators highlight displays of the museum's large collection of antique Nativity scenes: Look for the shepherds wearing Tyrolean hats. *Admission: 4,000 lire. Open Mar. 15–Oct., Mon.–Sat. 10–5; nativity scenes open Dec. 15–Feb. 10, Mon.–Sat. 2–5. Closed Dec. 24, 25.*

Casa Pfaundler, a Renaissance mansion located next to the parish church to the left of the Duomo, is a fitting reminder of the cultural mix of the region. The architecture, a blend of Italian and German elements, is as much a hybrid as the name.

At Bressanone you are no more than 45 kilometers (27 miles) north of Bolzano. The autostrada (A22) provides the best connection, but **32** there are two more important stops before you return. At **Chiusa** (Klausen), 18 kilometers (10 miles) south along A22, stop to see the narrow streets lined with houses built in the 15th and 16th centuries. Geraniums and begonias fill window boxes beneath the carved wooden shutters. Above the town is the Benedictine monastery of **Sabiona** (Saeben), built as a castle in the 10th century but occupying a site that was fortified in Roman times. The monastery buildings date from the late Middle Ages and are a mixture of Romanesque and Gothic architecture, surrounded by walls and turrets.

Just south of Chiusa on the autostrada, take a short detour east along S242 into the **Val Gardena** (Groedner Tal). Val Gardena provides some of the best views of the Dolomites and is one of Italy's most popular ski resorts. It is also home of the Ladins, descendants of soldiers sent by the Roman Emperor Tiberius to conquer the Celtic population of the area in the 1st century AD. Forgotten in the narrow cul-de-sacs of isolated mountain valleys, the Ladins have developed their own folk traditions and speak an ancient dialect that is derived from Latin and is similar to Romansch, which is spoken in some high valleys in Switzerland. Follow the valley for the 13 kilom-
33 eters (8 miles) to **Ortisei** (St. Ulrich), the best spot to catch a few

phrases of Ladin. Back again on the autostrada, a 20-kilometer (12-mile) drive will return you to Bolzano.

What to See and Do with Children

It's hard to go wrong with children in the Dolomites: The open spaces and the mountains are real attractions for them. The Italians love children, and many of the sports resorts (both summer and winter) have special children's facilities. Most ski resorts have ski schools for even very young children, and the multilingual teaching staffs make the learning experience enjoyable (*see* Sports, *below*).

Drive with the children through **Cornedo** (*see* Tour 3: The Great Dolomites Road, *above*) and tell the legend about King Laurin who—as the story goes—turned the rose-covered mountains to craggy peaks.

The **Museo degli Usi e Costumi della Provincia di Bolzano** (Ethnographic Museum) at Teodone near Brunico (*see* Tour 3: The Great Dolomites Road, *above*) is a hands-on museum designed to familiarize visitors with local customs and traditions.

No winter visit is complete without a visit to the nativity scenes at the **Museo Diocesano** (Diocesan Museum) in Bressanone (*see* Tour 3: The Great Dolomites Road, *above*).

Off the Beaten Track

On the **Renon** (Ritten) plateau, just above Bolzano and reachable by the funicular to Soprabolzano, are the **Earth Pyramids,** a bizarre geological formation where erosion has left a forest of tall, thin, needlelike spires of rock, each topped with a boulder. *The Soprabolzano funicular leaves from Via Renon, about 300 yards left from the Bolzano train station. At the top an electric train takes you on to Collalbo, where the Earth Pyramids are located.*

Five kilometers (3 miles) past Spondigna (Spondinig) in the Venosta Valley, turn left off S40 as it heads toward the Austrian border. A little road leads you to **Glorenza** (Glurns), a tiny village that looks much as it did in the Middle Ages, still surrounded by a high wall and turreted watchtowers. Local building ordinances set strict limits on new construction, and many streets are for pedestrians only.

From July to September at the pretty village of **Fiè** (Voels), just off A22, north of the Bolzano Nord exit, you can take the "Hay Cure" at Hotel Heubad (which means Hay Bath in German), a well-equipped hotel in a 16th-century building. The cure consists of burying yourself in warm hay composed of mountain herbs and grasses—a treatment devised by local peasants. The experience is said to be like having a sauna or mud bath, but be warned: This cure is under no circumstances to be taken by people with heart and circulation problems or people with pollen allergies. *Hotel-Pension Heubad, 39050 Fiè allo Scililar (Voels am Schlern), tel. 0471/725020, fax 0471/725425.*

Shopping

Shopping is fun in the Dolomites, where larger towns, such as Bolzano, Bressanone, and Brunico, have shops clustered in arcaded shopping streets designed to keep shoppers dry on rainy or snowy days. The ethnic mixture, with its strong Tyrolean influence, makes for local products and handicrafts that are quite different from those elsewhere in Italy. Tyrolean clothing—loden goods, lederhosen, dirndls, and linen suits with horn buttons—is a good buy and costs less than in neighboring Austria. Local handicrafts, such as embroidered goods, wood carvings, figures for nativity scenes, pottery, and handcrafted copper and iron objects, make good gifts.

Antiques **Trento** is the local center for antiques. The main dealers are **Antiquariato Corti** (Via Mantova 30), **Gasperetti** (Via Torre Verde 52), and **Antichità** (Piazza Santa Maria Maggiore 27).

Handicrafts In **Bolzano** the best store for locally made goods is **Artigiani Atesini** (Via Portici 39).

In **Trento,** go to Il Pozzo (Piazza Pasi 14/L) for handcrafted wooden objects; **Il Laboratorio** (Via Roma 12) specializes in terra-cotta pieces by local artists.

Food and Flea In **Bolzano,** the outdoor fruit and vegetable market is held in the
Markets central **Piazza delle Erbe** every morning (8–1) except Sunday. The big weekly flea market takes place Saturday morning in **Piazza della Vittoria,** just across the river.

Trento's small morning market is held in the center of town at **Piazza Lodron,** but the big shopping day is Thursday, when the weekly market spreads out around **Piazza d'Arogno,** next to the cathedral. A flea market is held in **Piazza d'Arogno** every third Sunday of the month; the same piazza is the scene of a handicrafts market every Friday and Saturday.

Sports

Cross-Country The Dolomites are an ideal place to learn or improve your cross-
Skiing country skiing (*sci di fondo* in Italian). The major Alpine resorts, and even many out-of-the-way villages, have prepared trails (usually loops marked off by kilometers) catering to differing degrees of ability. Two of the best are at **Ortisei** and **Dobbiaco.** You can have a lot of fun blazing new trails across virgin snow fields; you can usually get permission by asking at the nearest farmhouse or by inquiring at local tourist offices.

Golf **Campo Carlo Magno** (tel. 0465/41003) is a nine-hole course set in the mountains by Madonna di Campiglio, open July 1–September 15.

Hiking The Dolomites have a well-maintained network of trails for hiking and rock climbing, with *rifugi* (huts) located on the most difficult ascents. It is important to follow safety procedures and have all the latest information on trails and conditions. Two helpful organizations are the **Società degli Alpinisti Tridentini** (Via Manci 57, Trento, tel. 0461/986462) and **Club Alpino Italiano** (Piazza Erbe 46, Bolzano, tel. 0471/978172). Local tourist offices can provide information on less-demanding trails.

Skiing The Dolomites offer some of the best skiing in Europe, with some centers equipped for summer skiing. Generally the ski season runs from late November to April, by which time some people prefer to ski in shirtsleeves. The most comprehensive centers are **Cortina d'Ampezzo,** in the heart of the Dolomites to the east of Bolzano, and **Madonna di Campiglio,** west of Trento. These resorts are unashamedly upscale, but for your money you get the extras you expect from world-class centers: miles of interconnecting runs linked by cable cars and lifts, plus skating rinks, heated indoor pools, and lively après-ski activities.

For some of Cortina's charm, but at a fraction of the price, try the **Monte Rota** slopes, accessible from **Dobbiaco.**

Another comparatively inexpensive area is the **Badia Valley,** reached by heading south on S244 from Brunico.

Ortisei (St. Ulrich), just a few miles up the Val Gardena from the Adige Valley, is a popular skiing center, with lifts linking it to the Siusi range.

Stelvio, the focal point of Tour 2, is a year-round skiing center, with summer skiing on many of its runs.

Resorts call their bargain periods *settimane bianche* (white weeks); these are usually in January and February. Pre-Christmas, a period of unpredictable snow conditions can also trigger bargains in lift prices and accommodations.

Tennis Courts can be found in **Bressanone** (Lungoisarco Sinistro, tel. 0472/22992), **Brunico** (Lungofiume San Giorgio, tel. 0474/20444), **Cortina d'Ampezzo** (Via Sopiazes, tel. 0436/2937), and **Ortisei** (Roncadizza, tel. 0471/76019).

Dining and Lodging

Dining Encompassing the Germanic Alto Adige province and the Italian Trentino province, the Dolomites region combines Italian cuisine with local Tyrolean specialties, which are much like the dishes of Austria and central Europe. Local delicatessens teem with regional cheeses, pickles, salami, and smoked meats, while local bakeries present a wide selection of crusty dark rolls, caraway rye bread, and the like—perfect for picnics. Local dishes vary from one isolated mountain valley to the next. Don't miss speck, the local smoked ham. Other specialties include *canederli,* or *knoedel,* a type of dumpling with many variations, served either in broth or with a sauce; hot sauerkraut; ravioli made from rye flour, stuffed with spinach and fried; and apple or pear strudel. And—as befits a wine-producing region—the local vintages (and fruit brandies) are delicious. In the fall in the South Tyrol, when autumn colors beautify the mountains, it's a tradition to make a tour of the cozy country wine taverns to drink the new wine and eat hot roast chestnuts.

Highly recommended restaurants are indicated by a star ★.

Category	Cost*
$$$$	over 85,000 lire
$$$	60,000–85,000 lire
$$	30,000–60,000 lire
$	under 30,000 lire

per person, including house wine, service, and tax

Lodging Accommodations in the Dolomites range from refurbished castles to spic-and-span chalet guest houses, from stately 19th-century hotels to chic modern ski resorts. Even a small village may have scores of lodging places, many of them very inexpensive. Hotel information offices at train stations and tourist offices can help avoid the language problem if you arrive without reservations: Bolzano train station has a 24-hour hotel service, and tourist offices will give you a list of all the hotels in the area, arranged by location and price. We've tried to mention here a few hotels in towns that make good bases for travel, as well as some notable hotels found along the road. Remember that many hotels in ski resorts cater primarily to longer stays at full or half-board: It's wiser to book ski vacations as a package in advance. And a word of warning: While spring and fall are wonderful times to travel in the region, many mountain hotels are closed for a month or two after Easter and for about six weeks before Christmas.

Highly recommended lodgings are indicated by a star ★.

Category	Cost*
$$$$	over 300,000 lire
$$$	140,000–300,000 lire
$$	80,000–140,000 lire
$	under 80,000 lire

All prices are for a standard double room for two, including service and 9% IVA (13% for luxury hotels).

Bolzano (Bozen)
Dining
★

Grifone/Greif. More than just a routine hotel restaurant, the Grifone is a continuing favorite in its own right, known for fine food and service. It's especially pleasant to eat outside at tables set up on Piazza Walther. The menu, which changes daily, includes various local specialties, such as wine soup *(weinzuppe)*, made with consommé, cream, white wine, and cinnamon; *herrngröstl* (bite-size pieces of veal sautéed with potatoes and onions), served in the pan with cabbage salad; or *spinatspaetzli* (tiny spinach dumplings), served with butter and grated Parmesan cheese. The grilled fish is also good. *Hotel Grifone/Greif. Piazza Walther, tel. 0471/977056. No reservations. Dress: casual. Closed Sun. AE, DC, MC, V. $$$*

Abramo. Although outside Bolzano's attractive old center, this restaurant is the best in town. Chef Abramo Pantezi offers a variation of nouvelle cuisine in an attractive, elegantly modern setting designed to reflect Renaissance themes. Tables are set with crystal and silver. Specialties include fish dishes, such as *salmone allo champagne* (salmon in champagne sauce) and *tagliarini agli scampi* (thin noodles with shrimp). There's a vegetarian antipasto selection and a daily diet menu selected for calorie control. There's also an extensive wine cellar, which features even some top-quality California vintages. *Piazza Gries 16, tel. 0471/280141. Reservations advised. Dress: casual. AE, MC, V. Closed Sun. and Aug. 10–25. $$–$$$*

Belle Epoque. This is the fashionable restaurant of Park Hotel Laurin. Its furnishings live up to its name and include potted palms and chandeliers. During the summer months, the restaurant expands to include a grill restaurant in the hotel's lush, extensive park. The menu includes Italian and international cuisine, as well as local specialties, and the kitchen prides itself on serving seasonal dishes. In spring, you can sample half a dozen asparagus dishes, for example, while in the fall the menu offers game, including hare and venison served in a variety of ways. *Park Hotel Laurin. Via Laurino 4, tel. 0471/980500. No reservations. Jacket and tie advised. AE, DC, MC, V. Closed Sun. $$–$$$*

Flora's. In a medieval tower on Bolzano's market square, this tiny place has been a tavern for centuries, and it has been lovingly restored. There is no menu; you choose from a limited number of typical homey Tyrolean specialties, different every day. They may include canederli or *schlutzkrapfen* (ravioli). The desserts are homemade, too. The young owner takes pride in a selection of good wines. *Piazza delle Erbe 17, tel. 0471/974086. No reservations. Dress: casual. No credit cards. Closed Sun. $$*

Kaiserkron. Join the locals at this solid standby in the center of town. You'll find city burghers and their families eating well-prepared Italian, international, and South Tyrolean dishes under a low, vaulted ceiling or outdoors on an attractive summer terrace. The menu is heavy on grilled-meat dishes, but appetizers are interesting—especially the artichoke *(carciofo)* pâté, a delicious dark-green treat. The house wine is excellent. *Piazza della Mostra 1, tel. 0471/970770. No reservations. Dress: casual. AE, DC, MC, V. Closed Sat. dinner, Sun. $$*

Batzenhausl. A medieval building in the center of town houses this crowded *stube* (Tyrolean-style drinking hall). It's a popular hangout for the local intellectual set, who hold long, animated conversations over glasses of local wine and tasty local South Tyrolean specialties, such as herrengröstl and apple pancakes with ice cream. Try the fried Camembert. *Via Andreas Hofer 30, tel. 0471/976183. Reservations advised. Dress: casual. No credit cards. Closed lunch, Tues., and 2 weeks in July. $*

Cavallino Bianco/Weisses Roessl. This is another typical Tyrolean stube in the center of town, decorated with dark wood paneling, carved furniture, frescoes, and stuffed hunting trophies. A popular spot for local intellectuals and young people, it's also one of the few Bolzano restaurants that stays open until midnight. Waitresses in modified *trachten* (Tyrolean costume) serve local specialties, such as *kaseknoedel* (light cheese dumpling), *leberknoedel* (liver dumpling) soup, wurst, and *palaschinken* (sweet pancakelike crêpes). *Via dei Bottai (Bindergasse) 6, tel. 0471/973267. No reservations. Dress: casual. Closed Sat. dinner, Sun. No credit cards. $*

Lodging
★ **Grifone/Greif.** For at least five centuries, there's been a hotel on this spot, perfectly situated in the center of town on pedestrians-only Piazza Walther, looking across to the cathedral. You'll find a friendly atmosphere combined with old-fashioned elegance and a sense of history. The older wings have antique-style Tyrolean furnishings in some rooms, pleasant modern furnishings characterize the newer parts, and some back rooms have balconies looking past the hotel garden to the mountains. The hotel bar and restaurant set up tables and chairs right on Piazza Walther in the summer months. *Piazza Walther, tel. 0471/977056, fax 0471/980613. 130 rooms, 110 with bath. Facilities: garage, use of park and pool of Park Hotel Laurino. AE, DC, MC, V. $$$*

Park Hotel Laurino/Laurin. This big turn-of-the-century hotel, done in opulent art nouveau style, is set in a large, shady park, in the middle of town. Most rooms have stunning views of the park and the mountains beyond. Some rooms carry through the Belle Epoque decor; others are furnished in a classic modern hotel style. The Belle Epoque restaurant *(see above)*, with outdoor buffet in the summer, serves local specialties. *Via Laurino 4, tel. 0471/980500, fax 0471/970953. 95 rooms with bath. Facilities: pool, restaurant, park, garage. AE, DC, MC, V. $$$*

★ **Schloss Korb.** It's worth the 5-kilometer (3-mile) drive west from Bolzano to reach this remarkable hotel. It's set in a romantic 13th-century castle with crenellated roof and massive central tower, perched in a park amid vine-covered hills. Much of the ancient decor is preserved, and the public rooms are filled with Tyrolean antiques, elaborate wood carvings, old paintings, and attractive plants. The rooms are comfortably furnished—some tower rooms have the old Romanesque arched windows. *Missiano (5 km southwest of Bolza-*

no), tel. 0471/636000, fax 0471/636033. 56 rooms with bath. Facilities: heated indoor and outdoor pools, sauna, tennis courts. No credit cards. Closed Nov.–Easter. $$$

Luna/Mondschein. This central yet secluded hotel was built in 1798. Set in a lovely garden, it provides a tranquil, friendly atmosphere. The rooms are furnished in a comfortable, classic hotel style using wood paneling throughout. Some rooms overlooking the garden have balconies, but even the rooms overlooking the garage have good views of the mountains. The two restaurants include a typical Tyrolean *weinstube* that serves inexpensive local specialties in a cozy, convivial setting. *Via Piave 15, tel. 0471/975642, fax 0471/975577. 85 rooms with bath. Facilities: 2 restaurants, garden, garage. DC, MC, V. $$*

Magdalenerhof. Near the Renon cable car station, this family-run hotel has the appearance of a Tyrolean inn and is set in a garden surrounded by vineyards. Comfort and service are up to high local standards. *Via Rencio 48/a, tel. 0471/978267, fax 0471/981076. 21 rooms with bath. Facilities: restaurant, outdoor pool, garage. AE, DC, MC, V. $$*

Bressanone (Brixen)
Dining
★

Fink. Don't be discouraged by the name: This popular restaurant, under the arcades in the pedestrians-only center of town, has a friendly staff and features a good-value daily set menu. It has a rustic ambience upstairs with lots of wood paneling, and serves international as well as hearty Tyrolean specialties. Try the *carré di maiale gratinato* (pork roasted with cheese and served with cabbage and potatoes) or the *castrato alla paesana*, a kind of lamb stew. *Via Portici Minori 4, tel. 0472/34883. Reservations advised. Dress: casual. Closed Tues. dinner Oct.–June, Wed., and July. AE, DC, MC, V. $$*

Lodging

Dominik. Well equipped and modern, this hotel is centrally located but has a quiet garden and dining terrace. Most doubles are spacious and modern, with comfortable armchairs, ample baths, and balconies. The superior restaurant features local trout (in season). *Via Terzo di Sotto 13, tel. 0472/30144, fax 0472/36554. 29 rooms with bath. Facilities: indoor pool, park, garage, sauna. AE, MC, V. Closed Nov. 4–Easter. $$$*

★ **Elefante.** One of the best and most famous hotels in the region, this cozy inn is located in a historic 15th-century building: There's been a hotel on the site for more than 500 years. The hotel takes its name from an incident in 1550, when King John of Portugal stopped here for a few days while leading an elephant over the Alps as a present for Austria's Emperor Ferdinand. Each room is different, and many are decorated with antiques and paintings. The hotel is centrally located but is set in a large park with a swimming pool. Also in the park is the separate Villa Marzari, with 14 rooms. The hotel restaurant is known as one of the region's best (closed Mon.). *Via Rio Bianco 4, tel. 0472/32750, fax 0472/36579. 44 rooms with bath. Facilities: restaurant, pool, park. V. Closed Nov. 15–Dec. 28, Jan. 10–Feb. 28. $$–$$$*

Brunico (Bruneck)
Lodging

Andreas Hofer. There's a Tyrolean feel to this comfortable hotel set in a large garden outside the center of town. Traditional chalet-style balconies overlook the Pusteria Valley. The rooms have modern furnishings, and there are several rooms with special features for people with disabilities. The hotel restaurant is recommended. *Via Campo Tures 1, tel. 0474/31469, fax 0474/31283. 54 rooms with bath. Facilities: garden, restaurant, sauna, solarium. MC, V. Closed 2 weeks in May, Nov. 25–Dec. 12. $–$$*

Post. The best choice for lodging in the center of town is this homey, old, traditional hotel, recommended by locals, who also like its restaurant, café, and pastry shop. It has its own parking, which is important because of the pedestrians-only rules in effect throughout much of the central area. *Via Bastioni 9, tel. 0474/555127, fax 0474/ 31603. 60 rooms, 50 with bath. No credit cards. Closed Nov. $–$$*

Cortina d'Ampezzo

Dining

De la Poste. The exclusive restaurants of the hotel on Cortina's main square have a casually chic clientele and a lively atmosphere. There's an elegant, high-ceilinged main dining room with three big chandeliers where you can dine on soufflés and nouvelle cuisine dishes (every Friday fresh fish is served). There's also a more informal grill room with wood paneling and the family pewter collection. In ski season it's always crowded. *Piazza Roma 14, tel. 0436/4271. Reservations required. Jacket and tie required at dinner in both restaurants. AE, DC. $$$*

Tana della Volpe. Located near the Olympic ice skating rink, this popular restaurant has a bona fide Tyrolean ambience, with wood-paneled dining rooms and a local clientele. Here you can try Cortina specialties such as *zuppa di porcini* (wild mushroom soup), ravioli *di cervo* (stuffed with venison), and game. *Via dello Stadio 27/a, tel. 0436/867494. Reservations advised. Dress: casual. AE, DC, MC, V. Closed Wed. in May and Sept., closed June, Nov. $$–$$$*

Fanes. This restaurant in the Hotel Fanes outside town serves homey food in rustic elegance. Game is a specialty, with dishes including *camoscio* (chamois) cooked several ways and *capriolo in salmì con polenta* (roe deer stewed in red wine and served with polenta). *Hotel Fanes, Via Roma 136, tel. 0436/3427. Reservations advised. Dress: casual. AE, MC, DC, V. Closed Mon. $$*

Lodging

Europa. This traditional mountain hotel, in the center of town, has the warm family-style atmosphere typical of a chalet. Antiques including an antique wood stove decorate the interior. A roaring fire enlivens the bar. There's also a nightclub, disco, and grill room. *Corso Italia 207, tel. 0436/3221, fax 0436/868204. 54 rooms with bath. AE, DC, MC, V. Closed mid-Oct.–mid-Dec. $$$$*

Miramonti. This imposing and luxurious hotel, nearly a century old, has a magnificent mountain valley location about a kilometer (.6 mile) south of town. A touch of Old World formality accompanies the imperial Austrian design, and the interior decor carries the period style throughout. Most of the rooms have balconies and have been entirely redecorated. There's a restaurant, and in the cozy bar there's always a roaring fire in the hearth. *Localita Pezziè 103, tel. 0436/4201, fax 0436/867019. 106 rooms with bath, 7 suites and 5 junior suites. Facilities: shuttle bus every 15 min to town, pool, tennis courts, golf course, fitness center with sauna, massage, inhalation treatment. AE, DC, MC, V. Closed Easter–June 30, Sept. 15–Dec. 20. $$$$*

Cristallo. This large, imposing century-old hotel was built around the same time as the Miramonti and is set in a big park in the forest a half mile southeast of town. There's lots of wood paneling, and many of the spacious, comfortable rooms have fancy terraces or wrought-iron balconies that offer fine views. The restaurant is good and the stube is especially cozy. Entertainment includes a nightclub and piano bar. Room rates are for full- or half-board only. *Via R. Menardi 42, tel. 0436/4281, fax 0436/868058. 81 rooms with bath. Facilities: pool, tennis courts, 2 restaurants, nightclub, piano bar. AE, DC, MC, V. Closed Easter–June, Sept.–Dec. 19. $$$*

De la Poste. Skiers who want to be seen keep returning to this lively hotel on the main square in a pedestrian zone. It's been under the same family management since 1826, and the furnishings feature antiques in characteristic Dolomite style. Almost all rooms have wooden balconies. The hotel's main terrace bar, on the square, is always crowded and is one of Cortina's social centers. *Piazza Roma 62, tel. 0436/4271, fax 0436/868435. 83 rooms with bath. Facilities: restaurant, bar, safe in each room. AE, DC. Closed Oct. 20–Dec. 19. $$$*

Fanes. If you find Cortina's sophistication overbearing, get away from it all in this rustic-style hotel, which is set in a garden in the countryside at the southern outskirts of town. Many rooms have wooden balconies with fine views of the Campo range, and there's lots of wooden decor. Room rates are for full- or half-board only. *Via Roma 136, tel. 0436/3427, fax 0436/5027. 25 rooms with bath. AE, DC, MC, V. Closed Easter–June, Nov. 5–Dec. 21. $$$*

Dobbiaco (Toblach)
Lodging

Villa Santer. Take the Cortina Road to the mountains at the southern edge of town to reach this modern hotel. It's built and furnished in traditional Tyrolean style, with lots of wooden decoration and a balcony in every room. The restaurant and bar are dedicated to local specialties; there's more local color at the Tyrolean party held for guests once a week. *Via Alemagna 4, tel. 0474/72142, fax 0474/72797. 47 rooms with bath. Facilities: indoor pool, sauna, restaurant, bar. MC, V. Closed Easter–May 18, Oct. 15–Dec. 18. $$–$$$*

★ **Alpino Monte Rota/Alpengasthof Ratsberg.** To reach this hotel, you take the 10-minute cable car ride to Monte Rota. It is in traditional style, with the timeless look of local chalets. Front rooms have stunning mountain views from balconies, while those in the back look out over the dense mountain forest. You needn't take the cable car back down for sustenance: The Alpino has a good restaurant (which serves even some low-calorie dishes), a bar, and a Tyrolean-style stube. *Monte Rota 10, tel. 0474/72213, fax 0474/72916. 25 rooms with bath. Facilities: pool, sauna, restaurant, bar, lounge. MC, V. Closed Easter–May 30, Oct. 25–Dec. 20. $–$$*

Cristallo. Wood beams and paneling lend an Old Tyrolean tone to this small hotel set in a garden just outside town. The architecture and furnishings reflect the local preference for combining traditional chalet design with functional, but comfortable, modern furniture. Most rooms enjoy a panoramic view of the valley; some of the best rooms have balconies. Guests relax in the cozy and informal stube. *Viale Roma 11, tel. 0474/72138, fax 0474/72755. 30 rooms with bath. Facilities: indoor pool, restaurant, bar. MC, V. Closed Easter–May 15, mid-Oct.–mid-Dec. $–$$*

Madonna di Campiglio
Lodging
★

Golf. You'll have to make your way up to Campo Carlo Magno, the famous pass just north of town, to reach this grand hotel, which is the former summer residence of Hapsburg Emperor Franz Joseph. A modern wing has been added to the more-than-a-century-old original structure, but Old World charm remains: Rooms 114 and 214 are still decorated in the old imperial style. Other rooms are also elegantly maintained, and throughout are verandas, Persian carpets, and bay windows. The hotel is practically on the fairway of a golf course that draws a sophisticated summer crowd. There's a restaurant and piano bar. *Campo Carlo Magno, tel. 0465/41003, fax 0465/40294. 120 rooms with bath, 4 suites. Facilities: restaurant, bar, golf course, solarium, game room, shuttle bus to town. AE, DC, MC, V. Closed Apr.–June, Sept.–Nov. $$$$*

Savoia Palace. A major renovation in 1988 strengthened the Savoia Palace's reputation as the premier hotel in the center of this fashionable ski resort. The owners knew enough not to tamper with the decor—mountain-style furnishings with lots of carved wood—or the intimate atmosphere of the reception rooms. Two fireplaces blaze away in the bar, where guests recall the day's exploits on the ski slopes. The elegant restaurant serves a mixture of local specialties and hearty dishes drawing on Italian and Austrian influences.

Guests stay on full- or half-board terms only. *Via Dolomiti di Brenta, tel. 0465/41004, fax 0465/40549. 55 rooms with bath. Facilities: restaurant, bar. AE, DC. Closed Easter–June, Sept.–Nov. $$$$*

Grifone. A comfortable hotel that catches the sun, the Grifone has distinctive wood paneling on the outside, flower-decorated balconies, and rooms with views of the forested slopes. The restaurant serves home cooking as well as international dishes. *Via Vallesinella 7, tel. 0465/42002, fax 0465/40540. 40 rooms with bath. Facilities: restaurant, bar, solarium. AE, MC, V. Closed Apr. 15–June 30, Sept. 15–Dec. 4. $$*

Merano (Meran)

Dining

Andrea. This elegant showcase for fine cuisine and service is just off Merano's main shopping street, Via dei Portici, and right by a cable car station. In an atmosphere of relaxed modern elegance, enlivened by wood paneling and lots of green plants, you can dine on eye-pleasing specialties of both local and international cuisine, such as risotto *alle erbe* (with herbs), *filetto di vitello con salsa di alloro* (veal fillet with bay leaf sauce), or *canederli di ricotta su purea di frutta mista* (ricotta dumplings served with pureed fruit). A set menu (about 90,000 lire) offers a complete five-course dinner, including wines—and the wine cellar is also excellent. *Via Galilei 44, tel. 0473/237400. Reservations required. Jacket and tie advised. AE, DC, MC, V. Closed Mon. and 2 weeks in Feb. $$$*

Flora. There's room for only about 20 diners in this intimate candlelit restaurant under the historic arched arcades of Merano's ancient center. Chef Louis Oberstolz describes his imaginative cooking as "fresh, spontaneous, and natural, using only the finest ingredients." He offers a seven-course set menu. Among the specialties are *quaglia ripiena con fegato d'oca grasso* (boned quail stuffed with foie gras), an antipasto of various types of fish, and *Schlutzkrapfen* (fresh pasta ravioli with various fillings). *Via dei Portici 75, tel. 0473/231484. Reservations required. Dress: casual. AE, DC, MC, V. Closed lunch and Sun., mid-Jan.–mid-Feb. $$$*

★ **Tiffany Grill/Schloss Maur.** Stained-glass lamps and wood paneling create a warm art nouveau effect in these two restaurants of the Hotel Palace. The main restaurant is the height of elegance, with huge marble columns, high ceilings, and crystal chandeliers. In the summer, meals are served outdoors on the terrace overlooking the lovely park. The emphasis is on Italian and international cuisine, such as house specialty spaghetti *Schloss Maur* (served with a sauce of zucchini, sage, and green pepper) or roast saddle of lamb and lobster. The Tiffany Grill, which offers gourmet menus, is open only in the evening. *Hotel Palace, Via Cavour 2/4, tel. 0473/211300. Reservations required. Jacket and tie required. AE, DC, MC, V. Closed Sun. and July. $$$*

Terlano Putz. This local favorite is an old rustic stube under the arcades of Merano's old town. The wide menu focuses on seasonal dishes and offers Tyrolean specialties. Try *zuppa al vino bianco* (soup with white wine); crêpes with radicchio; or the various risottos, including one made with asparagus in the spring, and with Barolo wine later in the year. *Via dei Portici 231, tel. 0473/235571. Reservations advised. Dress: casual. No credit cards. Closed Wed. and mid-Feb.–mid-Mar. $–$$*

Lodging

★ **Palace Hotel.** Merano's grandest hotel is an opulent turn-of-the-century establishment providing top service and comfort. It is set in an extensive garden with an indoor-outdoor pool, and all rooms on the south side have balconies overlooking the park. The rooms are spacious, decorated in a stately modern classic design in restful colors. The public rooms are attractive and comfortable—there's a no-smoking lounge—with art nouveau touches, Tiffany glass, marble pillars, and high ceilings. The hotel is equipped with an impressive spa, featuring all sorts of baths, massages, mud treatments, and other cures. There is a lovely fountain serving thermal Merano water. *Via Cavour 2/4, tel. 0473/211300, fax 0473/234181. 120 rooms with bath. Facilities: indoor-outdoor pool, spa center, bar, restaurant, garden. AE, DC, MC, V. Closed Jan.–Feb., mid-Nov.–mid-Dec. $$$$*

Castel Freiburg. Set in a wooded valley about 7 kilometers (4.5 miles) south of town, Castel Freiburg is a romantic hideaway where guests feel pampered and welcome. A converted 14th-century castle, complete with tower, it is surrounded by its own park, stretching up to the forest. Reception rooms are full of antiques, and the guest rooms are individually furnished with color-coordinated fabrics and decorations. Although only some have terraces, all the rooms have good views of the mountains. A combination of an excellent restaurant and extensive sports facilities means that many guests remain on the premises for days on end. *Via Monte Franco, tel. 0473/244196, fax 0473/244488. 38 rooms with bath. Facilities: indoor and outdoor pools, children's playroom, restaurant, bar. AE, DC, MC, V. Closed Nov. 5–Apr. 15. $$$*

Schloss Rundegg. A romantic converted 12th-century castle with an original tower, Schloss Rundegg is furnished with antiques and rich fittings, such as Persian carpets. It's set in a park and functions as a fully equipped thermal spa. The restaurant even provides special diets for weight loss and other cures. Room 32, in the tower, has an interior staircase and 360-degree views. *Via Scena 2, tel. 0473/234100, fax 0473/237200. 30 rooms with bath. Facilities: pool, gym, sauna, spa, restaurant, bar. AE, DC, MC, V. Closed Jan. 6–31. $$$*

Castel Labers. Located on a hilltop amid forested slopes about 3 kilometers (1.8 miles) east of Merano's center, this hotel has a view of the town's gabled roofs and gardens. Actually a castle set in its own well-kept grounds, its red-tiled gables, towers and turrets give it an unmistakably Tyrolean look, heightened on the interior by dark ceiling beams, painted fresco decorations, and even crossed halberds on the walls. The hospitable Stapf-Neubert family owns the hotel and takes an active part in its management. In summer guests dine outdoors on the terrace and can enjoy a game of tennis or a dip in the hotel pool. *Via Labers 25, tel. 0473/234484, fax 0473/234146. 32 rooms with bath. Facilities: pool, garden, tennis court, restaurant. AE, DC, MC, V. Closed Nov.–Mar. $$*

Meranerhof. The hotel is located in the center of Merano, with spacious gardens overlooking the river. Plush gilt furniture and crystal chandeliers give the lobby an opulent look; bedrooms feature ample balconies with views of the city and mountains. The hotel restaurant is known for refined versions of regional dishes such as smoked trout and *insalata di mele* (apple salad). *Via Manzoni 1, tel. 0473/230230, fax 0473/233312. 68 rooms with bath. Facilities: pool, garden, restaurant (reservations advised, dress: casual but neat, closed Mon., $$), bar. AE, DC, MC, V. $$*

Minerva. Recommended by locals as a good spot for budget travelers, this is another turn-of-the-century hotel, built in 1909 and furnished in traditional period style. Set in a garden, it's about 10 minutes by foot from the town center, near several of the luxury hotels. Almost all rooms have balconies with views of the mountains. Full-board rates are economical. *Via Cavour 95, tel. 0473/236712. 44 rooms with bath. Facilities: restaurant, pool. AE, DC. Closed Nov.–Mar., except for 1 week Dec. 24–Jan.1. $$*

Naturno
(Naturns)
Lodging

Feldhof. You can savor the full splendor of the Venosta Valley, with its meadows and forests, from most rooms in this small, friendly hotel. The Feldhof is a modern hotel built in the traditional style and furnished in rustic elegance with antique furniture and lots of flowers. All rooms have a private safe, and most have balconies looking out over the hotel garden. The restaurant is for guests only. *Via Municipio 4, tel. 0473/87264, fax 0473/87263. 27 rooms with bath. Facilities: pool, sauna, solarium, thermal treatment center. No credit cards. Closed Nov. 5–Mar. 20. $–$$$*

Ortisei (St.
Ulrich)
Lodging

Aquila/Adler. Since 1810 there has always been a Hotel Aquila under the same family management in this popular Val Gardena sports center. Today it is regarded as one of the best in the valley. Set in a large park, the original building has been enlarged and renovated several times in the intervening 180 years, but retains a lot of the old atmosphere, looking something like a turreted castle. The Tyrolean character is carried through in special Tyrolean parties held once a week for guests. The rooms are spacious, and many have balconies or little terraces; some are suitable for disabled persons. *Via Rezia 7, tel. 0471/796203, fax 0471/796210. 94 rooms, most with bath. Facilities: pool, sauna, solarium, massage, tennis courts, fitness and beauty center, restaurant, bar. AE, DC, MC, V. Closed Easter– May 20, Nov. 1–mid-Dec. $$$*

Trento
Dining
★

Chiesa. Located near the castle in a building dating from about 1400, Chiesa is furnished with antiques and serves interesting dishes, some from centuries-old recipes. The *taglieri di Bernardo Cles*, for example, consists of coin-shaped pasta in a sauce of veal and lettuce—but no tomatoes: When the recipe was devised, tomatoes were not yet eaten in Italy. Other specialties include risotto *alle mele* (with apples), a hearty minestrone soup made of vegetables and barley, and the *Tonco de Pontesel*—a stew of mixed meat served with polenta, made according to a 15th-century recipe. *Via San Marco 64, tel. 0461/238766. Reservations advised. Jacket and tie required. AE, DC, MC, V. Closed Sun., Wed. dinner, and Aug. 15–31. $$$*

Le Due Spade. Near the Duomo, small and cozy, with wood paneling and a beautiful antique stove providing warmth on chilly days, this typical Tyrolean tavern has plenty of atmosphere. Given its popularity with locals, reservations are a must. The cuisine is local, too, and you can sample traditional *gnocchetti di ricotta* (ricotta cheese dumplings) and polenta *con funghi* (with mushroom sauce). *Via Don Rizzi 11, tel. 0461/234343. Reservations required. Dress: casual. AE, DC, MC, V. Closed Sun., Mon. dinner. $$–$$$*

Roma. Centrally located, about halfway between the Duomo and Buonconsiglio castle, this restaurant is one of the busiest in Trento, especially at lunch, when businesspeople come for satisfying, well-prepared dishes in traditional style. On the menu are homemade canederli and *spezzatino trentino* (meat stew). *Via San Simonino 6, tel. 0461/984150. Reservations advised. Dress: casual but neat. AE, DC, MC, V. Closed Sun. and Aug. $$*

Lodging

Accademia. This friendly character-filled hotel occupies an ancient house in the historic center of Trento, close to Piazza del Duomo. The public rooms retain the ancient vaulting, and the bedrooms are modern and comfortably equipped. There's a good restaurant and a courtyard garden. *Vicolo Colico 4, tel. 0461/233600, fax 0461/ 230174. 43 rooms with bath. Facilities: restaurant, garden, bar. AE, DC, MC, V. $$$*

The Arts and Nightlife

The Arts

Essentially rural in character, the Dolomites offer a rich selection of folk festivals, harvest fairs, and religious celebrations. Chief among these is Trento's week-long festival of San Vigilio (the last week of June), when marching bands and costumed choirs perform in the streets and squares of the heart of the city. The other major towns have similar festivals, but equally enjoyable are the more informal and low-key celebrations in the villages of the many valleys, sometimes amounting to nothing more than excuses for hard-working mountain farmers to get together for some local wine and song.

Folk Festivals **Bolzano.** Spring is heralded each May with large flower markets and with spin-off events, including concerts and folklore and art exhibits. Later, on August 24, is the Bartolomeo Horse Fair on Renon Mountain just northeast of the town. Hundreds of farmers converge for a day of serious trading and frivolous merriment.

Brunico. January 22 sees a dogsled race; locals turn up with flasks of hot mulled wine to back their favorites.

Merano. Local farmers put their horses to the test in the highly charged horse race that is the highlight of Easter Monday. On the second Sunday of October, Merano has a Grape Festival, with parades and wine tastings.

Ortisei. The Val Gardena comes alive with a parade of horse-drawn sleighs on January 1.

Trento. From late June to late September a regional "superfestival" spotlights historic castles as venues for performances and evocations of fact and legend. Trains taking passengers on excursions to the castles are part of it, as are music, costumes, and banquets.

Concerts **Bolzano** hosts the International Busoni Piano competition in late August. Concerts and recitals are held in halls and churches. Internationally acclaimed performers usually head the panel of judges.

Film **Trento** plays host each May to a month-long festival of films devoted to mountains and mountaineering.

Nightlife

The usual form of nightlife in this mountain region is to soak up the atmosphere in a Tyrolean-style stube, often the core of a hotel's entertainment or the focal point of an entire village. Wood-paneled and stocked with a range of local beers and wines, these establishments reflect the synthesis of Austrian and Italian cultures in the Dolomites. Beer is matched by wine, schnitzel by pasta, and zither-accompanied Austrian folk songs by the occasional Verdi aria. More sophisticated options are limited to the two chic ski resorts, Madonna di Campiglio and Cortina d'Ampezzo.

Discos **Cortina d'Ampezzo.** You can expect to mingle with the designer-clothing set at the VIP disco at the **Europa** hotel (*see* Dining and Lodging, *above*); nonguests are welcome, but don't expect to spend less than 40,000 lire.

Merano. The **Bristol** hotel is popular with locals as well as visitors.

Nightclub **Cortina d'Ampezzo.** The **Cristallo** hotel (*see* Lodging, *above*) has a nightclub that is open to nonguests.

12 Emilia-Romagna

Bologna to Rimini along the Via Emilia

Emilia-Romagna owes its beginnings to a road. In 187 BC the Romans laid out the Via Aemelia, a long highway running straight from the Adriatic port of Rimini to the central garrison town of Piacenza, and it was along this central spine that the primary towns of the region developed. The old Roman road still exists (S9), and a modern superhighway (A1 and A14) runs parallel to it. Most of the exploring in this chapter will be along either the old road or its modern counterpart.

Despite the unifying factor of the Via Emilia, as the highway is now called, the region has had a fragmented history. The eastern portion of the region, roughly the area from the city of Faenza to the coast, known as Romagna, has looked first to the east, and then to Rome, for art, political power, and, some say, national character. The western portion, Emilia, from Bologna to Piacenza, had a more northern, rather dour, sense of self-government and dissent. Italians say that in Romagna a stranger will be offered a glass of wine; in Emilia, a glass of water—if anything at all.

The principal city of the region is Bologna. It was founded by the Etruscans, but eventually came under the influence of the Roman Empire. The Romans established a garrison there, renaming the old Etruscan settlement Bononia, the Bologna of today.

It was after the fall of Rome that the region began its fragmentation. Romagna, centered in Ravenna, was ruled from Constantinople. Ravenna eventually became capital of the empire in the West, in the 5th century, passing to papal rule in the 8th century. The city today, however, is still filled with reminders of two centuries of Byzantine rule.

The other cities of the region, from the Middle Ages on, became the fiefs of important noble families—the Este in Ferrara and Modena, the Pallavicini in Piacenza, the Bentivoglio in Bologna, and the Malatesta in Rimini. Today all these cities bear the marks of their noble patrons. When in the 16th century the papacy managed to exert its power over the entire region, some of these cities were divided among the families of the reigning popes—hence the stamp of the Farnese family on Parma, Piacenza, and Ferrara.

The region was one of the first to join the quest for a unified Italy in the 19th century, pledging itself to the king of Italy and the forces of Garibaldi in the 1840s. Loyalty to the crown did not last long, however. The Italian socialist movement was born in the region, and throughout Italy Emilia-Romagna has been known for rebellion and dissent. Benito Mussolini was born here, although, in keeping with the political atmosphere of his home state, he was a firebrand socialist during the early part of his career. Despite being the birthplace of Il Duce, Emilia-Romagna did not take to fascism: It was in this region that the antifascist resistance was born, and during the war the region suffered terribly at the hands of the Fascists and the Nazis.

Despite a long history of bloodletting, turmoil, and rebellion, the arts—both decorative and culinary—have always flourished in Emilia-Romagna. The great families financed painters, sculptors, and writers (Dante found a haven in Ravenna after being expelled from his native Florence). In modern times, Emilia-Romagna has given to the arts such famous sons as painter Giorgio Morandi, author Giorgio Bassani (author of *Garden of the Finzi-Continis*), filmmaker Federico Fellini, and tenor Luciano Pavarotti.

Gourmets the world over would argue that Emilia-Romagna's greatest contribution to mankind has been gastronomic. Bologna is the acknowledged leading city of Italian cuisine. It is home to two of the most famous Italian delicacies—foods that, sadly, have been poorly treated outside their native city. What the world calls "baloney" the Bolognese call *mortadella*, a robust pork sausage spiced with whole peppercorns (if there aren't peppercorns in it, then it isn't mortadella), which bears no resemblance to the stuff sliced at the typical U.S. deli counter. The other famous dish is *spaghetti al ragù*, known to the world as *spaghetti bolognese*. The spaghetti with meat sauce dished around the world is a far cry from the real thing. In Bologna a ragù sauce is made with onions, carrots, minced pork and veal, butter, and fresh tomatoes, and is cooked for five or six hours in a special earthen pot. It is, in a word, exquisite. Few dining experiences in Italy can match the satisfaction of a properly cooked ragù.

Bologna is also the home of tortellini, lasagna, and *vitello alla bolognese*, a veal cutlet smothered with prosciutto and Parmesan cheese. The rest of the province has made substantial contributions to the kitchen. Parma is the home of Parma ham and the most famous of all Italian cheeses, Parmesan. Modena is the birthplace of *zampone* (stuffed pigs' feet, which tastes much better than it sounds) and *aceto balsamico*, the jet-black, fragrant herb vinegar that is now a must on the shelves of any self-respecting gourmet.

Essential Information

Important Addresses and Numbers

Tourist Information
Bologna (Gugliemo Marconi airport, tel. 051/381732; train station, tel. 051/246541; Piazza Maggiore 6, tel. 051/239–660).
Ferrara (Piazza Municipio 19, tel. 0532/209370 or 239269).
Modena (Via Scudari 30, tel. 059/222482).
Parma (Piazza Duomo 5, tel. 0521/234735).
Piacenza (Piazzetta Mercanti 7, tel. 0523/29324).
Ravenna (Via Salara 8, tel. 0544/35404).
Rimini (Piazzale Cesare Battisti, train station, tel. 0541/51331; Piazzale Indipendenza, waterfront, tel. 0541/51101).

Travel Agencies
Bologna (Marconi Tours, Via Marconi 47, tel. 051/235783).
Rimini (Urbinati, Viale Vespucci 127, tel. 0541/391660).

Emergencies
Police, tel. 112. **Ambulance,** tel. 113. **Doctors and Dentists,** tel. 113. **Late-Night Pharmacies,** tel. 051/192 for information.

Arriving and Departing by Plane

Bologna is an important business and convention center and is therefore served by air routes that link it with other Italian cities, as well as by direct flights to European capitals. The airport, **Guglielmo Marconi** is located at Borgo Panigale, 7 kilometers (4 miles) from town. Bus service connects it with a downtown air terminal at the central train station in Bologna proper. For air-traffic information call 051/311578.

Arriving and Departing by Train

Bologna is an important rail hub for the entire northern part of Italy and has frequent, fast train service to Rome, Milan, Florence, and Venice. For information about train departures call 051/246490.

Getting Around

By Car The Via Emilia (S9) runs through the heart of the region. It is a straight, modern low-lying road, the length of which can be traveled in a few hours. Ferrara and Ravenna are joined to it by good modern highways.

By Train The railway follows the Via Emilia, and all the cities mentioned here can be reached by train.

By Bus Private bus service links all the cities of Emilia-Romagna, with Bologna being the central hub. The Autostazione (bus terminal) is in Piazza XX Settembre, at the top of Via dell'Indipendenza; for information call 051/248374. City-run bus routes connect major towns with smaller villages and hamlets in the district, but routes are roundabout, and schedules vary from place to place.

Exploring Emilia-Romagna

A tour through Emilia-Romagna has something for everyone: great art, stirring history, fabulous food—even a day at the beach at the seaside resort of Rimini. The best way to see the region is to begin your tour in the west, in Piacenza, and to proceed east along the Via Emilia to the sea. The major towns are either on that route or just off it, the longest detours being no more than 30 or 40 miles off the main road.

Highlights for First-Time Visitors

Mosaics in church of San Vitale, Ravenna (Tour 2: Rimini, Ravenna, and Ferrara).

Tomb of Galla Placidia, Ravenna (Tour 2: Rimini, Ravenna, and Ferrara).

Tempio Malatestiano, Rimini (Tour 2: Rimini, Ravenna, and Ferrara).

Castello Estense, Ferrara (Tour 2: Rimini, Ravenna, and Ferrara).

Piazza del Duomo (including the Duomo, the baptistery, and the church of San Giovanni), Parma (Tour 1: From Piacenza to the Rubicon).

Farnese Theater and Palazzo della Pilotta, Parma (Tour 1: From Piacenza to the Rubicon).

Tour 1: From Piacenza to the Rubicon

Numbers in the margin correspond to points of interest on the Emilia-Romagna map.

❶ The city of **Piacenza** has always been associated with industry and commerce. Its position on the river Po has made it an important inland port since the earliest times—the Etruscans, then the Romans, had thriving settlements on this site. As you approach the city today, you could be forgiven for thinking that it holds little of interest. Piacenza is surrounded by ugly industrial suburbs (with particularly unlovely cement factories and a power station), but these enclose a delightfully unspoiled medieval downtown.

The heart of the city is **Piazza dei Cavalli** (Square of Horses), dominated by the massive Palazzo del Comune, a severe turreted and crenellated Gothic building of the 13th century. It was the seat of

Emilia-Romagna

town government during those times when Piacenza was not under the iron fist of a ruling family. The equestrian statues from which Piazza dei Cavalli takes its name are images of members of the last and greatest of the rulers of Piacenza. The statue on the right is Ranuccio Farnese; on the left is his father, Alessandro Farnese. Alessandro was a beloved ruler, enlightened and fair; Ranuccio, his successor, was less successful. Both statues are the work of Francesco Mochi, a master sculptor of the Baroque period.

Walk out of the piazza on Via XX Settembre, which leads to Piacenza's impressive **duomo** (cathedral), a rather grim-looking building dating from the mid-12th century. Attached to the massive bell tower is a *gabbia* (iron cage), where evildoers were exposed naked to the scorn (and missiles) of the crowd in the marketplace below. The interior of the cathedral is an odd mixture of Gothic and Baroque. Fine medieval stonework decorates the pillars and the crypt, and there are extravagant frescoes by 17th-century artist Guercino in the dome of the cupola. *Open daily 7–12, 4–7.*

The **Museo Civico,** the city-owned collection of Piacenzan art and antiquities, is housed in the vast Palazzo Farnese, which was started by the ruling family in 1558 but never completed. The museum was closed for many years for restoration and the reordering of the collection, but it is again open to the public. The highlight of this rather eclectic exhibit is the Etruscan Fegato di Piacenza, a bronze tablet in the shape of a *fegato* (liver), with the symbols of the gods of good and ill fortune marked on it. By comparing this master "liver" with one taken from the body of a freshly slaughtered sacrifice, the priests could predict the future. On a more humanistic note, the collection also contains a painting by Botticelli, the *Madonna with St. John the Baptist,* and a series of Roman bronzes and mosaics. There is also a collection of carriages, arms and armor, and other paraphernalia owned by the Farnese, giving a good idea of the splendor of that powerful family. *Piazza Cittadella. Admission: 4,500 lire. Open Tues., Wed., Fri. 9–12:30; Thurs. 9–12:30, 3:30–5:30; Sat. 9–12:30, 3–6; Sun. 9:30–12, 3:30–6:30.*

The area between Piacenza and Parma, 62 kilometers (37 miles) away, is opera country. In the quiet backwater towns north of the Via Emilia, the great Italian opera composer Giuseppe Verdi lived and worked. The composer of *Aïda, Rigoletto, La Traviata,* and *Otello* was born in a very simple farmhouse in the hamlet of Roncole ❷ and built the grand villa of **Sant'Agata** in the nearby town of **Busseto** when he had become world famous.

If you are driving from Piacenza, take S10 northeast for Cremona, but turn off it just a few miles out of Piacenza and follow the signs for S587 to the town of Cortemaggiore. From Cortemaggiore, turn onto a smaller rural road (not numbered) and follow the signs for Busseto, some 10 kilometers (6 miles) away. If you plan to visit all the area's Verdi's sights, invest in a 6,000-lire ticket valid for Villa Pallavicino, Palazzo Orlandi, Teatro Verdi, and Verdi's birthplace (but not Villa Sant'Agata).

In Busseto you can visit the **Villa Pallavicino,** where Verdi worked and lived with his mistress (later wife), Giuseppina Strepponi. There is a small Verdi museum here that displays such relics of the maestro as his piano, scores, composition books, walking sticks, and other bits of memorabilia. *Admission: 3,000 lire. Open Apr.–Nov., Tues.–Sun. 9:30–12:30 and 3–7.*

Palazzo Orlandi, owned for the past century by the Orlandi family, was also Verdi's home for a few years. Only a few of its stately rooms are open to the public. *Admission: 3,000 lire. Open Apr.–Nov., Tues.–Sun. 9:30–12:30, 3–7; Oct.–Mar., Tues.–Sun. 9:30–12, 2:30–5.*

In the center of town is the lovely **Teatro Verdi,** dedicated, as one may expect, to the works of the hamlet's famous son. It is a well-preserved 19th-century–style theater, and it's worth a look to get a feel for a place where Verdi worked. (Currently undergoing restoration. May be closed in 1995.) *Admission: 3,000 lire. Open Apr.–Sept., Tues.–Sun. 9:30–12:30, 3–7; Oct.–Mar., Tues.–Sun. 9:30–12, 2:30–5.*

Five kilometers (3 miles) north of Busseto is **Villa Sant'Agata,** the grand country home Verdi built for himself in 1849, where some of his greatest works were composed. For Verdi lovers, Sant'Agata is a shrine. *Admission: 5,000 lire. Open Apr. 1–Oct. 30, Tues.–Sun. 9–11:40, 3–6:40.*

The town of **Roncole,** the composer's birthplace, is a few kilometers east of Busseto. The simple farmhouse in which he was born is on the edge of town, as is the church in which he took some of his earliest steps in a musical career: He was the church organist here when still in his teens. *Verdi's birthplace. Admission: 3,000 lire. Open Apr.–Nov., Tues.–Sun. 9:30–12:30, 3–7.*

To reach Parma, the next stop on the tour, 30 kilometers (19 miles) from Busseto, take S588 south to the A1 or the Via Emilia and proceed east; or continue southeast from Roncole to either road.

❸ Parma is a delightful, dignified town that stands on the banks of a tributary of the river Po. Much of the historic center has been untouched by modern times, despite heavy damage during World War II, and with the efforts being made by the city fathers to control traffic, strolling Parma's cobbled streets is a charming experience. The traffic regulations, while a boon to pedestrians, are a nightmare for motorists. Every obstacle is put in the way of motor traffic—one-way streets, no-turning zones, and the like—so it is best to leave your car outside the center and see the town on foot.

Almost every major European power has had a hand in ruling Parma at one time or another. The Romans founded the city—it was little more than a garrison on the Via Emilia—and then a succession of feudal lords held sway here. In the 16th century came the ever-avaricious Farnese family (who are still the dukes of Parma), and then, in fast succession, the Spanish, French, and Austrians, with the Austrians taking over following the upheavals in central Europe after the fall of Napoleon. The French influence is strong. The great French novelist Stendahl lived in the city for several years and set his classic novel *The Charterhouse of Parma* here.

The **Piazza del Duomo**—site of the cathedral, the baptistery, the church of San Giovanni, and the palaces of the bishop and other notables—is the heart of the city. This square and its buildings make up one of the most harmonious, tranquil city centers in Italy. The focal point of the piazza is the magnificent 12th-century **Duomo,** with its two vigilant stone lions standing guard beside the main door. The arch of the entrance is decorated with figures representing the months of the year, a motif repeated inside the baptistery on the right-hand side of the square.

Some of the original artwork of the 1100s still exists in the church, notably the *Descent from the Cross,* a carving in the right transept, by Benedetto Antelami (1150–1230), a sculptor and architect whose masterwork is this cathedral's baptistery (*see below*). You can still feel the emotion the artist wished to convey in the simple figures.

It is odd to turn from this austere work of the 12th century to the exuberant fresco in the dome, the *Assumption of the Virgin,* by the 16th-century painter Antonio Correggio. The fresco was not well received when it was unveiled in 1530. "A mess of frogs' legs," the bishop of Parma is said to have called it. In contrast to the rather dark, somber interior of the cathedral, though, the beauty and light of the painting in the dome are a welcome relief. *Open daily 7–12, 3–7.*

The **Baptistery,** standing to the side of the Duomo, is a solemn and simple Romanesque building on the exterior and an uplifting Gothic building within. The doors of the baptistery are richly decorated with figures, animals, and flowers, and the interior is adorned with figures carved by Antelami, showing the months and seasons. *Admission: 3,000 lire. Open daily 9–12:30, 3–6.*

There is more painting by Correggio in the nearby church of **San Giovanni Evangelista,** a church with an elaborate Baroque facade and a Renaissance interior. Of the several works by Correggio in this church, it is his *St. John the Evangelist* (left transept) that is considered the finest. Also in this church (in the second and fourth chapels on the left) are works by Girolamo Parmigianino, a contemporary of Correggio's and, as his name suggests, a native of Parma. *Open daily 6:30–12, 3:30–8.*

Next door to the church, in the adjoining monastery, is a **pharmacy** where Benedictine monks used to mix medicines and herbals. The 16th-century decorations still survive, while the potions (the people of Parma swore they would cure almost every ill) are, alas, gone—the pharmacy stopped production in 1881. *Admission: 3,000 lire. Open daily 9–1:45.*

The **Galleria Nazionale** of Parma is the primary art gallery of the city, and it is housed in the vast, and rather grim looking, **Palazzo della Pilotta,** on the banks of the river. The palace was built about 1600 and is so big that from the air it is Parma's most recognizable sight—hence, the destruction done to it when it was bombed by Allied forces in 1944. Much of the building has been restored, but not all. The palazzo takes its name from the ballgame *pilotta,* a sort of handball played within the palace precincts in the 17th century.

To enter the art museum, which is on the ground floor of the palace, you pass through the magnificent and elaborately Baroque **Teatro Farnese,** built in 1628 and based on Palladio's theater in the northern Italian town of Vicenza. Built entirely of wood, the theater was burned badly during Allied bombing, but has been faultlessly restored.

The art gallery itself is large and contains many examples of works by the two best-known painters of Parma—Correggio and Parmigianino. There are also works by Fra Angelico, Leonardo da Vinci, El Greco, and Il Bronzino. *Admission: 10,000 lire. Open daily 9–1:45.*

Near the Palazzo della Pilotta, on Strada Garibaldi, is the **Camera del Correggio,** the former dining room of the abbess of the Convent of Saint Paul. It was extensively frescoed by Correggio, and, despite the religious character of the building, the decorations are entirely secular, with very worldly depictions of mythological scenes—the *Triumphs of the Goddess Diana,* the *Three Graces,* and the *Three Fates. Admission free. Open daily 9–1:45.*

Time Out Civilization in Parma is more than painting and architecture. To taste the delicacies that put Parma on the world culinary map, have a snack or buy the ingredients for a picnic at **Salumeria Melli** (Via della Repubblica 68) or **Specialità di Parma** (Via Farini 9/c).

Near the central Piazza Garibaldi is **Madonna della Steccata,** a delightful 16th-century domed church famous for a wonderful fresco cycle by Parmigianino. The painter took so long to complete it that his exasperated patrons imprisoned him briefly for breach of contract before releasing him to complete the work. *Open daily 9–12, 3–6.*

❹ Modena, 56 kilometers (35 miles) from Parma along Route A1, is an old town that's famous today for three very modern names. The luxury high-performance cars Maserati and Ferrari come from Modena, and so does the world-famous opera star Luciano Pavarotti.

The modern town that encircles the historic center is extensive, and, while the old quarter is small, it is filled with an Old World atmosphere, narrow medieval streets, and pleasant piazzas. Begin your exploration at the **Duomo** in the central Piazza Grande. The church is one of the finest examples of Romanesque architecture in the country and dates from the 12th century. As in Parma, the exterior is decorated with medieval sculptures showing scenes from the life of San Geminiano (patron saint of Modena) and fantastic beasts, as well as a realistic-looking scene of the sacking of a city by barbarian hordes, a reminder to the faithful to be ever vigilant in defense of the church. The bell tower is made of white marble and is known as *La Ghirlandina* (The Little Garland) because of its distinctive garland-shaped weather vane on the summit.

The interior of the church is very somber and is divided by an elaborately decorated gallery carved with scenes of the Passion of Christ. The carvings took 50 years to complete and are by an anonymous Modenese master of the 12th century. The tomb of San Geminiano is in the crypt. *Open daily 8–6.*

The principal museum of the town is housed in the **Palazzo dei Musei,** a short walk from the Duomo (follow Via Emilia—the old Roman road runs through the heart of the town—to Via di Sant'Agostino. The museum is in the piazza on the left). The collection was assembled in the mid-17th century by Francesco d'Este, Duke of Modena, and the gallery **Galleria Estense** is named in his honor. In the first room, there is a portrait bust of him by Bernini.

The duke was a man of many interests, as you can see from the galleries' collections of objets d'art—ivories, coins, medals, and bronzes, as well as works of art dating from the Renaissance to the Baroque. There are works here by Correggio, as well as by masters from other parts of Italy, such as the Venetians Tintoretto and Veronese, the Bolognese Reni and the Carracci brothers, and the Neapolitan Salvator Rosa.

The gallery also houses the Duke's **library,** a huge collection of illuminated books, of which the best known is the beautifully illustrated bible of the 15th century, the *Bible of Borso d'Este.* A map, dated 1501, was one of the first in the world to show Columbus's discovery of America. *Admission: 4,000 lire. Open Tues.–Sat. 9–2, Sun. 9–1.*

In Piazza Roma (follow the curved Via Ramazzini away from the Palazzo dei Musei), you'll find the huge Baroque **palace** of the dukes of Modena. It is now a military academy; once the province of the dukes only, it is still off-limits, except to flocks of cadets in elaborate uniforms. Behind the academy are Modena's large public gardens.

❺ Bologna, 38 kilometers (23 miles) from Modena, is the principal city of Emilia-Romagna and one of the most important cities in Italy. Through its long history, first as an Etruscan city, then a Roman one, then as an independent city-state in the Middle Ages, Bologna has always been a power in the north of Italy. Through the centuries, the city has acquired a number of nicknames: "Bologna the Learned," in honor of its ancient (the oldest in the world) university; "Bologna the Turreted," recalling the forest of medieval towers that once rose from the city center (two remarkable examples still exist); and "Bologna the Fat," a tribute to the preeminent position the city holds in the world of cuisine.

Wars, sackings, rebellions, and aerial bombing do not seem to have made much of an impression on the old center of the city: The narrow, cobblestoned streets are still there, as are the ancient churches, the massive palaces, the medieval towers, and the famous arcades that line many of the main thoroughfares of the town.

The streets are always bustling with students. The university was founded in the year 1050, and by the 13th century already had more than 10,000 students. It was a center for the teaching of law and theology, and it was ahead of its time in that many of the professors were women. Today the university has one of the most prominent business schools in Italy and has the finest faculty of medicine in the country. Marconi, the inventor of wireless telegraphy, first formulated his ground-breaking theories in the physics labs of the university.

The heart of the city is Piazza Maggiore and the adjacent Piazza del Nettuno. Grouped around these two squares are the imposing Basilica of San Petronio, the huge Palazzo Comunale, the Palazzo del Podestà, the Palazzo di Re Enzo, and the fountain of Neptune. It is one of the best groupings of public buildings in the entire country.

Numbers in the margin correspond to points of interest on the Bologna map.

❻ The **Basilica di San Petronio** was started in the 14th century, and work was still in progress on this vast building some 300 years later. It is still not finished, as you can see: The facade is partially decorated and lacks most of the marble facing that the architects planned on several hundred years ago. The main doorway was carved by the great Sienese master of the Renaissance, Jacopo della Quercia. Above the center of the door is a Madonna and Child, flanked by Saints Ambrose and Petronius, patrons of the city.

The interior of the basilica is huge and echoing, 432 feet long and 185 feet wide. It is so vast that it's sobering to note that originally the Bolognans had planned an even bigger church (you can still see the columns erected to support the larger church outside the east end) but decided on this "toned down" version in the interest of economy. The church museum contains models to show how the original, planned church would have looked. The most important artworks in the church are in the left aisle, frescoes by Giovanni di Modena, dating from the first years of the 1400s. Also in the left aisle, laid out in the pavement of the church, is a huge sundial, placed there in 1655, showing the time, date, and month. *Open daily summer, 7:30–6:30, winter, 7:30–5. Museo di San Petronio (inside church) open Mon., Wed., Fri.–Sun. 10–12:30.*

❼ The **Palazzo Comunale,** on the right as you face the church, is a mixture of styles and buildings, dating from the 13th to 15th centuries. When Bologna was an independent commune, this huge palace was the seat of government, a function it serves today. Over the door is a giant statue of Pope Gregory XIII, Bologna-born and most famous for his reorganization of the calendar—a system still in use today.

The Palazzo Comunale contains a picture gallery, the Collezioni Comunali d'Arte, which has paintings of the Middle Ages, as well as some Renaissance works by Luca Signorelli and Tintoretto. The best reason to see the collection, however, is to get a look at the views of the piazza from the upper stories of the palace. *Admission: 5,000 lire. Open Tues.–Sun. 10–6.*

❽ The **Palazzo del Podestà,** which faces the basilica, was built in 1484, and attached to it is the soaring Torre dell'Arengo. The bells in this tower have rung since 1453, whenever the city has celebrated, mourned, or called its citizens to arms.

❾ Next to the Palazzo del Podestà is the medieval **Palazzo di Re Enzo,** the building in which King Enzo of Sardinia was imprisoned for 23 years (until his death in 1272). He had been unwise enough to wage war on Bologna and was captured after the fierce battle of Fossalta in 1249. The palace has other unhappy associations: Common criminals received the last rites of the church in the tiny chapel in the courtyard before being taken out to execution in Piazza Maggiore.

Next to the Palazzo di Re Enzo is the elaborate Baroque **fountain** by the sculptor Giambologna. Given Bologna's landlocked position, the choice of subject—the God of the Sea, Neptune, and his attendant sirens and dolphins—seems rather odd. It was sculpted in 1566 and is known by the nickname Il Gigante (The Giant), which certainly fits.

The busy, chic Via Rizzoli runs from Piazza del Nettuno directly into the medieval section of the city, passing Piazza di Porta Ravegnana. Here are two of Bologna's famous towers: The taller, the **Torre degli Asinelli,** is 320 feet high and leans an alarming 7½-feet out of the perpendicular; the other tower, the **Torre Garisenda,** was shortened for safety in the 1500s. It is 165 feet high and tilts 10 feet. The Torre degli Asinelli can be climbed (500 steep stairs) and has a fine view of the city. *Admission: 3,000 lire. Open May–Sept., daily 9–6; Oct.– Apr., daily 9–5.*

The towers were built at the same time (1488) and are mentioned by Dante in the *Inferno.* They are the only two that remain of the more than 200 that once graced the city—every family of any importance had to have a tower as a symbol of its prestige and power.

From Piazza di Porta Ravegnana, turn right onto Via Santo Stefano. Four blocks along that street is the church of **Santo Stefano,** a remarkable building that is actually several churches contained in one building. The oldest, the church of Santi Vitale e Agricola, dates from the 8th century and contains a 14th-century nativity scene much loved by Bologna's children, who come at Christmastime to pay their respects to the baby Jesus. The church of San Sepolcro (12th century) contains the courtyard of Pontius Pilate, so named for the basin in the center of the court that's said to be the basin Pilate washed his hands in after condemning Christ. *Open daily summer, 9–12, 3:30–6:30; winter, 9–12, 3:30–5:30.*

There is also a museum here displaying various medieval religious works, where you can buy sundry items made by the monks, such as honey, shampoo, or jam. *Admission free. Open Mon.–Sat. 9–12, 3:30–5:30, Sun. 9–1, 3:30–5:30.*

Leaving the church, turn right on Via Farini, then, a few blocks farther along, turn left on Via Garibaldi. This leads you to the church of **San Domenico,** an interesting church that contains the tomb of St. Dominic, who died here in 1221. The tomb of the saint, called the Arca di San Domenico, is in the sixth chapel on the right. Many artists contributed to the decoration, notably Niccolò di Bari, who was so proud of his work here that he changed his name to Niccolò dell'Arca to recall this famous work. The young Michelangelo carved the angel on the right. In the right transept of the church is a tablet marking the last resting place of the hapless King Enzo, whose prison you saw in Piazza Maggiore. In the square in front of San Domenico are two curious tombs raised above the ground on pillars, commemorating two famous 14th-century lawyers. *Open daily 7–12, 3:30–7.*

Returning to Piazza di Porta Ravegnana, turn up the busy Via Zamboni and stop a few blocks up on the right to see the church of **San Giacomo Maggiore.** Inside is the burial chamber of the Bentivoglio family, the leading family in Bologna in the Middle Ages. The crypt is connected by underground passage to the Teatro Comunale, across the street—a rather odd feature, until you realize that the family palazzo of the Bentivoglio used to stand on that spot. The most notable tomb is that of Antonio Bentivoglio, carved by Jacopo della Quercia in 1435. We can tell his profession—lecturer in law—from the group of students carved on the base, all listening intently to their professor. *Open daily 8–12, 3:30–6.*

Continuing along Via Zamboni, you come to the principal art gallery
⓮ of the city and one of the most important in Italy, the **Pinacoteca
Nazionale.** The collection here includes many works by the immor-
tals of Italian painting, including Raphael's famous *Ecstasy of St.
Cecilia.* There is also a beautiful multipaneled painting by Giotto
and a Parmigianino *Madonna and Saints.* The centerpieces of the
collection, however, are the many rooms devoted to the two greatest
Bolognese painters, Guido Reni and Annibale Carracci, both masters of the late 16th century. Some of the most interesting paintings,
from a historical point of view, are by Giuseppe Crespi, a Bolognese
painter of the 18th century who avoided grand religious or historical
themes, preferring instead to paint scenes of daily life in his native
city. These small canvases give you an excellent idea of the boisterous, earthy life of Old Bologna. *Via delle Belle Arti 56, tel. 051/
243222. Admission: 6,000 lire. Open Tues.–Sat. 9–2, Sun. 9–1.*

⓯ The Pinacoteca Nazionale is on the edge of the **university** district,
and it is worth a walk through the adjoining streets to get a sense of
what an Italian university is like. There is no campus, as such, but a
jumble of buildings, some dating as far back as the 15th century,
with the bulk of them from the 17th and 18th centuries. This neighborhood, like neighborhoods in most college towns, has lots of bookshops, coffee shops, and cheap snack bars and restaurants. None of
them is particularly distinguished, but they all give a good idea of
student life in the city. Political slogans and sentiments are scrawled
on walls all around the university and tend, for the most part, to be
ferociously leftist.

Time Out For wonderful ice cream in the university district, try **Moline** (Via
delle Moline 13, closed Tues.), which has simple but delicious
cioccolata con panna (chocolate with heavy whipped cream) or a series of more adventurous flavors and delicate fruit ices.

From Bologna there are two choices of itineraries: Head north to
Ferrara and then east to Ravenna or continue along the Via Emilia,
stopping for short visits at some of the smaller towns en route to Rimini and the sea.

*Numbers in the margin correspond with points of interest on the
Emilia-Romagna map.*

If you have chosen the latter, the first port of call out of Bologna,
⓰ just off Via Emilia (S9), is the little hamlet of **Dozza,** 31 kilometers
(19 miles) away. It is a small village on a hill crowned with a splendid
restored medieval castle. Artists from all over Italy flock to the town
in September of odd years to take part in the mural competition—it
seems that every square foot of the town has been painted with colorful scenes done with varying degrees of skill. The castle is home to
the **Enoteca Regionale,** the wine "library" for the region. Here you
can sample the different vintages that come from the surrounding
countryside, particularly Dozza's own Albana, a white wine that
comes dry or sweet. *Tel. 0542/678089. Admission: 4,000 lire. Open
Apr.–Sept., Tues.–Sun. 10–12, 3–6; Oct.–Mar., Tues.–Sun. 10–
12, 2–5.*

Forty-nine kilometers (30 miles) from Bologna, along the Via
⓱ Emilia, is **Faenza,** a town that has been producing ceramics since the
12th century—its "faience" pottery is known the world over. In the
central **Piazza del Popolo** are dozens of shops selling the town's product. Faenza is also home to the **Museo delle Ceramiche,** one of the
largest ceramics museums in the world, covering the potter's art in
all phases of history and in all parts of the world. *Viale Baccarini.*

*Admission: 8,000 lire. Open Apr.–Oct., Tues.–Sat. 9:30–1, 3–6,
Sun. 9:30–1; Nov.–Mar., Tues.–Sat. 9:30–2.*

From Faenza continue on S9 to the town of **Forlì,** 14 kilometers (9
miles) away, and turn off onto the rural Route 9ter. This leads you
18 through hilly country to the small town of **Predappio,** the birthplace
of Benito Mussolini and Il Duce's final resting place. The cemetery
on the outskirts of town contains the crypt of the Mussolini family,
with the former dictator himself in the place of honor. A spotlit bust
glowers at visitors, and glass cases contain some of his decorations
and medals. It is a chilling place and has become the object of pilgrimage for the followers of fascism (young and old), who write
repugnant political slogans in the visitors' book. *Cimitero Municipale. Open daily 8 AM–sunset.*

Returning on S9, you pass through the modern towns of Forlimpo-
19 poli, Cesena, and Savignano. At **Savignano,** though, there is a reminder that no matter how new the towns might look, you are still
traveling in a place of great history—just outside the town is a small
stream, the Rubicone. Cross it and you, too, have crossed the Rubicon, the river made famous by Julius Caesar when, in 49 BC, he defied the Senate of Rome by bringing his army across the river and
plunging the country into civil war.

From here, the road leads on to the next three important destinations, Rimini, Ravenna, and Ferrara.

Tour 2: Rimini, Ravenna, and Ferrara

20 **Rimini** is the principal summer resort on the Adriatic Coast and one
of the most popular holiday destinations in Italy. Every summer,
beginning in June, the city is flooded with vacationers, not just from
Italy but from France, Austria, Germany, Scandinavia, and Great
Britain, as well. The city is given over almost exclusively to tourism,
with hundreds of hotels, grand and modest, and restaurants catering to virtually every national palate: You are just as likely to find a
bierkeller or an English tea shop as you are an Italian restaurant.
The waterfront is lined with beach clubs that rent a patch of sand, a
deck chair, and an umbrella by the day, week, month, or the entire
season. Hotels along the beach front have staked out their own private turf, so the chance of swimming (or even seeing the sea close
up) without paying for the privilege is slim.

In the off-season, Rimini, in common with resorts the world over, is
a ghost town. Some hotels and restaurants are open, but the majority are closed tight, hibernating until the return of the free-spending
tourists. Summers are so crowded here that it is most unwise to go
to Rimini without confirmed hotel reservations. For those who like
sun by day, disco by night, and hordes of frolicking teenagers, Rimini is the town for you; those who prefer more sedate vacations are
advised to stay away.

The new town has just about swallowed the old, but there are signs
here and there that tell of Rimini's long and turbulent history. Rimini stands at the junction of two great Roman consular roads: the Via
Aemilia, or Emilia as it is known now, and the Via Flaminia. In addition, in Roman times, it was an important port, making it a strategic
and commercial center. From the 13th century onward, the city was
controlled by the Malatesta family, an unpredictable group capable
of grand gestures and savage deeds. The famous lovers in Dante's
Inferno, Paolo and Francesca, were Malatestas. Paolo was the
brother of Gianciotto Malatesta; Francesca, Gianciotto's wife.

Gianciotto murdered them both for having betrayed him. Sigismondo Malatesta, lord of the city in the middle of the 15th century, was considered a learned man of great wit and culture. He also banished his first wife, strangled his second, and poisoned his third. He lived with his beautiful mistress, Isotta, until her death. He was so grief-stricken that he raised a magnificent monument in her honor, the **Tempio Malatestiano.** It is the principal sight in the town.

The oldest building in the city is the **Arco d'Augusto,** in Piazzale Giulio Cesare. It was erected in 27 BC, making it the oldest Roman arch in existence, and it marks the meeting of the Via Aemilia and the Via Flaminia. From there, walk along Corso Augusto to Piazza Tre Martiri (where, legend says, the mule carrying St. Anthony suddenly stopped and knelt in honor of the Holy Sacrament that was being carried past at the time) and turn right onto Via Quattro Novembre. One block up, also on the right side, is Sigismondo's memorial to his great love, Isotta, the Tempio Malatestiano.

Despite the irregular—from a church point of view—nature of Sigismondo's relationship with Isotta, the Tempio is today the **cathedral** of Rimini. The building was in fact originally a Franciscan church before Sigismondo took it over to make it into a monument to his beloved. The facade is a beautiful piece of Renaissance architecture by Leon Battista Alberti. It is in the shape of a Roman triumphal arch, and is considered to be one of Alberti's masterpieces.

The interior is light and spacious and contains the tombs of both the lovers. The intertwined I, for Isotta, and the S, for Sigismondo, are dotted about everywhere and look rather like "$" signs. The carvings of elephants and roses recall the coat-of-arms of the Malatesta family. Sigismondo's tomb, on the right of the entrance door, is some distance from Isotta's in the second chapel. (Her tomb is on the left wall of the chapel; the original inscription in marble had a pagan twist and was covered with another in bronze.) On the right, in what is now the Tempio's book and gift shop, is a wonderful but badly damaged fresco by Piero della Francesca showing Sigismondo paying homage to his patron saint. Over the main altar of the church is a crucifix attributed to Giotto. *Open daily 7–12, 3:30–7.*

There are two routes from Rimini to Ravenna. The coast road, S16, hugs the shoreline as far as Cervia before edging inland. While the distance, 52 kilometers (31 miles), is not great, the going along this route is slow. The coast north of Rimini is lined with dozens of small resort towns, only one having any charm, the seaport of Cesenatico; the others are mini-Riminis, and during the summer the narrow road is hopelessly clogged with traffic. A faster route is to head inland on A14 and then turn off onto the inland S71, which leads directly into Ravenna. The distance is 64 kilometers (39 miles).

㉑ About five kilometers (3 miles) southeast of Ravenna stands the church of **Sant'Apollinare in Classe.** It is landlocked now, but when the church was built, it stood in the center of the busy shipping port of Classis. The arch above and the area around the high altar are rich in mosaics. Those on the arch, older than those behind it, are considered superior to the rest. They show Christ in judgment and the 12 lambs of Christianity leaving the cities of Jerusalem and Bethlehem. In the apse is the figure of Sant'Apollinare himself, a bishop of Ravenna, and above him is a magnificent Transfiguration decorated with flowers, trees, and little birds. *Open daily winter, 9–12, 2–5; summer, 8:30–12, 2–6.*

㉒ **Ravenna** is a stately old city, still living on the dreams of its faded glory. The high point in Ravenna's long history was 1,500 years ago, when the city became the capital of the Roman Empire, but by then the empire was in its period of irreversible decline. The city was taken by the barbarian Ostrogoths in the 5th century; then, in the 6th, it was conquered by the Byzantines, who ruled the city from Constantinople.

Because Ravenna spent much of its history looking to the East, its greatest art treasures show much Byzantine influence: Above all, Ravenna is a city of mosaics, the finest in Western art. A single 7,000-lire ticket will admit you to six of Ravenna's most important monuments: the Tomb of Galla Placida, the church of San Vitale, the Neonian baptistery, and the church of Sant'Appollinare Nuovo, all described below, as well as the church of Spirito Santo and the Museo Arcivescovile e Cappella Sant'Andrea.

The **Tomb of Galla Placidia** and the church of **San Vitale** have the best-known, and most elaborate, mosaics in the city. The little tomb and the great church stand side by side, but the tomb predates the church by at least a hundred years. Galla Placidia was the sister of the last emperor of Rome, Honorius, the man who moved the imperial capital to Ravenna in AD 402. She is said to have been beautiful and strong willed, taking an active part in the governing of the crumbling empire. She was also one of the most active Christians of her day, endowing churches and supporting priests and their congregations throughout the realm. This tomb, built for her in the mid-5th century, is her monument.

Outside, the tomb is a rather uninspired building of red brick; within, however, the color and clarity of the mosaics that decorate the ceiling are startling. The deep blue and gold catch the light and seem to glitter. The central dome has symbols of Christ and the evangelists, and over the door is a depiction of the Good Shepherd. The Apostles, in groups of two (there are only eight of them, for some reason), ring the inner part of the dome. Notice the small doves at their feet, drinking from the water of faith. In the tiny transepts are some delightful pairs of deer (which represent souls), drinking from the fountain of resurrection. There are three sarcophagi in the tomb, and, it is thought, none of them contains the remains of Galla Placidia. She died in Rome in AD 450, and there is no record of her body having been transported back to the place where she wished to lie.

The mosaics of the Galla Placidia tomb are simple works that have not yet received the full impact of Byzantine influence. Quite the opposite is the case of the mosaics in the church of San Vitale, next door. The church was built in AD 547, after the Byzantines conquered the city, and it is decorated in an exclusively Byzantine style. In the area behind the altar are the most famous works in the church. These show accurate portraits of the emperor of the East, Justinian, attended by his court, and the bishop of Ravenna, Maximian. Facing him, across the chancel, is the emperor's wife, Theodora, with her entourage, holding a chalice containing the communion wine. From the elaborate headdresses and heavy cloaks of the emperor and empress, you can get a marvelous sense of the grandeur of the imperial court.

On the ceiling above the royal couple, ruling over all, is a mosaic of Christ the King. With him is the saint for whom the church is named, Vitale, and the founder of the church, Bishop Ecclesio, who holds a model of the building. *Tomb of Galla Placidia and Church of San Vitale. Via San Vitale off Via Salara, near Piazza del Popolo. Admission: 3,000 lire (ticket valid for both). Open summer, daily 9–7; winter, daily 9–4:30.*

Next to the church is the **Museo Nazionale** of Ravenna, housed in a former monastery. The collection contains artifacts of ancient Rome, Byzantine fabrics and carvings, and other pieces of early Christian art. *Admission: 6,000 lire. Open Tues.–Sun. 9–7.*

To reach another great mosaic site, the **Neonian baptistery,** return to Piazza del Popolo and walk along Via Battistero, toward Piazza John F. Kennedy. The baptistery, next door to the 18th-century cathedral, is a few blocks along on the left. In keeping with the purpose of the building, the great mosaic in the dome shows the baptism of Christ, and beneath that scene are the apostles. The lowest band of mosaics contains Christian symbols, the Throne of God and the Cross. *Admission: 3,000 lire (includes Museo Arcivescovile e Cappella Sant'Andrea). Open daily summer, 9–7; winter 9:30–4:30.*

A few blocks away, on Via Ricci, and next door to the large church of St. Francis, is a small neoclassical building containing the **tomb of Dante.** Exiled from his native Florence, the great poet, author of the *Divine Comedy,* died here in 1321. The Florentines have been trying to reclaim their famous son for hundreds of years, but the Ravennans refuse to give him up, arguing that Florence did not welcome Dante in life, so it doesn't deserve him in death. The site contains a small museum. *Admission: 3,000 lire; free on Sun. and holidays. Open summer, Tues.–Sun. 9–7; winter, Tues.–Sun. 9–12, 2–7.*

From the tomb of Dante, walk up Via Guaccimanni toward the busy Via Roma. At the intersection of the two streets, slightly to the left, is the last great mosaic site in the city proper, the church of **Sant'Apollinare Nuovo.** Since the left side of the church was reserved for women, it is only fitting that the mosaic decoration on that side is a scene of 22 virgins offering crowns to the Virgin Mary. On the right wall are 26 men carrying the crowns of martyrdom. They are approaching Christ, who is surrounded by angels. The mosaics in Sant'Apollinare Nuovo date from the early 6th century and are slightly older than the works in San Vitale. *Admission: 3,000 lire (includes the church of Spirito Santo). Open summer, daily 9–7; winter, daily 9:30–4:30.*

Seventy-four kilometers (46 miles) along S16 from Ravenna lies ❷❸ **Ferrara.** It is a city of turrets and towers, of a mighty castle protected by its deep moat, and historic palaces of great grandeur. Although the site has been inhabited since before Christ and was once the possession of Ravenna, the history of Ferrara begins in the 13th century, with the coming of the Este family. From 1259 until 1598 the city was ruled by the dukes of the Este family, and in those three and a half centuries the city was stamped indelibly with their mark.

It was during the Renaissance that the court of the Este came into full flower. In keeping with their time, the dukes could be politically ruthless—brother killed brother, son fought father—but they were avid scholars and enthusiastic patrons of the arts. Duke Niccolò III murdered his wife and her lover but was a man of cultivation. The greatest of all the dukes, Ercole I, tried to poison his nephew, who laid claim to the duchy (and when that didn't work, he beheaded him), but it is to this pitiless man that Ferrara owes its great beauty. One of the most celebrated names in Italian history, Lucrezia Borgia, married into the Este family—and it seems that her infamous reputation is not at all deserved. She was beloved by the Ferrarese people and was mourned greatly when she died. She is buried in the church of Corpus Domini in the city.

Naturally enough, the building that was the seat of Este power dominates the town: It is the massive **Castello Estense,** placed square in the center of the city in Piazza della Repubblica. It is a suitable symbol for the Este family: cold and menacing on the outside, lavishly decorated within. The public rooms are grand, but deep in the bowels of the fortress are chilling dungeons where enemies of the state were held in wretched conditions—a function these quarters served as recently as 1943, when antifascist prisoners were detained there.

The castle was begun in 1385, but work was going on as late as the 16th century. The Sala dei Giochi (the Games Room) is extravagantly decorated with walls painted to show pagan athletic scenes, and the Sala dell'Aurora to show the times of the day. Oddly enough, the one chapel that is on view is not Catholic, but Protestant (one of the few to survive the Counter-Reformation), placed here for the use of the Protestant Princess Renée of France, who married into the Este family in the 16th century. From the terraces of the castle, and from the hanging garden, reserved for the private use of the duchesses, are fine views of the town and surrounding countryside. *Admission: 6,000 lire. Open Tues.–Sat. 9–1, 2:30–6:30, Sun. 10–6.*

A few steps from the castle, along the Corso dei Martiri della Libertà, is the magnificent Gothic **Duomo,** with its facade of three tiers of arches and beautiful carvings over the central door. It was begun in 1135 and took more than a hundred years to complete. The interior does not live up to the expectations fostered by the facade. It was completely remodeled in the 17th century, and none of the original decoration remains in place. *Open daily 8–12, 3–7.*

The treasures of the old interior are preserved in the **cathedral museum** above the church (entrance inside). Here are some of the lifelike carvings taken from one of the doors of the Duomo, dating from the 13th century and showing the months of the year. Also in the museum are a statue of the Madonna by the Sienese master Jacopo della Quercia and two masterpieces by the Ferrarese painter Cosimo Tura, an *Annunciation* and *St. George Slaying the Dragon. Admission free, but donation accepted. Open summer, Mon.–Sat. 10–12, 3:30–6; winter, Mon.–Sat. 10–12, 3–5.*

The area behind the Duomo, the southern part of the city stretching between the Corso della Giovecca and the ramparts of the city above the river, is the oldest and most characteristic part of Ferrara. In this part of the old town various members of the Este family built themselves pleasure palaces, the most famous of which is the **Palazzo Schifanoia** (*schifanoia* means carefree—literally, "fleeing boredom"). Begun in the 14th century, the palace was remodeled in 1466 and is the first Renaissance palazzo in the city. The interior is lavishly decorated, particularly the Salone dei Mesi, with an extravagant series of frescoes showing the months of the year. The recently opened Sala degli Stucchi boasts a beautifully carved wooden ceiling from 1467, by Domenico di Paris, and an array of stuccos. The palazzo now houses the **Museo Civico** (City Museum), with its collection of coins, statuary, and paintings. *Via Scandiana 23. Admission: 5,000 lire, free 2nd Sun. and Mon. of each month. Open daily 9–7.*

Near the Palazzo Schifanoia, on Via XX Settembre, is the **Palazzo di Ludovico il Moro,** a magnificent 15th-century palace built for Ludovico Sforza, husband of Beatrice d'Este. The great, but unfinished, courtyard is the most interesting part of this luxurious palace, which also houses the region's **Museo Archeologico,** a repository of the relics of early man, the Etruscans, and Romans, found in the country surrounding the city. Unfortunately, the museum is closed indefinitely.

In the same neighborhood, on Via Scienze, is the peaceful palace called the **Palazzo del Paradiso.** In the courtyard is the tomb of the great writer Ariosto, author of the most popular work of literature of the Renaissance, the poem "Orlando Furioso." The building now houses the city library. *Admission free. Open weekdays 9–7:30, Sat. 9–1.*

The Estes were great patrons of Ariosto, and he passed a good deal of his life in Ferrara. **Ariosto's house** lies in the northern part of the city, at Via Ariosto 67. The interior has been converted into an office building and is not open to the public.

Not far from the Palazzo del Paradiso, on Via Savonarola, is a charming 15th-century house, the **Casa Romei.** Downstairs there are rooms with 15th-century frescoes and several sculptures collected from churches that have been destroyed. *Via Savonarola 30. Admission: 4,000 lire. Open Tues.–Sun. 8:30–2.*

On the busy Corso della Giovecca is the **Palazzina di Marfisa d'Este,** an elegant 16th-century home that belonged to Marfisa d'Este, a great patron of the arts. The house has painted ceilings, fine 16th-century furniture, and a garden containing a grotto and an outdoor theater. *Corso della Giovecca 170. Admission: 3,000 lire, free 2nd Sun. and Mon. of each month. Open daily summer, 9–12:30, 3–6; winter, daily 9–12:30, 2–5.*

Time Out For a good cup of cappuccino, a piece of pastry, or rich ice cream, try **Gelateria Nazionale** (28 Corso Martiri della Libertà 30, opposite the cathedral. Closed Thurs. and 2 weeks in Aug.).

From the castle, cross the Corso della Giovecca and walk up the wide Corso Ercole d'Este. At the corner of Corso Porta Mare is the **Palazzo dei Diamanti** (the Palace of Diamonds), so called for the 12,600 blocks of diamond-shaped stone that stud the facade. The palace was built in the 15th and 16th centuries and today contains an extensive art gallery devoted primarily to the painters of Ferrara. *Corso Ercole d'Este 21. Admission: 6,000 lire. Open Tues.–Sat. 9–2, Sun. 9–1.*

Sports

Golf **Chiesa Nuova di Monte San Pietro** (10 miles west of Bologna, tel. 051/969100).

Swimming There is a public swimming pool at Via Costa 174, Bologna (Tel. 051/617–9022. Open May–Sept., daily 9:30–7; Oct.–Apr., weekdays 1:30–3, Sun. 9–1).

Tennis **Virtus Tennis Club** (Via Galimberti 1, Bologna, tel. 051/412–408).

Dining and Lodging

Dining Bologna's reputation as the culinary capital of Italy is well deserved, but there is much fine dining to be had in the other cities of Emilia-Romagna as well. The inland part of the region takes its cue from Bologna, but each city has a traditional dish of its own. In Piacenza rice dishes predominate, particularly *risotto in padella* (rice simmered with fresh herbs and tomatoes). Parma is most famous for its ham; Modena, for meat products and the delicious balsamic vinegar;

Rimini, reflecting its position on the sea, is home to an elaborate fish stew called *brodetto;* Ferrara is famous for simple foods: pears, peaches, asparagus, and zucchini. Crumbly, fresh Parmesan cheese is produced throughout the region and can be picked up at bargain prices from the farms along the Via Emilia and other outlets.

The two most important pastas of the region are pasta al ragù, usually narrow egg noodles served with what is known the world over as Bolognese sauce, and the stuffed pasta called tortellini, which can be served with the ragù, in a cream sauce, or even in soups. Ravioli stuffed with ricotta cheese and spinach is a specialty of the area, as are the larger versions of the same thing: *agnolotti,* which can be stuffed with cheese but more frequently are filled with minced pork or beef, and *tortelli,* stuffed with squash.

The best-known wine of the region is Lambrusco, a sparkling red that has some admirers and many detractors. Some praise it for its tartness; others condemn it for the same quality. A lesser-known wine is Vino del Bosco, also a sparkling red, which comes from the region around Ferrara.

Highly recommended restaurants are indicated by a star ★.

Category	Cost*
$$$$	over 90,000 lire
$$$	60,000–90,000 lire
$$	30,000–60,000 lire
$	under 30,000 lire

per person, including first course, main course, dessert or fruit, and house wine

Lodging In Italy, the region of Emilia-Romagna has a reputation for an efficiency that outstrips most of the rest of the country. Consequently, even the smallest hotels are well run, with high levels of service and quality. Bologna is very much a businessperson's city, and most of the hotels cater to travelers of this type. There are, of course, smaller, more intimate hotels that cater to the tourist.

The business of Rimini is tourism. There are hundreds of hotels, grand ones with all sorts of luxury facilities and modest boarding houses with only a few rooms. Many offer full- or half-board plans—an economical alternative to eating in Rimini's many, but not particularly distinguished, restaurants. You should not go to Rimini during tourist season without confirmed hotel reservations: In July and August the city is filled to overflowing.

Highly recommended lodgings are indicated by a star ★.

Category	Cost*
$$$$	over 300,000 lire
$$$	160,000–300,000 lire
$$	100,000–160,000 lire
$	under 100,000 lire

All prices are for a standard double room for two, including service and tax.

Bologna
Dining

San Domenico. Located about 33 kilometers (20 miles) outside Bologna, in the town of Imola, San Domenico is the holder of a Michelin star and is always counted among the top 10 Italian restaurants—its partisans say it should be number one. It is an elegant place, well worth the trip from Bologna, and reservations must be made days in advance. Specialties of the house are the homemade pâté with truffles and a delicious breast of duck in a sauce of black olives. *Imola, Via Sacchi 1, tel. 054/229000. Reservations required. Jacket required. AE, DC, MC, V. Closed Mon. $$$$*

Al Pappagallo. Located almost directly beneath Bologna's famous Asinelli and Garisenda towers, the Pappagallo was once synonymous with gourmet eating in the city. Though competition has shifted the spotlight from it in recent years, it retains enough of its reputation and quality cuisine to merit at least one slap-up feast, served in a stylish, semiformal atmosphere. The first course specialty is *lasagna del Pappagallo*, made with veal, sirloin of pork, and wood mushrooms. For a main course, sample the *filetto di tacchino* (turkey stuffed with truffles, ham, and Parmesan). *Piazza della Mercanzia 3/c, tel. 051/232807. Reservations required. Jacket required. AE, DC, MC, V. Closed Sun. and Mon. lunch. $$$*

Rosteria Luciano. A changing list of daily specials augments what is already one of Bologna's most varied menus. Some of the best offerings are shrimp with pineapple, wild boar sausage, and excellent pork and veal roasts. Among the desserts is *ricottina al forno*—delicious, charcoal-flavored ricotta baked in the oven. *Via Nazario Sauro 19, tel. 051/231249. Reservations advised. Dress: casual. DC, MC, V. Closed Tues. dinner and Wed., Aug., Dec. 23–Jan. 2. $$$*

Bertino. Popularity has not spoiled this traditional neighborhood trattoria. Meals are simple but prepared with care: Try the *paglia e fieno* (yellow and green pasta) with sausage, or choose from the steaming tray of *bollito misto* (mixed boiled meats). *Via delle Lame 55, tel. 051/522230. Reservations not required. Dress: casual. AE, DC, MC, V. Closed Sun., Mon. dinner, Dec. 25, Jan. 1, and Aug. $$*

Da Carlo. Dining on the medieval terrace in summer is a treat in this attractive restaurant. Make sure to reserve a table outside. Specialties include delicate game, such as braised pigeon with artichokes. *Via Marchesana 6, tel. 051/233227. Reservations advised, especially in summer. Dress: casual. MC, V. Closed Tues. and Jan. 1–20, Aug. 23–Sept. 3–4. $$*

Da Cesari. Wine made by the owner's family, good pastas such as spaghetti *alla chitarra* (with asparagus and prosciutto), and entrées such as duck with lemon and wild radicchio make this one of the best restaurants in Bologna in its price category. *Via De Carbonesi 8, tel. 051/237710. Reservations advised. Dress: casual. AE, DC, MC, V. Closed Thurs. and Aug. $$*

Rosteria Antico Brunetti. This old wood-paneled restaurant, founded in 1873, is very close to Piazza Maggiore and serves mainly pizzas to a mixed clientele. The specialty here is fish and seafood, which can go on your pizza or in your pasta. Dining is on two floors, but even then the restaurant fills quickly. *Via Caduti di Cefalonia 5, tel. 051/234441. Reservations not required. Dress: casual. AE, DC, MC, V. Closed Wed. $$*

Ruggero. Unless it's Thursday or Friday, when fish is the best option, meat is the thing to order at this unassuming trattoria next to the Hotel Due Torri. On Monday the bollito misto is tender and tasty, as are the roasts and the famous Bolognese mortadella. *Via degli Usberti 6, tel. 051/236–056. Reservations advised. Dress: casual. AE, DC, MC, V. Closed Sat. lunch, Sun., and Aug. $$*

Victoria. This unpretentious but tastefully decorated trattoria/pizzeria off Via dell'Indipendenza usually has a line of people waiting for a table, so reserve ahead. Even if you can't, however, it's worth the wait. Although most people come for the wide choice of inexpensive pizzas, there is also a full menu of pasta, fish, and meat dishes. Beer, on tap or bottled, and wine are available. Try for a place in the internal room under the lovely 17th-century wooden ceiling. *Via Augusto Righi 9c, tel. 051/233548. Reservations advised. Dress: casual. AE, DC, MC, V. Closed Fri. $-$$*

Lodging
★ **Grand Hotel Baglioni.** Sixteenth-century frescoes by the Bolognese Carracci brothers are rarely seen outside a museum or church, but here they provide the stunning backdrop for the public rooms of one of Italy's most glamorous hotels. The rooms are warm and charming, and the staff is extremely attentive. The location is ideal, just a few steps from the central Piazza Maggiore. *Via Indipendenza 8, tel. 051/225445, fax 051/234840. 125 rooms with bath or shower. Facilities: restaurant, conference rooms, bar, garage. AE, DC, MC, V. $$$$*

★ **Corona d'Oro.** Once a medieval printing house, this centrally located hotel has been in business for more than a century. The public space is a delight, with a lyrical art nouveau decor, an atrium, and enough flowers for a wedding. The rooms are comfortable and air-conditioned. *Via Oberdan 12, tel. 051/236456, fax 051/262679. 35 rooms with shower. Facilities: bar, conference room. AE, DC, MC, V. Closed Aug. $$$*

Dei Commercianti. Close to San Petronio and recently renovated, Dei Commercianti provides comfort and a good location at reasonable prices. Ask for one of the rooms with a terrace—those on the upper floors have wonderful views. *Via dei Pignattari 11, tel. 051/233052, fax 051/224733. 35 rooms with shower. Facilities: bar, garage. AE, DC, MC, V. $$$*

Orologio. Under the same management as the Dei Commercianti, the Orologio is located in a quiet pedestrian zone and has been renovated. Top-floor rooms have good views of San Petronio. *Via IV Novembre 10, tel. 051/231253, fax 051/260552. 29 rooms with bath or shower. Facilities: bar, garage. AE, DC, MC, V. $$$*

Accademia. This small hotel is right in the middle of the university quarter, a comfortable base for exploring the area. The rooms are adequate, the staff friendly. *Via delle Belle Arti 6, tel. 051/263590 or 232318. 28 rooms, 24 with bath or shower. Facilities: parking. No credit cards. Closed 10 days in Aug. $-$$*

San Vitale. Modern furnishings and a garden distinguish this modest hostelry, which is a five-minute walk from the center of town. The service is courteous, and rooms are clean and bright. *Via San Vitale 94, tel. 051/225966, fax 051/531346. 15 rooms with shower. Facilities: garden. No credit cards. $*

Ferrara
Dining
★ **La Provvidenza.** One of the best-known restaurants in Ferrara, Provvidenza is a pleasant country-style inn with a lovely garden for summertime dining alfresco. The local specialties—like fish grilled over charcoal (Thursday and Friday only) and the bollito misto (Saturday and Sunday in winter)—are the best. *Corso Ercole d'Este 92, tel. 0532/205187. Reservations advised. Dress: casual. AE, DC, MC, V. Closed Mon. $$-$$$*

Le Grazie. In an atmospheric part of the old town, down a long cobbled street, this restaurant makes its own excellent pasta. Try the *tagliatelle con cuori di carciofo e noci* (pasta with artichoke hearts and nuts). Other dishes are local, as is the wine list. There is currently a 20,000-lire tourist menu offered here. *Via Vignatagliata 61, tel. 0532/761052. Reservations advised. Dress: casual. AE. Closed Tues. $-$$*

Lodging **Duchessa Isabella.** On a quiet street near Piazza Ariostea, this converted 16th-century mansion is the place for those who relish period atmosphere—the staff wears Old World dress, and a horse-drawn landau is available to guests for sightseeing. Scrupulous attention to the details of decor is evident everywhere, from the painted wooden ceiling in the elegant dining room to the sumptuously draped, and individually named, bedrooms and suites. Some may find the formality wearying and the tone somewhat bogus, but a stay here will definitely be memorable. *Via Palestro 70, tel. 0532/202121, fax 0532/202638. 28 rooms with bath. Facilities: restaurant, bar, garden, conference rooms, parking. AE, MC, V. $$$$*

★ **Ripagrande.** This hotel is in a meticulously restored 14th-century palace in the heart of old Ferrara. Although the public rooms are in authentic period style, most of the bedrooms are modern—chrome-and-glass-decorated boxes with little appeal. The suites, however, are more tasteful, and the rooms on the top floor have a terrace, beamed ceiling, and view of the city. The staff is very attentive, and there is a recommended restaurant, with outdoor eating in summer. *Via Ripagrande 21, tel. 0532/765250, fax 0532/764377. 40 rooms with bath or shower. Facilities: terrace bar, conference rooms, garage. AE, DC, MC, V. $$$*

San Paolo. Recently relocated to a quieter spot on the edge of the old city, San Paulo is the best inexpensive choice in town. The 10-minute walk from the heart of Ferrara's medieval quarter is effortless in a town so amenable to strolling, and there are some good restaurants in the vicinity. The rooms are outfitted in a modern style, and you can still hear the Duomo's bells chiming on a Sunday! *Via Baluardi 9, tel. 0532/762040. 20 rooms, 10 with shower. Facilities: bar, garden. No credit cards. $*

Modena **Borso d'Este.** One of the city's most highly regarded restaurants—
Dining particularly with the affluent youth—offers some delicious variations on old themes, like ravioli stuffed with game and Parmesan.
★ Other specialties include risotto *agli asparagi* and a mushroom tart with truffle sauce. *Piazza Roma 5, tel. 059/214114. Reservations required. Jacket and tie preferred. AE, DC, MC, V. Closed Sat. lunch, Sun., and Aug. $$$*

Fini. A dining institution in Modena, Fini is widely held to be the best restaurant the city has to offer. It is an elegant, traditional place, serving classics such as bollito misto in a piquant green sauce. Excellent local wines and homemade desserts. *Piazzale San Francesco, tel. 059/223314. Reservations required. Jacket and tie preferred. AE, DC, MC, V. Closed Mon., Tues., and July 27–Aug. 25, part of Dec. $$$*

Papillon. This cheerful, well-patronized trattoria on two floors makes no pretense of Old World character or sophistication, but you can still enjoy an excellent repast here. Fish is the top choice: Take your pick from a rich variety, such as *sogliola* (sole) or *triglie* (red mullet), according to season. Pizzas are also available. *Piazza Matteotti 40, tel. 059/222610. Reservations advised weekends. Dress: casual. AE, DC, MC, V. Closed Tues. $*

Lodging **Canal Grande.** Once a ducal palace, the Canal Grande offers large, airy, well-equipped rooms with minibar. The hotel's restaurant, La Secchia Rapita, is rated highly. *Corso Canalgrande 6, tel. 059/217160, fax 059/221674. 78 rooms with bath or shower. Facilities: restaurant, bar, garden, garage. AE, DC, MC, V. $$$*

La Torre. Not a particularly exciting accommodation, La Torre is nonetheless the best choice in this category in the center of town, just off the Via Emilia. Rooms are functional, well equipped, and comfortable; there is also a good restaurant. *Via Cervatta 5, tel. 059/*

222615, fax 059/216316. 26 rooms, 19 with shower. Facilities: restaurant, bar, garage. AE, DC, MC, V. $

Parma   **Croce di Malta.** The historic premises once housed a convent, then
Dining   an inn (there are still inexpensive rooms available here), before this
attractive restaurant with turn-of-the-century decor opened in
1984. It's in the heart of Parma, and the food is traditional local fare.
The homemade pasta is light and delicate; try tortelli with squash
filling or tagliatelle in any fashion. Second courses are well prepared
and filling versions of classic veal and cheese dishes. There is an inexpensive fixed-price menu at lunchtime. *Borgo Palmia 8, tel. 0521/
235643. Reservations advised. Dress: casual. AE, DC, MC, V.
Closed Sun. $$*

★   **La Greppia.** Here, at the best and most elegant restaurant in the
city, risotto with porcini mushrooms is excellent, as is the pâté in
Marsala wine, the *torta di melanzane* (eggplant pie), and the fried
porcini mushrooms. *Via Garibaldi 39A, tel. 0521/233686. Reserva-
tions required. Jacket required. AE, DC, MC, V. Closed Thurs.,
Fri., July and Dec. 24–Jan. 1. $$*

★   **Parma Rotta.** An old inn about 2 kilometers (1.25 miles) from downtown Parma, the Parma Rotta remains an informal neighborhood
trattoria serving hearty dishes like *pasta e fagioli* (bean and pasta
soup), roast pork, and spit-roasted lamb. *Via Langhirano 158, tel.
0521/581323. Reservations advised weekends. Dress: casual. AE,
DC, MC, V. Closed Sun. June–Aug., Mon. Sept.–May. $$*

Sant'Ambrogio. This is an informal restaurant in the center of town.
Duck and quail are the best bets, but try the *cotechino con crauti*
(boiled pork sausage with pickled cabbage), too. *Vicolo Cinque
Piaghe 1/a, tel. 0521/234482. Dress: casual. AE, DC, MC, V. Closed
Mon. $$*

Lodging   **Palace Hotel Maria Luigia.** A top-quality hotel convenient to old
Parma and the train station, the Maria Luigia has large, well-furnished rooms and is popular with business travelers. *Via Mentana
140, tel. 0521/281032, fax 0521/231126. 100 rooms with bath or shower. Facilities: restaurant, conference rooms, bar, garage. AE, DC,
MC, V. $$$*

Park Hotel Stendhal. Completely renovated, the Stendhal is again
one of the best hotels in Parma. It is on the edge of the historic cen-
ter of town and convenient for the tourist and business traveler
alike. Some rooms have views of the Palazzo della Pilotta. *Via Bodo-
ni 3, tel. 0521/208057, fax 0521/285655. 60 rooms with bath or show-
er. Facilities: restaurant, bar, conference rooms, garage. AE, DC,
MC, V. $$$*

Torino. A warm reception and pleasant surroundings are the best
reasons for staying in this relaxed hotel. It's well run, comfortable,
and located in a quiet pedestrian zone in the heart of town. *Via
Mazza 7, tel. 0521/281046, fax 0521/230725. 33 rooms with bath or
shower. Facilities: air-conditioning, bar, garage. AE, DC, MC, V.
Closed Aug. 1–25, Dec. 24–31. $$*

Piacenza   **Antica Osteria del Teatro.** Set on a lovely piazza in the center of town,
Dining   this restaurant is generally held to be the best in Piacenza. Try the
★   tortelli stuffed with ricotta, the roast duck, or the steamed sea bass.
*Via Verdi 16, tel. 0523/323777. Reservations advised. Dress: casual
but smart. AE, DC, MC, V. Closed Sun. dinner, Mon., and Aug.
1–Aug. 25, Jan. 1–Jan. 15. $$$*

Agnello. Central (on the corner of Piazza Cavalli), simple, and
cheap, Agnello is an excellent place to sit down and enjoy a lunchtime snack. Try the *tortelli alla Piacentina* (tortelli with ricotta and
spinach in a butter and cheese sauce), or, for a meat dish, *coniglio*

alla Cacciatora (rabbit). *Via Calzolai 2, tel. 0523/20874 or 320874. No credit cards. Closed Mon. $*

Ravenna **Tre Spade.** An old mill has been converted into this fine restaurant
Dining near the Duomo. The food is inventive and flawlessly served. The
★ *sella di lepre* (hare stuffed with liver pâté and polenta) and the roast
pheasant are wonderful. *Via G. Rasponi 37, tel. 0544/32382. Reservations required. Dress: casual. AE, DC, MC, V. Closed Sun. dinner in winter, Mon. and July 25–Aug. 20. $$$*

Ca' de Ven. A vaulted wine cellar in the heart of the old city, the Ca'
de Ven is a wonderful place for a hearty lunch or dinner. You sit at
long tables with the other diners and feast on platters of delicious
cold cuts; *piadine* (flat Romagna bread); and cold, heady white wine.
If you're here in chilly weather, try the wholesome pasta e fagioli.
*Via C. Ricci 24, tel. 0544/30163. No reservations. Dress: casual.
MC, V. Closed Mon. $*

Ristorante Scai. Roast meat and game are what this restaurant does
best, and a changing menu provides diners with pasta stuffed with
roe deer, as well as main courses of venison, duck, pig's feet, or rabbit. *Piazza Baracca 22 (close to the church of San Vitale, at the end
of Via Cavour), tel. 0544/212520. Reservations not necessary.
Dress: casual. AE, DC, MC, V. Closed Mon. $*

Lodging **Hotel Centrale Byron.** In the heart of Ravenna's old town, this is an
elegant, well-managed hotel, its rooms spacious and comfortably
furnished. Because its location is in a pedestrian zone, tranquillity is
assured, though you will have to leave your car in one of the nearby
garages. You can unload in front of the hotel, and the staff will guide
you to a garage. *Via IV Novembre 14, tel. 0544/33479. 54 rooms with
bath or shower. Facilities: bar. AE, DC, MC, V. $$$*

Al Guaciglio. Halfway between the train station and the town center, this small pensione offers neat rooms and a relaxed and friendly
atmosphere. There are no frills here, but it is a perfectly adequate
accommodation. *Via Brancaleone 42, tel. 0544/39403. 16 rooms, 9
with shower. Facilities: restaurant, bar. MC, V. $*

Rimini **Le Streghe.** A change of name and ownership has transformed this
Dining locale and given it a theme. The new name, The Witches, says it all:
Dimly lit to resemble, presumably, a coven place, it offers such
dishes as penne *al Lucifero* (with tuna and olives) and *pollo alla
Belzebu* (chicken with pepperoni, eggplant, hot peppers, and cognac, flambé). In addition to these piquant concoctions, there is a
more orthodox menu that features fish. However, return to the occult menu for the delicious dessert *nettare alle Streghe:* ice cream
whipped with eggs and liqueur. A good selection of wines is available, and there is also an economical fixed-price lunch. *Vicolo Santa
Chiara 105, tel. 0541/781148. Reservations advised weekends.
Dress: casual. DC, MC, V. Closed Wed. $$*

★ **Zio.** Nothing but seafood is served here, and all of it is good value for
the money. The *insalata frutti di mare* is an all-encompassing seafood antipasto; tortellini *al salmone* (stuffed pasta in a salmon
sauce), and simple grilled sole are also recommended. *Vicolo Santa
Chiara 18, tel. 0541/786160. Reservations advised on weekends and
in July and Aug. Dress: casual. DC, MC, V. Closed Wed. and July.
$$*

Rock Island. Formerly a seafood restaurant, now a busy pub and
panineria, the Rock Island is at the end of a pier right on the sea.
You can drink and snack here and take part in Rimini's raucous
nightlife. Steamy, loud, and full of young people, it's not for the
fainthearted. *Molo di Levante, tel. 0541/50178. Dress: casual. No
credit cards. Closed weekdays in winter. $*

Lodging **The Grand Hotel.** One of the leading resort hotels in Italy, the Grand
★ is a turn-of-the-century hotel set in a quiet park, within easy reach
of its own private beach. The rooms are large and airy, air-conditioned, and equipped with color TV and minibar. *Via Ramusio 1,
tel. 0541/56000, fax 0541/56866. 128 rooms with bath, 6 suites. Facilities: 2 pools, private beach, yacht and tennis clubs, sauna, restaurant, bars, nightclub, beauty salon, parking. AE, DC, MC, V. $$$$*
Club House Hotel. Ultramodern and right on the sea, the Club
House is a good hotel for summer vacations and is one of the few open
during the off-season. All rooms have balconies, minibar, and color
TV. *Viale Vespucci 52, tel. 0541/391460, fax 0541/391442. 28 rooms
with bath. Facilities: private beach, restaurant, bar, parking. AE,
DC, MC, V. $$$*
Annarita. Set back in a leafy, residential road leading off the main
Viale Vespucci, this is small but comfortable, mainly frequented by
a regular clientele: Availability may consequently be limited. Facili-
ties are rudimentary, rooms are basic, but the main benefits here
are its closeness to the beach promenade and the convenient price.
*Viale Misurata 24, tel. 0541/391044. 16 rooms with shower. Facili-
ties: restaurant, bar, parking. No credit cards. $*

The Arts

Bologna hosts a wide selection of orchestral and chamber music con-
certs, as well as an acclaimed opera season. The 18th-century Teatro
Comunale presents concerts by Italian and international orchestras
throughout the year, but opera dominates the theater's winter sea-
son. All events sell out quickly, so be sure to reserve seats early
(Largo Respighi 1, tel. 051/529999). The Teatro della Celebrazione is
the center for chamber music (Via Saragozza 236, tel. 051/614–
0886). Also check concert schedules for the Sala Bossi (Piazza Rossi-
ni 2, tel. 051/225559) and the Sala Mozart in the Accademia
Filarmonica, the principal music school of the city (Via Guerazzi 13,
tel. 051/222997).

Parma is the region's opera center, with performances held at the
Teatro Regio (tel. 0521/218910) on Via Garibaldi. Opera here is tak-
en just as seriously as in Milan, although tickets are a little easier to
come by. Playwright Dario Fo helped found the **Teatro Stabile di
Parma** (Viale Basetti 12, tel. 0521/230242), a theater whose produc-
tions still maintain a mixture of comedy and politics—though your
understanding of the themes will be limited without a knowledge of
Italian.

13 Umbria and the Marches

Perugia, Assisi, Urbino, Spoleto, and Orvieto

Umbria is the green heart of Italy. Blessed with steep, austere hills, deep valleys, and fast-flowing rivers, the region has not yet been swamped by tourism and has escaped the unplanned industrial expansion that afflicts much of central Italy. No town in Umbria boasts the extravagant wealth of art and architecture of Florence, Rome, or Venice, but this lack works in your favor. Cities can be experienced whole, rather than as a series of museums and churches, forced marches through 2,000 years of Western culture; in Umbria the visitor comes to know the towns as people live in them today.

This is not to suggest that the cultural cupboard is bare—far from it. Perugia, the capital of the region, and Assisi, Umbria's most famous city, are rich in art and architecture, as are Orvieto, Todi, and Spoleto. Virtually all the small towns in the region boast a castle, church, or museum worth a stop.

The earliest inhabitants of Umbria, the Umbri, were thought by the Romans to be the most ancient inhabitants of Italy. Little is known about them, since with the coming of Etruscan culture, the tribe fled into the mountains in the eastern portion of the region. The Etruscans, who founded some of the great cities of Umbria, were in turn supplanted by the Romans. Unlike Tuscany and other regions of central Italy, Umbria had few powerful medieval families to exert control over the cities in the Middle Ages—proximity to Rome ensured that Umbria would always be more or less under papal domination.

The relative political stability of the region did not mean that Umbria was left in peace. Located in the center of the country, it has for much of its history been a battlefield where armies from north and south clashed. Hannibal destroyed a Roman army on the shores of Lake Trasimeno, and the full and bloody course of the interminable Guelph-Ghibelline conflict of the Middle Ages was played out in Umbria. Dante considered it the most violent place in Italy. Trophies of war still decorate the facade of the Palazzo dei Priori in Perugia, and the little town of Gubbio continues a warlike rivalry begun in the Middle Ages—every year it challeges the Tuscan town of Sansepolcro to a crossbow tournament. Today, of course, the bowmen shoot at targets, but neither side has forgotten that 500 years ago its ancestors shot at each other.

In spite of—or perhaps because of—this bloodshed, Umbria has produced more than its share of Christian saints. The most famous is St. Francis, the decidedly unmartial saint whose life shaped the Church and the history of his time. His great shrine at Assisi is visited by hundreds of thousands of pilgrims each year. St. Clare, his devoted follower, was Umbria born, as were St. Benedict, St. Rita of Cascia, and, ironically, the shadowy patron saint of lovers, St. Valentine.

East of Umbria, the Marches—or Marche, in Italian—stretch between the hills of the southern Apennines down to the Adriatic sea. It is a scenic region of mountains and valleys, with great turreted castles standing on high peaks defending passes and roads—silent testament to the region's warlike past. The Marches have passed through numerous hands. First the Romans supplanted the native civilizations; then Charlemagne supplanted the Romans (and gave the region its name: It was divided into "Marks," or provinces, under the rule of the Holy Roman Emperor); then began the seemingly never-ending struggle between popes and local lords. Cesare Borgia succeeded in wresting control of the Marches from the local suzerains, annexing the region to the papacy of his father, Alexander VI.

Despite all this martial tussling, it was in the lonely mountain town of Urbino that the Renaissance came to its fullest flower; that small town became a haven of culture and learning that rivaled the greater, richer, and more powerful city of Florence, and even Rome itself.

Essential Information

Important Addresses and Numbers

Tourist Information **Ancona** (Via Thaon de Revel 4, tel. 071/33249; railway station, Piazza Fratelli Rosselli, tel. 071/41703).
Ascoli Piceno (Piazza del Popolo, tel. 0736/255250).
Assisi (Piazza del Comune 12, tel. 075/812534).
Gubbio (Piazza Oderisi 6, tel. 075/922–0693).
Loreto (Via Solari 3, tel. 071/977139).
Orvieto (Piazza del Duomo, tel. 0763/41772).
Perugia: Umbria's provincial tourist office (Via Mazzini 21, tel. 075/25341); Perugia's city tourist office (Piazza IV Novembre 3, tel. 075/572–3327).
Spoleto (Piazza della Libertà 7, tel. 0743/49890 or 220311).
Urbino (Piazza Duca Federico 35, tel. 0722/2441).

Emergencies **Police. Perugia** (Piazza dei Partigiani, tel. 113). **Assisi** (Piazza Matteotti 3, tel. 075/812239). **Spoleto** (Via Cerquiglia 36, tel. 0743/49044). **Orvieto** (Piazza Cahen, tel. 0763/42476).

Arriving and Departing

By Car On the western edge of the region is the Umbrian section of the Autostrada del Sole (A1), the principal north–south highway in Italy. It links Florence and Rome with the important Umbrian town of Orvieto and passes near Todi and Terni. The S3 intersects with A1 and leads on to Assisi and Urbino. The Adriatica superhighway (A14) runs north–south along the coast, linking the Marches to Bologna and Venice.

By Train The main rail line from Rome to Ancona passes through Narni, Terni, Spoleto, and Foligno. Travel time from Rome to Spoleto is a little less than 90 minutes on Intercity trains. The main Rome–Florence line stops at Orvieto, and, with a change of trains at the small town of Terontola, one can travel by rail from Rome or Florence to Perugia and Assisi.

By Bus Perugia and Orvieto are served by private bus services, leaving from Rome and Florence.

Getting Around

By Car Umbria has an excellent and modern road network. Central Umbria is served by a major highway, S75bis, which passes along the shore of Lake Trasimeno and ends in Perugia, the principal city of the region. Assisi, the most visited town in the region, is well served by the modern highway S75, which connects to S3 and 3bis, which cover the heart of the region. Major inland routes connect coastal A14 to large towns in the Marches, including Urbino, Jesi, Macerata, and Ascoli Piceno, but inland secondary roads in mountain areas can be tortuous and narrow.

By Train Branch lines link the central rail hub, Ancona, with the inland towns of Fabriano and Ascoli Piceno. In Umbria, a small, privately owned railway runs from Città di Castello in the north to Terni in the south.

By Bus There is good local bus service between all the major and minor towns of Umbria. Some of the routes in rural areas, especially in the Marches, are designed to serve as many destinations as possible and are, therefore, quite roundabout and slow. Schedules often change, so consult with local tourist offices before setting out.

Exploring Umbria and the Marches

The steep hills and deep valleys that make Umbria and the Marches so picturesque also make them difficult to explore. Driving routes must be chosen carefully to avoid tortuous mountain roads; major towns are not necessarily linked to each other by train, bus, or highway. A convenient base for exploring the region might be Perugia, the largest city in Umbria and the hub of Tour 1, but to see the region properly you would still need to stay overnight in other towns along the way. Tour 2 heads east across the Apennines to the Marches region; we begin exploring it in the hilltop city of Urbino, travel down to the Adriatic coast to visit Ancona, then climb back west into the hills to Loreto and Ascoli Piceno. Back in Umbria, Tour 3 concentrates on two memorable towns: Spoleto, site of the famous arts festival, south of Perugia; and Assisi, St. Francis's hometown, just east of Perugia. The final tour centers on Orvieto, built on a huge rock outcropping in western Umbria, southwest of Perugia.

Highlights for First-Time Visitors

Basilica of St. Francis, Assisi (Tour 3: Spoleto and Assisi).

Collegio del Cambio, Perugia (Tour 1: Perugia to Gubbio).

Duomo, Orvieto (Tour 4: Orvieto and Environs).

Duomo, Spoleto (Tour 3: Spoleto and Assisi).

Ducal Palace, Urbino (Tour 2: The Marches).

Fontana Maggiore and Palazzo dei Priori, Perugia (Tour 1: Perugia to Gubbio).

House of the Virgin Mary, Loreto (Tour 2: The Marches).

Palazzo dei Consoli, Gubbio (Tour 1: Perugia to Gubbio).

Piazza del Popolo, Ascoli Piceno (Tour 2: The Marches).

Tour 1: Perugia to Gubbio

Numbers in the margin correspond to points of interest on the Umbria and the Marches and Perugia maps.

❶ Perugia, the largest and richest of Umbria's cities, is an old and elegant place of great charm. Despite a rather grim crust of modern suburbs, Perugia's location on a series of hills high above the suburban plain has ensured that the medieval city remains almost completely intact. Perugia is the best-preserved hill town of its size, and few other places in Italy illustrate better the concept of the self-contained city-state that so shaped the course of Italian history.

The best approach to the city is by train—the station is located in the unlovely suburbs, but there are frequent buses running directly to Piazza d'Italia, the heart of the old town. If you are driving to Perugia, it is best to leave your car in one of the parking lots near the station and then take the bus or the escalator (which passes through fascinating subterranean excavations of the Roman foundations of the city) to the center of town.

The nerve center of the city is the broad, stately **Corso Vannucci,** a pedestrian street that runs from Piazza d'Italia to Piazza IV Novembre. As evening falls, Corso Vannucci is filled with Perugians out for their evening *passeggiata,* a pleasant predinner stroll that may include a pause for an aperitif at one of the many bars that line the street.

Time Out You can enjoy the lively comings and goings on Corso Vannucci from the vantage point of the **Bar Sandri** (Corso Vannucci 32). This fine old bar is a 19th-century relic with wood-paneled walls and an elaborately frescoed ceiling.

Corso Vannucci runs into Piazza IV Novembre, a pretty, sunny square dominated by the **Duomo** (Cathedral of San Lorenzo), the medieval **Palazzo dei Priori,** or seat of government, and the **Fontana Maggiore,** a fountain by Giovanni and Nicola Pisano that dates from the 13th century.

❷ The **Duomo** is a large and rather plain building dating from the Middle Ages but with many additions from the 15th and 16th centuries. The interior is vast and echoing, with little in the way of decoration. There are some elaborately carved choir stalls, executed by Giovanni Battista Bastone in 1520. The great relic of the church—the wedding ring of the Virgin Mary that the Perugians stole from the nearby town of Chiusi—is kept in a chapel in the left aisle. The ring is the size of a large bangle and is kept under lock (15 locks, actually) and key every day of the year except July 30, when it is exposed to view. *Duomo. Open daily 8–12, 4–7:30.*

In the adjoining **Museum of the Duomo** there is a large array of precious objects associated with the cathedral, including vestments, vessels, manuscripts, and gold work, as well as one outstanding piece of artwork, an early masterpiece by Luca Signorelli, the altarpiece showing the Madonna with St. John the Baptist, St. Onophrius, and St. Lawrence (1484). *Admission: 2,000 lire. Open Wed.–Fri. 9–12, Sat. 9–12, 3:30–5:30, Sun. 3:30–5:30.*

❸ The **Palazzo dei Priori** faces the Duomo across the piazza. It is an imposing building, begun in the 13th century, with an unusual staircase that fans out into the square. The facade is decorated with symbols of Perugia's pride and past power: The griffin is the symbol of the city; the lion denotes Perugia's allegiance to the Guelph (or papal) cause; and both figures support the heavy chains of the gates of Siena, which fell to Perugian forces in 1358.

❹ Attached to the Palazzo dei Priori, but entered from Corso Vannucci, is the **Collegio del Cambio,** a series of elaborate rooms that housed the meeting hall and chapel of the guild of bankers and money changers. The walls were frescoed from 1496 to 1500 by the most important Perugian painter of the Renaissance, Pietro Vannucci, better known as Perugino. The decorative program in the Collegio includes common religious themes, like the Nativity and the Transfiguration (on the end walls), but also figures intended to inspire the businessmen who congregated here. On the left wall are female fig-

Umbria and the Marches

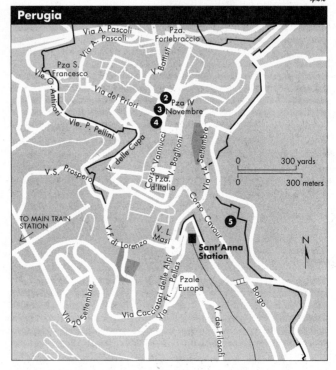

Perugia

ures representing the virtues, and beneath them the heroes and sages of antiquity. On the right wall are the Prophets and Sibyls— said to have been painted in part by Perugino's most famous pupil, Raphael, whose hand, the experts say, is most apparent in the figure of Fortitude. On one of the pilasters is a remarkably honest self-portrait of Perugino surmounted by a Latin inscription and contained in a faux frame. *Admission: 3,000 lire. Open Nov.–Feb., Tues.–Sat. 8–2, Sun. 9–12:30; Mar.–Oct., Tues.–Sat. 9–12:30, 2:30–5:30, Sun. 9–12:30.*

5 About a 10-minute walk south of the center along Corso Cavour leads to the **Archaeological Museum of Umbria,** which contains an excellent collection of Etruscan artifacts from throughout the region. Perugia was a flourishing Etruscan site long before it fell under Roman domination in 310 BC. (Other than this collection, little remains of Perugia's mysterious ancestors, although the Gate of Augustus, in Piazza Fortebraccio, the northern entrance to the city, is of Etruscan origin.) *Piazza Giordano Bruno. Admission: 4,000 lire. Open summer, Mon.–Sat. 9–1:30, 3–7, Sun. 9–1; winter, Mon.– Sat. 9–1:30, 2:30–6, Sun 9–1.*

6 Wine lovers are certain to want to visit **Torgiano,** 15 kilometers (9 miles) southeast of Perugia. It is home to the famous Lungarotti winery, best known for delicious Rubesco Lungarotti, San Giorgio, and chardonnay. The town is also home to a fascinating wine museum, which has a large collection of ancient wine vessels, presses, documents, and tools that tell the story of viticulture in Umbria and beyond. The museum traces the history of wine in all its uses—for drinking at the table, as medicine, and in mythology. *Corso Vittorio*

Emanuele 11. Admission: 3,000 lire. Open Apr.–Sept., daily 9–12, 3–8; Oct.–Mar., daily 9–1, 3–6.

7 The 40-kilometer (25-mile) trip from Perugia northeast to **Gubbio** follows S298 through rugged, mountainous terrain. There is something otherworldly about Gubbio, a small jewel of a medieval town tucked away in this mountainous corner of Umbria. Even at the height of summer, the cool serenity and silence of Gubbio's streets remain intact. The town is perched on the slopes of Mount Ingino, and the streets are dramatically steep.

Gubbio's relatively isolated position has kept it free of hordes of high-season visitors, but even during the busiest times of year the city lives up to its Italian nickname, The City of Silence. Parking in the central Piazza dei Quaranta Martiri (named for 40 hostages murdered by the Nazis in 1944) is easy and secure, and it is wise to leave your car there and explore the narrow streets on foot.

Walk up the main street of the town, Via della Repubblica (a steep climb) to Piazza della Signoria. This square is dominated by the magnificent **Palazzo dei Consoli,** a medieval building designed and built by a local architect known as Gattapone—a man still much admired by today's residents (every other hotel, restaurant, and bar has been named after him).

While the Palazzo dei Consoli is impressive, it is the piazza itself that is most striking. When approached from the thicket of medieval streets, the wide and majestic square is an eye-opener. The piazza juts out from the hillside like an enormous terrace, giving wonderful views of the town and surrounding countryside.

The Palazzo dei Consoli houses a small museum, famous chiefly for the Tavole Eugubine, bronze tablets written in an ancient Umbrian language. Also in the museum are the *ceri,* three 16-foot-high poles crowned with statues of saints Ubaldo, George, and Anthony. These heavy pillars are the focal point of the best-known event in Gubbio, the Festival of the Candles ("Ceri"), held every May 15. On that day, teams of Gubbio's young men, dressed in medieval costumes and carrying the ceri, race up the steep slopes of Mount Ingino to the Monastery of St. Ubaldo, high above the town. This festival, enacted faithfully every year since 1151, is a picturesque, if strenuous, way of thanking the patron saints of the town for their assistance in a miraculous Gubbian victory over a league of 11 other towns. *Admission: 4,000 lire. Open mid-Mar.–Sept., daily 9–12:30, 3:30–6; Oct.–mid-Mar., daily 9–1, 3–5.*

The **Duomo** and the **Palazzo Ducale** face each other across a narrow street on the highest tier of the town. The Duomo dates from the 13th century, with some Baroque additions—in particular, a lavishly decorated bishop's chapel. *Duomo. Open daily 9–12:30, 3–5.*

The Palazzo Ducale is a scaled-down copy of the Palazzo Ducale in Urbino (Gubbio was once the possession of that city's ruling family, the Montefeltro). Gubbio's palazzo contains a small museum and a fine courtyard. There are magnificent views from some of the public rooms. *Palazzo Ducale. Admission: 4,000 lire. Open daily 9–1:30.*

Time Out   Under the arches that support the Palazzo Ducale is the **Bar del Giardino Pubblico** (open May–Sept., daily 9–7), a bar set in the tiny public gardens, which seem to hang off the side of the mountain. It is a charming place for a cold drink and a rest after a tiring climb up to the Duomo and Palace.

Tour 2: The Marches

An excursion from Umbria into the region of the Marches is recommended for those who want to get off the beaten track and see a part of Italy rarely visited by foreigners. It must be admitted that traveling in the Marches is not as easy as in Umbria or Tuscany. Beyond the narrow coastal plain and away from major towns, the roads are steep and twisting. Train travel in the region is slow, and destinations are limited, although one can reach Ascoli Piceno by rail, and there's an efficient bus service from the coastal town of Pesaro to Urbino, the other principal tourist city of the region.

❽ Urbino is a majestic city, sitting atop a steep hill, with a skyline of towers and domes. It is something of a surprise to come upon it—the location is remote—and it is even stranger to reflect that this quiet country town was once a center of learning and culture almost without rival in western Europe. The town looks much as it did in the glory days of the 15th century, a cluster of warm brick and pale stone buildings, all topped with russet-colored tiled roofs. The focal point is the immense and beautiful Ducal Palace.

The tradition of learning in Urbino continues to this day. The city is the home of a small but prestigious Italian state university—one of the oldest in the world—and during term time the streets are filled with hordes of noisy students. It is very much a college town, with the usual array of bookshops, record stores, bars, and coffeehouses. During the summer, the Italian student population is replaced by foreigners who come to study Italian language and arts at several prestigious, private fine-arts academies.

Urbino's fame rests on the reputation of three of its native sons: Duke Federico da Montefeltro, the enlightened warrior-patron who built the Ducal Palace; Raphael, one of the most influential painters in history and an embodiment of the spirit of the Renaissance; and the architect Donato Bramante, who translated the philosophy of the Renaissance into buildings of grace and beauty. Why three of the greatest men of the age should have been born within a generation of one another in this remote town has never been explained. Oddly enough, there is little work by either Bramante or Raphael in the city, but the duke's influence can still be felt strongly, even now, some 500 years after his death.

The **Ducal Palace** holds the place of honor in the city, and in no other palace of its era are the principles of the Renaissance stated quite so clearly. If the Renaissance was, in ideal form, a celebration of the nobility of man and his works, of the light and purity of the soul, then there is no place in Italy, the birthplace of the Renaissance, where these tenets are better illustrated. From the moment you enter the peaceful courtyard, you know that you are in a place of grace and beauty, the harmony of the building reflecting the high ideals of the men who built it.

Today the palace houses the **National Museum of the Marches,** with a superb collection of paintings, sculpture, and other objets d'art, well arranged and properly lit. It would be hard to mention all the great works in this collection—some originally the possessions of the Montefeltro family, others brought to the museum from churches and palaces throughout the region—but there are a few that must be singled out. Of these, perhaps the most famous is Piero della Francesca's enigmatic work *The Flagellation of Christ.* Much has been written about this painting, and few experts agree on its meaning. Legend has it that the three figures in the foreground represent a murdered member of the Montefeltro family (the barefoot young man) and his two murderers. Others claim the painting is a heavily veiled criticism of certain parts of Christian Europe—the iconography is obscure and the history extremely complicated. All the experts agree, though, that the painting is one of Piero della Francesca's masterpieces. Piero himself thought so. It is one of the few works he signed (on the lowest step supporting Pilate's throne).

Other masterworks in the collection are Paolo Uccello's *Profanation of the Host*, Piero della Francesca's *Madonna of Senigallia*, and Titian's *Resurrection* and *Last Supper*. Duke Federico's study is an astonishingly elaborate, but tiny, room decorated with inlaid wood, said to be the work of Botticelli. *Piazza Duca Federico, tel. 0722/2760. Admission: 8,000 lire. Open Apr.–Sept., Mon.–Sat. 9–7, Sun. 9–1; Oct.–Mar., Mon.–Sat. 9–2, Sun. 9–1.*

The **house of the painter Raphael** really is the house in which he was born and in which he took his first steps in painting (under the direction of his artist father). There is some debate about the fresco of the Madonna that adorns the house. Some say it is by Raphael, others attribute it to the father—with Raphael's mother and the young painter himself standing in as models for the Madonna and Child. Either way, it's an interesting picture. *Via Raffaello. Admission: 5,000 lire. Open Apr.–Sept., Mon, Tues., Thurs.–Sat. 9–7, Sun. 9–1; Oct.–Mar., Mon., Tues., Thurs.–Sat. 9–2, Sun. 9–1.*

9 To reach **Ancona,** on the Adriatic coast, from Urbino, a distance of approximately 87 kilometers (54 miles), take the E78 or S3 to the superhighway A14, which runs along the coast but inland by a mile or so. The coast road, S16, is a congested two-lane highway with little to recommend it.

Ancona was probably once a lovely city. It is set on an elbow-shaped bluff (hence its name; ankon is Greek for "elbow") that juts out into the Adriatic. But Ancona was the object of serious aerial bombing during World War II—it was, and is, an important port city—and was reduced to rubble. The city has been rebuilt in the unfortunate postwar poured-concrete style, practical and inexpensive but certainly not pleasing. Unless you are taking a ferry to Venice, there is little reason to visit the city—with a few exceptions. Once in a while there are glimpses of the old architecture, as in the Duomo San Ciriaco and the Loggia dei Mercanti. In addition, Ancona can be the base for an excursion to Loreto or to Ascoli Piceno, farther down the Adriatic coast.

10 **Loreto** is an easy excursion from Ancona. To reach this small inland hill town, take A14 to the Loreto turnoff, a 24-kilometer (15-mile) drive south.

Loreto is famous for one of the best-loved shrines in the world, that of the **house of the Virgin Mary.** The legend is that angels moved the house from Nazareth, where the Virgin was living at the time of the Annunciation, to this hilltop in 1295. The reason for this sudden and divinely inspired move was that Nazareth had fallen into the hands of Muslim invaders, not suitable landlords, the angelic hosts felt. More recently, following archaeological excavations made at the behest of the Church, evidence has come to light proving that the house did once stand elsewhere and was brought to the hilltop by human means around the time the angels are said to have done the job.

The house itself consists of three rough stone walls contained within an elaborate marble tabernacle; built around this centerpiece is the giant basilica of the Holy House, which dominates the town. Millions of visitors come to the site every year (particularly at Easter and on the Feast of the Holy House, December 10), and the little town of Loreto can become uncomfortably crowded with pilgrims. Many great Italian architects, including Bramante, Sangallo, and Sansovino, contributed to the design of the basilica. Inside are a great many mediocre 19th- and 20th-century paintings but also some fine works by Renaissance masters such as Luca Signorelli and Melozzo da Forlì.

Nervous air travelers may take comfort in the fact that the Holy Virgin of Loreto is the patroness of air travelers and that Pope John Paul II has composed a prayer for a safe flight—available in the church in a half-dozen languages.

⑪ Ascoli Piceno, 105 kilometers (65 miles) from Ancona, is not a hill town. Rather, it sits in a valley, ringed by steep hills and cut by the fast-racing Tronto River. The town is almost unique in Italy, in that it seems to have its traffic problems—in the historic center, at any rate—pretty much under control; you can drive *around* the picturesque part of the city, but driving *through* it is most difficult. This feature makes Ascoli Piceno one of the most pleasant large towns in the country for exploring on foot. True, there is traffic, but you are not constantly assaulted by jams, noise, and exhaust fumes the way you are in other Italian cities.

The heart of the town is the majestic **Piazza del Popolo,** dominated by the Gothic church of San Francesco and the Palazzo del Popolo, a 13th-century town hall that contains a graceful Renaissance courtyard. The square itself functions as the living room of the entire city. At dusk each evening the piazza is packed with people standing in small groups, exchanging news and gossip as if at a cocktail party.

Time Out Ascoli Piceno is indelibly associated with the Meletti distillery situated on the outskirts of town. You can sample the aniseedlike spirit at the wood-paneled **Bar Centrale,** a small and cozy establishment that dates from the turn of the century, at Piazza del Popolo No. 9. For a light lunch or snack, pick up some delicious sandwiches and homemade pastries across the square at the **Pasticceria Angelini.**

The 175-kilometer (108-mile) drive to Spoleto takes you out of the Marches and back into Umbria. The route, S4 southwest to Rieti, then S79 north to Terni, then S3 into Spoleto, is roundabout but vastly preferable to a series of winding mountain roads that connect Ascoli Piceno with Umbria.

Tour 3: Spoleto and Assisi

⑫ Spoleto is an enchanting town perfectly situated in wooded countryside. "A little bit of heaven fallen to earth" it was once called, and it is not hard to understand the sentiment. "Quaint" may be an overused term, but it is the most appropriate word to describe this city still enclosed by stout medieval walls. The chief pleasure of Spoleto is that the city itself is the sight. There is no long tramp through museums and churches in store for you here; rather, you can enjoy the simple treat of walking through the maze of twisting streets and up and down cobbled stairways, enjoying the beauty of the town and its wonderful peace and quiet.

Quiet, that is, except when Spoleto is hosting the Festival of Two Worlds, an arts festival, held every year from mid-June to mid-July. During those two months the sleepy town is swamped with visitors who come to see world-class plays and operas, to hear concerts, and to see extensive exhibitions of paintings and sculpture. Hotels in the city and countryside are filled to overflowing, and the streets are packed with visitors. It is unwise to arrive in Spoleto during this period without confirmed hotel reservations. Furthermore, experiencing the town itself, rather than the festival, is very difficult during these months. Those who don't care for crowds are advised to stay away during the festival.

Even in the off-season, parking in the Old City is difficult. If you are traveling by car, it is best to park outside the walls. There is usually ample parking available near Piazza della Vittoria.

Spoleto is dominated by a huge castle that was built in 1359–63 by the Gubbio-born architect Gattapone. It was until recently a high-security prison, but is now undergoing restoration and is shortly due to open to the public. The castle was built to protect the town's most famous monument, the massive bridge known as the **Ponte delle Torri** (Bridge of the Towers), built by Gattapone on Roman foundations. This massive structure stands 262 feet above the gorge it spans and was built originally as an aqueduct. The bridge is open to pedestrians, and a walk over it affords marvelous views—looking down to the river below is the best way to appreciate the colossal dimensions of the bridge. The central span is actually higher than that of the dome of St. Peter's in Rome.

The bridge and castle stand at the highest point in the town. From there you can head downhill to the **Duomo**, set in a lovely square. The church facade is dourly Romanesque but with the pleasant light addition of a Renaissance loggia. The contrast between the heavy medieval work and the graceful later embellishment graphically demonstrates the difference, not only in style, but in philosophy, of the two eras. The earlier was strong but ungiving; the later, human and open-minded.

From Piazza del Duomo make your way to Piazza del Mercato, site of the old Roman forum and today the main square of the Old Town.

Time Out The square is lined with bars and delicatessens that serve good pastries and coffee. Parked in the square every day except Sunday is the van of a *porchetta* seller. These mobile snack bars are common to all central and northern Italy, and they serve only one product—roast pork. The whole pig is roasted on a spit, and slices are carved off to make delicious sandwiches on crusty rolls called *rosette*. The porchetta seller in Piazza del Mercato is particularly cheerful, and his portions are generous.

The **Arch of Drusus,** off the southern end of the square, was built by the Senate of Spoleto to honor the Roman general Drusus, son of the Emperor Tiberius.

North of Piazza del Mercato, past the picturesque Via Fontesecca, with its tempting shops selling local pottery and other handicrafts, is the church of **Sant'Eufemia** (in the courtyard of the archbishop's palace), an ancient, austere church built in the 11th century. Its most interesting feature is the gallery above the nave where female worshippers were required to sit—a holdover from the Eastern Church—one of the few such galleries in this part of Italy. *Open daily summer, 8–1, 4–8; winter, 8–1, 4–6.*

At the southern end of Corso Mazzini is a small but well-preserved **Roman theater,** used in summer for performances of Spoleto's arts festival. The theater was the site of one of the town's most macabre incidents. During the Middle Ages, Spoleto took the side of the Holy

Roman Emperor in the interminable struggle between Guelph (papal) and Ghibelline (imperial) factions over the question of who would control central and northern Italy. Four hundred of the pope's supporters were massacred in the theater, and their bodies were burned in an enormous pyre. It is not an episode of which Spoleto is proud, and, furthermore, the Guelphs were triumphant in the end. Spoleto was incorporated into the states of the Church in 1354. *Open Tues.–Sun. summer, 9–1:30, 3–6; winter, 9–1, 2:30–6. Closed holidays.*

On the outskirts of the city, just off Via Flaminia (S3), is the lovely church of **San Salvatore.** You may already have seen a lot of old churches in Italy, but few are as old as this one. It needed *renovation* in the 9th century—by that time it was already 600 years old. It is nestled under cypresses and surrounded by Spoleto's cemetery and is quiet, cool, and peaceful. The church was built by Eastern monks in the 4th century, and little has been added (or removed) since its renovation. San Salvatore has an air of timelessness and antiquity rarely found in churches so close to major towns. *Open daily 8–1, 4–6.*

Assisi is a total of 47 kilometers (30 miles) north and west of Spoleto on S3 and S75.

❸ The first sight of **Assisi** is memorable. The hill on which Assisi sits rises dramatically from the flat plain, and the town is dominated at the top of the mount by a medieval castle; on the lower slopes of the hill is the massive basilica of San Francesco, rising majestically on graceful arched supports.

Numbers in the margin correspond to points of interest on the Assisi map.

Except in the depths of the off-season, Assisi, the most famous and most visited city in Umbria, is always thronged with sightseers and pilgrims. Somehow, though, despite the press of visitors, there is an unspoiled quality to the city—although that charm can be taxed to the limit during major feasts of the church, like Christmas or Easter, or on the feast of the patron saint himself (October 4). But if you come to Assisi on a weekday or in the low season, you are sure to see this charming rose-colored town at its best.

St. Francis was born here in 1181, the son of a well-to-do merchant. He had, by his own account, a riotous youth but forsook the pleasures of the flesh quite early in life, adopting a life of austerity. His mystical approach to poverty, asceticism, and the beauty of man and nature struck a responsive chord in the medieval mind, and he quickly attracted a vast number of followers. He was a humble and unassuming man, and his compassion and humility brought him great love and veneration in his own lifetime. Without actively seeking power, as did many clerics of his day, he amassed great influence and political power, changing the history of the Catholic church. He was the first person to receive the stigmata (wounds in his hands, feet, and side corresponding to the torments of Christ on the cross), injuries that caused him great pain and suffering, which he bore with characteristic patience. Nonetheless, St. Francis welcomed the coming of "Sister Death," in 1226. Today the Franciscans are the largest of all the Catholic orders. And among the mass of clergy at Assisi, you can identify the saint's followers by their simple, coarse brown habits bound by belts of knotted rope.

❹ The **Basilica of San Francesco** is one of Italy's foremost monuments and was begun shortly after the saint's death. What St. Francis

Assisi

Basilica of
San Francesco, **14**
Hermitage of the
Carceri, **20**
Porta Nuova, **17**

San Damiano, **18**
Santa Chiara, **16**
Santa Maria degli
Angeli, **19**
Temple of Minerva, **15**

would have made of a church of such size, wealth, and grandeur—the opposite of all he preached and believed—is hard to imagine. His coffin, unearthed from its secret hiding place in 1818, is on display in the crypt below the lower church and is a place of piety. The basilica is not one church, but two huge structures built one over the other. The lower church is dim and full of candle-lit shadows, while the upper is a bright and airy place. Both are magnificently decorated artistic treasure houses, however, especially the upper church, where a fresco cycle by Giotto is a milestone in the history of Western art.

Visit the lower church first. The first chapel on the left of the nave was decorated by the Sienese master Simone Martini. Frescoed in 1322–26, the paintings show the life of St. Martin—the sharing of his cloak with the poor man, the saint's knighthood, and his death.

There is some dispute about the paintings in the third chapel on the right. Experts have argued for years as to their authorship, with many saying that they were done by Giotto. The paintings depict the life of St. Mary Magdalen. There is a similar dispute about the works above the high altar—some say they are by Giotto; others claim them for an anonymous pupil. They depict the marriage of St. Francis to poverty, chastity, and obedience.

In the right transept are frescoes by Cimabue, a Madonna and Saints, one of them St. Francis himself. In the left transept are some of the best-known works of the Sienese painter Pietro Lorenzetti. They depict the Madonna with Saints John and Francis, a Crucifixion, and a Descent from the Cross.

It is quite a contrast to climb the steps next to the altar and emerge into the bright sunlight and airy grace of the double-arched Renaissance cloister called the Cloister of the Dead. A door to the right leads to the treasury of the church and contains relics of St. Francis and other holy objects associated with the order.

The upper church is dominated by Giotto's 28 frescoes, each portraying incidents in the life of St. Francis. Although the artist was only in his twenties when he painted this cycle, the frescoes show that Giotto was the pivotal artist in the development of Western painting, breaking away from the stiff, unnatural styles of earlier generations and moving toward a realism and grace that reached its peak in the Renaissance. The paintings are viewed left to right, starting in the transept. The most beloved of all the scenes is probably that of *St. Francis Preaching to the Birds*, a touching painting that seems to sum up the gentle spirit of the saint. It stands in marked contrast to the scene of the dream of Innocent III. The pope dreams of a humble monk who will steady the church. Sure enough, in the panel next to the sleeping pope, you see a strong Francis supporting a church that seems to be on the verge of tumbling down. *Upper and lower churches. Open summer, Mon.–Sat. 6 AM–7 PM, Sun. 6 AM–7:30 PM; winter, Mon.–Sat. 6:30–12, 2–6, Sun. 6:30 AM–7 PM.*

⑮ Follow Via San Francesco from the Basilica up the hill to the central square of the town, Piazza del Comune. The **Temple of Minerva,** on the left, is made up of bits and pieces of a Roman temple that dates from the time of Augustus. It has been converted into a church. *Open daily 7–12, 4–7.*

⑯ Follow Corso Mazzini out of the square, heading toward the church of **Santa Chiara.** This 13th-century church is dedicated to St. Clare, one of the earliest and most fervent of St. Francis's followers and the founder of the order of the Poor Ladies, or Poor Clares, in imitation of the Franciscans. The church contains the body of the saint, and in the chapel of the Crucifix (on the right) is the cross that spoke to St. Francis and led him to a life of piety. A member of St. Clare's order is stationed before the cross and is heavily veiled in perpetual adoration of the image. *Open daily 8–1, 4–7.*

Walk past the church of Santa Chiara, along Via Borgo Aretino and ⑰ out through the walls of the gate called the **Porta Nuova.** From there, approximately 1 kilometer (.6 mile) farther on, you reach the ⑱ church of **San Damiano.** It was here that the crucifix spoke to St. Francis, saying "Vade, Francisce, et repara domum meam" ("Go, Francis, and repair my house"). It was also in this church, pleasantly situated in an olive grove, that St. Francis brought St. Clare into the religious life. The church became the first home of her order, and it, and its convent, simple and austere, give a far better idea of St. Francis and his movement than the great basilica. *Open daily 8–12:30, 2–6.*

Also on the outskirts of the town, on the plain near the train station, ⑲ is the church of **Santa Maria degli Angeli.** It is a Baroque building constructed over the **Porziuncola,** a little chapel restored by St. Francis. The shrine is much venerated because it was here, in the Transito chapel, then a humble cell, that St. Francis died. *Open daily 9–1, 4–7.*

⑳ Four kilometers (2½ miles) east of Assisi is the **Hermitage of the Carceri,** a monastery set in dense woodlands on the side of Mount Subasio. In the caves on the slope of the mountain, Francis and his followers established their first home, to which he returned often during his lifetime to pray and meditate. The church and monastery retain the tranquil contemplative air St. Francis so prized. *Open daily 8AM–sunset.*

Tour 4: Orvieto and Environs

Numbers in the margin correspond to points of interest on the Umbria and the Marches map.

Orvieto, on the western edge of Umbria, is 112 kilometers (70 miles) from Assisi and 86 kilometers (53 miles) from Perugia. The drive to Orvieto (on S3bis) is a pleasant one that cuts south through the center of the region and takes you through Todi, a lovely hill town. Todi has an extraordinary grouping of Gothic palaces and a medieval cathedral in its central Piazza del Popolo. At Todi, change to S448, which connects with the main north–south autostrada (A1).

㉑ **Orvieto,** 37 kilometers (23 miles) west of Todi, off A1, is one of Umbria's greatest cities. Its commanding, dramatic position on a great square rock is an amazing sight, dominating the countryside for miles in every direction. This natural fort was first settled by the Etruscans, but not even Orvieto's defenses could withstand the might of the Romans, who attacked, sacked, and destroyed the city in 283 BC. From that time, Orvieto has had close ties with Rome. It was solidly Guelph in the Middle Ages, and for several hundred years popes sought refuge in the city, at some times seeking protection from their enemies, at other times fleeing from the summer heat of Rome.

Orvieto's position on its rock has meant that little new building has ever been done here, giving the town an almost perfect medieval character. The jewel, the centerpiece of Orvieto, is its **Duomo,** set in the wide and airy Piazza del Duomo. The church, built to commemorate the Miracle of Bolsena, was started in 1290 and received the attention of some of the greatest architects and sculptors of the time. It was further embellished inside by great Renaissance artists. The facade is a prodigious work, covered with carvings and mosaics, the latter intricately ornamenting practically every pillar and post and also used in large representations of religious scenes (many of these were restored or redone in the 18th and 19th centuries). The bas-reliefs on the lower parts of the pillars were carved by Maitani, one of the original architects of the building, and show scenes from the Old Testament and some particularly gruesome renderings of the Last Judgment and Hell, as well as a more tranquil Paradise. (They have been covered with Plexiglas following some vandalizing in the 1960s.)

The vast interior of the cathedral is famous chiefly for the frescoes in the Cappella Nuova (the last chapel on the right, nearest the high altar). The earliest works here are above the altar and are by Fra Angelico. They show Christ in Glory and the Prophets. The major works in the chapel, however, are by Luca Signorelli and show a very graphic Last Judgment. The walls seem to be filled with muscular, writhing figures, and most critics draw a direct connection between these figures and the later Last Judgment of Michelangelo on the wall of the Sistine Chapel. Leonardo da Vinci, however, was less than impressed. He said that the figures, with their rippling muscles, reminded him of sacks "stuffed full of nuts."

Across the nave of the cathedral from the Cappella Nuova is the Cappella del Corporale. It houses the relics of the Miracle of Bolsena, the raison d'être for the Duomo. A priest in the nearby town of Bolsena suddenly found himself assailed by doubts about the transubstantiation—he could not bring himself to believe that the body of Christ was contained in the consecrated communion host. His doubts were put to rest, however, when a wafer he had just blessed suddenly started to drip blood. Drops of blood fell onto the linen covering the altar, and this cloth and the host itself are the principal relics of the miracle. They are contained in a sumptuous gold-and-enamel reliquary on the altar of this chapel and are displayed on the Feast of Corpus Christi and at Easter. *Duomo. Open daily 7–1, 3–sunset.*

To the right of the Duomo is the medieval **Palazzo dei Papi,** once the summer residence of popes, which contains the Archaeological Museum. *Admission free. Open May–Oct., Mon.–Sat. 9–1:30, 3–7, Sun. 9–1; Nov.–Apr., Mon.–Sat. 9–1:30, 2:30–6, Sun. 9–1.*

Time Out Orvieto is known for its wines, particularly the whites. Some of the finest wines in Umbria are produced here (Signorelli, when painting the Duomo, asked that part of his contract be paid in wine), and the rock on which the town sits is honeycombed with caves used to ferment the Trebbiano grapes that are used in making Orvieto vintages. Taking a glass of wine, therefore, at the **wine cellar** at No. 2, Piazza del Duomo, is as much a cultural experience as a refreshment stop. You'll find a good selection of sandwiches and snacks there as well.

The countryside southeast of Orvieto, heading toward the town of Narni, is rarely included in most travel itineraries—a pity, since the scenery and rustic charm of the small towns on the route make this one of the most pleasant parts of Umbria. It is also a manageable chunk of country that can be seen in a half-day's touring by car.

Drive southeast of Orvieto on S448 for 7.6 kilometers (4½ miles), then turn south onto a narrow country road that leads to the tiny medieval hamlet of **Baschi.** South of Baschi on S205, after 20 kilometers (12 miles), you'll come to **Lugnano in Teverina,** another picturesque town crowned with a beautiful Romanesque church, **Santa Maria Assunta.** *Open daily 9–1.*

What to See and Do with Children

Several of the region's historical pageants, like the **crossbow tournament** in Gubbio (usually the last Sunday in May; contact the Gubbio tourist agency, Piazza Oderisi 6, tel. 075/922–0693 for details) or the **Torneo della Quintana,** a medieval-style joust (the first Sunday in August) in Ascoli Piceno, are delightful for young and old alike.

The only attraction aimed directly at the younger set is **La Città della Domenica,** a Disney-style playground in the town of Montepulito, 8 kilometers (4.8 miles) west of Perugia on the secondary road that leads to Corciano. The 500 acres of parkland contain a variety of buildings based on familiar fairy-tale themes—Snow White's House, the Witches Wood—as well as a reptile house, a medieval museum, an exhibit of shells from all over the world, game rooms, and a choice of restaurants. *Tel. 075/754941. Admission: 16,500 lire adults, 13,900 lire children 4–10. Open Mar. 21–Sept. 19, daily 9–7; Sept. 20–Nov. 1, weekends and holidays 9–7; Nov. 2–Mar. 19 (exhibitions only), Sat. 2–7, Sun. 10–7.*

Off the Beaten Track

The area east of Umbria, known as the **Valnerina,** is the most beautiful of central Italy's many well-kept secrets. The roads that serve the rugged landscape are poor, but a drive through the region, even with all those time-consuming twists and turns, will be worth it to see forgotten medieval villages and dramatic mountain scenery. The first stop should be the **waterfalls at Marmore,** the highest falls in Europe. You'll find them a few miles east of Terni, on the road to Lake Piediluco and Rieti. The waters are diverted on weekdays to provide hydroelectric power for the town of Terni, so check with the tourist office (Viale C. Battisti 7/a, tel. 0744/43047) in Terni before heading there. On summer evenings, when the falls are in full spate, the cascading water is floodlit—and a delightful sight.

Close to the picturesque town of Ferentillo (northeast of Terni on S209) is the outstanding 8th-century abbey of **San Pietro in Valle.** There are fine frescoes in the nave of the church, and the cloister is graceful and peaceful. As a bonus, one of the abbey outbuildings houses a fine restaurant with moderate prices.

Farther east are the towns of **Norcia** and **Cascia;** Norcia is the most famous town for Umbrian food specialties. It is also the birthplace of St. Benedict. Cascia is the birthplace of the uncrowned patron saint of Italian women, St. Rita.

Shopping

Pottery and wine are the two most famous Umbrian exports, and examples of both commodities are excellent and unique to the region.

Gubbio, Perugia, and **Assisi** all produce ceramics, but those with the most flair are found in **Deruta,** south of Torgiano on S3bis. The red glazes of Gubbio pottery have been famous since medieval times. The secret of the original glaze died with its inventor some 500 years ago, but there are contemporary potters who produce a fair facsimile.

Perugia is a well-to-do town, and judging by the array of expensive shops on Corso Vannucci, the Perugians are not afraid to part with their money. The main streets of the town are lined with clothing shops selling the best-known Italian designers, either in luxurious boutiques or shops—such as Gucci, Ferragamo, Armani, and Fendi—run by the design firms themselves.

The best and most typical thing to buy in Perugia is, of course, some of the famous and delicious Perugina chocolate. *Cioccolato al latte* (milk chocolate) and *fondente* (dark chocolate) are available in tiny jewellike boxes or in giant gift boxes the size of serving trays. The most famous chocolates made by Perugina are the round chocolate-and nut-filled candies called Baci (Kisses), which come wrapped in silver paper and, like fortune cookies, contain romantic sentiments or sayings.

Orvieto is a center of woodworking, particularly fine inlays and veneers. The Corso Cavour has a number of artisan shops specializing in woodwork, the best known being the studio of the Michelangeli family, which is crammed with a variety of imaginatively designed objects ranging in size from a giant *armadio* (wardrobe) to a simple wooden spoon.

Minor arts, such as embroidery and lace making, flourish in Orvieto as well. One of the best shops for lace (*merletto*) is Duranti, at Via del Duomo 10.

Excellent Orvieto wines are justly prized throughout Italy and in foreign countries. The whites are fruity, with a tart aftertaste, and are made from the region's Trebbiano grapes. Orvieto also produces its own version of the Tuscan dessert wine *vin santo*. It is darker than its Tuscan cousin and is aged five years before bottling. The Lungarotti cellars at **Torgiano** sell the winery's award-winning reds and whites.

Sports

Hiking   Magnificent scenery makes Umbria fine hiking and mountaineering country. The area around Spoleto is particularly good, and the tourist office for the town (*see* Important Addresses and Numbers in Essential Information, *above*) will supply itineraries of walks and climbs to suit all ages and levels of ability.

Swimming   Lakes Trasimeno and Piediluco offer safe and clean bathing facilities. **Castiglione del Lago,** on Lake Trasimeno, has a public beach, with no strong undercurrents or hidden depths.

Dining and Lodging

Dining   Umbria is mountainous, and the cuisine of the region is typical of mountain people everywhere. The food is hearty and straightforward, with a stick-to-the-ribs quality that sees hard-working farmers and artisans through a long day's work and helps them make the steep climb home at night. Italians are generally thought not to eat much meat, but this is untrue of Italy in general and of Umbria in particular. Novelist Anthony Burgess once observed that a beefsteak in Italy is never *"una bistecca,"* but always *"una bella bistecca"*—a beautiful steak—and a simple steak in Umbria is almost always bella.

The region has made several important contributions to Italian cuisine. Particularly prized are black truffles from the area around Spoleto (signs warning against unlicensed truffle hunting are posted at the base of the grand Ponte delle Torri) and from the hills around the tiny town of Norcia. Norcia, in fact, exports truffles to France and hosts a truffle festival every year in November. Many regional dishes are given a grating of truffle before serving; unless the truffle is a really good one, however, its subtle taste may not come through. The local pasta specialty—thick, handmade spaghetti called *ciriole* or *strengozzi*—is good *al tartufo*, with a dressing of excellent local olive oil and truffles.

In addition, Norcia's pork products—especially sausages, *salami*, and *arista*—are so famous that pork butchers throughout Italy are called *norcini*, no matter where they hail from, and pork butcher shops are called *norcinerie*.

In the Marches, fish in various forms is the thing to look for. One of the characteristic dishes in Ancona is *brodetto*, a rich fish chowder containing as many as nine types of Adriatic saltwater fish. Ascoli Piceno, inland, is famous for two dishes: *olive ascolane* (stuffed olives rolled in batter and deep fried) and *vincisgrassi* (a local version of lasagne, far richer than you're likely to find elsewhere in Italy). Ascoli Piceno is also the home of the licorice-flavored liqueur *anisette*.

Highly recommended restaurants are indicated by a star ★.

Category	Cost*
$$$$	over 85,000 lire
$$$	60,000–85,000 lire
$$	25,000–60,000 lire
$	under 25,000 lire

per person, including first course, main course, dessert or fruit, and house wine

Lodging Virtually every historic town in Umbria has some kind of hotel, no matter how small the place may be. In most cases a small city boasts one or two hotels in a high price category and a few smaller, basic hotels in the inexpensive-to-moderate ($–$$) range. The cheaper the hotel, the fewer the services. Most basic hotels offer breakfast, but few have restaurants or bars.

A new and popular trend is the conversion of old villas and monasteries into first-class hotels. These tend to be outside the towns, in the countryside, and the splendor of the settings often outweighs the problem of getting into town. In all cases, these country hotels are comfortable, often luxurious, and offer a mixture of Old World charm and modern convenience.

Reservations at any hotel are recommended, and traveling in high season to Perugia, Assisi, Spoleto, Todi, or Orvieto without advance bookings is a chancy proposition.

Highly recommended hotels are indicated by a star ★.

Category	Cost*
$$$$	over 300,000 lire
$$$	160,000–300,000 lire
$$	100,000–160,000 lire
$	under 100,000 lire

All prices are for a standard double room for two, including tax, service, and breakfast.

Ancona
Dining

La Moretta. This family-run trattoria is located on the central Piazza del Plebiscito. In summer there is dining outside in the square, which has a fine view of the Baroque church of San Domenico. Among the specialties of La Moretta are *tagliatelle in salsa di ostriche* (pasta in an oyster sauce) and the famous brodetto fish stew. *Piazza del Plebiscito 52, tel. 071/202317. Reservations advised. Dress: casual. AE, DC, MC, V. Closed Sun., and Aug. 10–15, Dec. 26–Jan. 10. $$*

Lodging

Grand Hotel Palace. In the center of town, near the entrance to the port of Ancona, and widely held to be the best in town, this is an old-fashioned place well run by a courteous staff. *Lungomare Vanvitelli 24, tel. 071/201813, fax 071/207–4832. 41 rooms with bath. Facilities: restaurant, bar, garage. AE, DC, MC, V. $$$*

Hotel Roma e Pace. The only two reasons to stay in this hotel are the location and price. The rooms are ugly and cramped, and those facing the street are noisy (choose inward-facing ones). A historical note: In 1907 a Russian named Josef Dzhugashvili applied for a job here and was refused. He later found better-paying employment as supreme head of the Soviet Union under the name Stalin. *Via Leopardi 1, tel. 071/202007, fax 071/207–4736. 73 rooms with bath or shower. Facilities: restaurant, bar. AE, DC, MC, V. $$*

Ascoli Piceno
Dining
★

Ristorante Tornasacco. In this attractive family-run restaurant with rustic decor and vaulted brick ceilings, you can sample Ascoli's specialties, like *vincisgrassi* (pasta al forno in meat sauce) and *olive ascolane* (green olives stuffed with minced meat), as well as *maccheroncini alla contadina* (a homemade pasta in a thick meat sauce). *Piazza del Popolo 36, tel. 0736/254151. Dress: casual. Closed Fri. and June 15–30. AE, DC, MC, V. $$*

Lodging

Cantina dell'Arte. This newly renovated hotel is one of the few lodgings in the center of the Old Town. Although the service can be sloppy, the rooms are clean and well equipped with TV and telephone, representing excellent value for the money. There is a boisterous and inexpensive restaurant run by the same management across the road. *Rua della Lupa 8, tel. 0736/255744. 11 rooms with shower. No credit cards. $*

Assisi
Dining

Buca di San Francesco. This central restaurant is Assisi's busiest and most popular. The setting is lovely no matter what the season. In summer you dine outside in a cool green garden; in winter, in the cozy cellars of the restaurant. The food is first-rate, and the *filetto al rubesco* (fillet steak cooked in a hearty red wine) is the specialty of the house. *Via Brizi 1, tel. 075/812204. Reservations advised in high season (June–Sept.). Dress: casual. AE, DC, MC, V. Closed Mon. and July. $$*

La Fortezza. Parts of the walls of this modern restaurant were built by the Romans. The service is personable, and the kitchen reliable. A particular standout is *coniglio in salsa di asparagi* (rabbit in asparagus sauce). La Fortezza also has seven simple but clean guest rooms available. *Vicolo della Fortezza 19/b, tel. 075/812418. Reservations advised in high season. Dress: casual. AE, DC, MC, V. Closed Thurs. (except Aug.–Sept.), Feb.* $$

La Stalla. Just outside the town proper, this one-time stable has been turned into a simple and rustic restaurant. In summer, lunch and dinner are served outside under a delightful trellis shaded with vines and flowers. In keeping with the decor, the food is hearty country cooking. *Via Eremo delle Carceri 8, tel. 075/812317. Reservations advised in high season. Dress: casual. No credit cards. Closed Mon.* $$

Lodging **Hotel Subasio.** This hotel, close to the basilica of St. Francis, has counted Marlene Dietrich and Charlie Chaplin among its guests. It is housed in a converted monastery and has plenty of atmosphere. Some of the rooms remain a little monastic, but the views, comfortable old-fashioned sitting rooms, flowered terraces, and lovely garden more than make up for the simplicity. Ask for a room with a view of the valley. *Via Frate Elia 2, tel. 075/812206, fax 075/816691. 65 rooms with bath or shower. Facilities: garden, restaurant, bar, conference/reception rooms, baby-sitting, garage. AE, DC, MC, V.* $$$

★ **Hotel Umbra.** A 16th-century town house is home to this hotel, which is located in a tranquil part of the city, an area closed to traffic, near Piazza del Comune. The rooms are arranged as small apartments, with a tiny living room and terrace. *Via degli Archi 6, tel. 075/812240, fax 075/813653. 27 rooms with bath or shower. Facilities: restaurant (closed Tues.), bar. AE, DC, MC, V. Closed mid-Jan.–mid-Mar.* $$

San Francesco. This is a centrally located hotel in a renovated 16th-century building. Some of the rooms have a view of the basilica or the valley. *Via di San Francesco 48, tel. 075/812281, fax 075/816237. 45 rooms with bath or shower. Facilities: restaurant, bar. AE, DC, MC, V.* $$

Gubbio **Fornace di Mastro Giorgio.** This atmospheric restaurant is located in
Dining the medieval workshop of a famous master potter, one of Gubbio's most famous sons. The food is lighter than typical Umbrian fare, with the occasional southern dish, like *tiella barese* (a mixture of rice, mussels, and potatoes), added. *Via Mastro Giorgio 2, tel. 075/927-5740. Reservations advised in summer. Dress: casual. AE, DC, MC, V. Closed Sun. dinner and Mon.* $$

Grotta dell'Angelo. This rustic trattoria is in the lower part of the Old Town, near the main square and tourist information office. The menu features simple local specialties, including *capocollo* (a type of salami), strengozzi pasta, and *lasagna tartufate* (lasagne made with truffles). There are a few tables for outdoor dining. Inexpensive guest rooms are available here as well. *Via Gioia 47, tel. 075/927-3438. Reservations advised. Dress: casual. AE, DC, MC, V. Closed Tues. and Jan. 7–Feb. 7.* $$

Taverna del Lupo. It's one of the best restaurants in the city, as well as one of the largest—it seats 200 people and can get a bit hectic during the high season. Lasagne made in the Gubbian fashion, with ham and truffles, is the best pasta. You'll also find excellent desserts and an extensive wine cellar here. *Via G. Ansidei 21, tel. 075/927-4368. Reservations advised in high season. Dress: casual but neat. AE, DC, MC, V. Closed Mon. (except July–Aug.) and Jan.* $$

Lodging **Hotel Bosone.** Occupying the old central Palazzo Raffaelli, the Hotel Bosone has many rooms decorated with frescoes from the former palace. *Via XX Settembre 22, tel. 075/922-0688, fax 075/922-0552. 30 rooms with bath or shower. Facilities: restaurant, bar. AE, DC, MC, V.* $$

Hotel Gattapone. Right in the center of town is this hotel with wonderful views of the sea of rooftops. It is casual and family run, with good-size, modern, comfortable rooms, some with well-preserved timber-raftered ceilings. *Via Ansidei 6, tel. 075/927–2489, fax 075/ 927–1269. 13 rooms with bath or shower. AE, DC, MC, V. Closed Jan.* $

Orvieto **Le Grotte del Funaro.** This restaurant has an extraordinary location,
Dining deep in a series of caves within the volcanic rock beneath Orvieto.
★ Once you have negotiated the steep steps, typical Umbrian specialties, like tagliatelle *al vino rosso* (with red wine sauce) and grilled beef with truffles, await. Sample the fine Orvieto wines, either the whites or the lesser-known reds. *Via Ripa Serancia 41, tel. 0763/ 43276. Reservations advised. Dress: casual. AE, DC, MC, V. Closed Mon. and 2 weeks in July.* $$

★ **Maurizio.** In the heart of Orvieto, just opposite the cathedral, this warm and welcoming restaurant gets its share of tourists and has a local clientele as well. The decor is unusual, with wood sculptures by Orvieto craftsman Michelangeli. The menu offers hearty soups and homemade pastas such as *tronchetti* (a pasta roll with spinach and ricotta filling). *Via del Duomo 78, tel. 0763/41114. Reservations advised in summer. Dress: casual. AE, MC, V. Closed Tues. and 3 weeks in Jan.* $$

Lodging **Hotel La Badia.** This is one of the best-known country hotels in Umbria. The 700-year-old building, a former monastery, is set in rolling parkland that provides wonderful views of the valley and the town of Orvieto in the distance. Facilities include a swimming pool and several tennis courts. The rooms are well appointed. *Località La Badia 8.5 km (3½ mi) south of Orvieto, tel. 0763/90359, fax 0763/92796. 26 rooms with bath or shower. Facilities: restaurant, bar, conference rooms, tennis courts, pool, garage. AE, MC, V. Closed Jan.–Feb.* $$$

Hotel Maitani. The most deluxe hotel in the town of Orvieto itself, the Hotel Maitani is also centrally located. It is set in a 17th-century Baroque palazzo with a garden and a panoramic terrace but no restaurant. The rooms are old-fashioned but comfortable. *Via Maitani 5, tel. 0763/42011, fax 0763/42011. 40 rooms with bath or shower. Facilities: air-conditioning, bar, garage, conference rooms. AE, DC, MC, V.* $$$

Villa Bellago. This recently opened hotel outside the village of Baschi, 12 kilometers (7.5 miles) south of Orvieto, is run by a New York restaurateur and his wife. In a tranquil setting on a spit of land overlooking Lake Corbara, three farmhouses have been completely overhauled to include well-lighted and spacious guest rooms, a pool, a fully equipped gym, and a fine restaurant specializing in imaginatively prepared Umbrian and Tuscan dishes, with fresh fish always on the menu. *Baschi, S448, tel. 0744/950521, fax 0744/950524. 12 rooms with bath. Facilities: pool, gym, tennis court, bar, restaurant (closed Tues.). AE, DC, MC, V.* $$–$$$

Grand Hotel Reale. The best feature of this hotel is its location in the center of Orvieto, across a square that hosts a lively market. Facing the impressive Gothic-Romanesque Palazzo del Popolo, rooms are spacious and adequately furnished, if somewhat old-fashioned. *Piazza del Popolo 25, tel. 0763/41247, fax 0763/41247. 32 rooms with bath or shower. Facilities: restaurant, bar, garage. MC, V.* $$

Virgilio. The modest Hotel Virgilio is situated right in Piazza del Duomo, and the rooms with views of the cathedral are wonderful. The rooms are small but well furnished. *Piazza del Duomo 5, tel. 0763/41882. 13 rooms with bath or shower. Facilities: bar. No credit cards.* $$

Perugia **Il Falchetto.** Here you'll find exceptional food at reasonable prices—
Dining making this Perugia's best restaurant bargain. The service is smart
but relaxed, and the two dining rooms are medieval, with the kitch-
en and chef on view. The house specialty is *falchetti* (homemade
gnocchi with spinach and ricotta cheese). *Via Bartolo 20, tel. 075/
573–1675. Reservations advised. Dress: casual. AE, DC, MC, V.
Closed Mon. $$*

La Rosetta. This restaurant, in the hotel of the same name, is a
peaceful, elegant place. In the winter you dine inside under medi-
eval vaults; in summer, in the cool courtyard. The cuisine is simple
but reliable and flawlessly served. *Piazza d'Italia 19, tel. 075/572–
0841. Reservations advised. Dress: casual. AE, DC, MC, V. Closed
Mon. $$*

La Taverna. Signposted next to the Teatro Pavone, off Corso
Vannucci, medieval steps lead to this rustic restaurant on two levels,
where lots of wine bottles and artful clutter heighten the tavern atmosphere. The menu features regional specialties and better-known
Italian dishes. Good choices include *chitarrini* (pasta), with either
mushrooms (*funghi*) or pricier truffles (*tartufi*), and grilled meats.
*Via delle Streghe 8, tel. 075/572–4128. Dinner reservations advised.
Dress: casual. AE, DC, MC, V. Closed Mon. and 3 weeks in Jan.,
last week in July. $$*

Lodging **The Brufani Hotel.** The two hotels (this one and the Palace Hotel
Bellavista, below) in this 19th-century palazzo were once one. The
Brufani's public rooms and first-floor guest rooms have high ceilings
and are done in the grand style of the Belle Epoque. The second-
floor rooms are more modern, and many on both floors have a mar-
velous view of the Umbrian countryside or the city. *Piazza d'Italia
12, tel. 075/62541, fax 075/572–0210. 24 rooms with bath. Facilities:
restaurant, bar, air-conditioning, garage, 2 meeting rooms. AE,
DC, MC, V. $$$$*

★ **Locanda della Posta.** This luxuriously decorated small hotel in the
center of Perugia's historic district is a delight to behold, from its
faux-marble moldings, paneled doors, and tile bouquets in the baths
to the suede-upholstered elevator and fabric-covered walls. Archi-
tectural details of the 18th-century palazzo are beautiful, and views
of city rooftops from windows and balconies are soothing. Breakfast
is included here. *Corso Vannucci 97, tel. 075/572–8925, fax 075/572–
2413. 40 rooms with bath or shower. Facilities: breakfast room, sit-
ting room. AE, DC, MC, V. $$$*

Palace Hotel Bellavista. The rooms in this hotel are decorated in
splendid Belle Epoque grandeur, and many have a view over the
hills. The hotel's entrance is unimpressive, but the public rooms are
palatial. Weekly rates are available. *Piazza d'Italia 12, tel. 075/572–
0741, fax 075/572–9092. 81 rooms with bath or shower. Facilities:
conference facilities, bar, breakfast room. AE, DC, MC, V. $$*

Priori. On an alley leading off the main Corso Vannucci, this unpre-
tentious but elegant hotel has spacious and cheerful rooms with
modern furnishings. There is a panoramic terrace where breakfast
(included in the price) is served in summer. The hotel is difficult to
find if you're driving, but a car is an encumbrance wherever you are
in Perugia's historic center. *Via Vermiglioli 3, tel. 075/572–3378,
fax 075/572–3213. 48 rooms with bath or shower. Facilities: bar, ga-
rage. MC, V. $$*

Rosalba. This is a bright and friendly choice on the fringes of
Perugia's historic center. Rooms are scrupulously clean, and the
ones at the back enjoy a view. Although somewhat out of the way,
the hotel is only a matter of minutes from Corso Vannucci by virtue
of the nearby escalator stop, saving a good deal of legwork. Parking

is easy, too. *Via del Circo 7, tel. 075/572–8285. 11 rooms with shower. No credit cards. $*

Spoleto
Dining

Il Pentagramma. Just off the central Piazza della Libertà, this restaurant features such local dishes as *coda di bue alla spoletina* (oxtail) and *bocconcini di agnello tartufati* (lamb in a truffle sauce). *Via Martani 4, tel. 0743/223141. Reservations advised during the festival and on weekends. Dress: casual. AE, DC, MC, V. Closed Mon. $$*

Il Tartufo. Spoleto's most famous restaurant has a smart modern dining room on the second floor and a rustic dining room downstairs—both of which incorporate the ruins of a Roman villa. The traditional cooking is spiced up in summer to appeal to the cosmopolitan crowd who are attending (or performing in) the Festival of Two Worlds. As its name indicates, the restaurant specializes in dishes prepared with truffles, though there is a second menu from which you can choose items not containing this expensive delicacy. *Piazza Garibaldi 24 tel. 0743/40236. Reservations required during the festival and advised on weekends rest of year. Dress: casual but neat. AE, DC, MC, V. Closed Wed. and mid-July–1st week in Aug. $$*

Trattoria Panciolle. In the heart of Spoleto's medieval quarter, this restaurant has one of the most romantic settings you could wish for. Dining outside in summer is a delight in a small piazza filled with lime trees. Specialties include stringozzi with mushroom sauce and *agnello scottadito* (grilled lamb chops). Seven guest rooms are also available here. *Via del Duomo 3, tel. 0743/45598. Reservations advised. Dress: casual but neat. AE, MC, V. Closed Wed. $$*

Lodging

Dei Duchi. This excellent, well-run hotel is in the center of the town, near the Roman amphitheater. It's a favorite with performers in the Festival of Two Worlds. Some rooms have fine views of the city. *Viale Matteotti 4, tel. 0743/44541, fax 0743/44543. 51 rooms with bath or shower. Facilities: restaurant, bar, conference center, parking, garden. AE, DC, MC, V. $$$*

Hotel Gattapone. The tiny four-star Hotel Gattapone is situated at the top of the Old Town, near the Ponte delle Torri, and has wonderful views of the ancient bridge and the wooded slopes of Monteluco. The rooms are well furnished and tastefully decorated. *Via del Ponte 6, tel. 0743/223447, fax 0743/223448. 8 rooms with bath. Facilities: garden, bar. AE, DC, MC, V. $$$*

Nuovo Clitunno. A renovated 18th-century building houses this pleasant hotel, a five-minute walk from the town center. Bedrooms and public rooms, some with lovely timber-beamed ceilings, have a mixture of period as well as less characterful modern furniture. *Piazza Sordini 6, tel. 0743/223340, fax 0743/222663. 40 rooms with bath or shower. Facilities: restaurant, bar. AE, DC, MC, V. $$*

Urbino
Dining

La Vecchia Fornarina. These two small rooms just down from Urbino's central Piazza della Repubblica are often filled to capacity. The trattoria specializes in meaty country fare such as *coniglio in porchetta* (rabbit), and *vitello alle noci* or *ai porcini* (veal cooked with nuts or fresh mushrooms). There is also a good range of pasta dishes. *Via Mazzini 14, tel. 0722/320007. Reservations advised. Dress: casual. DC, MC, V. $$*

Lodging

Hotel San Giovanni. This hotel is located in the Old Town and is housed in a renovated medieval building. The rooms are basic, clean, and comfortable—with a wonderful view from No. 24 and No. 25—and there is a handy restaurant/pizzeria below. *Via Barocci 13, tel. 0722/2827. 33 rooms, 21 with shower. No credit cards. Closed July and Christmas week. $*

The Arts

The Festival of Two Worlds in Spoleto (mid-June–mid-July) features leading names in all branches of the arts—particularly music, opera, and theater—and draws thousands of visitors from all over the world. Tickets for all performances should be ordered in advance from the festival's box office (Via del Duomo 7, tel. 0743/220321). Information is available year-round from the festival's Rome office (Via Beccaria 18, tel. 06/321–0288).

There are other music festivals in Umbria throughout the year. The **Jazz Festival of Umbria** (July) and the **Festival of Sacred Music** (September) are both held in Perugia. Event and ticket information for both festivals can be obtained, year-round, from the Perugia Tourist Office (Piazza IV Novembre 3, tel. 075/572–3327).

The **Chamber Music Festival of Umbria** is held every August and September in the town of Città di Castello. For information, contact the tourist office (Via R. di Cesare 2/b, tel. 075/855–4817).

14 Campania

Naples, Pompeii, and the Amalfi Drive

Campania is a region of names to conjure with—Capri, Sorrento, Pompeii, Paestum—names evoking visions of cliff-shaded coves, sun-dappled waters, and mighty ruins. And Naples, a tumultuous, animated city, the very heart of Campania, stands guard over these treasures.

Campania stretches south in flat coastal plains and low mountains from Baia Domizia, Capua, and Caserta to Naples and Pompeii on the magnificent bay; past Capri and Ischia; along the rocky coast to Sorrento, Amalfi, and Salerno; and farther still past the Cilento promontory to Sapri and the Calabria border. Inland lie the bleak fringes of the Apennines and the rolling countryside around Benevento.

On each side of Naples, the earth fumes and grumbles, reminding natives and visitors alike that all this beauty was born of cataclysm. Toward Sorrento, Vesuvius smolders sleepily over the ruins of Herculaneum and Pompeii, while north of Naples, beyond Posillipo, the craters of the Solfatara spew steaming gases. And nearby are the dark, deep waters of Lake Averno, legendary entrance to Hades.

With these reminders of death and destruction so close at hand, it's no wonder that the southerner in general, and the Neapolitan in particular, chooses to take no chances, plunging enthusiastically into the task of living each moment to its fullest.

Campania was probably settled by the ancient Phoenicians, Cretans, and Greeks. Traces of their presence here date to approximately 1000 BC, some 300 years before the legendary founding of Rome. Herculaneum is said to have been established by Hercules himself, and as excavation of this once-great city—Greek and later Roman—progresses, further light will be thrown on the history of the whole Campania region.

The origin of Naples, once called Parthenope and later Neapolis, presumably can be traced to what are now the ruins of Cumae nearby, which legend tells us was already in existence in 800 BC. Here, in a dark vaulted chamber, the Cumaean Sybil rendered her oracles. Greek civilization flourished for hundreds of years all along this coastline, but there was nothing in the way of centralized government until centuries later, when the Roman Empire, uniting all Italy for the first time, surged southward and absorbed the Greek colonies with little opposition. The Romans were quick to appreciate the sybaritic possibilities of such a lovely land, and it was in this region that the wealthy of the empire built their palatial country residences. Generally, the peace of Campania was undisturbed during these centuries of Roman rule.

Naples and Campania, with the rest of Italy, decayed with the Roman Empire and collapsed into the abyss of the Middle Ages. Naples itself regained some importance under the rule of the Angevins in the latter part of the 13th century and continued its progress in the 1440s under Aragonese rule. The nobles who served under the Spanish viceroys in the 16th and 17th centuries, when their harsh rule made all Italy quail, enjoyed their pleasures, and taverns and gaming houses thrived, even as Spain milked the area with its taxes.

After a short-lived Austrian occupation, Naples became the capital of the Kingdom of the Two Sicilies, which the Bourbon kings established in 1738. Their rule was generally benevolent, as far as Campania was concerned, and their support of the papal authority in Rome was an important factor in the development of the rest of Italy. Their rule was important artistically, too, for not only did it contribute greatly to the architectural beauty of the region, but it attracted great musicians, artists, and writers, who were only too willing to enjoy the easy life of court in such magnificent natural surroundings.

Finally, Giuseppe Garibaldi launched his famous expedition, and in 1860 Naples was united with the rest of Italy.

Times were relatively tranquil through the years that followed—with tourists of one nation or another thronging to Capri, to Sorrento, to Amalfi, and, of course, to Naples—until World War II. Allied bombings did considerable damage in Naples and the bay area. At the fall of the fascist government, the sorely tried Neapolitans rose up against Nazi occupation troops and in four days of street fighting drove them out of the city. A monument to the *scugnizzo* (the typical Neapolitan street urchin) celebrates the youngsters who participated in the battle.

The war ended. Artists, tourists, writers, and ordinary lovers of beauty began to flow again into the Campania region that one ancient writer called "most blest by the Gods, most beloved by man." As the years have gone by, some parts have gained increased attention from the smart visitors, while others have lost the cachet they had. The balance is maintained, with a steady trend toward more and more tourist development.

Essential Information

Important Addresses and Numbers

Tourist Information The main EPT (provincial tourist board) offices for Campania are in Naples (Piazza dei Martiri 58, tel. 081/405311; Stazione Centrale, tel. 081/268779; Stazione Mergellina, tel. 081/761–2102; and Capodichino Airport, tel. 081/780–5761). These offices provide information on transportation, accommodations, and cultural events throughout the region. Local tourist offices in Campania are useful for information on festivals, changing opening hours, and maps of towns and villages.

Amalfi (Corso Roma 19, tel. 089/871107).
Benevento (Via Giustiniani 34, tel. 0824/25424).
Capri (Marina Grande pier, tel. 081/837–0634; Capri town, Piazza Umberto I, tel. 081/837–0686).
Caserta (Piazza Dante, tel. 0823/321137).
Naples (Piazza del Gesù, tel. 081/552–3328; hydrofoil station, Mergellina, summer only, tel. 081/761–4585).
Porto d'Ischia (Corso Vittoria Colonna 104, tel. 081/983066; Via Iasolino, Porto Salvo, tel. 081/991146).
Ravello (Piazza Duomo, tel. 089/857096).
Salerno (Piazza Amendola 8, tel. 089/224744).
Sorrento (Circolo Forestieri, Via De Maio 35, tel. 081/878–1115).

Emergencies **Police,** tel. 112.
Ambulance, tel. 081/752–0696 in Naples.
Doctors and Dentists, tel. 081/751–3177 in Naples.

Late-Night Pharmacies **Farmacia Helvethia** (Piazza Garibaldi 11, near the Stazione Centrale, Naples, tel. 081/554–8894).

Car Rental **Caserta.** *Avis* (Stazione FS, tel. 0823/443756).

Naples. *Avis* (Stazione Centrale, tel. 081/284041); *Hertz* (Piazza Garibaldi 69, tel. 081/206228).

Sorrento. *Avis* (Corso Italia 155, tel. 081/878–2459).

Arriving and Departing by Plane

Capodichino Airport (tel. 081/780–5763), 8 kilometers (5 miles) north of Naples, serves the Campania region. It handles domestic and international flights, including several flights daily between Naples and Rome (flight time: 45 minutes). Between May and September there is direct helicopter service (tel. 081/789–6273 or 584–1481) between Capodichino Airport and Capri or Ischia.

International travelers flying Alitalia to Rome's **Leonardo da Vinci Airport** can go directly from the airport to Naples' Mergellina train station via Alitalia's twice-daily airport train. Luggage is checked through to Naples, and meals are available on the train. Airport-train arrangements must be made when you buy your plane ticket. The service also operates in the other direction, returning from Naples to the da Vinci airport.

Arriving and Departing by Car, Train, and Bus

By Car Italy's main north–south route, A2 (also known as the Autostrada del Sole), connects the capital with Naples and Campania. In good traffic the ride takes less than three hours.

By Train There are trains every hour between Rome and Naples. Intercity trains make the trip in less than two hours. Trains take either the inland route (through Cassino) or go along the coast (via Formia). Intercity and express trains to Naples stop at Stazione Centrale (Central Station) on Piazza Garibaldi (tel. 081/553–4188).

By Bus **Cital,** a Rome-based line (tel. 06/474–7507) runs direct, air-conditioned buses from Rome to Pompeii, Sorrento, and Amalfi.

Getting Around

By Car Autostrada A3, a southern continuation of A2 from Rome, runs through Campania and into Calabria, to the south. It also connects with autostrada A16 to Bari, which passes Avellino and is linked with Benevento by expressway. Take S18 south from Naples for Ercolano (Herculaneum), Pompeii, and the Sorrento peninsula; for the Sorrento peninsula and the Amalfi Coast, exit at Castellammare di Stabia. To get to Paestum, take A3 to the Battipaglia exit and take the road to Capaccio Scalo/Paestum. All roads on the Sorrento peninsula and Amalfi Coast are narrow and tortuous, although they have outstanding views.

By Train Frequent local trains connect Naples with Caserta and Salerno. Travel time between Naples and Sorrento on the Circumvesuviana line (*see below*) is one hour. Benevento is on the main line between Naples and Foggia.

A network of suburban trains connects Naples with several points of interest. The **Circumflegrea** (tel. 081/551–3328) runs from Piazza Montesanto Station in Naples to the archaeological zone of Cumae, with three departures in the morning. The **Ferrovia Cumana** (tel. 081/551–3328) runs from Piazza Montesanto Station to Pozzuoli and Baia. The line used most by visitors is the **Circumvesuviana** (tel. 081/779–2444), which runs from Corso Garibaldi Station and stops at Stazione Centrale before continuing to Ercolano (Herculaneum), Pompeii, and Sorrento.

Naples has a **Metropolitana** (subway system). Although rather old, it provides frequent service and can be the fastest way to get around the traffic-clogged city.

By Bus There is an extensive network of local buses in Naples and throughout Campania. ACTP buses connect Naples with Caserta in one hour, leaving every 20 minutes from Piazza Garibaldi (tel. 081/700–5091). There are about six buses a day (except Sundays) from Piazza Garibaldi to Benevento. The trip takes 90 minutes.

SITA buses (tel. 081/552–2176) for Salerno leave every 30 minutes on weekdays and every two hours on Sundays from the SITA terminal on Via Pisanelli, near Piazza Municipio. SITA buses also serve the Amalfi Coast, connecting Sorrento with Salerno.

By Boat Hydrofoil and passenger and car ferries connect the islands of Capri and Ischia with Naples and Pozzuoli. Boats and hydrofoils for these islands, and for Sorrento, leave from the **Molo Beverello,** Piazza Municipio, near the Castel Nuovo, or from Mergellina, about 1.5 kilometers (1 mile) to the west.

Caremar (tel. 081/551–3882), **Lauro** (tel. 081/551–3236), and **Navigazione Libera del Golfo** (tel. 081/552–7209) have frequent passenger- and car-ferry services, as well as some hydrofoil services. **Alilauro** (tel. 081/761–1004) and **SNAV** (tel. 081/761–2348) also provide hydrofoil services. In the summer, these lines have a residents-only policy for cars.

Guided Tours

Orientation A number of operators offer one-, two-, and three-day tours of Campania, starting in Rome. These tours use 60-passenger air-conditioned buses, transferring to the islands by boat. Shorter tours feature Pompeii or Capri; longer tours usually take in both. For up-to-date information and fares, contact these offices in Rome: **Appian Line** (tel. 06/488–4151) or **CIT** (tel. 06/47941).

There is a wider choice of tours starting in Naples, all using English-speaking guides. These tours are either half- or full day, and cover the archaeological sites of Pompeii and Paestum, as well as one or more of the islands. Contact **CIT** (Piazza Municipio 70, tel. 081/552–5426), **Cima Tours** (Piazza Garibaldi 114, tel. 081/554–0646), or **Tourcar** (Piazza Matteotti 1, tel. 081/552–0429).

Exploring Campania

You have a few options in exploring Campania. If art and antiquity are high on your list, and if you have some sense of adventure, make Naples your base. Few fall in love with Naples at first sight, and many complain about its obvious flaws: urban decay and delinquency. But practically everyone who takes the time and trouble to discover its artistic riches and appreciate its vivacious atmosphere considers it worth the effort. Naples is near the most famous classical ruins, and, as capital of the region, it is also the most convenient base for your tours: It is connected by direct rail, road, and sea routes to nearly all the sights mentioned in this chapter.

If instead you're looking for dramatic scenery and want to enjoy it at a relaxed pace, plan to spend time either in touristy Sorrento, on the islands of Capri and Ischia, or on the beautiful Amalfi Coast. Be warned, though: These areas become quite crowded in July and August, when throngs of vacationing Italians arrive.

We have divided our exploring section into five separate tours. The first concentrates on the city and outlying districts of Naples. Naples is also the most convenient starting point for Tour 2 (to Herculaneum, Vesuvius, and Pompeii) and Tour 3 (inland to Caserta and Benevento). The last two tours, Tour 4 to the islands of Ischia and Capri and Tour 5 down the mainland coast past Amalfi, can be approached from Naples, but visitors may want to avoid the capital altogether.

Highlights for First-Time Visitors

Capodimonte (Tour 1: Naples and Its Bay).

Herculaneum (Tour 2: Herculaneum, Vesuvius, and Pompeii).

Mount Epomeo (Tour 4: Ischia and Capri).

Museo Archeologico (Tour 1: Naples and Its Bay).

Paestum's Temples (Tour 5: The Amalfi Drive: Sorrento to Salerno).

Pompeii (Tour 2: Herculaneum, Vesuvius, and Pompeii).

Positano (Tour 5: The Amalfi Drive: Sorrento to Salerno).

Ravello (Tour 5: The Amalfi Drive: Sorrento to Salerno).

Royal Palace (Tour 3: Caserta and Benevento).

Villa Jovis (Tour 4: Ischia and Capri).

Tour 1: Naples and Its Bay

Numbers in the margin correspond to points of interest on the Campania and Naples maps.

Is it the sense of doom, living in the shadow of Vesuvius, that makes the people of Naples so volatile, so seemingly blind to everything but the pain and pleasure of the moment? Poverty and overcrowding are the more likely causes, but whatever the reason, Naples is a difficult place for the casual tourist to like. The Committee of Ninety-Nine, formed to counter Naples's negative image, has its work cut out. If you have the time and if you're willing to work at it, you'll come to love Naples as a mother loves her reprobate son; but if you're only passing through and hoping to enjoy a hassle-free vacation, spend as little time here as you can.

Why visit Naples at all? First, Naples is the most sensible base—particularly if you're traveling by public transportation—from which to explore Pompeii, Herculaneum, Vesuvius, and the Phlegrean Fields. Second, it's the home of the Museo Archeologico Nazionale (National Archaeological Museum). The most important finds from Pompeii and Herculaneum are on display here—everything from sculpture to carbonized fruit—and seeing them will add to the pleasure of your trip to Pompeii and Herculaneum. Since the museum may be closed in the afternoon, depending on the time of year, spend the morning here and the afternoon visiting either the Phlegrean Fields or Herculaneum and Vesuvius. Spend the night back in Naples—perhaps at the world-famous San Carlo Opera House—and the following morning, set out for Pompeii.

❶ To visit **Naples,** you need a good sense of humor and a firm grip on your pocketbook and camera. Better still, leave all your valuables, including passport, in the hotel safe. You'll probably be doing a lot of walking, for buses are crowded and taxis get stalled in traffic. If you

Campania

Formia

Sessa
Aurunca

Teano

Dragoni

Carinola

Mondragone

Caiazzo

Capua

Volturno

Grazzanise

Caserta

Castel Volturno

S264

S79

Maddalon

S7

Villa Literno

Aversa

Calvano

Giugliano in C.

Casoria

Acerra

Pomigliano

A16

Naples
1 — **17**

Casamicciola
Terme

Cumae
20

Pozzuoli

19

18

Solfatara

Baia

S268

Ercolano

Vesuvius
22

21

Herculaneum

Scafati

Pompeii
23 — **41**

S18

Forio

Ischia

44

Porto
d'Ischia

Golfo di Napoli

Castellammare

S145

Sorrento
46

Positano
47

Tyrrhenian Sea

Capri
45

N

KEY

🚢 Ferry

0 ——— 10 miles

0 ——— 15 km

Golfo di Nápoli

Acquario, **17**
Capodimonte, **14**
Castel Nuovo, **2**
Castel dell'Ovo, **5**

Castel Sant'Elmo, **6**
Certosa di San
Martino, **7**
Duomo, **11**
Gesù Nuovo, **9**
Museo Archeologico
Nazionale, **8**

Museo Duca di
Martina, **15**
Palazzo Reale, **4**
San Lorenzo
Maggiore, **13**

Santa Chiara, **10**
Santa Maria
Donnaregina, **12**
Teatro San Carlo, **3**
Villa Pignatelli, **16**

come to Naples by car, park it in a garage as fast as you can, agree on the cost in advance, and then forget it for the duration of your stay (window smashing and theft are constant risks). Take the Metropolitana to distant destinations and use the funiculars to get up and down the hills. (Bus or funicular fares are 1,000 lire, or 1,500 lire for unlimited journeys between 8 AM and 2 PM; subway tickets cost 1,500 lire.)

2 A good place to start exploring is the **Castel Nuovo,** on Piazza Municipio, facing the harbor. Also known as the Maschio Angioino, this massive fortress was built by the Angevins (related to the French monarchy) in the 13th century and completely rebuilt by the Aragonese rulers (descendants of an illegitimate branch of Spain's ruling line) who succeeded them. The decorative marble triumphal arch that forms the entrance was erected during the Renaissance in honor of King Alfonso I of Aragón, and its rich bas-reliefs are credited to Francesco Laurana. Set incongruously into the castle's heavy stone walls, the arch is one of the finest works of its kind. Some rooms in the castle have recently been opened to the public and contain sculptures and frescoes from the 14th and 15th centuries (admission: 5,000 lire, open Mon.–Fri. 9–2, Sat. 9–1, closed Sun.). On the harbor behind it is the **Molo Beverello,** the pier from which boats and hydrofoils leave for Sorrento and the islands.

3 On the next block is the **Teatro San Carlo,** a large 18th-century theater redecorated in the white-and-gilt stucco of the neoclassical era. The theater was first built in 1737—40 years earlier than Milan's La Scala—though destroyed by fire and rebuilt in 1816. You can visit the impressive interior as part of a guided group, and visitors are sometimes allowed in during morning rehearsals.

Time Out Across the busy square is the imposing entrance to the glass-roofed turn-of-the-century **Galleria Umberto,** a shopping arcade where you can sit at one of several cafés and watch the vivacious Neapolitans as they go about their business.

4 Next to the Teatro San Carlo is the huge **Palazzo Reale** (Royal Palace). It dates from the early 1600s and was renovated and redecorated by successive rulers, including Napoleon's sister Caroline and her ill-fated husband, Joachim Murat, who reigned briefly in Naples after the French emperor had sent the Bourbons packing and before they returned to reclaim their kingdom. Don't miss seeing the royal apartments, sumptuously furnished and full of precious paintings, tapestries, porcelains, and other objets d'art. The monumental marble staircase gives you an idea of the scale on which Neapolitan rulers lived. *Piazza del Plebiscito, tel. 081/413888. Admission: 6,000 lire. Open Apr.–Oct., daily 9–7:30; Nov.–Mar., Mon.–Sat. 9–2, Sun. 9–1.*

Piazza del Plebiscito, the vast square next to the palace, was laid out by order of Murat, whose architect was clearly inspired by the colonnades of St. Peter's in Rome. The large church of San Francesco di Paola in the middle of the colonnades was added as a thanks offering for the Bourbon restoration by Ferdinand I, whose titles reflect the somewhat garbled history of the Kingdom of the Two Sicilies—made up of Naples (which included most of the southern Italian mainland) and of Sicily itself. They were united in the Middle Ages, then separated and unofficially reunited under the Spanish domination during the 16th and 17th centuries. In 1816, with Napoleon out of the way on St. Helena, Ferdinand IV of Naples, who also happened to be Ferdinand III of Sicily, officially merged the two kingdoms and proclaimed himself Ferdinand I of the Kingdom of Two Sicilies. His reactionary and repressive rule earned him a few more colorful titles among his rebellious subjects.

Follow Via Cesario Console along the waterfront, from the square to the port of Santa Lucia. At the end of a promontory you'll see the remains of **Castel dell'Ovo,** a 12th-century fortress built over the ruins of an ancient Roman villa. It commands a view of the whole harbor—proof, if you need it, that the Romans knew a premium location when they saw one. For the same reason, some of the city's top hotels share the same site.

Now take a deep breath, go back past Piazza del Plebiscito, and take Via Toledo (also known as Via Roma), one of the busiest commercial arteries in this perennially congested city.

Time Out | Walking up Via Toledo, you'll come upon **Caflisch** (Via Toledo 253), a historic café that has been renovated to accommodate a good Italian version of a fast-food counter.

Along the way, make a detour by way of the funicular from Piazza Montesanto up the Vomero Hill to **Castel Sant'Elmo,** a forbidding fortress built by the Spanish to dominate the port and the old city (open Tues.–Sun. 9–2). The Spanish garrison was quartered in now-decaying tenements aligned in a tight-knit grid along incredibly narrow alleys; this notorious slum district is still known as the Quartieri. Follow Via Tito Angelini from the upper station of the funicular to the **Certosa di San Martino,** a Carthusian monastery restored in the 17th century in exuberant Neapolitan Baroque style. Inside, the Museo Nazionale di San Martino has an oddly eclectic collection of ships' models, antique *presepi* (Christmas crèches), and Neapolitan landscape paintings, but you're here mainly to see the splendidly decorated church and annexes, the pretty garden, and the view from the balcony off Room 25. There's another fine view from the square in front of the Certosa. *Museo Nazionale di San Martino, tel. 081/578–1769. Admission: 6,000 lire. Open Tues.– Sun. 9–2.*

As you resume your walk up Via Toledo, you'll pass a great variety of shops and plenty of coffee bars where plump pastries are temptingly arranged. Students from the nearby music conservatory hang out in **Piazza Dante,** the semicircular hub of an area rich in inexpensive trattorias and pizzerias. On the other side of Piazza Dante, Via Toledo becomes Via Pessina, which leads straight to the **Museo Archeologico Nazionale,** a major attraction for anyone interested in antiquity and for those planning to visit Pompeii or Herculaneum. The huge red building, a cavalry barracks in the 16th century, is dusty and unkempt, but it holds one of the world's great collections of Greek and Roman antiquities, including such extraordinary sculptures as the colossal *Farnese Bull,* an exquisite Aphrodite attributed to the 4th-century BC Greek sculptor Praxiteles, and an equestrian statue of Roman Emperor Nerva. Vividly colored mosaics and countless artistic and household objects from Pompeii and Herculaneum provide insight into the life and art of ancient Rome. The most recent addition to the treasures on permanent display is an entire fresco sequence—more than 300 feet wide—discovered in 1765 in perfect condition at the Temple of Isis in Pompeii and now exhibited for the first time. Invest in an up-to-date printed museum guide, because exhibits are poorly labeled. *Piazza Museo, tel. 081/ 440166. Admission: 8,000 lire. Open May–Sept., Mon.–Sat. 9–7, Sun. 9–1; Oct.–Apr., Mon.–Sat. 9–2, Sun. 9–1.*

Retrace your steps to Via Toledo to explore the heart of the old city, where the arrow-straight Spaccanapoli, a street divided into tracts bearing several names, runs through Naples (*spacca* means "cut through") from west to east, beginning with Via Scura just west of Via Toledo and ending with Via Vicaria Vecchia just east of Via del Duomo, retracing one of the main arteries of the Greek, and later Roman, settlement. The tourist information office at **Piazza del Gesù** (*see* Important Addresses and Numbers in Essential Information, *above*) can provide pamphlets with itineraries tracing the city's development in ancient, medieval, and modern times.

9 The oddly faceted stone facade of the church of **Gesù Nuovo** was designed as part of a palace, but plans were changed as construction progressed, and it became the front of an elaborately decorated Ba-
10 roque church. Opposite is the monastery church of **Santa Chiara,** a Neapolitan landmark and the subject of a famous old song. It was built in the 1300s in Provençal Gothic style, and it's best known for the quiet charm of its cloister garden, with columns and benches sheathed in 18th-century ceramic tiles painted with delicate floral motifs and vivid landscapes. The entrance is off the courtyard at the left of the church. *Piazza Gesù Nuovo. Admission free. Open daily 7–12, 4–6:30.*

The next section of Spaccanapoli, **Via Benedetto Croce,** was named in honor of the illustrious philosopher who was born here in 1866, in the building at No. 12. Continue past peeling palaces, dark workshops where artisans ply their trades, and many churches and street shrines. Where the street changes to **Via San Biagio dei Librai,** the shops stage a special fair of hand-carved crèche figures during the weeks before Christmas.

11 Turn left onto Via del Duomo to the **Duomo.** It was established in the 1200s, but the building you see was erected a century later and has since undergone radical changes, especially during the Baroque age. Inside the cathedral, 110 ancient columns salvaged from pagan buildings are set into the piers supporting the 350-year-old wooden ceiling. Off the left aisle you step down into the 4th-century church of Santa Restituta, which was incorporated into the cathedral; though it was redecorated in the late 1600s in the prevalent Baroque style, a few very old mosaics remain in the baptistery and in a chapel on the left. On the right aisle of the cathedral, in the chapel of San Gennaro (open 8–noon), are multicolored marbles and frescoes honoring St. Januarius, miracle-working patron saint of Naples, whose altar and relics are encased in silver. Twice a year—on September 19, his feast day, and on the first Sunday in May, which commemorates the transference of his relics to Naples—his dried blood, contained in two sealed vials, is believed to liquefy during rites in his honor. These dates see the arrival of large numbers of devout Neapolitans offering up prayers in his memory.

About 100 yards ahead on each side of the cathedral are two of the
12 most interesting of the city's many churches, **Santa Maria**
13 **Donnaregina,** on Largo Donnaregina, to the north, and **San Lorenzo Maggiore,** to the southwest, on Via Tribunali. Both were built in the Middle Ages and decorated with 14th-century frescoes. Santa Maria Donnaregina has the towering Gothic funeral monument of Mary of Hungary, wife of Charles II of Anjou, who is said to have commissioned the frescoes in the church at a cost of 33 ounces of gold.

With San Lorenzo Maggiore on your left, walk down busy Via Tribunali to Porta Alba and Piazza Dante, at the junction with Via
14 Toledo. Here you can catch a taxi or Bus 109 to **Capodimonte,** the

royal palace built by the Bourbons in the 18th century in a vast park that served as the royal hunting preserve and later as the site of the Capodimonte porcelain works that the family established. Allow plenty of time for your visit to the palace; it's packed with works of art. Capodimonte's greatest attraction is the excellent collection of paintings well displayed in the Galleria Nazionale on the palace's top floor. Included are works from the 13th to the 18th centuries, including many familiar masterpieces by Dutch and Spanish masters, as well as by the great Italians. At the coffee bar halfway through, be sure to climb the stairs to the roof terrace for a sweeping view of the bay. Then continue through halls hung with dramatic Mannerist works of the 17th and 18th centuries, among them some stunning works by Caravaggio (1573–1610), originally hung in the city's churches. Downstairs are 19th-century Italian paintings and the royal apartments, where numerous portraits provide a close-up of the unmistakable Bourbon features, a challenge to any court painter. You'll also find beautiful antique furniture, most of it on the splashy scale so dear to the Bourbons, and a staggering collection of porcelain and majolica from the various royal residences. *Parco di Capodimonte, tel. 081/744–1307. Admission: 8,000 lire. Open Tues.–Sat. 9–2, Sun. 9–1.*

Another museum with a view—and with more porcelain—sits at the top of the funicular of Chiaia, which you can take from Via del Parco Margherita. The **Museo Duca di Martina** is set on the slopes of the Vomero hill, in a park known as Villa Floridiana. It houses a fine collection of European and Oriental porcelain and other objets d'art in a neoclassical residence built in the early 19th century by King Ferdinand I for his wife; their portraits greet you as you enter. Enjoy the view from the terrace behind the museum. *Via Cimarosa 77, tel. 081/578–8418. Admission: 4,000 lire. Open Tues.–Sat. 9–2, Sun. 9–1.*

Near the lower station of the Chiaia funicular is another small, dignified museum in the park of **Villa Pignatelli.** The low-key exhibits are of limited interest to anyone who doesn't like 19th-century furniture, but there's a collection of antique coaches and carriages in a pavilion on the grounds that is worth a look. And a stroll in the park is a pleasant respite from the noisy city streets. *Riviera di Chiaia 200, tel. 081/669675. Admission: 4,000 lire, park free. Open Tues.–Sat. 9–2, Sun. 9–1.*

For a change of pace, especially if you have children along, go to the **Acquario** (Aquarium) in the public gardens on Via Caracciolo. Founded by a German naturalist in the late 19th century, it's the oldest in Europe. About 200 species of fish and marine plants thrive in large tanks, undoubtedly better off here than in the highly polluted Bay of Naples, their natural habitat. *Viale A. Dohrn, tel. 081/583–3111. Admission: 3,000 lire adults, 1,500 lire children. Open May–Sept., Tues.–Sat. 9–5, Sun. 9–6; Oct.–Apr., Tues.–Sat. 9–5, Sun. 9–2.*

The remaining sights on this tour are outside the city limits but easy to reach from Naples; they can be treated as outings on their own.

The **Phlegrean Fields**—the fields of fire—was the name once given to the entire region west of Naples, including the island of Ischia. The whole area floats freely on a mass of molten lava very close to the surface. The fires are still smoldering. Greek and Roman notions of the Underworld were not the blind imaginings of a primitive people; they were the creations of poets and writers who stood on this very ground and wrote down what they saw.

Whether it's worth the half day it takes to tour these sites depends on your interests. If you've never seen volcanic activity, don't miss the **Solfatara,** the sunken crater of a volcano (it's quite safe if you stick to the path). The **Amphitheater** at **Pozzuoli** is fascinating because of its well-preserved underground passages and chambers, which give a good sense of how the wild animals were hoisted up into the arena. At **Lake Avernus** you'll be standing at the very spot that the ancients considered the entrance to Hades. The ruins at **Baia,** the resort town of the ancient Romans, won't mean too much unless you have more than a passing interest in antiquity. The **Oracle at Cumae** was as famous as the one at Delphi; if you've read *The Aeneid,* you'll want to enter the very cave described in Book VI, where Aeneas sought the Sibyl's aid for his journey to the Underworld.

⑱ To reach the **Solfatara** from Naples, take S7 Quater, Via Domiziana, west toward **Pozzuoli.** You'll see a sign to the Solfatara on your right, about 2 kilometers (1.3 miles) before Pozzuoli. The only eruption of this semiextinct volcano was in 1198. According to one legend, every crater in the Phlegrean Fields is one of the mouths of a hundred-headed dragon named Typhon that Zeus hurled down the crater of Epomeo on the island of Ischia. According to another, the sulfurous springs of the Solftare are poisonous discharges from the wounds the Titans received in their war with Zeus. Both legends, of course, are efforts to dramatize man's struggle to overcome the mysterious and dangerous forces of nature. *Admission: 4,500 lire. Open daily 9–one hour before sunset.*

⑲ The amphitheater at **Pozzuoli** (Anfiteatro Flavio) is slightly more than a mile farther west on S7. It's the third-largest arena in Italy, after the Colosseum and Santa Maria Capua Vetere, and could accommodate 40,000 spectators, who were sometimes treated to mock naval battles when the arena was filled with water. *Admission: 4,000 lire. Open daily 9–one hour before sunset.*

You may want to make a short side trip to Pozzuoli's harbor and imagine St. Paul landing here in AD 61 en route to Rome. His own ship had been wrecked off Malta, and he was brought here on the *Castor and Pollux*, a grain ship from Alexandria that was carrying corn from Egypt to Italy only 18 years before the eruption at Vesuvius.

To reach **Lake Avernus** (Lago d'Averno), continue west on S7 toward Cumae and then turn left (south) on the road to Baia. About a kilometer (.6 mile) along, turn right and follow signs to Lake Avernus. The best time to visit is at sunset or when the moon is rising. There's a restaurant on the west side, where you can dine on the terrace. Forested hills rise on three sides; the menacing cone of Monte Nuovo rises on the fourth. The smell of sulfur hangs over this sad, lonely landscape at the very gates of hell. No place evokes Homer, Virgil, and the cult of the Other World better than this silent, mysterious setting.

Before going on to Cumae, swing down the peninsula to the ancient city of **Baia** (5.8 kilometers, or 3.6 miles, from Pozzuoli). Now largely under the sea, it was once the most opulent and fashionable resort area of the Roman Empire, the place where Sulla, Pompey, Julius Caesar, Tiberius, Nero, and Cicero built their holiday villas. Petronius's *Satyricon* is a satire on the corruption and intrigue, the wonderful licentiousness of Roman life at Baia. (Petronius was hired to arrange parties and entertainments for Nero, so he was in a position to know.) It was here at Baia that Emperor Claudius built a great villa for his wife Messalina (who spent her nights indulging herself at public brothels); here that Agrippina poisoned her husband and was, in turn, murdered by her son Nero; here that Cleopatra was staying when Julius Caesar was murdered on the Ides of March. You can visit the excavations of the famous **baths.** *Via Fusaro 35, tel. 081/868–7592. Admission: 4,000 lire. Open Tues.– Sun. 9–one hour before sunset.*

Follow the loop around **Lake Miseno** (a volcanic crater believed by the ancients to be the Styx, across which Charon ferried the souls of the dead) and around **Lake Fusaro.** You'll pass some fine views of Pozzuoli Bay.

㉚ Cumae is perhaps the oldest Greek colony in Italy. In the 6th and 7th centuries BC, it overshadowed the Phlegrean Fields, including Naples. The **Sibyl's Cave** (Antro della Sibilla) is here—one of the most venerated sites in antiquity. In the 5th or 6th century BC, the Greeks hollowed the cave from the rock beneath the present ruins of Cumae's acropolis. Visitors walk through a dark, massive stone tunnel that opens into a vaulted chamber where the Sibyl rendered her oracles. Standing here, the sense of mystery, of communication with the invisible, is overwhelming. "This is the most romantic classical site in Italy," wrote H. V. Morton. "I would rather come here than to Pompeii."

Virgil wrote the epic *The Aeneid*, the story of the Trojan prince Aeneas's wanderings, partly to give Rome the historical legitimacy that Homer had given the Greeks. On his journey, Aeneas had to descend to the Underworld to speak to his father, and to find his way in, he needed the guidance of the Cumaean Sibyl.

Virgil did not dream up the Sibyl's cave or the entrance to Hades—he must have stood both in her chamber and along the rim of Lake Avernus, as you yourself will stand. When he wrote, "The way to hell is easy"—*Facilis descensus Averno*—it was because he knew the way. In Book VI of *The Aeneid*, Virgil described how Aeneas, arriving at Cumae, sought Apollo's throne (remains of the **Temple of Apollo** can still be seen) and "the deep hidden abode of the dread Sibyl,/An enormous cave . . ." *Via Acropoli, tel. 081/854–3060. Admission: 4,000 lire. Open Tues.–Sun. 9–one hour before sunset.*

The Sibyl was not necessarily a charlatan; she was a medium, a prophetess, an old woman whom the ancients believed could communicate with the Other World. The three most famous Sibyls were at Erythrae, Delphi, and Cumae. Foreign governments consulted the Sibyls before mounting campaigns. Wealthy aristocrats came to consult with their dead relatives. Businessmen came to get their dreams interpreted or to seek favorable omens before entering into financial agreements or setting off on journeys. Farmers came to remove curses on their cows. Love potions were a profitable source of revenue; women from Baia lined up for potions to slip into the wine of handsome charioteers who drove up and down the street in their gold-plated four-horsepower chariots.

With the coming of the Olympian gods, the earlier gods of the soil were discredited or given new roles and names. Ancient rites, such as those surrounding the Cumaean Sibyl, were carried out in secret and known as the Mysteries. The Romans—like the Soviets—tried in vain to replace these Mysteries by deifying the state in the person of its rulers. Yet even the Caesars appealed to forces of the Other World. And until the 4th century AD, the Sibyl was consulted by the Christian bishop of Rome.

Tour 2: Herculaneum, Vesuvius, and Pompeii

Volcanic ash and mud preserved the Roman towns of Herculaneum and Pompeii almost exactly as they were on the day Mount Vesuvius erupted in AD 79, leaving them not just archaeological ruins but testimonies of daily life in the ancient world. All three can be visited from either Naples or Sorrento, thanks to the Circumvesuviana (*see* Getting Around by Train in Essential Information, *above*), the suburban railway that provides fast, frequent, and economical service between Naples and Sorrento. If Naples is your base, your first stop is Herculaneum, at modern Ercolano; from Sorrento you will explore these sights in reverse order.

㉑ Ten kilometers (6 miles) south of Naples are the ruins of **Herculaneum,** which lie more than 60 feet below the town of Ercolano. The ruins are set among the acres of greenhouses that make this area one of Europe's principal flower-growing centers. The entrance to the site is a short walk south from the Circumvesuviana station. Hercules himself is said to have founded the town, which became a famous weekend retreat for the Roman elite. It had about 5,000 inhabitants when it was destroyed; many of them were fishermen, craftsmen, and artists. A lucky few patricians (aristocrats) owned villas overlooking the sea. Herculaneum was damaged by an earthquake in AD 63, and repairs were still being made 16 years later, when the gigantic eruption of Vesuvius (which also destroyed Pompeii) sent a fiery cloud of gas and pumice hurtling onto the town, which was completely buried under a tide of volcanic mud. This semiliquid mass seeped into the crevices and niches of every building, covering household objects and enveloping textiles and wood—sealing all in a compact, airtight tomb.

Casual excavation—and haphazard looting—began in the 18th century, but systematic digs were not initiated until the 1920s. Now less than half of Herculaneum has been excavated; with present-day Ercolano and the unlovely Resina Quarter (famous among bargain hunters as the area's largest secondhand clothing market) sitting on top of the site, progress is limited. From the ramp leading down to Herculaneum's neatly laid-out streets and well-preserved edifices, you get a good overall view of the site, as well as an idea of the amount of rock that had to be removed to bring it to light.

You could easily get lost in the streets of Pompeii, but not here. Most important buildings can be seen in about two hours. If you feel closer to the past at Herculaneum than at Pompeii, it's in part because there are fewer hawkers here. Also, though Herculaneum had only one-fourth the population of Pompeii and has only been partially excavated, what has been found is generally better preserved. In some cases, you can even see the original wooden beams, staircases, and furniture.

At the entrance you should pick up a map showing the gridlike layout of the dig. Decorations are especially delicate in the **House of the Mosaic Atrium,** with a pavement in a black-and-white checkerboard pattern, and in the **House of Neptune and Amphitrite,** named for the subjects of a still-bright mosaic on the wall of the nymphaeum (a recessed grotto with a fountain). Annexed to the latter house is a remarkably preserved wineshop, where *amphorae* (vases) still rest on carbonized wooden shelves. And in the **House of the Wooden Partition,** one of the best-preserved of all, there is a carbonized wooden partition with three doors. In the **Baths,** where there were separate sections for men and women, you can see benches; basins; and the hot, warm, and cold rooms, embellished with mosaics. The **House of**

the Bicentenary was a patrician residence with smaller rooms on the upper floor, which may have been rented out to artisan-tenants who were probably Christians because they left an emblem of the cross embedded in the wall. The *palaestra* (gymnasium) and 2,500-seat theater; the sumptuously decorated suburban baths; and the House of the Stags, with an elegant garden open to the sea breezes, are all evocative relics of a lively and luxurious way of life.

Until a few years ago it was believed that most of Herculaneum's inhabitants had managed to escape by sea, since few skeletons were found in the city. Excavations at Porta Marina, the gate in the sea wall leading to the beach, have revealed instead that many perished there, a few steps from the only escape route open to them. *Corso Ercolano, tel. 081/739-0963. Admission: 8,000 lire; children under 12 free. Open daily 9–one hour before sunset; ticket office closes 2 hours before sunset.*

❷❷ You can visit **Vesuvius** either before or after Herculaneum. If possible, save the mountain till after you've toured the buried city and learned to appreciate the volcano's awesome power. The most important factor is whether the summit is lost in mist—when it is, you'll be lucky to see your hand in front of your face. The volcano is visible from Naples, and everywhere else along the Bay of Naples; the best advice is, when you see the summit clearing—it tends to be clearer in the afternoon—head for it. The view then is magnificent, with the curve of the coast and the tiny white houses among the orange and lemon blossoms.

Reaching the crater takes some effort. From the Ercolano stop of the Circumvesuviana, take scheduled buses (departures at 10, noon, and 2) or your own car to the Seggovia station, the lower terminal of the defunct chair lift. (Though there's talk of putting it back in working order, no one is optimistic about the possibility.) From here you must climb the soft, slippery cinder track on foot, a 30-minute ascent, and you must pay about 4,500 lire for compulsory guide service, though the guides don't do much more than tell you to stay away from the edge of the crater. If you're not in shape, you'll probably find the climb tiring. Wear nonskid shoes (not sandals).

❷❸ **Pompeii** has its own stop (Pompeii–Villa Misteri) on the Circumvesuviana, close to the main entrance at the Porta Marina (there are other entrances to the excavations at the far end of the site, near the amphitheater). Ancient Pompeii was much larger than Herculaneum; a busy commercial center with a population of 10,000–20,000, it covered about 160 acres on the seaward end of the fertile Sarno plain.

Numbers in the margin correspond to points of interest on the Pompeii map.

In 80 BC the Roman General Sulla turned Pompeii into a Roman colony, where wealthy patricians came to escape the turmoil of city life. The town was laid out in a grid pattern, with two main intersecting streets. The wealthiest took a whole block for themselves; those less fortunate built a house and rented out the front rooms, facing the street, as shops. The facades of these houses were relatively plain and seldom hinted at the care and attention lavished on the private rooms within.

When a visitor entered, he passed the shops and entered an open area (atrium). In the back was a receiving room. Behind was another open area, called the peristyle, with rows of columns and perhaps a garden with a fountain. Only good friends ever saw this private part

Pompeii

N

| 0 | 200 yards |
| 0 | 200 meters |

Amphitheater, **41**
Antiquarium, **25**
Basilica, **27**
Casa di Menandro, **39**
Forum, **28**
Fullonica Stephani, **38**
House of the Faun, **30**

House of the Gilded Cupids, **35**
House of the Tragic Poet, **31**
House of the Vettii, **34**
Lupanare, **36**
Porta Ercolano, **32**
Porta Marina, **24**

Stabian Baths, **37**
Temple of Jupiter, **29**
Temple of Venus, **26**
Villa di Giulia Felice, **40**
Villa of the Mysteries, **33**

of the house, which was surrounded by the bedrooms and the dining area.

Pompeiian houses were designed around an inner garden so that families could turn their backs on the world outside. Today we install picture windows that break down visual barriers between ourselves and our neighbors; the people in these Roman towns had few windows, preferring to get their light from the central courtyard—the light within. How pleasant it must have been to come home from the forum or the baths to one's own secluded kingdom, with no visual reminders of a life outside one's own.

Not that public life was so intolerable. There were wineshops on almost every corner, and frequent shows at the amphitheater. The public fountains and toilets were fed by huge cisterns, connected by lead pipes beneath the sidewalks. Since garbage and rainwater collected in the streets of Pompeii, the sidewalks were raised, and huge stepping stones were placed at crossings so pedestrians could keep their feet dry. Herculaneum had better drainage, with an underground sewer that led to the sea.

The ratio of freemen to slaves was about three to two. A small, prosperous family had two or three slaves. Since all manual labor was considered degrading, the slaves did all housework and cooking, including the cutting of meat, which the family ate with spoons or with their hands. Everyone loved grapes, and figs were popular, too. Venison, chicken, and pork were the main dishes. Oranges weren't known, but people ate quinces (a good source of Vitamin C) to guard against scurvy. Bread was made from wheat and barley (rye and oats were unknown) and washed down with wine made from the grapes of the slopes of Vesuvius.

The government was considered a democracy, but women, children, gladiators, and Jews couldn't vote. They did, however, express their opinions on election day, as you'll see in campaign graffiti left on public walls.

Some 15,000 graffiti were found in Pompeii and Herculaneum. Many were political announcements—one person recommending another for office, for example, and spelling out his qualifications. Some were bills announcing upcoming events—a play at the theater, a fight among gladiators at the amphitheater. Others were public notices—that wine was on sale, that an apartment would be vacant on the Ides of March. A good many were personal, and give a human dimension to the disaster that not even the sights can equal. Here are a few:

At the Baths: "What is the use of having a Venus if she's made of marble?"

At a hotel: "I've wet my bed. My sin I bare. But why? you ask. No pot was anywhere."

At the entrance to the front lavatory at a private house: "May I always and everywhere be as potent with women as I was here."

In a back room at the Suburban Baths: "Apelles the waiter dined most pleasantly with Dexter the slave of the emperor, and they had a screw at the same time." (Did they do it with each other, or only at the same time? Homosexuality would not have been uncommon.)

The following route will help you locate the most interesting sights:

㉔ Enter through **Porta Marina**, so called because it faces the sea. It is near the **Pompeii–Villa Misteri Circumvesuviana Station.** On your

㉕ right is the **Antiquarium,** which contains casts of human bodies and a
㉖ ㉗ dog. Past the **Temple of Venus** is the **Basilica,** the law court and the
economic center of the city. These oblong buildings ending in a semicircular projection (apse) were the model for early Christian
churches, which had a nave (central aisle) and two side aisles separated by rows of columns. Standing in the Basilica, you can recognize the continuity between Roman and Christian architecture.

㉘ The Basilica opens onto the **Forum** (Foro), the public meeting place,
surrounded by temples and public buildings. It was here that elections were held and speeches and official announcements made—a
sort of Roman version of the village green. Turn left. At the far
㉙ (northern) end of the forum is the **Temple of Jupiter** (Tempio di
Giove). Walk around the right side of the temple, cross the street,
and continue north on **Via del Foro** (Forum Street). There is a **restaurant** on your left.

The next cross street becomes **Via delle Fortuna** to your right, and
Via delle Terme to your left. Turn right onto **Via della Fortuna.** On
㉚ your left is the **House of the Faun** (Casa del Fauno), one of the most
impressive examples of a luxurious private house, with wonderful
mosaics (originals in the National Archaeological Museum in Naples).

Retrace your steps along **Via della Fortuna** to **Via del Foro.** Cross the
street. You're now on **Via delle Terme.** The first entrance on the right
㉛ is the **House of the Tragic Poet** (Casa del Poeta Tragico). This is a
typical middle-class house from the last days of Pompeii. Over the
door is a mosaic of a chained dog and the inscription *Cave canem,*
"Beware of the dog." Continue west on Via delle Terme to the end.
Turn right and bear left along **Via Consolare.** Pass through the beau-
㉜ tiful **Porta Ercolano** (Gate of Herculaneum)—the main gate that led
to Herculaneum and Naples.

Now outside Pompeii, walk down **Via dei Sepolcri** (Street of the
Tombs), lined with tombs and cypresses. The road makes a sharp
㉝ left. At the four-way crossing, turn right to the **Villa of the Mysteries** (Villa dei Misteri). This patrician's villa contains what some consider the greatest surviving group of paintings from the ancient
world, telling the story of a young bride (Ariadne) being initiated
into the mysteries of the cult of Dionysus. Bacchus (Dionysus), the
god of wine, was popular in a town so devoted to the pleasures of the
flesh. But he also represented the triumph of the irrational—of all
those mysterious forces that no official state religion could fully sup-
press. The cult of Dionysus, like the cult of the Cumaean Sibyl, gave
people a sense of control over fate, and in its focus on the Other
World, helped pave the way for Christianity.

Return along **Via dei Sepolcri** to Pompeii. Retrace your steps down
Via Consolare, which joins with **Vicolo di Narciso.** Make your first
left onto **Vicolo di Mercurio.** Six blocks down is **Vicolo dei Vettii.**
㉞ Around the corner, to the left, is the **House of the Vettii** (Casa dei
Vetti). This is the best example of a rich middle-class merchant's
house, faithfully restored.

Return, back around the corner, to **Vicolo di Mercurio.** Continue
east one more block. You've now reached **Via Stabiana,** one of the
two major intersecting streets of the town. Around the corner to the
㉟ left is the **House of the Gilded Cupids,** an elegant, well-preserved
home with original marble decorations in the garden.

From the door of the house, turn right down Via Stabiana, go three
blocks, and turn right onto **Via Augustali.** Your first left will take

③⑥ you to the **Lupanare** (brothel) on **Vicolo del Lupanare**. On the walls are scenes of erotic games that clients could request. The beds have shoe marks left by visitors.

Continue south on Vicolo del Lupanare, turning left onto **Via dell'Abbondanza,** the other main street of the old town. On your left ③⑦ are the **Stabian Baths**. It was here that people came in the evening to drown the burdens of the day. The baths were heated by underground furnaces. The heat circulated among the stone pillars supporting the floor, rose through flues in the walls, and escaped through chimneys. The water temperature could be set for cold, lukewarm, and hot. Bathers took a lukewarm bath to prepare themselves for the hot room. A tepid bath came next, and then a plunge into cold water to tone up the skin. A vigorous massage with oil was followed by rest, reading, horseplay, and conversation.

Continue in the same direction, east on Via dell'Abbondanza (a left turn as you leave the baths). Two blocks down on your right is the ③⑧ **Fullonica Stephani,** a house converted into workshops for the cleaning of fabrics. All Roman citizens were required to wear togas in public, which weren't exactly easy to keep clean. It's not hard to imagine why there were more toga cleaners (fullers) in Pompeii than anything else, except perhaps bakers. The cloth was dunked in a tub full of water and chalk and stamped upon like so many grapes. Washed, the material was stretched across a wicker cage and exposed to sulfur fumes. The fuller carded it with a long brush, then placed it under a press. The harder the pressing, the whiter and brighter it became.

Go south, completely around the block. Behind the Fullonica ③⑨ Stephani is the entrance to the **Casa di Menandro,** a patrician's villa with many paintings and mosaics. Return to Via dell'Abbondanza. If you've had enough walking, turn left and go a few more blocks past the new restorations and then return to the Porta Marina, where your tour began. The recommended alternative is to turn right ④⓪ (east) on Via dell'Abbondanza to the **Villa di Giulia Felice** (House of Julia Felix), which has a large garden with a lovely portico. The wealthy lady living here ran a public bathhouse annex and rented out ground-floor rooms as shops.

④① Turn right past the villa and continue to the **Amphitheater** (Anfiteatro). The games here were between animals, between gladiators, and between animals and gladiators. There were also Olympic games and chariot races. The crowds rushed in as soon as the gates opened—women and slaves to the bleachers. When the Emperor or some other important person was in attendance, exotic animals— lions and tigers, panthers, elephants, and rhinos—were released. At "half time," birds of prey were set against hares, or dogs against porcupines; the animals were tied to each end of a rope so neither could escape. Most gladiators were slaves or prisoners, but a few were Germans or Syrians who enjoyed fighting. Teams of gladiators worked for impresarios, who hired them out to wealthy citizens, many of whom were running for office and hoping that the gory entertainment would buy them some votes. When a gladiator found himself at another's mercy, he extended a pleading hand to the president of the games. If the president turned his thumb up, the gladiator lived; if he turned his thumb down, the gladiator's throat was cut. The arena got pretty bloody after a night's entertainment and was sprinkled with red powder to camouflage the carnage. The victorious gladiator got money or a ribbon exempting him from further fights. If he was a slave, he was often set free. If the people of Pompeii had had trading cards, they would have collected portraits of gladiators; everyone had his favorite. Says one piece of graffiti: "Petronius Octavus fought thirty-four fights and then died, but Severus, a freedman, was victor in fifty-five fights and still lived; Nasica celebrates sixty victories." Pompeii had a gladiator school (Caserma dei Gladiatori), which you can visit on your way back to Porta Marina.

Return to Porta Marina, where your walk began, or exit through the **Ingresso Anfiteatro** and find a cab for the 1.6-kilometer (1-mile) trip back to Porta Marina. You could, of course, begin your trip at the Ingresso Anfiteatro and make the tour in the opposite direction. If you want a personal guide, you may have an easier time finding one here than at Porta Marina.

To get the most out of Pompeii, buy a detailed printed guide and map and allow plenty of time—at least three or four hours. You should have a pocketful of small change (500-lire coins) for tipping the guards who are on duty at the most important villas. They will unlock the gates for you, insist on explaining the attractions, show you some mild Pompeiian pornography if you ask for it, and expect a tip for their services. If you hire a guide, make sure he's registered and standing inside the gate. Agree beforehand on the length of the tour and the price. *Pompei Scavi, tel. 081/861-0744. Admission: 10,000 lire; children under 12 free. Open daily 9–one hour before sunset; ticket office closes 2 hours before sunset.*

Time Out | You can have lunch at the restaurant and cafeteria near the **Forum**, where there's a picnic area as well. There are also plenty of trattorias outside the entrances to the excavation.

Tour 3: Caserta and Benevento

Numbers in the margin correspond to points of interest on the Campania map.

A northward excursion from Naples takes you to Caserta, the Bourbons' version of Versailles, and if you proceed to Benevento, you'll view an almost perfectly preserved Roman arch. With the exception of some mountain scenery, there's not much else of interest on this route; Benevento was badly damaged by World War II bombings, and you will have to content yourself here with picking out the medieval and even older relics that have survived in the oldest part of the city. Both Caserta and Benevento can be reached by train from Naples. Daily bus service from Naples is quite frequent to Caserta, 28 kilometers (18 miles) away, less so to Benevento, 62 kilometers (39 miles) away. If you go by car, make a brief detour to the medieval hamlet of Caserta Vecchia on the hillside, where there is a very old cathedral and one or two good restaurants.

42 The **royal palace** at **Caserta**, known as the Reggia, will show you how Bourbon royalty lived in the mid-18th century. Architect Luigi Vanvitelli devoted 20 years to its construction under Bourbon ruler Charles II, whose son, Charles III, moved in when it was completed in 1774. Both king and architect were inspired by Versailles, and the rectangular palace was conceived on a massive scale, with four interconnecting courtyards, 1,200 rooms, and a vast park. Though not as well maintained as its French counterpart, the main staircase is suitably grand, and the **royal apartments** are sumptuous. It was here, in what Eisenhower called "a castle near Naples," that the Allied High Command had its headquarters in World War II, and here German forces in Italy surrendered in April 1945. Most enjoyable are the gardens and parks, particularly the Cascades, where a life-size Diana and her maidens stand. The park is the Reggia's main attraction, with pools and fountains stretching for more than a mile, formal Italian gardens and a delightful English garden. Some of the fountains are splendid and may be playing at full force now that the aqueduct built by the Bourbons has been repaired. If you don't like walking, a minibus makes a circuit of the grounds. *Piazza Carlo III. Admission: royal apartments, 6,000 lire; park, 4,000 lire; minibus, 1,500 lire. Royal apartments open Mon.–Wed. 9–1:30, Thurs.–Sat. 9–6:30, Sun. 9–12:30; park open daily 9–one hour before sunset. Royal apartments closed 2nd and 4th Mon. of each month and national holidays.*

Time Out **Mulini Reali** (Ponte di Sala, tel. 0823/301842, closed Tues.) is a restaurant set in an old mill. There's good pasta and fish at lunchtime, and the restaurant is located at an entrance to the English garden.

43 **Benevento,** 35 kilometers (21 miles) east, became the capital of the Lombards, a northern tribe that invaded and settled what is now Lombardy when they were ousted by Charlemagne in the 8th century. Tough and resourceful, the Lombards moved south and set up a new duchy in Benevento, later moving its seat south to Salerno, where they saw the potential of the fine natural harbor. Under papal rule in the 13th century, Benevento built a fine cathedral and endowed it with bronze doors that were a pinnacle of Romanesque art. The cathedral, doors, and a large part of the town were blasted by World War II bombs, so there's little left to see; fortunately, the majestic **Arch of Trajan** survived unscathed. To reach it, follow Viale Principe di Napoli from the station and take the first left after the river. The arch is a fine 2nd-century AD work, decorated with reliefs exalting the many accomplishments of Roman emperor Trajan, who sorted out Rome's finances, brought parts of the Middle East into the empire, and extended the Appian Way through Benevento to the Adriatic. From the arch, take Via Traiano and turn right onto Corso Garibaldi to get to the **duomo,** which has been rebuilt, with the remaining panels of the original bronze doors in the chapter library. Via Carlo, behind the cathedral, leads to the ruins of a **Roman Theater,** with a seating capacity of 20,000. The theater is still in good enough shape to host a summer opera and theater season. *Teatro Romano. Admission free. Open daily 9–one hour before sunset.*

Tour 4: Ischia and Capri

44 Capri wows you with its charm and beauty; **Ischia** takes time to cast its spell. An overnight stay is probably not long enough for the island to get into your blood. It does have its share of wine-growing villages beneath the lush volcanic slopes of Monte Epomeo and, unlike Capri, it enjoys a life of its own that survives when the tourists head home. But there are few signs of antiquity here, the architecture is unremarkable, the beaches are small and pebbly, there's little shopping beyond the high-trash gift shops that attract the German therapeutic trade, and most visitors are either German (off-season) or Italian (in-season). On the other hand, some of you will delight in discovering an island not yet overcome with tourists from the United States. Ischia also has some lovely hotel-resorts high in the mountains, offering therapeutic programs and rooms with breathtaking views. Should you want to plunk down in the sun for a few days and tune out the world, this is an ideal place to go; the mistake you shouldn't make is expecting Ischia to be an unspoiled, undiscovered Capri. When Augustus gave the Neapolitans Ischia for Capri, he knew what he was doing.

Unlike Capri, Ischia is volcanic in origin. From its hidden reservoir of seething molten matter come the thermal springs said to cure whatever ails you. As early as 1580, a doctor named Iasolino published a book about the mineral wells at Ischia. "If your eyebrows fall off," he wrote, "go and try the baths at Piaggia Romano. Are you unhappy about your complexion? You will find the cure in the waters of Santa Maria del Popolo. Are you deaf? Then go to Bagno d'Ulmitello. If you know anyone who is getting bald, anyone who suffers from elephantiasis, or another whose wife yearns for a child, take the three of them immediately to the Bagno di Vitara; they will bless you."

Today the island is covered with thermal baths surrounded by tropical gardens. Hydrofoils from Naples reach it in 45 minutes; the car ferry takes 90 minutes. The passenger-and-car ferry from Pozzuoli takes about 60 minutes. **Ischia Porto** is the largest town on the island and the usual point of debarkation. It's no workaday port, however, but a pretty resort with plenty of hotels and low flat-roofed houses arrayed on terraced hillsides above the water. Its narrow streets often become flights of steps that scale the hill, and its villas and gardens are framed by pines. If you're visiting Ischia for the day, your best bet is to recapture your youth at one of the mineral baths, such as the **Poseidon Gardens,** just south of the colorful port of Forio on the opposite side of the island, and then lose it at a harborfront restaurant in Ischia Porto or in **Forio.**

Most of the hotels are along the beach in the part of town called **Ischia Ponte,** which gets its name from the bridge *(ponte)* built by Alfonso of Aragón in 1438 to link the picturesque castle on a small islet offshore with the town and port. For a while, the castle was the home of Vittoria Colonna, poetess and platonic soulmate of Michelangelo, with whom she carried on a lengthy correspondence, and granddaughter of Renaissance Duke Federico da Montefeltro. If you choose to stay in Ischia Porto, you'll find a typical resort atmosphere; countless cafés, shops, and restaurants; and a half-mile stretch of fine sandy beach.

The **information office** is at the harbor. Remember that Ischia is off limits to visitors' cars from April through September; there's fairly good bus service, and you'll find plenty of taxis. One popular beach resort, just 5 kilometers (3 miles) west of Ischia Porto is **Casamicciola.** Next is chic and upscale **Lacco Ameno,** distinguished by a mushroom-shaped rock offshore and some of the island's best hotels. Here, too, you can enjoy the benefits of Ischia's therapeutic waters.

The far western and southern coasts of the island are more rugged and attractive. **Forio,** at the extreme west, is an ideal stop for lunch or dinner. The sybaritic hot pools of the **Poseidon Gardens** spa establishment are on the Citara beach, south of Forio. You can sit like a Roman senator on a stone chair recessed in the rock and let the hot water cascade over you—all very campy, and fun. **Sant'Angelo,** on the southern coast, is a charming village; the road doesn't reach all the way into town, so it's free of traffic, and it's a five-minute boat ride from the beach of Maronti, at the foot of cliffs. The inland towns of **Serrara, Fontana,** and **Barano** are all located high above the sea; Fontana, most elevated of the three, is the base for excursions to the top of **Mount Epomeo,** the long-dormant volcano that dominates the island landscape. You can reach its 788-meter (2,585-foot) peak in less than 1½ hours of relatively easy walking.

A good 35-kilometer (21-mile) road makes a circuit of the island; the ride takes most of a day at a leisurely pace, if you're stopping along the way to enjoy the views and perhaps have lunch. You can book a boat tour (20,000 lire) around the island at the booths in various ports along the coast; there's a one-hour stop at Sant'Angelo.

㊺ **Capri** (accent on the first syllable) is a pleasure island at the southern approach to the Bay of Naples. It's easy to reach by boat or hydrofoil from Naples and Sorrento all year and from the Amalfi Coast or Ischia during the summer months. The boat from Naples takes about 75 minutes; the hydrofoil, only about 40 minutes. In addition, there's direct helicopter service from Capodichino Airport in Naples (*see* Arriving and Departing by Plane in Essential Information, *above*). Note that from April 1 to October 31, no cars can be taken to the island.

The summer scene on Capri calls to mind the stampeding of bulls through the narrow streets of Pamplona: If you can visit in the spring or fall, do so. Yet even the crowds are not enough to destroy Capri's very special charm. The town is a Moorish opera set of shiny white houses, tiny squares, and narrow medieval alleyways hung with flowers. You can take a bus or the funicular to reach the town, which rests on top of rugged limestone cliffs, hundreds of feet above the sea.

The mood is modish but somehow unspoiled. The upper crust bakes in the sun in private villas; the secret is for you, too, to disappear while the day-trippers take over—offering yourself to the sun at your hotel pool or exploring the hidden corners of the island. Even in the height of summer, you can enjoy a degree of privacy on one of the many paved paths that wind around the island hundreds of feet above the sea. Unlike the other islands in the Bay of Naples, Capri is not of volcanic origin but is an integral part of the limestone chain of the Apennines, left above water when some subterranean cataclysm sank its connecting link with the mainland.

The Phoenicians were the earliest settlers of Capri. The Greeks arrived in the 4th century BC and were followed by the Romans, who made it their playground. Emperor Augustus vacationed here; Tiberius built 12 villas, scattered over the island, and here he spent the later years of his life, refusing to return to Rome even when he was near death. Capri was one of the strongholds of the 16th-century pirate Barbarossa, who first sacked it and then made a fortress of it. Moors and Greeks had previously established their citadels on its heights, and pirates from all corners of the world periodically raided it. In 1806 the British wanted to turn it into another Gibraltar and were beginning to build fortifications when the French took it away from them in 1808. However, the Roman influence has remained the strongest, reflecting a sybaritic way of life inherited from the Greek colonists on the mainland.

Capri has a reputation for being hideously expensive, and indeed some of its top-ranking hotels and restaurants are among the most costly in Italy. But plenty of moderately priced hotels and some inexpensive ones share the same fabulous views. There are also moderately priced trattorias off the beaten tourist track.

Thousands of legends concerning the life and loves of mythological creatures, Roman emperors, Saracen invaders, and modern eccentrics combine to give Capri a voluptuous allure—sensuous and intoxicating—like the island's rare and delicious white wine. (Most of the wine passed off as "local" on Capri comes from the much more extensive vineyards of Ischia.) Certainly, there are fewer pleasures more gratifying than gazing out at the sea from the quiet of a sun-dappled arbor while enjoying a glass of cold wine and flavorful *insalata caprese*, a minor work of art in itself, with smooth white mozzarella, fleshy red tomatoes, and bright green basil.

All boats for Capri dock at **Marina Grande,** where you can board an excursion boat for the 90-minute tour to the **Blue Grotto.** If you're pressed for time, however, skip this sometimes frustrating and disappointing excursion. You board one boat to get to the grotto, and you have to transfer to another, smaller, one in order to get inside the grotto. If there's a backup of boats waiting to get in, you'll be given precious little time to enjoy the gorgeous color of the water and its silvery reflections. *Cost, including 4,000-lire admission to the grotto: about 18,000 lire. Daily 9:30–two hours before sunset; departures less frequent in winter.*

As an alternative, take the approximately two-hour boat trip around the island—hassle free and very enjoyable. These excursions start at Marina Grande and are run by the Grotta Azzurra company. The cost is 17,200 lire. Make either of these boat trips in the morning, when light and visibility are better.

One of the town's two **tourist information offices** is on the pier where the boats from the mainland dock; ask for a brochure map *(Piantina)* showing the many walks you can take to get the best views and escape the crowds. You may have to wait in line for the cog railway (3,000 lire round trip) to the town of **Capri.** If it's not operating, there's bus and taxi service. From the upper station, walk out into Piazza Umberto I, much better known as the *Piazzetta*, the island's social center, *the* place to see and be seen, deliberately commercial and self-consciously picturesque at the same time. You can window-shop in expensive boutiques and browse in souvenir shops along Via Vittorio Emanuele, which leads south toward the many-domed **Certosa di San Giacomo.** The church and cloister of this much-restored monastery can be visited, and you should also pause long enough to enjoy the breathtaking view of Punta Tragara and the Faraglioni, three towering shoals, from the viewing stand at the edge of the cliff. *Via Certosa. Admission free. Open Tues.–Sun. 9–2.*

Beyond the monastery, Via Matteotti leads past bright shops and ice-cream stands to the **Giardini di Augusto** (Gardens of Augustus), a beautifully planted public garden with excellent views. From its terraces you can see the village of **Marina Piccola** below, where restaurants, cabanas, and swimming platforms huddle among the shoals. This is the best place on the island for swimming; you can reach it by bus or by following the steep and winding Via Krupp, actually a staircase cut into the rock, all the way down. (Friedrich Krupp, the German arms manufacturer, loved Capri and became one of the island's most generous benefactors.) Otherwise you swim off boats or take a hint from the family groups from Naples and Sorrento who swim off the unkempt but sandy beach at the end of Marina Grande past the cog railway station.

Time Out   Just down Via Roma from the Piazzetta is **Verginiello** (tel. 081/837–0944), one of the island's best-value restaurants for lunch. Try the calamari.

From the town of Capri, the 45-minute hike east to **Villa Jovis,** the grandest of those built by Tiberius, is strenuous but rewarding. Follow the signs for Villa Jovis, taking Via Le Botteghe from the Piazzetta, then continuing along Via Croce and Via Tiberio. At the end of a lane that climbs the steep hill, with pretty views all the way, you come to the precipice over which the emperor reputedly disposed of the victims of his perverse attentions. From a natural terrace above, near a chapel, are spectacular views of the entire Bay of Naples and (on clear days) part of the Gulf of Salerno. Below are the ruins of Tiberius's palace. Allow 45 minutes each way for the walk alone. *Via Tiberio. Admission: 4,000 lire. Open daily 9–one hour before sunset.*

A shorter, more level walk along Via Tragara leads to a belvedere overlooking the Faraglioni; another takes you out of the town of Capri on Via Matermania to the so-called Natural Arch, an unusual rock formation near a natural grotto that the Romans transformed into a shrine. The 20-minute walk from the piazzetta along picturesque Via Madre Serafina and Via Castello to the belvedere at Punta Cannone gives you a panoramic view of the island.

You can take a bus from Marina Grande (1,500 lire) or a taxi (about 15,000 lire one way; agree on the fare before starting out) up the tortuous road to **Anacapri,** the island's only other town. Here crowds are thickest around the square that is the starting point of the chair lift (6,000 lire) to the top of Mount Solaro. Elsewhere, Anacapri is quiet and appealing. Look for the church of **San Michele,** where a climb to the choir loft rewards one with a perspective of the magnificent 18th-century majolica tile floor showing the Garden of Eden. From Piazza della Vittoria, picturesque Via Capodimonte leads to **Villa San Michele,** charming former home of Swedish scientist Axel Munthe, now a museum of his antiques and furniture. *Via Axel Munthe. Admission: 5,000 lire. Open Nov.–Feb., daily 10:30–3:30; Mar., daily 9:30–4:30; Apr. and Oct., daily 9:30–5; May–Sept., daily 9–6.*

Anacapri is also good for walks: Try the 40-minute walk (each way) to the Migliara belvedere and another walk of about an hour each way to the ruins of the Roman villa of Damecuta. If walking is not your idea of happiness, just join the other sybarites sitting in the Piazzetta and remember that Augustus called Capri Apragopolis (City of Sweet Idleness) or, as the Italians would say, *dolce far niente* (pleasant idleness).

Tour 5: The Amalfi Drive: Sorrento to Salerno

This is the most romantic drive in Italy. The road is gouged from the side of rocky cliffs plunging into the sea. Small boats lie in sandy coves like so many brightly colored fish. Erosion has contorted the rocks into mythological shapes and hollowed out fairy grottoes where the air is turquoise and the water an icy blue. White villages, dripping with flowers, nestle in coves or climb like vines up the steep, terraced hills. The road must have a thousand turns, each with a different view, on its dizzying 69-kilometer (43-mile) journey from Sorrento to Salerno.

46 **Sorrento** is across the Bay of Naples, 50 kilometers (30 miles) from the city of Naples on autostrada A3 and S145; the Circumvesuviana railway, which stops at Herculaneum and Pompeii, provides another connection. The coast between Naples and Castellammare, where road and railway turn off onto the Sorrento peninsula, seems at times depressingly overbuilt and industrialized. Yet Vesuvius looms to the left, you can make out the 3,000-foot-high mass of Mount Faito ahead, and on a clear day you can see Capri off the tip of the peninsula. The scenery improves considerably as you near Sorrento, where the coastal plain is carved into russet cliffs rising perpendicularly from the sea. This is the Sorrento (north) side of the peninsula; on the other side is the Amalfi Coast, more dramatically scenic and somewhat less overcome by tourists in summer. Many prefer the charming towns on the Amalfi Coast to the tourist haven of Sorrento, but Sorrento has at least two advantages: the Circumvesuviana railway terminal and a fairly flat terrain. (Positano, and to a lesser extent Amalfi and Ravello, clings to hillsides and requires some strenuous walking.)

Until the mid-20th century Sorrento was a small, genteel resort favored by central European princes, English aristocrats, and American literati. Now the town has grown and spread out along the crest of its famous cliffs, and apartments stand where citrus groves once bloomed. Tour groups arrive by the busload, and their ranks are swollen by Italian vacationers in the peak summer season. Like most resorts, Sorrento is best off-season, either in spring and early autumn or in winter, when Campania's mild climate can make a stay pleasant anywhere along the coast. Another reason to avoid the peninsula during peak season is the heavy traffic on the single coast road, where cars and buses may be backed up for miles. Highlights of a visit to Sorrento include a stroll around town, with views of the Bay of Naples from the **Villa Comunale** or from the terrace behind the **Museo Correale.** The museum features a collection of decorative antiques, from ceramics to furniture to landscape paintings of the Neapolitan school. *Via Correale. Admission: 5,000 lire; gardens only: 3,000 lire. Open Apr.–Sept., Mon., Wed.–Sat. 9–12:30, 5–7, Sun. 9–12:30; Oct.–Mar., Mon., Wed.–Sat. 9–12:30, 3–5, Sun. 9–12:30.*

Around Piazza Tasso are a number of shops selling embroidered goods and intarsia (wood-inlay) work. Along narrow Via San Cesareo, where the air is pungent with the perfumes of fruit and vegetable stands, there are more shops selling local and Italian handicrafts.

Time Out | Just off Piazza Tasso is **Gigino** (Via degli Archi 15, closed Tues.), one of Sorrento's best-known inexpensive restaurants. Try the fixed-price menu at lunch.

Explore the town's churches and narrow alleys and follow Via Marina Grande, which turns into a pedestrian lane and stairway, to Sorrento's only real beach, where the fishermen pull up their boats. You can take a bus or walk a mile or so to Capo Sorrento, then follow the signs to the **Villa of Pollio Felice,** the scattered seaside remains of an ancient Roman villa, where you can swim off the rocks or simply admire the setting.

Before you leave Sorrento, consider a side trip west along the road that skirts the tip of the peninsula; if you enjoy dramatic seascapes, this will be worth the extra time.

❹❼ The most popular town along the Amalfi drive, particularly among Americans, is **Positano,** a village of white Moorish-type houses clinging dramatically to slopes around a small sheltered bay. When John Steinbeck lived here in 1953, he wrote that it was difficult to consider tourism an industry because "there are not enough [tourists]." Alas, Positano has since been discovered. The artists came first, and, as happens wherever artists go, the wealthy followed and the artists fled. What Steinbeck wrote, however, still applies: "Positano bites deep. It is a dream place that isn't quite real when you are there and becomes beckoningly real after you have gone. Its houses climb a hill so steep it would be a cliff except that stairs are cut in it. I believe that whereas most house foundations are vertical, in Positano they are horizontal. The small curving bay of unbelievably blue and green water laps gently on a beach of small pebbles. There is only one narrow street and it does not come down to the water. Everything else is stairs, some of them as steep as ladders. You do not walk to visit a friend, you either climb or slide."

In the 10th century Positano was part of Amalfi's Maritime Republic, which rivaled Venice as an important mercantile power. Its heyday was in the 16th and 17th centuries, when its ships traded in the Near and Middle East, carrying spices, silks, and precious woods. The coming of the steamship in the mid-19th century led to the town's decline, and some three-fourths of the town's 8,000 citizens emigrated to America, mostly to New York. One major job of Positano's mayor has been to find space in the overcrowded cemetery for New York Positanesi who want to spend eternity here.

What had been reduced to a forgotten fishing village is now the number-one attraction on the coast, with hotels for every budget, charming restaurants, and dozens of boutiques. From here, you can take hydrofoils to Capri during the summer, escorted bus rides to Ravello, and tours of the Emerald Grotto (*see below*).

Positano may not have a castle, but it does have another attraction that's bringing the town considerable wealth: stylish summer clothes. From January to March, buyers from all over the world come to Positano to buy the trend-setting handmade clothes that are sold in more than 200 boutiques. One-size loosefitting cotton dresses; full skirts, plain or covered with lace—some in light pastel colors with handprinted designs, others in bold block colors: bright oranges, pinks, and yellows. The choice is endless, and the prices— well, you're on vacation, and the same dresses would cost twice as much in New York or Rome.

If you're staying in Positano, check whether your hotel has a parking area. If not, you will have to pay for space in a parking lot, which is almost impossible to find during the high season, from Easter to September. The best bet for day-trippers is to get to Positano early enough so that space is still available. No matter how much time you spend in Positano, make sure you have some comfortable walking shoes—no heels, please!—and that your back and legs are strong enough to negotiate steps.

Thirteen kilometers (8 miles) along the coastal road from Positano, a short distance before Amalfi, you'll see signposts for the **Grotta Smeralda** (Emerald Grotto). You can park here and take an elevator down to the grotto, or you can drive on to Amalfi and return to the grotto by the more romantic route: via boat (boat tours leave from the Amalfi seafront approximately every two hours, according to demand; the charge is 10,000 lire per person). The grotto is named for its peculiar green light, which casts an eerie emerald glow over impressive formations of stalagmites and stalactites, many of them underwater. *Admission: 5,000 lire. Open summer, daily 9–5; winter, daily 10–4 (hours vary, so check before you go).*

Seventeen kilometers (11 miles) from Positano along the coast is **48** **Amalfi.** After Positano and Ravello, Amalfi is your third choice for a town to stay in along the drive. It would have to be a distant third, however, because of the congestion caused by tour buses, which make Amalfi the main stopping point on their excursions. The town is romantically situated at the mouth of a deep gorge and has some good-quality hotels and restaurants. It's also a convenient base for excursions to Capri and the Emerald Grotto.

During the Middle Ages, Amalfi was an independent maritime state—a little Republic of Venice—with a population of 50,000. The ship compass—trivia fans will be pleased to know—was invented here in 1302.

The main historical attraction is the **Duomo** (Cathedral of St. Andrew), which shows an interesting mix of Moorish and early-Gothic influences. The interior is a 10th-century Romanesque skeleton in an 18th-century Baroque dress. The transept (the transverse arms) and the choir are 13th century. The handsome 12th-century campanile (bell tower) has identical Gothic domes at each corner. Don't miss the beautiful late–13th-century Moorish cloister, with its slender double columns. At least one critic has called the cathedral's facade the ugliest piece of serious architecture in Italy—decide for yourself. The same critic snickers at the tourists who fail to note the cathedral's greatest treasure, the 11th-century bronze doors from Constantinople.

The parking problem here is as bad as that in Positano. The small lot in the center of town fills quickly; if you can afford the steep prices, make a luncheon reservation at one of the hotel restaurants and have your car parked for you.

The main street leads back through town from the cathedral to the mountains, and passes a ceramic workshop and some water-driven paper mills where handcrafted paper is made and sold. Though it's not always open, there's a paper museum where you can see exactly how the mills work.

Time Out Stop in at the **Pansa** pastry shop on Piazza del Duomo for a giant *sfogliatella* (a high-calorie meal in itself) or any of the other oven-fresh goodies.

Perched on a ridge high above Amalfi and the neighboring town of Atrani is **Ravello,** an enchanting village with stupendous views, quiet lanes, and two irresistibly romantic gardens—that of **Villa Rufolo,** where medieval ruins frame spectacular vistas, and **Villa Cimbrone,** a private estate open to the public with spectacular views of the entire Bay of Salerno.

Because Ravello is a long, steep drive from the sea, tour buses are discouraged and crowds are less overwhelming than at Positano and Amalfi. By early afternoon, the day-trippers have departed, and the town becomes one of the most restful settings in the world. There's very little to do except walk through peaceful gardens, admire the view, and exist.

The other towns on the Amalfi Coast between Atrani and Salerno have less charm, though the scenery is no less spectacular. In addition to the views, ceramics lovers will find the trip worthwhile for a chance to visit **Vietri sul Mare,** where well-known factories such as Solimene and Pinto have produced bright terra-cotta wares for hundreds of years. Vietri is the last stop on the Amalfi Coast, after which **Salerno,** spread out along its bay, is a sad testimony to years of neglect and overdevelopment. An imposing Romanesque cathedral is the only site most tourists consider worth seeing here. Built in 1085 and remodeled in the 18th century, it has Byzantine doors (1099) from Constantinople and an outstanding 12th-century pulpit.

In the new Diocesan Museum behind it is a collection of astounding medieval carved tablets. (Admission free.) A few blocks away in the recently restored **monastery of San Benedetto,** a museum holds a handsome bronze head of Apollo fished out of the bay in the 1930s.

Beyond Salerno, the road (S18) and train cut across 50 kilometers (30 miles) of flat coastal plain to one of Italy's most majestic sights: the remarkably well-preserved Greek temples of **Paestum.** S18 from the north passes the train station (Stazione di Paestum), which is about 800 yards from the ruins, through the perfectly preserved **Porta Sirena** archway. The ruins stand on the site of the ancient city of Poseidonia, founded by Greek colonists in the 7th century BC. When the Romans took over the colony in 273 BC and called it Paestum, they enlarged the settlement, adding an amphitheater and a forum. Much of the archaeological material found on the site is displayed in the **museum,** and several rooms are devoted to the unique tomb paintings discovered in the area, rare examples of Greek and pre-Roman pictorial art. About 200 yards from the museum (in front of the main entrance), framed by ranks of roses and oleanders, is the **Temple of Poseidon** (or Neptune), a magnificent Doric edifice, with 36 fluted columns and an extraordinarily well-preserved entablature (area above the capitals). Not even Greece itself possesses such a fine monument of Hellenic architecture. On the left of the temple is the so-called **Basilica,** the earliest of Paestum's standing edifices; it dates from very early in the 6th century BC. The name is an 18th-century misnomer, for the structure was in fact a temple sacred to Hera, the wife of Zeus. Behind it an ancient road leads to the **Forum** of the Roman era and the single column of the **Temple of Peace.** Beyond is the **Temple of Ceres.** Try to see the temples in the late afternoon, when the light enhances the deep gold of the stone and the air is sharp with the cries of the crows that nest high on the temples. *Admission: 8,000 lire for museum and temple area. Excavations open daily 9–one hour before sunset; museum open Tues.–Sun. 9– one hour before sunset.*

What to See and Do with Children

Campania is an ideal destination for those traveling with children. The locals follow the Italian tradition of doting on youngsters— which partly explains the number of *gelaterie* (ice-cream shops) and candy stores, even in the smallest towns. Most activities in Campania take place outdoors, so even at the ruins of Pompeii, Herculaneum, and Paestum children have an opportunity to play in the sun. They will also love the funiculars in Naples, Capri's cog railway, and the hydrofoils operating between the islands. The following sights are of particular interest to children.

Acquario (Tour 1: Naples and Its Bay).
Boat Tour Around Ischia (Tour 4: Ischia and Capri).
Certosa di San Martino (Tour 1: Naples and Its Bay).
Edenlandia. This is the largest amusement park in Campania. It's located in the Mostra d'Oltremare area of Naples, near San Paolo Stadium. *Viale Kennedy, tel. 081/239–1182. Admission free, individual fares for rides. Open all year.*
Grotto Smeralda (Tour 5: The Amalfi Drive: Sorrento to Salerno).
House of the Wooden Partition (Tour 2: Herculaneum, Vesuvius, and Pompeii).
Museo Archeologico Nazionale (Tour 1: Naples and Its Bay).
Museo Nazionale Ferroviario. Children love to see the old-fashioned engines, cars, and railroad equipment on display in the restored railway works, founded by the Bourbon rulers of Naples in the last cen-

tury. *Corso San Giovanni a Teduccio, tel. 081/472003. Admission free. Open Mon.–Sat. 8:30–2.*

Villa Jovis (Tour 4: Ischia and Capri).

Villa of the Mysteries (Tour 2: Herculaneum, Vesuvius, and Pompeii).

Off the Beaten Track

Cappella Sansevero. This chapel, located near San Domenico Maggiore, in Naples, features a masterful marble sculpture of the shrouded body of Christ by 18th-century Neapolitan sculptor Sammartino as well as other macabre works. *Via De Sanctis 19. Admission: 5,000 lire. Open Mon., Thurs.–Sat. 10–1, 5–7; Tues., Sun. 10–1.*

Catacombs of San Gennaro. Many of these catacombs in Naples predate the Christian era by two centuries. They are next to the huge **Madre di Buon Consiglio** church on Via Capodimonte. The church was inspired by St. Peter's in Rome. The niches and corridors of the catacombs are hung with early Christian paintings. *Via Capodimonte. Admission: 4,000 lire. Guided tours Fri., Sat., Sun. every 45 min 9:30–11:45.*

Seafront Tours. Evening boat tours take in the waterfront of Naples, from the port at Mergellina to Cape Posillipo, with a view of **Castel dell'Ovo** on the way back. *Tel. 081/661434. Fare: 6,000 lire. Runs July–Sept., departs daily at 6, 7, and 8 PM.*

Museo Campano. It's 33 kilometers (20 miles) north of Naples to Capua and this museum, whose collection includes Le Madri (Mothers), 200 eerily impressive stone votive statues representing highly stylized mother figures. They were found on the site of a sanctuary devoted to Matuta, the ancient goddess of childbirth, and date from the 7th to the 1st century BC. *Tel. 0823/961402. Admission: free. Open Tues.–Sat. 9–2, Sun. 9–1, closed Mon.*

Museo Filangieri. This Neapolitan museum contains a private collection of arms, armor, furniture, paintings, and fascinating memorabilia. It's housed in the Florentine-style Renaissance Palazzo Cuomo. *Via Duomo 288, tel. 081/203175. Admission: 4,000 lire. Open Tues.–Sat. 9–2, Sun. 9–1, closed Mon.*

Shopping

Leather goods, coral, jewelry, and cameos are some of the best items to buy in Campania. In Naples, where many of the top leather and fashion houses have their factories, you'll find good buys in bags, shoes, and clothing, but it's often wise to make purchases in shops rather than from street vendors. The coastal resorts have maintained some of their craft traditions, although some shops try to pass off poor-quality machine-made goods as handmade items.

Naples The **Galleria Umberto** (*see* Tour 1: Naples and Its Bay, *above*) is a good introduction to shopping in Naples; a wide variety of retail outlets trade in the four glass-roofed arcades. Other areas and streets are more specialized: The area immediately around **Piazza dei Martiri** is the heart of luxury shopping, with perfume shops, fashion outlets, and antiques on display. **Via Toledo** and **Via Chiaia** are better bets for bargains.

Positano The picturesque streets of this coastal resort are lined with **boutiques** selling **casual fashions** and **beachwear** in splashy colors and extravagant fabrics.

Sorrento This is the place to buy **embroidered table linens** and **crocheted lace.** Also, the wood-inlay art of **intarsia** is a centuries-old tradition here. Shops today offer everything from jewelry boxes to trays and coffee tables with intarsia decorations. **Ferdinando Corcione,** in his shop on Via San Francesco, gives demonstrations of his intarsia work, producing decorative plaques with classic or contemporary motifs.

Vietri sul This Amalfi Coast town is a major **ceramics** center, and its distinc-
Mare tive pottery, with sunny motifs and bright colors, is on sale in towns along the coast. Many small shops in Vietri sul Mare offer goods from local pottery workshops. You can pick over all kinds of dusty wares at the **Solimene** works.

Sports

Sun, sand, and sea combine in Campania to offer the visitor a number of sporting options, but be prepared to encounter pollution in some of the beaches nearest Naples (*see* Beaches, *below*). The top hotels often offer sports facilities, such as private beaches, swimming pools, and tennis courts, and many will allow nonresidents to use these facilities: Contact the hotels themselves or the local tourist office.

Bowling **Bowling Oltremare,** Viale Kennedy, Naples (tel. 081/624444).

Fishing For information on licenses and water quality, contact **Federazione Italiana Pesca Sportiva** (Piazza Santa Maria degli Angeli, Naples, tel. 081/764–4921).

Golf **Minigolf Kennedy** (Via Camillo Guerra 60, tel. 081/587–1386) is in the suburb of Chiaiano, west of Naples.

Horseback For riding in Campania, contact the **Centro Ippico Agnano** (Via
Riding Circumvallazione, Agnano, between Naples and Pozzuoli, tel. 081/570–2695).

Sailing **Nantic Coop** (Piazza Amedeo 15, Naples, tel. 081/415371).

Tennis Most top hotels have courts. Contact them or local tourist boards about their use. The following are public courts:

Benevento (Viale Atlantici, tel. 0824/29920).
Naples (Via Giochi del Mediterraneo, tel. 081/570–3910).
Ischia Porto (Lungomare Colombo, tel. 081/991013).

Water Skiing **Sci Nautico Partenopeo** (Lake Averno, Pozzuoli, tel. 081/866–2214).

Beaches

The waters of the Bay of Naples are notoriously polluted. The waters around Capri and some, but not all, of Ischia's beaches, offer clean swimming. Pollution is intermittent along the Amalfi Coast, where the deep waters are generally clean. Beaches in the Salerno area are best avoided; the water gets cleaner the farther south you go.

Dining and Lodging

Dining Campania's cuisine is simple and relies heavily on the bounty of the region's fertile farmland. Its tomatoes are exported all over the world, but to try them here is a new experience. Even during the winter you can find tomato sauce made with small sundried tomatoes plucked from bright red strands that you can see hanging outdoors on kitchen balconies. Pasta is a staple here, and spaghetti *al pomodoro* or *al filetto di pomodoro* (both with simple tomato sauces) and spaghetti *alle vongole* (with clam sauce, either white or red, depending on the cook's whims) appear on most menus.

This is the homeland of pizza, served mainly in its simpler versions: *alla napoletana*, with anchovies; *alla margherita*, with tomato and mozzarella; *alla marinara*, with tomato, garlic, and oregano. Locally produced mozzarella is used in many dishes; one of the most gratifying on a hot day is insalata caprese: slices of mozzarella and ripe red tomato, garnished with basil. *Melanzane* (eggplant) and even zucchini are served *alla parmigiana* (fried and layered with tomato sauce and mozzarella). Meat may be served *alla pizzaiola*, cooked in a tomato-and-garlic sauce. Fish and seafood in general can be expensive, though fried calamari and *totani* (cuttlefish) are usually reasonably priced. Among the region's wines, Gragnano, Falerno, Lacrima Cristi, and Greco di Tufo are fine whites. Ischia and Ravello also produce good white wine. Campania's best-known reds are Aglianico, Taurasi, and the red version of Falerno.

Restaurant prices in the region are generally a little lower than in Rome and northern Italy, though Capri restaurants can be very expensive. On the islands, the Sorrento peninsula, and the Amalfi Coast, restaurants may be open every day of the week during the season, but may close for long periods in the winter.

Highly recommended restaurants are indicated by a star ★.

Category	Cost*
$$$$	over 85,000 lire
$$$	60,000–85,000 lire
$$	25,000–60,000 lire
$	under 25,000 lire

per person, including house wine, service, and tax

Lodging Although Capri, Ischia, Sorrento, and the Amalfi Coast offer generally fine accommodations in all categories, good accommodations in Naples are scarce, so reserve well in advance. High-season rates apply at all coastal resorts in July and August. These rates extend from April/May through September at Sorrento and Amalfi Coast resorts, where Christmas and Easter also draw crowds and command top rates. Whereas coastal resorts elsewhere close up tight from fall to spring, at least some hotels and restaurants are open in Sorrento and on the Amalfi Coast year-round. It's always a good idea to book ahead, and it's imperative in high season. Campania hotel rates are generally lower than those in major tourist cities to the north, but rates in Capri's top hotels are at premium levels for Italy. On the other hand, even in Capri and especially along the Amalfi Coast, you can find charming little hotels with attractive rooms and wonderful views at very reasonable rates; just don't expect to find vacancies in August. During the summer, hotels on the coast almost always require that you take half-board if they serve meals. Local tourist information offices will help you find accommodations.

Highly recommended lodgings are indicated by a star ★.

Category	Cost*
$$$$	over 300,000 lire
$$$	160,000–300,000 lire
$$	100,000–160,000 lire
$	under 100,000 lire

All prices are for a standard double room for two, including service and 9% IVA (19% for luxury establishments).

Amalfi
Dining
★

La Caravella. You'll find this welcoming establishment tucked away under some arches lining the coast road, next to the medieval Arsenal, where Amalfi's mighty fleet once was provisioned. La Caravella has a nondescript entrance but a pleasant interior decorated in a medley of colors and paintings of Old Amalfi. It's small and intimate; specialties include *scialatielli* (homemade pasta with shellfish sauce) and *pesce al limone* (fish with lemon sauce). *Via M. Camera 12, tel. 089/871029. Reservations advised. Dress: casual. AE, MC, V. Closed Tues. and Nov. 10–30. $$*

Lodging
★

Santa Caterina. A large mansion perched above terraced and flowered hillsides on the coast road just outside Amalfi proper, the Santa Caterina is one of the best hotels on the entire coast, offering gracious living in a wonderfully scenic setting. The rooms are tastefully decorated; most have small terraces or balconies with great views. There are lovely lounges and terraces for relaxing, and an elevator whisks guests to the seaside saltwater pool, bar, and swimming area. On grounds lush with lemon and orange groves, there are two romantic villa annexes. *Strada Amalfitana 9, tel. 089/871012, fax 089/871351. 54 rooms with bath. Facilities: pool, swimming area, beach bar, restaurant, bar, parking. AE, DC, MC, V. $$$–$$$$*

Hotel Dei Cavalieri. This terraced, white Mediterranean-style hotel on the main road outside Amalfi has three villa annexes in grounds just across the road that extend all the way to a beach below. The bedrooms are air-conditioned and functionally furnished, with splashy majolica tile floors contributing a bright note throughout. An ample buffet breakfast is served, and, though half-board is mandatory during high season, you can dine either at the hotel or at several restaurants in Amalfi by special arrangement. *Via M. Comite 32, tel. 089/831333, fax 089/831354. 54 rooms with bath. Facilities: beach (via stairs), restaurant, bar, parking, garage, minibus to town. AE, DC, MC, V. $$–$$$*

Miramalfi. A modern building perched above the sea, the Miramalfi has wonderful views, simple but attractive decor, terraces, swimming pool, and a sunning/swimming area on the sea, as well as a quiet location just below the coast road, only a half mile from the center of town. Almost all rooms boast balconies with sea views. *Via Quasimodo 3, tel. 089/871588, fax 089/871588. 48 rooms with bath or shower. Facilities: restaurant, garden, private beach, pool, parking. AE, DC, MC, V. $$*

Anacapri
Lodging

Europa Palace Hotel. A modern resort atmosphere predominates at this large Mediterranean-style hotel set in lovely gardens. Each of four junior suites has a private swimming pool and terrace. The bedrooms are tastefully decorated in contemporary style, with white predominating; marble is featured in the bathrooms, and many rooms have balconies. The only minus is being in Anacapri, a bus or cab ride from the restaurants and shops in the town of Capri. *Via Axel Munthe, tel. 081/837-0955, fax 081/837-3191. 93 rooms with bath or shower. Facilities: pool, garden, air-conditioning, restaurant ($$), bar, parking. AE, DC, MC, V. Closed Nov.-Mar. $$$-$$$$*

San Michele. You'll find this large white villa-hotel next to Axel Munthe's Capri home. Surrounded by luxuriant gardens, the San Michele offers solid comfort and good value, along with spectacular views. The decor is contemporary, with some Neapolitan period pieces adding atmosphere. Most rooms have a terrace or balcony overlooking either the sea or island landscapes. *Via G. Orlandi 5, tel. 081/837-1427, fax 081/837-1420. 56 rooms with bath or shower. Facilities: pool, garden, 2 restaurants. AE, DC, MC, V. Closed Nov.-Mar. $$$*

Capri
Dining

La Pigna. Ensconced in a glassed-in veranda and offering outdoor dining in a garden shaded by lemon trees, the Pigna is one of Capri's favorite restaurants. The specialties are a house-produced wine, *farfalle impazzite* (pasta with seafood and tomato), and *aragosta alla luna caprese* (lobster). The cordial host organizes party evenings with feasts of seasonal specialties and seafood. *Via Lo Palazzo 30, tel. 081/837-0280. Dinner reservations required. Dress: casual. AE, DC, MC, V. Closed Tues. and Nov.-Easter. $$$*

★ **La Capannina.** Known as one of Capri's best restaurants, La Capannina is only a few steps from the busy social hub of the Piazzetta. It has a vine-draped veranda for dining outdoors by candlelight in a garden setting. The specialties, aside from an authentic Capri wine with the house label, are homemade ravioli *alla caprese* (with a cheese filling, tomato sauce, and basil) and regional dishes. *Via Le Botteghe 14, tel. 081/837-0732. Dinner reservations required. Dress: casual. AE. Closed Wed. (except Aug.) and Nov. 10–Mar. 15. $$-$$$*

Al Grottino. This small and friendly family-run restaurant, which is handy to the Piazzetta, has arched ceilings and lots of atmosphere; autographed photos of celebrity customers cover the walls. House specialties are *gnocchi* (dumplings) with tomato sauce and mozzarella, and *linguine ai gamberetti* (pasta with shrimp and tomato sauce). *Via Longano 27, tel. 081/837-0584. Dinner reservations required. Dress: casual. AE, MC, V. Closed Tues. and Nov. 3-Mar. 20. $$*

Lodging

Quisisana. Catering largely to Americans, this is the most luxurious and traditional hotel in the center of town. Spacious rooms are done in traditional or contemporary decor with some antique accents; many have arcaded balconies with views of the sea or the charming enclosed garden, in which there's a swimming pool. The bar and restaurant are casually elegant. *Via Camerelle 2, tel. 081/837-0788, fax 081/837-6080. 150 rooms with bath or shower. Facilities: garden, pool, sauna, tennis court, restaurant, bar. AE, DC, MC, V. Closed Nov.-mid-Mar. $$$$*

★ **Scalinatella.** The name means "little stairway," and that's how this charming but modern small hotel is built, on terraces following the slope of the hill, overlooking the gardens, pool, and sea. The bedrooms are intimate, with alcoves and fresh, bright colors; the bathrooms feature Jacuzzis. The hotel has a small bar but no restaurant. *Via Tragara 8, tel. 081/837-0633, fax 081/837-8291. 30 rooms with bath or shower. Facilities: pool, tennis court, garden, air-conditioning, bar. AE. Closed Nov.-Mar. 14. $$$$*

Villa Brunella. This quiet family-run gem nestles in a garden setting just below the lane leading to the Faraglioni. Comfortable and taste-fully furnished, the hotel also has spectacular views, a swimming pool, and a terrace restaurant known for good food. *Via Tragara 24, tel. 081/837–0122, fax 081/837–0430. 18 rooms with bath. Facilities: pool, bar, restaurant (tel. 081/837–0122; reservations required for nonguests. $$). AE, DC, MC, V. Closed Nov.–Mar. $$$*

Villa Sarah. This whitewashed Mediterranean building has a homey look and bright, simply furnished rooms. It's close enough to the Piazzetta (a 10-minute walk away) to give easy access to the goings-on there, while ensuring restful nights. There's a garden and small bar, but no restaurant. *Via Tiberio 3/a, tel. 081/837–0689, fax 081/837–7215. 20 rooms with bath. AE, MC, V. Closed Nov.–Mar. $$–$$$*

Villa Krupp. Among the hotels that are open all year, this historic hostelry—onetime home of Maxim Gorki, whose guests included Lenin—occupies a quiet location overlooking the Gardens of Augus-tus. Rooms are plain but spacious, and some have a balcony. *Via Matteotti 12, tel. 081/837–0362, fax 081/837–6489. 12 rooms with bath or shower. Facilities: garden. MC, V. $$*

Aida. A 10-minute walk from the center of town in a tiny lane that borders the Gardens of Augustus, the Aida offers a tranquil haven from Capri's bustle and hard sell. The staff is sociable, and the rooms, which look onto a small garden, are spacious, comfortably furnished, and immaculately clean. The beach, at Marina Piccola, is only 20 minutes away. *Via Birago, tel. 081/837–0366. 9 rooms, 5 with shower. No credit cards. Closed mid-Oct.–Apr. $–$$*

Caserta **Antica Locanda Massa 1848.** Near the Reggia, this large, informal
Dining restaurant is decorated in browns and white in 19th-century rustic style. In fair weather you eat alfresco under an arbor. The special-ties are linguine *al cartoccio* (pasta steamed with fresh tomato and shellfish) and *gazzerielli alla Borbone* (gnocchi with cheese and truffle sauce). *Via Mazzini 55, tel. 0823/321268. Reservations ad-vised. Dress: casual. AE, DC, MC, V. Closed Fri. and Aug. 5–20. $$*

La Castellana. Located in Casertavecchia, Caserta's medieval nu-cleus on the hillside overlooking the modern town, this tavern has atmosphere and hearty local specialties, such as *stringozzi alla castellana* (homemade pasta with a piquant tomato sauce served in individual casseroles) and *agnello alla castellana* (lamb sautéed in red wine). You dine inside or, in fair weather, under an arbor. *Via Torre 4, tel. 0823/371230. Reservations required weekends. Dress: casual. AE, DC, MC, V. Closed Thurs. (except Sept.). $$*

Ischia **Gennaro.** This small family restaurant on the seafront at Ischia
Dining Porto serves excellent fish in a convivial atmosphere. Specialties in-clude spaghetti con vongole and linguine *all'aragosta* (with lobster). *Via Porto 66, tel. 081/992917. Reservations advised weekends and July–Aug. AE, DC, MC, V. Closed Nov.–mid-Mar. and Tues., Mar., Apr., Oct. $$*

Lodging **Grand Hotel Punta Molino.** Right in the town of Ischia Porto, but set in a quiet zone near the sea and framed with pine trees and gardens, is one of the best hotels on the island. The decor is bright and con-temporary, with some luxury touches, and many rooms have sea views. There's a heated pool on one of the terraces. Half-board is re-quired. *Lungomare Colombo, tel. 081/991544, fax 081/991562. 82 rooms with bath or shower. Facilities: private beach, pool, spa treat-ments, garden, bar, restaurant, parking. AE, MC, DC, V. Closed Nov.–Apr. 24. $$$$*

★ **Villarosa.** You'll find this welcoming hotel in the heart of Ischia Porto and only a short walk from the beach. It is a gracious family-run villa with bright and airy rooms. There's a thermally heated pool in the villa garden. In high season, half board is required, and you must reserve well in advance. Prices fall into the lower end of this category. *Via Giacinto Gigante 3, tel. 081/991316, fax 081/ 992425. 37 rooms with bath or shower. Facilities: pool, garden, restaurant (for hotel guests only). AE, MC, V. Closed Nov.–Easter. $$$*

Del Postiglione. This attractive, pink Mediterranean-style edifice is smaller than it appears, with only 11 guest rooms. Its aura of under-stated luxury is created by marble floors, tropical plants adorning the outside, and generous balconies overlooking one of Ischia Porto's quiet back streets, a couple of minutes from the seafront. The rates are at the bottom of this category. *Via Giacinto Gigante 19, tel. 081/991579, fax 081/991579. 11 rooms with bath or shower. Facilities: restaurant, bar, baby-sitting. No credit cards. $$*

Lacco Ameno
Lodging
★

Regina Isabella. Tucked away in an exclusive corner of the beach in Lacco Ameno, Ischia's top luxury hotel has full resort facilities and pampers guests with spa treatments as well. The rooms are ample and decorated in warm Mediterranean colors. Most have terraces or balconies. Don't miss the fun of socializing with chic vacationers in the elegant bar or restaurant or at poolside. *Piazza Santa Restituta, tel. 081/994322, fax 081/986043. 134 rooms with bath or shower. Facilities: private beach, indoor and outdoor pools, tennis court, spa treatments, garden, restaurant, bar. AE, DC, MC, V. Closed Oct. 16–Apr. 14. $$$$*

Hotel San Montano. This modern hotel overlooks the sea in a quiet location. San Montano is decorated with nautical motifs and ceramic-tile floors. The rooms have compact English navy furnishings, color TV, and minibar. The San Montano has all resort facilities and provides spa treatments, too. *Via Montevico 1, tel. 081/994033, fax 081/980242. 67 rooms with bath or shower. Facilities: garden, pool, tennis courts, restaurant, spa treatments, parking. AE, DC, MC, V. Closed Nov.–Mar. $$$*

Naples
Dining

Casanova Grill. Soft lights and a trendy art-deco look set the tone in the Casanova Grill, the Hotel Excelsior's restaurant. The seasonal specialties and antipasti arranged on the buffet will whet your appetite for such traditional Neapolitan dishes as the simple spaghetti al pomodoro and the classic *carne alla pizzaiola* (meat with tomato and oregano). *Hotel Excelsior, Via Partenope 48, tel. 081/764–0111. Reservations advised. Jacket and tie advised at dinner. AE, DC, MC, V. $$$*

La Fazenda. Overlooking the sea at Marechiaro, in one of the city's most picturesque spots, this restaurant is a favorite for leisurely dining and an invitingly informal atmosphere. The pastas, many with vegetable sauces, are particularly good. The specialty is seafood, but you can also find a good, honest *bistecca* (beefsteak) here. Desserts are homemade. Note that you must take a taxi to get to La Fazenda. *Discesa Marechiaro 58, tel. 081/575–7420. Reservations advised. Dress: casual. V. Closed Mon. and Aug. 13–29. $$$*

★ **La Sacrestia.** Popular with Neapolitans because of its location and the quality of its food, La Sacrestia is set on the slopes of the Posillipo hill, with marvelous views of the city and bay. The specialties range from appetizing antipasti to linguine in *salsa di scorfano* (pasta in scorpion-fish sauce). Seafood has a place of honor on the menu, and there are interesting meat dishes as well. The setting in a patrician villa and the ambience are definitely upscale. *Via Orazio 116, tel. 081/761–1051. Reservations advised. Dress: jacket and tie*

preferred. AE, DC, MC, V. Closed Mon., Sun. in July, and Aug.
$$$

Bergantino. Near the central station, this bustling trattoria is a favorite with businesspeople. Courteous and efficient waiters serve a variety of classic Neapolitan dishes, including hearty *maccheroni con ragù* (pasta with meat sauce) or *sartù di riso* (rice casserole with bits of meat and cheese). Pizzas are also available here, and there is a 20,000-lire fixed-price menu at lunchtime. *Via Milano 16, tel. 081/ 553–9787. Reservations advised on weekends. Dress: casual. AE, MC, V. Closed Sun. and Aug. 10–20. $$*

Bersagliera. Most first-time visitors to Naples want to dine once on the Santa Lucia waterfront in the shadow of the medieval Castel dell'Ovo, and this is one of the best places to do so. It's touristy but fun, with an irresistible combination of spaghetti and mandolins. The menu offers uncomplicated classics, such as spaghetti *alla pescatora* (with seafood sauce) and melanzane alla parmigiana. *Borgo Marinaro 10, tel. 081/764–6016. Reservations advised. Dress: casual. AE, DC, MC, V. Closed Tues. $$*

Ciro a Santa Brigida. Centrally located off Via Toledo near the Castel Nuovo, Ciro is a straightforward restaurant popular with business travelers, artists, and journalists who are more interested in food than frills. In dining rooms on two levels, customers enjoy classic Neapolitan cuisine. Among the specialties: sartù di riso and *scaloppe alla Ciro* (veal with prosciutto and mozzarella). There's pizza, too. *Via Santa Brigida 71, tel. 081/552–4072. Reservations advised. Dress: casual. AE, DC, MC, V. Closed Sun. and Aug. $$*

Dante e Beatrice. A simple trattoria on central Piazza Dante, this popular spot features typical Neapolitan dishes in an unassuming setting. The menu may offer *pasta e fagioli* (very thick bean soup with pasta) and maccheroni al ragù. You can eat inexpensively here. *Piazza Dante 44, tel. 081/549–9438. Dinner reservations advised. Dress: casual. No credit cards. Closed Mon. and Aug. 24–31. $$*

Don Salvatore. Head just west to the little port of Mergellina to find an unpretentious-looking place known for good local dishes and seafood. Linguine *cosa nostra* (with shellfish) and other pastas with seafood sauces are specialties, and the *fritto misto* (mixed fried fish) is as light as a feather. *Via Mergellina 5, tel. 081/681817. Reservations advised. Dress: casual but neat. AE, DC, MC, V. Closed Wed. $$*

Lodging **Excelsior.** This CIGA hotel is located on the shore drive, with views of the bay from the front rooms. The lobby and lounges are lavish, with Oriental carpets and gilt or glass chandeliers. Off the large semicircular lounge are a chic little bar and the Casanova restaurant. The rooms are decorated either in CIGA's standard Empire style (with neoclassic furniture and brocades) or in more typically Neapolitan floral prints. *Via Partenope 48, tel. 081/764–0111, fax 081/764–9743. 102 rooms with bath or shower. Facilities: restaurant, bar, garage. AE, DC, MC, V. $$$$*

Jolly Ambassador. This hotel occupies the top 14 floors of the only skyscraper on the downtown skyline (if you don't count the business center beyond the station), and the bedrooms and roof garden-restaurant command sweeping views of Naples and the bay. Decorated in the uninspired but functional style of the Jolly chain, with dark brown and white predominating, it promises comfort and efficiency in a city where these are scarce commodities. *Via Medina 70, tel. 081/416000, fax 081/551–8010. 251 rooms with bath or shower. Facilities: restaurant, bar, garage. AE, DC, MC, V. $$$*

★ **Paradiso.** Stay here if you want something special a step or two off the beaten track. A modern air-conditioned building perched on the slopes of the hill above the port of Mergellina, the Paradiso is just a few minutes by taxi or funicular from downtown, and it has fabulous views from huge window walls in the lobby and all front rooms. The decor, in tones of blue and beige, is restful and attractive. Built-in furnishings of rosy wood with marble surfaces give the bedrooms a smart contemporary look. Though the rooms and bathrooms are smallish, they are well organized, with TV and minibar; about half have a balcony. Be sure to ask for a room with a view; there's no extra charge. There is a roof terrace for sitting, dining, and contemplating the entire bay as far as Vesuvius and beyond. *Via Catullo 11, tel. 081/761–4161, fax 081/761–3449. 74 rooms with bath or shower. Facilities: restaurant, bar, garage. AE, DC, MC, V. $$$*

Rex. This hotel, which is at the higher end of its price category, has a fairly quiet location near the Santa Lucia waterfront. Situated on the first two floors of an art nouveau building, it has no elevator; the decor ranges from 1950s modern to fake period pieces and even some folk art, haphazardly combined. Though it has no restaurant, there are many in the vicinity. *Via Palepoli 12, tel. 081/764–9389, fax 081/764–9227. 40 rooms, 37 with bath or shower. Facilities: bar, garage. AE, DC, MC, V. $$*

Ideal. Though far from living up to its name, this is nonetheless a useful stopover for anyone arriving by train and unwilling to venture too far into the city's confusion to find a hotel. Located in the square in front of the station, the rooms are mostly viewless, and some may be on the cramped side, but they are clean and functional. *Piazza Garibaldi 99, tel. 081/269237, fax 081/269237. 41 rooms, 30 with shower. AE, DC, MC, V. $*

Paestum
Dining and Lodging

Martini. Directly across the road from the Porta della Giustizia and only a few steps from the temples, the Martini has cottage-type rooms, each with minibar, in a garden setting. A pleasant restaurant serves local specialties and seafood: The home-produced ricotta and mozzarella are especially recommended. *Zona Archeologica, tel. 0828/811451, fax 0828/811600. 27 rooms with bath or shower. Facilities: beach ½ mile away, Sea Garden restaurant, garden, parking. Reservations advised. Dress: casual. AE, DC, MC, V. $*

Positano
Dining

Buca di Bacco. After an aperitif at the town's most famous and fashionable café downstairs, you dine on a veranda overlooking the beach. The specialties include spaghetti alle vongole and *grigliata mista* (mixed grilled seafood). *Via Rampa Teglia 8, tel. 089/875699. Dinner reservations advised. Dress: casual. AE, DC, MC, V. Closed Nov. 6–Mar. 31. $$*

Capurale. Among the popular restaurants on the beach promenade, this one just around the corner has the best food and lowest prices. Tables are set under vines on a breezy sidewalk in the summer, indoors and upstairs in winter. Spaghetti con melanzane and crêpes *al formaggio* (with cheese) are among the specialties. *Via Marina, tel. 089/875374. Reservations advised for outdoor tables and on weekends off-season. Dress: casual. AE, DC, MC, V. Closed Tues. Nov.–Mar. $$*

Lodging
★

San Pietro. Extraordinary is the word for this luxurious oasis for the affluent international set. Located outside the town, set high above the sea with garden terraces, the San Pietro has sumptuous Neapolitan Baroque decor and masses of flowers in the lounges, elegantly understated rooms (most with terraces), and marvelous views. There's a pool on an upper level, and an elevator whisks guests to the private beach and beach bar. The proprietors organize boating excursions and parties and provide car and minibus service into town. *Via Laurito, tel. 089/875455, fax 089/811449. 60 rooms with bath or* *shower. Facilities: pool, private beach and dock, hotel boat, tennis court, garden, restaurant, 2 bars, parking. AE, DC, MC, V. Closed Nov. 3–Mar. $$$$*

★ **Sirenuse.** A handsome 18th-century palazzo in the center of town is the setting for this luxury hotel in which bright tiled floors, precious antiques, and tasteful furnishings are featured in ample and luminous salons. The bedrooms have the same sense of spaciousness and comfort; most have splendid views from balconies and terraces. The top-floor suites have huge bathrooms and Jacuzzis. One side of a large terrace has an inviting swimming pool; on the other is an excellent restaurant—both share the hotel's view of the town, beach, and sea. *Via Cristoforo Colombo 30, tel. 089/875066, fax 089/811798. 60 rooms with bath or shower. Facilities: heated pool, restaurant, bar, sauna, parking. AE, DC, MC, V. $$$$*

Casa Albertina. One of the few hotels here that is open all year, Casa Albertina is a pleasant place with a friendly owner-manager. The rooms are bright with color, some have views, and you can enjoy the panorama from the terrace, where you can have breakfast or drinks in fair weather. It's a few steps up from one of the town's social hubs, the Bar De Martino. There's a restaurant and roof garden, and, except for the restaurant, rates are low in its category. *Via Tavolozza 4, tel. 089/875143, fax 089/811540. 21 rooms with bath or shower. Facilities: restaurant, bar, parking. AE, DC, MC, V. $$$*

Palazzo Murat. The location is perfect—in the heart of town, near the beachside promenade, but set in a quiet, walled garden. The old wing is a historic palazzo with tall windows and wrought-iron balconies; the new wing is a whitewashed Mediterranean building with arches and terraces. You can relax in antique-accented lounges or in the charming vine-draped patio, and since there's no restaurant, you will avoid the half-board requirement applied in most hotels here in high season. *Via dei Mulini 23, tel. 089/875177, fax 089/811419. 28 rooms with bath and shower. Facilities: garden, bar. AE, DC, MC, V. Closed Nov. 5–Mar. $$$*

Santa Caterina. There is more to this newly refurbished hotel than meets the eye: Rooms descend on three levels down the steep slope. The owners have made the most of the exquisite view of the town and seashore, which can be relished from each of the rooms as well as from the generous balconies and terraces. On street level (the top floor), there is also an excellent fish restaurant, well patronized by the locals. It's quite a hike to the beach—a good 15 minutes down the steps—but that's nothing new in Positano. *Via Pasitea 113. tel. 089/811513. 12 rooms, 6 with bath or shower. Facilities: restaurant, bar. AE, DC, MC, V. Closed Nov.–Mar. $*

Ravello **Cumpa Cosimo.** This family-run restaurant a few steps from the ca-
Dining thedral square offers a cordial welcome in three simple but attract-
★ ive dining rooms. There's no view, but the food is excellent. Among the specialties are cheese crêpes and roast lamb or kid. *Via Roma 44, tel. 089/857156. Reservations advised weekends and summer evenings. Dress: casual. AE, DC, MC, V. Closed Mon. Nov.–Mar. $$*

Lodging **Palumbo.** Occupying a 12th-century patrician palace furnished with antiques and endowed with modern comforts, this hotel has an elegant, warm atmosphere that gives you the feeling of being a guest in a lovely private home, under the personal care of courtly host Signor Vuilleumier. With lovely garden terraces, breathtaking views, and a sumptuous upstairs dining room, the hotel is a memorable one. *Palazzo Confalone, tel. 089/857244, fax 089/857347. 13 rooms with bath. Facilities: garden, restaurant, bar. AE, DC, MC, V. $$$$*

★ **Caruso Belvedere.** Charmingly old-fashioned, spacious, and comfortable, this rambling villa hotel has plenty of character and a full share of Ravello's spectacular views from its terraces and balconied rooms. Relax in the garden belvedere with its memorable views. The restaurant is known for fine food and locally produced house wine. *Via Toro 52, tel. 089/857111, fax 089/857372. 26 rooms with bath or shower. Facilities: garden, restaurant, bar. AE, DC, MC, V. $$$*

Villa Amore. A 10-minute walk from the main Piazza Duomo, this hotel is family-run, tidy, and comfortable, with a garden and an exhilarating view from most of its bedrooms. If you're looking for tranquillity, this is the place to find it, especially at dusk, when the valley is tinged with a glorious purple light. Furnishings are modest but modern. Full board is available here and may be required in the summer. Reserve ahead. *Via Santa Chiara, tel. 081/857135. 12 bedrooms with bath or shower. Facilities: garden, restaurant, bar. MC, V. $*

Sorrento
Dining

Antica Trattoria. An Old World dining room inside and garden tables in fair weather make this a pleasant place to enjoy the local cooking. The atmosphere is homey and hospitable. The specialties are classic spaghetti al pomodoro and melanzane alla parmigiana. *Via Giuliani 33, tel. 081/807–1082. Dinner reservations advised. Dress: casual but neat. No credit cards. Closed Mon., and Jan. 10–Feb. 10. $$*

Parrucchiano. Centrally located and popular, this is one of Sorrento's oldest and best restaurants. You walk up a few steps to glassed-in veranda dining rooms filled, like greenhouses, with vines and plants. The menu offers classic local specialties, among them *panzerotti* (pastry shells filled with tomato and mozzarella) and *scaloppe alla sorrentina* (veal with tomato and mozzarella). *Corso Italia 71, tel. 081/878–1321. Reservations advised weekends and Aug. Dress: casual. MC, V. Closed Wed. Nov.–May. $$*

Lodging
★

Cocumella. This hotel is set in a cliff-top garden in a quiet residential area on the edge of Sorrento (it's really in the adjacent town of Sant'Agnello). Occupying a historic old villa that was a monastery in the 17th century, it features a tasteful blend of antique and contemporary decor, with vaulted ceilings and archways, a dining veranda, and stunning tiled floors. It's exclusive and elegant without being stuffy. *Via Cocumella 7, tel. 081/878–2933, fax 081/878–3712. 60 rooms and suites with bath or shower. Facilities: garden, pool, elevator to swimming area, tennis court, restaurant, bar, parking. AE, DC, MC, V. Closed Jan.–Feb. $$$$*

Excelsior Vittoria. In the heart of Sorrento, but removed from the bustle of the main square, this historic hotel perches on the cliff. It has art nouveau decor and some quite grand, though faded, furnishings. Tenor Enrico Caruso's bedroom is preserved as a relic; the guest bedrooms are slightly less elegant but spacious and comfortable. The views are wonderful. Winter prices are 10% lower than high-season rates. *Piazza Tasso 34, tel. 081/807–1044, fax 081/877–1206. 106 rooms and suites with bath. Facilities: pool, garden, restaurant, bar. AE, DC, MC, V. $$$$*

Imperial Hotel Tramontano. The birthplace of the poet Torquato Tasso—the first of an impressive list of literary credentials—this palatial villa lies within a semitropical garden in the center of Sorrento. The sumptuous furnishings and Belle Epoque tone are set off by the spectacular views out to sea. *Via Veneto 1, tel. 081/878–2588, fax 081/807–2344. 120 rooms with bath or shower. Facilities: restaurant, bar, garden, private beach, parking, conference rooms. Closed Dec.–Mar. AE, DC, MC, V. $$$*

Eden. In a quiet but central location, the Eden has a garden and bright, though undistinguished, bedrooms. The lounge and lobby have more character. It's an unpretentious but friendly hotel, although it can get crowded in high season. *Via Correale 25, tel. 081/878–1909, fax 081/807–2016. 60 rooms with bath or shower. Facilities: restaurant, bar, parking, pool, garden. AE, DC, MC, V. Closed Nov.–Feb. $$*

City. The convenient location and excellent value for the money are the best reasons to stay in this modest establishment, close to the bus and train stations. Bedrooms are small and functional. The atmosphere is relaxed, and the management is always ready with information and advice. *Corso Italia 221, tel. 081/877–2210. 12 rooms with shower. MC, V. $*

The Arts and Nightlife

The Arts

Theater
One of the most impressive theater seasons is Pompeii's late-summer festival of the performing arts, known as the **Panatenee Pompeiane.** This series of classical plays takes place in July and August. For information, contact one of the three information offices: Naples (tel. 081/268779), Pompeii (tel. 081/863–1041), or Rome (tel. 06/488–3748).

Music
A classical music festival known as **International Music Weeks** takes place throughout May in Naples. Concerts are held at the **Teatro San Carlo,** the Teatro Mercadante, and in the neoclassic Villa Pignatelli. For information, contact the Teatro San Carlo box office (Via San Carlo 93/f, tel. 081/797–2331).

Informal music festivals take place all summer long in the resorts of **Capri, Sorrento, Amalfi,** and **Ravello.** Contact local tourist offices for details.

Film
Each December, the **International Cinema Convention** in Sorrento draws an elite collection of producers, directors, and stars in a less frantic atmosphere than that of the festival in Cannes. While much of the activity revolves around deal making, a number of previews are screened, and the town sees the festival as a shot of energy in the middle of the quiet season. For details contact the Sorrento tourist office (*see* Important Addresses and Numbers in Essential Information, *above*).

Opera
Naples has a full opera season from fall through spring. The **Teatro San Carlo** (*see above*), where the season runs from December to May, is one of Italy's top opera houses.

Arts Festivals
The festival **Settembre a Borgo** is held in the picturesque setting of Caserta Vecchia in September. For information, contact the Caserta tourist information office (tel. 0823/321137).

Nightlife

In these parts, as elsewhere in southern Italy, nightlife usually takes the form of outdoor living in cafés and restaurants with views of the passing parade. Piazzas are lively until late in fair weather, especially in resort towns on the islands and on the Sorrento peninsula. Capri's Piazzetta is a classic example. Entertainment in the coastal resorts is mainly seasonal.

Bars
Most of the best bars have the attraction of a good location (overlooking the Bay of Naples, for example) or comfortable setting; there is

sometimes music and dancing, but these establishments cannot truly be called nightclubs.

Gabbiano (Via Partenope 26, Naples, tel. 081/764–5717). Expect to be part of a sophisticated crowd at this fashionable watering hole; there is usually live music.

Circolo dei Forestieri (Via De Maio 35, Sorrento). Here you'll get a memorable view of the Bay of Naples from the terrace. Drinks are moderately priced, and there is live music in summer.

Villa Pompeiana (Via Marina Grande 6, Sorrento, tel. 081/877–2428). This bar, located next to the Bellevue Syrene Hotel, has a garden terrace and an indoor tavern with an ancient-Roman setting. There's music in summer.

Nightclubs **Rosolino** (Via Nazario Sauro 5–7, Naples, tel. 081/764–0513). This recent addition to the Neapolitan entertainment scene also has a quiet piano bar and a restaurant with some moderately priced meals.

L'Africana (Vettica Maggiore, Praiano). This is the premier nightclub on the Amalfi Coast and is built into a fantastic grotto above the sea. Praiano itself is only a couple miles east of Positano on the coast road.

Discos **Shaker** (Via Nazario Sauro 24, Naples, tel. 081/416775). This disco, located in the prime entertainment neighborhood of Naples, attracts a mixed crowd of locals and guests from the nearby hotels.

Papillon (Via Manzoni 207, Naples, tel. 081/769–0800). This club caters to a young crowd.

Special Events Capri's **New Year's Eve** celebrations last all evening with dancing and music culminating in a magnificent fireworks display. On **New Year's Day** there are marching bands, pageants, and all the vigorous revelry you would expect on this exuberant island.

15 Apulia

*Bari, Brindisi, and
the Gargano Peninsula*

It's a pity that all most tourists see of Apulia (called Puglia by the Italians—English-speakers are really using the Latin term) is the blur outside their car or train windows as they hurtle toward Bari or Brindisi for ferry connections to Greece.

This ancient land, the heel and spur of Italy's boot, contains some of the most unspoiled scenery, interesting artistic and historical sites, and finest beaches of the entire Italian peninsula. What's more, aside from the increasingly popular seaside resorts and a few major attractions, the region is still relatively free of tourists. Instead, your trip will take you through a sunbaked countryside where expanses of silvery olive trees and giant prickly-pear cactus fight their way through the rocky soil, as if in defiance of the relentless summer heat. Local buildings, too, do their best to dispel the effects of the sun: Whitewashed ports stand coolly over the turquoise Mediterranean, and the landscape is studded with strange dwellings, called *trulli*, which look like pointed igloos made of stone.

The trulli date to the Middle Ages, but Apulia had long before been inhabited, conquered, and visited by travelers. The Greeks and later the Romans were quick to recognize the importance of this strategic peninsula, and among the nations later to raid or colonize Apulia were the Normans, Moors, and Spaniards, each leaving a mark. Some of the most impressive buildings are the Romanesque churches and the powerful castles built by 13th-century Holy Roman Emperor Frederick II of Swabia (part of present-day Bavaria), King of Sicily and Jerusalem. One of the outstanding personalities of the Middle Ages, he was dubbed "Wonder of the World" for his wide-ranging interests in literature, science, mathematics, and nature.

All these interests can still be pursued in present-day Apulia, but less intellectual attractions include the inexpensive and hearty cuisine, which uses local seafood and produce, and picks the best from more than 2,000 years of foreign influences. Colorful local markets provide the chance to purchase local handicrafts ranging from lace, wood carvings, and baskets to ceramic pots and painted clay whistles. Hundreds of miles of beaches and an extensive cave complex let you explore, exercise, or just cool off.

Essential Information

Important Addresses and Numbers

Tourist Information	**Bari** (Piazza Moro 32a, tel. 080/524–2361). **Brindisi** (Piazza Dionisi, tel. 0831/521944). **Lecce** (Piazza Sant 'Oronzo, tel. 0832/304443). **Taranto** (Corso Umberto 113, tel. 099/432392). **Trani** (Via Cavour 140, tel. 0883/588830; kiosk in Piazza della Repubblica, tel. 0883/43295). **Vieste (Gargano)** (Piazza Kennedy, tel. 0884/708806).
Emergencies	**Police, Ambulance, Fire,** tel. 113. This number will also put you in touch with the First Aid Service (Pronto Soccorso). **Late-Night Pharmacies.** Pharmacies take turns remaining open late and on Sunday. A list of hours is posted on each *farmacia* (pharmacy).
Travel Agencies	**Bari.** *CIT* (Via Abate Gimma 157, tel. 080/521–3552); *Wagon Lits (Thomas Cook)* (Via Cardassi 85, tel. 080/554–0588).

Car Rental   **Bari.** *Avis* (Via Zuppetta 5/a, tel. 080/524–7154); *Hertz* (Piazza Moro 33, tel. 524–2250).

Brindisi. *Avis* (Via del Mare 50, tel. 0831/526407); *Hertz* (c/o Silver Travel, Corso Garibaldi 95, tel. 0831/528333).

Foggia. *Avis* (train station, tel. 0881/678912); *Hertz* (Via Monfalcone 39, tel. 0881/608400).

Taranto. *Avis* (Corso Umberto 61, tel. 099/432278); *Hertz* (Via Pupino 19, tel. 099/433763).

Arriving and Departing by Plane and Train

By Plane   Alitalia flies regularly from other Italian cities to Bari and Brindisi. **Palese Airport** is 8 kilometers (5 miles) west of Bari; **Papola Casale Airport** is 5 kilometers (3 miles) north of Brindisi. Regular bus services connect both airports with the cities.

By Train   Bari is a transit point for train connections with northern Italy.

Getting Around

By Car   This is probably the best way to get around Apulia and it is the only way to see some of the more remote sights. Apulia is linked with the Italian *autostrada* (superhighway) system, making it just a four- or five-hour drive from Rome to the Gargano Peninsula or Bari. Roads are good, and major cities are linked by fast autostrade. Secondary roads connect the whole region, while more direct—but sometimes less scenic—routes provide a convenient link between Bari, Brindisi, and Lecce. Don't plan on any night driving in the countryside because the roads can become confusing without the aid of landmarks or large towns.

By Train   Good train service, operated by **FS** (Italian State Railways), links Bari to Brindisi, Lecce, and Taranto, but smaller destinations can often be reached only by completing the trip on a connecting bus operated by the railroad. The private **Ferrovie Sud-Est** (FSE) line connects the trulli area and Martina Franca with Bari and Taranto, and the fishing port of Gallipoli with Lecce.

By Bus   Direct, if not always frequent, connections operate between most destinations in Apulia. In many cases the bus service is actually the backup to the train service (*see above*).

Guided Tours

The **CIT** office in Bari (*see* Important Addresses and Numbers, *above*) is the best connection for guided tours in Apulia, which is otherwise poorly served by tour operators. The CIT office can put you in touch with one of a number of local operators that offer everything from chauffeur-driven cars to inclusion in part of a longer excursion (such as southern Italy).

Exploring Apulia

Apulia's attractions are so varied and scattered that you may want to take a full week or more to explore it at a leisurely pace, selecting two or three bases in different parts of the region and taking day trips to nearby sights.

If you are mainly interested in spending time at the beach, the promontory of Gargano in the north boasts some of Apulia's best coastline, although there are pleasant beach resorts within easy reach of most of the region's attractions. Convenient travel bases include Alberobello or Martina Franca in the trulli country (the region of dome-shaped stone dwellings); Lecce, near the tip of the heel; and the small ports of Barletta, Molfetta, and Trani, up the coast from Bari.

The following tours go northwest from Bari up the Adriatic coast to Barletta, then continue to the promontory of Gargano, where white-washed coastal villages and turquoise water contrast sharply with the dense forests and pilgrimage towns of the interior. Then you head back inland toward the white villages of the trulli district, from which you proceed to Taranto, Brindisi, and down to the Baroque city of Lecce, close to the Salento shores.

A word of warning is needed if you are driving in Bari or Brindisi. These cities are notorious for purse-snatching, car thefts, and break-ins. Make sure you lock everything in the trunk, and find a guarded parking space if possible.

Highlights for First-Time Visitors

Alberobello and the Trulli (Tour 3: The Trulli District).

Appian Way Terminus, Brindisi (Tour 4: Across the Heel and South to Lecce).

Basilica di Santa Croce, Lecce (Tour 4: Across the Heel and South to Lecce).

Castel del Monte (Tour 3: The Trulli District).

Foresta Umbra (Tour 2: The Gargano Peninsula).

Monte Sant' Angelo (Tour 2: The Gargano Peninsula).

Museo Archeologico, Bari (Tour 1: Around Bari).

Museo Nazionale, Taranto (Tour 4: Across the Heel and South to Lecce).

Tour 1: Around Bari

Numbers in the margin correspond to points of interest on the Apulia and Bari maps.

① **Bari** is a big, hectic, rough-and-tumble port and a transit point for travelers catching ferries across the Adriatic to Greece. Most of the city is set out in a logical 19th-century grid pattern, following the designs of Joachim Murat, Napoleon's brother-in-law and the King of the Two Sicilies. The heart of the modern town is Piazza della Libertà, but just beyond it, across Corso Vittorio Emanuele, is the *città vecchia* (old town), a maze of narrow, crooked streets on the promontory that juts out between Bari's old and new ports. Here,
② overlooking the sea and just off Via Venezia, is the **Basilica di San Nicola** (St. Nicholas), built in the 11th century to house the bones of St. Nicholas, who is better known to us as St. Nick, or Santa Claus. His remains are said to have been stolen by Bari sailors from Myra, in what is now Turkey. The basilica, a solid and powerful construction, was the only building to survive the otherwise wholesale destruction of Bari by the Normans in 1152. *Open daily 9–12, 5–7.*

Follow the narrow Strada del Carmine from behind the basilica to
③ reach the **Cattedrale** (Cathedral), a century younger than the basilica. The seat of the local bishop, it was the scene of many significant political marriages between important families in the Middle Ages.

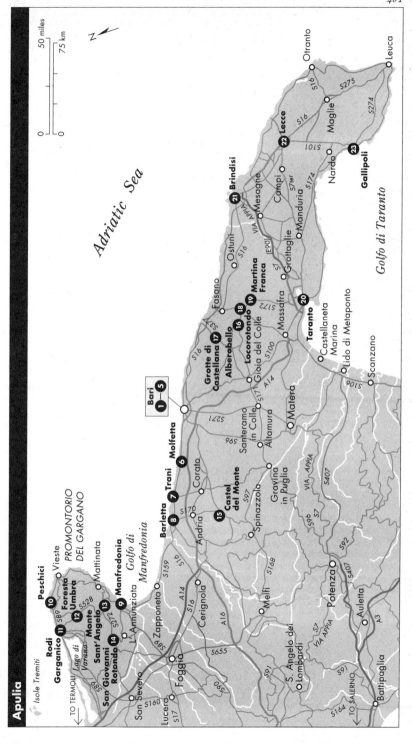

Apulia

Adriatic Sea

Isole Tremiti

TO TERMOLI

Rodi Garganico **10** **11**
Peschici **10**
Vieste
PROMONTORIO DEL GARGANO
Mattinata
Foresta Umbra **12**
Monte Sant'Angelo **13**
San Giovanni Rotondo **14**
Manfredonia **9**
Golfo di Manfredonia

Isole Tremiti
S89
S528
S272
S159
Lago di Varano
L'Amunziata
Zapponeta
S90
San Severo
S160
Lucera
S17
Foggia
S655
Cerignola
A16
A14
S16
S90
Melfi
S167
S168
Spinazzola
Gravina in Puglia
S96
VIA APPIA
S97
Altamura
Santeramo in Colle
S271
S96
Gioia del Colle
S100
S172
Matera
S7
S407
VIA APPIA
Castellaneta Marina
Lido di Metaponto
Castellaneta
Massafra
Taranto **20**
Golfo di Taranto
Scanzano
S106
Potenza
S92
Auletta
A3
S407
S. Angelo dei Lombardi
S91
VIA APPIA
S7
S91
TO SALERNO
Battipaglia
S164

Barletta **8**
Trani **7**
Molfetta **6**
Bari **1 — 5**
Corato
Andria
S170
Castel del Monte **15**
Ruvo
S98
Grotte di Castellana **17**
Alberobello **16**
Locorotondo **18**
Martina Franca **19**
Fasano
Ostuni
S16
S7ter
Campi
Mesagne
VIA APPIA
E90
Grottaglie
S7
Manduria
S7ter
Brindisi **21**
Lecce **22**
S16
S101
S16
Otranto
Maglie
Nardo
Gallipoli **23**
Leuca
S275
S274
S16

50 miles
75 km
0

Its solid architecture reflects the Romanesque style favored by the Normans of that period. *Open daily 9–12, 5–7.*

4 The huge **Castello** (Castle) looms behind the cathedral. The current building dates from the time of Holy Roman Emperor Frederick II, who rebuilt an existing Norman-Byzantine castle to his own exacting specifications. Designed more for powerful effect than for beauty, it looks out beyond the cathedral to the Porto Vecchio (Old Port), Bari's small harbor. Inside is an interesting collection of medieval Apulian art. *Admission: 4,000 lire. Open Tues.–Sun. 9–12, 3:30–5:30 (summer 4–7).*

From the castle, go south, crossing Piazza Massari and Piazza della **5** Libertà to take Via Cairoli to the **Museo Archeologico.** Inside is a fine collection of Apulian artifacts, including jewelry and weapons, some dating from the 7th century BC, that will leave you with a better understanding of why Apulia has been an important crossroads for more than 2,500 years. *Piazza Umberto I, tel. 080/521–1559. Admission free. Open Tues.–Sun. 9–12, 3:30–5:30 (summer 4–7).*

Time Out **Vecchia Bari** (Via Dante 47) is a good place for learning the secrets of Apulian cooking. Just take Via Sparano north one block from Piazza Umberto I, which is right behind the museum.

Leaving Bari, take the coastal road (S16) from the Castello northwest toward Molfetta, Trani, and Barletta, which have old ports reminiscent of Venetian ports such as Dubrovnik, across the Adriat-**6** ic Sea in Croatia. **Molfetta,** 25 kilometers (16 miles) from Bari, has an unusual 12th-century cathedral with distinct Byzantine features, such as the pyramid-shape covers to the three main domes. If you are in the area over Easter, don't miss Molfetta's colorful Holy Week processions.

❼ Trani, 18 kilometers (11 miles) farther, is the smallest of the three ports. Its old town has polished stone streets and buildings, medieval churches, and a harbor filled with fishing boats. The 11th-century **cathedral,** considered one of the finest in Apulia, is built on a spit of land jutting into the sea. Trani had a flourishing Jewish community in medieval times, and there is still a Via Sinagoga (Synagogue Street) in the old town. Two of the four synagogues that existed here still survive, as the 13th-century churches of **Santa Anna,** where there is still a Hebrew inscription, and **Santa Maria Scolanova.**

❽ In **Barletta,** 13 kilometers (8 miles) up the coast, don't miss the **Colossus,** a bronze statue over 15 feet tall, thought to be of the Byzantine Emperor Valentinian and dating from the 5th century AD. Part of Venice's booty after the sack of Byzantium's capital, Constantinople, in the 1200s, the Colossus was abandoned on the beach near Barletta when the ship carrying it to Venice foundered in a storm. It stands next to the church of San Sepolcro on Corso Vittorio Emanuele.

Tour 2: The Gargano Peninsula

Continue up the coast on S159 to the Gargano, the spur of Italy's boot, where the region's most attractive and popular beaches are found. Until a few years ago, this rocky peninsula of whitewashed coastal towns, wide sandy beaches, and craggy limestone cliffs topped by deep-green scrub pine was practically unknown: Some parts of the interior are still well off the usual tourist track. The beach-resort business has boomed in the past decade, though, and beaches can become crowded in midsummer.

❾ Manfredonia, a resort town on the southern side of the Gargano, is about 60 kilometers (37 miles) from Barletta. From there, take the winding coastal road (S89), which threads through miles of silvery olive groves interspersed with almond trees and prickly-pear cactus. Along the way you'll come across many local craftsmen's stalls selling homemade preserves, baskets, and carved olive-wood bowls and utensils. Vieste, a large town about 50 kilometers (30 miles) around on the tip of the spur, is the Gargano's main commercial cen-
❿ ⓫ ter. But continue on to the north shore resorts of **Peschici** and **Rodi Garganico,** whitewashed towns squeezed between the hills and the sea. You may want to make these your base for spending a few days exploring the beaches and coast.

Time Out   **Gabbiano** (Via Trieste 14) is a cheerful restaurant facing the sea in Rodi Garganico. Admire the view here while having a lunch of locally caught seafood.

Take S528 (midway between Peschici and Rodi Garganico) south to head back through the interior of the Gargano, where you'll discover a different world. In the middle of the peninsula is the majestic
⓬ Foresta Umbra (Shady Forest), a dense growth of beech, maple, sycamore, and oak generally found in more northerly climates, thriving here because of the altitude—3,200 feet above sea level. Between the trees are occasional dramatic vistas opening out over the Gulf of Manfredonia.

The interior is also important because of two centers for religious pilgrimage. Perched amid olive groves on the rugged white lime-
⓭ stone cliffs overlooking the gulf is the town of **Monte Sant'Angelo.**

Pilgrims have flocked here for nearly 1,500 years—among them, St. Francis of Assisi and the Crusaders setting off for the Holy Land from the then-flourishing port of Manfredonia. The town is centered on the **Sanctuary of San Michele,** built over the grotto where the Archangel Michael is believed to have appeared before shepherds in the year 490. Walk down a long series of steps to get to the grotto itself—on the walls you can see the hand tracings left by pilgrims as votive symbols. Steps lead left from the sanctuary down to the **Tomb of Rotari,** which is believed to have been a medieval baptistery, with some remarkable 12th-century reliefs. More steep steps lead up to the large ruined Norman castle, which dominates the town. Here you have the best chance to appreciate the intricate pattern of the streets and steps winding their way up the side of the valley. To the right, looking out from the castle, you can see the town's medieval quarter, the Rione Junno, a maze of little white houses squeezed into one corner of the narrow valley. To get there from the castle, take the steps down to Piazza Cappelletti and then turn right.

Time Out   Most shops in the Junno sell a local specialty called *ostia piena* (filled host), a pastry made with candied almonds and wafers similar to communion hosts. The best place to munch them is at the southern end of the Junno, by the Villa Comunale, where you can also savor the view of the Gulf of Manfredonia. Sunset is the best time for this treat.

⓮ About 25 kilometers (16 miles) west of Monte Sant'Angelo, along the winding S272, is the ancient village of **San Giovanni Rotondo,** a pilgrimage center that has grown up around the shrine and tomb of Padre Pio (1887–1968). The monk is revered for his pious life, for miraculous intercessions, and for having received the stigmata, the signs of Christ's wounds. The **Casa Sollievo della Sofferenza** (Foundation for the Mitigation of Suffering), supported through contributions from around the world, is a testament to the enduring appeal of this holy man.

A short ride south on S273, and then east (left) at L'Annunziata, will take you back to Manfredonia, where you can link up with the coastal road to return to Barletta.

Tour 3: The Trulli District

⓯ From Barletta, take S170 south for 30 kilometers (19 miles), through the important market town of Andria to **Castel del Monte,** one of Apulia's most impressive and mysterious monuments. Built on an isolated hill in the first half of the 13th century by Frederick II, Castel del Monte is a huge, bare, octagonal castle with eight towers: It can be seen for miles around and commands a stunning view. Very little is known about the structure, since virtually no records exist. It has none of the usual defense features associated with medieval castles, so it probably had little military significance. Some theories suggest it might have been built as a hunting lodge or may have served as an astronomical observatory or a stop for pilgrims on their quest for the Holy Grail. *Admission: 4,000 lire, children under 12 free. Open summer, Tues.–Sun. 9–6:30; winter, Tues.–Sun. 9–5.*

⓰ To reach **Alberobello,** the center of **trulli** country, continue on S170 south, then take S97 east to Gravina in Puglia, S96 east to Altamura, S171 east to Gioia del Colle, and then S604 to Alberobello.

The origins of the igloo-shaped trulli go back to the 13th century, and maybe further: The trulli are built of local limestone, without mortar, and with a hole in the top for smoke. Some are painted with mystical or religious symbols, some are isolated, and others are joined together with roofs on various levels. The trulli zone of Alberobello, where more than 1,000 trulli crowd together along steep, narrow streets, is a national monument. It is also one of the most popular tourist destinations in Apulia and a gold mine for people who enjoy shopping for souvenirs (*see* Shopping, *below*).

⑰ Near Alberobello, about 20 kilometers (12 miles) northwest, taking S172 then S377 toward the coast, is the **Grotte di Castellana,** a huge network of caves discovered in 1938. You can take one- or two-hour guided tours through the grottoes, which are filled with fantastically shaped stalagmites and stalactites: The grottoes constitute the largest network of caves on the Italian mainland. *Admission: 10,000 lire (1-hour tour) or 20,000 lire (2-hour tour). Open Apr.–Oct., daily 9–6:30; Nov.–Mar., daily 9:30–11:30, 2–5.*

⑱ Return to Alberobello, then continue on S172 southeast for 9 kilometers (5 miles) to **Locorotondo,** an attractive hillside town in the Itria Valley and still inside the trulli district. The *rotondo* in the town's name refers to the circular pattern of the houses, which is apparent from any vantage point at the top of the town.

⑲ Take S172 directly south for 6 kilometers (4 miles) to **Martina Franca,** an attractive town with a dazzling mixture of medieval and Baroque architecture in the light-colored local stone. Ornate balconies hang above the twisting, narrow streets, with little alleys leading off into the surrounding hills. Martina Franca was developed as a military stronghold in the 14th century, when a surrounding wall with 24 towers was built, but now all that remains of that role are the four gates that had been the only entrances to the town. Each July and August Martina Franca holds a music festival (*see* The Arts and Nightlife, *below*).

Tour 4: Across the Heel and South to Lecce

⑳ Take S172 from Martina Franca, or A14 and S7 from Bari, to reach **Taranto.** Taranto—the stress is on the first syllable—was an important port even in Roman times. It occupies an excellent position toward the back of the instep of the Italian boot, on a broad bay, the Mare Grande, which is connected to a small internal basin, the Mare Piccolo, by two narrow channels, one man-made and one natural. The old town is on an island between the larger and smaller bodies of water, while the modern city stretches inward along the mainland. Little remains of Taranto's past except the 14th-century church of San Domenico, at one end of the island, and the city's maritime heritage: Taranto is the home of a famous naval academy.

However, one shining beacon to shed light on the millennia of local history is the **Museo Nazionale,** where most of the large collection of prehistoric, Greek, and Roman artifacts come from the immediate vicinity. The museum is just over the bridge from the old town on the promontory. Some of the prehistoric items from Apulian tombs date to before 1000 BC, but more plentiful are the examples of intricate craftsmanship in the Greek jewelry from around 500 BC. The museum is a memorable testament to the importance of this ancient port, which has always taken full advantage of its unique trading position at the end of the Italian peninsula. *Corso Umberto 41, tel. 099/432113. Admission: 6,000 lire. Open daily 9–2, in summer also Tues.–Sun. 3–7. Closed national holidays.*

Time Out Overlooking the channel separating the old and new towns and just next to the bridge itself, **Barcaccia** (Corso Due Mari 22, closed Mon.) is a restaurant with a memorable view. It also has good seafood and pasta.

The modern E90 (S7) autostrada, which follows the course of the Via Appia (*see below*), makes short work of the 72-kilometer (45-mile) west–east crossing of Italy's heel. It's just as well, because this far south, the mountains run out of steam and the land is uniformly flat, although agriculturally quite important. Less than an hour from Taranto, but already on the eastern (Adriatic) coast, you will reach 🔞 **Brindisi,** long one of Italy's most important ports. (The first syllable, like that of Taranto, is stressed.)

Most people think of Brindisi only in terms of its ferry port, which links Italy with Greece. Although this impression fails to give credit to the broader importance of the city (it has a population of nearly 100,000), it is a present-day reminder of the role Brindisi has always played as gateway to the eastern Mediterranean and beyond. The core of the city is at the head of a deep channel, which branches into two harbors with the city between them. Look for the steeple of the **Duomo** (Cathedral) to get your bearings, but go beyond it and down the steps to the water's edge. Just to the left, along Viale Regina Margherita, you can see a tall **Roman column** and the base of another one next to it. These were built in the 2nd century AD and marked the end of the **Via Appia** (Appian Way), the Imperial Roman road from the capital to the important southern seaport. Brindisi has seen a constant flow of naval and mercantile traffic over the centuries, and in the Middle Ages was an important launching point for several Crusades to the Holy Lands.

Return to the Duomo to have a look at the mosaic floor in the apse; the floor dates from the 12th century, although much of the rest of the cathedral was rebuilt in the 18th. From the front of the Duomo take Via Tarantini away from the Roman columns; this leads on to Via Castello, where, about 500 yards from the Duomo, you turn right onto Via della Libertà. Just ahead is **Castello Svevo,** another of the defense fortifications built by the illustrious Frederick II in the 13th century. It guards the larger of the two inner harbors, and from the far side (the harbor-front side) you can look back on the Roman column and the jutting old section of the city.

The modern S16 whisks you along the 40 kilometers (25 miles) southeast to **Lecce,** the crowning jewel on the tour of Apulia. Although Lecce was founded before the time of the ancient Greeks, it is almost always associated with the term Lecce Baroque. This is because of a citywide impulse in the 17th century to redo the town in the Baroque fashion. But this was Baroque with a difference. While Baroque architecture is often heavy and monumental, here it took on a lighter, more fanciful tone. Just look at the **basilica di Santa Croce,** with the **palazzo della Prefettura** abutting it. While every column, window, pediment, and balcony is given a curling Baroque touch—and then an extra one for good measure—the overall effect is lighthearted. This is partly because the scale of the buildings is unintimidating and partly because the local stone used is a glowing honey color: It couldn't look menacing if it tried.

Coming out of the basilica, turn left, and 100 yards later, you reach **Piazza Sant'Oronzo,** in the middle of which is a Roman column of the same era and style as the one remaining in Brindisi. Next to the column is the **Roman amphitheater:** The shallow rows of seats suggest a small-scale version of the Roman Colosseum or Verona's arena.

Drive 37 kilometers (23 miles) south of Lecce on S101 to rejoin the
㉓ Gulf of Taranto at the town of **Gallipoli.** The modern section of town
lies on the mainland; turn right on the main street at the end of the
central square and cross a 17th-century bridge to the old town,
crowded onto its own small island in the gulf. The Greeks called it
Kallipolis, the Romans Anxa. Like the famous Turkish town of the
same name on the Dardanelles, the Italian Gallipoli occupies a strategic location and thus was repeatedly attacked through the centuries—by the Normans in 1071, the Venetians in 1484, the British in
1809. The historic quarter, a mesh of narrow alleys and squares, is
guarded by a formidable Aragonese **castello,** a massive fortification
that grew out of an earlier Byzantine fortress that you can still see at
the southeast corner. Other sights in town include the baroque
Duomo and the **church of La Purissima,** with its stuccoed interior as
elaborate as a wedding cake (note especially the tiled floor). To return to Taranto, take S174 back up the coast 93 kilometers (58
miles).

What to See and Do with Children

Children generally enjoy Apulia's archaeological diversions, such as
the Museo Archeologico in **Bari** and the Roman amphitheater in
Lecce, particularly if they are old enough to know something about
the ancient Greeks and Romans. Stop in **Barletta** to see the 15-foot-
tall Colossus, a Byzantine statue from the 5th century AD. The
igloolike trulli dwellings intrigue children, as do the mysterious
Castel del Monte and **Grotte di Castellana,** also in the trulli district.
Another grotto, in the town of **Monte Sant'Angelo,** the site of a supposed angelic visitation in 490, captures young imaginations. The
beaches and forests of the Gargano promontory are great places for
letting off steam, and many towns stage puppet shows in their public
gardens, which kids should enjoy. If you're visiting the area around
Easter time, young and old alike enjoy the Holy Week processions in
Molfetta.

Off the Beaten Track

Tremiti Islands. A ferry service from Termoli, north of the Gargano
(1 hour 40 minutes), and a hydrofoil service from Vieste, Peschici,
Rodi Garganico, and Manfredonia (40 minutes to 1 hour 40 minutes)
connect the mainland with these three small islands north of the
Gargano. Although somewhat crowded with Italian tourists in summer, they are famed for their sea caves, pine forests, and craggy
limestone formations. There are also interesting medieval churches
and fortifications on the islands.

Shopping

Apulia is rich in folk art, reflecting the influences of the many nations that have passed through the region or ruled it. Don't expect
too many high-fashion boutiques of the sort you'd find in Rome, Milan, Florence, or Venice. Instead, look for handmade goods, such as
pottery with traditional designs, and baskets, textiles, and carved
wood figures. These are on sale in shops and in open markets, where
some bargaining can enter into the purchase. The following are the
best towns and villages in which to pick up some fine handicrafts.

Alberobello **Rugs** and **fabrics** are the best bets here, but because of the town's
popularity with tourists, there is also a good deal of shoddy materi-

al. In the trulli zone, you'll find small shops selling hand-painted **clay figurines.**

Andria **Copper** objects and containers are made and sold here.

Lecce **Wrought-iron work** is the local specialty, but you should also look for works in **papier-mâché** (particularly nativity scenes).

Maglie **Fabrics** and **embroidery** are featured here.

Monte Sant'Angelo Local craftsmen make and sell **wooden utensils, furniture,** and **wrought-iron goods.** Shoemaker Domenico Palena displays his unique **leather sculptures** at his tiny shop in the Junno quarter.

Sports

Biking It's fun to see the hill towns and coastal villages on two wheels. You can rent bikes in most of the towns on our tours, but some of the recommended outlets are listed here.

Bari. *G.S. De Benedictus* (Via Nitti 23, tel. 080/574–4345).
Gioia del Colle. *G.S. Gioauto Renault* (Via Vittorio Emanuele, tel. 080/830417).
Manfredonia. *G.S. Cicli Castriotta* (Viale Beccarini 7, tel. 0884/23424).

Fishing For information on approved spots and license applications, contact **Federazione Italiana Pesca Sportiva** (Molo Pizzoli, Bari, tel. 080/524–7070).

Golf Apulia's only 18-hole golf course is the **Riva dei Tessali** (Marina di Ginosa, 40 kilometers [25 miles] west of Taranto along the coast road, tel. 099/643–9007).

Sailing Many of the larger coastal hotels offer guests the use of sailboats. Towns with clubs or municipal facilities include **Barletta** (Via Cristoforo Colombo, tel. 0883/33354); **Brindisi** (Lega Navale, Via Vespucci, tel. 0831/418824); and **Taranto** (Lega Navale, Lungomare Vittorio Emanuele II, tel. 099/93801).

Spelunking The **Grotte di Castellana** (tel. 080/896–5511) (*see* Tour 3: The Trulli District, *above*) are mainland Italy's largest cave complex.

Tennis Like sailing, tennis is offered at many of the larger hotels in Apulia. Public or club courts are located in **Brindisi** (Via Ciciriello, tel. 0831/521057); **Lecce** (Piazza Arco di Trionfo, tel. 0832/306142); and **Molfetta** (Via Dante Alighieri 5, tel. 080/911921).

Beaches

For the Italians and other tourists who return each summer, the sea is one of the major attractions of Apulia. The beaches along the **Gargano Peninsula,** although no longer "undiscovered," offer safe swimming and sandy beaches. The whole coastline between **Bari** and **Brindisi** is well served with beach facilities. In even the smallest villages you'll find beaches where there are changing rooms and—important in the blazing Apulian sun—beach umbrellas. If you don't mind venturing farther afield, try **Gallipoli,** on the south coast of the heel (take S101 from Lecce). The combination of historic town center and ample swimming and water-sports facilities makes it a good choice for families.

Dining and Lodging

Dining   Anyone who likes to eat will love traveling in Apulia. Southern cuisine is hearty and healthy, based on homemade pastas and cheeses, fresh vegetables, seafood, and local olive oil. Open markets and delicatessens burst with local fruits, vegetables, pastries, sausages, smoked meats, and cheeses.

Here you will find dishes unavailable elsewhere in Italy, such as *'ncapriata*, also called *favi e fogghi* (a delicious purée of fava beans served as a first course with a side dish of bitter chicory or other cooked vegetables). *Focaccia barese* (stuffed pizza) makes a great snack or lunch.

Apulia's pasta specialties include *orecchiette* (small, flat, oval pieces of pasta), *troccoli* (homemade noodles cut with a special ridged rolling pin), and *strascenate* (rectangles of pasta with one rough side and one smooth side). Among the many typical sauces is *salsa alla Sangiovanniello* (made with olive oil, capers, anchovies, parsley, and hot peppers), from Brindisi.

Don't miss the dairy products, such as ricotta and buttery *burrata* cheese, and remember that Apulia has a wealth of excellent local wines, ranging from the strong white wine of Martina Franca to the sweet red Aleatico di Puglia, and the sweet white Moscato di Trani to the rich, dry red Castel del Monte.

Highly recommended restaurants are indicated by a star ★.

Category	Cost*
$$$$	over 85,000 lire
$$$	60,000–85,000 lire
$$	25,000–60,000 lire
$	Under 25,000 lire

per person, including house wine, service, and tax

Lodging   There has been a rapid development of tourist facilities in some areas of Apulia, particularly along the miles of sandy beaches on the Gargano spur, now one of the most popular summer resorts for Italians. Here, and elsewhere on the coast, big white "Mediterranean"-style beach hotels have sprung up one after the other. Most are similar in design, price, and quality. In the busy season, many cater only to guests paying full board (lodging plus three meals per day at the hotel) or half-board (lodging plus breakfast and one other meal per day at the hotel) on longer stays, and it is best to make your reservations through a travel agent.

Elsewhere in Apulia, particularly outside the big cities, hotel accommodations are still limited, and those available are generally modest—both in amenities and price—though this may be more than compensated for by friendly service. Some places, such as Bari during the annual Trade Fair in September, will require reservations.

Many establishments, particularly the beach resorts, close during the winter months, so check for this also when choosing accommodations. And remember that in a region like this that gets blazing hot in summer and bitter cold in winter, air-conditioning and central heating are important.

Highly recommended lodgings are indicated by a star ★.

Category	Cost*
$$$$	over 300,000 lire
$$$	160,000–300,000 lire
$$	100,000–160,000 lire
$	under 100,000 lire

All prices are for a standard double room for two, including service and 9% IVA (19% for deluxe hotels).

Alberobello

Dining

Il Poeta Contadino. Proprietor Marco Leonardo serves "creative regional cooking" in this rustic-style restaurant. Set in the heart of the attractive trulli zone, it features an outdoor terrace and candlelit tables. Specialties to look for are fish platters and a house antipasto selection. *Via Indipendenza 21, tel. 080/721917. Lunch reservations advised. Dress: casual. AE, DC, MC, V. Closed Mon. and Jan. 7–Feb. 14. $$–$$$*

★ **Trullo d'Oro.** This welcoming restaurant occupies five trulli houses and is decorated in the rustic style, with dark wood beams, whitewashed walls, and an open hearth. Local country cooking includes dishes using horse meat as well as lamb and veal, vegetable and cheese antipasti, pasta dishes with crisp raw vegetables on the side, and almond pastries. Among the specialties are roast lamb with *lampasciuni* (a type of wild onion) and spaghetti *al trullo*, made with tomatoes, garlic, olive oil, *rughetta* (arugula, a bitter green), and four cheeses. *Via F. Cavallotti 29, tel. 080/721820. Reservations required. Dress: casual. AE, DC, MC, V. Closed Mon. $$*

Pugliese. A simple, homey restaurant with bare white walls in the trulli zone, Pugliese serves local dishes and has outdoor tables. Try the orecchiette with a sauce of cream, mushrooms, and pecorino (ewe's milk) cheese or *pannette alla Pugliese*, which has peppers, ground meat, mushrooms, and fresh tomatoes. *Via F. Gigante 4, tel. 080/721437. Reservations advised in high season. Dress: casual. AE, DC, MC, V. Closed Mon. during winter. $*

Lodging

Dei Trulli. Trulli-style cottages in a pine wood near the trulli zone make this a pleasant hotel, decorated with rustic furnishings including folk art rugs. There is a modestly priced restaurant serving local specialties. *Via Cadore 28, tel. 080/932–3555, fax 080/932–3560. 33 rooms with bath. Facilities: outdoor pool, minibars, garden. AE, MC, V. $$$*

Astoria. The undistinguished but comfortably modern Astoria is conveniently located near the train station and the trulli zone. Most rooms have big private balconies, and there is a garden as well as a moderately priced restaurant serving local dishes, such as homemade orecchiette and fava bean purée with chicory. *Viale Bari 11, tel. 080/932–3320, fax 080/721290. 47 rooms with bath or shower. Facilities: garden, restaurant, bar, parking. AE, DC, MC, V. $$*

Bari

Dining

Ristorante al Pescatore. This is one of Bari's best fish restaurants, located in the old town opposite the castle and just around the corner from the Duomo. The cooking is done outside, where (in summer) you can sit amid a cheerful clamor of quaffing and dining. Try the *céfalo* (mullet) if it is available, accompanied by crisp salad and a carafe of invigorating local wine. *Piazza Federico II di Svevia, tel. 080/523–7039. Reservations advised in high season. Dress: casual. AE, DC, MC, V. Closed Mon. $$*

Lodging **Sheraton Nicolaus.** This large, modern hotel on the edge of the city is easily reached by car from highway S16, which skirts the congested center of town. It caters mainly to businesspeople and is well-equipped for meetings, conferences, and banquets. Rooms are spacious and comfortable, with the usual Sheraton amenities. There's even an indoor swimming pool and sauna. *Via Agostino Ciasca 9, tel. 080/504-2626, fax 080/504-2058. 175 rooms with bath. Facilities: bar, restaurant, garden, garage. AE, DC, MC, V. $$$$*

Bristol. The Bristol is a good choice in the center of Bari's modern section, halfway between the train station and the old town. One of the few Bari hotels not geared exclusively to a business clientele, it has well-equipped first- and second-story rooms with modern furnishings. The pink decor and potted plants make for a pleasant, relaxed atmosphere. *Via Calefati 15, tel. 080/521-1503, fax 080/521-1503. 18 rooms with shower. AE, DC, MC, V. $$*

Barletta **Bacco.** Here is a place where you can dine in style. Elegantly furnished and centrally located, the Bacco has silver cutlery, crystal, and flowers and candles on each table; there is a piano bar in the evening. It serves innovative regional dishes, such as *gamberi al basilico* (shrimp with basil), *spigola ai frutti di mare* (sea bass with shellfish), and *capretto murgiano ai funghi cardoncelli* (goat with mushrooms). *Via Sipontina 10, tel. 0883/571000. Reservations advised. Jacket and tie required. AE, DC, MC, V. Closed Sun., Mon., and Dec. 27–Jan. 5, Aug. $$$$*

Dining
★

La Casaccia. Located near the castle, this simple restaurant serves home cooking and local dishes, such as homemade orecchiette and *penne piccanti* (spicy macaroni). *Via Cavour 40, tel. 0883/533719. Reservatons not required. Dress: casual. No credit cards. $$*

Brindisi **Majestic.** A modern hotel across from the train station and near the port, the Majestic is fully air-conditioned and furnished in comfortable, though uninspired, style, with carpeting on the walls and wooden furniture. Rooms 128, 228, and 328 have windows overlooking a public park. *Corso Umberto 151, tel. 0831/222941, fax 0831/524071. 68 rooms with bath. Facilities: parking, restaurant. AE, DC, MC, V. $$$*

Lodging

Mediterraneo. Comfort and a convenient central location are the advantages of this modern, air-conditioned hotel—though it is less accessible from the port than the Majestic. Most rooms have balconies, and there is a moderate restaurant. *Viale Aldo Moro 70, tel. 0831/82811, fax 0831/87858. 69 rooms with bath. Facilities: garage, restaurant. AE, DC, MC, V. $$*

Castel del Monte **Ostello di Federico.** This large, beautifully positioned restaurant, at the foot of the hill on which the castle rises, has a terrace overlooking splendid scenery, plus a bar, and a pizzeria with a wood oven. The restaurant serves local dishes, including *orecchiette a rape* (pasta with greens), and local cheeses, such as ricotta and creamy burrata. *Castel del Monte, tel. 0883/569877. Reservations preferred. Dress: casual. No credit cards. Closed Mon. $$*

Dining

Castellana Grotte **Al Parco Chiancafredda.** The refined ambience and cuisine of this restaurant, which is set apart from the tourist haunts in the area, make it pricier than its neighbors. But the food and service are worth the extra cost: Try such regional dishes as *sformato di verdura* (a kind of vegetable stew) and *agnello alla castellanese* (local lamb). *Via Chiancafredda 12, tel. 080/896-8710. Reservations preferred. Dress: casual. MC, V. Closed Tues. and Nov. $$*

Dining
★

Taverna degli Artisti. Located near the caves, this rustic tavern-style restaurant with a big garden specializes in local home cooking, such as roast lamb, homemade orecchiette, and dishes with fanciful names like *cannelloni all'Ernesto, timballo fine del mondo* (end-of-the-world timbale), and *involtini al purgatorio* (purgatory roulades). *Via Vito Matarrese 27, tel. 080/896–8234. Reservations not required. Dress: casual. No credit cards. Closed Thurs. Oct.–June and Dec. $$*

Castellaneta Marina
Lodging
★

Villa Giusy. About an hour's drive along the coast from Taranto, modern amenities blend with an old-fashioned flavor in this little resort hotel in a pinewood only 300 yards from a wide sandy beach. Most rooms have a balcony. There's an inexpensive restaurant serving local specialties; half or full board is required from 20 July to 20 August, at reasonable rates. *Via Sputnik 4, tel. 099/843–0031, fax 099/843–0031. 24 rooms with bath. Facilities: garden, pool, children's playground, restaurant. MC, V. $$*

Foggia
Dining
★

Mangiatoia. This rustic-style restaurant, on the main road to Bari, near the Foggia Agricultural Fairgrounds, has arches, hanging lamps, white walls, and wood-beamed ceilings that preserve some of the characteristics of the farmhouse it once was. Inside there's air-conditioning, but you can dine outdoors in a large garden, where tables made from wagon wheels surround an old well. Seafood is the specialty; fish and shellfish are displayed live in tanks. Chef Giovanni Prencipe will supply recipes for dishes, such as *spaghetti ai datteri di mare al cartoccio* (spaghetti with razor clams in bags), orecchiette with sauce and grated ricotta dura cheese, and fettucine in a creamy scampi sauce. *Via Virgilio 2, tel. 0881/634457. Reservations advised. AE, DC, MC, V. Closed Mon. $$*

San Giorgio. This lively pizzeria and restaurant near the train station has a predominantly young crowd. If you're not tempted by the sizzling pizzas (paid for by the meter!), you can choose from an array of pastas, such as the deliciously creamy *maccheroni alla Zozzone* (pasta with bacon, tomato sauce, Parmesan, and cream) and meat and fish main courses. There's a good-value fixed-price menu available for 18,000 lire. *Via Monfalcone 25, tel. 0881/677090. Reservations advised weekends. Dress: casual. MC, V. Closed Mon. $*

Lodging

Cicolella. Located near the station, this 1920s hotel has modern amenities and tastefully decorated rooms, a few of which have a balcony. There are also some suites that are particularly recommended, though these fall into the $$$$ category. There is also a $$ restaurant that specializes in international dishes; you can also find some well-prepared local dishes. *Via Ventiquattro Maggio 60, tel. 0881/688890, fax 0881/678984. 106 rooms with bath. Facilities: garage, restaurant, minibars. AE, DC, MC, V. $$$*

Gallipoli
Dining
★

Marechiaro. You have to cross a little bridge to this simple portside restaurant, which is actually not far from the town's historic center. It's built out onto the sea and decorated with wood paneling and flowers. Terraces right on the water provide panoramic views of the coast. Try the renowned *zuppa di pesce alla gallipolina* (fish stew made without tomatoes), succulent shellfish, and linguine with seafood. *Lungomare Marconi, tel. 0833/266143. Reservations advised weekends. Dress: casual. AE, DC, MC, V. Closed Tues. Oct.–May. $$*

Lodging
★

Costa Brada. The rooms all have terraces with sea views at the Costa Brada, a modern white beach hotel in classic Mediterranean design. The interiors are comfortable and tastefully decorated; rooms 110, 111, 113, and 114 are larger and directly overlook the beach. There is a beach snack bar and a restaurant specializing in seafood. The hotel accepts only half-board or full-board guests in the high season. *At Baia Verde beach, Litoranea Santa Maria di Leuca, tel. 0833/22551,* *fax 0833/22555. 87 rooms with bath. Facilities: indoor and outdoor pool, gymnasium, garden, tennis, sauna, restaurant, minibars. AE, DC, MC, V. $$$*

Le Sirenuse. There is a private beach and pinewoods at this gleaming white Mediterranean-style beach hotel complex. It is air-conditioned, with comfortable rooms whose terraces have good views of the coast. Half- or full-board is required in high season. *At Baia Verde beach, tel. 0833/273851, fax 0833/22539. 125 rooms with bath. Facilities: pool, garden, tennis, playground. MC, V. Closed Nov.– Mar. $$*

Gioia del Colle
Dining

Corte dei Sannaci. There is an appetizing mix of regional and nouvelle cuisine at this large rustic restaurant in a restored antique farmstead outside town. The service is friendly, and the waiters will help you choose from the many specials. For the main course, try the mixed grill of meats. *35 km (22 mi) south of Bari on SS100, tel. 080/ 998–1270. Reservations advised weekends. Dress: casual. AE, MC, V. Closed Tues. and Nov. $$*

Lecce
Dining

Guido & Figli. This is one of the busiest eateries in town, trading on its well-deserved reputation of quality food served in sympathetic surroundings. Located in spacious vaulted premises in the center of town (near the castle), the restaurant/pizzeria also offers an inexpensive self-service selection at lunchtime. In the evening, try such local dishes as orecchiette *ragutate* (pasta in a rich meat sauce) or linguine agli scampi. There is a wide choice of fish and meat, and for a real blowout, finish off with one of the homemade desserts. The only drawback may be slow service on weekends. *Via Venticinque Luglio 14, tel. 0832/305868. Reservations advised weekends. Dress: casual. AE, MC, V. Closed Mon. $$*

Taverna di Carlo V. The emphasis here is on nutritious, locally produced fare, served in an intimate, informal environment in the heart of Lecce. Among the traditional starters, you can choose *zuppa di farro e ceci* (grain and chickpea soup), while the *polpette leccesi al sugo* (meatballs) makes a good entrée. *Via Palmieri 46, tel. 0832/ 248818. Reservations not necessary. Dress: casual. DC, MC, V. Closed Sun. dinner, Mon., and a week in mid-Aug. $$*

Lodging

President. Located in the modern business center of town, this large and modern first-class hotel has comfortable rooms and a restaurant. Conference rooms and function rooms cater to the business clientele, which finds the President convenient and efficient. *Via Salandra 6, tel. 0832/311881, fax 0832/594321. 154 rooms with bath. Facilities: restaurant, parking. AE, DC, MC, V. $$$*

Risorgimento. An old-fashioned hotel in a converted palace in the heart of the Baroque old town, the Risorgimento combines historic charm and decor with modern comfort. There is a restaurant, cocktail lounge, and roof garden with a great view of the town. *Via Augusto Imperatore 19, tel. 0832/242125, fax 0832/245571. 57 rooms with bath or shower. Facilities: restaurant, conference rooms, roof garden. AE, DC, MC, V. $$*

Cappello. This is a popular choice close to the train station but outside the old city walls, about a 10-minute walk from the center of town. Rooms are small but clean and comfortable, equipped with telephone and television. Reservations are advised. *Via Montegrappa 4, tel. 0832/308881, fax 0832/301535. 32 rooms with bath or shower. Facilities: bar, garage. AE, DC, MC, V. $*

Manfredonia
Lodging

Gargano. The rooms in this typical big white beach hotel are decorated in blue and white and have terraces. The disco/bar keeps the atmosphere lively on summer evenings. Rates are at the bottom of the price category. *Viale Beccarini 2, tel. 0884/27621, fax 0884/*

26021. 46 rooms with bath or shower. Facilities: pool, restaurant, garage. MC, V. $$

Martina Franca
Dining
★

Arcobaleno. About 10 kilometers (6 miles) from Martina Franca, halfway to Ostuni, this restaurant is one of the best in the area. The specialty is an antipasto that offers as many as 12 tasty items, ranging from freshly prepared vegetable tidbits to marinated meats in a variety of sauces. The unusual pasta dishes are favorites, too. *Via Monte La Croce 105, Cisternino, tel. 080/718247. Reservations not necessary. Dress: casual. AE, MC, V. Closed Tues. $$*

La Tavernetta. This small restaurant with a vaulted ceiling in the old town center serves good home cooking and local specialties, starting with a pottery bowl full of local olives to nibble with the excellent house wine. Specialties include fava bean purée with cooked chicory and orecchiette with a side dish of *cocomero* (a vegetable that looks like a miniature round watermelon but tastes like a cross between a cucumber and a honeydew melon). Main-dish specialties include huge portions of mixed grilled lamb, liver, and spicy local sausage. *Corso Vittorio Emanuele 30, tel. 080/706323. Reservations not necessary. Dress: casual. No credit cards. Closed Mon. $$*

Lodging

Park Hotel San Michele. This garden hotel makes a pleasant base for excursions in the warm months when you can take a refreshing dip in the pool between jaunts. There are few frills, but the rooms have the basic comforts and many have views of the garden. It's favored by local businesspeople for meetings and dinners. *Viale Carella 9, tel. 080/880–7053, fax 080/880–8895. 86 rooms with bath or shower. Facilities: pool, restaurant, bar, parking. AE, DC, MC, V. $$*

Mattinata
Lodging

Baia delle Zagare. On the shore road around the Gargano Peninsula, north of Mattinata, Baia delle Zagare is a secluded, modern group of cottages overlooking an attractive inlet. An elevator takes you down to a private beach, and the hotel restaurant is good enough to keep you on the premises all day. (You're expected to take full board in August.) *Strada Litoranea (17 km [10 mi] northeast), tel. 0884/4155, fax 0884/4884. 144 rooms with shower. Facilities: pool, tennis, garden, restaurant. MC, V. Closed Oct.–May. $$–$$$*

Alba del Gargano. Although located in the center of town, the Alba provides a restful atmosphere; large balconies overlook a quiet courtyard garden and a frequent (and free) bus service connects with a private beach, where you can use the hotel's beach chairs and umbrellas. The hotel is modern, the rooms are comfortably furnished, and there is a good restaurant. *Corso Matino, tel. 0884/4771, fax 0884/4772. 43 rooms with shower. Facilities: garden, private beach, bar, restaurant, garage. AE, MC, V. $$*

Monte Sant'Angelo
Lodging

Hotel Rotary. This simple but welcoming modern hotel is set amid olive and almond groves just outside town. Each room has a terrace with a good view of the Gulf of Manfredonia. *Via per Pulsano, tel. 0884/62146. 24 rooms with shower. Facilities: restaurant. MC, V. $*

Ostuni
Dining
★

Chez Elio. Enjoy local dishes and a memorable view of the coastline from the terrace of this modern restaurant, which is set in green hills outside town. Inside, white walls and table linens contrast with decorative plants and bright flowers, giving a light, fresh atmosphere. Specialties include orecchiette with tomato sauce and *tagliatelle* noodles with blueberries. *Via dei Colli Selva 66, tel. 0831/302030. Reservations advised in summer. Dress: casual. AE, MC, V. Closed Mon. and Sept. $$*

Lodging

Incanto. A modest, modern hotel, it's located outside the old town, which you can admire from many rooms, along with the countryside and the sea in the distance. The decor and rooms are basic, but it's adequate as an overnight base for seeing the area. *Via dei Colli, tel. 0831/301781, fax 0831/338302. 74 rooms with shower. Facilities: parking, restaurant. AE, DC, MC, V. $$*

Peschici **Valle Clavia.** Olive and pine trees surround this modern, functional
Lodging hotel located near the beach. Ask for room 30, which has a view of the sea. There is a hotel restaurant. *Valle Clavia, tel. 0884/964209, fax 0884/964303. 51 rooms with bath. Facilities: garden, tennis court. MC, V. Closed Oct.–May. $$*

Rodi **Mizar.** Simple, comfortably furnished rooms with terraces look out
Garganico over the sea in this large Mediterranean-style hotel. Local seafood is
Lodging the attraction in the hotel restaurant. *Via Ippocampo, Lido del Sole, tel. 0884/97021, fax 0884/97022. 54 rooms with bath. Facilities: private beach, solarium, restaurant. AE, MC, V. Closed Oct.– May. $$*

Taranto **Grand Hotel Delfino.** A big, modern, well-equipped downtown hotel
Lodging catering to business clients, the Grand Hotel Delfino has airy rooms with balconies. The restaurant serves regional specialties, especially seafood. *Viale Virgilio, tel. 099/3205, fax 099/3205. 198 rooms with bath or shower. Facilities: garden, pool, minibars, restaurant. AE, DC, MC, V. $$$*

Trani **Antica Cattedrale.** Just in front of the cathedral, on a spit of land jut-
Dining ting out into the sea, the Antica Cattedrale has an antique flavor,
★ with stonework, vaulted ceilings, and terra-cotta tile floors. There are also tables outside. Regional specialties are presented imaginatively: Try the baked crêpes (similar to cannelloni); risotto made with salmon, crab, and cream; lobster; or grilled fish. *Piazza Archivio 2, tel. 0883/586568. Reservations required for Sunday lunch and dinner on summer weekends. AE, DC, MC, V. Closed Mon. $$*

Lodging **Royal.** Formerly known as the Holiday, this is an unpretentious modern hotel near the train station. Furnishings are comfortable, and there is a piano bar by the restaurant. *Via De Robertis 29, tel. 0883/588777, fax 0883/582224. 55 rooms with shower. Facilities: restaurant, bar, garage. AE, DC, MC, V. $$–$$$*
Trani. Like the Royal, the Trani is simple, modern, and near the station. It offers good-value accommodations and has a restaurant. *Corso Imbriani 137, tel. 0883/588010, fax 0883/587625. 51 rooms with bath. Facilities: restaurant. AE, DC, MC, V. $$*
Hotel al Duomo. Situated above the Antica Cattedrale restaurant, and under the same ownership, this small hotel occupies a 17th-century palazzo. The rooms are comfortable and well proportioned, but the best feature is the superb location opposite Trani's cathedral. *Piazza Duomo 2, tel. 0883/584527. 9 rooms with shower. Facilities: restaurant, bar, parking. AE, MC, V. $*

Vieste **Pizzomunno.** Probably the most luxurious resort on the Gargano,
Lodging Pizzomunno is right on the beach and is surrounded by a large park.
★ It is large, white, modern, well equipped, and air-conditioned. The rooms are ample and comfortable, and they all have terraces. There is a $$–$$$ restaurant specializing in fish, and there are many opportunities to unwind or try your hand at something a little more active, like tennis or archery. *Via Litoranea, tel. 0884/708741, fax 0884/707325. 183 rooms with bath. Facilities: pool, private beach, restaurant, movie theater, disco, handball and tennis courts, archery, water sports, fitness center, sauna, child care. AE, DC, MC, V. Closed Nov.–Mar. $$$$*

The Arts and Nightlife

The Arts

In keeping with the general atmosphere of Apulia, the arts take on a folk flavor, with processions on religious occasions more prevalent than performing arts in theaters or opera houses. Still, there are some good festivals and pageants to help broaden your experience of life in Italy's deep south. The best newspaper for listings is the daily *Gazzetta del Mezzogiorno*, which covers the entire region.

Theater Bari has the famous **Teatro Petruzzelli** (Corso Cavour, tel. 080/524–1761), which features performances of drama, opera, and ballet. At the time of this writing, work on the theater was not yet completed after a devastating fire in 1991.

Lecce is a good place to visit in July, when the public gardens are used for productions of drama and, sometimes, opera.

Music Lecce features a festival of Baroque music in September, when churches throughout the city serve as venues.

Martina Franca concentrates on music in its annual **Festival of the Itria Valley** each July and August.

Festivals and Pageants The **Disfida a Barletta,** held on the last Sunday in August, is a reenactment of an event of the same name, which took place in 1503. The *disfida* (challenge) was issued by 13 Italian officers to 13 French officers, after one of the French insulted the Italians by stating that Italy would always be under foreign domination. The Italians taught the rash Frenchman and his compatriots a lesson. Every Italian child learns this story at school.

The **City of Brindisi Festival** (July–September) is a citywide display of art and folklore.

Molfetta features **processions** on Good Friday and Easter Saturday.

Taranto also has Easter processions (Holy Thursday and Good Friday), called the **Procession of the Madonna Addolorata and of the Mysteries.**

Nightlife

Apulia is one of Italy's most rural regions, and even the cities have a marked provincial air to them. This can be frustrating for someone who expects the glamour of nightclubs and discos of the sort Milan and Rome have to offer. On the other hand, in the cafés surrounding the squares of most towns, you can have a ringside seat for that most Mediterranean of pageants—the *passeggiata*. Local people of all ages dress in their most stylish clothing and stroll through the streets, starting around sunset. This is Italian life at its most relaxed and, at the same time, most structured. No one is in a hurry; there is an air of laughter and conviviality; but young people will defer to their elders, and poorer people to those—the town doctor, lawyer, or monsignor—they consider to be their social superiors. And it's yours for the price of a cold drink at a sidewalk café.

16 Sicily

Arriving in Sicily for the first time, you may be surprised to see so many people with blond hair and blue eyes and to learn that two of the most popular boys' names are Ruggero (Roger) and Guglielmo (William), but that is what Sicily is all about. For 2,000 years it has been an island where unexpected contrasts somehow come together peacefully. Lying in a strategic position between Europe and Africa, Sicily at one time hosted two of the most advanced and enlightened capitals of Europe—a Greek one in Siracusa and an Arab-Norman one in Palermo. (The Normans are responsible for the blond-haired Rogers and blue-eyed Williams.) Sicily was one of the great melting pots of the ancient world and home to every great civilization that existed in the Mediterranean: Greek and Roman; then Arab and Norman; and, finally, French, Spanish, and Italian. Something of all of these peoples was absorbed into the island's artistic heritage, a rich tapestry of art and architecture that includes massive Romanesque cathedrals, two of the best-preserved Greek temples in the world, Roman amphitheaters, and delightful Baroque palaces and churches.

Modern Sicily is still a land of surprising contrasts. The traditional graciousness and nobility of the Sicilian people exist side by side with the atrocities and destructive influences of the Mafia, and only recently do events suggest that the Mafia's grip on the island can be loosened. Alongside some of the most exquisite architecture in the world are the shabby products of some of the worst speculation imaginable. In recent years, Sicily, like much of the Mediterranean coast, has experienced a boom in tourism and a surge in condominium development that has only begun to be checked. The chic boutiques purveying lace and linen in jet-set resort towns like Taormina give no clue to the poverty in which their wares are produced.

In Homer's *Odyssey*, Sicily represented the unknown end of the world, yet the region eventually became the center of the known world under the Normans, who recognized a paradise in its deep blue skies and temperate climate, its lush vegetation, and rich marine life. Much of this paradise does still exist today. Add to it Sicily's unique cuisine—another harmony of elements—which mingles Arab and Greek spices with Spanish and French dishes, using some of the world's tastiest seafood, and you can understand why those who came here were often reluctant to leave.

You do not have to be paranoid about safety in Sicily, but you do have to be careful: Do not flaunt your gold jewelry, and keep your handbag securely strapped across your chest. Leaving valuables visible in your car while you go sightseeing is, naturally, inviting trouble. Be careful; then enjoy the company of the Sicilians. You will find them to be friendly and often willing to go out of their way to help tourists. It doesn't matter if you don't speak Italian or speak only a little: They aren't usually offended if your pronunciation isn't perfect—as is sometimes the case elsewhere in Europe—and they will never submit you to a grammar lesson in the middle of the street. One of the reasons for this, no doubt, is the fact that many Sicilians or their close relatives have themselves been strangers in foreign lands, and empathy goes a long way.

Essential Information

Important Addresses and Numbers

Tourist
Information

Aeolian Islands (Corso Vittorio Emanuele 202, Lipari, tel. 090/988–0095).

Agrigento (Viale della Vittoria 255, tel. 0922/401352; Via Atenea 123, tel. 0922/20454).

Caltagirone (Palazzo Libertini, tel. 0933/53809).

Caltanisetta (Corso Vittorio Emanuele 109, tel. 0934/26560).

Catania (Largo Paisiello 5, tel. 095/312124; rail station, tel. 095/531802; airport, tel. 095/341900).

Cefalù (Corso Ruggero 77, tel. 0921/21050).

Enna (Piazza Garibaldi 1, tel. 0935/500901; Piazza Napoleone Colajanni 6, tel. 0935/26119).

Erice (Via Conte Pepoli 55, tel. 0923/869388).

Marsala (Via Garibaldi 45, tel. 0923/714097).

Messina (Via Calabria 301/b, tel. 090/675356; Piazza Cairoli 45, tel. 090/293–3541).

Monreale (Piazza Duomo, tel. 091/656–4270).

Palermo (Piazza Castelnuovo 35, tel. 091/583847; Stazione Centrale, tel. 091/616–5914).

Piazza Armerina (Via Cavour 15, tel. 0935/680201).

Siracusa (Via San Sebastiano 43, tel. 0931/461477; Via Maestranza 33, tel. 0931/65201; at the entrance to the Archaeological Park, tel. 0931/60510).

Taormina (Largo Santa Caterina, Palazzo Corvaia, tel. 0942/23243; Corso Umberto 144, tel. 0942/23243).

Trapani (Piazza Saturno, tel. 0923/29000; Via Vito Sorba 15, tel. 0923/27273).

Arriving and Departing by Plane

Sicily can be reached from all major cities via Rome, Milan, or Naples. Planes land at **Punta Raisi Airport,** 32 kilometers (20 miles) west of Palermo (tel. 091/591698), or at Catania's **Fontanarossa Airport** (tel. 095/341900), 5 kilometers (3 miles) south of the city. At both, there is bus service into the center of town. During the high season, there are also direct charter flights to Sicily from New York, London, and Paris.

Arriving and Departing by Car, Train, and Boat

By Car and
Ferry

Frequent **car ferries** cross the strait between Villa San Giovanni in Calabria and Messina on the island. The crossing usually takes about half an hour, but during the summer months there can be considerable delays. From Naples, overnight car ferries operate daily to Palermo and once a week to Catania and Siracusa; there is also an overnight ferry from Genoa to Palermo.

By Train

There are direct **express trains** from Milan and Rome to Palermo, Catania, and Siracusa. The Rome–Palermo journey takes at least 11 hours. After Naples, the run is mostly along the coast, so try to book a window seat on the right. At Villa San Giovanni, in Calabria, the train is separated and loaded onto a ferryboat to cross the strait to Messina.

By Passenger
Boat

Besides the ferries mentioned above (*see* By Car and Ferry, *above*), **hydrofoils** (*aliscafi*), which carry passengers only, also cross the strait in about 30 minutes.

Getting Around

By Car Renting a car is definitely the best way to travel in Sicily because the trains are unreliable and slow, and the buses, though faster and air-conditioned in summer, can be subject to delays and strikes. Modern highways circle and bisect the island, making all main cities easily reachable. Cars can be rented at airports and downtown locations in every major city.

By Train Main lines connect Messina, Taormina, Siracusa, and Palermo. Secondary lines are generally very slow and unreliable. The Messina–Palermo run, along the northern coast, is especially scenic.

By Bus Air-conditioned coaches connect major and minor cities and are often faster and more convenient than local trains but slightly more expensive.

Guided Tours

Orientation City tours are provided by the Italian tour operator **CIT** in all major cities. CIT also arranges complete tours of Sicily, which range from seven-day tours of the island's major sights to a four-day minitour. Departures are once a week from Palermo in a comfortable air-conditioned coach with an English-speaking guide. The cost includes all meals and accommodations in three- or four-star hotels. CIT has offices in Palermo (Via della Libertà 12, tel. 091/586333), Catania (Via Mario Sangiorgi 49, tel. 095/538134), Taormina (Corso Umberto 101, tel. 0942/23301), New York (342 Madison Ave., Room 207, New York, NY 10173, tel. 212/697–2100 or 800/248–8687), and Croydon, England (3–5 Lansdowne Rd., tel. 081/686–0677).

Special-Interest **Amelia Tours** (280 Old Country Rd., Hicksville, NY 11801, tel. 516/433–0696 or 800/SICILY–1) has a carefully prepared program for Sicily, emphasizing the cultural life of the region.

Exploring Sicily

Sicily is about 180 kilometers (112 miles) north to south and 270 kilometers (168 miles) across. The best way to visit it is to travel counterclockwise along the coast by car, bus, or train, making occasional detours inland. Plan to spend three nights in Palermo, one in Agrigento, two in Siracusa, and three at Taormina. If you can, add a few days to explore some inland towns, such as Caltagirone and Enna, and to visit the rugged Aeolian islands off the northeast coast and the larger islands of Pantelleria in the southwest or Ustica in the northwest, which are paradises for swimming and skin-diving enthusiasts.

The following tours trace a loop around the island that begins in the capital city of Palermo, meeting point of Sicily's Arab and Norman cultures; moves west and south to the stunning Greek cities of Selinunte and Agrigento; dips inland to see the remarkable Roman mosaics at Piazza Armerina; continues southeast to Siracusa, once the rival of ancient Greece; skirts the base of volcanic Mt. Etna to the enchanting mountaintop town of Taormina; and ends in Messina, where ferryboats connect Sicily to the Italian mainland.

Highlights for First-Time Visitors

Catania (Tour 3: Eastern Sicily).

Cathedral in Piazza del Duomo, Siracusa (Tour 3: Eastern Sicily).

Cefalù (Tour 1: Palermo and Environs).

Imperial Roman Villa, Casale (Tour 3: Eastern Sicily).

Mt. Etna (Tour 3: Eastern Sicily).

National Archaeological Museum, Palermo (Tour 1: Palermo and Environs).

Palazzo dei Normanni, Palermo (Tour 1: Palermo and Environs).

Taormina (Tour 3: Eastern Sicily).

Valley of the Temples (Tour 2: The Western Coast to Agrigento).

Tour 1: Palermo and Environs

Numbers in the margin correspond to points of interest on the Sicily and Palermo maps.

❶ Our tour begins in **Palermo.** Once the intellectual capital of southern Europe, the city has always been at the crossroads of civilization. Favorably located on a crescent-shaped bay at the foot of Monte Pellegrino, it has attracted almost every people and culture touching the Mediterranean world. To Palermo's credit, it has absorbed these diverse cultures into a unique personality that is at once Arab and Christian, Byzantine and Roman, Norman and Italian.

Palermo was first colonized by Phoenician traders in the 6th century BC, but it was their descendants, the Carthaginians, who built the important fortress here that caught the covetous eye of the Romans. After the First Punic War, the Romans took control of the city, in the 3rd century BC. After several invasions by the Vandals, Sicily was settled by Arabs, who made the country an emirate and made Palermo a showpiece capital that rivaled both Cordoba and Cairo in Oriental splendor. Nestled in the fertile Conca d'Oro (Golden Conch) plain; full of orange, lemon, and carob groves; and enclosed by limestone hills, Palermo became a magical world of palaces and mosques, minarets and palm trees.

It was so attractive and sophisticated a city that the Norman ruler Roger de Hauteville decided to conquer it and make it his capital (1061). The Norman occupation of Sicily resulted in the Golden Age of Palermo (from 1072 to 1194), a remarkable period of enlightenment and learning in which the arts flourished. The city of Palermo, which in the 11th century counted more than 300,000 inhabitants, became the center of the Norman court in all Europe and one of the most important ports of trade between East and West.

Eventually the Normans were replaced by the Swabian ruler Frederick II, the Holy Roman Emperor, and incorporated into the Kingdom of the Two Sicilies. You will also see evidence in Palermo of the Baroque art and architecture of the Spanish viceroys, who came to power after the bloody Sicilian Vespers uprising of 1282, in which the French Angevin dynasty was overthrown. The Aragonese viceroys also brought the Inquisition to Palermo, which some historians believe helped foster the protective secret societies that eventually evolved into today's Mafia.

TO SARDINIA

TO TUNIS

TO SARDINIA

I. di Ustica

TO LIVORNO, GENOA

TO NAPLES

Tyrr

San Vito
lo Capo

*Golfo di
Castellammare*

Mondello

Palermo
1—**11**

S113

Erice
15

Monreale
12

Trapani

16

Termini

Mt. S.
Calogero

A19

*I.
Favignana*

Segesta
14

S188

A29

Corleone

S121

18

Marsala

S115

Castelvetrano

S115

S118

17 **Pantelleria**

S189

Caltan

19

Selinunte

Sciacca

S640

Agrigento
20—**27**

S115

Mediterranean Sea

N

Licata

0   20 miles

0   30 km

TO LINOSA

TO LAMPEDUSA

Stromboli 41

Panarea 40

Alicudi 42 Filicudi 43

Salina 39

AEOLIAN ISLANDS

Lipari 37

Vulcano 38

...enian Sea

TO NAPLES

Golfo di Gióia

Milazzo

Capo d'Orlando

S113

Patti

A20

Messina 36

Reggio

Cefalù

13

Santo Stefano
di Camastra

S113

S117

Castelmola

35

Taormina

A18

Bronte

Mt. Etna 34

Adrano

Biancavilla

Acireale

Paterno

...etta

28

Enna

S192

A19

Catania 33

Golfo di
Catania

Ionian Sea

29 Piazza
Armerina

Imperial Roman 30
Villa at Casale

S288

31

Caltagirone

S124

Gela

Palazzolo
Acreide

Euryalus

Golfo di Gela

Comiso

S124

32

Siracusa

Ragusa

Noto

Avola

Modica

S115

Golfo
di Noto

Capo
Passero

TO MALTA

Palermo

Duomo, **4**
International Museum
of Marionettes, **10**
Martorana, **8**
Palazzo Abatellis, **9**
Palazzo dei
Normanni, **2**
Quattro Canti, **5**

Regional
Archaeological
Museum, **11**
San Cataldo, **7**
San Giovanni degli
Eremiti, **3**
Santa Caterina, **6**

Palermo's main attractions are easily reached on foot, though you may choose to spend a morning taking a city bus tour to help you get oriented. The tourist attractions are scattered along three major streets: Corso Vittorio Emanuele, Via Maqueda, and Via Roma. The tourist information office in Piazza Castelnuovo will give you a map and a valuable handout that lists opening and closing times, which sometimes change with the seasons.

❷ At the far end of the Corso, away from the harbor, is the **Palazzo dei Normanni** (Norman Royal Palace), now the seat of the Sicilian Parliament. The palace was, unfortunately, closed to the public for security reasons in 1992, but the **Cappella Palatina** (Palatine Chapel) inside, one of Italy's greatest art treasures, happily remains open. Built by Roger II in 1132, this is a dazzling example of the unique harmony of artistic elements that came together under the Normans. In it, the skill of French and Sicilian masons was brought to bear on the decorative purity of Arab ornamentation and the splendor of Greek Byzantine mosaics. The interior is covered with glittering mosaics and capped by a splendid Arab honeycomb stalactite wooden ceiling. Biblical stories blend happily with scenes of Arab life—look for one showing a picnic in a harem—and Norman court pageantry. Stylized Moorish palm branches run along the walls below the mosaics and recall the battlements on Norman castles—each one a different mosaic composition.

Upstairs are the royal apartments, including the Sala di Ruggero (King Roger's Hall), decorated with medieval murals of hunting scenes. Tour guides escort you around these halls, which once hosted one of the most splendid courts in Europe. French, Latin, and Arabic were spoken here, and Arab astronomers and poets exchanged ideas with Latin and Greek scholars in what must have been one of the most unique marriages of culture in the Western world. *Cappella Palatina, Piazza Indipendenza. Admission free. Open Mon.–Fri. 9–12, 3–5, Sat. 9–12, Sun. 9–10, 12–1. Closed during religious services and for weddings.*

❸ To the left of the front of Palazzo dei Normanni, along Via Benedettini, you'll see the five pink domes of the church of **San Giovanni degli Eremiti,** one of the most picturesque of Palermo's churches. The 12th-century church was built by the Normans on the sight of an earlier mosque—one of 200 that once stood in Palermo. The emirs ruled Palermo for almost two centuries and brought to it their passion for lush gardens and fountains. One is reminded of this while sitting in San Giovanni's delightful cloister of twin half-columns, surrounded by palm trees, jasmine, oleander, and citrus trees. *Open Tues., Wed., Fri. 9–1, 3–5; Mon., Thurs., Sat. 9–2; Sun. 9–1.*

❹ Returning to Corso Vittorio Emanuele and going east, you will soon see the **Duomo,** which is a prime example of Palermitan eclecticism. Its turrets, towers, dome, and arches come together in the kind of meeting of diverse elements that King Roger, whose tomb is inside along with that of Frederick II, fostered during his reign. Be sure to walk outside and look at the back of the apse, which is gracefully decorated with interlacing Arab arches, inlaid with limestone and black volcanic tufa. *Open daily 9:30–12, 4–5:30.*

❺ Farther down the Corso is **Quattro Canti** (Four Corners), actually the intersection with Via Maqueda. Here four Baroque palaces from the Spanish rule meet at concave corners, each with its own fountain, Spanish ruler, patron saint, and representation of one of the four seasons.

Just to the right is Piazza Pretoria, with a lavishly decorated fountain, originally intended for a Florentine villa. Its abundance of nude figures so shocked some Palermitans when it was unveiled in 1575 that it got the nickname "the fountain of shame." It is even more shameful at night, when it is illuminated.

If you cross to the far side of the fountain and continue to the right, ❻ you'll reach Piazza Bellini and the splendid Baroque church of **Santa Caterina** (1596). Its walls are covered in decorative 17th-century inlays of precious marble.

Across the piazza and up a staircase are two churches that form a ❼ delightful Norman complex. The orange-red domes belong to **San Cataldo** (1160), whose spare but intense interior, punctuated by antique Greek columns, retains much of its original medieval simplici- ❽ ty. The other church, with an elegant campanile, is the **Martorana,** which was erected in 1143 but had its interior altered considerably during the Baroque period. High along the western wall, however, is some of the oldest mosaic artwork of the Norman period. Near the entrance is an interesting mosaic of Roger being crowned by Christ. In it, Roger is dressed in a bejeweled Byzantine stole, reflecting the Norman court's penchant for all things Byzantine. Archangels along the ceiling wear the same stole, wrapped around their shoulders and arms. Like the archangels, the Norman monarchs liked to think of themselves as emissaries from heaven, engaged in defending Christianity by ridding the island of infidel invaders. *La Martorana open Mon.–Sat. 8:30–1, 3:30–7:30 (3:30–5:30 in winter), Sun. 8:30–1; to visit San Cataldo, see the custodian of La Martorana.*

❾ Heading toward the port, take Via Alloro to the **Palazzo Abatellis,** which houses the Regional Gallery of Sicily. Among its treasures is an Annunciation (1474) by Sicily's prominent Renaissance master, Antonello da Messina, and an arresting fresco by an unknown painter, titled *The Triumph of Death,* a macabre depiction of the plague years. *Via Alloro 4, tel. 091/616–4317. Admission: 2,000 lire. Open Tues., Thurs., Fri. 9–1:30, 3–7:30 (3–5 in winter); Mon., Sat. 9–1:30; Sun. 9–12:30.*

❿ Nearby is the **International Museum of Marionettes,** with an impressive display of Sicilian and European puppets. The traditional Sicilian *pupi* (marionettes), with their glittering armor and fierce expressions, have become a symbol of Norman Sicily. Plots center on the chivalric legends of the troubadours, who, before the puppet theater, kept alive tales of Norman heroes in Sicily, such as Orlando Furioso and William the Bad. *Via Butera 1, tel. 091/328060. Admission: 2,000 lire. Open Mon., Wed., Fri. 9–1, 4–7; Thurs., Sat. 9–1.*

Return to Corso Vittorio Emanuele and walk toward Via Roma. Before you get there, you will come upon the outdoor market that spreads out into a maze of side streets around Piazza Domenico. This is the **Vucciria**—a dialect word that means "voices" or "hubbub." It's easy to see why. Hawkers everywhere deliver their unceasing chants from behind stands brimming with mounds of olives, blood oranges, wild fennel, and long-stemmed artichokes. One of them goes at the trunk of a swordfish with a cleaver, while across the way another holds up a giant squid or dangles an octopus. All the time, the din continues. It may be Palermo, but this is really the Casbah.

Time Out   The **Vucciria** is full of stalls selling street food. Everything from *calzoni* (deep-fried meat- or cheese-filled pockets of dough) to *panelle* (chickpea-flour fritters). If you want to try something typically Palermitan that is a bit adventurous but delicious, look for a stall with a big cast-iron pot selling *guasteddi* (fresh buns filled with thin strips of calf's spleen, ricotta cheese, and a delicious hot sauce).

⑪ Back on Via Roma, the **Regional Archaeological Museum** has a small but excellent collection. Especially interesting are the examples of prehistoric cave drawings and a marvelously reconstructed Doric frieze from the Greek Temple at Selinunte that gives you a good idea of the high level of artistic culture attained by the Greek colonists in Sicily some 2,500 years ago. *Piazza Olivella 4, tel. 091/587825. Admission: 2,000 lire. Open Tues., Fri. 9–1:30, 3–6, Mon., Wed., Thurs., Sat. 9:30–1:30, Sun. 9–12:30.*

There are several interesting day trips you can make from Palermo. **⑫** Don't miss the splendid cathedral of **Monreale,** about 10 kilometers (6 miles) southwest of the city. It is lavishly decorated with mosaics depicting events from the old and new testaments. Bring 500-lire coins to illuminate the mosaics. There are 130 pictures, covering 6,000 square yards. Be sure to see the rear exterior and the graceful Romanesque cloister to the left, laced with intricate arches, mosaic-inlaid twin columns, and capitals that represent one of the richest collections of Sicilian medieval sculpture. In a corner by the stylized palm tree fountain, look for a capital showing William II offering the cathedral to the Virgin. *Cathedral, tel. 091/640–4413. Open winter, daily 8:30–12:30, 3:30–6:30; summer 9–7. Cloister, tel. 091/640–4403. Admission: 2,000 lire. Open winter, Mon., Fri., Sat. 9–1, Tues., Wed., Thurs. 9–1, 3–7, Sun. 9–12; summer, Mon.–Sat. 9–7, Sun. 9–1.*

⑬ **Cefalù,** about 70 kilometers (42 miles) east of Palermo, along the coast, is a charming town built on a spur jutting out into the sea and dominated by a massive 12th-century Romanesque **Duomo** that is one of the finest Norman cathedrals in Italy. King Roger began it in 1131 as a thanks offering for having been saved here from a shipwreck. Its mosaics rival those of Monreale. Both cathedrals are dominated by colossal mosaic figures of the Byzantine Pantocratic Christ, high in the bowl of their apses. The Monreale figure is an austere and powerful image, emphasizing the divinity of Christ, while the Cefalù Christ, softer and more compassionate, seems to stress his humanity. *Cathedral, tel. 0921/21141. Open daily 9–12, 4–6 (summer 3:30–8). No shorts or beachwear.*

Cefalù has become a popular summer resort, and the traffic going in and out of town can be heavy. You may want to take the 50-minute train ride or 40-minute bus ride from Palermo instead.

Tour 2: The Western Coast to Agrigento

⑭ About 85 kilometers (50 miles) southwest of Palermo is **Segesta,** where one of the most impressive Greek **temples** in the world is located—on the side of a windswept barren hill overlooking a valley of wild fennel. Virtually intact, the temple is considered by some to be finer, in its proportions and setting, than any Doric temple left standing. The Greeks started the temple in the 5th century BC but never finished it. The walls and roof are missing, and the columns were never fluted. Just over half a mile away, near the top of the hill, are the remains of a fine Greek theater, with impressive views, especially at sunset, of nearby Monte Erice and the sea.

⑮ Continue west about 30 kilometers (18 miles) and then up 2,450 feet to **Erice,** an enchanting medieval mountaintop aerie of castles and palaces, fountains and cobblestone streets. Erice was the ancient

Eryx and was dedicated to a fertility goddess, whom the Phoenicians called Astarte; the Greeks, Aphrodite; and the Romans, Venus. According to Virgil, Aeneas built a temple to the goddess here, but it was destroyed when the Arabs took over and renamed the place Mohammed's Mountain. When the Normans arrived, they built a castle where today there is a public park with benches and belvederes, from which there are striking views of Trapani, the Egadi islands, and, on a *very* clear day, Cape Bon and the Tunisian coast.

Time Out *Cassata di Erice,* a sponge cake filled with either ricotta cheese or almond paste and chocolate cream, then covered with pistachio icing and elaborately decorated with candied fruit flowers, is a dignified version of the famous Sicilian dessert, which is of Arabic origin. Try a slice (a little goes a long way) at any of the pastry shops along Via Vittorio Emanuele or in Piazza Umberto I.

⑯ The modern town of **Trapani,** below Erice, is the departure point for ferries to the Egadi islands and the island of Pantelleria, near the African coast. This rugged western end of Sicily is reminiscent of the terrain in American westerns—as it well should be, for many "spaghetti westerns" were filmed here. If you are familiar with North African couscous, Trapani is the place to try the Sicilian version, which is made with fish instead of meat. The result is a kind of fish stew with semolina, spiced with cinnamon, saffron, and black pepper.

⑰ **Pantelleria,** near the Tunisian coast, is one of Sicily's most evocative islands, although many find its starkness unappealing. Its volcanic formations, scant patches of forest, prehistoric tombs, and dramatic seascapes constitute an otherworldly landscape. From its grapes—the *zibibbo* (a strain of *moscato*)—the locals make an amber-colored dessert wine and a strong, sweet wine called Tanit. Daily ferries and hydrofoils connect the island with Trapani.

⑱ From Trapani take the main coastal road 30 kilometers (18 miles) south to **Marsala,** a quiet seaside town that is world famous for its rich-colored, sweet-tasting wine. In 1773 a British merchant named John Woodhouse happened upon Marsala and discovered that the wine there was as good as the port the British had long imported from Portugal. Two other wine merchants, Whitaker and Ingram, rushed in, and by 1800 Marsala was exporting its wine all over the British Empire.

⑲ Continue southeast on the main road, through Castelvetrano, and south to **Selinunte,** where an overwhelming array of ruined Greek temples is perched on a plateau overlooking the Mediterranean. The city was one of the most superb colonies of ancient Greece. The original complex held seven temples scattered over two sites separated by a harbor. Of the seven, only one—reconstructed in 1958—still stands. Founded in the 7th century BC, Selinunte became the rich and prosperous rival of Segesta, which in 409 BC turned to the Carthaginians for help. The Carthaginians sent an army commanded by Hannibal to raze the city. The temples were demolished, the city was laid flat, and 16,000 of Selinunte's inhabitants were slaughtered. The beautiful metopes preserved in Palermo's Archaeological Museum come from the frieze of Temple E here. There is also a small museum at the site that contains other excavated pieces. Selinunte is named after a local variety of wild celery that in spring still grows profusely among the ruined columns and overturned capitals. *Ad-*

mission to site and museum: 2,000 lire. Open daily 9–one hour before sunset.

About 100 kilometers (60 miles) farther east along the highway, the ⑳ golden temples of **Agrigento** appear on a rise to your left. Agrigento, or Akragas as the Greeks called it, was settled by the Greeks in 580 BC and grew wealthy through trade with Carthage, just across the Mediterranean. Despite attacks from the Carthaginians at the end of the 5th century BC, the city survived through the Roman era, the Middle Ages (when it came under Arab and Norman rule), and into the modern age, and structures from all these eras sit side-by-side in Agrigento today. The birthplace of both the ancient Greek philosopher Empedocles and the modern Italian playwright Luigi Pirandello, Agrigento is a study in contrasts, but its chief attraction, the Valley of the Temples, remains one of the most impressive classical sites in all of Italy.

Numbers in the margin correspond to points of interest on the Agrigento map.

Coming upon the **Valley of the Temples** for the first time is always a memorable moment—whether in the sunshine of spring, when they are surrounded by blossoming almond trees, or at night, when they are floodlit. Even in winter, when the vegetation is limited—perfectly limited—to century plants *(agaves)* and gnarled gray olive trees, it is easy to understand why Pindar called Agrigento "the most beautiful city built by mortal men." Exiting from the highway, walk down from the parking lot on Via dei Templi and turn left. The ㉑ first temple you encounter as you enter the complex is the **Temple of Hercules**—eight pillars of the oldest temple in Agrigento, built dur- ㉒ ing the 5th century BC. Up the hill is the **Temple of Concord,** one of the best-preserved Doric temples in the world and certainly the most impressive in Sicily. In the late afternoon, as the sun descends below the horizon, the temple's sandstone begins to change from honey-gold to pink russet, and the vertical lines of the fluted columns and their triangular pediment sharpen against the fading skyline. The columns were probably once covered by brightly painted stucco. Follow the road that climbs around to the left, and you'll ㉓ reach the **Temple of Juno,** which commands an exquisite view of the valley, especially at sunset. If you look carefully, you can see red fire-marks on some of the columns—the result of the Carthaginian attack in 406 BC, which destroyed the city. Return to the parking lot in the Piazzale dei Templi (where there is a bar selling drinks and ice cream) and cross to the opposite side of the road, where the ruins ㉔ continue. First is the **Temple of Jupiter,** the largest temple ever planned in Sicily. Though never completed, it was considered the eighth wonder of the world. The nearby sleeping giant is a copy of one of the 38 colossal Atlas figures, or telamones, that supported the temple's immense roof. The last temple is the much-photographed ㉕ **Temple of Castor and Pollux,** whose four columns supporting part of an entablature have become a symbol of Agrigento, even though they were reconstructed in 1836, and probably from diverse buildings. At the end of Via dei Templi, where it turns left and becomes ㉖ Via Petrarca, stands the **National Archaeological Museum,** which contains one of the original telamones, an impressive collection of Greek vases dating from the 7th century BC, and models of what the temples once looked like. *Contrada San Nicola, tel. 0922/29008. Admission free. Open Sun.–Fri. 9–1, Sat. 9–3.*

㉗ On the opposite side of the road from the museum is the **Hellenistic and Roman Quarter,** which consists of four parallel streets, running north and south, that have been uncovered, along with the founda-

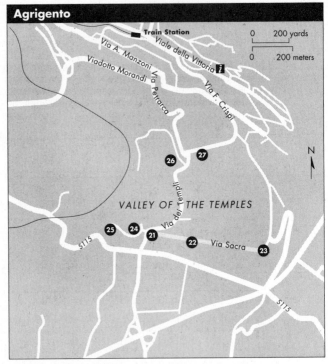

tions of some houses from the Roman settlement (2nd century BC). Some of these streets still have their original mosaic pavements.

Time Out — There is little reason to go up the hill to the rather dreary modern city of Agrigento, where speculation keeps threatening to encroach upon the Valley of the Temples below—except to ring the doorbell at the **convent of Santo Spirito** on the Salita di Santo Spirito off Via Porcello and try the sweet cake, *kus-kus*, made of pistachio nuts and chocolate, that the nuns there prepare.

On the first weekend in February, Agrigento hosts an Almond Blossom Festival, with international folk dances, a costumed parade, and the sale of marzipan and other sweets made from almonds.

Tour 3: Eastern Sicily

Numbers in the margin correspond to points of interest on the Sicily map.

From Palermo, follow A19 east and south about 150 kilometers (93 miles); from Agrigento, cut inland and follow the road upland, through Caltanissetta, about 105 kilometers (63 miles) to **Enna,** a fortress city of narrow winding streets that is home to an impressive castle built by Frederick II. The views from here of the flat interior and Mt. Etna in the distance are exceptional.

Turn south, through the pine and eucalyptus woods and low farmland, to **Piazza Armerina,** a tiny Baroque town with an exceptionally well-preserved and well-presented example of a sumptuous Roman emperor's country house. The **Imperial Roman Villa at Casale,** about

6 kilometers (4 miles) southwest of the city, is made up of four groups of buildings on different levels and is thought to have been a hunting lodge of the Emperor Maximianus Heraclius (4th century AD). The excavations were not begun until 1950, and all the wall decorations and vaulting have been lost. However, some of the best mosaics of the Roman world cover 3,500 square meters under a shelter shaped to give an idea of the layout of the original buildings. The mosaics were probably made by Carthaginian artisans, because they are similar to those in the Tunis Bardo Museum. The entrance was through a triumphal arch that led into an atrium surrounded by a portico of columns. Through this, the *thermae*, or bathhouse, is reached. It is colorfully decorated with mosaic nymphs, a Neptune, and slaves massaging bathers. The Peristyle leads to the main villa, where in the Salone del Circo you look down on mosaics that illustrate Roman circus sports. Another apartment shows hunting scenes of tigers, elephants, and ostriches; the gym shows young girls exercising; the private apartments are covered with scenes from Greek and Roman mythology; and Room 38 even has a touch of eroticism. In August, Piazza Armerina has a costumed horse race, called the Palio dei Normanni, to celebrate the city's prosperity under the Normans. *Tel. 0935/680036. Admission: 2,000 lire. Open daily 9–two hours before sunset.*

31 **Caltagirone,** about 30 kilometers (18 miles) southeast of Piazza Armerina, is a leader in the Sicilian ceramics industry and a charming Baroque town built over three hills, with majolica balustrades, tile-decorated windowsills, and a monumental **tile staircase** of 142 steps—each decorated with a different pattern. On the feast of San Giacomo (July 24), the staircase is illuminated with candles that form a tapestry design over the steps. It is the result of months of work preparing the 4,000 *coppi*, or cylinders of colored paper that hold oil lamps. At 9:30 PM on July 24, a squad of hundreds of boys springs into action to light the lamps, so that the staircase flares up all at once. There is an interesting **Ceramics Museum** in the public gardens, which were designed by Basile, the master of Sicilian Art Nouveau. The exhibits in the museum trace the history of the craft from specimens excavated from the earliest settlements, through the influential Arab period, to the present. *Museo Regionale della Ceramica, Giardino Pubblico. Admission free. Open Tues.–Sat. 9–2, Sun 9–1.*

About 100 kilometers (60 miles) east of Caltagirone on the winding but scenic S124 you arrive at the Ionian Sea. Greek Sicily began along this coast, and some of the finest examples of Baroque art and architecture also were created here, particularly in **Siracusa.** The **32** city was founded in 734 BC by Greek colonists from Corinth and soon grew to rival, and even surpass, Athens in splendor and power. Siracusa became the largest, wealthiest city-state in Magna Grecia and the bulwark of Greek civilization. Although it suffered from tyrannical rule, kings such as Dionysius filled their courts in the 5th century BC with Greeks of the highest artistic stature—among them, Pindar, Aeschylus, and Archimedes. The Athenians did not welcome the rise of Siracusa and sent a fleet to destroy the rival city, but the natives outsmarted them in what was one of the greatest naval battles of ancient history (413 BC). Siracusa continued to prosper until it was conquered two centuries later by the Romans.

There are essentially two areas to explore in Siracusa—the Archaeological Park, on the mainland, and the island of Ortygia, the ancient city first inhabited by the Greeks, which juts out into the Ionian sea and is connected to the mainland by two small bridges. The **Archaeo-**

logical Park, at the western edge of town, contains the ruins of a fine Roman amphitheater and the most complete Greek theater existing from antiquity. A comparison of these two structures reveals much about the differences between the Greek and Roman personalities. The Greek theater, in which the plays of Aeschylus premiered, was hewn out of the hillside rock in the 5th century BC. All the seats converge upon a single point—the stage—which had the natural scenery and the sky as its background. Drama as a kind of religious ritual was the intention here. In the Roman amphitheater, however, the emphasis was on the spectacle of combative sports and the circus. The arena is one of the largest of its kind and was built around the 2nd century AD. The corridor where gladiators and beasts entered the ring is still intact, and the seats, some of which still bear the occupants' names, were hauled in and constructed on the site from huge slabs of limestone. A crowd-pleasing show, and not the elevation of men's minds, was the intention here. Climb to the top of the seating area in the Greek theater, which could accommodate 15,000, for a fine view. In May and June of even-numbered years, performances of Greek tragedies are held here. If the Archaeological Park is closed, go up Viale G. Rizzo from Viale Teracati, to the belvedere overlooking the ruins, which are floodlit at night.

Near the entrance to the park is the gigantic altar of Hieron, which was once used by the Greeks for sacrifices involving hundreds of animals at a time. Just beyond the ticket office, you will come upon a lush tropical garden full of palm and citrus trees. This is the Latomie del Paradiso, a series of quarries that served as prisons for the defeated Athenians, who were enslaved; the quarries once rang with the sound of their chisels and hammers. At one end is the Orecchio di Dionisio, with an ear-shaped entrance and unusual acoustics inside, as you'll discover if you clap your hands. The legend is that Dionysius used to listen in at the top of the quarry to hear what the slaves were plotting below. *Viale Augusto, tel. 0931/66206. Admission: 2,000 lire. Open daily 9–two hours before sunset.*

Not far from the Archaeological Park, off Viale Teocrito, are the **catacombs** of San Giovanni, one of the earliest-known Christian sites in the city. Inside the crypt of San Marciano is an altar where St. Paul preached on his way through Sicily to Rome. The frescoes in this small chapel are still bright and fresh, though some date from the 4th century AD. *Piazza San Giovanni. Admission: 2,000 lire. Open mid-Mar.–mid-Nov., daily 10–12, 4–6; mid-Nov.–mid-Mar., daily 10–12.*

Continue walking east, toward the sea, along Viale Teocrito, and you'll soon come to the **papyrus studio** at No. 80, where you can see papyruses being prepared from reeds and then see the scrolls painted—an ancient tradition in Siracusa. Siracusa, it seems, has the only climate outside the Nile Valley in which the papyrus plant—from which we get our word *paper*—thrives.

Nearby is the splendid **Archaeological Museum.** Its impressive collection is arranged by region around a central atrium and ranges from neolithic pottery to fine Greek statues and vases. You will want to compare the Landolina Venus—a headless, stout goddess of love who rises out of the sea in measured modesty (she is a 1st-century Roman copy of the Greek original)—with the much earlier (300 BC) elegant Greek statue of Hercules in Section C. Of a completely different type is a marvelous fanged Gorgon, its tongue sticking out, that once adorned the cornice of the temple of Athena in order to ward off evildoers. The pieces are generally well lit, and there are also several interesting, instructive exhibits. One depicts the Temple of Apollo, the oldest Doric temple in Sicily, on the island of Ortygia. *Viale Teocrito, tel. 0931/464022. Admission: 2,000 lire. Open Tues.–Sun. 9–2. Closed 2nd and 4th Sun. of every month.*

The central part of Siracusa is a modern city, with Corso Gelone its main shopping street. At its southern end, Corso Umberto leads to the **Ortygia Island** bridge, which crosses a pretty harbor lined with fish restaurants. In the piazza on the other side of the bridge, you'll find the ruins of the **Temple of Apollo** depicted in the Archaeological Museum. In fact, little of this noble Doric temple still remains today, except for some crumbled walls and shattered columns that survive along with a fragment (the window in the south wall) of a Norman church that was built much later on the same spot. Apart from this ancient Greek relic, Ortygia is composed almost entirely of warm, restrained Baroque buildings. This uniformity is the result of an earthquake in 1693 that necessitated major rebuilding at a time when the Baroque was very popular. Wander into the back streets— especially along Via della Maestranza or Via Veneto—and notice the bulbous wrought-iron balconies (said to have been invented to accommodate ladies' billowing skirts), the window-surrounds and cornices of buildings decorated with mermaids and gargoyles, and the stucco decoration on Palazzo Lantieri on Via Roma.

Ortygia has two main piazzas: Piazza Archimede and Piazza del Duomo. Piazza Archimede is easily recognized because of its Baroque fountain of fainting sea nymphs and dancing jets of water. The bars here are popular meeting and sitting places. **Piazza del Duomo,** one of the most beautiful piazzas in Italy, is a short walk away. The **cathedral** is an archive of island history, beginning with the bottommost excavations that have unearthed remnants of Sicily's distant past, when the Siculi inhabitants worshiped their deities here. During the 5th century BC, the Greeks built a temple to Athena over it, and in the 7th century, Siracusa's first Christian cathedral was built on top of the Greek structure. The elegant columns of the original temple were incorporated into the present structure and are clearly visible, embedded in the exterior wall along Via Minerva. The Greek columns were also used to dramatic advantage inside, where on one side they form chapels connected by elegant wrought-iron gates. The Baroque facade, added in 1700, displays a harmonious rhythm of concaves and convexes. The piazza in front is encircled by pink and white oleanders and surrounded by elegant buildings ornamented with filigree grillwork. In the right corner of the piazza is the elegant **Palazzo Beneventano del Bosco,** with an impressive interior courtyard ending in a grand winding staircase. At the opposite end is the tiny Baroque church of **Santa Lucia alla Badia,** with an engaging wrought-iron balcony and pleasing facade. The feast of the city's patroness Santa Lucia (St. Lucy) is held on December 13, when a splendid silver statue of the saint is carried from the cathedral to the church on the site of her martyrdom, near the Catacombs of San Giovanni. A torchlight procession and band music accompany the bearers.

Walk down Via delle Vergini, behind the church, and turn onto Via Capodieci, where the **National Museum** is housed inside Palazzo Bellomo, a lovely Catalan-Gothic building with mullioned windows and an elegant exterior staircase. Among the select group of paintings and sculptures inside is a Santa Lucia by Caravaggio and a damaged, but still brilliant, Annunciation by Antonello da Messina. *Via Capodieci 14, tel. 0931/65343. Admission: 2,000 lire. Open Mon.– Sat. 9–2, Sun. 9–1.*

Walk in the opposite direction, down Via Capodieci to the promenade along the harbor, and you'll come to the **Fountain of Arethusa,** a freshwater spring next to the sea. This anomaly is explained by a Greek legend that tells how the nymph Arethusa was changed into a fountain by the goddess Artemis (Diana) when she tried to escape the advances of the river god Alpheus. She fled from Greece, into the sea, with Alpheus in close pursuit, and emerged in Sicily at this spring. Supposedly even today, if you throw a cup into the river Alpheus in Greece, it will emerge here at this fountain, which at present is home to a few tired ducks and some dull-colored carp—but no cups. Steps lead to the tree-lined promenade along the harbor front, where you can buy a drink and watch the ships come in. Or, you can walk out to the far end of the island, to the **Castello Maniace,** now an army barracks but once a castle of Frederick II, from which there are fine views of the sea.

North of the city, on the highlands that overlook the sea, Dionysius created the fortress of **Euryalus** with the help of Archimedes, as protection against the Carthaginians. This astonishing boat-shaped structure once covered 15,000 square yards. Its intricate maze of tunnels is fascinating, and the view from the heights is superb. *8 km (5 mi) northwest of Siracusa. Open 9–one hour before sunset.*

From Siracusa it is a 60-kilometer (36-mile) drive up the coast to
33 Sicily's second city, **Catania.** The chief wonder of Catania is that it is there at all. Its successive populations were deported by one Greek tyrant, sold into slavery by another, and driven out by the Carthaginians. Every time the city got back on its feet, it was struck by a new calamity: Plague decimated the population in the Middle Ages, a mile-wide stream of lava from Mt. Etna swallowed most of the city in 1663, and 25 years later a disastrous earthquake forced the Catanese to begin again. Today the city needs much renovation. Traffic flows in ever-increasing volume and adds to the smog from the industrial zone between Catania and Siracusa, but the views of Mt. Etna from Catania are superb. To Etna, Catania also owes a fertile surrounding plain and its site on nine successive layers of lava. Many of Catania's buildings are constructed from solidified lava, and the black lava stone has given the city a singular appearance. As a result, Catania is known as the city of lava and oranges. Catania's greatest native son is the composer Vincenzo Bellini, whose operas have thrilled audiences since their premieres about 170 years ago. His home, now the **Bellini Museum,** in Piazza San Francesco, preserves memorabilia of the man and his work. *Piazza San Francesco 3. Admission free. Open Mon.–Sat. 9–1:30, Sun. 9–12:30.*

The **Villa Bellini,** Catania's public gardens, is to the north just off Via Etnea, and on clear days has lovely views of snow-capped Etna. The **Duomo,** at the opposite end of Via Etnea, is a fine work by Vaccarini (1736), as is the obelisk-balancing elephant carved out of lava stone in the piazza in front. Bellini is buried inside the cathedral. Also inside is the sumptuous chapel of St. Agatha, Catania's patron saint, who is credited with having held off, more than once, the fiery flows of lava that threatened the city. During the festival of her feast day (Feb. 3–5), huge 5-meter, highly ornate carved wooden *cannelore* (large bundles of candles) are paraded through the streets at night.

Time Out If you haven't had a cannolo yet in Sicily, the pastry shops along Via Etnea are good places to try one of these wafer tubes filled with silky smooth ricotta cheese. If you're in need of something more substantial, duck into one of the trattorias along this street and order a dish of *pasta alla Norma*. It's named after one of Bellini's most famous operas and consists of short pasta with a rich eggplant-and-tomato sauce, garnished with basil leaves and grated dry ricotta cheese.

Catania is the departure point for excursions around—but not always to the top of—**Mt. Etna.** Buses leave from in front of the train station in early morning, or you can take the Circumetnea railroad around the volcano's base. Etna is one of the world's major active volcanoes and is the largest and highest in Europe. The cone of the crater rises to 3,340 meters (10,958 feet) above sea level. It has erupted nine times in the past three decades, most spectacularly in 1971 and 1983, when rivers of molten lava destroyed the two highest stations of the cable car that rises from the town of Sapienza. Travel in the proximity of the crater depends at the moment on Etna's temperament, but you can walk up and down the enormous lava dunes and wander over its moonlike surface of dead craters. The rings of vegetation change markedly as you rise, with vineyards and pine trees gradually giving way to broom and lichen.

On the other side of Mt. Etna lies the medieval mountaintop town of **Taormina.** The town's natural beauty is so great that even the considerable overdevelopment that it has suffered in the past 50 years cannot spoil its grandeur. The view of the sea and Etna from its jagged cactus-covered cliffs is as close to perfection as a panorama can get, especially on clear days, when the snowcapped volcano's white puffs of smoke are etched against the blue sky. Writers have extolled Taormina's beauty almost since its founding in the 6th century BC by Greeks from Naples. Goethe and D. H. Lawrence were among its enthusiasts. The Greeks put a high premium on finding impressive locations to stage their dramas, and Taormina's **Greek Theater** occupies one of the finest sites of any such theater. It was built during the 3rd century BC and rebuilt by the Romans during the 2nd century AD. Its acoustics are exceptional: Even today a stage whisper can be heard in the last rows. In summer, Taormina hosts an arts festival of music, cinema, and dance events, many of which are held in the Greek Theater. *Via Teatro Greco. Admission: 2,000 lire. Open daily 9–two hours before sunset.*

The main street in town is Corso Umberto, which is lined with smart boutiques and antiques shops. There are also the inevitable, and all too numerous, shops selling cheap pottery and jewelry made from Etna's black lava stone, but Piazza 9 Aprile, along the Corso, commands wonderful views and is the perfect place to sit and have a cappuccino. The town's many 14th- and 15th-century palaces have been carefully preserved; especially beautiful is the **Palazzo Corvaja,** with characteristic black lava and white limestone inlays. Today, it houses the tourist office (open weekdays 8–2 and 2:30–7:30, Sat. 8–noon). The medieval **Castello San Pancrazio** (admission free), enticingly perched on an adjoining cliff above the town, can be reached by footpath or car. If your passion for heights hasn't been exhausted, visit **Castelmola,** the tiny town above Taormina, where the Bar Turrisi makes its own refreshing almond wine—the perfect complement to the spectacular 360-degree panorama.

Time Out If you are a devotee of marzipan (almond paste), you should not leave Taormina without trying it at either the **Bar Tamako** in Piazza 9 Aprile or at one of the pastry shops along the Corso. The marzipan is shaped like various fruits, including the ubiquitous *fico d'India* (prickly pear), which grows wild along the slopes of Taormina.

The road between Taormina and Messina, about 50 kilometers (30 miles) north, is bordered by lush vegetation on one side and the sea on the other. The coast here has many inlets punctuated by gigantic odd-shaped rocks. It was along this coast, legend says, that the giant one-eyed cyclòpes hurled their boulders down on Ulysses and his terrified men as they fled to sea and on to their next adventure in Homer's *Odyssey*.

36 Messina's ancient history is a series of disasters, but the city nevertheless managed to develop a fine university and a thriving cultural environment. But at 5 o'clock in the morning on December 28, 1908, Messina changed from a flourishing metropolis of 120,000 to a heap of rubble, shaken to pieces by an earthquake that turned into a tidal wave and left 80,000 dead and the city almost completely leveled. As you approach the sickle-shape bay, from which ferries connect Sicily with the mainland, you see nothing to alert you to the relatively recent disaster, except that the 3,000-year-old city looks modern. The somewhat flat look is a precaution of seismic planning: Tall buildings are not permitted. The cathedral has been entirely rebuilt (it was originally constructed by the Norman King Roger II in 1197, and the reconstruction has maintained much of the original plan, including a handsome crown of Norman battlements, an enormous oven apse, and a splendid wood-beam ceiling). The adjoining bell tower—of a much later date—is one of the city's principal attractions. It contains one of the largest and most complex mechanical clocks in the world, constructed in 1933 with a host of gilded automatons—a roaring lion, a crowing rooster, and numerous biblical figures—that go into action every day at the stroke of noon.

Messina is the birthplace of the great Renaissance painter Antonello da Messina, whose *Polyptych of the Rosary* (1473) can be seen along with two large Caravaggios in the **Regional Museum,** located along the sea in the northern outskirts of the city. *Viale della Libertà, tel. 090/361292. Admission: 2,000 lire. Open Mon., Wed., Fri. 9–1:30, Tues., Thurs., Sat. 9–1:30, 3–5:30, Sun. and holidays 9–12:30.*

Time Out   **Pippo Nunnari,** on the corner of Via Ugo Bassi and Via Pellegrino, near Piazza Cairoli, would be the epitome of a Sicilian deli, if such a thing existed. Here you can sample or take away such typical Sicilian snacks as *arancini* (deep-fried breaded rice balls filled with cheese), mozzarella in *carrozza* (deep-fried bread pockets), and pizza covered with thin slices of potato and rosemary. The restaurant next door, under the same proprietor, is good, too.

Tour 4: The Aeolian Islands

Just off Sicily's northeast coast lies an archipelago of seven beautiful islands of volcanic origin. The **Aeolian Islands** were named after Aeolus, the Greek god of the winds, who is said to keep all the Earth's winds stuffed in a bag in his cave here. The islands are reachable by hydrofoil from Messina, Palermo, and Milazzo. The latter also has a ferryboat service to the islands, as do Palermo and Naples, but on a less frequent schedule. In summer there are numerous boats and hydrofoil excursions connecting the individual islands. The Aeolians are a fascinating world of grottoes and clear-water caves carved by the waves through the centuries. They are ideal for snorkeling or scuba diving. All Sicily's islands—and these seven in particular—are extremely popular in summer, and some of them are unpleasant-
37 ly overcrowded in July and August. **Lipari** is the largest of the Aeolians and the one most developed for tourism. Local buses circle

the island and provide wonderful views of Sicily and the other islands. Take a bus ride away from Lipari's distinctive pastel-colored houses and into its fields of spiky agaves to the northernmost tip of the island, Aquacalda, where there are interesting pumice and obsidian quarries. Or take a bus west to San Calogero, where there are hot springs and mud baths. From the red lava base of the island a plateau rises that is crowned with a 16th-century castle and a 17th-century cathedral. Next door is the **Archaeological Museum,** one of the best in Europe, with an intelligently arranged collection of prehistoric finds—some dating as far back as 4,000 BC—from various sites in the archipelago. *Tel. 090/981–1031. Admission free. Open Mon.–Sat. 9–2, Sun. and holidays 9–1.*

㊳ Vulcano, true to its name, has plenty of fumaroles sending up jets of hot vapor, but the volcano here has long been dormant. You can ascend to the crater (386 meters [about 1,266 feet] above sea level) on muleback for a wonderful view or take boat rides into the grottoes around the base. From Capo Grillo there is a view of all the Aeolians.

㊴ Salina, the second-largest island, is also the most fertile—which accounts for its good wine, the golden Malvasia. Excursions go up Mt. Fossa delle Felci, which rises to over 3,000 feet. It is also the highest of the islands, and the vineyards and fishing villages along its slopes add to its charm.

㊵ Panarea has some of the most dramatic scenery of the islands: wild caves carved out of the rock and dazzling flora. The exceptionally clear water and the richness of life on the seabed make Panarea especially suitable for underwater exploration. There is a small Bronze Age village at Capo Milazzese.

㊶ Stromboli consists entirely of the cone of an active volcano. The view from the sea—especially at night, as an endless stream of glowing red-hot lava flows into the water—is unforgettable. Stromboli is in a constant state of mild dissatisfaction, and every now and then its anger flares up, so authorities insist that you climb to the top (924 meters [about 3,031 feet] above sea level) only with a guide. The climb takes about four hours.

㊷ ㊸ Alicudi and **Filicudi** are just dots in the sea, but each has a hotel, and some local families put up guests. Filicudi is famous for its unusual volcanic rock formations and the enchanting Grotta del Bue Marino (Grotto of the Sea Ox). At Capo Graziano there is a prehistoric village. Alicudi is the farthest outpost of the Aeolians—it remains sparsely inhabited, wild, and at peace.

Time Out | The bars in the Aeolian islands, and especially those on Lipari, are known for their *granite:* dishes of shaved ice made by freezing the juice and pulp of fresh fruit. These are not snowcones doused with sickeningly sweet syrups but fruit drinks made from fresh strawberries, melon, peaches, and other fruits. Whenever the need arises for a real thirst-quencher, order a lemon granita and keep adding water from the glass or pitcher that usually accompanies your order. Many Sicilians begin the hot summer days with a *granita di caffè,* a coffee ice topped with whipped cream, into which they dunk their breakfast rolls. You can have one any time of day.

What to See and Do with Children

Almost every major city in Sicily has a theater giving performances of the world-famous **pupi siciliani** (Sicilian marionettes). The most popular are in Palermo, Acireale, and Taormina. Stories center on heroes from the Norman fables, distressed damsels, and Saracen invaders. Even if you can't understand Italian, the action is fast and furious, so it's easy to figure out what's going on. Palermo has an **International Museum** dedicated to these and other types of marionettes (*see* Tour 1: Western Sicily, *above*). If you are in Sicily at **Carnival** time (about 45 days before Easter), Acireale, near Catania, has one of the best carnivals in Italy, with dozens of colorful torch-lit floats with papier-mâché characters aboard that are pulled through the streets by costumed revelers.

Off the Beaten Track

Behind Palermo's Duomo, on Via Papireto, is the **flea market,** a good place to hunt for antique marionettes of the Norman cavaliers or for brilliantly colored pieces from the *carretti siciliani* (Sicilian carts). This is also the antiques-store neighborhood, which spreads to the next street, Corso Amedeo.

One of Agrigento's native sons was the distinguished dramatist **Luigi Pirandello** (1867–1936), whose plays, such as *Six Characters in Search of an Author*, express the fundamental ambiguity of life. Pirandello is buried under a pine tree behind the house where he was born, in Piazzale Caos, a few miles west of town. His **house** has been made into a museum of Pirandello memorabilia. Every year a festival of Pirandello's plays is held in Agrigento from late July to early August. *Admission free. Open Mon.–Sat. 9–12, 3–7 (winter 3–5).*

From Messina, a hydrofoil will speed you across the strait to **Reggio di Calabria,** on the toe of the boot, where two larger-than-life-size 5th-century Greek bronze statues are exhibited in the excellent **National Museum of Magna Grecia.** The statues—known as the **Riace bronzes**—were found by accident by an amateur deep-sea diver off the coast of Calabria in 1972 and are worth going out of your way to see. *Corso Garibaldi, Piazza De Nava, tel. 0965/812255. Admission: 6,000 lire. Open Mon. 9–1, Tues.–Sat. 9–1, 3:30–7, Sun. 9–12:30.*

Shopping

Sicily is one of the leaders in the Italian **ceramics** industry, with important factories at **Caltagirone,** in the interior, and **Santo Stefano di Camastra,** along the northern coast between Messina and Cefalù. Colorful Sicilian folk pottery can still be bought at bargain prices. Fratantoni, on Via Nazionale, in Santo Stefano di Camastra, has a wide selection and also some unusual pieces, such as gigantic ceramic heads—of Norman knights and Saracens—that can be used as planters. Branciforti in Caltagirone (Scala Santa Maria del Monte 3) produces elegant designs based on traditional motifs from the 10th to the 19th centuries. If you seek more modern designs, De Simone, whose Picasso-like faces on plates and pitchers are popular abroad, has an outlet at Via Messina Marina 633, and in Palermo at Piazza Leoni 2 and Via Stabile 133.

Place mats, tablecloths, napkins, and **clothing** decorated with fine petitpoint are good buys in **Cefalù, Taormina,** and **Erice,** but they are not cheap. Make sure that any linen you buy is produced in Sicily and not on another continent.

Collectors have been combing Sicily for years for pieces of the colorful **carretti siciliani** (Sicilian carts). Before the automobile, these were the major form of transportation in Sicily, and they were decorated in bright primary colors and in primitive styles, with scenes from the Norman troubadour tales. The axles of these carts were ornamented with open filigree work, which was also brightly painted. Pieces sometimes appear at better antiques shops, such as Chez le Francais, in **Taormina** (Piazza San Domenico 6). Modern "adaptations" are available at the **Palermo** flea market (Via Papireto, behind the Duomo).

Sports

Camping Sicily has excellent camping facilities on both the main island and its satellite islands. The two best are **El Bahira,** in San Vito Lo Capo (tel. 0923/972577), and **Bazia,** in Furnari Marini, west of Milazzo (tel. 0941/81235). Both have restaurants and showers, as well as swimming pools, tennis courts, and discos.

Scuba Diving The island of **Ustica,** north of Palermo, is an international center for scuba diving and snorkeling. Its rugged coast is dotted with grottoes that are washed by crystal-clear waters and filled with an incredible variety of interesting marine life. In July Ustica hosts an International Meeting of Marine Fishing that attracts sportsmen as well as marine biologists from all over the world.

Skiing Skiing is becoming a very popular sport in Sicily. Ski areas can be found on the slopes on the north side of Mt. Etna. The most popular is at **Linguaglossa,** located in a magnificent pine forest about 45 kilometers (27 miles) from Catania. The other area for skiing in Sicily is in the **Le Madonie** mountains, south of Cefalù.

Beaches

There is a surfeit of beaches in Sicily, but many of them are too rocky, too crowded, or too dirty to be enjoyed for long. Among the exceptions are **Mondello,** near Palermo, a popular sandy beach on a tiny peninsula jutting out into the Mediterranean; **Sant'Alessio** and **Santa Teresa,** north of Taormina (the beaches just below Taormina itself are disappointing); and **Capo San Vito,** on the northern coast, near Erice, a sandy beach on a promontory overlooking a bay in the Gulf of Castellammare.

Dining and Lodging

Dining Sicilian cooking reflects the different Mediterranean influences that have left their mark on the island. Fish, vegetables, and grains are used in imaginative combinations, sometimes served with Italian pastas and sometimes with Arab ingredients, such as *couscous* (steamed semolina). Sweet and sour tastes are deftly mingled, and each cook has a distinctive touch, so that *caponata* (an antipasto of eggplant, capers, olives, and, in eastern Sicily, peppers) is different at each restaurant.

Sicily has always been one of Italy's poorest areas, so meat is seen rarely on menus. When it *is* featured, it is usually prepared *alla brace* (skewered) or in *falso magro* (a thin slice of meat rolled around sausage, onion, bacon, bits of egg, and cheese).

Seafood from Sicilian waters is the best and most varied in all Italy. *Tonno* (tuna) is a staple in many coastal areas, while *pesce spada*

(swordfish) is equally common, if more expensive. Try *ricci* (sea ur-
chins), which are a specialty of Mondello, near Palermo. Fish sauces
for pasta are also noteworthy: *Pasta con le sarde* is made with fresh
sardines, olive oil, anchovies, raisins, and pine nuts, and has the distinctive flavor of wild fennel. In Catania, spaghetti alla Norma,
named for the heroine in the opera by local composer Vincenzo Bellini, has a sauce of tomatoes and fried eggplant. Desserts from Sicily
are famous. *Cassata siciliana* is a rich combination of candied fruit,
marzipan, and icing. *Gelato* (ice cream) is excellent and is usually
homemade, sometimes in the form of *granita di limone*, a kind of
lemon slush. Gooey cakes and very sweet desserts help raise the
blood-sugar level, and the high priests of nouvelle cuisine would
probably keel over if faced with a typical Sicilian dessert, like chestnut ice cream covered with hot *zabaglione* (rich, foamy custard laced
with Marsala).

The sweet dessert wine, Marsala, is Sicily's most famous, but there
is a range of other local wines, from the dark red Faro to the sparkling dry Regaleali, which is excellent with fish.

Highly recommended restaurants are indicated by a star ★.

Category	Cost*
$$$$	over 85,000 lire
$$$	60,000–85,000 lire
$$	25,000–60,000 lire
$	under 25,000 lire

per person, including house wine, service, and tax

Lodging Though Sicily is Italy's largest region, it has some of the most remote countryside and only a limited number of good-quality hotels.
The major cities and resorts of Palermo, Taormina, and Agrigento
are the only spots with a real range of accommodations. There are,
of course, some superb establishments, such as converted villas
with views over the sea or well-equipped modern hotels, but it is
best not to expect to come across some charming spot in the middle
of nowhere. If you want to get away from the major centers, make
reservations well in advance.

Hotels in the Very Expensive bracket provide comfort and services
to match those in other Italian regions; they are usually older, more
established hotels. In the $$–$$$ range, you'll find newer hotels
built to cater to the increased tourist trade of the past 20 years.
Chains, such as Jolly Hotels, are predictable but reliable. Inexpensive establishments are usually family-run and offer a basic level of
comfort: Although the bathroom will be clean, it will probably also
be down the hall.

Highly recommended lodgings are indicated by a star ★.

Category	Cost*
$$$$	over 300,000 lire
$$$	160,000–300,000 lire

$$	100,000–160,000 lire
$	under 100,000 lire

All prices are for a standard double room for two, including service and 9% IVA (19% for luxury establishments).

Agrigento
Dining

Caprice. The specialty of this popular restaurant in the temple area is meat prepared alla brace, although there is also a good selection of seafood, particularly pesce spada. The waiters are proud to explain some of the less familiar entries on the wine list, which is relatively extensive. *Via Panoramica dei Templi 51, tel. 0922/26469. Reservations advised. Dress: casual. AE, DC, MC, V. Closed Fri. and July 1–15. $$*

Taverna Mosè. This restaurant is popular with sightseers from nearby temples, so it can get busy in the early evening, when it becomes too dark for temple exploring. The atmosphere is bustling, with waiters shouting orders at each other and at the kitchen. The house specialties are homemade sausages and grilled fish, and the wine list is comprehensive. *Contrada San Biagio, tel. 0922/26778. Reservations not necessary. Dress: casual. No credit cards. Closed Mon. $$*

Vigneto. Unless you make reservations at this popular restaurant, it's best to arrive early to snag one of the good tables on the terrace, which has a memorable view of the temples. The menu changes, with daily specials reflecting whatever is in season or is freshest at the fish market. *Arrosti* (roast meats) are always a good bet. *Via Cavaleri Magazzeni 11, tel. 0922/414319. Reservations advised. Dress: casual. No credit cards. Closed Tues. and Nov. 1–30. $$*

Lodging

Jolly dei Templi. Guests travel 8 kilometers (5 miles) southeast of town to Villagio Mosè to stay in this member of the Jolly hotel chain. Rooms are large, bright, and airy, and if there's a sense of having seen it all before, you probably have—in one of the other Jolly hotels or in any well-equipped U.S. motel. That is the price to pay for what are always comfortable, hassle-free accommodations. The Pirandello restaurant is excellent, so you won't have to head into Agrigento to dine. *Parco Angeli, Villagio Mosè, tel. 0922/606144, fax 0922/606685. 144 rooms with bath. Facilities: pool, restaurant, bar. AE, DC, MC, V. $$$*

★ **Villa Athena.** There is much demand for this well-furnished former villa, so make reservations as early as possible. Many rooms—they're all different—have terraces looking out on the large gardens and the swimming pool. The temple zone is an easy walk from the hotel, and there is a convivial atmosphere in the bar, where a multinational crowd swaps stories and advice. *Via dei Templi 33, tel. 0922/596288, fax 0922/402180. 41 rooms with bath or shower. Facilities: pool, garden, restaurant, bar. AE, MC, V. $$$*

Castelmola
Dining
★

Il Faro. Castelmola is a small village above Taormina, and as you dine in this family-run country restaurant, sitting under a grape arbor, you have an excellent view of the wild cliffs and sea. Meat dishes are recommended alla brace, particularly *pollo* (chicken) and *coniglio* (rabbit). Piera and Francesco, the owners, provide an antipasto with homegrown vegetables. Start your meal with *bruschetta all' ortolana* (country bread toasted with olive oil, topped with tomatoes and onions). *Via Rotabile, Contrada Petralia, tel. 0942/28193. Reservations advised. Dress: casual. No credit cards. Closed Wed. $$*

Catania **Costa Azzurra.** This seafood restaurant is in the Ognina district, just
Dining north of the center and on the way to the Taormina road. Reserve a
★ table on the veranda by the edge of the sea. There are good views of
the harbor. The *fritto misto* (mixed grill) can be ordered as an antipasto or a main course, and the pesce spada steak is a simple classic—served grilled with a large slice of lemon. *Via De Cristofaro 4,
tel. 095/494920. Reservations advised. Jacket and tie required. AE,
DC, MC, V. Closed Mon. $$$*

Pagano. This restaurant, located behind the Hotel Excelsior, has
been around a long time (since the 1950s) and remains a favorite
with locals for genuine Catanese cooking. Seafood is the specialty,
but it's the unpretentious kind that won't send the check into the
stratosphere. Try *insalata di polipo* (octopus salad) as a starter and
then *sarde* or *acciughe* (sardines or anchovies) in a variety of sauces.
Like the sober, rather dated decor, the service is formal. *Via De
Roberto 37, tel. 095/537045, Reservations advised. Dress: casual.
AE, DC, MC, V. Closed Sat. and Aug. $$*

Lodging **Excelsior.** Ask for a room facing Piazza Verga, a neat tree-lined
square in this quiet but central district of Catania. The Excelsior has
air-conditioning and sound-insulating windows in all rooms. The
rooftop garden is one of Catania's most chic meeting places, and the
American Bar should provide solace to anyone pining for a Manhat-
tan. *Piazza Verga 39, tel. 095/537071, fax 095/537015. 167 rooms
with bath. Facilities: rooftop garden, restaurant, 2 bars, garage.
AE, DC, MC, V. $$$*

Savona. A good central choice, the Savona is an efficiently run and
well-maintained hotel a stone's throw from Piazza del Duomo. The
rooms are spacious and comfortable, solidly furnished, and
equipped with TV and telephones. Prices include a Continental
breakfast. Parking may be a problem. *Via Vittorio Emanuele 210,
tel. 095/326982, fax 095/715–8169. 25 rooms, 15 with shower. Facili-
ties: bar, breakfast room. No credit cards. $*

Cefalù **La Brace.** There is a lively atmosphere in this bistro-style restau-
Dining rant located near the cathedral in the center of town. Graceful ceil-
ing arches and rustic walls lend an informal air that makes it popular
with tourists. Stick to the excellent grills, and save room for the
homemade desserts, such as cassata siciliana. *Via Venticinque
Novembre 10, tel. 0921/23570. Reservations advised. Dress: casual.
AE, DC, MC, V. Closed Mon. and Dec.–Jan. $$*

Gabbiano. The name, meaning "seagull," is appropriate for a har-
borside restaurant decorated with a nautical theme and specializing
in seafood. The house specialties are *involtini di pesce spada*
(swordfish rolls) and spaghetti *alla marinara* (with a spicy sauce of
tomatoes, garlic, and onions). *Via Lungomare Giardina 17, tel.
0921/21495. Reservations advised. Dress: casual but neat. AE, DC,
MC, V. Closed Wed. $$*

Lodging **Baia del Capitano.** The peaceful district of Mazzaforno, about 5 ki-
★ lometers (3 miles) outside town, is the setting for this handsome ho-
tel, which has a surprising number of extras, considering its size.
The building is less than 25 years old, but it blends in with the tradi-
tional homes nearby. The colorful gardens, extending to the sur-
rounding olive groves, are ideal for quiet reading or an afternoon
siesta in the shade. A good sandy beach is an easy walk away, but
many guests choose to stay by the pool and have drinks on the ter-
race. The rooms are large and quiet. *Contrada Mazzaforno,
Mazzaforno, tel. 0921/20005, fax 0921/20163. 39 rooms with bath or
shower. Facilities: pool, game room, terrace, tennis court, garden,
restaurant, bar. AE, MC, V. $$–$$$*

Le Calette. This seaside hotel is popular with Scandinavians and Germans, who know a good place to sunbathe when they see one. The modern hotel is surrounded by gardens on the three sides that don't face the sea, and guests can use the private beach. The rooms are bright and airy; those facing the sea escape the hot Sicilian sun. The Caldura district, where Le Calette is located, is a little more than a mile from the center of town. *Contrada Caldura, tel. 0921/ 24144, fax 0921/23688. 50 rooms with shower. Facilities: private beach, pool, restaurant, bar, garden, disco. AE, DC, MC, V. Closed Nov.–Apr. $$*

★ **Kalura.** Caldura is also the setting for this modern hotel, which shares the advantages of Le Calette but is a bit harder to reach without a car. Taxis from Cefalù take only a few minutes, though. The Kalura is on a small promontory, making it something of a retreat. Sports facilities keep you from getting too sedentary, and the private beach is ideal for swimming. Most rooms have views of the sea, and the decor is bright and cheerful. *Contrada Caldura, tel. 0921/ 21354, fax 0921/20548. 75 rooms with bath or shower. Facilities: private beach, pool, tennis court, restaurant, bar, garden. AE, DC, MC, V. $$*

Erice **La Taverna di Re Aceste.** This popular restaurant is named for
Dining Acestus, the first king of Erice, and the house specialty, *cuscus*
★ *Aceste* (a spicy Arab-influenced semolina-and-seafood mixture) is in his honor, as are the murals along the walls. The chef also has a special pesto dish made with wild herbs. Try the grilled fish, but ask for the price, since you'll be paying by weight, not per order. The waiters are helpful and will guide you through the daily specials and the wine list. *Viale Conte Pepoli, tel. 0923/869084. Reservations advised. Dress: casual but neat. AE, DC, MC, V. Closed Wed. and Nov. $$*

Lodging **Ermione.** Spectacular views and cool breezes are the rewards of a visit to Erice, and this 1960s hotel overlooking the Tyrrhenian Sea is in a position to offer both. Nearly every room has a good view, although some would say that the terrace bar has the most panoramic vista. The hotel restaurant is popular locally, with fish couscous a standout. *Via Pineta Comunale 43, tel. 0923/869138, fax 0923/ 869587. 46 rooms with bath or shower. Facilities: terrace, pool, restaurant, bar, garden, garage. AE, DC, MC, V. $$*

★ **Moderno.** Local craft work and some antiques decorate the gracious rooms of this intimate and well-run hotel on the cobblestone streets of the medieval town. Some rooms are in the modern annex. The main building, with a fire blazing in the lounge in winter, is one attraction; the restaurant, serving seafood pastas and homemade desserts, is another. Ask for a room facing the sea. *Via Vittorio Emanuele 63, tel. 0923/869300, fax 0923/869139. 40 rooms with bath or shower. Facilities: restaurant, bar, tavern, garage, terrace. AE, DC, MC, V. $$*

Messina **Alberto.** Many visitors to Messina make it a priority to reserve a ta-
Dining ble at this deluxe restaurant and are willing to splurge even if
★ they're budgeting. If you're adventurous, and not too worried about the cost, ask the waiter to order for you: You'll get a succession of courses linked by a common theme of seafood. À la carte items are also delicious, particularly the *fettuccine con ortaggi e crostacei* (pasta with peas, celery, and shellfish) and the involtini di pesce spada. Have some vintage Marsala with one of the rich homemade desserts. *Via Ghibellina 95, tel. 090/710711. Reservations required. Jacket and tie required. AE, DC, MC, V. Closed Sun. and Aug. $$$*
Pippo Nunnari. Traditional Sicilian cooking is complemented by the

refined decor, with antiques and rich fabrics. A favorite Sicilian appetizer is a selection of arancini (rice balls filled with meat or cheese); you can also have the risotto di mare, whose ingredients change with each day's catch of fish. Don't be embarrassed about ordering the *bistecca* (steak) here: It's charcoal grilled and renowned locally. Pippo has a specialty shop next door—ideal for picnic supplies. *Via Ugo Bassi 157, tel. 090/293–8584. Reservations advised. Dress: casual but neat. AE, MC, V. Closed Mon. and July 1–15. $$–$$$*

Monreale **La Botte.** It's worth the short drive or inexpensive taxi fare to reach
Dining this good-value restaurant, which features local specialties. Dine alfresco on daily specials, such as spaghetti *alla brigantesca* (with fresh tuna, capers, olives, tomato, parsley, and white wine), or regular favorites, such as stuffed involtini. Local wines are a good bet. *Contrada Lenzitti 416, S186, tel. 091/414051. Reservations advised weekends. Dress: casual but neat. AE, DC, MC, V. Closed lunch weekdays except by reservation and in June. Closed Mon. and July–Aug. $$*

Noto **Il Giglio.** Seafood dishes with a Spanish touch are the specialty at
Dining this pleasant trattoria in the center of town run by Maria Luz Corruchaga and her husband, Corrado. Particularly recommended are pasta *al nero di seppia* (with cuttlefish) and *zuppa di vongole e cozze* (clam and mussel soup). You'll also find paella on the menu. *Piazza Municipio, tel. 0931/838640. Reservations advised weekends. Dress: casual. MC, V. $*

Palazzolo **Da Alfredo.** This one-man show (Alfredo is the owner/chef) is located
Acreide on one of the most attractive streets of this Baroque town between
Dining Caltagirone and Siracusa. Specialties depend on the season, the availability of ingredients at the local markets, and the whims of Alfredo himself. Homemade pasta, such as tubular penne and cheese-filled ravioli, are specialties, and the sauces are hearty and spicy. *Via Duca d'Aosta 27, tel. 0931/883266. Reservations advised weekends. Dress: casual. AE. Closed Wed. $*

Palermo **Charleston.** You'll feel pampered by the discreet service and elegant
Dining surroundings in this famous Palermo restaurant located on a quiet
★ square in the heart of the city. Impeccably dressed waiters coast effortlessly through the high-ceiling rooms, offering help with the extensive menu and wine list. Specialties run the gamut of Sicilian and international dishes, with an emphasis on seafood, in keeping with the cuisine of the island. Try the spaghetti *all'aragosta*, with its delicious lobster sauce, or the pesce spada *arrosto* (roast swordfish), but leave room for the sweet, rich house dessert, *torta Charleston*. The whole restaurant operation moves 5 miles north to Mondello from June 16 to September 25: The Mondello premises occupy a pavilion on the sea. *Charleston (Sept. 26–June 15), Piazza Ungheria 30, tel. 091/321366; Charleston le Terrazze (June 16–Sept. 25) Viale Regina Elena, Mondello, tel. 091/450171. Reservations required. Jacket and tie required. AE, DC, MC, V. Closed Sun. $$$*

★ **Da Renato.** There is an excellent view of the harbor from this top-quality restaurant along the sea road toward Cefalù. It's enough out of the way to make it the insider's choice, and the clientele consists mainly of well-heeled locals who know their way around a good seafood menu. *Frutti di mare* (mixed seafoods) makes a good antipasto, and the *zuppa di mare* (fish soup) is hearty enough to be a meal in itself. Grills are also recommended. *Via Messina Marina 224, tel. 091/630–2881. Reservations advised weekends. Dress: casual but neat. AE, MC, V. Closed Wed. and Aug. 10–25. $$$*

Gourmand's. A chic clientele frequents this modern restaurant, with its high-tech decor (lots of metal and primary colors) and nouvelle cuisine–influenced menu. Pesce spada *affumicato* (smoked swordfish) goes well with a bottle of local Regaleali. Gourmand's is in the northern end of Palermo, near Piazza Castelnuovo. *Via della Libertà 37/e, tel. 091/323431. Reservations required. Jacket and tie required. AE, DC, MC, V. Closed Sun. $$$*

Lo Scudiero. The antipasto and the *assaggini* (sample portions) of the various pastas give you a delicious introduction to Sicilian cuisine: The courteous waiters are also ambassadors for local cooking. Lo Scudiero has a subdued atmosphere, which will be appreciated in this noisy city. Try some of the nonseafood items on the menu—the meat dishes are excellent, especially the bistecca. The fritto misto contains meats and seasonal vegetables. *Via Turati 7, tel. 091/ 581628. Reservations advised. Dress: casual. AE, DC, MC, V. Closed Sun. $$*

Strascinu. The specialty in this informal and busy restaurant is pasta con le sarde, the famous Arab-Sicilian blend of fresh sardines, wild fennel fronds, sultanas, and pine nuts. *Viale Regione Siciliana 2286, tel. 091/401292. Reservations advised. Dress: casual but neat. AE, DC. Closed Mon. and July 15–31. $$*

Antica Focacceria San Francesco. On the square in front of the church of San Francesco, off Corso Vittorio Emanuele in the heart of Palermo, this place is an institution, as you can see from the turn-of-the-century wooden cabinets and fixtures of what is still a neighborhood bakery. But it also bakes and fries the snacks that locals love—and from which you can well make an inexpensive meal. Try arancini and panelle (chickpea fritters) or pizza right out of the oven. You can sit at marble-topped tables while you eat, or take food out if you wish. Beverages, including wine and beer, are available. *Via Paternostro 58, tel. 091/320264. No reservations. Dress: casual. No credit cards. Closed Mon. $*

★ **Shangai.** There is nothing Chinese about this Palermo institution in the busy Vucciria market. It's on a terrace above the market (the source of all the ingredients): Look down and order your fish from the displays below, and it will be hoisted up in a wicker basket. The atmosphere is jovial and frantic, with lots of teasing and shouting. Fritto misto (usually fish here) is always a good bet. *Vicolo Mezzani 34, tel. 091/589702. No reservations. Dress: casual. No credit cards. Closed Sun. $*

Toto. A neighbor of the Shangai in the bustling Vucciria market, Toto is one of the plainest trattorias in town, serving fresh fish in a variety of ways, including alla brace, as fritto misto, and in zuppa di pesce. Ask Toto to sing—he may even do magic tricks. At times this place makes even the Shangai look staid. *Via dei Coltellieri 5, no phone. No reservations. Dress: casual. No credit cards. Open lunch only. Closed Sun. $*

Lodging
★ **Villa Igiea.** A short taxi ride through some rough-looking districts of Palermo takes you to this oasis of luxury and comfort, situated in its own tropical garden at the edge of the bay. It's difficult to imagine that you're so close to busy Palermo as you meander through the grounds, which include an ancient Greek temple at the water's edge. The large rooms (many with terraces overlooking the gardens and the sea) are furnished individually, the most attractive with an Italian art nouveau flavor. Spacious lobbies and public rooms give onto a terrace with its own restaurant. Sports facilities help make this elegant villa a self-contained enclave in frenetic Palermo. *Via Belmonte 43, tel. 091/543744, fax 091/547654. 6 suites and 117 rooms with bath. Facilities: pool, tennis court, restaurant, terrace bar, American cocktail bar. AE, DC, MC, V. $$$$*

Grande Albergo e delle Palme. There is a faded charm about this *grande dame*, whose public rooms suggest the elegant life of Palermo society before World War I, when tea dances and balls were held here. Guest rooms are uneven—some are charming period pieces stuffed with antiques and heavy fabrics, others are dark and cramped. There is an American-style cocktail bar and a rooftop terrace with good views of Palermo. *Via Roma 396, tel. 091/583933, fax 091/331545. 5 suites and 187 rooms with bath or shower. Facilities: restaurant, piano bar, rooftop terrace, parking. AE, DC, MC, V. $$$*

★ **Mondello Palace.** The beach resort of Mondello is just north of Palermo and is a perennial favorite because of its cleaner air and less rushed atmosphere. The Mondello Palace is the leading hotel in the resort, making the best use of its location near the beach. The private beach has cabins and changing rooms for the use of Mondello Palace guests, and most of the hotel rooms have a balcony with a view over the sea. The rooms are well equipped and large, with bright fabrics and large beds. In summer there's a choice of two popular restaurants—one in the hotel and one on the nearby wharf. *Viale Principe di Scalea, Mondello Lido, tel. 091/450001, fax 091/450657. 8 suites and 91 rooms with bath or shower. Facilities: pool, private beach, gardens, restaurant, bar. AE, MC, V. $$$*

Mediterraneo. An uninspiring hotel, it is nonetheless a useful, conveniently located base for exploring Palermo's sights. From the large air-conditioned lobby furnished in 1970s style, elevators ascend five stories to rather boxy rooms without much of a view, though well equipped with TV and telephone. *Via Rosolino Pilo 43, tel. 091/581133, fax 091/586974. 106 rooms with bath or shower. Facilities: restaurant, bar, garage. AE, DC, MC, V. $$*

Principe di Belmonte. This is a tasteful choice among Palermo's cheaper hotels. It is family-run and friendly and centrally located—a convenient walk both from the port and Piazza Castelnuovo—but is on a relatively quiet street. Advance reservations are advised. *Via Principe di Belmonte 25, tel. 091/331065. 17 rooms, 14 with shower. Facilities: bar. AE, DC, MC, V. $*

Piazza Armerina
Dining

Centrale da Totò. Centrally located, this reliable trattoria is often crowded with both sightseers and locals. The emphasis is on a family clientele, rather than intimate or expense-account dining, and the portions reflect this *mangia, mangia* outlook. Try the *pappardelle alla Centrale*, a rich, filling pasta dish made with tomato sauce and fresh vegetables. *Via Mazzini 29, tel. 0935/680153. No reservations. Dress: casual. No credit cards. Closed Mon. $*

Siracusa
Dining
★

Ionico. Enjoy seaside dining in the coastal Santa Lucia district. Chef/proprietor Pasquale Giudice cooks meals to order or will suggest a specialty from a selection of market-fresh ingredients. Try the pasta *con acciughe e il pan grattato* (in an anchovy sauce). *Riviera Dionisio il Grande 194, tel. 0931/65540. Reservations advised. Dress: casual. AE, DC, MC, V. Closed Tues. and Aug. 15–31. $$$*

Archimede. The antipasto misto should whet your appetite for the predominantly seafood menu of this small establishment in the Old Town. Risotto di mare and pesce spada are specialties, but the menu veers away from seafood when game is in season. Order the coniglio if you see it on the menu. *Via Gemmellaro 8, tel. 0931/69701. Reservations advised. Dress: casual. AE, MC, V. $$*

Arlecchino. A bustling bohemian atmosphere pervades this restaurant, located midway between the archaeological zone and the Old Town. It's popular with artists and students, always a sign of good value. The Palermo-born proprietor serves specialties from his hometown, such as risotto *ai granchi* (with crab) and homemade cassata for dessert. Try for a table on the terrace. *Via dei Tolomei 5, tel. 0931/66386. Reservations not required. Dress: casual. AE, DC, MC, V. Closed Mon. and Aug. $$*

Minosse. You'll find this small, old-fashioned restaurant in the heart of Siracusa's Città Vecchia. Fish is the specialty, and it comes broiled, baked, stuffed, and skewered. For an introduction to the local seafood, try the antipasto misto di frutti di mare. Ask for the daily special as your main course, or try the pesce spada alla brace. The zuppa di pesce is a local favorite. *Via Mirabella 6, tel. 0931/66366. Reservations advised weekends. Dress: casual. AE, MC, V. Closed Mon. $$*

Lodging **Forte Agip.** This standard motel, with modern comforts (color TV and minibar in all rooms) is across the street from the archaeological zone. The rooms are bright and clean, and the restaurant serves some local specialties as well as classic hotel food. *Viale Teracati 30, tel. 0931/463232, fax 0931/67115. Facilities: restaurant, bar, parking. AE, DC, MC, V. $$$*

Jolly Hotel. The rooms are uniformly comfortable in this member of the Jolly hotel chain, Italy's answer to Holiday Inns. The big advantage, apart from knowing that the plugs work and the rooms are soundproofed, is the location. The hotel is less than a quarter mile from the train station and within easy walking distance of the archaeological zone. *Corso Gelone 45, tel. 0931/461111, fax 0931/461126. 100 rooms with bath or shower. Facilities: garden, restaurant, bar, parking. AE, DC, MC, V. $$$*

Taormina **Delfino.** This seaside restaurant is across the road from the cable car
Dining station in Mazzarò, to the east of Taormina proper. Seafood takes
★ pride of place here, from hearty starters, such as the zuppa di pesce or risotto marinara, to main courses, such as *gamberetti* (shrimp) *alla brace*. Arrive early or reserve to get one of the best tables overlooking the sea. *Via Nazionale, Mazzarò, tel. 0942/23004. Dress: casual but neat. Reservations advised. AE, DC, MC, V. Closed Nov.– Mar. 15. $$–$$$*

Luraleo. You can dine indoors by candlelight or in the vine-covered garden in summer. The food here is of a high standard, with the accent on fish—sample the risotto with salmon and pistachios, a specialty of the house. There is a rich selection of antipasti. *Via Bagnoli Croci 27, tel. 0942/24279. Reservations advised. MC, V. Closed Jan. $$*

Lodging **San Domenico Palace.** The panoramic views from this converted
★ 15th-century convent will stay in your mind long after you're gone. Luxury and comfort are bywords in this deluxe hotel, which has managed to sneak a number of unobtrusive 20th-century comforts into its furnishings (such as wheelchair access and climate control). The essentially Renaissance flavor remains, however, from the cloisters to the chapel, which is now a bar. The rooms in the front of the hotel have sweeping views of the bay; those in back look out over the gardens, with Etna visible in the distance. The rooms are decorated with antiques and are brimming with fresh flowers. *Piazza San Domenico 5, tel. 0942/23701, fax 0942/625506. 101 rooms with bath. Facilities: 2 restaurants, 2 bars, pool, gardens, terrace, piano bar. AE, DC, MC, V. $$$$*

Jolly Diodoro. Located high on a cliff near the Greek amphitheater, this Jolly hotel shares the view with the much more expensive San Domenico Palace. Another departure from the sometimes functional Jolly format is the relaxing and colorful garden, where you can have a drink and watch the play of light over the sea. *Via Bagnoli Croce 75, tel. 0942/23312, fax 0942/23391. 103 rooms with bath or* shower. *Facilities: pool, garden, restaurant, bar, parking. AE, DC, MC, V. $$$*

Villa Fiorita. This converted private home near the Greek amphitheater has excellent views of the coast from nearly every room. The rooms vary in size and furnishings, but most are bright and colorful, with large windows that let in the sea breezes. Prices are reasonable for a hotel with a swimming pool and small garden. *Via Pirandello 39, tel. 0942/24122, fax 0942/625967. 24 rooms with bath or shower. Facilities: garden, pool, garage. AE, MC, V. Closed Jan.–Easter. $$*

Trapani
Dining
★ **P & G.** Couscous is a specialty of this small, popular restaurant on a quiet street between the train station and the Villa Margherita public gardens. The couscous features fish in summer and meat in winter. A mixed grill of meats in a zesty orange sauce will revive any appetite suffering from fish fatigue. Wash it all down with a bottle of Donnafugata, a good white from the Rallo vineyards at Marsala. *Via Spalti 1, tel. 0923/547701. Reservations advised. Dress: neat but casual. AE, DC, MC, V. Closed Sun. and Aug., Dec. 25–Jan. 2. $$*

The Arts

Opera **Teatro Bellini** (Piazza Bellini, Catania, tel. 095/312020) hosts an opera season from October to mid-June, attracting top singers and productions to the birthplace of the great operatic composer Vincenzo Bellini.

In May and June, Siracusa's impressive **Teatro Greco** will be the setting for performances of classical drama and comedy; the festival is held in even-numbered years only. For information, call 0931/67415.

Concerts The churches and theaters of Taormina are the venues for the summer festival of **classical music,** held each year from May to September. For information, call 0942/23751.

Events The **Palio dei Normanni,** a medieval tournament with participants dressed in 14th-century fashion, takes place on August 13 in Piazza Armerina.

From July 11 to 15, Palermo stages a **street fair** in honor of its patron saint, Santa Rosalia. There are fireworks displays in the evenings.

Messina stages a **folklore parade** of huge traditional effigies, called Giganti, each year on August 13 and 14.

Epiphany (Jan. 6) is celebrated with Byzantine rites and a procession of townspeople in local costume through the streets of Piana degli Albanesi, near Palermo. The village, 24 kilometers (15 miles) south of the island's capital, is named for the Albanian immigrants who first settled there, bringing with them the Byzantine Catholic rites.

Theater Taormina's **Greco-Roman Theater** is the setting for regular theatrical performances from July to September. For information, call 0942/23220.

Palermo's **Teatro Biondo** (tel. 091/588755) is Sicily's foremost theater, featuring a winter season of plays from November to May.

Cinema Taormina hosts an international **film festival** each July in the grand setting of the Roman amphitheater. For information, call 0942/23220.

17 Sardinia

The second-largest island in the Mediterranean—just smaller than Sicily—Sardinia is about 180 kilometers (112 miles) from mainland Italy and very much off the beaten track. A Phoenician stronghold in ancient times and later a Spanish dominion, Sardinia doesn't seem typically "Italian" in its color and flavor. It lies just a bit too far from the mainland—from imperial and papal Rome and from the palaces of the Savoy dynasty—to have been transformed by the events that forged a national character. Yet Giuseppe Garibaldi, the charismatic national hero who led his troops in fervid campaigns to unify Italy in the mid-19th century, chose to spend his last years in relative isolation on the small island of Caprera, just off the coast of Sardinia.

Although Sardinia (Sardegna in Italian) is now less than an hour by air and only several hours by boat from mainland Italy, it is removed from the mainstream of tourism except for a brief two-month period in the summer, when vacationing Italians take its beautiful coasts and clean waters by storm. This is a good reason not to visit Sardinia in July or August. May and October are the best touring months. In June and September the coasts are not too crowded, and ribbons of sandy beaches welcome sun worshipers. These are the best months if you want to combine sightseeing with sunbathing. Winter in the north of the island is cold and rainy but is mild and generally sunny in the south. The interior is *never* crowded; Italian tourists in Sardinia come for the sea, not for rugged and deserted mountain scenery.

Sardinia closely resembles Corsica, the French island across the 16-kilometer (10-mile)-wide windswept Strait of Bonifacio to the north. A dense bush, or *macchia*, barely penetrable in some districts, covers large areas. The terrain is rough, like the short, sturdy shepherds you see in the highlands—impassive figures engaged in one of the few gainful occupations that the stony land allows. Shaggy flocks of sheep and goats are familiar features in the Sardinian landscape, just as their meat and cheese are staples of the island's cuisine. Aside from the chic opulence of the Costa Smeralda, there's little sophistication in Sardinia. The sprawling cities of Cagliari and Sassari have a distinctly provincial air. Newer hotels may seem a little old-fashioned, and hotels—of any vintage—are hard to find inland. There's little traffic on the roads, and trains, buses, and people in general move at a gentle pace. There are hamlets where women swathed in black shawls and long, full skirts look with suspicion upon strangers passing through. Sardinians are courteous but remote, perhaps because of their innate dignity.

Like mainland Italians, the Sardinians are of varied origin. On the northwest coast, fine traceries of ironwork around a balcony underscore the Spanish influence. In the northeast, the inhabitants boast Genoese or Pisan ancestry, and the headlands display the ruined fortresses of the ancient duchy of Malaspina on the Italian mainland. As you explore the southern coast, you'll come upon the physiognomies, customs, dialects, place names, and holy buildings of the Turks, the Moors, the Phoenicians, the Austrians, and the mainland Italians. If there are any pure Sards—or Sardinians—left, perhaps they can be found in the south-central mountains, south of Nuoro, under the 6,000-foot crests of the Gennargentu massif, in the rugged country still ironically called Barbagia, "Land of Strangers."

People visit Sardinia for landscapes, rather than cathedrals or monuments; for easy-going excursions with plenty of detours, rather than a highly organized itinerary; for a low-key entertainment scene that highlights folklore, rather than brilliant or expensive nightlife. And, speaking of expense, the cost of living on Sardinia, as on most islands, is somewhat higher than on the mainland. On the other hand, if you're willing to rough it, you'll find low-cost lodgings at modest inns along your way.

Sardinia is not as large as some other regions, but its mountainous terrain makes some drives through deserted country seem very long, indeed. The main highway linking Cagliari with Sassari was begun in 1820 by the Savoy ruler Carlo Felice; designated Highway 131, but still referred to as the Carlo Felice Highway (after its founder) by the islanders, it heads northwest through the fertile Campidano plain for 216 kilometers (134 miles) to Sassari. The entire island is about 260 kilometers (162 miles) from north to south, and roughly 120 kilometers (75 miles) across. A fairly comprehensive tour taking in the coastline and interior can be accomplished in five to seven days.

Essential Information

Important Addresses and Numbers

Tourist Information **Alghero** (Piazza Porta Terra 9, tel. 079/979054).
Cagliari (Piazza Matteotti 9, tel. 070/669255; Elmas Airport, tel. 070/240200).
Nuoro (Piazza Italia 19, tel. 0784/30083).
Olbia (Via Catello Piro, tel. 0789/21453; City Hall, Golfo Aranci, tel. 0789/46915 [summer only]; Costa Smeralda Airport, tel. 0789/52600).
Oristano (Via Cagliari 276, tel. 0783/74191).
Sassari (Via Viale Umberto 72, tel. 079/233534).

Emergencies **Police.** Tel. 112, 113.
Hospital. In Cagliari, tel. 070/60181.
Ambulance. In Cagliari, tel. 070/656979.
Late-Night Pharmacy. On a rota basis: Information on current schedules is pinned up on any pharmacy door or can be obtained by phoning 192.

Travel Agency **Cagliari** (Viaggi Orru, Via Roma 95, tel. 070/657954).

Car Rental **Cagliari.** *Avis* (train station, tel. 070/668128; airport, tel. 070/240081). *Hertz* (Piazza Matteotti 1, tel. 070/668105; airport, tel. 070/240037).
Olbia. *Avis* (Via Genova 67, tel. 0789/22420; airport, tel. 0789/69540). *Hertz* (Via Regina Elena 34, tel. 0789/21733; airport, tel. 0789/66024).
Sassari. *Avis* (Via Mazzini 2, tel. 079/235547). *Maggiore* (Viale Italia 3, tel. 079/235507).

Arriving and Departing by Plane

Airports and Airlines Alitalia and Alisarda connect Rome, Milan, Pisa, and other cities on the mainland and in southern Europe with Sardinia. Flying is by far the fastest and easiest way to get to the island. The Rome–Cagliari flight takes about an hour. Sardinia's major airports are at Cagliari and Alghero, with another, smaller one, at Olbia, providing access to the Costa Smeralda.

Cagliari airport at Elmas is about 6 kilometers (4 miles) from the center of town, and there is a regular bus service from the airport to Piazza Matteotti, in front of the train station. For information, call 070/240047.

Alghero's Fertilia airport is 13 kilometers (8 miles) from the city. A bus links the airport with the air terminal on Corso Vittorio Emanuele II. For information, call 079/935033.

Costa Smeralda Airport is 4 kilometers (2½ miles) outside Olbia. For information, call 0789/52600.

Arriving and Departing by Boat

Large modern ferries run by **Tirrenia Lines, Navarma Lines,** and the **FS** (Italian State Railways) connect the island with the mainland. Tirrenia (tel. 06/474–2043) sails to several ports in Sardinia from Genoa, Civitavecchia, Naples, Palermo, and Trapani. Navarma (tel. 0565/918101) transports passengers and cars between Livorno and Olbia. FS ferries carry trains as well as passengers and cars; they sail from Civitavecchia to Golfo Aranci, near Olbia. For information, call 0766/23273 on the mainland, or 0789/46800 in Golfo Aranci. The Civitavecchia–Olbia/Golfo Aranci run takes about eight hours and there are overnight sailings. Depending on the season, the service is scheduled two or three times a week; reservations are essential in the summer.

Getting Around

By Car The best way to get around Sardinia is to drive. The roads are generally in good condition, but bear in mind that such roadside conveniences as gas stations and refreshment stands are infrequent on some routes, especially in the east. Cars may be taken on board most of the ferry lines connecting Sardinia with the mainland.

By Train There are fairly good connections between Olbia, Cagliari, Sassari, and Oristano. You can reach Nuoro via Macomer; Alghero is reached via Sassari. Service on the few other local lines is infrequent and slow. The fastest train between Olbia and Cagliari takes more than four hours. A local train connects Golfo Aranci, the FS port for the train ferry, with Olbia and takes 20 minutes.

By Bus Cagliari is linked with the other towns of Sardinia by a network of buses. Local destinations are served by ARST (tel. 070/409–8324), and the major cities, excluding Olbia, by PANI (tel. 070/652326). The heart of the Sardinian bus system is the **Stazione Autolinee** in Cagliari's Piazza Matteotti, across the square from the main tourist office. You can pick up a schedule and route map from either of these sources; if you can't find a convenient bus service, you can go to the west side of the square to the main train station. City buses in Cagliari and Sassari operate on the same system as those on the mainland: Buy your ticket first, at a tobacco shop or machine, and cancel it on the bus by slipping it into the machine until the ticket is punched. Fares are low for these local services, about 1,300 lire.

Guided Tours

Orientation The following guided tours are good introductions to Sardinia; all include travel from the Italian mainland, as well as travel and accommodations on Sardinia. They should be booked through a travel agent.

Chiariva offers two group tours of Sardinia by bus with guide. A nine-day tour leaves from Genoa; an eight-day tour departs from Rome. Both operate from April to September.

Aviatour has a similar eight-day tour leaving from either Milan or Rome. The tour also runs from April to September only.

Appian Line can arrange a fly-drive package on the Costa Smeralda; transportation is by air, the rental car is picked up at the airport at Olbia. Accommodations are in good, but not outlandishly expensive, hotels on this famous coastline for the rich.

Exploring Sardinia

The best way to see Sardinia is by car, because driving is the only way to travel to and through the island's most interesting sights. Local transportation is not geared to the needs of tourists, so you can see more in less time if you have a car. If you don't, your best bet is to establish yourself in one of the larger towns and make excursions to as many attractions as time and schedules allow. We have divided the country into three exploring tours, each of which has at least one town large enough to act as a touring base.

Tour 1 covers Sardinia's capital, Cagliari, and the surrounding area along the south coast. This is a good introduction to the rugged countryside and fascinating archaeology of the island. All the attractions are within easy reach of Cagliari.

Tour 2 begins the northward exploration of Sardinia, heading into the hinterland of the Barbagia region, where traditional Sardinian customs are maintained in remote hilltop villages. Here, rare species of wildlife share the rocky uplands with sturdy medieval churches and mysterious *nuraghi*—ancient stone citadels left by prehistoric people. Oristano, the medieval center of Sardinian nationalism, is on the island's west coast and makes a good center for exploring this region.

The last tour continues northward, taking in the sunny resorts of Alghero, the Spanish-influenced port on the west coast, and the Costa Smeralda, the luxury resort complex developed by the Aga Khan on the northeast corner of Sardinia.

Tour 1: Cagliari and Environs

Numbers in the margin correspond to points of interest on the Sardinia and Cagliari maps.

1 A good place to start exploring Sardinia is **Cagliari** in the south, reached by plane or boat from the mainland. The island's capital, it has impressive Italianate architecture and churches in a variety of styles; it's clear that medieval Spanish conquerors from Aragón were here, as well as Austrians and Italians. Cagliari (the stress is on the first syllable) is Sardinia's largest city, characterized by a busy commercial center and waterfront with broad, tree-lined avenues, as well as by the typically narrow streets of the old town on a hill.

2 Begin your visit at the **Museo Archeologico,** within the walls of the castle that the Pisans erected on the city's heights in the early 1300s to ward off attacks from the Aragonese and Catalans, from what is now Spain. The museum contains some intriguing pieces, especially bronze statuettes from the tombs and dwellings of Sardinia's earliest inhabitants, who remain a prehistorical enigma. These aboriginal people left scarcely a clue to their origins. Ancient writers called them the nuraghic people, from the name of their stone dwellings, the nuraghi, containing features unique to Sardinia, just as the Az-

Sardinia

tec pyramids are to Mexico. Archaeologists date the nuraghi from about 1300–1200 BC, a time when the ancient Israelites were establishing themselves in Canaan, when the Greeks were besieging Troy, when the Minoan civilization collapsed in Crete, when the Ramses Pharaohs reigned in Egypt, and when many migrations were taking place along the shores and water routes of the Mediterranean. During the next 1,000 years, the nuraghic people gradually withdrew into the island's highland fastnesses to avoid more disciplined and better-armed invaders. (The only weapons they knew, say the chroniclers, were hurled stones and boulders rolled down from the hilltops.) Their civilization eventually succumbed when the Romans, following on the heels of Carthaginian invaders, conquered the island in the 3rd century BC. Artifacts from Nuraghic, Carthaginian, and Roman times make up the museum's collections. *Cittadella dei Musei, Piazza Arsenale, tel. 070/655911. Admission: 4,000 lire. Open daily 9–6:30.*

3 4 Outside the museum is the medieval **Tower of San Pancrazio,** which was part of the imposing Pisan defenses; its twin, the **Tower of the Elephant,** is at the seaward end of the bastions. Take Via Martini **5** about 200 yards to Piazza Palazzo. Here you'll find the **cathedral,** which has been extensively rebuilt and restored. The tiers of columns on the facade echo those of medieval Pisan churches, but only the center portal is an authentic relic of that era. All around the church are the narrow streets of the Spanish quarter, where humble dwellings still open directly onto the sidewalk and the wash is hung out to dry on elaborate wrought-iron balconies. This is the most interesting part of the city, so take time to wander through it, making your way to the Elephant Tower and the Bastion of St. Remy, better

6 known as the **Terrazza Umberto I.** A monumental neoclassic staircase and arcade was added in the 19th century to the bastion built by the Spaniards 400 years earlier. It offers a magnificent view over the city and port, the sandy beaches, and the lagoons shimmering in the sun that are characteristic of the landscape around Cagliari and Oristano. Sunset, viewed from the Terrazza Umberto I, can be a memorable sight.

7 Cagliari has a **Roman amphitheater** (below the Museo Archeologico), some very old churches, and a few good restaurants near the waterfront (*see* Dining and Lodging, *below*), but once you have seen the main attractions, you will probably be ready to explore its surrounding areas.

The eastern route takes you through some dismal industrial suburbs on the road that leads to the scenic coast and beaches of Capo Boi and **8** Capo Carbonara; **Villasimius** ranks as the chief resort here.

It's more interesting, though, to head in the other direction from Cagliari. The area southwest of the capital has its share of fine scenery and good beaches—resort villages sprawl along the coast, and **9** the Is Molas championship golf course near **Pula** has won tributes from Tom Watson, Jack Nicklaus, and other professionals. On the marshy shoreline between Cagliari Airport and Pula, huge flocks of flamingos are a common sight.

The real attraction here is archaeological: On a narrow promontory less than 3 kilometers (2 miles) outside the town of Pula is **Nora,** the site of a Phoenician, then Carthaginian, and later Roman settlement. Extensive excavations here have shed light on life in this ancient city from the 8th century BC onward. Many of the exhibits in Cagliari's archaeological museum were found here. An old Roman road passes the moss-covered ruins of temples, an amphitheater, and a small Roman theater. You can make out the channels through which hot air rose to warm the Roman baths; watch for the difference between the simple mosaic pavements laid by the Carthaginians and the more elaborate designs of the Roman mosaics. Taking in the views from Nora, you also see why the Phoenicians chose the site for their settlement. They always scouted for locations with good harbors, cliffs to shelter their crafts from the wind, and a position such as a promontory, which they could defend from attack by local tribes. If the sea is calm, look under the clear waters along the shore for more ruins of the ancient city, submerged by earthquakes, rough seas, and erosion. *Admission: 4,000 lire. Excavations open Apr.–Oct., daily 9 AM–7:30 PM; Nov.–Mar., Mon.–Sat. 9–12, 2–5, Sun. 9–5.*

Use the same ticket to visit the small archaeological museum, with finds from the Nora site, in the nearby village of Pula. *Corso Vittorio Emanuele 28, Pula, tel. 070/920–9610. Open same times as excavations at Nora.*

Time Out Take advantage of the coastal location to have a seafood lunch at **Urru** (Via Tirso). Grilled fish specials depend on the day's catch.

The little Romanesque church of **Sant'Efisio,** at the base of the Nora promontory, plays a part in one of the island's most colorful annual events. Efisio, the patron saint of Sardinia, was a 3rd-century Roman soldier who converted to Christianity. A procession in early May accompanies a statue of the saint all the way from Cagliari and back again. The processional round trip takes four days, with festive stops along the way, and culminates in a parade down Cagliari's main avenue that rivals the St. Patrick's Day parade in New York. If you're in Sardinia from May 1 to May 4, don't miss it.

Off the southwest coast are two islands that are popular picnic spots with good beaches. You can drive over a causeway to **Sant'Antioco,** where the most hectic activity seems to be the silent repairing of nets by local fishermen who have already handled their daily catch. A ferry at the small northern port of Calasetta connects Sant'Antioco with the smaller island of **San Pietro.** This is a favorite of wealthy Cagliarians, many of whom have built weekend cottages here.

Tour 2: Oristano, Nuoro, and the Barbagia

From Cagliari head north on the Carlo Felice highway toward Oristano, making a detour to the fascinating nuraghe of **Su Nuraxi,** off the main road outside the quiet little town of **Barumini.** You could spend hours clambering over this extraordinary structure of concentric rings of stone walls, chambers, passages, wells, and beehive tower, and it's a good idea to take a flashlight along for peering into dark corners. This nuraghe is probably about half its original height, and some of the smaller towers around the main one have been reduced by pillaging and erosion to mere circles of stones on the ground. The nuraghi were fortified villages, prehistoric versions of medieval walled towns and the forts of the American West. Though this particular type of construction is unique to Sardinia, similar buildings dating from the same era are found in other parts of the Mediterranean, such as Cyprus and the Balearic islands off Spain. Of the 7,000 nuraghi on Sardinia, Su Nuraxi is the most impressive, with those of Sant'Antine and Losa, both near Macomer, close runners-up. *1 kilometer (½ mile) west of Barumini. Admission free. Open daily 9–2.*

Just north of Barumini is the **Giara di Gesturi,** a basalt plateau that is home to some of the island's more exotic wildlife, including a species of wild dwarf horse. Another rare species to be found in the Giara is the mouflon, a wild sheep distinguishable from its domesticated counterpart by its long curving horns and skittishness when confronted by any human, however well intentioned. Long hunted for their decorative horns, the mouflon are now an endangered species, with only a few surviving on Sardinia and neighboring Corsica.

Oristano, on the west coast of the island, shone in the Middle Ages, when it was capital of the Giudicato of Arborea, an independent duchy led by Sardinia's Joan of Arc, Eleanora di Arborea. In the 14th century Eleanora inherited the difficult task of defending the duchy's freedom, constantly undermined by the superior military might of the Spanish troops from Aragón. Although the duchy eventually reverted to Aragonese rule, Eleanora made a lasting contribution to Sardinia by implementing a code of law that was adopted throughout the island and remained in effect until Sardinia's unification with Italy in 1847. Now an important but slow-paced agricultural center, Oristano is the scene of livestock fairs and a rousing series of horse races, called Sa Sartiglia, marking the end of the Carnival season in February.

Time Out Join the locals at the **Forchetta d'Oro** (Via Giovanni XXIII 8) for a lunch of pasta with cuttlefish sauce.

Close by to the west, you can see the extensive marshlands of **Cabras,** where fishermen pole round-bottomed rush boats through shallow ponds teeming with eels and crayfish. While there, take time to drive 10 kilometers (6 miles) west, along the road marked San Giovanni di Sinis, to visit the ruins of the Carthaginian city of **Tharros,** with its strategic position on the scenic Sinis peninsula. Like Nora to the south (*see* Tour 1: Cagliari and Environs, *above*), the site was chosen because it commanded the best views of the harbor and could provide an easy escape route if inland tribes threatened.

On your way to Tharros, you'll pass the ghost town of **San Salvatore,** revived in the 1960s as a location for spaghetti westerns and later abandoned again. The saloon of the movie set still stands. Farther along, among the dunes, are large rush huts formerly used by fishermen and now much in demand as back-to-nature vacation homes. The 5th-century church of **San Giovanni di Sinis,** also on the peninsula, is the oldest Christian church in Sardinia.

⑮ Head northeast for **Nuoro,** a shabby provincial capital locked in a gorge in the harsh mountainous area that culminates in **Gennargentu,** the island's highest massif (6,000 feet). The only things likely to interest you in Nuoro are the views from the park on Sant'Onofrio hill and the exhibits in the **Museo della Vita e delle Tradizioni Popolari Sarde** (Museum of Sardinian Life and Folklore), where you can see local costumes, domestic and agricultural implements, and traditional jewelry. *Via Mereu 56, tel. 0784/31426. Admission: 3,000 lire. Open Tues.–Sat. 9–1, 3–7, Sun. 9–1.*

Make an excursion a couple of miles east to **Mount Ortobene** (2,900 feet), for some dizzying views over the gulch below Nuoro. Here you can also visit up close the imposing statue of Christ the Redeemer that overlooks the city. Picnic tables make this a handy spot for an al fresco lunch stop.

From Nuoro, strike out south into the **Barbagia** region for the mountain scenery and a glimpse of Sardinia's most primitive district. Life in some villages has not changed much since the Middle Ages. Here a rigidly patriarchal society perpetuates the unrelenting practice of vendetta, and strangers are advised to mind their own business. Tortuous roads wind and loop their way through the scenery; towns are small and undistinguished, their social fabric seemingly impervious to the 20th century. On feast days the elaborate regional costumes are taken out of mothballs and worn as an explicit statement of community identity. You can see one of the most characteristic of these celebrations in local costume on the Feast of St. John, June 24,
⑯ at **Fonni,** highest town on the island and base for excursions by car to Monte Spada and the Bruncu Spina refuge on the Gennargentu massif.

Head west on road 129 from Nuoro to Bosa, where you turn right into hilly and arid scrub country, with its abundance of cactus and juniper. Pines and olive trees shelter low buildings from the steady winds that make these parts ideal for sailing and unfit for agriculture. About the only cash crop here is cork from the cork trees dotting the landscape. Yet in the low valleys and along the river beds, masses of oleanders bloom in the summer, creating avenues of color.

⑰ Among the larger centers on the northwest coast is **Alghero,** which is an appealing walled town with a distinct Spanish flavor. It was built and inhabited in the 14th century by the Aragonese and Catalans, who constructed seaside ramparts and sturdy towers encompassing an inviting nucleus of narrow, winding streets. Rich wrought-iron scrollwork decorates balconies and screens windows; Spanish motifs appear in stone portals and in bell towers. The dialect spoken here is a version of Catalan, not Italian: Locals find it easier to converse in Barcelona than in Rome. Alghero is a popular resort, near broad sandy beaches and the spectacular heights of **Capo Caccia,** an imposing limestone headland to the west. At the base of the sheer cliff, the pounding sea has carved an entrance to the vast **Grotto of Neptune,** a fantastic, fabulous cavern, which you must visit with a guide. By land, you can reach the entrance at the base of the cliff by descending the more than 600 steps of the aptly named *escala del cabirol* (mountain goat's stairway), a dizzying enterprise—and the ascent is just as daunting. *Admission 10,000 lire. Open Easter–Oct. 15, daily 9–6; Oct. 16–one week before Easter, daily 9–2. Guided tour starts on the hour.*

The excursion by sea is much less fatiguing but is not possible when seas are rough. Boats leave the port of Alghero four times daily, every hour or so in peak season, and the journey takes three hours. *Navisarda, tel. 079/975599. Fare: 15,000 lire; admission to grotto: 3,000 lire. Daily Apr.–Oct.*

Time Out | Hungry landlubbers need go only **Dieci Metri** (Ten Meters; Vicolo Adami 47, off Via Roma), from the center of Alghero for a nourishing meal of seafood and local wine.

⑱ Inland and northeast of Alghero is **Sassari,** important as a university town and an administrative center. It has little to interest a visitor other than an old and ornate cathedral and an archaeological museum. Sassari is the hub of several highways and secondary roads leading to various scenic coastal resorts, among them Stintino and ⑲ **Castelsardo,** which is a walled seaside citadel and a delight for basket lovers. Roadside stands and shops in the old town sell tons of island handicrafts: rugs, wrought iron—and baskets, in myriad ⑳ shapes and colors. **Santa Teresa di Gallura,** at the northern tip of Sardinia, has the relaxed, carefree air of an authentic fishing village-turned-resort. From nearby Palau you can visit the archipela- ㉑ go of **La Maddalena,** seven granite islands embellished with lush green scrub and wind-bent pines. Pilgrims pay homage to Garibaldi's tomb on the grounds of his hideaway on Caprera, one of the islands.

Sardinia's northeastern coast is fringed with low cliffs, inlets, and small bays. This landscape has become an upscale vacationland, with glossy resorts, such as Baia Sardinia and Porto Rotondo, just outside the confines of the famed Costa Smeralda, developed by the Aga Khan, who discovered its charms—and potential—by accident in 1965, when his yacht ran in for shelter from a storm. The Costa Smeralda is still dominated by his personality; its attractions remain geared to those who can measure themselves by the yardstick of his fabled riches. Sardinia's most expensive hotels are here, and the ㉒ world's most magnificent yachts anchor in the waters of **Porto Cervo.** The trend has been to keep this enclave of the really rich an exclusive haven, by encouraging more multimillionaires to build discreetly luxurious villas and planning four more golf courses to be built for them.

All along the coast, carefully tended lush vegetation surrounds vacation villages and the more elaborate villa colonies that have sprung up over the past decade in a range of spurious architectural styles best described as bogus Mediterranean. Set amid the resorts ㉓ is **Olbia,** a lively little seaport, not heavily industrialized, at the ㉔ head of a long, wide bay. At the bay's mouth is **Golfo Aranci,** a blossoming resort and debarkation point for FS ferries from the mainland.

What to See and Do with Children

Sardinia is a vast playground where children can roam, explore, and swim in season. There's nothing like a long hike along deserted beaches or through herb-scented hills to send them to bed early. Let them clamber over the nuraghi and poke into the countless *domus de janas* (witches' houses) and *tombe di giganti* (giants' tombs), fancifully named grottoes hewn in the rock by the island's prehistoric inhabitants. They served as burial places, but with a little imagination you can elaborate on their names and make up some good fairy tales. There are plenty around **Sassari,** at **Anghelu Ruhu,** and near **Dorgali.** Take the children to see the **Elephant Rock** near Castelsardo; hollowed out by primitive man to become a domus de janas, it resembles an elephant, trunk and all. Go to see the Wild West film-set village at **San Salvatore** near Oristano (*see* Tour 2: Oristano, Nuoro, and the Barbagia, *above*). Visit the folk museum at **Nuoro** (*see* Tour 2, *above*).

Off the Beaten Track

Considering that all Sardinia is off the beaten track for most tourists, practically everything you do or see here comprises the unusual. But if your curiosity prods you to even more esoteric experiences, you could go just inland of Sant'Antioco to explore the rugged, once-booming mining country around **Carbonia,** a town built by Mussolini in 1938 to serve as the administrative center for the coal miners and their families. With its overpowering fascist architecture, it has been called an urban UFO set down in the Sardinian landscape. Nearby **Iglesias** is an authentic Sardinian town, with a medieval cathedral; traveling east past Domusnovas on the Cagliari-Iglesias highway, you can detour and drive right through an immense cave, the **Grotta di San Giovanni.**

Visit **San Sperate,** near Cagliari; practically every wall in town has been brightened with *murales* (mural paintings) by local artists and some well-known Italian painters, transforming the entire town into a modern art gallery. You can see more of the murales in the Barbagia district, at the village of **Orgosolo.**

If you have the stamina, take the rickety old train that runs on a single-gauge track between Cagliari and **Arbatax,** midway up the east coast. If all goes well, it takes about nine hours to cover the approximately 250 kilometers (155 miles) of track, guaranteeing you a look at the Sardinia few tourists ever see. The train rattles up into the Barbagia district through some breathtaking mountain scenery, then eases down into the desert landscape inland of Arbatax, where the trip ends on the dock next to the fishing boats. The train is run by the Ferrovie Complementari, and the ticket costs less than 15,000 lire. For information, call 070/491304.

Shopping

Sardinia is handicrafts heaven. Locally produced goods include bright woolen shawls and rugs, handcarved wooden objects, gold filigree jewelry in traditional forms, coral jewelry, and, above all, handwoven baskets in all shapes and sizes. The best place in Cagliari to get an idea of what's available is at **ISOLA** (Via Bacaredda 184, tel. 070/400707), a government-sponsored exhibition of island handi-crafts; most of the items on display are also for sale. ISOLA pro-motes pilot centers for arts and crafts in remote areas where Sardinian handicrafts are produced. You can find ISOLA centers at **Castelsardo** (Lungomare Colombo) and **Sant'Antioco** (Lungomare Vespucci). Larger towns have a complete range of Sardinian handi-crafts, but elsewhere on the island the small towns and villages con-form to the centuries-old tradition of specializing in one item.

Handicrafts **Alghero.** Coral, still harvested in the bay, and gold jewelry are the traditional handicrafts.

Aritzo. This mountain village, high up in the Barbagia, produces handcrafted wooden utensils and furniture.

Castelsardo. The specialty is a brightly colored basket made of dwarf palms.

Dorgali. This east-coast port is a rug- and tapestry-producing cen-ter.

Isili. Handwoven rugs and hammered copperware are the special-ties of this village just east of Su Nuraxi.

Nuoro. Wooden masks, made for local festivals, make unusual souve-nirs.

Oristano. Ceramics are featured in the small craft shops here.

Santa Teresa di Gallura. Contemporary pottery utilizing traditional motifs sells well, especially among the rich along the Costa Smeralda.

Tonara. Special candies are made from honey and nougat.

Sports

Fishing Check locally for regulations on deep-sea fishing. Underwater fish-ing is restricted to the daylight hours, and no more than five kilos of fish and shellfish may be taken. No oxygen tanks or nets may be used for underwater fishing. Freshwater fishing is good along the Flumendosa, Tirso, Rio Mannu, and other rivers rising in the moun-tainous interior and in the artificial basins of Flumendosa and Omodeo. For information on obtaining a license, write to **Assessor-ato Regionale alla Difesa dell'Ambiente,** Via Biasi 7/9, 09100, Cagliari (tel. 070/606–6620).

Golf Sardinia has two world-class golf courses, with four more planned for the Costa Smeralda, where the **Pevero Golf Club** course was de-signed by Robert Trent Jones. The club is on the Bay of Pevero, near Porto Cervo (tel. 0789/96210). The 18-hole **Is Molas** course is at San-ta Margherita di Pula (tel. 070/920–9165); the adjacent Is Molas Golf Hotel (tel. 070/924–1006) offers special golfing vacations.

Horseback Riding The **Associazione Nazionale di Turismo Equestre** (Via Carso 35a, Sassari, tel. 079/299889) can provide information on renting mounts and joining riding parties with itineraries along the coast or into the heart of the island. The **Centro Vacanze Alabirdi** at Arborea, near Oristano (tel. 0783/800512) and the **Centro Vacanze Su Gologone** at Oliena (tel. 0784/287512) offer riding vacations.

Sailing A popular sport in Sardinia, sailing is enjoyed all along the coast. The **Lega Navale Italiana** at Marina Piccola in Cagliari (tel. 070/303794) will furnish information on the island's facilities. The **Yacht Club Costa Smeralda** at Porto Cervo (tel. 0789/91332) admits tempo-rary members.

Tennis Most resort hotels have their own tennis courts, many of which are open to guests. The **Porto Cervo Tennis Club** on the Costa Smeralda is open year-round, and membership is available to visitors on a daily or weekly basis (Porto Cervo, tel. 0789/92244). The **Federazione Italiana Tennis** (Via Palestrina 46, Cagliari, tel. 070/494468) can provide information about local competitions.

Spectator Sports

Yachting You can see the very rich engage in one of their favorite sports at the posh resorts of Costa Smeralda each August, when a number of regattas are held.

Beaches

Sardinia's beaches are among the best in the Mediterranean; its waters are among the cleanest, with the exception of those in the immediate vicinity of Cagliari, Arbatax, and Porto Torres. The beach resorts of the Costa Smeralda are exclusive and expensive, but elsewhere on the island you can find a wide range of beaches.

Most agree that the most beautiful beaches on the island are those of **Cala Luna** and **Cala Sisina,** hidden among the rocky cliffs near Baunei and Dorgali, on the eastern coast; they can be reached only by boat from Cala Gonone or Arbatax, and can definitely be considered remote. For more accessible beaches with more amenities, go to **Santa Margherita di Pula,** near Cagliari, where there are several hotels; to **Villasimius** and the **Costa Rei,** on the southeastern coast; or to the sandy coves sheltered by wind-carved granite boulders on the northern coast in the Gallura district and the archipelago of La Maddalena. There are also beaches around Olbia, Alghero, and on the Costa Paradiso, near Castelsardo.

Dining and Lodging

Dining In the island's restaurants you'll find that Sardinian regional cuisine is basically Italian, with interesting local variations. Meat dishes are usually veal, lamb, or *porcheddu* (roast suckling pig). On the coast, seafood is king and is served in great variety. *Langouste* or *aragosta* (lobster) is a specialty of the northern coast; it can be expensive. Foreign conquerors left legacies of bouillabaisse (known here as *zimino),* couscous, and paella, but there are native pastas: *malloreddus,* small shells of pasta di semola (bran pasta) sometimes flavored with saffron, and *culingiones,* the Sardinian version of ravioli. Sharp cheese made of sheep's milk (pecorino) and thin crispy bread called *carta di musica* are typical island fare. Try the *sebadas* (fried cheese-filled ravioli doused with honey) for dessert. The red wines are sturdy and strong, with the whites tending to a light and delicate quality. Amber-colored Vernaccia is dry and heady.

Highly recommended restaurants are indicated by a star ★.

Category	Cost*
$$$$	over 85,000 lire
$$$	60,000–85,000 lire
$$	35,000–60,000 lire
$	under 35,000 lire

per person, including house wine, service, and tax

Lodging The island's most luxurious hotels are on the Costa Smeralda; they have magnificent resort facilities but close up from fall to spring and are too out of the way to be good touring bases. Other, equally attractive coastal areas have seen a spate of new resort hotels and villa colonies sprout up, but they, too, close from October through April, which narrows the choice of hotels considerably during the other months. In the cities suggested as touring bases, you can expect to find standards of comfort slightly below those of the mainland; the best accommodations may be offered by commercial hotels with little atmosphere. Service is usually courteous and competent, with perhaps the exception of the seasonal resort hotels, where the staff is likely to change from year to year. In smaller towns throughout the island, you'll find modest hotels offering basic accommodations, restrained but genuine hospitality, and low rates.

Highly recommended lodgings are indicated by a star ★.

Category	Cost*
$$$$	over 300,000 lire
$$$	160,000–300,000 lire
$$	100,000–160,000 lire
$	under 100,000 lire

All prices are for a standard double room for two, including service and 9% VAT (19% for luxury hotels).

Alghero **La Lepanto.** White stucco and wrought-iron grilles set a Spanish
Dining tone in Alghero's top seafood restaurant. The specialty is *aragosta* cooked in a variety of ways, including *alla catalana* (with tomato and onions). For starters, try risotto *con vongole* (with clams and tomato sauce). *Via Carlo Alberto 135, tel. 079/979116. Dinner reservations advised. Dress: casual. AE, DC, MC, V. Closed Sun. dinner and Mon. Oct.–May. $$*

Da Pietro. On a narrow street in the picturesque old town near Largo San Francesco, this seafood restaurant has vaulted ceilings and a bustling atmosphere. The menu features *bucatini all'algherese* (pasta with a sauce of clams, capers, and tomatoes) and baked fish *con Vernaccia* (with white wine sauce); there are some meat dishes, too. *Via Ambrogio Machin 18, tel. 079/979645. Dinner reservations advised. Dress: casual. AE, DC, MC, V. Closed Wed. Oct.–May and 2 weeks at Christmas. $*

Lodging **Carlos V (Carlos Quinto).** Located on the shore boulevard about half a mile from the center of town, this hillside hotel is modern but attractive, with porticoes and terraces, one of which has a swimming pool. Smallish but bright rooms all have a balcony, many with sea view. Low season rates are a bargain. *Lungomare Valencia 24, tel. 079/979501, fax 079/980298. 110 rooms with bath or shower. Facilities: pool, tennis court, garden, restaurant, parking. AE, MC, V. $$$*

Villa Las Tronas. The villa is a former royal mansion on a rocky bluff above the sea but still near the center of town. It has turn-of-the-century atmosphere, modern comforts, and great views across the water to the old town. Rates are at the lower level of this category. *Lungomare Valencia 1, tel. 079/981818, fax 079/981044. 30 rooms in main building, 7 in annex, all with bath or shower. Facilities: pool, garden, restaurant (summer only), private beach, parking. AE, DC, MC, V. $$$*

San Francesco. Centrally located in Alghero's Spanish quarter, this hotel occupies the convent that was once attached to the church of San Francesco. The rooms are grouped around the 14th-century cloister and though somewhat cramped are modern and quiet. Breakfast is available at an extra charge. *Via Machin 2, tel. 079/ 979258, fax 079/979258. 21 rooms with shower. Facilities: bar, conference rooms. MC, V. $*

Cagliari **Dal Corsaro.** This popular restaurant just by the waterfront is one of
Dining the island's most popular eating places, so reservations are essential. The decor is informal, in tune with the cordial welcome. The menu features seafood and meat specialties, such as seafood antipasto and porcheddu (roast suckling pig). *Viale Regina Margherita 28, tel. 070/664318. Reservations advised. Dress: casual but neat. AE, DC, MC, V. Closed Sun. $$$*

Il Gatto. "The Cat," located near the train station and the central Piazza del Carmine, is popular with locals. Follow their lead and make sure you have reservations because the restaurant can fill up quickly. It serves some of the best Sardinian seafood, such as the risotto with shellfish, but for a change of pace try the *boccone del Gatto* (stuffed chicken breast). *Viale Trieste 15, tel. 070/663596. Reservations advised. Dress: casual. AE, DC, MC, V. Closed Sun. $$*

Lodging **Panorama.** Despite the obtrusive and ugly exterior, this useful hotel in downtown Cagliari is geared toward the business class. Rooms are functional, spacious, and comfortable: Try to reserve one on the upper of the nine floors and enjoy the view over the harbor and bay. Rates are low in the category. *Viale Armando Diaz 231, tel. 070/ 307691, fax 070/305413. 97 rooms with bath or shower. Facilities: restaurant, bar, outdoor pool, garden, garage, conference rooms. AE, DC, MC, V. $$$*

Moderno. A good overnight stop, the Moderno is convenient to the train station and the harbor, but don't expect atmosphere or more than adequate comfort. In compensation, rates are at the lower end of the category. *Via Roma 159, tel. 070/660286, fax 070/660260. 93 rooms with bath or shower. AE, DC, MC, V. $$*

Costa **Cala di Volpe.** Built to resemble an ancient village, this establish-
Smeralda ment is in a secluded position on a bay. The decor is rustic-elegant,
Lodging with beamed ceilings, Sardinian art and craftwork, and porticoes overlooking the sea. The presidential suite in the highest tower has a private pool. *Cala di Volpe, tel. 0789/96083, fax 0789/96442. 125 rooms and suites with bath or shower. Facilities: saltwater pool, launch to private beach, tennis courts, access to Pevero Golf Club, garden, hairdresser, disco, restaurant, bar. AE, DC, MC, V. Closed Oct.–mid-May. $$$$*

Cervo. Low Mediterranean buildings surround a large swimming pool and garden in the heart of the Costa Smeralda's Porto Cervo. This complex is next to the marina and piazzetta and is popular with people who like to be seen. The rooms are large and most have a terrace. *Porto Cervo, tel. 0789/92003, fax 0789/92593. 95 rooms with bath or shower. Facilities: pool, garden, launch to private beach, access to Porto Cervo Tennis Club and Pevero Golf Club, hairdresser, terrace restaurant, piano bar. AE, DC, MC, V. Closed Oct.–mid-May. $$$$*

Nibaru. In a secluded inlet set in lush gardens, this hotel enjoys all the best features of the Costa Smeralda at comparatively low rates. Guests are just a few yards from the sea and some superb swimming spots and also within easy access to the Pevero Golf Club and the tennis courts of Porto Cervo. The buildings here are pinkish-red brick with tiled roofs. Each room has a balcony and view of the sea.

Cala di Volpe, tel. 0789/96038, fax 0789/96474. 45 rooms with bath. Facilities: restaurant, bar, pool, garden. AE, DC, MC, V. Closed Oct.–Apr. $$$

Olbia **De Plam.** Though aesthetically unimpressive, this seafront hotel can
Lodging at least boast the best views in Olbia. The rooms are furnished in a motel style that is functional if not particularly memorable. The location is convenient to the port (though still a taxi ride away), and the town center is a short walk. *Via de Filippi 33, tel. 0789/25777, fax 0789/22648. 60 rooms with bath or shower. Facilities: restaurant, bar, parking, air-conditioning, conference rooms. MC, V. $$*

Oliena **Su Gologone.** Oliena is near Nuoro, and this well-known restaurant
Dining is worth a detour for an authentic Sardinian meal in a bustling inn
★ that attracts tourists in droves but manages to maintain its friendly atmosphere. The island specialties include *maccarones de busa* (thick homemade pasta), culingiones, porcheddu, and sebadas. Wash it all down with some Vernaccia. Rooms are also available here. *Località Su Gologone, tel. 0784/287512. Reservations advised weekends.. Dress: casual. AE, DC, MC, V. $$$*

Oristano **Il Faro.** Locals and visiting gourmets consider this elegant restau-
Dining rant to be one of the best in the area, as it offers authentic and well-
★ prepared local dishes that change with the season. There's *capretto allo spiedo* (spit-roasted goat) in the winter and an aromatic *zuppa di fave* (fava bean soup with bacon and fennel) in the spring. Seafood is featured throughout the year. *Via Bellini 25, tel. 0783/70002. Reservations advised. Dress: casual. AE, DC, MC, V. Closed Sun. dinner, Mon., and Jan. 1–15, July 1–15. $$$*
Salvatore. In this classic seafood restaurant you can sample seafood from the tidal ponds of Cabras and Santa Giusta just outside Oristano. Specialties are spaghetti *alla bottarga* (with smoked fish roe) and grilled *anguilla* (eel). *Vico Mariano 2, tel. 0783/71309. Reservations advised. Dress: casual. MC, V. Closed Sun. and last 2 weeks in Aug. $$*

Lodging **Cama.** Located near the train station, the hotel is also within walking distance of Oristano's interesting old town center. A parking lot and garage make it convenient for drivers. Another feature is air-conditioning, not always found in hotels of this category. *Via Vittorio Veneto 119, tel. 0783/74374, fax 0783/74375. 54 rooms with bath or shower. Facilities: restaurant, garage. MC, V. $*
Mistral. This hotel, in the same price category as the Cama, is more appealing, but it's located on the edge of town, so you'll probably need a car to reach it. The rooms are bright and air-conditioned, and some have views of the mysterious nuraghe countryside to the east. The restaurant serves good seafood specialties. **Mistral 2** is a large annex consisting of a convention center with a swimming pool in the center of town. *Via Martiri di Belfiore, tel. 0783/212505, fax 0783/210058. 48 rooms with bath or shower. Facilities: restaurant, bar. AE, DC, MC, V. $*

Santa **Is Morus.** A luxurious enclave, the Is Morus is on a sandy cove and
Margherita di offers all the amenities of a fine beach resort, with low, attractive
Pula buildings shaded by pinewoods, plus the option of golfing at the fine
Lodging Is Molas course, about 11 kilometers (7 miles) away. *Santa*
★ *Margherita, tel. 070/921171, fax 070/921596. 85 rooms with bath or shower. Facilities: pool, miniature golf, tennis, hairdresser, terrace restaurant, bar, private beach, parking. AE, DC, MC, V. Closed Nov.–Easter. $$$–$$$$*
Flamingo. Also directly on the beach and in a shady setting, this resort hotel features a main building and several two-story cottages

nestled among the pines. *Santa Margherita, tel. 070/920–8361, fax 070/920–8359. 134 rooms with bath or shower. Facilities: pool, tennis court, miniature golf, private beach, sauna, restaurant, disco, bar, parking. AE, DC, MC, V. Closed Oct. 16–May 9. $$$*

Santa Teresa di Gallura
Dining
★

Canne al Vento. This cheerful, family-run restaurant on the edge of town is popular with visitors who want authentic island cuisine. Try the local specialty, *zuppa cuata* (bread, cheese, and tomato soup), porcheddu, or seafood. Twenty-two inexpensive guest rooms (with shower), in the $ category, are available here. *Via Nazionale 23, tel. 0789/754219. Reservations advised. Dress: casual. MC, V. Closed Sat. (except summer) and Oct.–Nov. $$*

Lodging

Corallaro. This hotel offers comfortable, pleasing accommodations in a panoramic spot overlooking the sea, not far from the center of town. *Via Nazionale 85, tel. 0789/755431, fax 0789/755431. 22 rooms with bath or shower. Facilities: pool, tennis court, garden, restaurant. AE, MC, V. $$*

The Arts and Nightlife

The Arts

As one of Italy's most (perhaps *the* most) remote regions, Sardinia is not really a prime spot for sophisticated visual or performing arts. This same remoteness, however, can prove fruitful if you're interested in sampling some of the culture that has developed here, sometimes natively inspired, sometimes drawing on the influences of the traders and invaders who have left their mark on the islands over the millennia. Sardinia's own brand of Catholicism—occasionally bordering on the grotesque—can be witnessed in the local *feste*, or festivals. Ostensibly, the festivals celebrate a saintly or religious occasion, but often they are imbued with an almost pagan atmosphere.

Festivals and Pageants

Cagliari. The **Feste del Mare** (Festivals of the Sea) are held each year on the first Sunday in April. The **Festa di Sant'Efisio** (May 1) offers a chance to take part in a festival of Sardinian folklore.

Nuoro. The **Festa del Redentore** (Feast of the Redeemer) is held on the next-to-last Sunday in August.

Oristano. The Sartiglia festival, on the last Sunday of Carnival season, includes rich costumes and a ritual joust. Each summer, the town holds an **arts and crafts** exhibition, with local foods and wines given prominence. Contact the tourist office (*see* Important Addresses and Numbers in Essential Information, *above*) for information.

Music

Cagliari's **university** (Via Università) has concerts throughout the academic year.

Nightlife

Nightlife in much of Sardinia means a quiet drink before turning in early, tired out from the day's outdoor activity. But as if to make up for the sleepy atmosphere of most of the island, the **Costa Smeralda** sparkles most nights in the summer. Be prepared to part with a tidy sum if you visit the Costa, but if that doesn't deter you, go to the complex at **Porto Cervo** (*see* Dining and Lodging, *above*) for a selection of high-class bars, restaurants, and discos.

Conversion Tables

Distance

Kilometers/Miles To change kilometers to miles, multiply kilometers by .621
To change miles to kilometers, multiply miles by 1.61

Km to Mi	Mi to Km
1 = .62	1 = 1.6
2 = 1.2	2 = 3.2
3 = 1.9	3 = 4.8
4 = 2.5	4 = 6.4
5 = 3.1	5 = 8.1
6 = 3.7	6 = 9.7
7 = 4.3	7 = 11.3
8 = 5.0	8 = 12.9
9 = 5.6	9 = 14.5

Meters/Feet To change meters to feet, multiply meters by 3.28
To change feet to meters, multiply feet by .305

Meters to Feet	Feet to Meters
1 = 3.3	1 = .31
2 = 6.6	2 = .61
3 = 9.8	3 = .92
4 = 13.1	4 = 1.2
5 = 16.4	5 = 1.5
6 = 19.7	6 = 1.8
7 = 23.0	7 = 2.1
8 = 26.2	8 = 2.4
9 = 29.5	9 = 2.7

Weight

Kilograms/Pounds To change kilograms to pounds, multiply by 2.20
To change pounds to kilograms, multiply by .453

Kilos to Pounds	Pounds to Kilos
1 = 2.2	1 = .45
2 = 4.4	2 = .91
3 = 6.6	3 = 1.4
4 = 8.8	4 = 1.8
5 = 11.0	5 = 2.3
6 = 13.2	6 = 2.7
7 = 15.4	7 = 3.2

8 = 17.6	8 = 3.6
9 = 19.8	9 = 4.1

Grams/Ounces To change grams to ounces, multiply grams by .035
To change ounces to grams, multiply ounces by 28.4

Grams to Ounces	Ounces to Grams
1 = .04	1 = 28
2 = .07	2 = 57
3 = .11	3 = 85
4 = .14	4 = 114
5 = .18	5 = 142
6 = .21	6 = 170
7 = .25	7 = 199
8 = .28	8 = 227
9 = .32	9 = 256

Liquid Volume

Liters/U.S. Gallons To change liters to U.S. gallons, multiply liters by .264
To change U.S. gallons to liters, multiply gallons by 3.79

Liters to U.S. Gallons	U.S. Gallons to Liters
1 = .26	1 = 3.8
2 = .53	2 = 7.6
3 = .79	3 = 11.4
4 = 1.1	4 = 15.2
5 = 1.3	5 = 19.0
6 = 1.6	6 = 22.7
7 = 1.8	7 = 26.5
8 = 2.1	8 = 30.3
9 = 2.4	9 = 34.1

Clothing Sizes

Men Suits To change American suit sizes to Italian suit sizes, add 10 to the American suit size.
To change Italian suit sizes to American suit sizes, subtract 10 from the Italian suit size.

U.S. Size	36	38	40	42	44	46	48
Italian Size	46	48	50	52	54	56	58

Shirts To change American shirt sizes to Italian shirt sizes, multiply the American shirt size by 2 and add 8.
To change Italian shirt sizes to American shirt sizes, subtract 8 from the Italian shirt size and divide by 2.

U.S. Size	14	14½	15	15½	16	16½	17	17½
Italian Size	36	37	38	39	40	41	42	43

Shoes Italian shoe sizes vary in their relation to American shoe sizes.

U.S. Size	7½	8	8½/9	9½/10	10½/11	11½/12	12½
Italian Size	38	39	40	41	42	43	44

Women To change U.S. dress/coat sizes to Italian dress/coat sizes, add 28 to
Dresses and the U.S. dress/coat size.
Coats To change Italian dress/coat sizes to U.S. dress/coat sizes, subtract
28 from the Italian dress/coat size.

U.S. Size	4	6	8	10	12	14	16
Italian Size	32	34	36	38	40	42	44

Blouses and To change U.S. blouse/sweater sizes to Italian blouse/sweater sizes,
Sweaters add 8 to the U.S. blouse/sweater size.
To change Italian blouse/sweater sizes to U.S. blouse/sweater sizes,
subtract 8 from the Italian blouse/sweater size.

U.S. Size	30	32	34	36	38	40	42
Italian Size	38	40	42	44	46	48	50

Shoes Italian shoe sizes vary in their relation to U.S. shoe sizes.

U.S. Size	5/5½	6	6½/7	7½	8	8½	9
Italian Size	35	36	37	38	38½	39	40

Italian Vocabulary

Words & Phrases

	English	*Italian*	*Pronunciation*
Basics	Yes/no	Sí/No	see/no
	Please	Per favore	pear fa-**vo**-ray
	Yes, please	Sí grazie	see **grah**-tsee-ay
	Thank you	Grazie	**grah**-tsee-ay
	You're welcome	Prego	**pray**-go
	Excuse me, sorry	Scusi	**skoo**-zee
	Sorry!	Mi spiace!	mee spee-**ah**-chay
	Good morning/ afternoon	Buon giorno	bwohn **jor**-no
	Goodevening	Buona sera	**bwoh**-na say-ra
	Goodbye	Arrivederci	a-ree-vah-**dare**-chee
	Mr.(Sir)	Signore	see-**nyo**-ray
	Mrs. (Ma'am)	Signora	see-**nyo**-ra
	Miss	Signorina	see-nyo-**ree**-na
	Pleased to meet you	Piacere	pee-ah-**chair**-ray
	How are you?	Come sta?	ko-may **sta**
	Very well, thanks	Bene, grazie	**ben**-ay **grah**-tsee-ay
	And you?	E lei?	ay **lay**-ee
	Hello (over the phone)	Pronto?	**proan**-to
Numbers	one	uno	**oo**-no
	two	due	**doo**-ay
	three	tre	tray
	four	quattro	**kwah**-tro
	five	cinque	**cheen**-kway
	six	sei	say
	seven	sette	**set**-ay
	eight	otto	**oh**-to
	nine	nove	**no**-vay
	ten	dieci	dee-**eh**-chee
	eleven	undici	**oon**-dee-chee
	twelve	dodici	**doe**-dee-chee
	thirteen	tredici	**tray**-dee-chee
	fourteen	quattordici	kwa-**tore**-dee-chee
	fifteen	quindici	**kwin**-dee-chee
	sixteen	sedici	**say**-dee-chee
	seventeen	diciassette	dee-cha-**set**-ay
	eighteen	diciotto	dee-**cho**-to
	nineteen	diciannove	dee-cha-**no**-vay
	twenty	venti	**vain**-tee
	twenty-one	ventuno	vain-**too**-no
	twenty-two	ventidue	vayn-tee-**doo**-ay
	thirty	trenta	**train**-ta
	forty	quaranta	kwa-**rahn**-ta
	fifty	cinquanta	cheen-**kwahn**-ta
	sixty	sessanta	seh-**sahn**-ta
	seventy	settanta	seh-**tahn**-ta
	eighty	ottanta	o-**tahn**-ta
	ninety	novanta	no-**vahn**-ta
	one hundred	cento	**chen**-to

| | ten thousand | diecimila | dee-eh-chee-**mee**-la |
| | one hundred thousand | centomila | chen-to-**mee**-la |

Colors	black	nero	**neh**-ro
	blue	azzurro	a-**tsu**-ro
	brown	marrone	mah-**ro**-nay
	green	verde	**vehr**-day
	pink	rosa	**ro**-za
	purple	porpora	**por**-por-a
	orange	arancio	a-**rahn**-cho
	red	rosso	**ros**-so
	white	bianco	bee-**ang**-ko
	yellow	giallo	**ja**-lo

Days of the week	Monday	lunedì	**loo**-neh-dee
	Tuesday	martedì	**mahr**-teh-dee
	Wednesday	mercoledì	**mare**-co-leh-dee
	Thursday	giovedì	**jo**-veh-dee
	Friday	venerdì	**ven**-air-dee
	Saturday	sabato	**sah**-ba-toe
	Sunday	domenica	doe-**men**-ee-ca

Months	January	gennaio	jeh-**nah**-yo
	February	febbraio	feh-**brah**-yo
	March	marzo	**mahr**-tso
	April	aprile	a-**pree**-lay
	May	maggio	**mah**-jo
	June	giugno	**joon**-yo
	July	luglio	**loo**-lee-o
	August	agosto	ah-**goo**-sto
	September	settembre	seh-**tem**-bray
	October	ottobre	o-**toe**-bray
	November	novembre	no-**vem**-bray
	December	dicembre	dee-**chem**-bray

Useful phrases	Do you speak English?	Parla inglese?	**par**-la een-**glay**-zay
	I don't speak Italian	Non parlo italiano	non **par**-lo ee-tal-**yah**-no
	I don't understand	Non capisco	non ka-**peess**-ko
	Can you please repeat?	Può ripetere?	pwo ree-**pet**-ay-ray
	Slowly!	Lentamente!	**len**-ta-men-tay
	I don't know	Non lo so	noan lo **so**
	I'm American/	Sono americano/a	**so**-no a-may-ree-
	British	Sono inglese	**ka**-no/a **so**-no een-**glay**-zay
	What's your name?	Come si chiama?	**ko**-may see kee-**ah**-ma
	My name is . . .	Mi chiamo . . .	mee kee-**ah**-mo
	What time is it?	Che ore sono?	kay **o**-ray **so**-no
	How?	Come?	**ko**-may
	When?	Quando?	**kwan**-doe

Yesterday/today/ tomorrow	Ieri/oggi/ domani	**yer**-ee/**o**-jee/ do-**mah**-nee
This morning/ afternoon	Stamattina/Oggi pomeriggio	sta-ma-**tee**-na/**o**-jee po-mer-**ee**-jo
Tonight	Stasera	sta-**ser**-a
What?	Che cosa?	kay **ko**-za
What is it?	Che cos'è?	kay ko-**zay**
Why?	Perché?	pear-**kay**
Who?	Chi?	kee
Where is . . .	Dov'è . . .	doe-**veh**
the bus stop?	la fermata dell'autobus?	la fer-**ma**-ta del ow-toe-**booss**
the train station?	la stazione?	la sta-tsee-**oh**-nay
the subway station?	la metropolitana?	la may-tro-po-lee-**ta**-na
the terminal?	il terminal?	eel ter-mee-**nahl**
the post office?	l'ufficio postale?	loo-**fee**-cho po-**sta**-lay
the bank?	la banca?	la **bahn**-ka
the . . . hotel?	l'hotel . . . ?	lo-**tel**
the store?	il negozio?	ell nay-**go**-tsee-o
the cashier?	la cassa?	la **ka**-sa
the . . . museum?	il museo . . . ?	eel moo-**zay**-o
the hospital?	l'ospedale?	lo-spay-**dah**-lay
the first aid station?	il pronto soccorso?	eel **pron**-to so-**kor**-so
the elevator?	l'ascensore?	la-shen-**so**-ray
a telephone?	un telefono?	oon tay-**lay**-fo-no
Where are the rest rooms?	Dov'è il bagno?	doe-**vay** eel **bahn**-yo
Here/there Left/right	Qui/là A sinistra/a destra	kwee/la a see-**neess**-tra/ a **des**-tra
Straight ahead	Avanti dritto	a-**vahn**-tee **dree**-to
Is it near/far?	È vicino?/lontano?	ay vee-**chee**-no/ lon-**tah**-no
I'd like . . .	Vorrei . . .	vo-**ray**
a room	una camera	**oo**-na **ka**-may-ra
the key	la chiave	la kee-**ah**-vay
a newspaper	un giornale	oon jor-**na**-lay
a stamp	un francobollo	oon frahn-ko-**bo**-lo
I'd like to buy . . .	Vorrei comprare . . .	vo-**ray** kom-**pra**-ray
a cigar	un sigaro	oon see-**ga**-ro
cigarettes	delle sigarette	day-lay see-ga-**ret**-ay
some matches	dei fiammiferi	day-ee fee-ah-**mee**-fer-ee
some soap	una saponetta	**oo**-na sa-po-**net**-a
a city plan	una pianta della città	**oo**-na **pyahn**-ta day-la chee-**ta**
a road map of . . .	una carta stradale di . . .	**oo**-na **cart**-a stra-**dah**-lay dee

a country map	una carta geografica	**oo**-na **cart**-a jay-o-**grah**-fee-ka
a magazine	una rivista	**oo**-na ree-**veess**-ta
envelopes	delle buste	**day**-lay **booss**-tay
writing paper	della carta da lettere	**day**-la **cart**-a da **let**-air-ay
a postcard	una cartolina	**oo**-na car-toe-**lee**-na
a guidebook	una guida turistica	**oo**-na **gwee**-da too-**reess**-tee-ka

How much is it?	Quanto costa?	**kwahn**-toe **coast**-a
It's expensive/ cheap	È caro/economico	ay **car**-o/ay-ko-**no**-mee-ko
A little/a lot	Poco/tanto	**po**-ko/**tahn**-to
More/less	Più/meno	pee-**oo**/**may**-no
Enough/too (much)	Abbastanza/troppo	a-bas-**tahn**-sa/**tro**-po
I am sick	Sto male	sto **ma**-lay
Please call a doctor	Chiami un dottore	kee-**ah**-mee oon doe-**toe**-ray
Help!	Aiuto!	a-**yoo**-toe
Stop!	Alt!	ahlt
Fire!	Al fuoco!	ahl **fwo**-ko
Caution!/Look out!	Attenzione!	a-ten-**syon**-ay

Dining Out

A bottle of . . .	Una bottiglia di . . .	**oo**-na bo-**tee**-lee-ah dee
A cup of . . .	Una tazza di . . .	**oo**-na **tah**-tsa dee
A glass of . . .	Un bicchiere di . . .	oon bee-key-**air**-ay dee
Ashtray	Il portacenere	eel por-ta-**chen**-ay-ray
Bill/check	Il conto	eel **cone**-toe
Bread	Il pane	eel **pa**-nay
Breakfast	La prima colazione	la **pree**-ma ko-la-**tsee**-oh-nay
Cheers!	Cin cin!	cheen cheen
Cocktail/aperitif	L'aperitivo	la-pay-ree-**tee**-vo
Dinner	La cena	la **chen**-a
Enjoy!	Buon appetito	bwone a-pay-**tee**-toe
Fixed-price menu	Menù a prezzo fisso	may-**noo** a **pret**-so **fee**-so
Fork	La forchetta	la for-**ket**-a
I am diabetic	Ho il diabete	o eel dee-a-**bay**-tay
I am on a diet	Sono a dieta	**so**-no a dee-**et**-a

I am vegetarian	Sono vegetariano/a	**so**-no vay-jay-ta-ree-**ah**-no/a
I cannot eat . . .	Non posso mangiare . . .	non **po**-so man-**ja**-ray
I'd like to order	Vorrei ordinare	vo-**ray** or-dee-**nah**-ray
I'd like . . .	Vorrei . . .	vo-**ray**
I'm hungry/thirsty	Ho fame/sete	o **fa**-may/**set**-ay
Is service included?	Il servizio è incluso?	eel ser-**vee**-tzee-o ay een-**kloo**-zo
It's good/bad	È buono/cattivo	ay **bwo**-no/ka-tee-vo
It's hot/cold	È caldo/freddo	ay **kahl**-doe/**fred**-o
Knife	Il coltello	eel kol-**tel**-o
Lunch	Il pranzo	eel **prahnt**-so
Menu	Il menù	eel may-**noo**
Napkin	Il tovagliolo	eel toe-va-lee-**oh**-lo
Please give me . . .	Mi dia . . .	mee **dee**-a
Salt	Il sale	eel **sah**-lay
Spoon	Il cucchiaio	eel koo-kee-**ah**-yo
Sugar	Lo zucchero	lo **tsoo**-ker-o
Waiter/Waitress	Cameriere/ cameriera	ka-mare-**yer**-ay/ ka-mare-**yer**-a
Wine list	La lista dei vini	la **lee**-sta **day**-ee **vee**-nee

Menu Guide

English	Italian
Set menu	Menù a prezzo fisso
Dish of the day	Piatto del giorno
Specialty of the house	Specialità della casa
Local specialties	Specialità locali
Extra charge	Extra . . .
In season	Di stagione
Cover charge/Service charge	Coperto/Servizio

Breakfast

Butter	Burro
Croissant	Cornetto
Eggs	Uova
Honey	Miele
Jam/Marmalade	Marmellata
Roll	Panino
Toast	Pane tostato

Starters

Assorted cold cuts	Affettati misti
Assorted seafood	Antipasto di pesce
Assorted appetizers	Antipasto misto
Toasted rounds of bread, fried or toasted in oil	Crostini/Crostoni
Diced-potato and vegetable salad with mayonnaise	Insalata russa
Eggplant parmigiana	Melanzane alla parmigiana
Fried mozzarella sandwich	Mozzarella in carrozza
Ham and melon	Prosciutto e melone
Cooked sausages and cured meats	Salumi cotti
Filled pastry shells	Vol-au-vents

Soups

"Angel hair," thin noodle soup	Capelli d'angelo
Cream of . . .	Crema di . . .
Pasta-and-bean soup	Pasta e fagioli
Egg-drop and parmesan cheese soup	Stracciatella

Pasta, Rice, and Pizza

Filled pasta	Agnolotti/ravioli/tortellini
Potato dumplings	Gnocchi
Semolina dumplings	Gnocchi alla romana
Pasta	Pasta
with four cheeses	*ai quattro formaggi*
with basil/cheese/pine nuts/garlic sauce	*al pesto*
with tomato-based meat sauce	*al ragù*
with tomato sauce	*al sugo* or *al pomodoro*
with butter	*in bianco* or *al burro*
with egg, parmesan cheese, and pepper	*alla carbonara*
green (spinach-based) pasta	*verde*

Rice	Riso
Rice dish	Risotto
with mushrooms	*ai funghi*
with saffron	*alla milanese*
Noodles	Tagliatelle
Pizza	Pizza
Pizza with seafood, cheese, artichokes, and ham in four different sections	Pizza quattro stagioni
Pizza with tomato and mozzarella	Pizza margherita
Pizza with oil, garlic, and oregano	Pizza marinara

Fish and Seafood

Anchovies	Acciughe
Bass	Persico
Carp	Carpa
Clams	Vongole
Cod	Merluzzo
Crab	Granchio
Eel	Anguilla
Lobster	Aragosta
Mackerel	Sgombro
Mullet	Triglia
Mussels	Cozze
Octopus	Polpo
Oysters	Ostriche
Pike	Luccio
Prawns	Gamberoni
Salmon	Salmone
Shrimp	Scampi
Shrimps	Gamberetti
Sole	Sogliola
Squid	Calamari
Swordfish	Pescespada
Trout	Trota
Tuna	Tonno

Methods of Preparation

Baked	Al forno
Cold, with vinegar sauce	In carpione
Fish stew	Zuppa di pesce
Fried	Fritto
Grilled (usually charcoal)	Alla griglia
Seafood salad	In insalata
Smoked	Affumicato
Stuffed	Ripieno

Meat

Boar	Cinghiale
Brain	Cervella
Braised meat with wine	Brasato
Chop	Costoletta
Duck	Anatra
Lamb	Agnello
Baby lamb	Abbacchio
Liver	Fegato
Pheasant	Fagiano
Pork roast	Arista

Rabbit	Coniglio
Steak	Bistecca
Sliced raw steak with sauce	Carpaccio
Mixed boiled meat	Bollito misto

Methods of Preparation

Battered with eggs and crumbs and fried	. . . alla milanese
Grilled	. . . ai ferri
Grilled (usually charcoal)	. . . alla griglia
Raw, with lemon/egg sauce	. . . alla tartara
Roasted	. . . arrosto
Very rare	. . . al sangue
Well done	. . . ben cotta
With ham and cheese	. . . alla valdostana
With parmesan cheese and tomatoes	. . . alla parmigiana

Vegetables

Artichokes	Carciofi
Asparagus	Asparagi
Beans	Fagioli
Brussels sprouts	Cavolini di Bruxelles
Cabbage	Cavolo
Carrots	Carote
Cauliflower	Cavolfiore
Cucumber	Cetriolo
Eggplants	Melanzane
Green beans	Fagiolini
Leeks	Porri
Lentils	Lenticchie
Lettuce	Lattuga
Mushrooms	Funghi
Onions	Cipolle
Peas	Piselli
Peppers	Peperoni
Potatoes	Patate
Roasted potatoes	*Patate arroste*
Boiled potatoes	*Patate bollite*
Fried potatoes	*Patate fritte*
Small, roasted potatoes	*Patatine novelle*
Mashed potatoes	*Purè di patate*
Radishes	Rapanelli
Salad	Insalata
vegetable	*mista*
green	*verde*
Spinach	Spinaci
Tomatoes	Pomodori
Zucchini	Zucchini

Sauces, Herbs, and Spices

Basil	Basilico
Bay leaf	Lauro
Chervil	Cerfoglio
Dill	Aneto
Garlic	Aglio
Hot dip with anchovies (for vegetables)	Bagna cauda

Marjoram	Maggiorana
Mayonnaise	Maionese
Mustard	Mostarda *or* senape
Oil	Olio
Parsley-based sauce	Salsa verde
Pepper	Pepe
Rosemary	Rosmarino
Tartar sauce	Salsa tartara
Vinegar	Aceto
White sauce	Besciamella

Cheeses

Fresh:	Caprino fresco
	Mascarpone
	Mozzarella
	Ricotta
Mild:	Caciotta
	Caprino
	Fontina
	Grana
	Provola
	Provolone dolce
	Robiola
	Scamorza
Sharp:	Asiago
	Gorgonzola
	Groviera
	Pecorino
	Provolone piccante
	Taleggio
	Toma

Fruits and Nuts

Almonds	Mandorle
Apple	Mela
Apricot	Albicocca
Banana	Banana
Blackberries	More
Black currant	Ribes nero
Blueberries	Mirtilli
Cherries	Ciliege
Chestnuts	Castagne
Coconut	Noce di cocco
Dates	Datteri
Figs	Fichi
Green grapes	Uva bianca
Black grapes	Uva nera
Grapefruit	Pompelmo
Hazelnuts	Nocciole
Lemon	Limone
Melon	Melone
Nectarine	Nocepesca
Orange	Arancia
Pear	Pera
Peach	Pesca
Pineapple	Ananas
Plum	Prugna/Susina
Prune	Prugna secca

Raisins	Uva passa
Raspberries	Lamponi
Red currant	Ribes
Strawberries	Fragole
Tangerine	Mandarino
Walnuts	Noci
Watermelon	Anguria/Cocomero
Dried fruit	Frutta secca
Fresh fruit	Frutta fresca
Fruit salad	Macedonia di frutta

Desserts

Custard filled pastry, with candied fruit	Cannoli
Ricotta filled pastry shells with sugar glaze	Cannoli alla siciliana
Ice cream with candied fruit	Cassata
Ricotta filled cake with sugar glaze	Cassata siciliana
Chocolate	Cioccolato
Cup of ice cream	Coppa gelato
Caramel custard	Crème caramel
Pie	Crostata
Fruit pie	Crostata di frutta
Ice cream	Gelato
Flaked pastry	Millefoglie
Chestnuts and whipped-cream cake	Montebianco
Whipped cream	Panna montata
Pastries	Paste
Sherbet	Sorbetto
Chocolate coated ice cream	Tartufo
Fruit tart	Torta di frutta
Apple tart	Torta di mele
Ice-cream cake	Torta gelata
Vanilla	Vaniglia
Egg-based cream with sugar and Marsala wine	Zabaione
Ice-cream filled cake	Zuccotto

Alcoholic Drinks

On the rocks	Con ghiaccio
Straight	Liscio
With soda	Con seltz
Beer	Birra
light/dark	*chiara/scura*
Bitter cordial	Amaro
Brandy	Cognac
Cordial	Liquore
Aniseed cordial	Sambuca
Martini	Cocktail Martini
Port	Porto
Vermouth	Vermut/Martini
Wine	Vino
blush	*rosé*
dry	*secco*
full-bodied	*corposo*
light	*leggero*
red	*rosso*

sparkling	spumante
sweet	dolce
very dry	brut
white	bianco
Light wine	Vinello

Bottle	Bottiglia
Carafe	Caraffa
Flask	Fiasco

Nonalcoholic Drinks

Mineral water	Acqua minerale
carbonated	gassata
still	non gassata
Tap water	Acqua naturale
Tonic water	Acqua tonica

Coffee with steamed milk	Cappuccino
Espresso	Caffè espresso
with milk	macchiato
decaffeinated	decaffeinato
lighter espresso	lungo
with cordial	corretto
Fruit juice	Succo di frutta
Hot chocolate	Cioccolata calda
Lemonade	Limonata
Milk	Latte
Orangeade	Aranciata
Tea	Tè
with milk/lemon	col latte/col limone
iced	freddo

Index

Personal Itinerary

Departure *Date*

Time

Transportation

Arrival *Date*   *Time*

Departure *Date*   *Time*

Transportation

Accommodations

Arrival *Date*   *Time*

Departure *Date*   *Time*

Transportation

Accommodations

Arrival *Date*   *Time*

Departure *Date*   *Time*

Transportation

Accommodations

Personal Itinerary

Arrival *Date*   *Time*

Departure *Date*   *Time*

Transportation

Accommodations

Arrival *Date*   *Time*

Departure *Date*   *Time*

Transportation

Accommodations

Arrival *Date*   *Time*

Departure *Date*   *Time*

Transportation

Accommodations

Arrival *Date*   *Time*

Departure *Date*   *Time*

Transportation

Accommodations

Personal Itinerary

Arrival *Date*   *Time*

Departure *Date*   *Time*

Transportation

Accommodations

Arrival *Date*   *Time*

Departure *Date*   *Time*

Transportation

Accommodations

Arrival *Date*   *Time*

Departure *Date*   *Time*

Transportation

Accommodations

Arrival *Date*   *Time*

Departure *Date*   *Time*

Transportation

Accommodations

Personal Itinerary

Arrival *Date*   *Time*

Departure *Date*   *Time*

Transportation

Accommodations

Arrival *Date*   *Time*

Departure *Date*   *Time*

Transportation

Accommodations

Arrival *Date*   *Time*

Departure *Date*   *Time*

Transportation

Accommodations

Arrival *Date*   *Time*

Departure *Date*   *Time*

Transportation

Accommodations

Personal Itinerary

Arrival *Date*   *Time*

Departure *Date*   *Time*

Transportation

Accommodations

Arrival *Date*   *Time*

Departure *Date*   *Time*

Transportation

Accommodations

Arrival *Date*   *Time*

Departure *Date*   *Time*

Transportation

Accommodations

Arrival *Date*   *Time*

Departure *Date*   *Time*

Transportation

Accommodations

Addresses

Name   Name

Address   Address

Telephone   Telephone

Name   Name

Address   Address

Telephone   Telephone

Name   Name

Address   Address

Telephone   Telephone

Name   Name

Address   Address

Telephone   Telephone

Name   Name

Address   Address

Telephone   Telephone

Name   Name

Address   Address

Telephone   Telephone

Name   Name

Address   Address

Telephone   Telephone

Name   Name

Address   Address

Telephone   Telephone

Addresses

Name	*Name*
Address	*Address*
Telephone	*Telephone*
Name	*Name*
Address	*Address*
Telephone	*Telephone*
Name	*Name*
Address	*Address*
Telephone	*Telephone*
Name	*Name*
Address	*Address*
Telephone	*Telephone*
Name	*Name*
Address	*Address*
Telephone	*Telephone*
Name	*Name*
Address	*Address*
Telephone	*Telephone*
Name	*Name*
Address	*Address*
Telephone	*Telephone*
Name	*Name*
Address	*Address*
Telephone	*Telephone*

Addresses

Name	*Name*
Address	*Address*
Telephone	*Telephone*
Name	*Name*
Address	*Address*
Telephone	*Telephone*
Name	*Name*
Address	*Address*
Telephone	*Telephone*
Name	*Name*
Address	*Address*
Telephone	*Telephone*
Name	*Name*
Address	*Address*
Telephone	*Telephone*
Name	*Name*
Address	*Address*
Telephone	*Telephone*
Name	*Name*
Address	*Address*
Telephone	*Telephone*
Name	*Name*
Address	*Address*
Telephone	*Telephone*

Notes

Escape to ancient cities and exotic

islands *with CNN Travel Guide, a*

wealth of valuable advice. Host Valerie Voss will take you

to all of your favorite destinations,

including those off the beaten path.

Tune into your passport to the world.

CNN TRAVEL GUIDE
SATURDAY 12:30 PM ET   SUNDAY 4:30 PM ET

The only guide to explore a Disney World® you've never seen before:

The one for grown-ups.

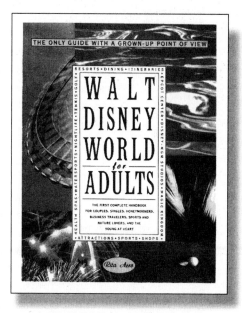

0-679-02490-5 $14.00 ($18.50 Can)

This is the only guide written specifically for the millions of adults who visit Walt Disney World® each year <u>without</u> kids. Upscale, sophisticated, packed full of facts and maps, *Walt Disney World® for Adults* provides up-to-date information on hotels, restaurants, sports facilities, and health clubs, as well as unique itineraries for adults. With *Walt Disney World® for Adults* in hand, you'll get the most out of one of the world's most fascinating, most complex playgrounds.

At bookstores everywhere, or call **1-800-533-6478**.

Fodor's Travel Guides

Available at bookstores everywhere, or call 1–800–533–6478, 24 hours a day.

U.S. Guides

Alaska

Arizona

Boston

California

Cape Cod, Martha's Vineyard, Nantucket

The Carolinas & the Georgia Coast

Chicago

Colorado

Florida

Hawaii

Las Vegas, Reno, Tahoe

Los Angeles

Maine, Vermont, New Hampshire

Maui

Miami & the Keys

New England

New Orleans

New York City

Pacific North Coast

Philadelphia & the Pennsylvania Dutch Country

The Rockies

San Diego

San Francisco

Santa Fe, Taos, Albuquerque

Seattle & Vancouver

The South

The U.S. & British Virgin Islands

USA

The Upper Great Lakes Region

Virginia & Maryland

Waikiki

Walt Disney World and the Orlando Area

Washington, D.C.

Foreign Guides

Acapulco, Ixtapa, Zihuatanejo

Australia & New Zealand

Austria

The Bahamas

Baja & Mexico's Pacific Coast Resorts

Barbados

Berlin

Bermuda

Brittany & Normandy

Budapest

Canada

Cancún, Cozumel, Yucatán Peninsula

Caribbean

China

Costa Rica, Belize, Guatemala

The Czech Republic & Slovakia

Eastern Europe

Egypt

Euro Disney

Europe

Florence, Tuscany & Umbria

France

Germany

Great Britain

Greece

Hong Kong

India

Ireland

Israel

Italy

Japan

Kenya & Tanzania

Korea

London

Madrid & Barcelona

Mexico

Montréal & Québec City

Morocco

Moscow & St. Petersburg

The Netherlands, Belgium & Luxembourg

New Zealand

Norway

Nova Scotia, Prince Edward Island & New Brunswick

Paris

Portugal

Provence & the Riviera

Rome

Russia & the Baltic Countries

Scandinavia

Scotland

Singapore

South America

Southeast Asia

Spain

Sweden

Switzerland

Thailand

Tokyo

Toronto

Turkey

Vienna & the Danube Valley

Special Series

Fodor's Affordables

Caribbean

Europe

Florida

France

Germany

Great Britain

Italy

London

Paris

**Fodor's Bed &
Breakfast and
Country Inns Guides**

America's Best B&Bs

California

Canada's Great
Country Inns

Cottages, B&Bs and
Country Inns of
England and Wales

Mid-Atlantic Region

New England

The Pacific
Northwest

The South

The Southwest

The Upper Great
Lakes Region

The Berkeley Guides

California

Central America

Eastern Europe

Europe

France

Germany & Austria

Great Britain &
Ireland

Italy

London

Mexico

Pacific Northwest &
Alaska

Paris

San Francisco

**Fodor's Exploring
Guides**

Australia

Boston &
New England

Britain

California

The Caribbean

Florence & Tuscany

Florida

France

Germany

Ireland

Italy

London

Mexico

New York City

Paris

Prague

Rome

Scotland

Singapore & Malaysia

Spain

Thailand

Turkey

Fodor's Flashmaps

Boston

New York

Washington, D.C.

Fodor's Pocket Guides

Acapulco

Bahamas

Barbados

Jamaica

London

New York City

Paris

Puerto Rico

San Francisco

Washington, D.C.

Fodor's Sports

Cycling

Golf Digest's Best
Places to Play

Hiking

The Insider's Guide
to the Best Canadian
Skiing

Running

Sailing

Skiing in the USA &
Canada

USA Today's Complete
Four Sports Stadium
Guide

**Fodor's Three-In-Ones
(guidebook, language
cassette, and phrase
book)**

France

Germany

Italy

Mexico

Spain

**Fodor's
Special-Interest
Guides**

Complete Guide to
America's National
Parks

Condé Nast Traveler
Caribbean Resort and
Cruise Ship Finder

Cruises and Ports
of Call

Euro Disney

France by Train

Halliday's New
England Food
Explorer

Healthy Escapes

Italy by Train

London Companion

Shadow Traffic's New
York Shortcuts and
Traffic Tips

Sunday in New York

Sunday in San
Francisco

Touring Europe

Touring USA:
Eastern Edition

Walt Disney World and
the Orlando Area

Walt Disney World
for Adults

**Fodor's Vacation
Planners**

Great American
Learning Vacations

Great American
Sports & Adventure
Vacations

Great American
Vacations

Great American
Vacations for Travelers
with Disabilities

National Parks and
Seashores of the East

National Parks
of the West

**The Wall Street
Journal Guides to
Business Travel**

AT LAST

YOUR OWN PERSONALIZED LIST
OF WHAT'S GOING ON IN THE
CITIES YOU'RE VISITING.

KEYED TO THE DAYS WHEN
YOU'LL BE THERE, CUSTOMIZED
FOR YOUR INTERESTS,
AND SENT TO YOU BEFORE YOU
LEAVE HOME.

GET THE INSIDER'S
PERSPECTIVE. . .

UP-TO-THE-MINUTE
ACCURATE
EASY TO ORDER
DELIVERED WHEN YOU NEED IT

Now there is a revolutionary way to get customized, time-sensitive travel information just before your trip.

Now you can obtain detailed information about what's going on in each city you'll be visiting <u>before</u> you leave home—up-to-the-minute, objective information about the events and activities that interest you most.

Travel Updates contain the kind of time-sensitive insider information you can get only from local contacts – or from city magazines and newspapers once you arrive. But now you can have the same information before you leave for your trip.

The choice is yours: current art exhibits, theater, music festivals and special concerts, sporting events, antiques and flower shows, shopping, fitness, and more.

The information comes from hundreds of correspondents and thousands of sources worldwide. Updated continuously, it's like having your own personal concierge or friend in the city.

You specify the cities and when you'll be there. We'll do the rest — personalizing the information for you the way no guidebook can.

It's the perfect extension to your Fodor's guide and the best way to make the most of your valuable travel time.

**Use Order Form on back
or call 1-800-799-9609**

Your Itinerary:
Customized reports available for 160 destinations

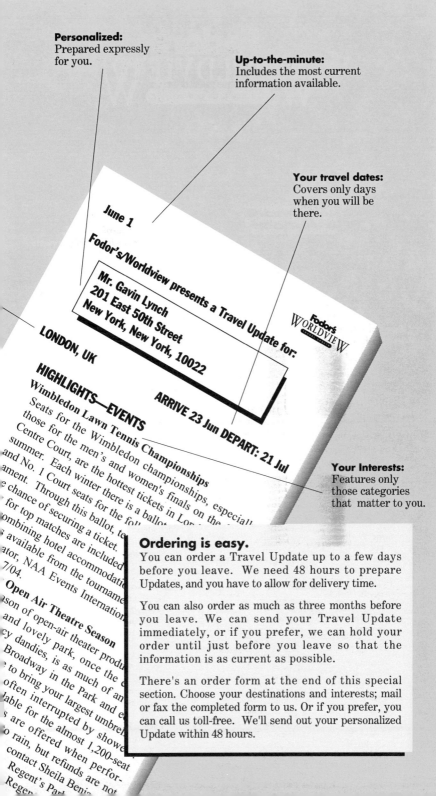

Personalized:
Prepared expressly for you.

Up-to-the-minute:
Includes the most current information available.

Your travel dates:
Covers only days when you will be there.

June 1

Fodor's/Worldview presents a Travel Update for:

Mr. Gavin Lynch
201 East 50th Street
New York, New York, 10022

Fodor's
WORLDVIEW

LONDON, UK

ARRIVE 23 Jun DEPART: 21 Jul

Your Interests:
Features only those categories that matter to you.

HIGHLIGHTS—EVENTS

Wimbledon Lawn Tennis Championships

Seats for the Wimbledon championships, especially those for the men's and women's finals on the Centre Court, are the hottest tickets in Lon summer. Each winter there is a ballot and No. 1 Court seats for the foll ament. Through this ballot, te chance of securing a ticket. for top matches are included ombining hotel accommodati s available from the tournam ator, NAA Events Internam 7/04.

Open Air Theatre Season

ason of open-air theater produ and lovely park, once the cy dandies, is as much of an Broadway in the Park and e to bring your largest umbrel often interrupted by showe able for the almost 1,200-seat s are offered when perfor o rain, but refunds are not contact Sheila Beni Regent's Par Regen

Ordering is easy.

You can order a Travel Update up to a few days before you leave. We need 48 hours to prepare Updates, and you have to allow for delivery time.

You can also order as much as three months before you leave. We can send your Travel Update immediately, or if you prefer, we can hold your order until just before you leave so that the information is as current as possible.

There's an order form at the end of this special section. Choose your destinations and interests; mail or fax the completed form to us. Or if you prefer, you can call us toll-free. We'll send out your personalized Update within 48 hours.

**Special concerts—
who's performing
what and where**

**One-of-a-kind,
one-time-only events**

**Special interest,
in-depth listings**

Children — Events

Angel Canal Festival
The festivities include a children's funfair, entertainers, a boat rally and displays on the water. Regent's Canal. Islington. N1. Tube: Angel. Tel: 267 9100. 11:30am-5:30pm. 7/04.

Blackheath Summer Kite Festival
Stunt kite displays with parachuting teddy bears and trade stands. Free admission. SE3. BR: Blackheath. 10am. 6/27.

Megabugs
Children will delight in this infestation of giant robotic insects, including a praying mantis 60 times life size. Mon-Sat 10am-6pm; Sun 11am-6pm. Admission 4.50 pounds. Natural History Museum, Cromwell Road. SW7. Tube: South Kensington. Tel: 938 9123. Ends 10/01.

Childminders
This establishment employs only women, providing nurses and qualified nannies to

Music — Jazz & Blues

Tito Puente's Golden Men of Latin Jazz
The father of mambo and Cuban rumba king comes to town. Royal Festival Hall. South Bank. SE1. Tube: Waterloo. Tel: 928 8800. 8pm. 7/15.

Georgie Fame and The New York Band
Riding a popular tide with his latest album, the smoky-voiced Fame and his keyboard are on a tour yet again. The Grand. Clapham Junction. SW11. BR: Clapham Junction. Tel: 738 9000. 7:30pm. 7/07.

Jacques Loussier Play Bach Trio
The French jazz classicist and colleagues. Kenwood Lakeside. Hampstead Lane. Kenwood. NW3. Tube: Golders Green, then bus 210. Tel: 413 1443. 7pm. 7/10.

Tony Bennett and Ronnie Scott
Royal Festival Hall. South Bank. SE1. Tube: Waterloo. Tel: 928 8800. 8pm. 7/11.

Santana
Royal Festival Hall. South Bank. SE1. Tube: Waterloo. Tel: 928 8800. 8pm. 7/12.

Count Basie Orchestra and Nancy Wilson Trio
Royal Festival Hall. South Bank. SE1. Tube: Waterloo. Tel: 928 8800. 8pm. 7/14.

King Pleasure and the Biscuit Boys
Royal Festival Hall. South Bank. SE1. Tube: Waterloo. Tel: 928 8800. 6:30 and 9pm. 7/16.

Al Green and the London Community Gospel Choir
Royal Festival Hall. South Bank. SE1. Tube: Waterloo. Tel: 928 8800. 8pm. 7/13.

BB King and Linda Hopkins
Mother of the blues and successor to Bessie Smith, Hopkins meets up with "Blues Boy" ... Hall. South Bank. SE

Music — Classical

Marylebone Sinfonia
Kenneth Gowen conducts music by Puc... and Rossini. Queen Elizabeth Hall. So... Bank. SE1. Tube: Waterloo. Tel: 928 88... 7:45pm. 7/16.

London Philharmonic
Franz Welser-Moest and George Benja... conduct selections by Alexander Go... Messiaen, and some of Benjamin's own ... positions. Queen Elizabeth Hall. South F... SE1. Tube: Waterloo. Tel: 928 8800. 8pm...

London Pro Arte Orchestra and Forest C...
Murray Stewart conducts selection... Rossini, Haydn and Jonathan Willcocks. Queen Elizabeth Hall. South Bank. Tube: Waterloo. Tel: 928 8800. 7:45pm.

Kensington Symphony Orchestra
... ll Keeble conducts Dvorak's D

Here's what you get . . .

Detailed information about what's going on — precisely when you'll be there.

Reviews by local critics

Show openings during your visit

Handy pocket-size booklet

Exhibitions & Shows—Antique & Flower
Westminster Antiques Fair
Over 50 stands with pre-1830 furniture and other Victorian and earlier items. Thu-Fri 11am-8pm; Sat-Sun 11am-6pm. Admission 4 pounds, children free. Old Royal Horticultural Hall. Vincent Square. SW1. Tel: 0444/48 25 14. 6-24 thru 6/27.

Royal Horticultural Society Flower Show
The show includes displays of carnations, summer fruit and vegetables. Tue 11am-7pm; Wed 10am-5pm. Admission Tue 4 pounds, Wed 2 pounds. Royal Horticultural Halls. Greycoat Street and Vincent Square. SW1. Tube: Victoria. 7/20 thru 7/21.

Hampton Court Palace International Flower Show
Major international garden and flower show taking place in conjunction with

Theater — Musical
Sunset Boulevard
In June, the four Andrew Lloyd Webber musicals which dominated London's stages in the 1980s (Cats, Starlight Express, Phantom of the Opera and Aspects of Love) are joined by the composer's latest work, a show rumored to have his best music to date. The 1950 Billy Wilder film about a helpless young writer who is drawn into the world of a possessive, aging silent screen star offers rich opportunities for Webber's evolving style. Soaring, aching melodies, lush technical effects and psychological thrills are all expected. Patti Lupone stars. Mon-Sat at 8pm; matinee Thu-Sat at 3pm. In-person sales only at the box office; credit card bookings, Tel: 344 0055. Admission 15-32.50 pounds. Adelphi Theatre. The Strand. WC2. Tube: Charing Cross. Tel: 836 7611. Starts: 6/21.

Leonardo A Portrait of Love
A new musical about the great Renaissance artist and inventor comes in for a London pre-___ tested by a brief run at Oxford's Old ___. The work explores ___

Spectator Sports — Other Sports
Greyhound Racing: Wembley Stadium
This dog track offers good views of greyhound racing held on Mon, Wed and Fri. No credit cards. Stadium Way. Wembley. HA9. Tube: Wembley Park. Tel: 902 8833.

Benson & Hedges Cricket Cup Final
Lord's Cricket Ground. St. John's Wood Road. NW8. Tube: St. John's Wood. Tel: 289 1611. 11am. 7/10.

Business-Fax & Overnight Mail
Post Office, Trafalgar Square Branch
Offers a network of fax services, the Intelpost system, throughout the country and abroad. Mon-Sat 8am-8pm, Sun 9am-5pm. William IV Street. WC2. Tube: Ch___

Fodor's
WORLDVIEW
TRAVEL UPDATE

London, England
Arriving: June 23
Departing: July 21

Interest Categories

For <u>your</u> personalized Travel Update, choose the categories you're most interested in from this list. Every Travel Update automatically provides you with *Event Highlights* - the best of what's happening during the dates of your trip.

1.	**Business Services**	Fax & Overnight Mail, Computer Rentals, Photocopying, Protocol, Secretarial, Messenger, Translation Services

Dining

2.	**All Day Dining**	Breakfast & Brunch, Cafes & Tea Rooms, Late-Night Dining
3.	**Local Cuisine**	In Every Price Range—from Budget Restaurants to the Special Splurge
4.	**European Cuisine**	Continental, French, Italian
5.	**Asian Cuisine**	Chinese, Far Eastern, Japanese, Other
6.	**Americas Cuisine**	American, Mexican & Latin
7.	**Nightlife**	Bars, Dance Clubs, Casinos, Comedy Clubs, Ethnic, Pubs & Beer Halls
8.	**Entertainment**	Theater—Comedy, Drama, English Language, Musicals, Dance, Ticket Agencies
9.	**Music**	Country/Western/Folk, Classical, Traditional & Ethnic, Opera, Jazz & Blues, Pop, Rock
10.	**Children's Activities**	Events, Attractions
11.	**Tours**	Local Tours, Day Trips, Overnight Excursions, Cruises
12.	**Exhibitions, Festivals & Shows**	Antiques & Flower, History & Cultural, Art Exhibitions, Fairs & Craft Shows, Music & Art Festivals
13.	**Shopping**	Districts & Malls, Markets, Regional Specialities
14.	**Fitness**	Bicycling, Health Clubs, Hiking, Jogging
15.	**Recreational Sports**	Boating/Sailing, Fishing, Golf, Ice Skating, Skiing, Snorkeling/Scuba, Swimming, Tennis & Racquet
16.	**Spectator Sports**	Auto Racing, Baseball, Basketball, Boating & Sailing, Football, Golf, Horse Racing, Ice Hockey, Rugby, Soccer, Tennis, Track & Field, Other Sports

Please note that interest category content will vary by season, destination, and length of stay.

Destinations

The Fodor's/Worldview Travel Update covers more than 160 destinations worldwide. Choose the destinations that match your itinerary from this list. (Choose bulleted destinations only.)

Europe
- Amsterdam
- Athens
- Barcelona
- Berlin
- Brussels
- Budapest
- Copenhagen
- Dublin
- Edinburgh
- Florence
- Frankfurt
- French Riviera
- Geneva
- Glasgow
- Istanbul
- Lausanne
- Lisbon
- London
- Madrid
- Milan
- Moscow
- Munich
- Oslo
- Paris
- Prague
- Provence
- Rome
- Salzburg
- Seville
- St. Petersburg
- Stockholm
- Venice
- Vienna
- Zurich

United States (Mainland)
- Albuquerque
- Atlanta
- Atlantic City
- Baltimore
- Boston
* Branson, MO
* Charleston, SC
- Chicago
- Cincinnati
- Cleveland
- Dallas/Ft. Worth
- Denver
- Detroit
- Houston
* Indianapolis
- Kansas City
- Las Vegas
- Los Angeles
- Memphis

- Miami
- Milwaukee
- Minneapolis/ St. Paul
* Nashville
- New Orleans
- New York City
- Orlando
- Palm Springs
- Philadelphia
- Phoenix
- Pittsburgh
- Portland
* Reno/ Lake Tahoe
- St. Louis
- Salt Lake City
- San Antonio
- San Diego
- San Francisco
* Santa Fe
- Seattle
- Tampa
- Washington, DC

Alaska
- Alaskan Destinations

Hawaii
- Honolulu
- Island of Hawaii
- Kauai
- Maui

Canada
- Quebec City
- Montreal
- Ottawa
- Toronto
- Vancouver

Bahamas
- Abaco
- Eleuthera/ Harbour Island
- Exuma
- Freeport
- Nassau & Paradise Island

Bermuda
- Bermuda Countryside
- Hamilton

British Leeward Islands
- Anguilla

- Antigua & Barbuda
- St. Kitts & Nevis

British Virgin Islands
- Tortola & Virgin Gorda

British Windward Islands
- Barbados
- Dominica
- Grenada
- St. Lucia
- St. Vincent
- Trinidad & Tobago

Cayman Islands
- The Caymans

Dominican Republic
- Santo Domingo

Dutch Leeward Islands
- Aruba
- Bonaire
- Curacao

Dutch Windward Island
- St. Maarten/ St. Martin

French West Indies
- Guadeloupe
- Martinique
- St. Barthelemy

Jamaica
- Kingston
- Montego Bay
- Negril
- Ocho Rios

Puerto Rico
- Ponce
- San Juan

Turks & Caicos
- Grand Turk/ Providenciales

U.S. Virgin Islands
- St. Croix
- St. John
- St. Thomas

Mexico
- Acapulco
- Cancun & Isla Mujeres
- Cozumel
- Guadalajara
- Ixtapa & Zihuatanejo
- Los Cabos
- Mazatlan
- Mexico City
- Monterrey
- Oaxaca
- Puerto Vallarta

South/Central America
* Buenos Aires
* Caracas
* Rio de Janeiro
* San Jose, Costa Rica
* Sao Paulo

Middle East
* Jerusalem

Australia & New Zealand
- Auckland
- Melbourne
* South Island
- Sydney

China
- Beijing
- Guangzhou
- Shanghai

Japan
- Kyoto
- Nagoya
- Osaka
- Tokyo
- Yokohama

Pacific Rim/Other
* Bali
- Bangkok
- Hong Kong & Macau
- Manila
- Seoul
- Singapore
- Taipei

* Destinations available by 1/1/95

Fodor's WORLDVIEW **Order Form**

THIS TRAVEL UPDATE IS FOR (Please print):

Name

Address

City	State	Country	ZIP

Tel # (   )   -   **Fax #** (   )   -

Title of this Fodor's guide:

Store and location where guide was purchased:

INDICATE YOUR DESTINATIONS/DATES: You can order up to three (3) destinations from the previous page. Fill in your arrival and departure dates for each destination. **Your Travel Update itinerary (all destinations selected) cannot exceed 30 days from beginning to end.**

			Month	Day		Month	Day
(Sample)	*LONDON*	From:	**6**	/ **21**	To:	**6**	/ **30**
1		From:	/		To:	/	
2		From:	/		To:	/	
3		From:	/		To:	/	

CHOOSE YOUR INTERESTS: Select up to eight (8) categories from the list of interest categories shown on the previous page and circle the numbers below:

1 2 3 4 5 6 7 8 9 10 11 12 13 14 15 16

CHOOSE WHEN YOU WANT YOUR TRAVEL UPDATE DELIVERED (Check one):
❑ Please send my Travel Update immediately.
❑ Please hold my order until a few weeks before my trip to include the most up-to-date information.
  Completed orders will be sent within 48 hours. Allow 7-10 days for U.S. mail delivery.

ADD UP YOUR ORDER HERE. *SPECIAL OFFER FOR FODOR'S PURCHASERS ONLY!*

	Suggested Retail Price	Your Price	This Order
First destination ordered	$ 9.95	$ 7.95	$ 7.95
Second destination (if applicable)	$ 6.95	$ 4.95	+
Third destination (if applicable)	$ 6.95	$ 4.95	+

DELIVERY CHARGE (Check one and enter amount below)

	Within U.S. & Canada	Outside U.S. & Canada
First Class Mail	❑ $2.50	❑ $5.00
FAX	❑ $5.00	❑ $10.00
Priority Delivery	❑ $15.00	❑ $27.00

ENTER DELIVERY CHARGE FROM ABOVE: +

TOTAL: $

METHOD OF PAYMENT IN U.S. FUNDS ONLY (Check one):
❑ AmEx   ❑ MC   ❑ Visa   ❑ Discover   ❑ Personal Check (U. S. & Canada only)
❑ Money Order/ International Money Order

  Make check or money order payable to: Fodor's Worldview Travel Update

Credit Card | | | | | | | | | | | | | | | | **Expiration Date:** | | | |

Authorized Signature

SEND THIS COMPLETED FORM WITH PAYMENT TO:
Fodor's Worldview Travel Update, 114 Sansome Street, Suite 700, San Francisco, CA 94104

OR CALL OR FAX US 24-HOURS A DAY
Telephone **1-800-799-9609** • Fax **1-800-799-9619** (From within the U.S. & Canada)
(Outside the U.S. & Canada: Telephone 415-616-9988 • Fax 415-616-9989)

(Please have this guide in front of you when you call so we can verify purchase.)
Code: FTG   Offer valid until 12/31/95